How Students Learn

HISTORY, MATHEMATICS, AND SCIENCE
IN THE CLASSROOM

Committee on *How People Learn,* A Targeted Report for Teachers

M. Suzanne Donovan and John D. Bransford, *Editors*

Division of Behavioral and Social Sciences and Education

NATIONAL RESEARCH COUNCIL
OF THE NATIONAL ACADEMIES

THE NATIONAL ACADEMIES PRESS
Washington, D.C.
www.nap.edu

THE NATIONAL ACADEMIES PRESS • 500 Fifth Street, N.W. • Washington, D.C. 20001

NOTICE: The project that is the subject of this report was approved by the Governing Board of the National Research Council, whose members are drawn from the councils of the National Academy of Sciences, the National Academy of Engineering, and the Institute of Medicine. The members of the committee responsible for the report were chosen for their special competences and with regard for appropriate balance.

This study was supported by Award No. R215U990024 between the National Academy of Sciences and the U.S. Department of Education. Any opinions, findings, conclusions, or recommendations expressed in this publication are those of the author(s) and do not necessarily reflect the views of the organizations or agencies that provided support for the project.

Library of Congress Cataloging-in-Publication Data

National Research Council (U.S.). Committee on How People Learn, A Targeted Report for Teachers.
  How students learn : history, mathematics, and science in the classroom / Committee on How People Learn, A Targeted Report for Teachers ; M. Suzanne Donovan and John D. Bransford, editors.
    p. cm.
  "Division of Behavioral and Social Sciences and Education."
  Includes bibliographical references and index.
  ISBN 0-309-07433-9 (hardcover) — ISBN 0-309-08948-4 (pbk.) —
ISBN 0-309-08949-2 (pbk.) — ISBN 0-309-08950-6 (pbk.) 1. Learning. 2.
Classroom management. 3. Curriculum planning. I. Donovan, Suzanne.
II. Bransford, John. III. Title.
  LB1060.N38 2005
  370.15'23—dc22

                            2004026246

Additional copies of this report are available from the National Academies Press, 500 Fifth Street, N.W., Lockbox 285, Washington, DC 20055; (800) 624-6242 or (202) 334-3313 (in the Washington metropolitan area); Internet, http://www.nap.edu

Printed in the United States of America.

Suggested citation: National Research Council. (2005). *How Students Learn: History, Mathematics, and Science in the Classroom.* Committee on *How People Learn*, A Targeted Report for Teachers, M.S. Donovan and J.D. Bransford, Editors. Division of Behavioral and Social Sciences and Education. Washington, DC: The National Academies Press.

First Printing, November 2004
Second Printing, May 2005
Third Printing, November 2005

THE NATIONAL ACADEMIES
Advisers to the Nation on Science, Engineering, and Medicine

The **National Academy of Sciences** is a private, nonprofit, self-perpetuating society of distinguished scholars engaged in scientific and engineering research, dedicated to the furtherance of science and technology and to their use for the general welfare. Upon the authority of the charter granted to it by the Congress in 1863, the Academy has a mandate that requires it to advise the federal government on scientific and technical matters. Dr. Bruce M. Alberts is president of the National Academy of Sciences.

The **National Academy of Engineering** was established in 1964, under the charter of the National Academy of Sciences, as a parallel organization of outstanding engineers. It is autonomous in its administration and in the selection of its members, sharing with the National Academy of Sciences the responsibility for advising the federal government. The National Academy of Engineering also sponsors engineering programs aimed at meeting national needs, encourages education and research, and recognizes the superior achievements of engineers. Dr. Wm. A. Wulf is president of the National Academy of Engineering.

The **Institute of Medicine** was established in 1970 by the National Academy of Sciences to secure the services of eminent members of appropriate professions in the examination of policy matters pertaining to the health of the public. The Institute acts under the responsibility given to the National Academy of Sciences by its congressional charter to be an adviser to the federal government and, upon its own initiative, to identify issues of medical care, research, and education. Dr. Harvey V. Fineberg is president of the Institute of Medicine.

The **National Research Council** was organized by the National Academy of Sciences in 1916 to associate the broad community of science and technology with the Academy's purposes of furthering knowledge and advising the federal government. Functioning in accordance with general policies determined by the Academy, the Council has become the principal operating agency of both the National Academy of Sciences and the National Academy of Engineering in providing services to the government, the public, and the scientific and engineering communities. The Council is administered jointly by both Academies and the Institute of Medicine. Dr. Bruce M. Alberts and Dr. Wm. A. Wulf are chair and vice chair, respectively, of the National Research Council.

www.national-academies.org

COMMITTEE ON *HOW PEOPLE LEARN*: A TARGETED REPORT FOR TEACHERS

JOHN D. BRANSFORD (*Chair*), College of Education, University of Washington
SUSAN CAREY, Department of Psychology, Harvard University
KIERAN EGAN, Department of Education, Simon Fraser University, Burnaby, Canada
SUZANNE WILSON, School of Education, Michigan State University
SAMUEL S. WINEBURG, Department of Education, Stanford University

M. SUZANNE DONOVAN, *Study Director*
SUSAN R. MCCUTCHEN, *Research Associate*
ALLISON E. SHOUP, *Senior Project Assistant*
ELIZABETH B. TOWNSEND, *Senior Project Assistant*

Preface

This book has its roots in the report of the Committee on Developments in the Science of Learning, *How People Learn: Brain, Mind, Experience and School* (National Research Council, 1999, National Academy Press). That report presented an illuminating review of research in a variety of fields that has advanced understanding of human learning. The report also made an important attempt to draw from that body of knowledge implications for teaching. A follow-on study by a second committee explored what research and development would need to be done, and how it would need to be communicated, to be especially useful to teachers, principals, superintendents, and policy makers: *How People Learn: Bridging Research and Practice* (National Research Council, 1999). These two individual reports were combined to produce an expanded edition of *How People Learn* (National Research Council, 2000). We refer to this volume as *HPL*.

In the present book, the goal is to take the *HPL* work to the next step: to provide examples of how the principles and findings on learning can be used to guide the teaching of a set of topics that commonly appear in the K-12 curriculum. As was the case in the original work (1999), the book focuses on three subject areas: history, mathematics, and science. Each area is treated at three levels: elementary, middle, and high school. Distinguished researchers who have extensive experience in teaching or in partnering with teachers were invited to contribute the chapters. The committee shaped the goals for the volume, and commented—sometimes extensively—on the draft chapters as they were written and revised. The principles of *HPL* are embedded in each chapter, though there are differences from one chapter to the next in how explicitly they are discussed.

Taking this next step to elaborate the *HPL* principles in context poses a potential problem that we wish to address at the outset. The meaning and relevance of the principles for classroom teaching can be made clearer with specific examples. At the same time, however, many of the specifics of a particular example could be replaced with others that are also consistent with the *HPL* principles. In looking at a single example, it can be difficult to distinguish what is necessary to effective teaching from what is effective but easily replaced. With this in mind, it is critical that the teaching and learning examples in each chapter be seen as illustrative, not as blueprints for the "right" way to teach.

We can imagine, by analogy, that engineering students will better grasp the relationship between the laws of physics and the construction of effective supports for a bridge if they see some examples of well-designed bridges, accompanied by explanations for the choices of the critical design features. The challenging engineering task of crossing the entrance of the San Francisco Bay, for example, may bring the relationship between physical laws, physical constraints, and engineering solutions into clear and meaningful focus. But there are some design elements of the Golden Gate Bridge that could be replaced with others that serve the same end, and people may well differ on which among a set of good designs creates the most appealing bridge.

To say that the Golden Gate Bridge is a good example of a suspension bridge does not mean it is the only, or the best possible, design for a suspension bridge. If one has many successful suspension bridges to compare, the design features that are required for success, and those that are replaceable, become more apparent. And the requirements that are uniform across contexts, and the requirements that change with context, are more easily revealed.

The chapters in this volume highlight different approaches to addressing the same fundamental principles of learning. It would be ideal to be able to provide two or more "*HPL* compatible" approaches to teaching the same topic (for example, the study of light in elementary school). However, we cannot provide that level of specific variability in this already lengthy volume. Nevertheless, we hope that common features across chapters, and the variation in approach among the chapters, are sufficient to provide instructive insights into the principles laid out in *How People Learn*.

This volume could not have come to life without the help and dedication of many people, and we are grateful to them. First and foremost, the committee acknowledges the contributions of Robbie Case, who was to have contributed to the mathematics chapters in this volume. Robbie was at the height of a very productive career when his life came to an unexpected end in May 2000. Robbie combined the very best in disciplinary research and attention to the incorporation of research findings into classroom tools to support teaching and learning. In this respect, he was a model for researchers interested in supporting improved educational practice. The mathematics chapters in this volume are marked by Robbie Case's influence.

The financial support of our sponsors, the U.S. Department of Education and the President's Circle of the National Academy of Sciences, was essential. We appreciate both their support and their patience during the unexpectedly long period required to shape and produce so extensive a volume with so many different contributors. Our thanks to C. Kent McGuire, former assistant secretary of the Office of Education Research and Improvement for providing the initial grant for this project, and to his successor and now director of the National Institute for Education Sciences, Grover J. Whitehurst; thanks are due as well to Patricia O'Connell Ross, Jill Edwards Staton, Michael Kestner, and Linda Jones at the Department of Education for working with us throughout, and providing the time required to produce a quality product.

This report is a somewhat unusual undertaking for the National Research Council in that the committee members did not author the report chapters, but served as advisers to the chapter authors. The contributions of committee members were extraordinary. In a first meeting the committee and chapter authors worked together to plan the volume. The committee then read each draft chapter, and provided extensive, and remarkably productive, feedback to chapter authors. As drafts were revised, committee members reviewed them again, pointing out concerns and proposing potential solutions. Their generosity and their commitment to the goal of this project are noteworthy.

Alexandra Wigdor, director of the Division on Education, Labor, and Human Performance when this project was begun, provided ongoing guidance and experienced assistance with revisions. Rona Brière brought her special skills in editing the entire volume. Our thanks go to Allison E. Shoup, who was senior project assistant, supporting the project through much of its life; to Susan R. McCutchen, who prepared the manuscript for review; to Claudia Sauls and Candice Crawford, who prepared the final manuscript; and to Deborah Johnson, Sandra Smotherman, and Elizabeth B. Townsend, who willingly provided additional support when needed. Kirsten Sampson Snyder handled the report review process, and Yvonne Wise handled report production—both challenging tasks for a report of this size and complexity. We are grateful for their help.

This report has been reviewed in draft form by individuals chosen for their diverse perspectives and technical expertise, in accordance with procedures approved by the National Research Council's Report Review Committee. The purpose of this independent review is to provide candid and critical comments that will assist the institution in making its published report as sound as possible and to ensure that the report meets institutional standards for objectivity, evidence, and responsiveness to the study charge. The review comments and draft manuscript remain confidential to protect the integrity of the deliberative process. We thank the following individuals for their review of this report: Jo Boaler, Mathematics Education, School of Education, Stanford University; Miriam L. Clifford, Mathematics Department, Carroll College, Waukesha, Wisconsin; O.L. Davis, Curriculum and Instruction, The University of Texas at Austin; Patricia B. Dodge, Science Teacher, Essex Middle School, Essex Junction, Vermont; Carol T. Hines, History Teacher, Darrel C. Swope Middle School, Reno, Nevada; Janis Lariviere, UTeach—Science and Mathematics Teacher Preparation, The University of Texas at Austin; Gaea Leinhardt, Learning Research and Development Center and School of Education, University of Pittsburgh; Alan M. Lesgold, Office of the Provost, University of Pittsburgh; Marcia C. Linn, Education in Mathematics, Science, and Technology, University of California, Berkeley; Kathleen Metz, Cognition and Development, Graduate School of Education, University of California, Berkeley; Thomas Romberg, National Center for Research in Mathematics and Science Education, University of Wisconsin–Madison; and Peter Seixas, Centre for the Study of Historical Consciousness, University of British Columbia.

Although the reviewers listed above have provided many constructive comments and suggestions, they did not see the final draft of the report before its release. The review of this report was overseen by Alan M. Lesgold, University of Pittsburgh. Appointed by the National Research Council, he was responsible for making certain that an independent examination of this report was carried out in accordance with institutional procedures and that all review comments were carefully considered. Responsibility for the final content of this report rests entirely with the authors, the committee, and the institution.

John D. Bransford, *Chair*
M. Suzanne Donovan, *Study Director*

Contents

Part I:
History

Part II:
Mathematics

Part III:
Science

A Final Synthesis:
Revisiting the Three Learning Principles

How Students Learn

HISTORY, MATHEMATICS, AND SCIENCE
IN THE CLASSROOM

Introduction

M. Suzanne Donovan and John D. Bransford

More than any other species, people are designed to be flexible learners and, from infancy, are active agents in acquiring knowledge and skills. People can invent, record, accumulate, and pass on organized bodies of knowledge that help them understand, shape, exploit, and ornament their environment. Much that each human being knows about the world is acquired informally, but mastery of the accumulated knowledge of generations requires intentional learning, often accomplished in a formal educational setting.

Decades of work in the cognitive and developmental sciences has provided the foundation for an emerging science of learning. This foundation offers conceptions of learning processes and the development of competent performance that can help teachers support their students in the acquisition of knowledge that is the province of formal education. The research literature was synthesized in the National Research Council report *How People Learn: Brain, Mind, Experience, and School.*[1] In this volume, we focus on three fundamental and well-established principles of learning that are highlighted in *How People Learn* and are particularly important for teachers to understand and be able to incorporate in their teaching:

1. Students come to the classroom with preconceptions about how the world works. If their initial understanding is not engaged, they may fail to grasp the new concepts and information, or they may learn them for purposes of a test but revert to their preconceptions outside the classroom.

2. To develop competence in an area of inquiry, students must (a) have a deep foundation of factual knowledge, (b) understand facts and ideas in the context of a conceptual framework, and (c) organize knowledge in ways that facilitate retrieval and application.

3. A "metacognitive" approach to instruction can help students learn to take control of their own learning by defining learning goals and monitoring their progress in achieving them.

A FISH STORY

The images from a children's story, *Fish Is Fish*,[2] help convey the essence of the above principles. In the story, a young fish is very curious about the world outside the water. His good friend the frog, on returning from the land, tells the fish about it excitedly:

> *"I have been about the world—hopping here and there,"*
> *said the frog, "and I have seen extraordinary things."*
> *"Like what?" asked the fish.*
> *"Birds," said the frog mysteriously. "Birds!" And he told the*
> *fish about the birds, who had wings, and two legs, and*
> *many, many colors. As the frog talked, his friend saw the*
> *birds fly through his mind like large feathered fish.*

The frog continues with descriptions of cows, which the fish imagines as black-and-white spotted fish with horns and udders, and humans, which the fish imagines as fish walking upright and dressed in clothing. Illustrations below from Leo Lionni's *Fish Is Fish* © 1970. Copyright renewed 1998 by Leo Lionni. Used by permission of Random House Children's Books, a division of Random House, Inc.

Principle #1: Engaging Prior Understandings

What Lionni's story captures so effectively is a fundamental insight about learning: *new understandings are constructed on a foundation of existing understandings and experiences.* With research techniques that permit the study of learning in infancy and tools that allow for observation of activity in the brain, we understand as never before how actively humans engage in learning from the earliest days of life (see Box 1-1). The understandings children carry with them into the classroom, even before the start of formal schooling, will shape significantly how they make sense of what they are

BOX 1-1 The Development of Physical Concepts in Infancy

Research studies have demonstrated that infants as young as 3 to 4 months of age develop understandings and expectations about the physical world. For example, they understand that objects need support to prevent them from falling to the ground, that stationary objects may be displaced when they come into contact with moving objects, and that objects at rest must be propelled into motion.[3]

In research by Needham and Baillargeon,[4] infants were shown a table on which a box rested. A gloved hand reached out from a window beside the table and placed another box in one of two locations: on top of the first box (the possible event), and beyond the box—creating the impression that the box was suspended in midair. In this and similar studies, infants look reliably longer at the impossible events, suggesting an awareness and a set of expectations regarding what is and is not physically possible.

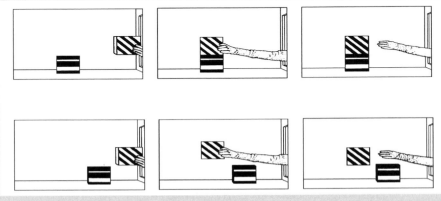

SOURCE: Needham and Baillargeon (1993). Reprinted with permission from Elsevier.

BOX 1-2 Misconceptions About Momentum

Andrea DiSessa[5] conducted a study in which he compared the performance of college physics students at a top technological university with that of elementary schoolchildren on a task involving momentum. He instructed both sets of students to play a computerized game that required them to direct a simulated object (a dynaturtle) so that it would hit a target, and to do so with minimum speed at impact. Participants were introduced to the game and given a hands-on trial that allowed them to apply a few taps with a wooden mallet to a ball on a table before they began.

DiSessa found that both groups of students failed miserably at the task. Despite their training, college physics majors—just like the elementary school children—applied the force when the object was just below the target, failing to take momentum into account. Further investigation with one college student revealed that she knew the relevant physical properties and formulas and would have performed well on a written exam. Yet in the context of the game, she fell back on her untrained conceptions of how the physical world works.

taught. Just as the fish constructed an image of a human as a modified fish, children use what they know to shape their new understandings.

While prior learning is a powerful support for further learning, it can also lead to the development of conceptions that can act as barriers to learning. For example, when told that the earth is round, children may look to reconcile this information with their experience with balls. It seems obvious that one would fall off a round object. Researchers have found that some children solve the paradox by envisioning the earth as a pancake, a "round" shape with a surface on which people could walk without falling off.[6]

How People Learn summarizes a number of studies demonstrating the active, preconception-driven learning that is evident in humans from infancy through adulthood.[7] Preconceptions developed from everyday experiences are often difficult for teachers to change because they generally work well enough in day-to-day contexts. But they can impose serious constraints on understanding formal disciplines. College physics students who do well on classroom exams on the laws of motion, for example, often revert to their untrained, erroneous models outside the classroom. When they are confronted with tasks that require putting their knowledge to use, they fail to take momentum into account, just as do elementary students who have had no physics training (see Box 1-2). If students' preconceptions are not addressed directly, they often memorize content (e.g., formulas in physics), yet still use their experience-based preconceptions to act in the world.

Principle #2: The Essential Role of Factual Knowledge and Conceptual Frameworks in Understanding

The *Fish Is Fish* story also draws attention to the kinds of knowledge, factual and conceptual, needed to support learning with understanding. The frog in the story provides information to the fish about humans, birds, and cows that is accurate and relevant, yet clearly insufficient. Feathers, legs, udders, and sport coats are surface features that distinguish each species. But if the fish (endowed now with human thinking capacity) is to understand how the land species are different from fish and different from each other, these surface features will not be of much help. Some additional, critical concepts are needed—for example, the concept of adaptation. Species that move through the medium of air rather than water have a different mobility challenge. And species that are warm-blooded, unlike those that are cold-blooded, must maintain their body temperature. It will take more explaining of course, but if the fish is to see a bird as something other than a fish with feathers and wings and a human as something other than an upright fish with clothing, then feathers and clothing must be seen as adaptations that help solve the problem of maintaining body temperature, and upright posture and wings must be seen as different solutions to the problem of mobility outside water.

Conceptual information such as a theory of adaptation represents a kind of knowledge that is unlikely to be induced from everyday experiences. It typically takes generations of inquiry to develop this sort of knowledge, and people usually need some help (e.g., interactions with "knowledgeable others") to grasp such organizing concepts.[8]

Lionni's fish, not understanding the described features of the land animals as adaptations to a terrestrial environment, leaps from the water to experience life on land for himself. Since he can neither breathe nor maneuver on land, the fish must be saved by the amphibious frog. The point is well illustrated: learning with understanding affects our ability to apply what is learned (see Box 1-3).

This concept of learning with understanding has two parts: (1) factual knowledge (e.g., about characteristics of different species) must be placed in a conceptual framework (about adaptation) to be well understood; and (2) concepts are given meaning by multiple representations that are rich in factual detail. Competent performance is built on neither factual nor conceptual understanding alone; the concepts take on meaning in the knowledge-rich contexts in which they are applied. In the context of Lionni's story, the general concept of adaptation can be clarified when placed in the context of the specific features of humans, cows, and birds that make the abstract concept of adaptation meaningful.

BOX 1-3 Learning with Understanding Supports Knowledge Use in New Situations

In one of the most famous early studies comparing the effects of "learning a procedure" with "learning with understanding," two groups of children practiced throwing darts at a target underwater.[9] One group received an explanation of refraction of light, which causes the apparent location of the target to be deceptive. The other group only practiced dart throwing, without the explanation. Both groups did equally well on the practice task, which involved a target 12 inches under water. But the group that had been instructed about the abstract principle did much better when they had to transfer to a situation in which the target was under only 4 inches of water. Because they understood what they were doing, the group that had received instruction about the refraction of light could adjust their behavior to the new task.

This essential link between the factual knowledge base and a conceptual framework can help illuminate a persistent debate in education: whether we need to emphasize "big ideas" more and facts less, or are producing graduates with a factual knowledge base that is unacceptably thin. While these concerns appear to be at odds, knowledge of facts and knowledge of important organizing ideas are mutually supportive. Studies of experts and novices—in chess, engineering, and many other domains—demonstrate that experts know considerably more relevant detail than novices in tasks within their domain and have better memory for these details (see Box 1-4). But the reason they remember more is that what novices see as separate pieces of information, experts see as organized sets of ideas.

Engineering experts, for example, can look briefly at a complex mass of circuitry and recognize it as an amplifier, and so can reproduce many of its circuits from memory using that one idea. Novices see each circuit separately, and thus remember far fewer in total. Important concepts, such as that of an amplifier, structure both what experts notice and what they are able to store in memory. Using concepts to organize information stored in memory allows for much more effective retrieval and application. Thus, the issue is not whether to emphasize facts or "big ideas" (conceptual knowledge); both are needed. Memory of factual knowledge is enhanced by conceptual knowledge, and conceptual knowledge is clarified as it is used to help organize constellations of important details. Teaching for understanding, then, requires that the core concepts such as adaptation that organize the knowledge of experts also organize instruction. This does not mean that that factual knowledge now typically taught, such as the characteristics of fish, birds, and mammals, must be replaced. Rather, that factual information is given new meaning and a new organization in memory because those features are seen as adaptive characteristics.

BOX 1-4   Experts Remember Considerably More Relevant Detail Than Novices in Tasks Within Their Domain

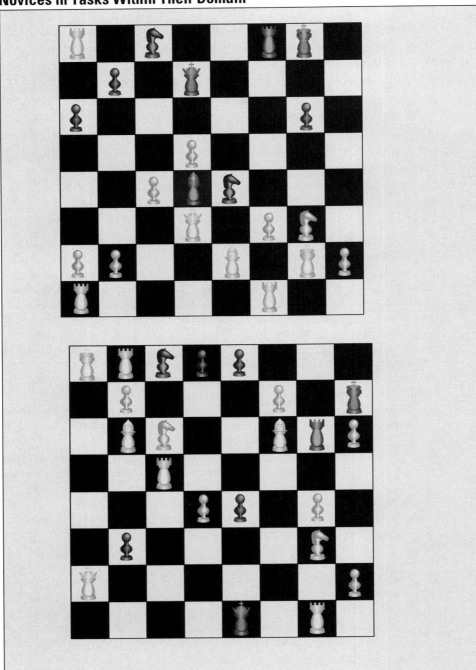

In one study, a chess master, a Class A player (good but not a master), and a novice were given 5 seconds to view a chess board position from the middle of a chess game (see below).

After 5 seconds the board was covered, and each participant attempted to reconstruct the board position on another board. This procedure was repeated for multiple trials until everyone received a perfect score. On the first trial, the master player correctly placed many more pieces than the Class A player, who in turn placed more than the novice: 16, 8, and 4, respectively. (See data graphed below.)

However, these results occurred only when the chess pieces were arranged in configurations that conformed to meaningful games of chess. When chess pieces were randomized and presented for 5 seconds, the recall of the chess master and Class A player was the same as that of the novice—they all placed 2 to 3 positions correctly. The apparent difference in memory capacity is due to a difference in pattern recognition. What the expert can remember as a single meaningful pattern, novices must remember as separate, unrelated items.

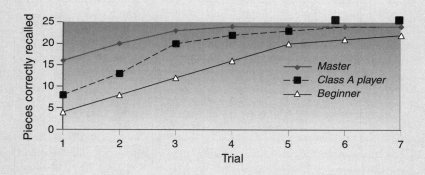

SOURCE: Chase and Simon (1973). Reprinted with permission from Elsevier.

Principle #3: The Importance of Self-Monitoring

Hero though he is for saving the fish's life, the frog in Lionni's story gets poor marks as a teacher. But the burden of learning does not fall on the teacher alone. Even the best instructional efforts can be successful only if the student can make use of the opportunity to learn. Helping students become effective learners is at the heart of the third key principle: a "metacognitive" or self-monitoring approach can help students develop the ability to take control of their own learning, consciously define learning goals, and monitor their progress in achieving them. Some teachers introduce the idea of metacognition to their students by saying, "You are the owners and operators of your own brain, but it came without an instruction book. We need to learn how we learn."

"Meta" is a prefix that can mean after, along with, or beyond. In the psychological literature, "metacognition" is used to refer to people's knowledge about themselves as information processors. This includes knowledge about what we need to do in order to learn and remember information (e.g., most adults know that they need to rehearse an unfamiliar phone number to keep it active in short-term memory while they walk across the room to dial the phone). And it includes the ability to monitor our current understanding to make sure we understand (see Box 1-5). Other examples include monitoring the degree to which we have been helpful to a group working on a project.[10]

BOX 1-5 Metacognitive Monitoring: An Example

Read the following passage from a literary critic, and pay attention to the strategies you use to comprehend:

If a serious literary critic were to write a favorable, full-length review of How Could I Tell Mother She Frightened My Boyfriends Away, Grace Plumbuster's new story, his startled readers would assume that he had gone mad, or that Grace Plumbuster was his editor's wife.

Most good readers have to back up several times in order to grasp the meaning of this passage. In contrast, poor readers tend to simply read it all the way through without pausing and asking if the passage makes sense. Needless to say, when asked to paraphrase the passage they fall short.

SOURCE: Whimbey and Whimbey (1975, p. 42).

In Lionni's story, the fish accepted the information about life on land rather passively. Had he been monitoring his understanding and actively comparing it with what he already knew, he might have noted that putting on a hat and jacket would be rather uncomfortable for a fish and would slow his swimming in the worst way. Had he been more engaged in figuring out what the frog meant, he might have asked why humans would make themselves uncomfortable and compromise their mobility. A good answer to his questions might have set the stage for learning about differences between humans and fish, and ultimately about the notion of adaptation. The concept of metacognition includes an awareness of the need to ask how new knowledge relates to or challenges what one already knows—questions that stimulate additional inquiry that helps guide further learning.[11]

The early work on metacognition was conducted with young children in laboratory contexts.[12] In studies of "metamemory," for example, young children might be shown a series of pictures (e.g., drum, tree, cup) and asked to remember them after 15 seconds of delay (with the pictures no longer visible). Adults who receive this task spontaneously rehearse during the 15-second interval. Many of the children did not. When they were explicitly told to rehearse, they would do so, and their memory was very good. But when the children took part in subsequent trials and were not reminded to rehearse, many failed to rehearse even though they were highly motivated to perform well in the memory test. These findings suggest that the children had not made the "metamemory" connection between their rehearsal strategies and their short-term memory abilities.[13]

Over time, research on metacognition (of which metamemory is considered a subset) moved from laboratory settings to the classroom. One of the most striking applications of a metacognitive approach to instruction was pioneered by Palincsar and Brown in the context of "reciprocal teaching."[14] Middle school students worked in groups (guided by a teacher) to help one another learn to read with understanding. A key to achieving this goal involves the ability to monitor one's ongoing comprehension and to initiate strategies such as rereading or asking questions when one's comprehension falters. (Box 1-5 illustrates this point.) When implemented appropriately, reciprocal teaching has been shown to have strong effects on improving students' abilities to read with understanding in order to learn.

Appropriate kinds of self-monitoring and reflection have been demonstrated to support learning with understanding in a variety of areas. In one study,[15] for example, students who were directed to engage in self-explanation as they solved mathematics problems developed deeper conceptual understanding than did students who solved those same problems but did not engage in self-explanation. This was true even though the common time limitation on both groups meant that the self-explaining students solved fewer problems in total.

Helping students become more metacognitive about their own thinking and learning is closely tied to teaching practices that emphasize self-assessment. The early work of Thorndike[16] demonstrated that feedback is important for learning. However, there is a difference between responding to feedback that someone else provides and actively seeking feedback in order to assess one's current levels of thinking and understanding. Providing support for self-assessment is an important component of effective teaching. This can include giving students opportunities to test their ideas by building things and seeing whether they work, performing experiments that seek to falsify hypotheses, and so forth. Support for self-assessment is also provided by opportunities for discussion where teachers and students can express different views and explore which ones appear to make the most sense. Such questioning models the kind of dialogue that effective learners internalize. Helping students explicitly understand that a major purpose of these activities is to support metacognitive learning is an important component of successful teaching strategies.[17]

Supporting students to become aware of and engaged in their own learning will serve them well in all learning endeavors. To be optimally effective, however, some metacognitive strategies need to be taught in the context of individual subject areas. For example, guiding one's learning in a particular subject area requires awareness of the disciplinary standards for knowing. To illustrate, asking the question "What is the evidence for this claim?" is relevant whether one is studying history, science, or mathematics. However, what counts as evidence often differs. In mathematics, for example, formal proof is very important. In science, formal proofs are used when possible, but empirical observations and experimental data also play a major role. In history, multiple sources of evidence are sought and attention to the perspective from which an author writes and to the purpose of the writing is particularly important. Overall, knowledge of the discipline one is studying affects people's abilities to monitor their own understanding and evaluate others' claims effectively.

LEARNING ENVIRONMENTS AND THE DESIGN OF INSTRUCTION

The key principles of learning discussed above can be organized into a framework for thinking about teaching, learning, and the design of classroom and school environments. In *How People Learn*, four design characteristics are described that can be used as lenses to evaluate the effectiveness of teaching and learning environments. These lenses are not themselves research findings; rather, they are implications drawn from the research base:

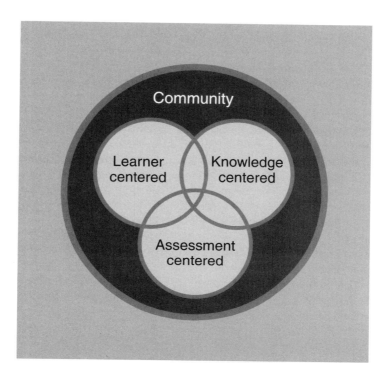

FIGURE 1-1 Perspectives on learning environments.

- The *learner-centered lens* encourages attention to preconceptions, and begins instruction with what students think and know.
- The *knowledge-centered lens* focuses on what is to be taught, why it is taught, and what mastery looks like.
- The *assessment-centered lens* emphasizes the need to provide frequent opportunities to make students' thinking and learning visible as a guide for both the teacher and the student in learning and instruction.
- The *community-centered lens* encourages a culture of questioning, respect, and risk taking.

These aspects of the classroom environment are illustrated in Figure 1-1 and are discussed below.

Learner-Centered Classroom Environments

Instruction must begin with close attention to students' ideas, knowledge, skills, and attitudes, which provide the foundation on which new learning builds. Sometimes, as in the case of Lionni's fish, learners' existing ideas lead to misconceptions. More important, however, those existing conceptions can also provide a path to new understandings. Lionni's fish mistakenly projects the model of a fish onto humans, birds, and cows. But the fish does know a lot about being a fish, and that experience can provide a starting point for understanding adaptation. How do the scales and fins of a fish help it survive? How would clothing and feathers affect a fish? The fish's existing knowledge and experience provide a route to understanding adaptation in other species. Similarly, the ideas and experiences of students provide a route to new understandings both about and beyond their experience.

Sometimes the experiences relevant to teaching would appear to be similar for all students: the ways in which forces act on a falling ball or feather, for example. But students in any classroom are likely to differ in how much they have been encouraged to observe, think about, or talk about a falling ball or feather. Differences may be larger still when the subject is a social rather than a natural phenomenon because the experiences themselves, as well as norms regarding reflection, expression, and interaction, differ for children from different families, communities, and cultures. Finally, students' expectations regarding their own performances, including what it means to be intelligent, can differ in ways that affect their persistence in and engagement with learning.

Being learner-centered, then, involves paying attention to students' backgrounds and cultural values, as well as to their abilities. To build effectively on what learners bring to the classroom, teachers must pay close attention to individual students' starting points and to their progress on learning tasks. They must present students with "just-manageable difficulties"—challenging enough to maintain engagement and yet not so challenging as to lead to discouragement. They must find the strengths that will help students connect with the information being taught. Unless these connections are made explicitly, they often remain inert and so do not support subsequent learning.

Knowledge-Centered Classroom Environments

While the learner-centered aspects of the classroom environment focus on the student as the starting point, the knowledge-centered aspects focus on what is taught (subject matter), why it is taught (understanding), how the knowledge should be organized to support the development of expertise (curriculum), and what competence or mastery looks like (learning goals). Several important questions arise when one adopts the knowledge-centered lens:

- What is it important for students to know and be able to do?
- What are the core concepts that organize our understanding of this subject matter, and what concrete cases and detailed knowledge will allow students to master those concepts effectively?
- [The knowledge-centered lens overlaps with the assessment-centered lens (discussed below) when we ask], How will we know when students achieve mastery?[18] This question overlaps the knowledge-centered and assessment-centered lenses.

An important point that emerges from the expert–novice literature is the need to emphasize *connected* knowledge that is organized around the foundational ideas of a discipline. Research on expertise shows that it is the organization of knowledge that underlies experts' abilities to understand and solve problems.[19] Bruner, one of the founding fathers of the new science of learning, has long argued the importance of this insight to education:[20]

> The curriculum of a subject should be determined by the most fundamental understanding that can be achieved of the underlying principles that give structure to a subject. Teaching specific topics or skills without making clear their context in the broader fundamental structure of a field of knowledge is uneconomical. . . . An understanding of fundamental principles and ideas appears to be the main road to adequate transfer of training. To understand something as a specific instance of a more general case—which is what understanding a more fundamental structure means—is to have learned not only a specific thing but also a model for understanding other things like it that one may encounter.

Knowledge-centered and learner-centered environments intersect when educators take seriously the idea that students must be supported to develop expertise over time; it is not sufficient to simply provide them with expert models and expect them to learn. For example, intentionally organizing subject matter to allow students to follow a path of "progressive differentiation" (e.g., from qualitative understanding to more precise quantitative understanding of a particular phenomenon) involves a simultaneous focus on the structure of the knowledge to be mastered and the learning process of students.[21]

In a comparative study of the teaching of mathematics in China and the United States, Ma sought to understand why Chinese students outperform students from the United States in elementary mathematics, even though teachers in China often have less formal education. What she documents is that Chinese teachers are far more likely to identify core mathematical concepts (such as decomposing a number in subtraction with regrouping), to plan instruction to support mastery of the skills and knowledge required for conceptual understanding, and to use those concepts to develop clear connections across topics (see Box 1-6).

If identifying a set of "enduring connected ideas" is critical to effective educational design, it is a task not just for teachers, but also for the developers of curricula, text books, and other instructional materials; universities and other teacher preparation institutions; and the public and private groups involved in developing subject matter standards for students and their teachers. There is some good work already in place, but much more needs to be done. Indeed, an American Association for the Advancement of Science review of middle school and high school science textbooks found that although a great deal of detailed and sophisticated material was presented, very little attention was given to the concepts that support an understanding of the discipline.[22]

Each of the chapters in this volume describes core ideas in a subject area that support conceptual understanding and that connect the particular topic discussed to the larger discipline: the concepts of historical evidence and perspective in history; the concepts of proportionality and dependence in mathematics; and the concepts of scientific evidence and modeling in science. Because textbooks sometimes focus primarily on facts and details and neglect organizing principles, creating a knowledge-centered classroom will often require that a teacher go beyond the textbook to help students see a structure to the knowledge, mainly by introducing them to essential concepts. These chapters provide examples of how this might be done.

Assessment-Centered Classroom Environments

Formative assessments—ongoing assessments designed to make students' thinking visible to both teachers and students—are essential. Assessments are a central feature of both a learner-centered and a knowledge-centered classroom. They permit the teacher to grasp students' preconceptions, which is critical to working with and building on those notions. Once the knowledge to be learned is well defined, assessment is required to monitor student progress (in mastering concepts as well as factual information), to understand where students are in the developmental path from informal to formal thinking, and to design instruction that is responsive to student progress.

An important feature of the assessment-centered classroom is assessment that supports learning by providing students with opportunities to revise and improve their thinking.[23] Such assessments help students see their own progress over time and point to problems that need to be addressed in instruction. They may be quite informal. A physics teacher, for example, reports showing students who are about to study structure a video clip of a bridge collapsing. He asks his students why they think the bridge collapsed. In giving their answers, the students reveal their preconceptions about structure. Differences in their answers provide puzzles that engage the students in self-questioning. As the students study structure, they can mark their changing understanding against their initial beliefs. Assessment in this sense provides a starting point for additional instruction rather than a summative ending. Formative assessments are often referred to as "classroom-based assessments" because, as compared with standardized assessments, they are most likely to occur in the context of the classrooms. However, many classroom-based assessments are summative rather than formative (they are used to provide grades at the end of a unit with no opportunities to revise). In addition, one can use standardized assessments in a formative manner (e.g., to help teachers identify areas where students need special help).

Ultimately, students need to develop metacognitive abilities—the habits of mind necessary to assess their own progress—rather than relying solely on external indicators. A number of studies show that achievement improves when students are encouraged to assess their own contributions and work.[24] It is also important to help students assess the kinds of strategies they are using to learn and solve problems. For example, in quantitative courses such as physics, many students simply focus on formulas and fail to think first about the problem to be solved and its relation to key ideas in the discipline (e.g., Newton's second law). When students are helped to do the latter, their performance on new problems greatly improves.[25]

The classroom interactions described in the following chapters provide many examples of formative assessment in action, though these interactions are often not referred to as assessments. Early activities or problems given to students are designed to make student thinking public and, therefore, observable by teachers. Work in groups and class discussions provide students with the opportunity to ask each other questions and revise their own thinking. In some cases, the formative assessments are formal; in elementary mathematics, for example, the number knowledge test allows teachers to quickly assess the current mastery level of a student in order to guide the choice of the subsequent instructional activities. But even when informal, the teaching described in those chapters involves frequent opportunities for both teachers and students to assess understanding and its progress over time.

Community-Centered Classroom Environments

A community-centered approach requires the development of norms for the classroom and school, as well as connections to the outside world,

BOX 1-6 Organizing Knowledge Around Core Concepts: Subtraction with Regrouping[26]

A study by Ma[27] compares the knowledge of elementary mathematics of teachers in the United States and in China. She gives the teachers the following scenario (p. 1):

> Look at these questions (52 – 25; 91 – 79 etc.). How would you approach these problems if you were teaching second grade? What would you say pupils would need to understand or be able to do before they could start learning subtraction with regrouping?

The responses of teachers were wide-ranging, reflecting very different levels of understanding of the core mathematical concepts. Some teachers focused on the need for students to learn the *procedure* for subtraction with regrouping (p. 2):

> Whereas there is a number like 21 – 9, they would need to know that you cannot subtract 9 from 1, then in turn you have to borrow a 10 from the tens space, and when you borrow that 1, it equals 10, you cross out the 2 that you had, you turn it into a 10, you now have 11 – 9, you do that subtraction problem then you have the 1 left and you bring it down.

Some teachers in both the United States and China saw the knowledge to be mastered as procedural, though the proportion who held this view was considerably higher in the United States. Many teachers in both countries believed students needed a conceptual understanding, but within this group there were considerable differences. Some teachers wanted children to think through what they were doing, while others wanted them to understand core mathematical concepts. The difference can be seen in the two explanations below.

> They have to understand what the number 64 means. . . . I would show that the number 64, and the number 5 tens and 14 ones, equal the 64. I would try to draw the comparison between that because when you are doing regrouping it is not so much knowing the facts, it is the regrouping part that has to be understood. The regrouping right from the beginning.

This explanation is more conceptual than the first and helps students think more deeply about the subtraction problem. But it does not make clear to students the more fundamental concept of the place value system that allows the subtraction problems to be connected to other areas of mathematics. In the place value system, numbers are "composed" of tens. Students already have been taught to compose tens as 10 ones, and hundreds as 10 tens. A Chinese teacher explains as follows (p. 11):

> What is the rate for composing a higher value unit? The answer is simple: 10. Ask students how many ones there are in a 10, or ask them what the rate for composing a higher value unit is, their answers will be the same: 10. However, the effect of the two questions on their learning is not the

same. When you remind students that 1 ten equals 10 ones, you tell them the fact that is used in the procedure. And, this somehow confines them to the fact. When you require them to think about the rate for composing a higher value unit, you lead them to a theory that explains the fact as well as the procedure. Such an understanding is more powerful than a specific fact. It can be applied to more situations. Once they realize that the rate of composing a higher value unit, 10 is the reason why we decompose a ten into 10 ones, they will apply it to other situations. You don't need to remind them again that 1 hundred equals 10 tens when in the future they learn subtraction with three-digit numbers. They will be able to figure it out on their own.

Emphasizing core concepts does not imply less of an emphasis on mastery of procedures or algorithms. Rather, it suggests that procedural knowledge and skills be *organized around core concepts*. Ma describes those Chinese teachers who emphasize core concepts as seeing the knowledge in "packages" in which the concepts and skills are related. While the packages differed somewhat from teacher to teacher, the knowledge "pieces" to be included were the same. She illustrates a knowledge package for subtraction with regrouping, which is reproduced below (p. 19).

The two shaded elements in the knowledge package are considered critical. "Addition and subtraction within 20" is seen as the ability that anchors more complex problem solving with larger numbers. That ability is viewed as both conceptual and procedural. "Composing and decomposing a higher value unit" is the core concept that ties this set of problems to the mathematics students have done in the past and to all other areas of mathematics they will learn in the future.

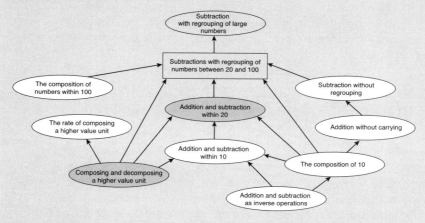

SOURCE: Ma (1999). Illustration reprinted with permission of Lawrence Erlbaum Associates.

that support core learning values. Learning is influenced in fundamental ways by the context in which it takes place. Every community, including classrooms and schools, operates with a set of norms, a culture—explicit or implicit—that influences interactions among individuals. This culture, in turn, mediates learning. The principles of *How People Learn* have important implications for classroom culture. Consider the finding that new learning builds on existing conceptions, for example. If classroom norms encourage and reward students only for being "right," we would expect students to hesitate when asked to reveal their unschooled thinking. And yet revealing preconceptions and changing ideas in the course of instruction is a critical component of effective learning and responsive teaching. A focus on student thinking requires classroom norms that encourage the expression of ideas (tentative and certain, partially and fully formed), as well as risk taking. It requires that mistakes be viewed not as revelations of inadequacy, but as helpful contributions in the search for understanding.[28]

Similarly, effective approaches to teaching metacognitive strategies rely on initial teacher modeling of the monitoring process, with a gradual shift to students. Through asking questions of other students, skills at monitoring understanding are honed, and through answering the questions of fellow students, understanding of what one has communicated effectively is strengthened. To those ends, classroom norms that encourage questioning and allow students to try the role of the questioner (sometimes reserved for teachers) are important.

While the chapters in this volume make few direct references to learning communities, they are filled with descriptions of interactions revealing classroom cultures that support learning with understanding. In these classrooms, students are encouraged to question; there is much discussion among students who work to solve problems in groups. Teachers ask many probing questions, and incorrect or naïve answers to questions are explored with interest, as are different strategies for analyzing a problem and reaching a solution.

PUTTING THE PRINCIPLES TO WORK IN THE CLASSROOM

Although the key findings from the research literature reviewed above have clear implications for practice, they are not at a level of specificity that would allow them to be immediately useful to teachers. While teachers may fully grasp the importance of working with students' prior conceptions, they need to know the typical conceptions of students with respect to the topic about to be taught. For example, it may help science teachers to know that students harbor misconceptions that can be problematic, but those teachers will be in a much better position to teach a unit on light if they know specifically what misconceptions students typically exhibit when learning about light.

Moreover, while teachers may be fully convinced that knowledge should be organized around important concepts, the concepts that help organize their particular topic may not be at all clear. History teachers may know that they are to teach certain eras, for example, but they often have little support in identifying core concepts that will allow students to understand the era more deeply than would be required to reproduce a set of facts. To make this observation is in no way to fault teachers. Indeed, as the group involved in this project engaged in the discussion, drafting, and review of various chapters of this volume, it became clear that the relevant core concepts in specific areas are not always obvious, transparent, or uncontested.

Finally, approaches to supporting metacognition can be quite difficult to carry out in classroom contexts. Some approaches to instruction reduce metacognition to its simplest form, such as making note of the subtitles in a text and what they signal about what is to come, or rereading for meaning. The more challenging tasks of metacognition are difficult to reduce to an instructional recipe: to help students develop the habits of mind to reflect spontaneously on their own thinking and problem solving, to encourage them to activate relevant background knowledge and monitor their understanding, and to support them in trying the lens through which those in a particular discipline view the world. The teacher–student interactions described in the chapters of this volume and the discipline-specific examples of supporting students in monitoring their thinking give texture to the instructional challenge that a list of metacognitive strategies could not.

INTENT AND ORGANIZATION OF THIS VOLUME

In the preface, we note that this volume is intended to take the work of *How People Learn* a next step in specificity: to provide examples of how its principles and findings might be incorporated in the teaching of a set of topics that frequently appear in the K–12 curriculum. The goal is to provide for teachers what we have argued above is critical to effective learning—the application of concepts (about learning) in enough different, concrete contexts to give them deeper meaning.

To this end, we invited contributions from a variety of researchers with extensive experience in teaching or partnering with teachers, whose work incorporates the ideas highlighted in *How People Learn*. The chapter authors were given leeway in the extent to which the three learning principles and the four classroom characteristics described above were treated explicitly or implicitly. Most of the authors chose to emphasize the three learning principles explicitly as they described their lessons and findings. The four design characteristics of the *How People Learn* framework (Figure 1-1) are implicitly represented in the activities sketched in each of the chapters but often not discussed explicitly. Interested readers can map these discussions to the *How People Learn* framework if they desire.

The chapters that follow explore the application of core learning principles in three content areas and at three different grade levels. The text is organized into parts by discipline, and each part begins with a chapter that considers the learning principles in the context of the discipline generally. The chapters that follow then explore particular topics. While we began with a common description of our goal, we had no common model from which to work. One can point to excellent research papers on principles of learning, but the chapters in this volume are far more focused on teaching a particular topic. There are also examples of excellent curricula, but the goal of these chapters is to give far more attention to the principles of learning and their incorporation into teaching than is typical of curriculum materials. Thus the authors were charting new territory as they undertook this task, and each found a somewhat different path. As a result, the character of each of the three sections (history, mathematics, and science) differs considerably.

The history part contains three chapters (2 through 4). The first of these treats the principles of learning as they apply to the discipline of history in impressive depth. Elementary and middle school history are treated together at length in Chapter 3, a decision that permits the authors to demonstrate progression in the sophistication with which the same concepts can be discussed at different grade levels. Chapter 4 on high school history also focuses on the treatment of particular concepts that fall under the general topic of exploration and discovery. Because there is no agreed-upon sequence of topics in history during the K–12 years, using a single broad topic allows for a clearer focus on the nature of the investigations in which students might engage at different grade levels.

The mathematics part consists of four chapters. Chapter 5 presents an introduction to the principles as they apply to mathematics generally. The three chapters that follow treat important topics at the three different grade levels: whole number in elementary school (Chapter 6), rational number in middle school (Chapter 7), and functions in high school (Chapter 8). These three topics are routinely covered in K–12 curricula in this sequence and represent the major conceptual shifts required of students in mathematics.

Following the introductory Chapter 9, the science part treats three very different topics: light and shadow at the elementary school level (Chapter 10), gravity at the middle school level (Chapter 11), and genetics and evolution at the high school level (Chapter 12). The sequence of K–12 science topics in the United States is far less predictable than that of mathematics. The topics in this part of the volume were chosen at the three grade levels for the opportunities they provide to explore the learning principles of interest, rather than for their common representation in a standard curricular sequence. Light as a topic might just as well appear in middle or high school as in elementary school, for example, and physics is generally taught either in middle school or high school.

The reader will find that the chapters in this volume differ a great deal from one to the next. In inviting contributions, we drew on the expertise and talents of individuals whose work has differed not only in topic, but in the aspects of learning investigated most deeply. For example, the introductory chapter in the history part (Chapter 2) gives more detailed treatment of the principles as they relate to the discipline of history than do the introductory chapters in the other two disciplines. This treatment reflects the research program undertaken by Peter J. Lee and his colleagues, which has systematically explored student conceptions about history and its core concepts. Annemarie Sullivan Palincsar, one of the authors of the elementary science chapter, has done extensive work on metacognition, and the chapter by Magnusson and Palincsar (Chapter 10) is particularly strong in its emphasis on supporting the development of metacognitive skills in students.

Mathematics chapter authors Sharon Griffin, Joan Moss, and Mindy Kalchman all worked closely with Robbie Case, whose untimely death prevented his intended participation in this volume. Case and his colleagues did extensive research on central conceptual structures in mathematics, making the treatment of core conceptual understandings a strength of these chapters. Chapters authored by teachers (Chapter 4 by Robert B. Bain and Chapter 11 by James Minstrell and Pamela Kraus) are particularly strong in the classroom experience they bring to student–teacher interactions and the familiarity with the challenges of teaching they communicate. And the chapters written by authors who have done extensive work on curriculum development (Chapter 5 by Karen C. Fuson, Mindy Kalchman, and John D. Bransford, Chapter 6 by Sharon Griffin, and Chapter 12 by James Stewart, Jennifer L. Cartier, and Cynthia M. Passmore) exhibit strengths in drawing connections among concepts across a topic area. The work of Rosalyn Ashby, Peter J. Lee, and Denis Shemilt in Chapter 3 looks at the development of the concepts of a discipline (in this case history) over the span of school years in more depth than does any other chapter.

These differences we take to be a varied set of strengths. We did not attempt to impose uniformity across chapters, since we believed that the authors could make their greatest individual contributions by emphasizing their specific areas of expertise. For this reason, we urge readers to cross the disciplines and take lessons from one that might be applied to others.

The major focus of the volume is student learning. It is clear that successful and sustainable changes in educational practice also require learning by others, including teachers, principals, superintendents, parents, and community members. For the present volume, however, student learning is the focus, and issues of adult learning are left for others to take up.

The willingness of the chapter authors to accept this task represents an outstanding contribution to the field. First, all the authors devoted considerable time to this effort—more than any of them had anticipated initially. Second, they did so knowing that some readers will disagree with virtually every teaching decision discussed in these chapters. But by making their thinking visible and inviting discussion, they are helping the field progress as a whole. The examples discussed in this volume are not offered as "the" way to teach, but as approaches to instruction that in some important respects are designed to incorporate the principles of learning highlighted in *How People Learn* and that can serve as valuable examples for further discussion.

In 1960, Nobel laureate Richard Feynman, who was well known as an extraordinary teacher, delivered a series of lectures in introductory physics that were recorded and preserved. Feynman's focus was on the fundamental principles of physics, not the fundamental principles of learning. But his lessons apply nonetheless. He emphasized how little the fundamental principles of physics "as we now understand them" tell us about the complexity of the world despite the enormous importance of the insights they offer. Feynman offered an effective analogy for the relationship between understanding general principles identified through scientific efforts and understanding the far more complex set of behaviors for which those principles provide only a broad set of constraints:[29]

> We can imagine that this complicated array of moving things which constitutes "the world" is something like a great chess game being played by the gods, and we are observers of the game. We do not know what the rules of the game are; all we are allowed to do is to *watch* the playing. Of course, if we watch long enough, we may eventually catch on to a few of the rules. *The rules of the game* are what we mean by *fundamental physics*. Even if we knew every rule, however, we might not be able to understand why a particular move is made in the game, merely because it is too complicated and our minds are limited. If you play chess you must know that it is easy to learn all the rules, and yet it is often very hard to select the best move or to understand why a player moves as he does. . . . Aside from not knowing all of the rules, what we really can explain in terms of those rules is very limited, because almost all situations are so enormously complicated that we cannot follow the plays of the game using the rules, much less tell what is going to happen next. (p. 24)

The individual chapters in this volume might be viewed as presentations of the strategies taken by individuals (or teams) who understand the rules of the teaching and learning "game" *as we now understand them*. Feynman's metaphor is helpful in two respects. First, what each chapter offers goes well beyond the science of learning and relies on creativity in strategy development. And yet what we know from research thus far is critical in defining the constraints on strategy development. Second, what we expect to learn from a well-played game (in this case, what we expect to learn from well-conceptualized instruction) is not how to reproduce it. Rather, we look for insights about playing/teaching well that can be brought to one's own game. Even if we could replicate every move, this would be of little help. In an actual game, the best move must be identified in response to another party's move. In just such a fashion, a teacher's "game" must respond to the rather unpredictable "moves" of the students in the classroom whose learning is the target.

This, then, is not a "how to" book, but a discussion of strategies that incorporate the rules of the game as we currently understand them. The science of learning is a young, emerging one. We expect our understanding to evolve as we design new learning opportunities and observe the outcomes, as we study learning among children in different contexts and from different backgrounds, and as emerging research techniques and opportunities provide new insights. These chapters, then, might best be viewed as part of a conversation begun some years ago with the first *How People Learn* volume. By clarifying ideas through a set of rich examples, we hope to encourage the continuation of a productive dialogue well into the future.

NOTES

1. National Research Council, 2000.
2. Lionni, 1970.
3. National Research Council, 2000, p. 84.
4. Needham and Baillargeon, 1993.
5. diSessa, 1982.
6. Vosniadou and Brewer, 1989.
7. Carey and Gelman, 1991; Driver et al., 1994.
8. Hanson, 1970.
9. Judd, 1908; see a conceptual replication by Hendrickson and Schroeder, 1941.
10. White and Fredrickson, 1998.
11. Bransford and Schwartz, 1999.
12. Brown, 1975; Flavell, 1973.
13. Keeney et al., 1967.
14. Palincsar and Brown, 1984.
15. Aleven and Koedinger, 2002.
16. Thorndike, 1913.
17. Brown et al., 1983.
18. Wood and Sellers, 1997.
19. National Research Council, 2000, Chapter 2.
20. Bruner, 1960, pp. 6, 25, 31.

21. National Research Council, 2000.
22. American Association for the Advancement of Science Project 2061 Website. http://www.project2061.org/curriculum.html.
23. Barron et al., 1998; Black and William, 1989; Hunt and Minstrell, 1994; Vye et al., 1998.
24. Lin and Lehman, 1999; National Research Council, 2000; White and Fredrickson, 1998.
25. Leonard et al., 1996.
26. National Research Council, 2003, pp. 78-79.
27. Ma, 1999.
28. Brown and Campione, 1994; Cobb et al., 1992.
29. Feynman, 1995, p. 24.

REFERENCES

Aleven, V., and Koedinger, K. (2002). An effective metacognitive strategy—Learning by doing and explaining with a computer-based cognitive tutor. *Cognitive Science, 26*, 147-179.

American Association for the Advancement of Science. (2004). About *Project 2061.* Available: http://www.project2061.org/about/default/htm. [August 11, 2004].

Barron, B.J., Schwartz, D.L., Vye, N.J., Moore, A., Petrosino, A., Zech, L., Bransford, J.D., and Cognition and Technology Group at Vanderbilt. (1998). Doing with understanding: Lessons from research on problem and project-based learning. *Journal of Learning Sciences, 7*(3 and 4), 271-312.

Black, P., and William, D. (1989). Assessment and classroom learning. *Special Issue of Assessment in Education: Principles, Policy and Practice, 5*(1), 7-75.

Bransford, J.D., and Schwartz, D.L. (1999). Rethinking transfer: A simple proposal with multiple implications. *Review of Research in Education, 24*(40), 61-100.

Brown, A.L. (1975). The development of memory: Knowing about knowing and knowing how to know. In H.W. Reese (Ed.), *Advances in child development and behavior* (p. 10). New York: Academic Press.

Brown, A.L., and Campione, J.C. (1994). Guided discovery in a community of learners. In K. McGilly (Ed.), *Classroom lessons: Integrating cognitive theory and classroom practices.* Cambridge, MA: MIT Press.

Brown, A.L., Bransford, J.D., Ferrara, R.A., and Campione J.C. (1983). Learning, remembering, and understanding. In J.H. Flavell and E.M Markman (Eds.), *Handbook of child psychology: Cognitive development volume 3* (pp. 78-166). New York: Wiley.

Bruner, J. (1960). *The process of education.* Cambridge, MA: Harvard University Press.

Carey, S., and Gelman, R. (1991). *The epigenesis of mind: Essays on biology and cognition.* Mahwah, NJ: Lawrence Erlbaum Associates.

Chase, W.G., and Simon, H.A. (1973). Perception in chess. *Cognitive Psychology, 4*(1), 55-81.

Cobb P., Yackel, E., and Wood, T. (1992). A constructivist alternative to the representational view of mind in mathematics education. *Journal for Research in Mathematics Education, 19*, 99-114.

Cognition and Technology Group at Vanderbilt. (1996). Looking at technology in context: A framework for understanding technology and education research. In D.C. Berliner and R.C. Calfee (Eds.), *The handbook of educational psychology* (pp. 807-840). New York: Simon and Schuster-MacMillan.

diSessa, A. (1982). Unlearning Aristotelian physics: A study of knowledge-based learning. *Cognitive Science, 6*(2), 37-75.

Driver, R., Squires, A., Rushworth, P., and Wood-Robinson, V. (1994). *Making sense out of secondary science.* London, England: Routledge Press.

Feynman, R.P. (1995). *Six easy pieces: Essentials of physics explained by its most brilliant teacher.* Reading, MA: Perseus Books.

Flavell, J.H. (1973). Metacognitive aspects of problem-solving. In L.B. Resnick (Ed.), *The nature of intelligence.* Mahwah, NJ: Lawrence Erlbaum Associates.

Hanson, N.R. (1970). A picture theory of theory meaning. In R.G. Colodny (Ed.), *The nature and function of scientific theories* (pp. 233-274). Pittsburgh, PA: University of Pittsburgh Press.

Hendrickson, G., and Schroeder, W.H. (1941). Transfer training in learning to hit a submerged target. *Journal of Educational Psychology, 32,* 205-213.

Hunt, E., and Minstrell, J. (1994). A cognitive approach to the teaching of physics. In K. McGilly (Ed.), *Classroom lessons: Integrating cognitive theory and classroom practice* (pp. 51-74). Cambridge, MA: MIT Press.

Judd, C.H. (1908). The relation of special training to general intelligence. *Educational Review, 36,* 28-42.

Keeney, T.J., Cannizzo, S.R., and Flavell, J.H. (1967). Spontaneous and induced verbal rehearsal in a recall task. *Child Development, 38,* 953-966.

Leonard, W.J., Dufresne, R.J., and Mestre, J.P. (1996). Using qualitative problem solving strategies to highlight the role of conceptual knowledge in solving problems. *American Journal of Physics, 64,* 1495-1503.

Lin, X.D., and Lehman, J. (1999). Supporting learning of variable control in a computer-based biology environment: Effects of prompting college students to reflect on their own thinking. *Journal of Research in Science Teaching, 36*(7), 837-858.

Lionni, L. (1970). *Fish is fish.* New York: Scholastic Press.

Ma, L. (1999). *Knowing and teaching elementary mathematics.* Mahwah, NJ: Lawrence Erlbaum Associates.

National Research Council. (1999). *How people learn: Brain, mind, experience, and school.* Committee on Developments in the Science of Learning. J. D. Bransford, A.L. Brown, and R.R. Cocking (Eds.). Commission on Behavioral and Social Sciences and Education. Washington, DC: National Academy Press.

National Research Council. (2000). *How people learn: Brain, mind, experience, and school, Expanded edition.* Committee on Developments in the Science of Learning and Committee on Learning Research and Educational Practice. J.D. Bransford, A. Brown, and R.R. Cocking (Eds.). Commission on Behavioral and Social Sciences and Education. Washington, DC: National Academy Press.

National Research Council. (2003). *Learning and instruction: A SERP research agenda.* Panel on Learning and Instruction, Strategic Education Research Partnership. M.S. Donovan and J.W. Pellegrino (Eds.). Division of Behavioral and Social Sciences and Education. Washington, DC: The National Academies Press.

Needham, A., and Baillargeon, R. (1993). Intuitions about support in 4 1/2 month-old-infants. *Cognition, 47*(2), 121-148.

Palincsar, A.S., and Brown, A.L. (1984). Reciprocal teaching of comprehension monitoring activities. *Cognition and Instruction, 1*, 117-175.

Thorndike, E.L. (1913). *Educational psychology* (Vols. 1 and 2). New York: Columbia University Press.

Vosniadou, S., and Brewer, W.F. (1989). *The concept of the Earth's shape: A study of conceptual change in childhood.* Unpublished manuscript. Champaign, IL: Center for the Study of Reading, University of Illinois.

Vye, N.J., Schwartz, D.L., Bransford, J.D., Barron, B.J., Zech, L., and Cognitive and Technology Group at Vanderbilt. (1998). SMART environments that support monitoring, reflection, and revision. In D. Hacker, J. Dunlosky, and A. Graessner (Eds.), *Metacognition in educational theory and practice.* Mahwah, NJ: Lawrence Erlbaum Associates.

Whimbey, A., and Whimbey, L.S. (1975). *Intelligence can be taught.* New York: Dutton.

White, B.Y., and Fredrickson, J.R. (1998). Inquiry, modeling, and metacognition: Making science accessible to all students. *Cognition and Instruction, 16*(1), 3-118.

Wood, T., and Sellers, P. (1997). Deepening the analysis: Longitudinal assessment of a problem-centered mathematics program. *Journal for Research in Mathematics Education, 28*, 163-186.

Part I

HISTORY

2

Putting Principles into Practice: Understanding History

Peter J. Lee

A major principle emerging from the work on *How People Learn* is that students do not come to their classrooms empty-handed. They bring with them ideas based on their own experience of how the world works and how people are likely to behave. Such ideas can be helpful to history teachers, but they can also create problems because ideas that work well in the everyday world are not always applicable to the study of history. The very fact that we are dealing with the past makes it easy for misconceptions to arise (soldiers and farmers are not the same now as in the seventeenth century, and "liberty" did not have the same meaning for people then as it does today). But problems with everyday ideas can go deeper. Students also have ideas about how we know about the past. If they believe, for example, that we can know nothing unless we were there to see it, they will have difficulty seeing how history is possible at all. They will think that because we cannot go back in time and see what happened, historians must just be guessing or, worse, making it up. If, as teachers, we do not know what ideas our students are working with, we cannot address such misconceptions. Even when we think we are making a difference, students may simply be assimilating what we say into their existing preconceptions.

Another principle of *How People Learn* is that students need a firm foundation of factual knowledge ordered around the key concepts of the discipline. Some of the key concepts for the study of history are concerned with the content or substance of history—with the way people and societies work. These substantive concepts include, for example, political concepts such as state, government, and power, and economic concepts such as trade, wealth, and tax. But understanding history also involves concepts of a different kind, such as evidence, cause, and change.

Historians talk and write about things that go on in the world. Their histories are full of pioneers, politicians, and preachers, or of battles, bureaucracies, and banks. They give their readers explanations, they use evidence, and they write accounts, but their books are not about the idea of explanation, or the notion of evidence, or what kind of thing a historical account is. Rather, they use their own (usually sophisticated) understandings of evidence or explanation to write books about Columbus or the Maya or the American Revolution. Nevertheless, concepts such as evidence lie at the heart of history as a discipline. They shape our understanding of what it is to "do" history and allow us to organize our content knowledge (see Box 2-1).

There is no convenient agreed-upon term for this knowledge of the discipline. It is sometimes called "metahistorical"—literally, "beyond history"—because the knowledge involved is not part of what historians study, but knowledge of the kind of study in which they are involved. Another term sometimes used is "second-order" knowledge, denoting a layer of knowledge that lies behind the production of the actual content or substance of history. Finally, because the knowledge involved is built into the discipline of history, rather than what historians find out, another term used is "disciplinary" knowledge. In this chapter, all three terms are used interchangeably to refer to ideas about "doing history." It is important to stress that the intent here is not to suggest that students in school will be doing history at the same level or even in the same way as historians. The point is rather that students bring to school tacit ideas of what history is, and that we must address these ideas if we are to help them make progress in understanding what teachers and historians say about the past.

Once we start to include ideas of this kind among the key concepts of the discipline, we can see that they also provide a basis for enabling students to think about their own learning. We thereby arrive at the third principle emphasized in *How People Learn*—the importance of metacognitive strategies (see Chapter 1). Monitoring one's own learning in history means, among other things, knowing what questions to ask of sources and why caution is required in understanding people of the past. It means knowing what to look for in evaluating a historical account of the past, which in turn requires understanding that historians' accounts are related to questions and themes. In short, it means having some sense of what counts as "doing" history.

In Box 2-1, for example, Angela is implicitly asking whether her group is making the right moves in its attempt to explain why World War II started. She is using her knowledge of what counts as a good explanation in history to question how well the group really understands why the war began. In this way, metahistorical (disciplinary) concepts allow students to begin to monitor their understanding of particular events in the past. As metacognitive strategies of this kind become explicit, they play an increasingly important role in learning.

This introductory chapter first explores students' preconceptions about history, pointing out some key concepts involved in making sense of the discipline. It considers students' ideas of time and change, of how we know about the past, of how we explain historical events and processes, and of what historical accounts are, and why they so often differ (second-order ideas). The discussion then turns to students' preconceptions of how political and economic activities work (substantive concepts). Of course, students' ideas change as their experience grows and they encounter new problems; this means we need to consider how we might expect students' ideas to develop as we teach them. Although there is a growing volume of research on students' ideas about history, one that is expanding particularly rapidly in the United States, it is important to remember that there has been much less work of this kind in history than in science or mathematics.[1] Research conducted in the United States and Europe over the past three decades appears to suggest that some of the key concepts of history (the discipline) are counterintuitive, and that some of the working assumptions about history used by students are much more powerful than others and may be developed in a systematic way over the years spent studying history in schools. The chapter ends with an exposition of how teachers can present history to their students in a way that works to develop historical understanding.

HISTORY AND EVERYDAY IDEAS

What do we mean by saying that history is "counterintuitive"? The "intuitions" at stake here are the everyday ideas students bring to history lessons. They are the ideas that students use to make sense of everyday life, and on the whole they work very well for that purpose. But people doing history are looking at things differently from the way we handle them for practical daily living.

Take the example of telling the truth. If a youngster gets home late and her mother asks where she has been, the child has a choice between "telling the truth" and "telling a lie." From the child's point of view, what has happened is a fixed, given past, which she knows very well; the only issue is whether she tells it the way it was. Often children learn what counts as "telling the truth" in just this kind of situation, where the known past functions as a touchstone; it is as if what one says can be held up against the past to see if it measures up. This idea works fine in some everyday situations, but in history the past is not given, and we cannot hold what we are saying up against the real past to see whether it matches. The inferential discipline

BOX 2-1 Understanding the Past and Understanding the Discipline of History

The three (British) seventh-grade students in the excerpt below are discussing why World War II started and whether it could have been avoided without thus far having studied this at school. All they have to work with from school history is their knowledge of World War I, along with anything they know from outside school. To understand what is going on here, we need to distinguish between two different kinds of knowledge about history: knowledge of what happened, of the *content* of history, and knowledge about the *discipline* of history itself.

Angela	I think Hitler was a madman, and I think that's what . . .
Susan	He was . . . a complete nutter, he should have been put in a . . . um . . .
Angela	He wanted a super-race of blond, blue-eyed people to rule the world.
Susan	Yeah—that followed him. . . .
Angela	I mean, but he was a short, fat, dark-haired sort of person.
Susan	. . . little person.
Katie	Could it be avoided? I don't think it could have.
Angela	No.
Katie	If Hitler hadn't started . . . I mean I can't blame it on him, but if he hadn't started that and provoked . . . you know . . . us . . . if, to say, you know, that's wrong . . .
Susan	It would have been [avoided]. . . .
Katie	Yeah, it would have been, but it wasn't.
Susan	Yeah, if you think about it, *every* war could've been avoided.
Angela	I reckon if Hitler hadn't come on the scene that would never have happened.
Katie	Oh yeah, yes, yes.
Angela	There must've been other *underlying* things, like World War I we found out there was lots of underlying causes, not only . . . Franz Ferdinand being shot. . . .
Susan	Yeah.
Angela	. . . but loads of other stuff as well.
Katie	Oh yeah, I don't think he was so far . . .

Angela	Yeah, there must've been a few other main currents. . . .
Katie	But, like that Franz Ferdinand, he didn't get, that was the main starting point for it all, that really blew it up. . . .
Angela	But I don't know whether . . . because we don't know any underlying causes. If Hitler *hadn't* been there, I don't know whether it could've been avoided or not.
Susan	Yeah but most wars can be avoided anyway, I mean if you think about it we could've avoided the First World War and *any* war . . .
Katie	. . . by discussing it.
Susan	Exactly.
Katie	Yeah, you can avoid it, but I don't think . . .
Angela	Yeah but not everybody's willing to discuss. . . .

SOURCE: Lee and Ashby (1984).

In discussing World War II, the three girls try to use what they have learned at school about World War I. Their knowledge points in two different directions. What they know about the events suggests to them that "most wars can be avoided" if people discuss their problems, so Susan and probably Katie think that World War II could have been avoided by reasonable negotiation. They have learned a "lesson" from their study of one passage of the past and, sensibly enough, try to apply it to another. Unfortunately the "lesson" does not hold. Angela has learned a different kind of knowledge from her earlier study of World War I, and it leads her to treat her friends' lesson with caution. She has learned that a historical explanation is likely to require more than a single immediate cause, and that "underlying causes" may also be at work. So even if there had been no Hitler, we need to know more about international relations between the wars before we can say that World War II could have been avoided. Angela's knowledge of how explanations are given in the discipline of history provides her with a more powerful way of thinking about why things happen. She knows what to look for.

of history has evolved precisely because, beyond the reach of living memory, the real past cannot play any direct role in our accounts of it. History depends on the interrogation of sources of evidence, which do not of themselves provide an unproblematic picture of the past.

Everyday ideas about a past that is given can make it difficult for students to understand basic features of doing history. For example, how is it possible for historians to give differing accounts of the same piece of history? (See Box 2-2.) Students' common sense tells them that the historians must be getting things wrong somewhere.

Differences in the Power of Ideas

The everyday idea of telling the truth is often closely linked to a very recent past in which people remember what they did or saw. Some students behave as if they believe the past is somehow just there, and it has never really occurred to them to wonder how we know about it. In Box 2-2, Kirsty, like many other fifth and sixth graders, does not even raise the question of how we could know about the past.

Other youngsters are only too well aware that this question may be problematic. Allison, a fifth grader, states the difficulty quite clearly: "You cannot really decide unless you were there." If one thinks like this, history becomes impossible. If knowing something depends on having seen it (or better still, having done it), one can never say anything worthwhile about most of the past. Many students stop here, wondering what the point of history is. However, while some working assumptions make history appear to students to be a futile exercise, others allow its study to go forward.

Samantha (fifth grade):

Why are there different dates?
  No one knows, because no one was around then, so they both can be wrong.
How could you decide when the Empire ended?
  If you found an old diary or something it might help.
Does it matter if there are two different dates?
  Yes, because you can get mixed up and confused.

We can see here both the problem and initial steps toward a solution. Samantha appears to agree with Allison when she writes, "No one knows, because no one was around then." But Samantha, unlike Allison, sees the beginnings of a way out for historians. Perhaps someone told it the way it was and wrote it down, and we could find it: "If you found an old diary or something it might help." This view remains very limiting because it still sees the past as fixed, but it does make history possible. If we have true reports, historians are in business.

Of course, many students see that truthful testimony may not be easy to come by. They are well aware that people have reasons for saying what they say and the way they say it. As Brian (eighth grade) remarks, "I don't think we could find out definitely [when the Empire ended] because there are only biased stories left." Students who decide that we cannot rely on reports because they are biased or give only opinions are almost back to square one. If history is possible only when people (eyewitnesses or agents) tell us truthfully what happened, its study once more comes to a stop.

It is only when students understand that historians can ask questions about historical sources that those sources were not designed to answer, and that much of the evidence used by historians was not intended to report anything, that they are freed from dependence on truthful testimony. Much of what holds interest for historians (such as, What explains American economic supremacy in the postwar years? Did the changing role of women in the second half of the twentieth century strengthen or weaken American social cohesion?) could not have been "eyewitnessed" by anyone, not even by us if we could return by time machine. Once students begin to operate with a concept of evidence as something inferential and see eyewitnesses not as handing down history but as providing evidence, history can resume once again; it becomes an intelligible, even a powerful, way of thinking about the past.

The Progression of Ideas

Insofar as some of the ideas students hold are more powerful than others, we may talk about progression in the way students understand the discipline of history. For example, changes in students' ideas about our access to the past allow us to discern a pattern of progression of ideas about *evidence*. Working from less to more powerful ideas, we find a given past with no questions arising about how we can know; a notion of testimony, with questions about how truthful a report may be; and a concept of evidence, whereby questions can be asked that no one was intending to answer.[2] (Medieval garbage dumps were not constructed to fool historians.) Once we are able to think in terms of a progression of ideas in history, we can see how students' understandings can gradually be extended. In some cases we can accomplish this by enabling students to discover how prior conceptions break down in the face of historical problems. However workable the idea of a given past may be in everyday life, for instance, it is a misconception in history. In other cases we can build more directly on existing ideas. Thus testimony is important to historians, even if it must be used as evidence rather than simply being accepted or rejected. The goal is to

BOX 2-2 Two Different Ideas About Historical Accounts

In research by Project CHATA (Concepts of History and Teaching Approaches) into students' understanding of how there can be different historical accounts of the same events, 320 British students in grades 2, 5, 6, and 8 were given three pairs of stories and asked how it is possible for there to be two different history stories about the same thing. Each pair of stories was about a different topic, and the two stories making up any particular pair were the same length and ran side by side down a single page. Specially drawn cartoons illustrated key themes and steps in the story. Younger children tended to say that the two stories in each pair were "the same" because they were "about the same thing" but were just "told differently." Many of the students considered that the pairs of stories were different because no one has enough knowledge. Older students tended to emphasize the role of the author, some relying on relatively simple ideas of lies and bias as distorting stories, and others taking a more sophisticated view about the inevitability and legitimacy of a point of view. About 20 percent of the older students pointed out that stories answer different questions and fit different parameters (not their word). They did not see historical accounts as copies of the past and thought it natural that such accounts should differ.

One pair of stories had to do with the end of the Roman Empire, each claiming it ended at a different date. The first story, dealing mainly with the barbarian incursions, ended with the fall of the Empire in the West in 476. The second, which concentrated on the Empire's administrative problems, took the story up to the fall of Constantinople in 1453. Below are two (written) responses to the task.

Kirsty (fifth grade):
Why are there different dates?
One of the stories must be wrong.
How could you decide when the Empire ended?
See what books or encyclopedias say.
Does it matter if there are two different dates?
Yes, because if someone reads it and it has the wrong date in it then they will be wrong and might go round telling people. *

Kirsty's view of history is that if there is more than one account, one must be wrong. The past is given (in books), and she is sure that if historians read the same books and are honest, they will come up with the same story "because they will do the same things and they are not lying." Everyday ideas are apparent here, but they do not help Kirsty solve the problem she faces. We can see how different things look for someone who has a more sophisticated understanding of what a historical account is if we read Lara's response to the same problem.

> *Lara (eighth grade):*
> *Why are there different dates?*
> > *Because there is no definite way of telling when it ended. Some think it is when its city was captured or when it was first invaded or some other time.*
> *How could you decide when the Empire ended?*
> > *By setting a fixed thing what happened for example when its capitals were taken, or when it was totally annihilated or something and then finding the date.*
> *Could there be other possible times when the Empire ended?*
> > *Yes, because it depends on what you think ended it, whether it was the taking of Rome or Constantinople or when it was first invaded or some other time.*

Where Kirsty sees the past as given, Lara understands that it has to be reconstructed in that statements about the end of the Roman Empire are judgments about the past, not just descriptions of events in it. This means that a historical account is not fixed by the past, but something that historians must work at, deciding on a theme and timescale. Thus the problem of the date of the end of the Roman Empire is not a matter of finding an already given right answer but of deciding what, within the parameters of a particular account, counts as the end. Knowing when the Roman Empire ended is not like knowing when Columbus reached America.

---

*All responses in this chapter not otherwise attributed are unpublished examples of responses from Project CHATA. For published CHATA work, see, for example, Lee and Ashby (2000).

help students develop more powerful ideas that make the study of history an intelligible task, even in the face of disagreement and uncertainty, whether encountered in school or in the multiple histories at large in the wider world.

Grounds for Caution

Some caution is needed here. The notion of getting students to understand the discipline of history may appear to make life absurdly difficult for adolescents, let alone fourth graders. It is perhaps appropriate, therefore, to clarify at this juncture what we are *not* saying. We are not saying that teaching history is about training mini-historians. Second-order, disciplinary understandings of the kind we are talking about are not all-or-nothing understandings. Historians no doubt learned some science at school or college, but their understanding of science is not likely to be in the same league as that of a professional physicist. This does not mean their understanding is equivalent to that of a 7-year-old, nor does it mean such understanding is useless. Developing students' understanding of history is worthwhile without implying any grandiose claims.

It is also important to recognize that learning to understand the discipline does not replace the goal of understanding particular periods of the past. The substantive history (the "content" of the curriculum) that students are required to study is important, and so there will always be arguments about what is to be included, what should be omitted, and whether there is too much to cover. Regardless of what must be taught, however, understanding the kind of knowledge history is, its evidentially based facts and its stories and explanations, is as much a part of what it means to know some history as is knowing about the chosen periods of study, whatever these may be. Better understanding of key second-order ideas can help students make sense of any new topics they encounter. Although the quantity of research evidence available on the transfer of disciplinary ideas from one topic to another is relatively small, an evaluation of the Schools Council History Project in the United Kingdom suggests that teaching for transfer can be successful.[3] In light of the principles of *How People Learn*, this should not be entirely unexpected.

The point of learning history is that students can make sense of the past, and doing so means knowing some historical content. But understanding the discipline allows more serious engagement with the substantive history students study and enables them to do things with their historical knowledge. This is why such an understanding is sometimes described in terms of *skills*. However, the term is misleading. Skills are commonly single-track activities, such as riding a bicycle, which may be learned and improved through practice. The understandings at stake in history are complex and demand reflection. Students are unlikely to acquire second-order understandings by practice alone; they need to think about what they are doing and the extent to which they understand it. This kind of metacognitive approach is essential for learning history effectively. Building ideas that can be used effectively is a task that requires continuous monitoring and thinking on the part of both teacher and student.

The Ideas We Need to Address

Historians give temporal order to the past, explain why events and processes took place as they did, and write accounts of the past; they base everything they do on the evidence available. In this section we examine some key second-order concepts that give shape to the discipline of history: *time, change, empathy* (roughly, understanding people in the past), and *cause*, as well as *evidence* and *accounts*, mentioned earlier in passing. With any such list of second-order concepts, it is important to remember that we are using labels that refer to an adult concept to cover a whole range of understandings. When we talk about a concept such as *evidence*, as we have already seen, some of these understandings will fall far short of the kind of ideas we eventually want our students to grasp. For many students, what we present to them as *evidence* will be thought of as *information* or *testimony*. Thus if we say of a particular lesson that one of its purposes is "to teach students about evidence," we are thinking of where we want the students to arrive, not how they may actually be operating. The same considerations apply to anything we say about other ideas.

Time

The concepts of time and change are clearly central to history. Time in history is measured through a conventional system of dates, and the importance of dates is that they allow students to order past events and processes in terms of sequence and duration. The latter is particularly important if students are to understand that processes in history (for example, urbanization or shifts in the attitudes of Europeans and Native Americans toward each other) may be long-drawn-out and cannot be treated as if they were events taking place at a particular moment.

Teachers at the elementary level often say their students have no concept of time. This may mean that children foreshorten the passage of time in waiting for some anticipated event or that they cannot "work" clock time (perhaps their counting skills are defective, or they do not understand the analogue symbolism of a clock face). It seldom means that even very young children have failed to internalize their everyday basic temporal structures, such as day and night or breakfast, lunch, and dinner, let alone patterns of work and play. But they may have trouble estimating the long duration of passages of the past, and once again the attempt to transfer common-sense ideas about time from everyday life to history may pose problems.

For example, when English first-grade students were asked to sort paired pictures of people and objects into piles labeled "from long ago" and "from now," a significant majority were influenced by such factors as the physical condition of the objects portrayed and the state of the pictures. When a picture of a 7-year-old in a Victorian Little Lord Fauntleroy suit was paired with a modern photograph of an old man, most students said the Victorian picture was "from now." A picture of a beat-up and dirty modern car would be placed on the "from long ago" pile when paired with a photograph of a bright and shiny museum stagecoach. The pairing of clean and crisp pictures with bent, faded, and dog-eared pictures proved to be almost as distracting. It is clear that for these first graders, the historical distinction between long ago and now had been assimilated into the common-sense distinctions of old versus young and old versus new.[4]

With time, as with other ideas, history can be counterintuitive. Several features of history show the limits of a "clock time" understanding. Even apparently conventional terms are not always what they appear to be. Notoriously, a century in history is not necessarily a hundred years when used as an adjective (as in "eighteenth-century music"). The nineteenth century may be held to have closed with the start of the Great War of 1914–1918 or with the entry of America into the war and the beginning of the "American Century." The reason there are alternative possibilities and even disputes about such matters is obvious enough: historians clump and partition segments of time not as bits of time but as events, processes, and states of affairs that appear to belong together from certain perspectives. Thus the eighteenth century may be shorter musically than it is architecturally. Start and end dates are debatable, such that it makes no sense to argue over the beginning and end of any conventionally designated century. Much the same could be said about decades. When, for example, did "the 1960s" begin?

Of course, none of this means the conventional time markers and their normal mathematical relationships are unimportant in history or that they do not need to be understood, only that they must be supplemented by other ideas. The problem with centuries or decades is that they are linked to ideas of *period* in history (see Box 2-3). Knowing historical periods and being able to use them depends on knowing some of the history from which they are constructed. It means knowing the themes historians have chosen as a basis for thinking about the past. It may also mean knowing how people saw themselves, which presupposes that students recognize the distance of the past from our thinking as well as our time. For this reason, as well as the fact that it requires a good deal of knowledge, a sense of period is a difficult achievement for students, one that tends to come late in their study of history.[5]

BOX 2-3 **Periods in History**

Periods in history are not necessarily transparent, as this example from Sweden indicates. The students are responding to the teacher's question about which historical period came after the Renaissance.

Student	The Baroque Period.
Teacher	In the fine arts, yes.
Student	The Age of Greatness.
Teacher	Yes, but that was in Sweden.
Student	The Age of Freedom.
Teacher	That came a bit later.
Student	The Age of Monarchic Absolutism.
Teacher	Yes, or the Age of Autocracy. What's the period that we're reading about now?
Student	The Age of Freedom.
Teacher	In Sweden, yes.
Student	The Age of Enlightenment.
Teacher	Yes.

Halldén, who reports this exchange, comments, "It is tragic-comical that, in this particular case, the concepts that are supposed to help the students grasp the continuity of history become a problem in themselves." He adds, "It is highly probable that this is not an exceptional case."

SOURCE: Halldén (1994).

Change

Events are not in themselves changes, although this is exactly how many students see things. For children, the everyday model of change can often be simple. One minute "nothing" is happening, and then something does happen (often, someone does something). So there has been a change, and the change is that an event has taken place. It is a natural step to think of the event as a change.[6]

History tends to deal with longer scales than the moment-to-moment scale of everyday life, and historians are unlikely to subscribe to the notion of "nothing" happening. The idea that nothing happens is typically an everyday-life notion, rooted in highly conventional and agreed-upon ideas about what counts as interesting. Historians also operate with criteria of importance that include or exclude events, but these criteria are likely to be contested. Instead of the idea that no events occurred, historians are apt to work with the notion of *continuity*. This notion presupposes two other key ideas—*state of affairs* and *theme*. Change in history is generally to be understood in terms of changes in states of affairs; it is not equivalent to the occurrence of events. Consider the change from a state of affairs in which a class does not trust a teacher to one in which it does. There may be no event that could be singled out as marking the change, just a long and gradual process. Similarly in history, changes in population density, the role of the automobile industry in the economy, or attitudes toward minority cultures may change without any landmark event denoting a point in time in which the change took place. If students see changes as events, the idea of gradual, unintended changes in situations or in the context of actions and events is not available to them. Change is likely to be regarded as episodic, intentional (and hence rational or stupid), and able to be telescoped into a small compass (see Box 2-4).

As students become aware that historians must choose themes to write about (it is not possible to write about everything at once), they can begin to think in terms of patterns of change. What was changing? How? Was it changing a lot or just a little? Answering such questions involves concepts such as the *direction* and *pace* of change. One of the key understandings for students is that changes can run in different directions both between and within themes. Suppose the theme is subsistence and food production. For societies in Western Europe over a long period, food became more reliable, relatively cheaper (compared with income), more easily obtained, and available in a wider variety. Of course, in a parallel theme dealing with changes in the environment, there were costs. Here once again, students' preconceptions can cause problems. There is some evidence from research that students tend to think of the direction of change as automatically involving progress, and that this tendency may be more marked in the United States than in some other countries.[7] This misconception can lead to a condescending attitude toward the past, while also making it more difficult to grasp the complexities of change.

Two of the most common ideas likely to be encountered among students are the notion that everything gets better and that the past can be viewed in terms of deficits. Kenny (fourth grade) suggests some examples of progress:

> Better cars, they've gone from women [now] getting the
> exact same thing as men; now black people have gone from
> being horrible people to being—they're the best athletes in

BOX 2-4 Change as Progressive, Rational, and Limited in Time

Keith Barton spent a year in two Cincinnati classrooms, observing, discussing lessons with the teachers, and interviewing students. In his formal interviewing he showed pictures from different periods of American history to pairs of fourth and fifth graders and asked them to put the pictures in order, explaining their reasons as they did so.

He found that students envisaged change as something linear and "generally beneficial." They tended to think of change as being spatially and temporally limited in scope and "conceived of history as involving a limited number of discrete events, rather than lengthy and extensive processes." They "thought of change as having come about for logical reasons" and believed that people in the past decided to make changes because they realized, usually in the face of some particular event, that change would improve matters. Hence Jenny, a fourth-grade student, explained the end of witch trials like this:

When they accused like the mayor's wife or somebody's wife that they were a witch, and he said, "This has gone too far, we've killed enough innocent people, I want you to let everyone go, my wife is not a witch, and this has just gone too far," and then, just like that, everybody just forgot, and they didn't accuse people of witches anymore.

Jenny has turned a process of change into an event. Someone important made a rational decision that everyone accepted forthwith.

SOURCES: Barton (1996), Lee and Ashby (2001).

the world, they've gone from bad to good—and the cars have gone from bad to good; everything has gotten better than before.[8]

The idea of progress is reinforced by the idea—a very natural one acquired in part, no doubt, from parents and grandparents—of a deficit past. "Milk used to come in bottles because they didn't have cardboard." It was delivered to people's houses because "they didn't have many stores back then." Bicycles looked different because "they hadn't come up with the ideas yet."[9]

Patterns of change also provide a context for attributing *significance* in history. Significance can be attributed to changes within themes. A key idea for students is that the same change may have differing significance within different themes.[10] The significance of change in food marketing, for example, may differ for a theme of changes in health and one of patterns of working life and employment.

Empathy

One kind of explanation in history involves showing that what people did in the past makes sense in terms of their ideas about the world. This kind of explanation is often called *empathy*. Here we run into some problems. The word "empathy" has more than one meaning, and it tends to be used only because finding a single word that does the job better is difficult. (Other labels are "historical understanding" and "perspective taking"; however, the former is too broad, and the latter tends to get confused with "multiple perspectives," which is more a matter of the points of view from which accounts are constructed.) The use of the word "empathy" in history education is to some extent stipulative (that is, the word is assigned a particular meaning, whatever other meanings it may have in the world outside history education). To that extent it is jargon, but there is no harm in this if it helps professionals reach a consensus on what they are talking about.

The central idea here is that people in the past did not all share our way of looking at the world. For this reason, when writing or reading history we must understand the ideas, beliefs, and values with which different groups of people in the past made sense of the opportunities and constraints that formed the context within which they lived and made decisions about what to do. Thus empathy in the study of history is the understanding of past institutions, social practices, or actions as making sense in light of the way people saw things. Why, for example, would a free peasant agree to become a serf in the Middle Ages? Southern (1953, pp. 109-110) explains an act that appears almost perverse to us now by showing how it could fit into a pattern of beliefs and values: "There was nothing abhorrent in the idea of servitude—everything depended on its object. All men by sin have lost the dignity of freedom and have made themselves, in varying degrees, slaves of their passions. . . ." He quotes St. Anselm:

> Is not every man born to labor as a bird to flight? . . . . So if all men labor and serve, and the serf is a freeman of the Lord, and the freeman is a serf of Christ, what does it matter apart from pride—either to the world or to God—who is called a serf and who is called free?

Southern continues:

It is easy to see that from this point of view secular serfdom had no terrors. The burdens and restrictions it imposed were of featherweight compared with those imposed by the radical servitude of unredeemed nature. At best, this human

> *servitude was a preparatory discipline . . . at worst, it added*
> *only one more lord . . . to an array of lordly passions under*
> *which human nature already groaned. . . .*

Southern's explanation—and of course this is only a short excerpt, not a full explanation even of the narrow issue of why people might *choose* serf-dom—relies on the reconstruction of past beliefs and values using historical evidence. Empathy is not a special faculty for getting into other people's minds, but an understanding we achieve if we entertain ideas very different from our own. "Entertaining" ideas here denotes more an achievement than a special sort of process. It is where we arrive when, on the basis of evidence, we can say how someone might have seen things. It requires hard thinking and use of the evidence we have in a valid way. Empathy, however, is not just having the inert knowledge that people saw things in the way they did, but also being able to use that knowledge to make sense of what was done. This is not a matter of having an emotional bond. In history we must empathize with ideas we might oppose in the unlikely event we came across exactly the same ideas in the present. If understanding people in the past required shared feelings, history would be impossible. Understanding the hopes of the Pilgrims means entertaining their beliefs and values and knowing that they had those hopes. But we cannot now share the hopes—feel them ourselves—even if we want to, because to hope for something means to see it as a possible outcome, and our hindsight allows us to know that the outcome did not occur. Similarly, we cannot experience the fear felt by people in Britain in 1940 that Hitler might triumph and occupy their country. The same holds for a great deal of history.

None of this is to say that we do not want students to care about people in the past. If they treat people in the past as less than fully human and do not respond to those people's hopes and fears, they have hardly begun to understand what history is about.[11] But people in the past can appear to be strange and sometimes to do peculiar things (things we would not do) and so it is not always easy for students to accord them respect.

Partly because students tend to think about people in the past as not having what we have, and partly because they encounter decisions or ways of behaving that are difficult to make sense of, they tend to write off people in the past as not as smart as we are. (Evidence for the ideas described below goes back nearly 30 years and appears to have survived through a variety of changes in teaching.)[12] Students are quite capable of assuming that people in the past did not understand or do very basic things. A highly intelligent eighth grader, puzzling out why the Saxons might have used the ordeal of cold water to discover whether someone was guilty of a crime, declares, "But *we* know that nowadays if you ain't got air you're dead, but they didn't." An exchange between two eighth graders, this time about the ordeal of hot water, shows a similar disposition to write off the past:[13]

Sophie	And what about the boiling water, the boiling water—that could be hotter one time than another. I know it boils at 100 degrees centigrade, but um . . .
Mark	They wouldn't be able to get it that high, would they, in them times.

Another common way of dealing with the strange activities of human beings of the past is to assimilate those activities with our own. Often this is done in routine, even stereotypical ways. Mark, a fifth grader, explains why European monarchs paid for overseas ventures to the New World:[14] "They were greedy and wanted gold and more land, and sometimes they wanted jewels and different things." This sort of explanation is almost standard for monarchs and emperors, regardless of the period involved. Claudius invaded Britain for much the same reason:[15] "to get the pearls, the tin and the gold," or because "he wanted more land." Of course, assimilation can be more sophisticated than these examples, but may still leave problems unresolved. When, to return to our earlier example, students do not simply write off the Saxon ordeal but instead construe it as either a "punishment" or a "deterrent," they often remain dissatisfied with their own explanation.

At a higher level, students begin to think carefully about the particular situation in which people found themselves. What exactly were the circumstances in which they had to make decisions about what to do? This thinking can involve careful exploration, in which a variety of elements of the situation are related to one another. But although students who think like this make considerable efforts to understand why people in the past did what they did, they still tend to think in terms of present ideas (see Box 2-5).

Some students, however, will recognize that people in the past not only found themselves in different situations from those of today, but also thought differently, as is evident in this eighth grader's explanation of trial by ordeal:[16]

> I think that the Saxons used the ordeal partly because of their belief in God. I think that the Saxons believed that as the ordeal was the judgment of God, and because God had power over everyone, God would heal your hand or make you sink if you were innocent, or make you float or your hand not heal if you were guilty. I think that the Saxons believed that God would save you, and God was saying if you were guilty or innocent.

The ordeal becomes intelligible as a different way of thinking about things from our own, and our job in doing history is to understand it in past terms as well as ours. Occasionally, students even in the second or third grade think like this, but given the way parents and grandparents introduce children to the differences between the past and the present, as well as prevailing ideas about "progress," we are more likely to encounter assumptions about a deficit past. Nevertheless, with teaching that aims to develop sensitivity to past ways of thinking, one can expect to find students making moves such as the one Sarah (a fifth grader) makes in trying to work out why the Helots did not rebel against their Spartan masters:

> *We're given the training of freedom, right, we're given this ever since we grew up, and we have had freedom, in different ways. But these people never had freedom at all, so they can't imagine life without being enslaves [sic] right? They don't know what it's like, they'd be scared of it.*[17]

There is an element of condescension in this view, perhaps. But what appears to her fellow students as craven weakness on the part of the Helots in failing to rebel despite great numerical superiority, Sarah recognizes as an intelligible position.

Cause

Not all explanations in history are concerned with understanding people's reasons for acting or thinking as they did. We often want to explain why something happened that no one intended. Actions have unintended consequences, or simply fail to achieve their purposes. Historians also explain why large-scale events or processes occurred (for example, the Renaissance, the Industrial Revolution, or American westward expansion). In such cases, understanding what people were trying to do—their reasons for action—can be only part of an explanation of how events turned out, and we are likely to have to start talking in terms of *causes*. Students who have noticed this sometimes take a step too far and dismiss intentions as irrelevant since "they didn't happen." (No one intended World War I, so what people were trying to do is irrelevant.) When asked whether knowledge of people's plans is important to historians even if the plans go wrong, a typical response of students thinking this way is:[18] "No! 'Cos they didn't cause anything then if they went wrong."

Students often treat causes as special events that make new events happen in much the same way as individual people do things: causes act the way human agents act. When one fails to do something, nothing happens; similarly, if no causes act, nothing happens. It is as if the alternative to something happening is not something different occurring, but a hole being left in history.[19] Students thinking like this misconceive the explanatory task,

BOX 2-5   Exploring the Logic of the Situation

Even young children may sometimes give quite sophisticated explanations of apparently puzzling actions in the past, but they tend to rely on our modern ways of thinking to explain why people did as they did.

Twenty-three second graders in three schools in England were interviewed to explore how far and in what ways their ideas about history changed as they went through school. The CHATA researchers interviewed them twice in grade 2 and again at the end of grades 3 and 4. The students were asked to explain actions that appeared puzzling according to modern ways of thinking. They were given information about the people concerned and the circumstances they faced, including the broader context of the situation. The materials also included information about ideas and values held by people at the time.

In grade 2, 6 children were baffled in the face of a puzzling action, and 12 gave explanations of action in personal terms (e.g., the emperor Claudius ordered the invasion of Britain because he "wanted gold"). By grade 4 there was a shift: 2 children remained baffled, but more than half had moved to or beyond explanations appealing to roles (e.g., explaining the invasion by appeal to the kinds of things that *emperors* do). Four children explained by examining the situation in which people were acting.

One fourth grader (Carol) tried to reconstruct the situation and values of Elizabeth I to explain why she delayed so long in ordering the execution of Mary, Queen of Scots, in a way not characteristic of many eighth graders.*

Carol	Well, there're a number of reasons. Well, one, Mary was Elizabeth's cousin, and she couldn't desert her just like that, even though, well, their differences; and also I think she wanted to hold the favor of the Catholics in England and Scotland for as long as she could, and also, she didn't want to have a civil war, as I said, she didn't really have the money to, er, well, get together an army to fight.
Interviewer	So, erm, hang on . . . so she wanted to avoid civil war?
Carol	Yes.

Interviewer	Who would she have had the civil war with?
Carol	Well, as she was a Protestant, she might have had a civil war with the Catholics.
Interviewer	Ah, right, right, anything else?
Carol	Er, well, it partly . . . it might have been to do with the other countries, the Catholic countries, France, Spain, Holland. And she might have, even though they weren't sort of joined together, united as friends, I think she wanted to avoid a war, at least very bad relations with those countries.
Interviewer	Right . . . and why would she want to avoid a war with those?
Carol	Well, as I said before, there's the money, the . . . she wanted to keep, and also, well, I suspect she wanted to keep on good relations with the whole of Europe.
Interviewer	Right, any other points?
Carol	Er, not really. I don't think so, at least.
Interviewer	No, Ok. Does anything puzzle you about Elizabeth delaying for so long?
Carol	No, no.
Interviewer	Nothing at all?
Carol	No.

Carol's achievement here is considerable. She takes into account Elizabeth's relationship with Mary, the possibility of clashes between Protestants and Catholics at home, the danger of war with other European countries, and the financial burdens of war. But none of these considerations goes beyond present-day ways of thinking about Elizabeth's decisions. Despite having relevant information at hand, Carol does not, for example, take account of Elizabeth's reluctance to execute another monarch, and shows no sign of understanding what a serious step this would be.

---

*Interview from unpublished CHATA longitudinal study, Lee, Dickinson, and Ashby (1996b).

seeing it as explaining, for example, why the Civil War happened as opposed to "nothing" happening. But the task for historians is to explain why the Civil War occurred rather than other possibilities (such as a compromise solution or the gradual demise of slavery).

Another idea connected with seeing causes as special kinds of events is that causes are discrete entities, acting independently from each other. Construed this way, they can be thought of as piling up so that eventually there are enough causes to make something happen. Hence students make lists, and the more causes are on the list, the more likely the event is to happen. (The bigger the event, the longer the list needs to be.[20]) Some students, while still seeing causes as discrete events, go beyond the idea of a list and link the causes together as a linear chain. The first event impacts on the second, which in turn causes the third, and so on down a line. Should a textbook tackle the question of why Europeans went exploring with brief sections on the Renaissance, the rise of nation states, demand for luxury goods, and technological developments, some students will see these as interchangeable items. Others will try to order them in a linear chain, seeing the Renaissance as leading to nation states, which in turn led to demand for luxury goods, which in turn led to technological changes in navigation and ship design. This is a more powerful idea than simply piling causes up, but still makes it difficult for students to cope with the complex interactions that lie at the heart of historical explanations.[21]

The notion of causes as discrete events makes it difficult for students to understand explanations as dealing with relationships among a network of events, processes, and states of affairs, rather than a series of cumulative blows delivered to propel an outcome forward. In the textbook example of the question of why Europeans went exploring, the Renaissance helps explain developments in technology and astronomy, the rise of the nation state helps explain both demand for luxury goods from the east and the technological developments, and those technological developments in turn made it possible to meet and indirectly further stimulated the demand. There is a network of relationships involved, not a simple chain. In historical explanations, the relationships among the elements matter as much as the elements themselves—it is how they came together that determined whether the event we want to explain happened, rather than something else. Within this network of interacting elements, a key idea is that there are some elements without which the event we are explaining would not have occurred. This idea provides a basis for understanding that historians tend to select necessary conditions of events from the wider (sufficient) set. If these necessary conditions had not been present, the event we are explaining would not have happened; it is often these that are picked out as the "causes." This in turn gives students a means of thinking about how to test explanations. If causes in history are usually necessary conditions and necessary conditions

BOX 2-6 **Causes as Necessary Conditions**

Researchers in Project CHATA gave British students in grades 2, 5, 6, and 8 cartoon and text material on Roman and British life prior to the Roman conquest of Britain and a short story describing Claudius's invasion. They were then given two explanations of why the Romans were able to take over most of Britain. One said, "The Romans were really able to take over most of Britain because the Roman Empire was rich and properly looked after." The other said, "The Romans were really able to take over most of Britain because they beat the Britons at the battle by the River Medway." They were then asked how we could decide whether one explanation is better than another.

James, an eighth grader, shows that he is thinking of causes as necessary conditions. (He replies using his own labels—A and B for the two rival causes he is considering and X for the event he was asked to explain.)

If without A, X doesn't happen, but it does [happen] even without B, then A is more important than B.
If point A [the Roman Empire was rich and properly looked after] wasn't true, could the Roman takeover of Britain still happen?
If point B [the Romans beat the Britons in a battle by the River Medway] wasn't true could the Roman takeover of Britain still happen?
A good explanation would mean the Roman takeover of Britain couldn't really happen while a bad explanation wouldn't stop it happening even if the explanation wasn't there/wasn't true.

In a further example, in which James is testing the explanation that the Romans took over Britain because they had good weapons, he asks:

If the Romans didn't have good weapons, would they have been able to take over Britain anyway? If they could, then [the suggested explanation] is wrong.

SOURCES: Lee (2001, p. 80), originally in Lee and Ashby (1998).

are the ones that must be present for the event to happen, we can test an explanation by asking whether the event could have happened without the causes selected to explain it (see Box 2-6).

Historical explanations place some relationships in the foreground as causes and treat others as background conditions. A "cause" in history is frequently chosen because it is something that might have been different or is not to be found in other ("normal") situations. This perspective, too, connects with everyday life, but this time more helpfully. The cause of a rail disaster is not the fact that the train was traveling at 80 mph but that the rail was broken, or the driver went past the signal telling him to stop. Our ideas about what is normal help us decide what is a background condition and what is a cause. Trains often run at 80 mph without coming off the rails. But a broken rail is not present in those cases in which the incident did not happen, and drivers might be expected to stop when signals tell them to. Thus it is these states of affairs, events, or actions that tend to be identified as "causes."

It is easy for students to assimilate this distinction between background conditions and causes into the everyday distinction between long- and short-term causes. When they do so, they are likely to try to differentiate causes by attempting to assign them dates, fastening on arbitrary cut-off points between long and short instead of understanding the more context-related ways in which we pick "causes" out from the mass of interconnected antecedents to particular events.

If students think of causes as discrete events that act to produce results, they have difficulty recognizing that it is the questions we choose to ask about the past that push some factors into the background and pull others to the foreground to be treated as causes. We select as a cause something absent in other, comparison cases. The question of why the Roman Empire in the west fell is a classic case. The question may be answered in at least two different ways: first, "when it had successfully resisted attack for hundreds of years," and second, "when it didn't end in the east." In the first case we look for events or processes that were present in the fifth century but not (to the same degree) earlier. In the second we look for factors present in the west in the fifth century but not at that time in the east. What counts as a cause here, rather than a background condition, is determined in part by what question we ask.[22]

Evidence

We have already noted the way some ideas about how the past can be understood bring the study of history to a halt while others allow it to move forward. The concept of *evidence* is central to history because it is only through the use of evidence that history becomes possible. Even when students ask themselves how we know about what happened, however, it does not follow that they will recognize source material as evidence to be used differently from the notes or textbook accounts they may encounter on other occasions.

Research suggests that for some students, the question of how we can know about the past does not arise.[23] Younger students in particular are likely to assume that history is just known; it is simply information in authoritative books, such as encyclopedias. Forced to consider the question of *how* we know, they may slip into an infinite regress (bigger and better books) or assume that a witness or participant wrote down what happened on "bits of paper," in diaries, or in letters, or even carved it into the walls of caves (see Box 2-7). The assumption that the past is given on authority makes any encounter with multiple sources problematic. If sources are simply correct or incorrect information, all we can do is accept or reject what is proffered. Sources either get things right, or they do not. Common sense suggests that if two sources say one thing and a third says something different, the third must be wrong. And once one knows which sources are right, why bother with reading two that say the same thing?

The idea that what we can say about the past depends on eyewitnesses can provoke apparently similar reasoning, although it has a different significance. Students still count sources to decide what to believe (the majority wins), but there is an implicit understanding that the question of how we know about the past is at stake. We may still just have to accept or reject what we are told (after all, we were not there, so how else can we know), but we have a more sophisticated basis for making a choice. We can begin to ask questions about whether the witnesses agree, whether they are truthful or not, and even whether they were in a position to know. Once students ask such questions, further questions arise about why people lie or distort the truth in partisan and selective ways. Here a further everyday idea comes into play—the notion of bias.

The trouble is that students are likely to hold well-established everyday ideas about personal bias, which often surface in the statement "He would say that, wouldn't he." Students know only too well that people have their own agendas and may twist what they say to fit them or that people tend to take sides, whether personally or as part of a social group. One study found that even many students aged 16–18 who were taught about the importance of detecting bias in historical sources behaved as though bias were a fixed property of a source that rendered it useless. Once they managed to find any sign of a point of view, the students jettisoned the source; there was no point in considering it further.[24] This kind of idea again rests on the assumption that historians can repeat only what past sources have truthfully reported. And since students know that most people's reports must be taken with a grain of salt, they regard history as a dubious activity.

The preconception that history is dependent on true reports also encourages students to think of the reliability of a source as a fixed property, rather than something that changes for different questions. This notion in turn can lead students to take the historian's distinction between primary

BOX 2-7 Finding Out About the Past: Received Information or Evidence?

Denis Shemilt explored U.K. students' ideas about evidence. He found that for some students the question of how we know about the past does not arise, whereas others understand that historians used evidence to produce knowledge about the past. Research conducted under Project CHATA more than a decade later found very similar patterns of ideas.

When students stick with common-sense ideas they can run into difficulties. This is clear in the following excerpt, in which Annie, a ninth-grade student, responds after being asked how she knew that Hitler started World War II:

Annie	I've read it.
Interviewer	How did the author [of the book] know?
Annie	He might have been in the war or have been alive and knew what happened.
Interviewer	How do people who write books know about cave men?
Annie	The same . . . only they've to copy the books out again and translate some of 'em.
Interviewer	Are you saying that cave men wrote history books?
Annie	No, they'd carve it on the rocks.

Contrast this with Jim, an eighth grader, who can see that sources must be interrogated if we are to say anything about the past.

Interviewer	Is there anything you have to be careful about when you're using sources to find out what's happened?

and secondary sources to mean that the latter are less reliable than the former. The recognition that someone writing a long time after an event has occurred is not in as good a position to know about it as someone writing at the time is useful as a broad principle. The danger is that students will mistakenly generalize the principle to historians, as if their histories were also reports from the past rather than attempts to construct pictures of the past on the basis of evidence. This misconception is all the easier to fall into

Jim	You have to think about how reliable they're going to be . . . either if they're a long time after the event they, they're not likely to be, erm, primary sources of evidence, there's going to be more passed on either by reading something or having a story told to you, which if its told you it's less likely to be accurate because details. . . .
Interviewer	. . . Details go in the telling?
Jim	Yeah, and also if it's a particularly biased piece of evidence [we] might have to look at it and compare it to another piece of evidence, and it might not be much good on its own to get information, just opinion—it would only be good if you wanted an opinion of how people saw the event.
Interviewer	Right.
Jim	So you have to look at what context you're looking at the evidence in and what you want to find out from it.

Jim makes the point that reports can be damaged in transmission over time, and shows he is aware that we must weigh how far we can trust reports about the past. However, he also distinguishes the value of a source as a report of what happened from its value as a means of shedding light on a different kind of question—how people saw what happened. He is beginning to show signs of recognizing that we can ask questions about the past that the sources we have were not meant to answer.

SOURCES: Shemilt (1987); Lee, Dickinson, and Ashby (1996a).

when both contemporary reports and historians' inferential arguments are called "sources."

In any case, the distinction is a difficult one, and presupposes that students already understand it is the questions we decide to ask that determine whether something is a primary or a secondary source. Thus Gibbon's book *The History of the Decline and Fall of the Roman Empire* may be either a primary or a secondary source, depending on whether we are asking questions about Rome or about eighteenth-century ideas. Much the same sort of issue arises for Frederick Jackson Turner's argument before the American Historical Association in 1893 that the frontier was closed. Even the idea that a primary source is contemporary with whatever it addresses encounters difficulties with something like Bede's *History*. In the face of these difficulties, some students develop their own categories; as one sixth grader said:[25] "I can tell this is a primary source because it doesn't make any sense."

A crucial step for students in shedding everyday preconceptions and making real headway in understanding historical evidence is therefore to replace the idea that we are dependent on reports with the idea that we can construct a picture of the past by inference. Historians are not simply forced to choose between two reports, but can work out their own picture, which may differ from both.[26] With this understanding goes the recognition that we can know things about the past that no witness has reported. What matters is the question we are asking. Gibbon and Turner were not *reporting* anything about the beliefs and values of their time, but historians may use what they said (and other evidence) to produce an account of those beliefs and values. Jim, in Box 2-7, shows signs of thinking like this when he says you have to remember what you want to find out from any piece of evidence you are using.

Once students understand two parallel distinctions—between relic and record and between intentional and unintentional evidence—they can escape from the trap set by some of their everyday preconceptions. A record is a source that intends to tell us, or someone else, something about some event, process, or state of affairs. Relics are sources that were not intended to tell us what happened, or sources that are used by an investigator to answer a particular question in ways that do not depend on what they intend to report but on what they were part of. Coins, tools, and acts of Congress do not report the past to us, and so cannot be more or less "reliable." They are the traces of human activities, and we can use them to draw inferences about the past. Even deliberate reports of the past can be used to answer questions in this way when we do not ask about what they meant to report, but what they show about the activity of which they were a part.

One final point is worth making in connection with students' ideas about evidence. Common sense dictates that claims must be *backed up*, so students understandably look for evidence that does this: the more, the better. This is perfectly acceptable, but students also need to understand that however much evidence they gather in support of a claim, one piece can be enough to refute it. Learning to try to disconfirm claims may be difficult initially, but disconfirmation can be a highly efficient strategy in the face of a multiplicity of claims. We say "can be" because in history matters are seldom clear-cut, so the single piece of knockout evidence may be difficult to find, and there is always a danger that students will try to short-circuit difficult problems demanding judgment simply by trying to discredit whatever is put before them.

Accounts

The concept of a historical *account* is related to that of evidence. Whereas with evidence the focus tends to be on the establishment of particular facts, with accounts we are more concerned with how students view historical narratives or representations of whole passages of the past.

Many younger students appear to work with the idea that what makes a "true story" true is that all the component singular factual statements within it are true. As a first move in distinguishing between true stories and fiction, this idea is reasonable enough, but as a characterization of a true story, it will not stand up even in everyday life. All the component singular factual statements in an account may be true, but the meaning of the account may still be highly contestable. The meaning of a story is more than the sum of its parts. In history this point is of great importance, as the following account demonstrates.

Adolf Hitler

In 1933 Adolf Hitler came to power in Germany. In elections held soon after he became chancellor, he won a massive majority of the votes. Pictures taken during his chancellorship suggest his popularity with the German people. He presided over an increasingly prosperous nation. A treaty signed with France in 1940 enabled Hitler to organize defenses for Germany along the Channel coast, and for a time Germany was the most militarily secure power in Europe. Hitler expressed on many occasions his desire to live peacefully with the rest of Europe, but in 1944 Germany was invaded from all sides by Britain, the United States, and the Soviet Union. Unable to defeat this invasion of his homeland by superior numbers, Hitler took his own life as the invading Russian armies devastated Berlin. He is still regarded as one of the most important and significant figures of the twentieth century.

Every component statement in this account is true, but the story would not be accepted by most people as a "true story," and no historian would regard it as a valid account. Given that its title indicates a general survey of what is important about Hitler and his political career, the most obvious defect is the omission of clearly germane material that would give a different implicit meaning to the story. Moreover, what is said carries implications that would normally be specifically ruled out if they did not hold. If we are told that a politician won a massive majority, this normally means that voters had choices and were not under duress. The point of saying, without qualification, that someone has expressed a desire to live at peace is that it shows what he or she wants, and Hitler did not—in any straightforward sense—want peace. The account puts matters in ways that would normally suggest certain relationships, but in this case the relationships are highly questionable.

Students tend to deal with the problem that true statements do not guarantee acceptable historical accounts by using concepts employed in everyday life. If accounts are not clearly and unambiguously true or untrue, they must be matters of opinion. This view carries with it the idea that it is impossible to choose between conflicting accounts and, for some students, the idea that therefore anything goes. History is reduced to an arena in which opinions are freely exercised, like dogs in the park.[27]

Another preconception that can cause difficulties for students is the idea that a true account is a copy of the past rather than something more like a picture, or better still, a theory. If students think true stories are copies of the past, there will obviously be a problem when different stories exist. One way students explain this is by saying that different stories must arise when historians make mistakes. Another explanation is that part of the story has not been found. It is as if stories lie hidden like mosaics buried beneath the sands, waiting to be uncovered, but when historians sweep aside the sand, they find that some pieces are missing. Either way, the view is that historians do not know the real story (see Box 2-8).

Some students think alternative historical accounts are created when people deliberately distort the truth, usually because they are "biased." The everyday idea of bias as something like taking sides allows students to attempt to solve the problem by looking for accounts written by someone neutral. This approach makes sense for everyday clashes between two people with clear interests in some practical outcome (Who started the fight?), but it does not work for history, where alternative accounts may have nothing to do with taking sides over a practical issue. The ideal of neutrality is sometimes broadened into writing from a "perspective-free" stance.[28]

Such ideas will cause difficulties for students until they can see that stories are not so much copies of the past as ways of looking at it. The key notion here is that stories order and make sense of the past; they do not reproduce it. There can be no "complete" story of the past, only accounts within the parameters authors unavoidably set when they decide which questions to ask (see Deirdre in Box 2-8). All this means that accounts demand selection, and therefore a position from which selection is made. A point of view is not merely legitimate but necessary; perspective-free accounts are not possible. Research suggests that some students already understand this point by the end of eighth grade.[29] They know we can assess the relative merits of alternative accounts by asking the right questions. What are the accounts claiming to tell us? What questions are they asking? Are they dealing with the same themes? Are they covering the same time span?

How do they relate to other accounts we accept and to other things we know?

SUBSTANTIVE CONCEPTS

Second-order, disciplinary concepts such as *change* and *evidence*, discussed above, are involved in any history, whatever the content. Other concepts, such as *trade, nation, sachem, protestant, slave, treaty*, or *president*, are encountered in dealing with particular kinds of historical content. They are part of what we might call the *substance* of history, and so it is natural to call them "substantive concepts."

Such concepts belong to many different kinds of human activity—economic, political, social, and cultural. They are numerous and fit together in many different ways, which makes it difficult to form a coherent picture of student presuppositions about these concepts. As teachers, however, we tend to be much more aware of the substantive preconceptions students bring to lessons than of their disciplinary ideas. As part of the content of history, substantive concepts are usually central to what we think of ourselves as teaching, and if we forget to pay attention to students' ideas, they often remind us by revealing the misconceptions that can be so frustrating (and sometimes entertaining).

Concepts are not the same as names and dates. It is important to remember that understanding concepts—such as *colony, market*, or *migration*—involves knowing a rule (what makes something a migration, for example) and being able to identify instances of that rule. The substantive concepts we encounter in history can come from any walk of life or any discipline, but each denotes a cluster of *kinds* of things in the world. Names and dates are not like this; they are particulars that students must know about as individual items. Moreover, names are not limited to people. Some denote particular things, such as the Constitution, or France, or Wounded Knee. Some, like the American Revolution, denote a cluster of events and processes not because they are one kind of thing, but because they make up a greater whole to which we wish to assign a name. Of course, *constitution* is a concept that we want students to understand and apply across a range of cases, but the Constitution is the name of one particular case. Similarly while *revolution* is a general concept, the American Revolution is the name of a particular instance, although in this case exactly what it denotes can be disputed. This kind of dispute is a frequent occurrence in history (consider the Renaissance, the Age of Discovery, and the Industrial Revolution), and one that we need to help students understand if they are to be able to make sense of differences in historical accounts.

Substantive concepts in history involve a complication not often encountered in the practical concepts of everyday life: their meaning shifts

BOX 2-8 Historical Accounts Are Not Copies of the Past

While some students think of history stories as copies of the past (provided we know enough to get things right), others think of them as alternative ways of answering questions and making sense of the past.

In CHATA research exploring students' ideas about historical accounts, researchers gave 320 students in grades 2, 5, 6, and 8 two different stories of the Saxon invasion of Britain, one concentrating on the arrival of the Saxons and one taking the story right through the period of settlement. The students were then asked to say whether they agreed or disagreed with the following statement:

History really happened, and it only happened **one** *way, so there can only be* **one** proper *story about the Saxons in Britain.*

Amy, a second grader, was interviewed:

Interviewer	You said "because it happened or we wouldn't know it." So, do you think history only happened one way?
Amy	Yes.
Interviewer	Yeah? And do you think there's only one proper history story about the Saxons in Britain?
Amy	Yes.
Interviewer	How come we've got all these other different stories then, Amy, do you think?
Amy	Because they don't know which one's the real one.
Interviewer	Right.
Amy	And they just make them up.

over time as well as space. An eighteenth-century king is not the same as a fifteenth- or a twenty-first-century king, and students who think they are likely to behave in the same way and have the same powers and roles are likely to become confused. Conceptions of presidents, church leaders, and even the wealthy or beautiful differ in different times. Thus while students can learn, for example, what a president is, they may run into difficulty if they gain this knowledge in the context of Thomas Jefferson and go on to assume when they deal with Lyndon Johnson and the Great Society that

Interviewer   Who makes them up?

Amy   The historians.

Amy is convinced that if there is more than one story, there must be something wrong. Not all students go as far as Amy in their dismissal of historians, but many share her view that if only one thing happened, there can only be one story. Annabelle, a sixth grader, writes:

Something in history can only happen one way. I got up this morning. I wouldn't be right if I wrote I slept in. Things only happen one way and nobody can change that.

These students think of history stories as copying the past: one past gives one true story.

Deirdre, an eighth grader, takes a very different view. She recognizes that different stories fit different questions and is therefore able to see that there can be more than one historical account of the "same" events:

Yes, history really did happen. Yes, there was an outcome. But lots of different factors and things may have affected it. A history story may emphasize one particular point, but it doesn't mean that that is the only correct history story. They can say different things to answer certain questions. They can go into more detail on a certain point. They may leave out certain points but it doesn't mean it is right or wrong. There can be many different history stories about one thing.

SOURCE: Lee (2001).

presidents are just presidents. The full significance of Jefferson can be understood only through the historical accounts of his presidency. Indeed, learning about historical particulars always involves studying historical accounts; in other words, it means knowing some historical content.

The concepts that enable us to operate in the world are not neatly defined, closed capsules. We cannot expect students to learn definitions and examples, however thoroughly, on a particular occasion and then simply apply them to other cases. Students' social concepts emerge out of current ways of life and fit into patterns of behavior that may not be fully understood, but are so "normal" that for students they are just the way things are. Students carry these concepts with them into the past. Apparently harmless concepts, such as *town* or *painter*, can be burdened with present associations, never deliberately taught, that may cause serious difficulties. When students learn of the Pilgrims coming upon an abandoned Native American "town," some assume that the Pilgrims were on to a good thing: at least they would quickly find shelter in some of the empty buildings. But even when a concept is not one that is salient in their everyday lives, students may assimilate it into known patterns of behavior that are. One of the first things beginner history teachers learn is that for most youngsters, a monk is likely to be a pretty safe source of evidence. How could it be otherwise? Monks spent their time worshipping God and living a Christian life. Clearly they would not tell lies.

Research suggests that while there may be differences in the development of relevant political and economic concepts in different societies, there may be commonalities in the United States and Western Europe.[30] There is some evidence from Europe that between second and fifth grade, the idea of someone in charge, a "boss," develops, although politicians are often not distinguished from other forms of boss. Students are likely at this age to think of people in power giving commands through direct personal contact.[31] Research provides some support for a pattern in which political and military affairs are understood by students first as the actions of individuals or collectives without structure (such as a crowd) and later in terms of systems and structures (such as armies and nation states).[32] A recent study found that before fourth grade, many Italian students believe wars are begun by individual fighters and end when people are too tired to go on or are enslaved or killed.[33] From the fourth grade on, students are more likely to see war as a clash between nation states and to believe that political authorities begin and end hostilities. Even within a particular society and school system, however, students' political concepts may develop in very different ways, depending on what experiences they have had, as well as on what they have been taught.[34]

In economic matters (money, profit making, banking, ownership, poverty, and wealth), students tend to transition from ideas based on moral norms to more overtly economic ideas in which people and actions are considered in terms of their potential as opportunities to increase personal wealth. Youngsters tend to think that shopkeepers exist to make people happy and will be pleased if prices drop, since that means people can save their money. By fourth grade, most students should be beginning to integrate ideas about, for example, buying and selling, so as to understand the workings of economic life. But an understanding of these things at the level of everyday life does not necessarily carry over into other areas. Ninth or tenth graders may have difficulty understanding how banks make profits, and the fact that sixth graders can cite profit as a motive for starting a factory does not necessarily mean they understand how shops, let alone factories, make profits[35] (see Box 2-9).

We need to remember that even when students have a quite sophisticated understanding of political and economic concepts, they may find it difficult to transfer those concepts from one case to another in history. A consequence of changes in the meaning of concepts in history is that learning history means paying attention to details and to contexts because they often determine what can and cannot be transferred. This is a point made at the beginning of the chapter in describing students who tried to apply ideas about the origins of World War I to the origins of World War II. (Both World Wars I and II are historical particulars, of course, even though both fall under the concept of *war*.) In short, students need to know some substantive history well: they need to have a deep foundation of factual and conceptual knowledge and to understand these facts and ideas in a broader framework. The qualification "some" history is important because what students do know must be manageable. And for what students know to be manageable, it must be organized so they can access and use it, knowing how to make cautious and realistic assessments about how far and in what circumstances it is applicable. We therefore need to consider the kind of history that will allow this to be achieved.

HISTORY THAT WORKS

In the previous section, the focus shifted from second-order understandings of the kind of discipline history is to substantive understandings of the content of history. Students certainly need to know some history well if they are to see, first, that there are nuances and complications within any particular topic or period that may or may not apply outside it, and, second, that however much they know, it may still be necessary to know more. But as they begin to make connections between how people in the past saw things on the one hand and actions, policies, and institutions on the other, it becomes possible for even young students to begin to appreciate something of the complexity of historical understanding. For such understandings to develop, a topic (and preferably more than one) must be studied in depth. But not everything has to be thus studied. As long as the scope and scale of a particular in-depth study are workable, students can be introduced to the kinds of thinking required. Here such concepts as *empathy* and *evidence* are central, and time must be allowed for students to begin to develop their ideas of how we can make claims about and understand the past.

While understanding something in depth is a necessary part of learning history, however, it is not enough. Moving from one in-depth topic to an-

BOX 2-9 Substantive Concepts in History: Payment for Work

As part of a broad investigation of students' ideas about a range of economic concepts, Berti and Bombi interviewed 60 Italian students aged 6 to 14 to explore their understanding of payment for work. They found that some second graders envisaged payment for work as an exchange between just two figures: one person providing goods or services and another consuming them. They saw "pay" as an exchange of money, but had no clear idea of the direction of the exchange, seeing the relationship as comparable to that of friends who give each other money. ("Change" was seen as money given to the purchaser of goods, and the youngsters thought it may often be more than is tendered in the first place.) Chiara (age 6) explained how people get money at the drugstore.

> *When you go to get medicine, then the money they give you for the medicine you keep for getting something to eat.*

The interviewer asked whether her father, who owned a drugstore, gave people more or less or the same amount as they gave him. Chiara replied:

> *My daddy gives them different amounts. . . . [He] gives more than they gave.*

Most third graders understood payment for work in terms of a "boss" figure paying people for work, seen either as a private owner of a business or the council or state (understood as a much richer version of the private owner). They knew that the money goes from boss to worker, but did not necessarily understand how the boss acquires the money used to pay the workers or whether the boss is also paid.

Massimo (age $6^1/_2$), having said that people who organize work pay the workers, explained how these people in turn get their money:

> Massimo   Sometimes they get it from home, maybe they ask their wife for it and . . . sometimes they find it in their wallet, if they don't have much then they go and get it from those who have.

Interviewer	And the man who pays the bus-driver, how does he come to have the money?
Massimo	He could go to the bank and get it.
Interviewer	What is the bank?
Massimo	Where they go and put money, and when they need it they go and take it. . . .
Interviewer	To get the money does this man have to put some in the bank already or does the bank give him some all the same?
Massimo	The bank gives it to him.

More than half the fifth graders and all the seventh graders could fit the idea of payment for work into a framework of relationships whereby bosses, too, receive money from other business people or customers who buy goods and services from their business. Giovanni (aged 10 $\frac{1}{2}$) was asked who pays factory workers:

Giovanni	The owner of the factory.
Interviewer	And how does he get the money?
Giovanni	Because while others work to produce various objects, the owner sells them at a higher price, then he gives a small percentage to the workers, and he himself keeps the greater part of the money he's made.

Of course, American children may not have exactly the same ideas as Italian children. The point is not that all students, in whatever culture, will have the same range of ideas, although this is a possibility in Western industrialized countries; research in Britain, for example, appears broadly to fit the pattern suggested by Berti and Bombi. The importance of research of this kind is that it makes us aware that we cannot assume students share adults' assumptions (even at a very basic level) about how the economic, social, and political worlds work. Teaching history without recognizing this may have serious consequences for students' ability to make sense of the history they encounter.

SOURCE: Berti and Bombi (1988, pp. 32, 34, 38).

other and illuminating each in the historical spotlight only begins to develop historical understanding if such topics are set in a wider historical framework. Students will be unable to make much sense of historical change if they examine only brief passages of the past in depth. The snapshots of different periods they acquire will differ, but it will be impossible to say why the changes occurred. Moreover, if students need study only short periods of history, they will have no opportunity to come to grips with a central characteristic of historical accounts—that the significance of changes or events varies with timescale and theme. A long-run study is therefore essential for students both to understand the kind of discipline history is and to acquire a usable framework of the past.

Working through a narrative sequence of events of the history of the United States may not be the most effective way of helping students acquire a framework that can be adjusted to accommodate to or assimilate new knowledge. To provide something students can use and think about, we may need to teach a big picture quite quickly, in a matter of two or three weeks, and keep coming back to it. Such a framework focuses on large-scale patterns of change, encompassing students' in-depth studies so they are not simply isolated topics. For a temporally extended topic such as migration, exploration, and encounter, students can derive a broad picture of migration to and within America, at first picking out just the main phases of population movement to America (the land bridge crossings, the Arctic hunters, the Europeans). As in-depth studies of Native American settlement and later European arrivals (including Columbus, later Spanish exploration, Virginia, and the Pilgrims) are taught, they can be fit into this broad picture. But if it is to be a usable framework, the original broad picture will have to be adapted and made richer as it expands to include new in-depth studies. The original three phases will become more complex. Patterns of movement within America can be taught (again quickly), and changes in population movement from outside can be studied, so that, for example, differences in the kind of European migration over time are recognized.

Such a framework is not just a long narrative of events and cannot be organized in the same way as an in-depth study, bringing together all aspects of life in their complex interrelations. Instead the framework must allow students to think in terms of long-run themes, at first rather isolated from one another, but increasingly linked as students' understanding increases. Population change, migration, and cultural encounter provide themes for a framework, but these themes will be taught at the level of a big picture of change. It is the in-depth studies nesting within the framework that allow students to explore how the themes play out at the level of events.

If such a framework is to avoid overloading students with information, it must give them a range of large-scale organizing concepts for patterning change. It is the ability of such concepts as *internal* and *external migration*, *population density,* and *life expectancy* to "clump" information in meaningful ways that allow students to handle "the long run" in history rather than becoming overwhelmed by a mass of detail. The in-depth studies chosen to nest in the long-run study remind students that the details of those studies' complex interrelations matter too, and can serve as tests for the adequacy of the framework developed in the long-run study. But the latter must concentrate on the big picture, not degenerate into a series of impoverished would-be in-depth studies. Part of learning history is learning the effect of scale, and the difference between big generalizations (which can admit of exceptions) and singular factual statements.

Taking stock of the ideas presented thus far, we can say that students' substantive knowledge of history should be organized in a usable form so they can relate it to other parts of the past and to the present. This means students need to acquire a usable framework of the past, a big picture organized by substantive concepts they increasingly understand and can reflect upon. It also means they need an in-depth knowledge of contained (not overlong) passages of the past, with time to explore the way of life and world view of the people they are studying. This in turn allows them to begin to be aware of the complex interrelations involved and to be thoughtful and reflective about analogies they draw with other times and places. But learning history also requires an understanding of history as a discipline, evidenced in students' increasing understanding of key second-order concepts. Without this understanding, students lack the tools to reflect on their own knowledge, its strengths, and its limits.

Any picture of the past to which students are introduced inside school is likely to encounter rival and often opposed accounts in the wider world outside.[36] As soon as singular factual statements are organized into historical accounts, they acquire meanings within the stories in which they figure. Such stories may already be part of students' apparatus for thinking about the world before they encounter competing accounts in school. Teaching multiple perspectives, or critiquing particular accounts, is a valuable step toward facing up to students' predicament, but it is not enough.

To understand this point, consider these students' responses when faced with two alternative historical accounts. Laurence, an eighth grader, insists that the differences between the stories do not matter "because it is good to see how other people thought on the subject and then make your own mind up. Everyone is allowed to hold on to his own opinions, and no matter what the evidence, people believe different things." Briony, another eighth grader, claims that the differences are just a matter of opinion, and it does not matter "because it's up to you to express your opinion unless there are sufficient facts that prove a story. . . . I think it really is a matter of opinion." Rosie, a sixth grader, says accounts will differ "because some people are biased and therefore have different opinions of how it happened. . . . People are always going to have different opinions of how something happened." If students think like this, multiple perspectives are simply different opinions, and people can believe what they want. Xiao Ming, also in the sixth grade, sums up: "There can be many different opinions from historians so there can be different stories. Of course one *has* to be true but we don't know which one." Critiquing accounts will not make much sense to Xiao Ming when, despite our critiques, we can never know which is true.

Without explicit teaching and reflection on the nature of historical evidence and historical accounts, as well as the different ways in which various types of claims can be tested for validity, multiple perspectives become just another reason for not taking history seriously. If students are to go beyond helpless shoulder shrugging in the face of contested histories, they must have an intellectual toolkit that is up to the task. There is a danger that "toolkit" implies something overly mechanistic, so that it is simply a matter of applying the tool to get the job done. Such a simple analogy is not intended here. What is meant is that some tasks are possible only if certain tools are available, and in this case the tools are conceptual. Students need the best tools we can give them, understandings that enable them to think clearly about, for example, what kind of evidence is needed to support a particular kind of claim or what questions are being addressed in competing accounts. Once they understand that accounts are not copies of the past but constructions that answer a limited range of questions within a chosen set of boundaries, students can begin to understand how several valid accounts can coexist without threatening the possibility of historical knowledge or leading to a descent into vicious relativism.

Students have ideas about the past, and about history, regardless of what and how we teach them. The past is inescapable; it is built into our ways of thinking about ourselves. What would we say of someone who, when asked what the United States is, could define it only as a geographical entity? Our notion of what the United States is incorporates a past; it is a time-worm. Nor should we think that, because we are often told students do not know this or that piece of information about the United States, they have no version of its past. They certainly have one, but the question is whether it is the best we can give them. And while "the best" here does not mean "the one best story," because there is no such thing, the fact that there is not just one best story most certainly does not mean that any story will do. What we should give our students is the best means available for making sense of and weighing the multiplicity of pasts they are offered in various accounts. To this end, students must learn to understand the discipline of history—the one offering school can make that the busy world outside cannot. Schools could hardly have a more important task.

The study of history is often portrayed as learning an exciting—and sometimes not so exciting—story. This chapter has attempted to show that there is more to learning history than this. But we are not thereby absolved from asking how the history we teach can engage our students and what they might feel about what they are getting from it. History offers students (albeit at second hand) strange worlds, exciting events, and people facing seemingly overwhelming challenges. It shows students the dark and the light sides of humanity. It is one of the central ways of coming to understand what it is to be human because in showing what human beings have done and suffered, it shows what kind of creatures we are. The past is, as has often been said, a foreign country.[37] Its strangeness provides endless puzzles and endless opportunities for students to widen their understanding of people and their activities. An important part of understanding what appears strange is the disposition to recognize that we must try to understand the situations in which people found themselves and the beliefs and values they brought to bear on their problems. If students fail to see that there is anything to understand or do not care whether they understand or not, history will appear to be a senseless parade of past incompetence and a catalogue of alien and unintelligible practices. Empathy, in the very specific senses discussed earlier in this chapter, is central here. Historical imagination needs tools.

History can also offer another very human motivation—a sense of mystery and adventure. One source of adventure is to follow the experiences of people who were moving into unknown territory. Such study can be quite literal, when focused on people who explored lands they had not known existed, or metaphorical, when focused on those who attempted what no one had done before in some aspect of life. In the case of one of the topics discussed in the next chapter—the Pilgrims—the sense of the precariousness of their situation and the sheer scale of the challenges they faced has long been understood by teachers to offer obvious opportunities for the engagement of students' imagination. For older students, a dawning understanding of the enormity of the choices Native Americans had to make, in circumstances in which the future could only be guessed at, can offer a more complex and morally difficult stimulus to the imagination. But beyond adventure, strangeness, and a sense of awesome challenges, there is mystery. Young children—and many adults—love the mystery of the unknown. The voyage of St. Brendan (a topic in the next chapter) appeals to just this sense of mystery. What happened so long ago? What can we make of such a weird but sometimes plausible tale? Even better, the mystery arises in circumstances in which St. Brendan was having real adventures, too.

Of course, if history is the tale of things known, a fixed story that simply must be learned, then mystery can be reduced to waiting for the next installment. If we teach history as simply a set of facts to be imparted to our pupils, the mystery is a phony one. The teacher knows the answers, so where is the mystery? It can only be in deciphering the workings of the teacher's mind, in finding out what he or she wants to hear—in short, in getting the right answer. In history there are unending opportunities for students to be given tasks that leave room for them to maneuver, and to be more or less successful in finding a valid answer to an open question. Knowing the facts then becomes an urgent and meaningful business because they are essential for beginning to answer the question, and the question is worthwhile because it is a real question.

For a long time, and not just in history, schools have tended to keep a kind of secret knowledge from all but their oldest and most able students. Knowledge is contested, is provisional, and is subject to continuous change. Mystery never stops, and there is always a job for the next generation to do. The authors of this and the following chapter still remember, as one of the high points of their teaching lives, the excitement of the moment when a group of students whose main subject was science realized that science was not "all sewn up." In learning the history of medicine, they came to see—quite suddenly—that the whole way in which scientists approached and understood disease had undergone major shifts. *They* had a future in science beyond tweaking the textbooks. If they could devise new questions, they could begin new projects. Knowledge was not closed but open and open to them, too, if they mastered what was known well enough to understand what was not.

As we learn more, we should begin to see that mystery does not fade away as we come to know things. The more we know, the more questions there are, and the more there is that we need to understand. History must look like this to students as well. There is excitement in finding oneself in a richer, more open world than one thought one inhabited, but there is even more excitement in suddenly finding oneself empowered by a flash of understanding. It is not only that one has some stake in the answers and the right to a view. One can actually see that it is precisely what one is learning that gives one the right to the view, as well as the means to improve upon it. Understandings of this kind must be taught precisely because they are not things one picks up in everyday life. Generations of people have had to fashion the conceptual tools that really make a difference in the way we see the world. The only institutions whose central task is to hand those tools on and encourage the next generation to develop them are schools and universities, and the only people whose professional job it is to do this are teachers.

NOTES

1. This reservation is important, but it should also be pointed out that there has been considerable agreement among independent research teams in the United Kingdom; moreover, some recent U.S. work, as well as research in places as diverse as Portugal, Spain, and Taiwan, appears to point in a similar direction.

    There is a strong U.S. tradition of research into the ways in which the meaning of particular history stories and topics is viewed by school students, but there has been rather less focus on students' understanding of the discipline. Where such research has been undertaken, many of the researchers, such as Jim Voss, have worked mainly with college students. However, Keith Barton, Linda Levstik, and Bruce VanSledright have all done extensive research on the ideas of younger school students. Peter Seixas in Canada has carried out wide-ranging research with older school students. Sam Wineburg has worked with school and college students and with historians, and has recently begun to pay particular attention to ideas acquired outside school. Other U.S. researchers, such as Gaea Leinhardt, have investigated the differing approaches of history teachers to classroom history teaching, and investigation of students' understanding of textbooks has been widespread.

    Students' understanding of second-order concepts has been explored by Isabel Barca and Marilia Gago in Portugal; Lis Cercadillo, Mario Carretero, and Margarita Limón in Spain; and Irene Nakou in Greece. Research in this area outside the United States and Europe is also beginning to expand. Early findings from a Taiwanese study by Liu Ching Cheng and Lin Tsu Shu suggest that students in Taiwan share many ideas about historical accounts with British and Portuguese students. Mario Carretero has carried out some of his research in Argentina, and Angela Bermudez and Rosario Jaramillo have investigated ideas about causation in Colombia.

    Lists of this kind can only hint at the range of work, and any brief selection of names is necessarily invidious. This list, for example, omits a whole new generation of U.S. researchers whose work is beginning to be published. (See, for example, the authors in O.L. Davis Jr., Elizabeth Anne Yeager, and Stuart Foster (Eds.). *Historical Empathy and Perspective Taking in the Social Studies,* Lanham, MD: Roman and Littlefield, 2001.)
2. Lee et al., 1996a.
3. Shemilt, 1980.
4. Shemilt, 1994.
5. Shemilt, 1983, pp. 11-13.
6. Ibid, 1983, p. 7.
7. Barton, 1999, 2001.
8. Barton, 1996, p. 61.
9. Ibid, 1996, p. 56.
10. Cercadillo, 2000, 2001.
11. Levstik, 2002; Walsh, 1992.
12. Dickinson and Lee, 1978, 1984; Shemilt, 1984; Ashby and Lee, 1987; Lee et al., 1997; Lee and Ashby, 2001.
13. Ashby and Lee, 1987, p. 71.

14. Brophy and VanSledright, 1997, p. 130.
15. Lee et al., 1997, p. 236.
16. Lee et al., 1996a, 1997.
17. Dickinson and Lee, 1984, p. 134.
18. Shemilt, 1980, p. 33.
19. Shemilt, 2000, pp. 89-92.
20. Shemilt, 1980, pp. 30-32.
21. Lee et al., 1998.
22. Martin, 1989, pp. 58-61.
23. Shemilt, 1987; Lee et al., 1996a.
24. Thomas, 1993.
25. Ashby, 1993.
26. Wineburg, 1998; Wineburg and Fournier, 1994.
27. Lee and Ashby, 2000.
28. Barca, 1997; Cercadillo, 2000.
29. Lee and Ashby, 2000.
30. Furnham, 1992; Berti, 1994; Delval, 1992; Torney-Purta, 1992.
31. Berti and Andriolo, 2001.
32. Berti and Vanni, 2002.
33. Ibid., 2002.
34. Berti and Andriolo, 2001.
35. Furnham, 1992, pp. 19, 25, 26.
36. Seixas, 1993; Penuel and Wertsch, 1998; Wertsch and Rozin, 1998; Wineburg, 2000.
37. Lowenthal, 1985.

REFERENCES

Ashby, R. (1993). *Pilot study on students' use of evidence.* Unpublished study, Essex, England.

Ashby, R., and Lee, P.J. (1987). Children's concepts of empathy and understanding in history. In C. Portal (Ed.), *The history curriculum for teachers.* London, England: Falmer Press.

Barca, I. (1997). *Adolescent ideas about provisional historical explanation.* (Portuguese translation for publishing at CEEP.) Braga, Portugal: Universidade do Minho.

Barton, K.C. (1996). Narrative simplifications in elementary students' historical thinking. In J. Brophy (Ed.), *Advances in research on teaching: Teaching and learning history, vol. 6.* Greenwich, CT: JAI Press.

Barton, K.C. (1999). *Best not to forget them: Positionality and students' ideas about significance in Northern Ireland.* Paper presented at the Annual Meeting of the American Educational Research Association, Montreal.

Barton, K.C. (2001). A sociocultural perspective on children's understanding of historical change: Comparative findings from Northern Ireland and the United States. *American Educational Research Journal, 38,* 881-891.

Berti, A.E. (1994). Children's understanding of the concept of the state. In M. Carretero and J.F. Voss (Eds.), *Cognitive and instructional processes in history and the social sciences.* Mahwah, NJ: Lawrence Erlbaum Associates.

Berti, A.E., and Andriolo, A. (2001). Third graders' understanding of core political concepts (law, nation-state, government) before and after teaching. *Genetic, Social and General Psychology Monograph, 127*(4), 346-377.

Berti, A.E., and Bombi, A.S. (1988). *The child's construction of economics.* Cambridge, MA: Cambridge University Press.

Berti, A.E., and Vanni, E. (2002). Italian children's understanding of war: A domain specific approach. *Social Development, 9*(4), 479-496.

Brophy, J., and VanSledright, B. (1997). *Teaching and learning history in elementary schools.* New York: Teachers College Press.

Cercadillo, L. (2000). *Significance in history: Students' ideas in England and Spain.* Unpublished doctoral thesis, University of London.

Cercadillo, L. (2001). Significance in history: Students' ideas in England and Spain. In A.K. Dickinson, P. Gordon, and P.J. Lee (Eds.), *Raising standards in history education: International review of history education volume 3.* Portland, OR: Woburn Press.

Delval, J. (1992). Stages in the child's construction of social knowledge. In M. Carretero and J.F. Voss (Eds.), *Cognitive and instructional processes in history and the social sciences.* Mahwah, NJ: Lawrence Erlbaum Associates.

Dickinson, A.K., and Lee, P.J. (1978). Understanding and research. In A.K. Dickinson and P.J. Lee (Eds.), *History teaching and historical understanding* (pp. 94-120). London, England: Heinemann.

Dickinson, A.K., and Lee, P.J. (1984). Making sense of history. In A. K. Dickinson, P.J. Lee, and P.J. Rogers (Eds.), *Learning history* (pp. 117-153). London, England: Heinemann.

Furnham, A. (1992). Young people's understanding of politics and economics. In M. Carretero and J.F. Voss (Eds.), *Cognitive and instructional processes in history and the social sciences* (pp. 19, 25, 26). Mahwah, NJ: Lawrence Erlbaum Associates.

Halldén, O., (1994). Constructing the learning task in history instruction. In M. Carretero and J.F. Voss (Eds.), *Cognitive and instructional processes in history and the social sciences* (p. 187). Mahwah, NJ: Lawrence Erlbaum Associates.

Lee, P. (2001). History in an information culture. *International Journal of Historical Teaching Learning and Research, 1*(2). Also available: http://www.ex.ac.uk/historyresource/journal2/journalstart.htm [Accessed January 14, 2003].

Lee, P.J., and Ashby, R. (1984). *Making sense of the Second World War.* Unpublished study of seventh grade students' historical explanations carried out in 1984 in Essex, England. Data were collected using video recordings of groups of three students discussing possible explanations, with no adults present, University of London Institute of Education.

Lee, P.J., and Ashby, R. (1998). *History in an information culture.* Paper presented at the Annual Meeting of the American Educational Research Association, San Diego, CA.

Lee, P.J., and Ashby, R. (2000). Progression in historical understanding among students ages 7-14. In P.N. Stearns, P. Seixas, and S. Wineburg (Eds.), *Knowing, teaching and learning history.* New York: University Press.

Lee, P.J., and Ashby, R. (2001). Empathy, perspective taking and rational understanding. In O.L. Davis Jr., S. Foster, and E. Yaeger (Eds.), *Historical empathy and perspective taking in the social studies.* Boulder, CO: Rowman and Littlefield.

Lee, P.J., Dickinson, A.K., and Ashby, R. (1996a). Progression in children's ideas about history. In M. Hughes (Ed.), *Progression in learning.* Bristol, PA: Multilingual Matters.

Lee, P.J., Dickinson, A.K., and Ashby, R. (1996b). Research carried out by Project CHATA (Concepts of history and teaching approaches), funded by the Economic and Social Research Council, Essex, England, 1991-1996.

Lee, P.J., Dickinson, A.K., and Ashby, R. (1997). "Just another emperor": Understanding action in the past. *International Journal of Educational Research, 27*(3), 233-244.

Lee, P.J., Dickinson, A.K., and Ashby, R. (1998). Researching children's ideas about history. In J.F. Voss and M. Carretero (Eds), *International review of history education: Learning and reasoning in history, vol. 2.* Portland, OR: Woburn Press.

Levstik, L., (2002). *Two kinds of empathy: Reasoned analysis and emotional response in historical thinking.* Paper presented at the Annual Meeting of the American Educational Research Association, New Orleans, LA.

Lowenthal, D. (1985). *The past is a foreign country.* Cambridge, MA: Cambridge University Press.

Martin, R. (1989). *The past within us.* Princeton, NJ: Princeton University Press.

Penuel, W.R., and Wertsch, J. (1998). Historical representation as mediated action: Official history as a tool. In J.F. Voss and M. Carretero (Eds.), *International review of history education: Learning and reasoning in history, vol. 2.* Portland, OR: Woburn Press.

Seixas, P. (1993). Popular film and young people's understanding of the history of Native-white relations, *The History Teacher, 3*(May), 351-370.

Shemilt, D. (1980). *History 13-16 evaluation study.* Edinburgh, Scotland: Holmes McDougall.

Shemilt, D. (1983). The devil's locomotive. *History and Theory, XXII*(4), 1-18.

Shemilt, D. (1984). Beauty and the philosopher: Empathy in history and the classroom. In A.K. Dickinson, P.J. Lee, and P.J. Rogers (Eds.), *Learning history.* London, England: Heinemann.

Shemilt, D. (1987). Adolescent ideas about evidence and methodology in history. In C. Portal (Ed.), *The history curriculum for teachers.* London, England: Falmer Press.

Shemilt, D. (1994). Unpublished research, University of Leeds, United Kingdom.

Shemilt, D. (2000). The Caliph's coin: The currency of narrative frameworks in history teaching. In P.N. Stearns, P. Seixas, and S. Wineberg (Eds.), *Knowing, teaching and learning history.* New York: University Press.

Southern, R.W. (1953). *The making of the Middle Ages.* New Haven, CT: Yale University Press.

Thomas, J. (1993). *How students aged 16-19 learn to handle different interpretations of the past.* Unpublished study, University of London Institute of Education, 1990–1993.

Torney-Purta, J. (1992). Dimensions of adolescents' reasoning about political and historical issues: Ontological switches, developmental processes, and situated learning. In M. Carretero and J.F. Voss (Eds.), *Cognitive and instructional processes in history and the social sciences.* Mahwah, NJ: Lawrence Erlbaum Associates.

Walsh, P. (1992). History and love of the past. In P. Lee, J. Slater, P. Walsh, and J. White (Eds.), *The aims of school history: The national curriculum and beyond.* London, England: Tufnell Press.

Wertsch, J.V., and Rozin, M. (1998). The Russian revolution: Official and unofficial accounts. In J.F. Voss and M. Carretero (Eds.), *International review of history education: Learning and reasoning in history, vol. 2.* London, England: Woburn Press.

Wineburg, S. (1998). Reading Abraham Lincoln: An expert/expert study in the interpretation of historical texts. *Cognitive Science, 22*(3), 319-346.

Wineburg, S. (2000). Making historical sense. In P.N. Stearns, P. Seixas, and S. Wineburg (Eds.), *Knowing, teaching and learning history.* New York: New York University Press.

Wineburg, S., and Fournier, J. (1994). Contextualized thinking in history. In M. Carretero and J.F. Voss (Eds.), *Cognitive and instructional processes in history and the social sciences.* Mahwah, NJ: Lawrence Erlbaum Associates.

3

Putting Principles into Practice: Teaching and Planning

Rosalyn Ashby, Peter J. Lee, and Denis Shemilt

It has been argued thus far that the learning of history can be accelerated and deepened through consistent application of the key findings from *How People Learn*, and that these findings should be applied in ways that acknowledge what is distinctive about the historical enterprise and the particular challenges it poses to students (see Chapter 2).

The first key finding of *How People Learn* emphasizes the importance of students' preconceptions. Teachers must take account not only of what students manifestly do not know, but also of what they think they know. This finding is confirmed in the study of history by both research and experience.[1] Much of the gap between what we teach and what students learn is attributable to the fact that students link new knowledge about the past to preexisting but inappropriate knowledge derived from everyday life. Thus, for example, an account of the growth of medieval towns may be linked to existing knowledge about the growth of trees; that is, students assume medieval buildings got bigger, and so the towns grew. More significant still, students have critical misconceptions—about how we know about the past, about the relationship between historical accounts and the past they represent, about what counts as an answer to a "why" or a "how" question, and so on—that are more difficult to access but that impact profoundly the ways in which students construe what they are taught. To the extent that we are able to identify the preconceptions held by students, we may preempt misunderstandings about the substantive past and, more important, seek to modify and develop the conceptual tools students need to make sense of history.

The second key finding of *How People Learn* emphasizes the importance of providing students with conceptual structures and tools with which to organize and manipulate factual knowledge. Students must have a deep foundation of factual knowledge, but this is not tantamount to saying that they must learn all there is to know about any topic or set of topics. Because history is an information-rich subject, it is easy for students to flounder in a sea of facts that cannot be contained or controlled. And because history is about people and events that are halfway recognizable, it can sometimes be viewed as a series of weird soap operas. Thus, the foundations of factual knowledge must be deep in the sense that its layers of historicity are understood; in other words, the rules by which communities work and people interact are likely to shift according to time and place. In addition, as is argued in Chapter 2, the substantive facts and ideas of history must be understood in the context of a conceptual framework that includes second-order concepts such as those associated with time, change, empathy, and cause, as well as evidence and accounts. Indeed, it has been argued that the systematic development of such concepts is essential for students to be able to organize knowledge in ways that facilitate retrieval and application.

The third key finding of *How People Learn* emphasizes the importance of metacognitive approaches that enable students to reflect on and control their own learning. This finding relates to the development of second-order concepts noted above. Students can acquire and refine the conceptual tools necessary to organize and manipulate information only to a limited extent until they are explicitly aware of what they are doing. In order, for example, to determine that a given source is reliable for some purposes but not for others, or to decide that a source can yield evidence of things that it purports to neither say nor show, students must be able not merely to draw inferences, but also to know that they are doing so and to make those inferences objects of consciousness that are evaluated against rules. This level of metacognitive awareness is unlikely to be achieved in the lower grades, but its achievement may be accelerated if teachers of third and fourth graders focus their attention on such questions as "How do we know?" "Is this possible?" and "If this could have happened, can we say that it did happen?"

This chapter examines what these three key findings entail for the ways in which we work with students in the classroom and for the strategies used to plan history teaching. The first section sets the stage for what follows by addressing the issue of the extent to which these findings can realistically be applied in the classroom. The next two sections demonstrate the applicability of the findings by presenting two detailed example classroom case studies.

THE REALITY TEST

The three key findings of *How People Learn* and the arguments advanced in the preceding chapter may be thought to reflect too favorable a view of the realities of teaching in some classrooms. Indeed, we may not always have carte blanche in what is taught, but feel obliged to work within the narrow space between national standards on the one hand and locally adopted textbooks on the other. In consequence, the second key finding may appear to presume that we have more freedom in what we teach than is always allowed us. Worse still, the emphasis placed in the previous chapter and in the first key finding on the identification and systematic development of preconceptions and second-order concepts assumes that we have more in-depth knowledge of how and what students think than may be the case. At the start of the school year, we may know names and test scores but little else. Students must still be taught even if we lack in-depth analysis of their existing knowledge of pre-Columbian civilization or their ability to empathize with predecessors. Last but not least, the exhortation to take "a metacognitive approach to instruction" may appear overly optimistic for some students, who by the end of the year still have not acquired any kind of coherent story. What chance do they have of becoming metacognitively aware?

These are fair points, and can serve as acid tests of the value of what is presented below. At the same time, the reader must keep in mind that a chapter such as this cannot provide a simple recipe for instant success, as any experienced history teacher will know only too well. A lesson plan for unknown children in unknown classrooms invites disaster. This is not just because all students are different personalities; both research and experience tell us there are more specific reasons. Individual students have different prior conceptions of history, the past, and how things happen in the world. In addition, students at any given age are likely to be working with a wide range of ideas (see Box 3-1). We can make some informed predictions about what ideas are likely to be prevalent among students in a particular grade, but research makes it clear that in any given class, some students are likely to be thinking in much more sophisticated ways, perhaps even using the sorts of ideas more common among students many years older. Likewise, some will be operating with much simpler ideas.

Moreover, if we talk here about "fourth graders" and "youngsters" or "seventh graders" and "older students," we are not implying that changes in ideas are an automatic consequence of age. Many seventh graders will happily go on thinking in much the same ways as fourth graders if they are not made aware of the problems their everyday ideas create. Teachers are not the only impetus for changing students' ideas, but it is part of our job as teachers to act as if we were. Because we cannot predict the starting points of any particular class of students, the discussion of example lesson tasks in the following case studies must be qualified by "ifs," alternatives, and conditional moves. At the same time, however, practical moves with real teaching materials used by the authors and by serving teachers in both the United Kingdom and the United States are suggested.[2] They nevertheless remain

BOX 3-1 The 7-Year Gap

The CHATA research discussed in Chapter 2 reveals the conceptual understandings of *some* 8-year-old students to be more advanced than those of *many* 14-year-olds. For example, when asked to explain why one account of the Roman invasion of Britain conflicts with another, *some* 7- and 8-year-olds suggest that the authors may have chosen to record "different facts" because they were asking different questions about the invasion, while *many* 14-year-olds claim that one or other author "made mistakes" in their account. It follows that when working with typical mixed-ability classes, teachers must accommodate a "7-year gap" between the ideas of the lowest- and highest-attaining students.

Two other CHATA findings are significant in this connection. First, ideas about different second-order concepts do not develop in lockstep. A student's understanding of evidence and accounts may be the most advanced in the class, but her grasp of causal and empathetic explanation may not be as good, and her understanding of time and change may even be below the class average. Second, students' ideas about history do not develop as a necessary consequence of maturation. Many seventh and eighth graders are happy with their mental furniture and see no need to rearrange or replace it. To some extent, this is because they lack metacognitive awareness and conclude that they "are no good at history." It is one of the more difficult jobs of teachers to show such students how they can "get good" at the subject, albeit at the cost and effort of ongoing mental makeover.[3]

examples only, and do not offer "the best way" to teach these or any other topics.

Two case studies are presented in this chapter. Each involves a specific task—comprising teaching materials and questions—in the context of how the task might be used in developing students' ideas about historical evidence. The focus of the first case study is a familiar topic, "The Pilgrim Fathers and Native Americans"; the second deals with a more unusual topic, "St. Brendan's Voyage." It might appear illogical to start with the Pilgrim Fathers, since the topic chronologically precedes the Brendan voyage. The fact that the task in the Brendan case study is written for fourth graders, while that in the Pilgrims case study is for sixth graders, may make the order appear even more wayward.

Given appropriate teaching, we would expect sixth graders on the whole to outperform fourth graders in their understanding of historical evidence. If their teaching has been designed to develop their understanding of evidence, older students will, on the whole, apply more powerful ideas than younger ones. However, we have already seen that the "7-year gap" means there is considerable variation in students' ideas, and in any case, students' ideas will depend in part on what they have already learned. Moreover, historical questions can be answered at very different levels of sophistication, so that students from a range of different grades can profitably tackle the same materials and questions. Students need not wait until they reach a certain grade to benefit from trying to weigh the evidence for the claim that St. Brendan reached America a thousand years before Columbus, but more conceptually sophisticated students will give different answers than less sophisticated ones.

Of course, the language we use in designing our questions and materials is likely to set limits on the range of students who will be able to work with them, and we cannot expect young students to have the same understanding of the adult world—even in the present—as older students. Thus, it still makes sense to talk of designing tasks for a particular grade, at least as far as setting limits below which use of the task would be unwise. But if we encounter students from sixth or seventh grade who have not developed ideas about evidence that we would normally begin to teach in fourth grade, we might profitably use the "fourth-grade" task with them.

We therefore begin with the Pilgrim Fathers and Native Americans case study, on the grounds that it will be a much more familiar topic for most teachers than the Brendan voyage. The discussion of evidence work in this first case study assumes that reference is made to a standard textbook and that we have no privileged knowledge about student preconceptions and misconceptions. The case study aims to illustrate, first, how it is possible to identify and work with student preconceptions during the process of teaching; second, how student ideas about a second-order concept, that of *evidence*, can be developed in ways that support, not supplant, the teaching of substantive history; and third, how it is possible to promote metacognitive awareness among students who have no special ideas and abilities.

While the materials and questions in the Pilgrim Fathers and Native Americans case study are designed for students who already have some acquaintance with ideas about evidence, the aim of the second case study—on St. Brendan's Voyage—is to introduce less sophisticated students to some key ideas about evidence in the context of an adventure without losing them in masses of content. There is also a difference in focus between the two case studies. Discussion of the first emphasizes the identification and refinement of previously acquired ideas about evidence, whereas the second case study concentrates on the teaching of students who have yet to reach first base and, in particular, who cannot yet make clear and stable distinctions between well-founded and speculative accounts of the past.

Although the tasks in the two case studies were designed with students in grade 4 (St. Brendan) and grade 6 (Pilgrim Fathers) in mind, materials and questions from both can be and have been used from grades 4 through 8 and beyond. This notwithstanding, decisions about how—and even whether—materials and questions are used with given classes must be informed by the ideas the students are already working with and the kind of responses we expect. In any case, nothing in what follows is about learning that can be accomplished in a single or even several short sessions. Even when students appear to have understood what has been taught in one context, we will need to return to it in other topics. Changes in students' ideas take time, patience, and planning.

WORKING WITH EVIDENCE: PILGRIM FATHERS AND NATIVE AMERICANS

Exploring the Basis for Textbook Claims and the Nature of Sources

The choice of the arrival of the Pilgrims as a topic for discussion here implies no claims about what should or should not be taught. However, it is clearly a popular topic in textbooks, and one with which readers are likely to be familiar. It is also relevant to the broader topics, such as "Exploration and Encounter" and "The Settlement of New England" that are regularly taught. Moreover, it is a topic that offers opportunities to explore the Pilgrims' significance for later generations in America, and supports an examination of the complex relationships between the newcomers and the native inhabitants that can help break down stereotyping. There is also a very rich record available from the testimony of the Pilgrims that can provide worthwhile and exciting learning opportunities, particularly in connection with understanding the nature of historical evidence.

The questions in the Pilgrims' task work at two levels. First, they can expose the assumptions students appear to be working with, and second, as a consequence, they provide the teacher with a basis for a learning dialogue with the students.[4] As will be seen, such a dialogue can challenge the misconceptions that become apparent and encourage the development of more powerful ideas, while at the same time providing the teacher with information about future learning needs. Testimony of the kind provided in the materials associated with this task needs to be understood evidentially, and part of the teacher's task is to encourage students to think in more complex ways about the experiences, ideas, and beliefs of these "eyewitnesses."

The source materials can interact with the textbook so as to transport students from the security of a few historical particulars and descriptions of the arrival of the Mayflower in Cape Cod Bay in 1620 to the more precarious circumstances of William Bradford and John Pory and the early seventeenth-century world they inhabited. The time and place can be richly explored through the materials left behind, and the legacy of the events considered through their impact on later societies. The search for access to this world through these materials is likely to be halting and problematic for young students; good storytellers may well be tempted to believe they can open it up to their students without involving the testimony of those involved more directly. Working with students, who are happy to grapple with the difficulties inherent in materials of this kind, provides us with a different perspective. Learning experiences of any kind, however, need structures, with clear objectives.

An approach of this kind can be used for a wide range of age and ability groups. The format can remain the same but the task made to differ in its language level; the nature, length, and quantity of the sources used; and the extent of visual material needed to support ideas. The task was initially designed for sixth graders but was taught to U.K. sixth and eighth graders as a whole-class lesson. The examples quoted are of two kinds: written answers to the teachers' whole-class questions, and excerpts from a recorded follow-up discussion with a small group of three sixth graders. (The small-group recording offers a more detailed picture than written answers can provide of how students responded to the questions.) U.K. students' perspective on the Pilgrims is likely to differ from that of equivalent students in the United States, but the focus here is on students' evidential understanding.

Five sources have been chosen. The extracts taken from William Bradford's journal have been set out separately in Sources 1 and 3, separating the arrival of the Mayflower from the expedition ashore, so as to allow students easier access. The extracts have also been edited to limit the difficulty for these 12- and 15-year-olds.

The three written sources provide testimony from William Bradford about the arrival and settlement of the Pilgrims at Plymouth in 1620 and testimony from John Pory, a visitor to the settlement in 1622. Through these sources, the teacher is able to explore students' existing understandings of "eyewitness" accounts, and to encourage students to look behind this testimony to consider the circumstances, ideas, and beliefs of the people directly involved.

The two paintings depicting the arrival of the Pilgrims allow the teacher to explore and challenge students' misconceptions about these sources as a record of the actual events of the time. They also give the teacher an opportunity to encourage students to recognize that while the paintings may not provide evidence of the events of 1620, they do provide evidence of the significance attached to the arrival of the Pilgrims in 1620 by later generations.

The Pilgrims' task begins by presenting students with extracts from their textbooks and a map showing them the location where the action takes place. The second textbook extract provides an opportunity to introduce the testimony of William Bradford and the evidence it may not have been intended to provide.

How do we know about the arrival of the Pilgrims in America? The Mayflower finds land, and the Pilgrims look for a place to settle.

One textbook tells us:

> On November 11, 1620, after 10 weeks at sea, a small, storm-battered English vessel rounded the tip of Cape Cod and dropped its anchor in the quiet harbor of what is now Provincetown, Massachusetts. The people in the ship were too tired and sick to travel farther. While the Mayflower swung at anchor in Provincetown harbor, a landing party looked for a place to settle. These men explored a small bay on the western edge of Cape Cod. They found a swift-running stream with clear, fresh drinking water. The area seemed ideal for a settlement. In December, the Pilgrims anchored the Mayflower in the bay and began building Plymouth Plantation.[5]

Another textbook tells us:

> They found a spot on the inner shore of Cape Cod Bay and promptly named it for the town from which they had sailed—Plymouth. At Plymouth the Pilgrims found abandoned cornfields. Their leader, William Bradford, sadly described their situation. "What could they see," he wrote, "but a hideous and desolate wilderness…what could now sustain them but the spirit of God and his grace?"[6]

Here is a map to help you locate the places the textbook is talking about.

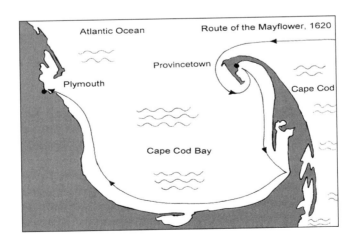

Once the students are familiar with this basic material from the textbooks, the teacher can give them a briefing sheet. This briefing sheet has three main purposes: to introduce the students to their inquiry, to encourage an enthusiasm for the work, and to provide them with an ultimate goal—the production of their own *substantiated* account of the arrival of the Mayflower and the decision to settle in Plymouth. The briefing sheet enables the students to focus on the instructions, to which they can return if necessary; the teacher works through the instructions with the class, clarifying, checking understanding, and reinforcing them as necessary.

Source 1: An extract taken from William Bradford's personal journal, finished in 1650. Bradford was one of the leaders of the English Separatists whom we now call the Pilgrims.

Having arrived in a good harbor, and brought safe to land, they fell upon their knees and blessed God who had delivered them. They had no friends to welcome them and no inns to refresh their weather beaten bodies; no houses to go to for food. When St. Paul (in the bible) was shipwrecked the barbarians were kind to him and his friends but the barbarians here when they met with the Separatists and their friends were readier to fill their sides full of arrows. And it was winter, and they knew the winters here to be subject to fierce storms, and dangerous to travel to known places, much more to search an unknown coast. They could only see a desolate wilderness, full of wild beasts and wild men—and what multitudes there might be of them they knew not. What could now sustain them but the Spirit of God and his Grace?

Source 2: "The Mayflower on Her Arrival in Plymouth Harbor" by William Formsby Halsall. Painted in Massachusetts in 1882.

Briefing Sheet

Things for you to think about and things for you to do

How do the people who wrote the textbooks know about these events when they happened nearly 400 years ago?

The second of these textbook writers gives us a clue about how they found out.

◆ Can you spot it?

The first textbook tells us more than the second textbook, but the second textbook helps us understand how the writer knew about the Pilgrims' arrival.

◆ You are going to carry out your own inquiry about "The Arrival of the Pilgrims" so that you can write your own version in a way that shows how you know these things.

Your inquiry will involve looking carefully at some *sources* and doing some hard thinking.

Source 3: Another extract taken from William Bradford's personal journal, finished in 1650.

Arrived at Cape Cod on the 11th of November and a few people volunteered to look for a place to live. It was thought there might be some danger but sixteen people were given permission to explore. They were well armed and led by Captain Standish. They set off on the 15th of November; and when they had marched about a mile by the seaside, they spotted five or six persons with a dog coming towards them, who were savages; but they fled from them and ran up into the woods, and the English followed them, partly to

Source: A source is something that has survived from the past that we can use to find out about the past. Sources help us work things out that we wouldn't otherwise know.

✦ Read the sources carefully, and as you do this, write down questions that come to your mind.

(These questions will be useful to your teacher because they will help her understand how you are thinking.)

✦ Then answer the questions your teacher thought about, set out on a separate sheet.

(While you are answering your teacher's questions, she will collect your questions and think about how to find answers to them.)

Words you might need to know about:

Pilgrims: These people were looking for a place to live so that they could worship God in their own way without interference. They were called Separatists at the time because they separated themselves from the official ideas the priests in England taught about God. Later people called them the Pilgrims, and sometimes the Pilgrim Fathers.
Shallop: A small boat. This was used to get close to land because the Mayflower could not safely go into shallow water.

see if they could speak with them, and partly to discover if there might be more of them lying in ambush. But the Indians left the woods and ran away on the sands as hard as they could so they followed them by the track of their feet for several miles. When it was night they set up a guard and rested in quiet that night; and the next morning followed their track till they had headed a great creek and so left the sands and turned another way into the woods. They followed them by guess, hoping to find their dwellings; but they soon lost both them and themselves. At length they found water and refreshed themselves, being the first New England water they had drunk.

*Then they changed their direction to get to the other shore,
and on the way found a pond of clear, fresh water, and
shortly after a large area of clear ground where the Indians
had formerly set corn, and some of their graves. And further
on they saw new stubble where corn had been set the same
year; also they found where lately a house had been, where
some planks and a great kettle was remaining, and heaps of
sand newly paddled with their hands. Which, they digging
up, found in them Indian baskets filled with corn of different
colors, which seemed to them a very goodly sight (having
never seen any such before). This was near the place of the
river they thought they might find and they found it where it
opened itself into two arms with a high cliff of sand in the
entrance but more like creeks of salt water than fresh, and
they saw a good harbor for their shallop. Then they returned
to the ship lest the others might be in fear of their safety;
and took with them part of the corn and buried up the rest.*

**Source 4: "The Landing of the Pilgrims" by Michael Felice
Corne. Painted in Salem, Massachusetts, between 1803 and
1806.**

**Source 5: Written by John Pory, an official from the settle-
ment at Jamestown, farther south in Virginia, after he had
visited Plymouth in 1622.**

Whether it was because of the wind or the backwardness of their ship's captain they did not arrive where they had planned. Instead they reached the harbor of Cape Cod, called Pawmet by the Indians. After some dangerous errors and mistakes, they stumbled by accident upon the harbor of Plymouth where it pleased Almighty God (who had better provided for them than they could imagine) to land them where there was an old town, which several years before had been abandoned by the Indians. So they quietly and justly settled down there without having to push any of the natives out, so not so much as one drop of blood was shed. Even the savages themselves did not claim any title to it so that the right of those planters to it is altogether unquestionable. The harbor is good for shipping both small and great being land-locked on all sides. The town is seated on the ascent of a hill. There is plenty both of fish and fowl every day in the year and I know no place in the world that can match it.

The briefing sheet is designed to encourage students to record their own questions during their initial examination of the sources. This is done to make transparent any difficulties the students might encounter with the sources, and to encourage them to generate their own questions as part of the longer-term goal of developing their independent learning strategies. After their initial perusal of the sources and the recording of their own questions, the students are asked to respond to their teacher's questions. It is useful to explain to the students that these questions may well look similar to those they have raised themselves, demonstrating that questions are not necessarily the special province of the teacher. Normally the teacher will promise to collate the questions raised by the students and pursue answers to them in the following session. Students may raise the point that none of the sources directly record the thoughts of the native population at the time; this creates the opportunity to ask the students to think about why that is and what those thoughts might have been.

Students' written responses to the teacher's questions are used to provide the teacher first with an understanding of the students' preconceptions about evidence, and second with an opportunity to begin a learning dialogue about the nature of these sources and their potential as evidence (see questions 1, 2, 3, and 4). In addition, the questions provide a means to support the first steps in developing students' understanding of the beliefs that influenced the Pilgrims' actions (see questions 5 and 6). These questions are simply examples, and there are many other ways in which the selected sources could be used to both diagnose and develop students' thinking.

Teacher Question 1.

The first textbook writer describes the Mayflower's arrival. He tells us that "a small storm-battered English vessel rounded the tip of Cape Cod." Source 2 is a painting showing the Mayflower arriving at Cape Cod. We know that when the ship's master sailed it back to England, it quickly fell into disrepair and rotted. So how would the person painting the picture in Source 2 have been able to work out what the Mayflower looked like?

What is this question trying to find out about students' existing understanding?

The question is designed to check whether students understand that

    (a) The painter is not an eyewitness to the arrival of the Mayflower.
    (b) There was a time difference between the source and the event.
    (c) The Mayflower was not available to the painter as a relic from the time.

The question also probes whether students understand the ways in which the painter might have knowledge of the Mayflower, and whether they see the painting as providing direct information about the arrival of the Mayflower or as evidence of its significance to later generations.

What is this question trying to encourage students to reflect on as a means of developing their understanding?

The question is trying to develop students' understanding of evidence by encouraging them to see:
    (a) That the painting is better evidence of the *significance* than the *fact* of the Mayflower's arrival.
    (b) That the absence of relic evidence or of trustworthy descriptions by eyewitnesses is not an insoluble problem. We can find good grounds for saying what the Mayflower could not have looked like and for working out its probable appearance.
    (c) That it is possible to work out the extent to which the representation of the Mayflower should be trusted by checking whether it is typical of ships of the period.

The responses of two particular groups of students—aged 12 and 15—to some of the questions exemplify the kinds of moves students make. (If no age is given for a quotation, the example comes from the younger group.)

You need to be able to see for yourself.

Simon assumed that the painter might have seen the Mayflower before it left England, ignoring the time gap between the painting and the event it depicted. He claimed that "the person who drew the picture knew what the boat looked like because he might have seen it in the port before she set sail for America." Jennifer, recognizing a time difference, believed there would still be something left of the Mayflower, and was convinced that "the person painting the picture in Source 2 was able to work out what the Mayflower looked like by visiting the remains." Some 12-year-olds saw that the painter could not have been an eyewitness, but argued that it was therefore not possible to know what the ship looked like. As Adam explained, "The person painting Source 2 wouldn't have known what the Mayflower had looked like as he wasn't even there."

If you weren't there to see for yourself, then you need access to someone who was.

Typically, many students felt the need to connect the painter with the subject matter of the painting by creating a direct link with an eyewitness. Peter said, "The painter could have got the information from a person who actually saw the Mayflower." In saying this, however, Peter stretched the age of the possible witness to an improbable extent to accommodate his thinking, while simultaneously shrinking the amount of time that passed between 1620 and the production of the painting in 1882. "Since it was a hundred years after, there may have been people alive from the vessel to describe it." The importance to *some* students of an eyewitness as a way of knowing about the past is clearly considerable.

Contact could be maintained with the eyewitness by means of knowledge handed down through the generations.

Students can, of course, be more realistic about the time difference. Elliot pointed out that the painting "was painted 262 years after the voyage." He looked for a different kind of link to the original witness, the handing down of knowledge within a linear sequence. He suggested, "It must have been told by the voyagers to their children, and then to their children, and then to their children, what it looked like." He recognized that this might have created difficulties for the artist and claimed, "The painter is probably drawing partly from what he's been told and partly from his imagination." In a similar vein, Edward recognized the difficulty of both a drawing of the Mayflower surviving over a long period of time and this kind of information being available as oral evidence over such a long period. He wrote:

> *I don't think he could have [worked out what the Mayflower looked like]. The only way he could was if there was a drawing that had remained for over 250 years which is unlikely. It also says that the artist painted it in 1882 so it couldn't have been spread about by word of mouth.*

In recognizing the problems, however, Edward provided no solution for how we might check the appearance of the Mayflower and thus the accuracy of the information in the painting. The absence of a direct link and uncertainties of transmission make a determination of accuracy difficult.

You can use a scissors-and-paste approach.

When faced with the difficulties of direct access or transmission error, many students operate with a scissors-and-paste approach to piece together what is available and what they can trust. Robert explained that "the person who painted it knew what the Mayflower looked like because another artist had probably provided it in Britain and he altered the angle and scenery." He was working with the idea that the picture of the Mayflower needs to be an exact copy of its arrival in the bay, almost a photograph of the event, and saw the possibility of piecing information together to produce this result. Robert believed that the details of the ship might have been available to the artist through a previous picture of the Mayflower in England, but that the American painter would have been able to create the setting needed to portray this event, perhaps from his own personal geographical knowledge.

You have to work it out from other sources or knowledge available to you.

The awareness of a broader range of records available to the historian can help students recognize that we are not left totally helpless without eyewitnesses (or indeed, as some believe, without the recovery of the Mayflower itself). Julie, aged 15, suggested, "The artist may have studied pictures of other early seventeenth-century ships and drawn one. The painter might have incorporated knowledge from these into his painting." Melanie, also 15, claimed in her written answer to this question, "There would have been blueprints, paintings and maybe even a sister ship to the Mayflower."

Students' need for a direct link with the events, however, can remain very strong. Peter was particularly keen on having access to something tangible from the period.

Peter	They have this age testing machine and they can test how old things are.
Teacher	What would they be testing with that?
Peter	Maybe things on the ship.
Matthew	Yes, but then that would only tell us when it was manufactured and not when it circled round Cape Cod, and it still wouldn't tell us what it looked like.
Peter	Well that would be in William Bradford's diary.
Matthew	I think it was based on what was probably a regular design and all that would have changed was mast shapes so it could have been like a regular ship.
Peter	The archaeologists might have got it up from the sea, with all sorts of cranes and things.
Matthew	But it had rotted.
Peter	Well the basic shape might be there just not all the fine details.

Even when he came under pressure from his teacher and Matthew, Peter remained convinced that the recovery of the ship or a direct description of it is essential. He was clearly familiar with the way in which science, archaeology, and technology might assist the historian.

Teacher Question 2.

In Source 3, William Bradford is talking about the first people who went ashore. He tells us that it wasn't until they had "marched about a mile by the seaside" that "they spotted five or six persons with a dog coming towards them." He tells us they "fled and ran away into the woods, and the English followed them." But Source 4 shows the Native Americans waiting on the shore to meet them. How do I solve this confusion?

What is this question trying to find out about students' existing understanding?

The question explores whether students are making decisions simply on the basis of whether someone was there or not (Bradford was, the artist wasn't), or they understand that people's intentions in producing the sources also need to be taken into account.

What is this question trying to encourage students to reflect on as a means of developing their understanding?

The question is designed to encourage students to reflect on:
    (a) Whether, and under what circumstances, the accuracy of the picture matters.
    (b) What the artist was trying to portray about the encounter between the Pilgrims and the Native Americans.
    (c) Whether the encounter portrayed by Bradford would have been described in the same way by the native people at the time.

Trust the source who was in a position to know.

We must expect many students, convinced of the need for an eyewitness, to respond in a direct and uncomplicated way to this question. George, for example, wrote, "William Bradford was there and the painter wasn't." Given the claim being made, this is a perfectly justifiable answer. Jack also made the point about Bradford being in a position to know, and explained the conflicting information in the painting by pointing out that stories change over time:

> *I think that Source 3 was right, as he was one of the leaders of the Pilgrims. In his own personal diary he was probably writing the events that happened when they happened, whereas Source 4 was drawn almost 200 years after the events. Over 200 years stories change.*

These students did not question whether Bradford was among the actual party that first went ashore. They made the assumption that he was there. The idea of "being there" is often generalized by students and taken as sufficient to validate a great deal. Sometimes they use "from the time" regardless of the distance between the person providing testimony and the event itself. In this case, however, the students made a legitimate distinction.

You need to understand the purpose of the artist.

In pursuing this question with students, an important goal is to help them understand that the painting is not meant to be a photographic image of an exact moment in time, and that although it is "just a painting," it can often yield information about how past events were seen by later generations.

Some 12-year-olds considered the artist's purpose in relation to the information contained in the painting. Daniel, for example, said, "I think that the Indians are in the picture to show that they were there first, and that they were watching for them even if they weren't seen." Daniel's response is interesting in two ways. First, it suggests a specific purpose on the part of the artist, showing that Daniel was aware that this intent must be considered if the painting is to be understood. Second, the response introduced a perspective not yet suggested by the text extracts and the sources, nor at this stage by the questions. Daniel was sensitive to the position of the Native Americans. In the questions he had recorded when first looking at the sources, he had written about the painting (Source 4), "Were the Indians watching them from the land?" About John Pory's testimony (Source 5), he raised the question, "Why didn't the native Indians attack them?"

When Adam began to muse on the production of both paintings (Sources 2 and 4) in a follow-up classroom discussion, the teacher used Daniel's written response to explore the issue further.

| Adam | It's funny that it's done in Massachusetts the same as the other one. |
| Teacher | Yes. Let me just run this past you all and see what you think about this. This answer by someone in your class says, "In this picture I think the Indians are in the picture to show that they were there first, and that they were watching for them, even if they weren't seen." |

Matthew recognized the point being made when the teacher confronted the students with Daniel's response, and he elaborated on it. Although both Matthew and Daniel were making assumptions about the artist's actual intentions, they clearly recognized that the artist was not necessarily attempting a historical reconstruction.

| Matthew | I think that's very good 'cos art isn't always total fact it's usually symbolism because you couldn't put tiny men on there showing that they are far away, it could very well symbolize, yeah, that these Native Americans are here first and its not really the Pilgrims' land at all. |
| Adam | I think the Indians would be very territorial, like protect their land and their territories and say, like, "This is my territory, go away!" |

The teacher probed the students' ideas further by getting them to consider the possibility that the painting might provide evidence of the importance of the event to future generations, and might not necessarily be an attempt to recognize the Native Americans' first claim to the land.

Teacher	You remember the part where we said that those who arrived on the Mayflower become known as the Pilgrim Fathers later on. And that kind of means that the painting might really be trying to say these people are really important because they established, it was the beginning, they are the "Fathers" who made this part of America what it was at the time the painting was done. So what might the artist want to portray about these people—the Pilgrim Fathers? Would the painter be concerned to portray the Native Americans' position? Would the historical accuracy matter that much in this case?
Matthew	Like they would want to show them as great because they founded the white part of America.
Adam	Maybe it was to make the Pilgrims look good.
Peter	Yeah, make the Pilgrims look like they are fending off the Indians, make the Pilgrims look good.

Matthew took the point further, and an awareness of past attitudes and perspectives came into play.

Matthew	I think this painting could be somewhat racial and that they are kind of trying to say that these Pilgrims are the white fathers and that the Native Americans shouldn't be there, its just for these people which isn't fair, its very racial, but that's what could be portrayed—it could be a racial statement.
Teacher	That's interesting, but what would we need to know to interpret the painting? It may not have been intended to be racial, but merely to focus on the arrival of the Pilgrims, and the Native Americans are just there as part of the scenery. The racial aspect may be more unconscious than we are supposing, or the artist may have wanted to reflect this as a peaceful encounter.

Adam	You would need to know about the painter who actually painted it. You need some background information.
Peter	Then we could find out the truth about what it's saying.
Teacher	Would the information you need be just information about the painter? What else would you need to know?
Matthew	What period of time it was painted and whereabouts it was painted. They could be changed with society, like giving in to society [meaning agreeing with predominant ideas?] because, like, most people in Salem, Massachusetts, which is where this was painted, were white, so he wanted to portray the white people as the great greats . . . or however you want to interpret it.
Teacher	There was some very good thinking there actually, and I think you got us on to that point, didn't you, Matthew, about symbolism, and therefore what you're saying to me seems to be that the painting is not supposed to be *exactly* what happened at the time but may be more about what it means to people later on, and at a particular time and place.

In this excerpt, the teacher sought to discover whether Matthew was close to adopting a more subtle approach than his initial position had suggested, and his response showed a growing awareness of the complexities of interpreting the intentions of the painter and the kind of knowledge one needs about the society in which the painter was working (see Box 3-2). This is a strong hint that Matthew will be able to use any new information and source materials judiciously and to understand the significance of the Mayflower's arrival for future generations. The materials to be used in future lessons with these particular students will need to explore the different relationships among groups of people at the time and the complexities of the Mayflower legacy.

Teacher Question 3.

The writer of Source 5 tells us, "The harbor is good for shipping both small and great, being landlocked on all sides" and "The town is seated on the ascent of a hill." How did the writer know this?

BOX 3-2 Interpreting Sources in Context

The disposition to interpret historical data with reference to the social contexts within which they were produced and intended to be used is slow to develop and, even when developed, may be difficult to activate. Working with a group of "college-bound" seniors who "represented the successes of our educational system," Sam Wineburg found that they were disposed to take at face value a "patently polemical" account of the skirmish between British soldiers and colonial farmers at Lexington Green in 1775. Wineburg concludes that these able seniors "failed to see the text as a social instrument skillfully crafted to achieve a social end."[7]

It is necessary to account for the disparity in ideas and assumptions between the "college-bound" seniors and the more sophisticated sixth graders who engaged with the Pilgrim Fathers materials and tasks. Three factors are significant in this connection. First, it may be easier for students to construe pictorial rather than textual sources within a supplied or inferred context of social meanings and intentions. Second, the text used by Wineburg carried the received authority of a textbook account and, as Wineburg notes, "the textbook, not the eyewitness accounts, emerged as the primary source." Teaching of the sixth graders, on the other hand, had systematically diminished the credibility of the Mayflower painting by pointing out that the artists could not possibly have witnessed the events depicted. Third, and perhaps most significant, the teachers who worked with the Pilgrim Fathers materials and tasks had the development of students' understanding of evidence concepts as their principal objective. The seniors, as Wineburg observes, should not be "overly" criticized since "these aspects of text, while central to the skilled reading of history, are rarely addressed in school curricula."

Teacher Question 4.

John Pory, the writer of Source 5, tells us that when the Pilgrims reached the harbor of Cape Cod, they found "an old town, which several years before had been abandoned by the Indians." The writer was not one of the people who arrived on the Mayflower, so how did he know this?

What are these questions trying to find out about students' existing understanding?

These two questions work together. They are designed to check whether students understand that "being in a position to know" is not just a matter of whether someone was there at the time, but also depends on the kind of knowledge we are asking about.

What are these questions trying to encourage students to reflect on as a means of developing their understanding?

The questions encourage students to:
(a) Recognize that different kinds of information may be given in people's testimony.
(b) Think about how these differences affect the way we can verify testimony (using other sources in some cases, and judging likelihood and plausibility in others).
(c) Think about why the circumstances at Plymouth might be important to John Pory and perhaps speculate about the nature of his visit.

These kinds of reflections can encourage students to move beyond the face value of testimony and begin to draw inferences, getting sources to yield what they did not set out to reveal.

You need to make distinctions among kinds of claims.

Pory's claim in Source 5 that "the harbor is good for shipping both small and great, being landlocked on all sides" and that "the town is seated on the ascent of a hill" are based on his own observation of the geographic advantages of Plymouth during his visit in 1622. Students who have become familiar with source work are likely to look at the source caption and recognize this. Pory's claim that the town was one that "several years before had been abandoned by the Indians" is, however, of a different kind, and may well have rested on word of mouth from either the native population or more likely the Pilgrims' own story of their arrival, told to him during his visit. The circumstances at Plymouth may indeed have reached him by word of mouth at Jamestown, but his written account of Plymouth is in the context of his visit. The advantages of Plymouth's geographic location and the Pilgrims' relationships with the Native Americans would no doubt have been a subject of discussion between someone from Jamestown and the leaders of the Plymouth settlement, and Pory's account helps the teacher introduce students to the importance of these advantages for the Plymouth settlers.

We should expect many 12-year-olds, and perhaps most 15-year-olds, to be able to distinguish between the different claims addressed in these two questions. Jonathan's written answers demonstrated his ability to make this distinction:

> *Question 3: The writer of Source 5 would know this because he visited Plymouth two years after the Pilgrims' settlement and not many changes of this kind would have happened.*
>
> *Question 4: John Pory probably asked William Bradford about this because they were both in Plymouth in the same decade.*

Jonathan understood that Plymouth's geography was unlikely to change quickly and that Pory would have been able to see these features for himself. He was also aware, like many in his age group, that Pory's knowledge base for the second claim might have depended on what others at Plymouth had told him.

Generalizing.

Some students will suggest William Bradford's journal as the basis for John Pory's knowledge of Plymouth and pay little attention to the information attached to Source 5 about the visit to Plymouth in 1622, or decide that this information is not relevant to the question. David's responses are illustrative:

> *Question 3: The writer would have known this by the personal diary of William Bradford which they found.*
>
> *Question 4: He could have known this because of the diary of William Bradford.*

Students like David may not take into account that Bradford's journal was not published until 1650, and may therefore not ask themselves whether Bradford would have shown Pory any records he had made or whether, during a visit in the circumstances of early settlement, these things would have been an important matter for discussion between the two men (and indeed others). David did not get behind this source to the circumstances surrounding its production. If he had looked at the source caption, he did not use it to inform his response.

Another kind of response is to recognize that a site visit could provide this kind of evidence, but not to think about the difference between the geographic features of the site, which are unlikely to have deteriorated, and the signs of an abandoned town, which may well have been obliterated by the activities of the 2 years between the arrival of the Pilgrims and Pory's visit. The concept of "town" here is also likely to be important: if students imagine a Native American settlement as consisting of brick or stone buildings, an answer such as Vincent's makes more sense.

Question 3: The writer might have known this by going to the site and finding ruins.

Question 4: This question has the same answer as question 3.

Vincent was presumably assuming that Patuxet (the name used by the native population for the abandoned town on which the Plymouth Plantation was built) would still have been visible in the way the ruins of a modern town might be. Although there may have been signs of a settlement, it is more plausible that the abandoned town would have been an important topic of the conversations that took place between Pory and the settlers, particularly given the comparative advantage an "abandoned town" had for the Pilgrims in their relationship with the native population.

If we return to one of the groups of students reflecting on these questions with their teacher and look at a substantial portion of their discussion, the importance of understanding exactly what students mean becomes very clear. Unless we know the distinctions that matter here—the ones that indicate crucial steps in students' understanding—we can blur students' ideas and fail to help them move forward.

In discussion with his teacher, Peter—forever enthusiastic—suggested a range of possible sources that Pory might have used as a basis for his claims, while Matthew tried to pin down the circumstances of the visit, and made a distinction between what Pory would have been able to see for himself and what he might have been told by the people of Plymouth. Adam challenged Pory's second claim by suggesting it rested on hearsay. Their teacher triggered this discussion by focusing on questions 3 and 4.

Teacher	We need to look at Source 5. It says the harbor is good for shipping both small and great, being landlocked on all sides. Some people asked about what landlocked meant. Do you understand what that means now?
All	Yes.
Teacher	Pory also tells us that the town is seated on the ascent of a hill. And one question there is how does he know that? And a further question is that he also tells us that when the Pilgrims reached the harbor of Cape Cod they found an old town, which several years before had been abandoned by the Indians. So I want to know how the writer knew that, because he wasn't on the Mayflower. Can you explain *each* of those to me?

Peter	Well maybe for the second one it could have been that the leader, William Bradford, maybe it was in his journal, and maybe also that he's been to see that place and he has found signs of markings, like Indian words and statues of their gods.
Matthew	Yeah because it says here "Written by John Pory an official from the settlement at Jamestown, further south in Virginia, after he has visited Plymouth in 1622," so he had actually visited, so that explains the geographical point, and then it could have been from word of mouth from the people who were actually on the Mayflower so they are talking to each other. That's how he finds out about the old town that several years had been abandoned by the Indians.
Adam	Yeah, that's probably true but that doesn't make his source as reliable as it could be then, because his source is not based on pure facts, it's probably not based on pure fact, it's probably based on word of mouth and what he's been told.

Perhaps Adam used the phrase "not based on pure facts" in an attempt to distinguish between the physical environment available for all to see, and as a consequence easily testable, and the kind of knowledge that comes secondhand to someone, resting on another's word about what he or she had seen or heard. The teacher checked the students' understanding of this distinction, but it was Matthew who responded.

Teacher	Which one of these things can you say that for? Both of those questions?
Matthew	No. I believe like I said before, that where it says the harbor is good for shipping both small and great, being landlocked on both sides, you can see through your eyes, so you don't need to be told about that, but in order to be told about the old town it has to have been by word of mouth which can sometimes be twisted like we managed to find that paintings can be twisted by social . . . surroundings.
Peter	Even if he did get it by word of mouth people do twist the truth as you go along.
Adam	Like *Pass it on*.

This discussion goes beyond the parameters of questions 3 and 4 in a search for some general principles. Matthew's notion of "twisting the truth" appears to appeal to a familiar, everyday understanding of intentional distortion, but his reference to "social surroundings" may indicate an understanding that "twisting" may be less deliberate. Adam's analogy with the game *Pass it on* reflects the same ambiguity between transmission errors as a consequence of the very nature of word-of-mouth information and deliberate distortion (although Peter's comment was clearly about the latter).

The teacher explored how far the students could think more precisely about intentions, because the second of John Pory's claims is not of the sort likely to have come about through a deliberate attempt to twist the truth. The students nevertheless continued to pursue the issue of deliberate distortion.

Teacher	If you are going to use the word "twist," can you make distinctions between the kind of things people are likely to twist and those they aren't?
Peter	If it was something important and they didn't want anybody to find out about it they twist it so they think it was something else.
Matthew	It depends who they are supporting, um, say the Pilgrims did something really bad. Say they murdered Indians while they were sleeping just out of want for their land, they would make it sound a bit better, like that the Indians did so many horrible things to them that they didn't actually do, so that it was even a good deed to go and murder them while they were sleeping.
Adam	They wouldn't even say they were sleeping. They would say the Indians came to them so they killed them in battle and so they were great warriors.

These speculations brought Peter back to the sources they were examining. Despite the previous discussion about the status of the painting in Source 4, he used this source as a stimulus to articulate his concerns about the Native American perspective.

Peter	Yeah, and you know where it says abandoned by the Indians, well in Source 4 it shows that the Indians were actually still there, so whether

	maybe the Indians were slaughtered or maybe they were hiding, because they did not want those people to come over and take the land and change their cultures, and then these people just found their land, and they are threatened by it, and they think they are going to take over their culture.
Adam	Yeah, leading on from what Matt says about the way they exaggerate things, it says they was abandoned but the people could have done, like, invaded their culture and slaughtered them, and therefore they would say there were no Indians there so it was abandoned to make them sound, like, not so bad.
Matthew	So it would be to look like they were great.
Peter	Supposedly.
Matthew	In American people's eyes they *were*, because they founded their land and would see it as their land.

The students had begun to think of the general context of what an encounter of this kind might mean to the Native Americans, and as a consequence found it difficult to believe in the convenience of the "abandoned" town (all the more convenient if the "town" is still conceived of as a collection of permanent structures in which the new arrivals could find shelter). They also believed that the Pilgrims would have felt some need to justify their claim to Plymouth. At this point, the students, as well as their teacher, had begun to recognize the need for material that would enable some of these questions and assumptions to be pursued.

Teacher	Well, before you can answer all those kinds of questions you need to know some more things perhaps, some more background information.
All	Yeah.
Teacher	But just let me get clear what you are saying that you have got in this source written by John Pory. You made the important point didn't you, that some things he could have seen for himself, but that he would not have been able to see for himself the bit about the abandoned town, and you are saying he might have heard about that from the people who were there. The point then that Matthew is making is that it would be difficult to see *that*

> first hand, and that he would be relying on the Pilgrims for that information, and so Matthew is just saying that there might be an issue here, that he might be a bit worried about doing that and that it may not be quite right. It may be that if we know something more about John Pory and the Pilgrims we can think about this point further.

You need to get behind the record to the concerns of the people who produced them.

The teacher then pursued the further objective involved in these questions—that concerned with thinking about the kinds of things particular people might record. An attempt was made to encourage the students to consider why the advantages at Plymouth had a particular resonance with John Pory.

Teacher	Why is Pory concerned with these things anyway, this kind of information? Why would he record *this kind* of information? If I told you that he came from the settlement farther south, and that the settlement farther south, when *they* got to America there wasn't any abandoned land and they were having a lot of problems. So why might that make him want to mention this?
Adam	Probably to let his settlement know, and they have probably got friends and allies, that they *have* got abandoned land, and maybe they could share with those who haven't actually got any.

It is clear that the knowledge base with which students are working is unlikely to be sufficient to pursue this matter further at this stage. The need for additional information exists on a more or less continuous basis in history lessons. It is vital in this task not to crowd out the evidence objectives by providing too many factual details too soon, but at this point it is difficult to advance understanding without further contextual understanding. Some details can be provided without risk, as the students will be in a position to assimilate them and use them effectively to shed light on the problems they have already identified. These details have a context that will give them meaning.

The teacher, aware of these difficulties and of the overall scheme of work, was able to tell the students that a comparative study of the settlements at Plymouth and Jamestown would be part of their future work and would shed light on John Pory's concerns. In addition, she explained that the following lesson would use further source material to explore other matters: the circumstances of the abandoned town; the relationship between the Pilgrims and the Wampanoags, who lived in the immediate area; and the changing nature of the relationships between the settlers and the native populations with the arrival of a Mr. Weston and his attempt to create a settlement at Wessagusett. The teacher also knew (but did not tell the students at this time) that they would be learning about the changes in these relationships in the context of patterns of white penetration into the lands populated by the native peoples of the eastern lands of North America over a longer time span.

Understanding what is likely to get recorded and under what circumstances: diaries.

Students in the sixth, seventh, and eighth grades tend to be quite aware that we depend on traces from the past in order to say anything about it; as we have seen, however, they are likely to assume that if this testimony is less than accurate, we will face difficulty. When testimony is still the main idea in the students' toolkit, one of the first things they suggest as a good source for historians is a diary. The following exchange indicates why.

Teacher	Perhaps we could come back to the things in William Bradford's diary because several people in the class asked how Bradford knew the Native Americans—Bradford calls them barbarians—were ready to fill them full of arrows. The question people wrote down when they were looking at this source was, "How did he know they were ready to do this?" So what I want you to do is to try to shed some light on this for us.
Adam	It's very strange really because you know when you write a diary, no one would lie to a diary because that would be just like lying to yourself. It would be a ridiculous thing to do.
Peter	I think he might lie in his diary, maybe because he knows that one day or another, people some how or another are going to find his diary, and he wants to, maybe, twist this so that people hear what he wants them to think.

The teacher had returned to William Bradford's testimony to encourage the students to consider how the language of such a text can help us recreate the circumstances in which records are made and hence the subject matter that is likely to be recorded, and to examine the further question of how a diary becomes a publication. The aim was to see how far the students were thinking beyond the simplistic dichotomy of "telling the truth" or "lying" that came out in the exchange between Adam and Peter. The students were aware that we can make moves that go beyond testimony, but it is precisely testimony that they confronted in this material. The teaching objective was therefore to help them see that even when we have testimony, we have to use it in quite subtle ways. In other words, we have to use it as *evidence*, not just as testimony. This means thinking about how the testimony arose. The teacher explored the students' ideas to provide herself with an informed starting point for the next exercise.

Teacher	What about us thinking about the way diaries get written, we need to think about the circumstances in which diaries get written.
Matthew	Yes, because you're not exactly, it's like talking to a really good friend, because mostly people start it off like "Dear Diary" so they're not really leaving it for someone else to find. It's just like having someone to talk to, because I know they are not there, but you just feel better after you have written it down.
Teacher	Do you think people might write their diary up every day?
Adam	Well some people do, like Anne Frank, she did.
Teacher	But she was in a room with nothing else—she was restricted in what else she could be doing. In what sort of circumstances might people not write their diary up every day?
Matthew	Oh, if there is something exciting happening they probably wouldn't do it so when they were on the ship then he probably would have filled it in, but by the time they had landed he would probably be so excited he wouldn't, that would be the last thing on his mind, he probably wouldn't be able to do those things.
Adam	And if he did it would be like dear diary too excited to write we just did this and that, right see you tomorrow, so he might have written it a lot later.

Teacher	It would be nice to go into this further, but we are not going to have time to do that today. But what I was trying to do was to get you to think about how when the Pilgrims arrived they had an awful lot of things to cope with because they had had this dreadful journey, they were exhausted, and clearly some of them are very ill or dying, and maybe William Bradford was very busy when they arrived. He might not have had time to write up his diary on a regular basis, and if you write a diary later on, what are you likely to write about compared with if you write a diary every day?
Adam	Pick out all the good points, because if you have had some really down times you don't want to make it worse by writing about the bad things.
Peter	And I think if you write in your diary every day you just write what happened today, and if you, say, write up a date a week later you think, "Wait a minute! I'll only write this," because you don't want people going through your stuff and finding this. "I want them to find good things."
Teacher	Do you think he is just writing this out personally for his own benefit? I mean this is a man who eventually becomes the Governor of Plymouth.
Matthew	I suppose it could be for both, because personally, like, maybe other people know what Indians are really like, and maybe they all put their ideas and extracts into this diary so that it can be passed down so that everyone can remember the story of the Pilgrims and we do now. Maybe they had plans so that everyone would remember who they were and what they did.
Adam	And how great they were.
Teacher	So in the extract you were looking at, by William Bradford, Source 1, what does it say at the top?
Adam	I think he sort of writes it in the past tense, he says "having arrived."

Teacher	And what does it actually say about the source?
Adam	Personal journal finished in 1650, and they arrived in 1620, so that's, like, a 30-year diary.
Peter	I don't think anyone would have a 30-year diary.
Matthew	Well if he is a great man . . .
Peter	Maybe it's not for personal use, because for personal use it would be more like a child, and when you are 20 you are more mature, so you wouldn't really bother. Not many adults keep diaries for personal use, so maybe he just thought, "Oh, I will leave it for future generations."
Teacher	If you know you are a small group of people who have gone all the way across the Atlantic Ocean creating a new settlement . . .
Matthew	Yeah, you are going to want people to take notice of it. If there is a small number they might not even survive, or like reproduce and they are going to want other people who come to the land to think, "Oh my God, these people were great," and, like, other people from the past, like, think that if you won a battle God was on your side so they might think, "Oh my God, God was on their side so he must be the true God!," so he is increasing their religion which would still make their name.
Peter	And it may even have worked because like in America they have carved out of rock the foreheads of the forefathers so it probably even worked.

The teacher was aware that in future lessons, her students would need to develop more subtle understandings about the nature of diary accounts, their relationship to record keeping, and the level of awareness of authors of these accounts with respect to the possible legacies they were creating. In particular, the students would need to understand the responsibility that William Bradford, as governor of a settlement of this nature, would have had for keeping particular kinds of records. Within this context, they would need to be able to differentiate, even within the same document, among different kinds of information and whether the document is being used as a record or relic source.

Ideas, Beliefs, and Attitudes

Although the focus of the Pilgrims' task as discussed here is on the concept of *evidence*, an important connection exists between that concept and some aspects of *empathy*. If students are to know what a source may be used to argue, they need to understand two closely related things. First, they must understand what sort of thing a source is as an object that has social meaning at a particular time—in this case a diary (or, more precisely, a journal). Second, they must be able to begin to understand the ways of seeing the world, and the associated values, manifested by the source.

In the above discussion, Matthew introduced an opportunity to consider how religious beliefs, particularly that of "providence," actually work. In explaining that winning a battle would actually be evidence of God being on your side, Matthew also suggested that successes of this kind would reinforce such a belief. This is a complex understanding, and it will be valuable to him when in further studies he is asked to give explanations of some of the later actions of the European settlers on the eastern coast of America. The Pilgrims' task contains two questions that would provide an introduction to such later work. The first is a simple question asking students to use Sources 1 and 5 to identify who the Pilgrims believed was helping them when they arrived at Cape Cod.

Teacher Question 5.

The writer of Source 1 and the writer of Source 5 seem to share the same beliefs about who was helping the Pilgrims when they arrived at Cape Cod. Who did they think was helping them?

What is this question trying to find out about students' existing understanding?

This question explores students' understanding of:

(a) The distinction between how people at the time would explain the advantages they had and how we might explain these things now.

(b) How Bradford's and Pory's beliefs provided them with an explanation of their circumstances.

What is this question trying to encourage students to reflect on as a means of developing their understanding?

The question encourages students to:

(a) Reflect on how the interrogation of sources can give us access to understandings beyond the immediate information that the source intended to provide.

(b) Think about the distinction between the way in which the Pilgrim Fathers would have explained what was happening and the way in which we might explain it.

This question is also an opportunity to introduce the specific idea of "providence."

A majority of sixth graders were able to identify God as the agency the Pilgrims believed was helping them, but another response we are likely to encounter is that it was the Native Americans who really helped the settlers. In many ways, students are quite right to say this (and indeed in the evidence work that followed, the students were introduced to Squanto), but the issue here was how the Pilgrims would have seen things, and in particular how they would have interpreted the help they received from the Native Americans as the manifestation of divine providence. Later the students often emphasized the practical support the Pilgrims received as a consequence of either the good will of the native population or the food stores of the native population that the Pilgrims found. Sean, for example, wrote, "I think the Indians helped them because why would they suddenly have a grudge with someone they just met." This response was illuminating because it turned the question into one about who *he* thought provided the help, rather than one about who the writers of the sources thought was helping. In claiming that "in Source 1 and 5 they have the Native Americans helping them," Colin was being less than precise, but appeared to have picked up the discovery of the supplies from Source 3, together with Pory's remarks to the effect that the native population made no objection to the settlement in Plymouth, and to have seen this as important practical help.

Other students made the distinction between our way of seeing things and the beliefs of people such as Bradford and Pory. These students were ready to recognize that it is *past* ideas that count here. Alex drew inferences from the religious practices of the Pilgrims to their beliefs. She wrote, "They thought God was helping them as they blessed God when they arrived." Janine, aged 15, saw as a routine consequence of their religion that they would believe the help was from God: "They thought that God was helping them because the Pilgrims were supposed to be very religious so God would help them." In discussion with Peter, Matthew, and Adam, the teacher explored this question further.

Matthew	I think that is pretty obvious. I'm sure they believed it was God helping them; it's quite easy to figure that out. [He then quoted Bradford.] "They fell upon their knees and blessed God who had delivered them."
Adam	And then it says, backing up Matt's idea, in Source 5, "After some accidents and mistakes he stumbled on the harbor of Plymouth where it pleased Almighty God who had better provided for them than they could imagine."
Teacher	What do you think he meant by "than they could imagine"?
Adam	I think he means, like, they got better land than him because they got an abandoned town, so John Pory's group in South Virginia didn't have that, so God had provided them better.
Peter	And in those times most things were based round religion, religion was very important in those days.
Teacher	What kind of religion is this that you are talking about?
All	Catholic? Christians?
Teacher	Did you read the bottom of that page about the Pilgrims? [pointing to the definition of Pilgrims on the briefing sheet]
Adam	Oh no. They're Protestants, and they're getting away from the English church because they don't want to abide by their laws.
Teacher	Do you know the word "providence"? If I said people believed in "divine providence" would you know what I meant? If I said you believe that God lets you know whether what you are doing is OK, would you know what I meant?
Adam	Like in a vision?
Teacher	What kind of things could you use to decide how God is going to let you know?
Adam	He could come to you in a dream.
Teacher	What is God likely to do to people that please him?
Matthew	Give them good weather and be nice to them.
Adam	Give them what they want.
Teacher	So how do you know?

Adam	If you have got a good life.
Teacher	Yes, if something good happens to you.
Adam	Then you know.
Teacher	How are you going to see that?
Adam	As an act of God.

The teacher drew their attention to the particulars of the Pilgrims' situation.

Teacher	Right, so what about this abandoned village?
Matthew	To them it's like an act of God because its more than they could have imagined possible.
Peter	They might have said, like English kings, they say, like God chose me to be king. So the Pilgrims could be saying, well, God has told me that I have to live here.

Teacher Question 6.

Why did religious people like the Pilgrims think they had the right to take over land that wasn't theirs?

What is this question trying to find out about students' existing understanding?

This question explores the extent to which students:

(a) Make stereotypical assumptions about religious beliefs.

(b) Are able to use their understanding about the Pilgrims' religious beliefs to explain the Pilgrims' actions in this particular case.

What is this question trying to encourage students to reflect on as a means of developing their understanding?

The question is designed to:

(a) Open up a discussion of the different ways in which past events can be explained.

(b) Develop an understanding that the Pilgrims' values and practices were not the same as ours and help explain what they did.

This question of how people see things is important for understanding what to make of evidence and is central to any kind of empathy (whether understanding patterns of belief and values or explaining particular actions; see Box 3-3). The Pilgrims' task allows this understanding to be taken further, and question 6 pursues one major thread, presenting students with a paradox.

Students' answers to question 6 revealed attempts to make what today appears to be rather indefensible behavior less unpalatable. Sean explained:

> *The Pilgrims wanted to discover more land and find out what the world looked like. They were not aiming to take over land when they set off, they were just aiming to discover more land and find out if the land around them was inhabited or if they were the only people existing along with other people they knew existed such as the French and Scandinavians.*

Sean actually avoided explaining the relevant action of the Pilgrims, or at least justified it as not intentional, suggesting that the Pilgrims were in fact part of a larger movement of people who were benign explorers.

In the small-group discussion we have been following, the teacher drew the attention of Peter, Adam, and Matthew to this question.

Teacher	Let's think about this right they think they have to take the land.
Adam	They believe they had the right like Peter said, because they needed to get away and after some errors and accidents like they stumbled across a harbor, whether it was because of the wind or the backwardness of their ship's captain they did not arrive where they had planned, so they therefore believed that God did not want them to live where they had planned, so whether it was the ship's captain or the wind, God changed it around, so that instead they reached the harbor of Cape Cod, so therefore they believed that God wanted them to live there.

Peter took this argument further, suggesting they would need to justify the action in terms of the Native Americans' religious "failings," and Matthew was concerned that their religious beliefs should not go unrecognized. Peter, however, reinforced the point more precisely by talking about how the Pilgrims might justify their action in their own terms, rather than according to the way we would look at this situation now.

BOX 3-3 Did People Think Like Us in the Past?

A major step for young students of history is to recognize that they cannot rely on our modern ways of thinking to explain why people in the past acted as they did.

In action research in U.K. schools carried out by Dickinson and Lee and by Ashby and Lee, groups of three students in grades 5 to 8 were asked to explain why the Anglo-Saxons used the ordeal to find out whether someone was guilty or innocent of a crime.[8] Their discussions were recorded on videotape.

Some students dismissed the ordeal as absurd, but others tried to make sense of it by turning it from a form of trial into a method of punishment aimed at deterrence. Their reaction was that, given any reasonable—i.e., modern—ideas and values, it could not have been a trial, so it must have been something else. If it was so deliberately unfair (by our standards), then it must have been doing what *we* would do if *we* behaved like that. As one group of eighth graders said, "If this is as unfair as we seem to make out it is, no one's going to steal anything," because they will be "scared they'll get caught." Students thinking like this cease to think of the ordeal as part of a trial, and reduce it to a form of deterrent. Some students slip into calling the ordeal a "punishment."

Another move made by students is to recognize that the Anglo-Saxons held different religious beliefs from ours, but then to treat this as part of the problem: the ordeal is the sort of absurd thing you would expect from their religion.

A few eighth graders, however, not only were able to use the different ideas held by the Anglo-Saxons to explain why the ordeal took the form it did, but were even prepared to switch perspective to judge present institutions in what they thought of as Anglo-Saxon terms.

Tim | They'd probably say that their system then, with God, is better than ours, because, well people can muck around with the truth, but God . . .
Lawrence | But God doesn't.
Tim | They'd probably say theirs was better than ours.

Peter | They might have even thought that God was punishing the Indians because the Indians weren't very religious.
Matthew | Weren't they, they had Gods, other Gods, didn't they?
Adam | Yes, they had statues and things, totem poles and things?

| Peter | The Pilgrims could have said in, like, their defense, that you have not been worshiping the right God, so you have been bad, so you can go away. |

The Language of Sources, Interpretation, and Other Perspectives

At the end of the discussion with Peter, Adam, and Matthew, their teacher wanted them to consider more carefully the different ways in which actions may be interpreted.

Teacher	Do you think when Bradford talks of the group of native people as "running away" that the native people would have described it as "running away"?
Adam	I wouldn't think so. I think they would say [sic] it as "going back to your tribe to tell them what was happening."
Matthew	To tell them.
Adam	They might say, "We've got white people with different ideas and a strange language. We need back-up, we've got to get ready for these people or otherwise they could change our entire habitat our entire . . ."
Teacher	So you are saying that if you don't attack someone as soon as they land and you go away, you don't have to see that as "running away." I know I'm probably putting words in your mouth here, but would you see this kind of "running away" as being scared or being sensible?
Matthew	Being sensible because like it says they were greeted by five or six people with a dog, and how are five or six people and a dog going to take on the people with the firearms?
Peter	Maybe they can sense, like, these people are dangerous so it might be a mixture of both really.
Teacher	So sensible people have to work out what's going on before they make decisions?
Peter	Well maybe it's a mixture of being sensible and being scared.

Teacher	Have you heard that expression, "Fools rush in where angels fear to tread"?
Adam	Yes. Angels are smart so they back off but fools they rush in and get killed.
Teacher	So this may have been not "running away" in the way we might understand it, as it is described, but making sure that they could assess the situation in their own way in their own time.

In the absence of testimony from the Native Americans, this conversation about how to understand a relatively concrete and simple action opens up the possibility of helping students think about the way our picture of the actions of the Native Americans is mediated by the cultural assumptions of the settlers.

The exploratory approach exemplified by this task and the ensuing dialogue enables us to gauge our students' understanding of historical evidence, particularly their understanding of how to use testimony as evidence. We can then engage more confidently in direct teaching, knowing that we have a clearer understanding of the ideas with which particular students are working. The evidence work was not, of course, detached from gaining knowledge of the topic. In fact, the richness of the sources generated a great deal of excitement and a wealth of questions. Students were keen to know more about what happened: to understand the opportunities that were available to the Pilgrims, the nature of the difficulties they faced, and how they dealt with those difficulties. They raised questions about the native population: Who were they? What kinds of beliefs and ideas did they hold? How did they live? Were they friendly? How did they feel about the arrival of the Pilgrims? Did they mind them taking the corn? Did they help them? Did they attack them? Did they feel threatened? While some waited with anticipation for the next lesson, others went off to search the Web for answers to their questions. Work focused on developing ideas about how evidence had simultaneously opened up opportunities to explore the historical content. It was as if, in grappling with the sources, they had acquired a vested interest in knowing.

WORKING WITH EVIDENCE: THE ST. BRENDAN'S VOYAGE TASK

The Pilgrim Fathers' case study exemplifies how several important things can be happening at once in the classroom. Developing an understanding of key second-order concepts and learning about the past can go hand in hand. At the same time as they are learning about evidence, students can acquire knowledge ranging from relatively straightforward matters, such as the physical conditions the Pilgrims faced on their arrival in America, to more sophisticated ideas, such as seventeenth-century conceptions of Providence.

We can try to understand students' ideas and at the same time build on or reshape those ideas. As we probe students' use of source materials to discover their preconceptions about how one can know about the past, we have an opportunity to develop their understanding of testimony by encouraging them to think about how it may have arisen. Encouraging such thinking in turn opens up new opportunities to consider what kinds of beliefs are involved, so that the students begin to consider the nature of the source. Students capable of discussing these matters are not far from an understanding of how sources may be used as evidence.

Of course, the ideas about evidence that surface in the Pilgrims' case study give us only a snapshot of students' ideas at one point in time. Such ideas may be more or less well consolidated and stable; they may be accessible to students in one context but not in another. We cannot assume that any changes that take place in one lesson have been fully grasped, so it will be important to return to them in other encounters with history. Still more important, the ideas we uncover in our probing will depend partly on what has been taught in previous grades. The students' ideas might have been different if their earlier teaching had been different.[9] The point is not that someone might have taught the students about the Pilgrims already in an earlier grade, but that they could have begun to learn about evidence much earlier, through different content—something exciting that we think is appropriate for youngsters and still fits into our overall content framework (in this case that of migrations, explorations, and encounters). Equally, we may sometimes want to help a group of older students who happen not to have had the opportunity to confront ideas about historical evidence, or whose understanding remains weak.

The St. Brendan task is an example of one possible way in which we might begin much earlier than sixth grade to develop students' ideas about how one can know the past. The story of St. Brendan's voyage in the sixth century allows us to raise the question, "Did an Irish monk land in America about 1,000 years before Columbus?" This is a question of the kind many students enjoy, and the different layers of evidence available make it highly suitable for addressing the problems of making valid statements about the past. As historical "content," its importance lies in helping students see that— even if it were true that Brendan reached America—"firsts" of this kind often lead nowhere. However, the discussion here focuses not on historical significance, but on learning about historical evidence, and serves only as an example of how such a task might work, not a prescription to be followed as "the right way to teach."

The story of St. Brendan may appear to be a matter of peripheral interest to a grand theme such as migration, exploration, and encounter, but it is possible to use very small amounts of content to tackle big ideas. We must avoid swamping *any* students with content, but this is especially important with younger or less sophisticated students. They need space to think, and teachers need time to help them. The purpose of the St. Brendan task is to develop students' ideas of historical evidence, not to give them large quantities of information. We must not repeatedly ambush students with things they *do not* know when the point of the task is to equip them with ideas to help them think more effectively about what they *do* know. This is an important reason why the—relatively—self-contained St. Brendan story is used. The voyage of St. Brendan is also useful because it is likely to be unfamiliar to students (see Box 3-4).

The St. Brendan task is designed primarily for young students from fourth grade up. (How far up will depend on what targets we set; students can respond to open-ended questions at very different levels.) It differs significantly from the Pilgrims' task, in part because it is designed to put teaching first rather than to aid in the "diagnosis" of students' ideas. Nonetheless, teaching and diagnosis must go hand in hand.

Preparing for the Task

Before proceeding with the St. Brendan task, we must consider both the preconceptions the students will be bringing to the task and just what we might achieve with them.

The student quotations used in the Brendan case study are from written work done after whole-class teaching in the United States and the United Kingdom, and also from recorded oral work with small groups. The group work (with U.K. children) was important because it allowed students' discussions to be recorded so as to give an accurate and detailed picture of some of what was said, and as a result, the majority of the examples are taken from the recordings. But it is important to emphasize that the Brendan task is not designed particularly for group work, and has been used in the United States and the United Kingdom with full classes from grades 2 to 6.

Preconceptions About How We Know About the Past

Research and experience suggest that the preconceptions we are likely to encounter will be something along the following lines.[10] Many students between fourth and sixth grades will not have thought about how we know of the past and will have no settled ideas about how we can gain such knowledge. They may treat the matter as being about *where we find the information*—which books or encyclopedias we consult or whom we ask—

BOX 3-4 The Dangers of What Appears to Be Familiar

Students are frequently resistant to teachers' attempts to change their ideas. One reason for this is their lack of metacognitive awareness, which can make it difficult for them to distinguish between what they think they already know about a topic and new information presented by a teacher or inferred from evidence.

VanSledright set out as researcher and teacher to teach fifth graders American history, while at the same time developing their understanding of historical enquiry.[11] He presented the students with Hakim's conjecture that local Powhatan Indians withheld food and supplies from Jamestown, perhaps laying siege to the stockade for much of the winter of 1609–1610. He provided the students with primary source materials and a framework for questioning those materials. The task was to test Hakim's claim. VanSledright reports the difficulties some students experienced in having to put aside their everyday ideas and prior assumptions to focus on the available evidence.

Having picked up on the testimony of Governor George Percy—who spoke of "great plenty" in 1605 in contrast to Captain John Smith, who reported starvation at Jamestown in 1624—the students resolved this conflict by depicting Percy as someone covering up the truth. Many of the students used the testimony as evidence that Percy had survived the famine. Ignoring the temporal context (perhaps influenced by Disney's character in "Pocahontas," the rather fat and greedy Governor Ratcliffe, whose dog was called Percy) the students decided that George Percy had hoarded and eaten all the food and was therefore responsible for the famine. This position was difficult to shake. As VanSledright tells us, "Given the documents at our disposal, it was likely that either poor leadership in hunting and gathering food over the winter or a siege by the Powhatans was a more palatable, evidence-based interpretation of the Starving Time. However, the die appeared to be cast. The popularity of 'liar Percy,' who hoarded food for himself, became the interpretive mantra of all but . . . four students."

It follows that much may be gained by working with topics that are completely new to students and do not figure in folk histories, and about which films—by Disney or anyone else—have not been made.

not about what evidence we examine. Others will have given the matter some thought and will assume *we cannot really know because we were not there.* For some students, this is where their thinking will stop.

A majority of the students who have thought about how we gain knowledge of the past are likely to think that true reports (typically diaries or accounts handed down in families) may allow us to know what happened.

But many will recognize that there may be problems in obtaining such reports. Typically they will point out that people do not always tell the truth. They are also likely to suggest the possibility of transmission errors (a conception modeled on the party whispering game, where a message changes as it is passed on). They may also assume that we cannot know whether reports are true or not. Older students—and some fourth graders—may mention exaggeration and bias as additional problems. Even among those students who have some idea about links with the past, many will think the only way to check the truth of reports properly would be to go back into the past to witness what happened; thus in the end, these students, too, are likely to come back to the position that we cannot really know about the past because we were not there.

Box 3-5 summarizes the range of student assumptions about how we know of the past that we are likely to encounter in our teaching. Our goal is to help students see that knowing about the past is a problem of working things out using evidence, but we may have to be content with less: if some students move from seeing the problem in terms of information to thinking of it in terms of testimony, we will have achieved something important.

BOX 3-5 Common Student Assumptions About How We Know of the Past

It's an information problem.	Where do we find the stuff?
It's a problem about access to the past.	We can't know because we weren't there. We didn't see it.
It's a problem about finding true reports.	We can know about what happened, but only if we can find something where someone "told it like it was." They would probably have had to see it happen.
It's a problem about trusting "true" reports.	We can't really know if someone did tell the truth, and anyway things get changed as they are passed down. People tell lies and exaggerate. Some are biased.
It's a problem about working things out using evidence.	We don't depend on people telling us what happened. We can work it out from clues we have, even if no one told us what happened. We can ask questions of a source that it wasn't intended to answer.

What Are We Trying to Achieve?

As teachers we could choose to do all sorts of things with the Brendan story, but in this discussion we focus on some key shifts in ideas. First is the shift from the idea that we just have *information* about the past that is usually true (but sometimes false) to the idea that any claim about the past needs testing and some sort of backup. Second is the shift from the idea that we cannot say anything about the past unless someone from the time left us a true report (testimony) to the idea that we have to work out what happened using evidence.

By the end of the Brendan task, fourth graders who started with little experience of working with historical evidence should understand (at least in this context) that the past is not given information, fixed by books or authorities; that we have no direct access to the past; and that we do not rely on someone from the time telling us truthfully what happened. Nonetheless, we can work out what happened; indeed, a discipline called "history" exists precisely because we *have* to work it out. Students should also understand that often we cannot be certain about what happened, but this does not mean guessing is sufficient: when we cannot be certain, we can still produce stronger or weaker arguments about what answers make most sense. This understanding is likely to remain highly unsophisticated after just one task, and students will find it difficult to articulate what counts as a "stronger" or "weaker" argument. This is why it is important to return frequently and explicitly to what makes an argument work or fail in a range of contexts.

This level of understanding is likely to be enough for many fourth-grade students. However, some youngsters may already be working with much more sophisticated ideas than most of their classmates, and eventually we want *all* our students to go beyond the above shifts in ideas. Thus it is worth thinking about how to take students' ideas about evidence a little further should such opportunities arise.

Only when we are clear about the question we are asking can we say what evidence is available, and it is our question that allows us to begin to consider whether a source of evidence is reliable. People often talk of written sources as more or less "reliable" as though these accounts are reports to be judged on what they are deliberately telling us—mere testimony that we must accept or reject (whether in part or as a whole). Students often think of reliability as inherent in the source instead of asking themselves, "Reliable for what?" We might expect some students to go further, and understand that we can ask a question that is not about what the source is reporting at all. All this indicates the importance of helping students understand that it is *questions* that lie at the heart of using evidence. Students also tend to think of reliability as an all-or-nothing property of a source rather than as a judge-ment about how far the source can be used as evidence to answer a particular question. They should understand that some questions place heavier burdens on a source than others. In other words, the burden of proof resting on a source varies according to both the nature of the source and the demands and precision of the question. For example, answers to the question, "Did Bjarni Herjólfsson accidentally reach Labrador in the tenth century?" may impose a greater burden of proof on a source than does the question, "Could the Vikings have reached America?"

Students can begin to tackle these problems by considering something close to their lives. How reliable is a school report? Can we answer that question without knowing what it is supposed to be evidence for? Is it as reliable for providing evidence of a student's school behavior as for providing evidence of the teacher's attitude toward the student? Many fourth graders are well able to appreciate the importance of the question we ask if we begin with everyday examples:

Teacher	If I say "Here's your teacher's report, on you, what are the things I *can* learn about you, and what sort of things *can't* I find about you from this report?" what would you say?
Jeff	You could learn how we act around our teacher.
Carly	If we chat, and not listen.
Teacher	What wouldn't we be able to learn?
Jeff	How we act at home, what sort of games we play on our Playstation.

An extension of these ideas is that our questions need not ask about what the source is trying to tell us. Moreover, some sources are not trying to give us any kind of true story about something that happened; they are relics of an activity, not reports on it.

Teacher	OK, supposing I get one of your exercise books. Is there anything in it about you? There's nothing in it telling a story about you? Does that mean I couldn't say anything about you on the basis of what's in the book?
Carly	Our handwriting and spelling . . .
Jeff	You could say I'm not very good at writing.
Teacher	So if a historian picked up your exercise book, she could tell something about you even if you weren't trying to tell her anything.

The Brendan task actually sidesteps talk about "reliability," precisely because it can too easily lead youngsters to think in terms of accepting or rejecting something as a true or false report rather than thinking about how to use it as evidence. There is a sense in which it is doubly misleading to think of the Brendan story as a true report of something. How could this story possibly be testimony that Brendan reached America? There was no "America" when the story was written, so no one could write a report of his reaching it. This is another reason why the whole tenor of the task is one of working out the best answer we can get to what is our (twenty-first-century) question.

If the Brendan task were used with students in the seventh grade and beyond, we would be thinking in terms of more sophisticated understanding (even fourth or third graders who started with more powerful ideas than those we assumed in the previous section would be capable of making real gains here). In particular, it would be worth developing the idea that to make sense of a piece of evidence, we must know what kind of thing it is. The account of the voyage of St. Brendan is not a failed attempt to give a factual report of an exploration, but a story about a saint. There is not a necessary conflict between its inclusion of supernatural events and its having a basis in fact, because if the author were writing for an audience that expected wonders, their absence would simply weaken the story. So even in the unlikely event that the writer had access to an oral tradition that gave a detailed account of a more modern kind, we would scarcely expect the story to have been written in that way. The teaching target, then, is to help students see that we cannot decide whether the Brendan story will help answer the question "Did Brendan get to America?" by dismissing it as a "made-up" story, any more than they can simply accept it as a "true story." We are trying to get them beyond this simple dichotomy and encourage them to ask, "What kind of story is this?"

How can we know what inferences we are entitled to draw from a source? At this point, we are touching on ideas generally labeled "empathy" or "perspective taking." The link between evidence and empathy is the general principle that, if we are to be able to use any particular source of evidence to answer a question, we must know what kind of thing the source is. And we cannot know what kind of thing a source is if we do not know what it meant to the people who produced it. Only if we understand that a source is, say, a piece of religious exhortation rather than a news report can we avoid making serious mistakes in the way we argue from it. And knowing what a source is means knowing what people at the time saw it as, which in turn requires knowing about people's world view at the time. Students may find it easy to deal with this issue in the context of everyday items with which they are familiar, especially if those items have a place in the students' culture that is not always obvious to adults. For example, students would likely have little trouble in seeing how a future historian who assumed that a high-status brand of sneaker was just a shoe might find it difficult to understand how someone would commit a crime to obtain it.

However, a task designed to tackle students' ideas about understanding people in the past would have to offer them more material about Brendan's world than is required in the evidence task on which we are focusing here. We must not confuse our goals by attempting too much at once, and in any case, there are other specific ideas that students need to learn in connection with empathy. It is enough in the Brendan task to help students see that they need to ask what kind of story they are dealing with before they can safely use it as evidence.

Preconceptions About People, Society, and How the World Works

It is much more difficult to predict what assumptions students will have about the substantive past than what they will assume about the discipline of history. This is so because in the former case, so many assumptions are possible in so many different areas, even with relatively circumscribed content such as the Brendan story.

The problem of identifying students' assumptions is complicated enough when we confine ourselves to their ideas about what is physically possible. Some will expect wooden objects to last for thousands of years and think it possible for submarines to search the entire seabed of the Atlantic in a week or two to find the remains of a small wood-and-leather boat. Many will have no idea what an ocean current is or why it might have made a difference in what destination a sailing boat with a steering oar could reach. Some will imagine icebergs to be rather small objects, a few yards across. (And of course few will know the location of the Faroe Islands, Iceland, or Newfoundland. Here, however, it is easier for the teacher to list essential knowledge and make sure it is available.)

Predicting students' prior conceptions is even more difficult when it comes to ideas about what people do. The one thing we can be fairly sure of is that students will assume people in the past thought as we do. Thus in teaching about Brendan, we are likely to find students arguing that the story may have been exaggerated so that it was more exciting, and that one reason for this was that the writer could make a better profit. Behind this argument, of course, is a picture of a world that has always had widely available books, mass literacy, and a capitalist economic system.

What all this means is that as teachers we need to be sensitive to students' substantive assumptions as we proceed—hence the importance of lessons in which students have room to express their ideas so that there is some chance of discovering what those ideas are. But it is important to remember with something like the Brendan task, which is designed to develop understandings about the discipline of history, that not all students' substantive misconceptions actually matter for the task at hand. For this task, the focus is their thinking about how we know about the past, not on correcting every minor misconception about geography or even about how society works.

Working Through the Task

The Question

We begin with the question:

Did an Irish monk land in America about 1,000 years before Columbus?

As teachers we need to be very clear in our own minds about the question right from the start, even if it is not necessarily sensible to pursue this with the students as an abstract issue at the outset. This particular question is asking about what happened, not just what was possible. Since in history it is always the question that decides what can be evidence and how that evidence can be used, this is an important point.

We tell the students that they are going to look at some important historical sources and that they will use these sources as evidence to try to obtain the best answer they can to the question. The idea of "the best answer you can get" is something that can be woven into the discussion as it proceeds.[12] By the end of the task, we will want all the students at least to understand that "the best answer" means the one for which we have the best evidence. Some students will be able to think in more sophisticated terms— perhaps something more like "the answer that makes the best sense of the most evidence and is not knocked out by anything."

The Story

We next give students an introduction to the story of St. Brendan's voyage and the story itself to read. (This material can be read by the teacher, but preferably should not be read around the class by students since doing so tends to break up the picture, especially if the students read in a halting manner.) Issues about the meaning of words or sentences can be addressed at the end, but not in a way that preempts interpretation. For example, there should be no hint that the supernatural elements in the story might also be interpreted naturalistically or that they are somehow signs of the story's being discredited or "untrue." At this stage, we normally try to avoid offering any views of our own on the nature of the story or its veracity. We need to find out how our students see it.

Introduction: The Story of St. Brendan

(All the underlined words are explained at the end.)

Sometime between the year 900 and the year 1000, someone wrote down an amazing story. It was written in the <u>Latin</u> language.

The story described how an Irish <u>monk</u> called St. Brendan went on a long voyage lasting 7 years to a land called the <u>Land of Promise</u>. We know that Brendan lived in Ireland between (roughly) 486 and 578. There are things in the story that make some people think Brendan might have crossed the Atlantic Ocean and reached America.

It is quite likely that the story comes from even earlier times than 900, but we don't know that. There are more than 120 versions of the story in Latin and more in other languages. They all say almost the same things.

— —

Time Line

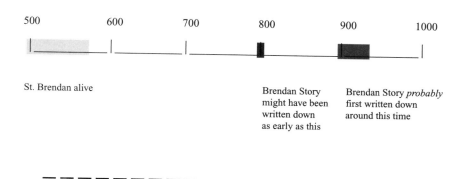

| 500 | 600 | 700 | 800 | 900 | 1000 |

St. Brendan alive

Brendan Story might have been written down as early as this

Brendan Story *probably* first written down around this time

— —

The Voyage of St. Brendan

(This is a shortened version of the story. It misses out some of the adventures of St. Brendan and his crew of monks. All the underlined words are explained at the end.)

St. Brendan lived at Clonfert in Ireland. He was head of a <u>community</u> of 3000 <u>monks</u>. One day a monk called Barrind visited Brendan and told him about a <u>Land of Promise</u> across the sea in the west. It was a wonderful place, special to God.

Brendan decided to go and find this Land of Promise. He and his monks built a boat with a wooden frame, covered in <u>tanned</u> leather. He put food and drink in the boat to last for 40 days, and also spare leather and fat for greasing it.

1. An Irish boat, copied from a carving done on a stone pillar some time between 700 and 800.

Brendan set out with 17 other monks and sailed west. After 15 days they landed on a tall rocky island. A dog led them to a settlement, where they found a meal waiting for them. They stayed for 3 days without seeing anyone, but food was always set out on the table for them.

Next they landed on an island with lots of streams, all full of fish. It was called the Island of Sheep, because flocks of sheep roamed over it all year round. A man gave them food.

Then they visited another island that was rocky and bare. They made a fire to cook food, when suddenly the "island" began to move. The monks quickly jumped into their boat, just in time to see the "island" swim off with the fire still burning. St. Brendan told the monks that it was the biggest fish in the ocean, and its name was "Jasconius."

2. The monks land on Jasconius. A picture painted between 600 and 700 years after Brendan's time.

After this the monks sailed to an island called The Paradise of Birds. They hauled their boat almost a mile up a narrow stream, and found a huge tree covered in white birds. A bird flew down and told Brendan that the birds were men's spirits, and that he would have to search 7 years to find the Land of Promise. The birds sang hymns and chanted prayers at the right times of day. A man called the Steward brought food across to the monks. (He was the man who had given them food on the Island of Sheep.)

The monks were at sea for 3 months before they came to another island. They were so exhausted that they could hardly row the boat against the wind. On the island they found monks who had agreed to keep silent (so that they could concentrate on thinking about God). The monks had been there 80 years, and none of them had been ill. They showed Brendan how their lamps were lit by a miraculous flaming arrow each evening.

The monks had many adventures before they found the Land of Promise. Many times they found themselves back at the Island of Sheep. But they still continued their search. Once they found a column of <u>crystal</u> sticking up out of the sea. It was surrounded by a <u>mesh</u> that was the color of silver and as hard as <u>marble</u>. They found an opening in the mesh and took the boat close to the column. St Brendan and his monks measured the column. Its four sides were each 700 yards long. The monks then took hold of the mesh and pulled the boat out to the open sea.

3. A modern picture of what we think Brendan's boat might look like.

Another day the monks were blown towards an island, and Brendan was worried. He heard the sound of a <u>forge</u>, with the thud of a hammer on an <u>anvil</u>. As the monks came near the island, an islander came out and threw molten metal and hot stones at them. A lump flew 200 yards over their heads and fell into the sea. The sea round it boiled, and smoke rose up. Then more islanders rushed down to the shore and threw hot stones at the monks. Soon it looked as if the whole island was on fire. The sea boiled, the air was filled with a howling sound, and there was a terrible smell. Brendan told his monks they had reached the edge of Hell. They sailed away as fast as they could.

In the end the Steward from the Isle of Sheep had to help them find the Land of Promise. They left the Isle of Sheep again, and after 40 days at sea they sailed into a great fog. The Steward said the fog always encircled the Land of Promise.

At last they saw a great light, and the boat came to the shore. The land was full of fruit trees. They explored for 40 days, but still did not come to the end of the land they were exploring. Finally they reached a big river, which Brendan said they would not be able to cross. A man came to them, spoke to them by name, and said the land would eventually be made known to all people at a time when Christians were being persecuted.

Brendan gathered samples of fruits, and sailed home with his monks.

Explanation of Words in the Story

Latin

Latin was the language people used for writing in Brendan's time. Almost the only people in Europe who could write were Christian monks and priests. Christian priests continued to use Latin for most of their writing for more than 1,000 years after Brendan's time.

Monk

Monks are men who spend their lives studying God, worshipping him, and trying to do what God wants. They live together in communities called monasteries, helping each other and worshipping God together.

Communities

Communities are groups of people who live or work together.

Land of Promise

This means a land where everything is right for people to live a great life. It's the sort of land where it is easy to find food, where all the plants and flowers are beautiful and grow well, and the climate is comfortable.

Tanned leather

This was specially toughened leather. It was soaked in juice from the bark of oak trees to make it stronger.

Column

A column is shaped like a pillar or a fat post, usually taller than it is wide.

Crystal

The monks meant the column was hard, bright, and semitransparent.

Mesh

A mesh is like the sort of pattern you get with a net: squares with lines or gaps between them.

Marble

This is a very hard kind of stone, often used for expensive buildings or for gravestones.

Forge

A forge is where blacksmiths make tools or weapons out of hot iron.

Anvil

This is a big block (usually made of iron) that blacksmiths use. When they are beating some hot iron into shape with a hammer (to make a tool or a weapon), they rest the hot iron on the anvil.

Working Things Out for Ourselves

Once the students have read the story and preferably had a chance to talk to each other about it, we can ask, "What do you think? Did St. Brendan get to America? What's your hunch?" After time for a free discussion, part of the point of which is to discover the way students are thinking about how we know the past or about how the Brendan story might be tested, we can press for justifications. "How can we take this further? What kind of backup can you give for your hunches? It needs to be something that might persuade someone else."

The first target is to build the idea that claims about the past cannot be taken simply as (given) information, true or false. We have to be able to justify them, and this may raise problems for us. The kinds of moves students are making will need to be made explicit and weighed. What exactly are they doing to test the claim here? What is helpful? What does not work? Are they treating the sources simply as information? (See Box 3-6.)

We need to encourage students to think about their own strategies and arguments as much as about Brendan. Some group work may be valuable here, although whole-class discussion can be highly effective if students are used to really listening to each other.

We also want to begin to counter the idea that we are totally dependent on someone in the past telling us a true story. We can try to make students

BOX 3-6 **Going Beyond Face Value**

When they start using historical evidence, students seldom pay much attention to the provenance of the sources, especially when they are looking at pictures. But faced with a paradox and a little encouragement to look more closely, they can often take major steps beyond treating sources as information.

Teacher	The boat was made of leather wasn't it? So how come *that* boat [points to Jasconius picture] is made of wood? Before you answer, just read what it says under the picture.
Don	So if it was painted after all *them* years, perhaps the painter never knew what his boat looked like, he just thinks, "Cor blimey, I don't know what to paint, so I might as well just pretend his boat's wood."
Rachel	The painter wouldn't know that his boat was made of leather 'cos the painter weren't a scientist, and he would've had to read something like this, what we've read, to find out.
Jilly	Because it was 700 years later, they didn't think, like, you'd have leather boats in that time, because they would've had wooden boats.

BOX 3-7 **Being Aware of How You Are Thinking**

Youngsters are not generally accustomed to thinking about the kind of knowledge they have and how they are using it, so although they are well aware of the concrete suggestions they have made, getting them to consider these ideas reflexively may be difficult.

Teacher	You've given some good reasons. Where were they coming from?
Sonny	My brain?
Joe	What we've learned.
Teacher	Well, let's look at the things Sonny was saying, because what he actually said was they'd have run out of food, because if you count the number of days they were on the voyage. . . . Now, what sort of test is that? Where's that idea come from? What is it that you know, to have asked that question?
Sonny	I just wondered how could they survive without food.
Teacher	OK, but what is it that you know, to make that a good question?
Charlene	Because in this story it said nothing about food.
Teacher	Right, but why is Sonny right to say, "Hang on a minute, they haven't got enough food"? Where does that knowledge come from that he has?
Joe	It says in the first part they only had enough food and drink for 40 days.
Teacher	So he's looked very closely at the story, but then he's testing it by asking a question that's not from knowledge about the story. What's it knowledge about? When you say, "Could they have survived without food?", what knowledge are you using?
Joe	Oh! Using the knowledge that everyone knows that you can't survive without food!

This exchange among third graders is the start of a process, not a secure achievement at this point.

aware of the kinds of criteria they are already using that are not dependent on authority (given information) or on testimony (see Box 3-7). They raise such questions as "Could this incident have happened?", "Do birds sing hymns?", and "Isn't the Atlantic a bit rough for a little leather boat?" The fifth graders in the following (written) examples provide plenty for their teacher to go on, but the key point to emphasize is that we are not completely helpless if someone is not "telling the truth."

| Greg | I think St. Brendan did get to America. But the story would sound more real if they took out all of the talk birds. You could find out by going to a library, and if the library doesn't have it, ask somebody else. |
| Barbara | I'm not sure [if Brendan got to America]. To me he could have just sailed to another part of Ireland he didn't know about. I don't even think this story is true, because the stewardess [sic] was also before them, so he could have reached "America" before them. When they first met him, how did they know they weren't already in America? The way the story is told just sounds fake. If no one had been to America, how did they know about it, and why did it take so long to write about it? If we wanted to find out, we would have to take everybody who thought about this back in time, because one person could lie. |

Many students, like these third graders, distinguish between "true stories" and "fake" or "made-up stories."

Charlene	If they wrote it like 300 years after he'd done something, it couldn't, it might not be true 'cos they don't actually know.
Joe	How would they know this would've happened all those years after?
Sonny	The story could be carried on by other people.
Charlene	But it might be made up.
Sonny	It might be not true, it might be, like . . .
Charlene	Made up. It might be, what do they call, is it fiction or nonfiction?
Teacher	It's fiction if it's made up.
Charlene	Yeah, fiction.

We need to be sure students are clear that factual stories try to say true things, whereas fiction is invented, and does not have to be true. But this is just making sure that everyone is starting from the same point because, as noted earlier, we need to get students beyond this simple dichotomy. Youngsters often have problems in conceptualizing something that is not straight-forwardly true or untrue. Take the following discussion among third graders.

Teacher	What sort of story do you think this is?
Ricky	I think it's like sort of true, and not true, sort of story, between that.
Teacher	Half way between true and not true? And why do you think that?
Ricky	It might be, in that bit, they, he might [much hesitation and repetition of start of sentence] . . . I don't know what I'm going to say now [laughs].
Teacher	[Laughs] No, keep going. . . .Sounded interesting.
Ricky	I'll start again. I think it's between that because he might not get there, and it's like sort of made up, some of this, I think.
Teacher	What makes you think some of it is made up?
Ricky	Because there couldn't be a giant fish—there's no giant fishes around now.
Lenny	You know that fish, it could be a whale-shark.

The idea that Brendan may possibly have reached America or that his doing so may be more or less likely tends to be expressed in terms of Brendan going part of the way. Halfway between true and made up is turned into part of the way to America.

Bill	He could've gone somewhere near America.
Steve	He might have done it to Canada.
Naomi	Yeah, but America just doesn't fit.
Steve	I think it was Canada.
Teacher	They're including all that as America. It's the continent of North America, not the country—there wasn't one called America then.
Naomi	I think it was round about America but not America.
Teacher	So where was it then? That's not a good move, because now you've got a worse problem, because you've got to say where it could have been, and there isn't anywhere it could have been.
Steve	What's under America?

Teacher	More of America.
Bill	Mexico! Might be Mexico.
Steve	Could've gone to Cuba.
Teacher	But if he got that far, he could have got to America.
Bill	America's so *big*. He could've gone *that* side of the world [pointing to Indian Ocean].

Note that the problem here is not that the students' geography is shaky (although that may be true), but that they have a desperate need to find something Brendan might have reached that is not America. If the story cannot be accepted but cannot be dismissed, the answer must be that Brendan got part of the way, or even went a different way. This notion is a proxy for talk of possibility or likelihood. Mitch, a fifth grader, may be thinking in this way when he suggests, "I think it's not possible because he might have went in circles, there might have been another way to get to America to go the opposite way, or it might not work because of the wind and currents."

Much of the discussion will be based on plausibility, partly because the task is deliberately designed so that initially it gives little else to go on; thus students are able to make judgments without having to master a mass of material. They generally will not use the word "plausible," but it is valuable to introduce the term here to make them more aware of their own thinking. As students are introduced to new evidence, we can then keep returning to the question, "How plausible do you think the story is now?"

Most students at this stage talk in terms of "everyday" plausibility—what would be plausible if the story were written today. Ideas that appeal to what was likely then do not usually emerge until later, when we turn to the kind of story the Brendan voyage is. The distinction is highly sophisticated, but occasionally a few students will hint at it. Such responses need reinforcing—not necessarily at this point if doing so discourages other responses, but as something to return to should the chance arise.

Thinking About the Story from the Outside

To build on the general ideas students use to make their first judgment about Brendan's voyage, we can ask a simpler question: "Is it even *possible* that a boat like Brendan's could make a journey across an ocean?" Because we want to know how the students are thinking, we can also ask, "How could we find out?"

If the students are to make good progress in answering these questions, they will need to consider more specific knowledge, namely other relevant things we know about Brendan and his times. But students often suggest making a copy of the Brendan boat to see what it can do, and because Tim Severin did exactly that, this is a good time to introduce his reconstruction and his crossing of the North Atlantic.[13] Shirley, a fifth grader, immediately saw the possibilities: "I don't think Brendan got to America. We could find out by remaking the events, finding how possible each is and when they might have been."

How far could a leather boat have managed to sail?

In the 1970s someone made a leather boat just like the one St. Brendan would have used and tried to sail it from Ireland to America. He was called Tim Severin, and he and four other sailors sailed from Ireland to Iceland in the summer of 1976, and then from Iceland to Newfoundland in the summer of 1977. They had to sail through some rough seas, and past icebergs but the boat did not sink and they made it successfully!

Below is a photograph of Tim Severin's reconstruction of a boat from Brendan's time. The picture shows the boat just as it reached the coast of Newfoundland.

Scientists think that the climate was probably warmer in the times when Brendan was sailing than it is now. Brendan might not have met such gales and rough seas as Tim Severin did on his voyage.

What do we know about the sort of boat St. Brendan would have used?

The boat Brendan would have used would have been made of specially toughened leather, sewn over a wooden frame. The boat would have used sails on the open sea, and people would have rowed it with oars when it was near the land.

Below is an Irish boat, copied from a carving done on a stone pillar sometime between 700 and 800.

Map 1. The North Atlantic Ocean, where St. Brendan would probably have had to go if he did get to America.

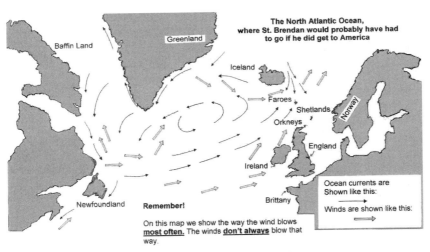

The North Atlantic Ocean, where St. Brendan would probably have had to go if he did get to America

Baffin Land

Greenland

Iceland

Faroes

Shetlands

Orkneys

Norway

England

Ireland

Newfoundland

Brittany

Remember!

On this map we show the way the wind blows **most often.** The winds **don't always** blow that way.

Currents are just as important as the wind for fixing which way it's easiest for a boat to go. And on days when there isn't much wind, currents are even more important.

Ocean currents are Shown like this:

Winds are shown like this:

Map 2. Places we think it likely that St. Brendan visited.

What do we know, or think might be true, about St. Brendan?

- *We know Brendan lived in Ireland between (roughly) 486 and 578.*
- *We know he sailed to Iona, an island several miles off the west coast of Scotland.*
- *We think it is very likely that he sailed to Brittany in France.*
- *We think it is possible he visited the islands beyond the north of Scotland.*
- *We know many Irish monks made voyages in the seas near Ireland at this time.*

Map 1 is especially useful at this juncture since we want to add material to allow students to think about the story in the context of more particular historical knowledge. It is obviously important to check that students have some conception of the size of the Atlantic. But more important, without Map 1, they tend to dismiss the evidence of the sea journeys offered in Map 2 on the grounds that America is so much farther on a direct route that the shorter voyages are irrelevant. Map 1 shows what kind of journey might have taken place. It allows students to see the relationships among the islands that might have broken up Brendan's journey, and how winds and ocean currents would have dictated that he take precisely that kind of route.

Even so, some fourth graders will not see the connections to be made without careful teaching.

Having looked at the further evidence shown above, Shirley (fifth grade) commented, "Yes, it is possible because Tim Severin did it, but you need rations and tools." Students from third grade up can be very suspicious of such a reconstruction, pointing out that Tim Severin knew where he was going, and St. Brendan did not. For third graders, the fact that Tim Severin had a crew of only four represents a crucial difference because they would have eaten less food than a larger crew.

Some students will find it difficult to grasp the idea that because it may have been *possible* for a boat like Brendan's to reach America, this tells us nothing about whether it *did* do so. (Of course, recognizing the possibility makes the question of whether it *did* do so one that may be worth asking.) We can ask students directly: "Tim Severin's voyage proves that a leather boat can sail across the Atlantic. Does that prove that Brendan did make it to America?" Joe, a third grader, *wants* Brendan to have made it, and shifts from a claim about what was possible to a claim about what Brendan actually did:

Joe	This is proof. This is proof of it.
Teacher	What, Tim Severin's copy is the proof?
Joe	Yeah, it . . .
Teacher	What does it prove?
Joe	It proves, like, that he did go from Ireland to America, to the Land of Promise, and if *he* did it, then probably Brendan did it.
Teacher	That *who* did?
Joe	Brendan.
Teacher	It's proof that Brendan *did* go?
Joe	Yeah, it's proof.

The issue of what weight the evidence will bear can be raised at this point: the Severin voyage is strong evidence if our question is whether the voyage was possible, but carries much less weight if the question is whether Brendan actually reached America. This is a difficult idea, but it is accessible to many fourth graders, particularly if something like Cartoon 1 (provided by Phil Suggitt) is used to reinforce the point.

In this example, Charlene, a third grader, doesn't immediately understand what is involved when the teacher asks her to use the idea in another context but then suddenly sees how it works:

Cartoon 1.

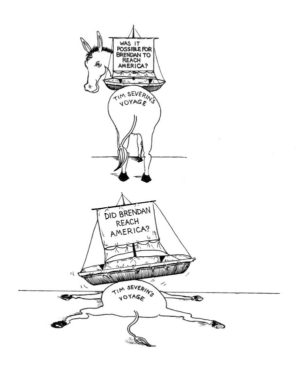

| Teacher | Tim Severin's voyage, what did we think it did prove? |
| Charlene | That Tim Severin got there, but Brendan might've not. |

The teacher then asks what questions their exercise books will and will not answer.

Charlene	I don't know what you mean.
Teacher	I'm looking at your exercise book now. What questions *can* I ask that it *will* answer for me?
Joe	It will answer if we are, a nice character—no! If we are messy!
Teacher	And what *won't* it answer?
Charlene	It won't answer, like, if I'm, if I get along with my Mum or my brother, or if I don't.
Teacher	Your exercise book's like the donkey. If we ask it the question about what your writing's like, or what you were doing on a certain day in class, it can carry those questions.

Charlene	Mmm [agrees].
Teacher	If we ask it the question "How do you get on with your Mum?". . .
Charlene	It'd collapse!

Once they get used to the idea, students begin to use it themselves, as in this example, also from third grade.

Teacher	Because it's a story about a saint, will it let us say anything about whether Brendan got to America or not? What do you think?
Ricky	I think that story would collapse.
Lenny	I don't think it would collapse for whether he got to America or not, because, um I need to check on the map [hunts for map], Newfoundland, well, that's part of America, isn't it, and he got to Newfoundland.

We can pursue this concept further by asking what difference the evidence about Brendan's *known* seagoing (Map 2 and the factual statements linked to it) makes to the weight Tim Severin's voyage will bear for our big question. Common reactions include the claim that Brendan probably did get *somewhere* (substituting "halfway there" for "possibly got there") and, depending on prior learning, comments about how far Viking or Roman ships managed to sail, with conclusions (positive or negative) about what that meant for Brendan's leather boat.

Thinking About the Story from the Inside

The students have already been thinking about the internal evidence (i.e., the evidence that can be found in the story itself), of course, and some may already have introduced natural explanations for the supernatural events in the story. But we now require a closer and more systematic consideration of the story. Two sets of questions start things off:

Make a list of the three things in the story that would best back up the claim that Brendan reached America. How do they back up the claim?

What parts of the story make the claim that Brendan reached America a shaky one? Pick the three things that seem to you hardest to accept. How do they make it hard for us to believe that the story shows that Brendan reached America?

These questions can produce widely varying results. Some students are skeptical from the start, whereas others want Brendan to have succeeded. Both groups find the second question much easier than the first. As an answer to the first question, fruit trees do not amount to much! The only way to see the evidence inside the story as supporting the claim that Brendan reached America is (1) to interpret key events in the story naturalistically, and then (2) to use evidence from outside the story to show how those events fit the route Brendan is most likely to have taken. One powerful line of argument is the difficulty of finding an alternative destination that fits as well as America. If any of the story is to be treated seriously as an actual voyage, what other destination could fit the events better? This kind of understanding appears to be tacit in some youngsters' comments, but to see its importance and be able to articulate it involves sophisticated thinking, generally done spontaneously only by older students.

To bring out the way in which events in the story fit the most likely route, students need to be conscious of alternative ways of seeing some key events. For this purpose, the materials used in this example focus on the crystal column and the "edge of Hell." The first step is to raise the general issue of how we interpret things, using a concrete example—the duck-rabbit and the bird-antelope. (See Cartoons 2 and 3, provided by Phil Suggitt.)

Before we take a closer look at bits of the story, we need to think about how we make sense of things we see or things we read. What do these two pictures show?

Cartoons 2 and 3.

Strictly speaking, because these examples depend on perception and not on how we understand text, they are different from history. There is a danger here. There is no right answer in *any* sense, and nothing turns on which answer is chosen. The danger is that students may think this is true of interpretation in history. It is important to stress that in the case of Brendan, we are trying to decide what happened, and we have something to go on. Students can be reminded that they have already used material from outside the story. If handled carefully, the analogy, despite its defects, is close enough to engage fourth graders, and it creates considerable excitement and amusement among younger students.

The bird-antelope raises questions about the shaded area on its neck. Is this fur or feathers? The answer depends on the interpretation of the whole picture; the details are too ambiguous to settle the issue. We go back and forth between the shading and the overall shape to decide what the animal is. Something analogous applies with Brendan: the way we view the story will help determine how we view particular incidents within it, and vice versa. However, it would not be wise to pursue this point unless the students are already making sense of the basic issue—that some things can be interpreted in more than one way. The next step is to ask the students to look again at the paragraph in the story about the crystal column. Some students will already have seen that the column may have been an iceberg, although many fourth graders do not think of this interpretation at first. If we ask, "Can you think of two different ways this part of the story could be interpreted?" and then provide the pictures below as either a confirmation or a revelation, we can give a concrete example of interpretation, categorizing the pictures as supernatural and natural interpretations. (See Cartoons 4 and 5, provided by Phil Suggitt.)

Cartoons 4 and 5.

This material often provokes exchanges such as the following (fourth grade):

Bill	I think it's a fairy tale, like, a bit like Cinderella and the Fairy Godmother, like . . .
Naomi	Like the birds and spirits and that sort of thing.
Steve	If you reckon it's a fairy tale, you don't see people trying to kill you in fairy tales, do you . . .

Bill	*Some* fairy tales there are—Little Red Riding Hood—the wolf tries to eat you.
Naomi	I think it's a *kind* of fairy tale.
Bill	A fairy tale, 'cos people throwing molten hot rocks, wouldn't they actually burn their hands?
Steve	But it could've been real people, and it could've been a volcano, and the crystal could've been an iceberg, and the fish could've been a whale, and the talking birds [long pause] parrots [triumphantly].
Bill	[Contemptuously] How can you get white parrots? Must be a one-in-a-million chance to see a white parrot.

The "jug" or chalice in the supernatural picture provokes questions and enables us to complicate matters a bit. The fuller version of the story allows the teacher to raise a note of caution about jumping to conclusions.

Before you come to a decision, you ought to look at a fuller version of what the writer actually wrote, not just the summary you've had to work with so far. Here it is.

One day after they had said Mass, they saw a column in the sea. It did not appear to be far away, and yet it took them three days to get near it. When the Man of God came near to it, he couldn't see the top, because it was so high. It was higher than the sky. All around the column was an open-meshed net, with openings so large the boat could pass through the gaps. They didn't know what the net was made of. It was silver in color, but seemed to be harder than marble. The column itself was of clearest crystal. The monks pulled on the meshes of the net to get the boat through it. There was a space about a mile wide between the net and the column. They sailed all day along one side of the column, and could still feel the heat of the sun through its shadow. The Man of God kept measuring, and the side was 700 yards long. It took four days to measure all four sides. On the fourth day they saw an ornamental church plate and jug in a window of the column. They were made of the same material as the column. Saint Brendan took hold of the plate and the jug, and said, "Our Lord Jesus has shown us a miracle, and given me these two gifts so that other people will believe us."

The Mass (which can be explained simply as a religious service) and the title "the Man of God" for St. Brendan both help to emphasize that the story is connected with religious beliefs and is not just a "factual report" of what happened. We can ask, "Has this changed the way you think we should interpret the crystal column, or not? Why?"

We then give the same treatment to the "Hell" passage. The students reread the relevant paragraph of the story, and then we ask, "Is this piece of the story natural or supernatural?" Once again two pictures emphasize the basic point, but this time they are rapidly followed by some new information. It is this information that opens up the possibility of interpreting three major incidents in the voyage, in addition to the iceberg, as indicating just the kinds of things that might have been encountered on a voyage that followed prevailing Atlantic winds and currents. (See Cartoons 6 and 7, provided by Pill Suggitt.)

Cartoons 6 and 7.

Some facts we have good reasons to be sure about

- *The Faroe Islands have had large flocks of sheep on them for a very long time.*
- *Iceland has active volcanoes on it that still erupt even nowadays.*
- *There is very often fog in the area near Newfoundland.*

Some fourth graders will initially deny that that there could be volcanoes in Iceland because volcanoes are hot and Iceland is cold, so it is important not to allow this misconception to make nonsense of the kind of progress we are trying to make. The questions we ask to this end can be straightforward, reinforcing the importance of interpretation: "How should we interpret the visit to the island that Brendan said was Hell? Could the Isle of Sheep have been a real place?" Students quickly appreciate the idea that there may be a case to be made for saying that Brendan passed the Faroes and Iceland, encountered an iceberg somewhere during his journey, and ended up in the fogs close to Newfoundland. For some students, the result is a huge step in understanding. In the following example, Joe, a third grader, begins to see that his earlier ideas were too simple:

Joe	Brendan's gone from Ireland, to the Faroes, named it the Island of Sheep, then went to Iceland, called it [pauses] . . .
Teacher	Called it Hell.
Charlene	Why?
Teacher	Because Hell's supposed to be very hot and smoky and smelling.
Joe	Called it Hell, and saw the people throwing rocks at him which was really a volcano, and then on the way saw the iceberg, which they thought was the crystal column but really it was the iceberg, and then they saw the fog and then they got lost, then came to Newfoundland, and the whole thing is part true, part fiction.
Teacher	Right. But you started by saying it was *all* made up.
Joe	It's not *all* made up. The person going from there to there [points to map] is true. But all

	this [edge of Hell, etc.], all that rubbish is not true.
Teacher	So, why would that be there if it was true that he made that trip? Why would they put it in those other funny ways?
Joe	They put the miracles in because they thought, they would think, that it'd be true.

In the last sentence there are signs that Joe is beginning to see that having miracles in the story might have made sense at the time. This is a big step for a third-grade student.

At this point, we have to be careful that students do not think the matter is sewn up. Rereading the passages about the hymn-singing birds, Jasconius, and the arrow that miraculously lit the lamps is a useful way of reminding students that whatever they say about the story must explain these things as well.

Finding Out What Kind of Story the Brendan Story Is

The problem can now be put to students as follows. If we say this story is just a made-up tale, we have to explain why it appears to make sense as a voyage in the Atlantic Ocean. If we say the story describes a real voyage because we can interpret apparently supernatural events as really being natural, we have to explain the things that do not fit so easily. What this means is that we need to help students consider what kind of story they are dealing with. Doing so raises matters that not all fourth graders can grasp, but it is worth introducing them here even though we will need to return to them in other lessons on other topics. Indeed, none of the ideas dealt with in this material can be assumed to stay with students after just one lesson; all need to be woven into a series of lessons.[14]

The goal here is to help students understand that if we are to know what weight this story can bear as evidence of Brendan's reaching America, we need to know what its writer was trying to accomplish and the conventions of the time (see Box 3-8). If it is a story intended to show what a splendid saint Brendan was, we should expect it to be "embroidered" with supernatural events whether they had a natural basis or not. Just because *we* treat magical events as implausible, we should not expect people *then* to have done the same. Indeed, as a story about a saint, it would be highly implausible without such events. If the students now look at some more evidence, we can ask, "What sort of story is this?"

BOX 3-8 We Can Believe Historical Films When People in Them Behave As We Would

The tendency to assume that people in the past shared our ways of thinking and acting has been found among students in Canada as well as in the United States and the United Kingdom.

Peter Seixas asked Canadian tenth graders to watch selected scenes from two popular films dealing with the relations between Native Americans and whites in the 1860s—*The Searchers* and *Dances with Wolves*.[15] The 10 students were asked to explain the differences between the films and to say which gave a more accurate picture of life for Native Americans and for the whites in the west in the 1860s.

The interpretative framework of *Dances with Wolves* coincided with students' own assumptions: they agreed with its portrayal of Indian and white lives and the picture it gave of relationships between the two groups, and they saw its modern cinematic techniques and the "realistic" portrayal of how people act as making it more believable. Having limited knowledge of the topic, in assessing the film they fell back on their general knowledge of human nature and their sense of a believable narrative. Seixas suggests that, "Ironically, the more a 'historical' film presents life in the past as being similar to life in the present, the more believable it is to these students."

The Searchers, with its dated cinematic conventions and acting, provoked the students into thinking about the status of the film, whereas when they had watched *Dances with Wolves* they had treated it as a window on the past. The conventions of *The Searchers* were dismissed as "the more primitive techniques of an earlier age," but students had more difficulty dealing with its interpretative stance. Seixas emphasizes the importance of confronting students with interpretative stances that differ from their own as a means of challenging and developing ideas about historical films by making the apparent "transparency" of films that accord with our present preconceptions more problematic.

What are writings from those days (500–1000) usually like?

They generally don't give many of the details we might expect (times, dates, or where things happened) and are often vague about exactly what happened. When they give details, they often say different things about the same event.

Often people who wrote in these times weren't trying to get the details right. They weren't writing news reports. They might have been trying to show how a good person ought to live, or how God helped good people and punished bad ones. Other times they might be telling the story of a great hero.

A very common sort of Irish story was the "imram," which was a made-up tale about a sea voyage. People liked hearing such stories. But most imrams were probably written later than the time when the story of St. Brendan's voyage was written.

Some people think "The Voyage of St. Brendan" is different from the usual writings of the time. For instance, one lady who is an expert on writings from 500 to 1,000 is puzzled because "The Voyage of St. Brendan" doesn't keep going on about Brendan doing miracles. She says that when writings from this time are about saints, most of them make sure to have the saint doing lots of miracles. (That is because they wanted to show how good a saint he or she was, and how powerful God is.) But in "The Voyage of St. Brendan," Brendan doesn't do miracles himself.

The material demands a good deal of thought, but with some guidance, fourth-grade students can begin to incorporate it into their arguments:

Bill	I wonder what the entire thing comes to? Nine years and 7 years and 40 days and another 40 days and . . .
Teacher	It adds up to a long time, yes, but it's a bit like . . . What about it saying the iceberg reached the sky, the crystal column reached the sky?
Naomi	It means it's *really* tall.
Teacher	So when it says 40 days and 40 nights?
Steve	It means really long.
Teacher	I mean, if they're not *trying* to tell us how long something takes, then maybe it's a mistake for us to say, "Hang on, lets add all these up and see what they come to," because they're not even *trying*. It's a bit like stories about "Long, long ago. . . ."
Bill	They don't actually tell us when it was, do they? So it's a bit like this, *they* don't actually tell us how long the journey was.
Teacher	That's right. That's what it says here in this bit look [pointing to the students' sheet]—What are writings like in those days?—most stories were like that in those days, they didn't give all the exact figures, they didn't *have* to add up.
Bill	Yeah.

We can now introduce the notion of "embroidering" a story as changing the way it is presented to make it more acceptable to its audience and ask, "Why do people embroider stories? Might people at the time this story was written have had different reasons from ours for embroidering?" We should try to avoid introducing such words as "exaggerate" or "distort," and especially such ideas as "making it exciting." These notions would preempt the everyday ways in which students will already be thinking about the audience, exemplified in the following fourth graders' exchange:

Teacher	What *sort* of story do you think it is?
Steve	A legend, or [pauses] . . .
Teacher	Why would somebody have written a story like this?
Steve	To be famous?
Bill	Or he could make a profit on it selling his story.

The issue here is that our embroidering of a story may be done in different ways and for different reasons from those of people at the time the story took its present form. Our questions must help students rethink their assumptions: "Who is the hero of this story? What sort of person is he? What were saints supposed to be like? If you believed in miracles and supernatural events, what would tell you if someone was a saint? What could someone writing this story (more than a thousand years ago) put in it that would show everyone Brendan was a saint?" Finally, we can ask, "Would embroidering a story like this one make it more or less plausible to people living then? Why?"

At this point we are asking students to grasp, albeit in a simple way, first, that people in the past thought differently from us, and second, that to make sense of what we want to use as evidence, we have to understand how they thought. In doing so, we are touching on empathy, and we need to remember what ideas our students are likely to be working with. Many of them will willingly recognize that people then believed in supernatural events, but see this simply as proof that in those days, people were pretty stupid and therefore gullible (see Box 3-9). Such a deficit view of the past (see also Chapter 2) does not necessarily stop third graders from beginning to understand that the Brendan story may be rather different from a modern travel account.

Teacher	What sort of story was he trying to write?
Ricky	It might be one that he thought, like, if it was a volcano that he made it like *people* throwing it, so like volcanoes are natural things, and he changed them to people, and that, Jesus and everything else like that.

BOX 3-9 The Deficit Past

The idea that people in the past could not do what we can and were not as clever as we are is very stubborn, even in the face of strong pressure. It is worth quoting part of a long exchange among fourth graders to show just *how* stubborn.

Teacher	Could we learn anything from the Brendan story that it's not trying to tell us?
Carly	They weren't very clever.
Teacher	Why?
Carly	'Cos they couldn't make oars, to row the boat.
Jeff:	They did use oars, in the picture.
Carly	Oh, did they? [finds picture] Oh yeah!
Teacher	What do you think then, do you think people then were not as clever as us, or about the same, or cleverer, or what?
Jeff	They can't figure out about volcanoes, and icebergs, and that.
Teacher	So they're not as clever as us?
Jeff	No.
Teacher	You all think that then, do you?
Carly	Not as clever.
David	Technology [points to mini-disc recorder] . . .
Teacher	Does that make me cleverer than you?
David	The people who made it.
Teacher	So you can make one of those, can you?
All	No.
Teacher	So you're as stupid as they were, are you?
Carly	[Laughing] No!
David	We know how to use it.
Carly	They didn't know how to use it.

Teacher	Why would he want to do that?
Ricky	So it's more interesting, and something to do about God.
Teacher	Why would he want to make it something about God?

Teacher	So do you think that if I had Brendan here, it'd take more than 5 minutes to teach him how to make it work?
Carly	No, he'd probably get it straight away, but he couldn't [pauses] . . .
Teacher	This man may have got to America. He could write in Latin—can you write in Latin?
All	No.
Teacher	Well, are you stupider than Brendan then?
Carly	No, but he can't write English!
Jeff	Yeah!
Teacher	So not being able to write English or Latin doesn't make you stupid. So why does knowing which buttons to press on one of those make you cleverer than Brendan?
Carly	*We're* making cars, and *they* just had to walk.
Teacher	And that makes them stupid?
Carly	No . . . [Laughs]
Jeff:	Not *as* clever.
Teacher	What do you mean by being "clever" then?
David	Smart.

The connection between willingness to underestimate people in the past and a deficit picture of the past derived from a technological idea of progress is quite apparent here. The students repeatedly accepted that their argument was inadequate, but kept returning to it anyway. This exchange continued for some time, but there was little sign that it did any more than modify the edges of the students' ideas. Deeper changes require specifically targeted tasks and frequent return to the issue in a variety of contexts.

Ricky	'Cos he said he's a Man of God.
Teacher	Why try to find the Land of Promise? Why go to all this trouble?
Lenny	Because monks are normally very, worship God a lot, and the Island of Promise was to do with God too.

Teacher	Why do you think somebody would write this story then? What do you think they were trying to show?
Lenny	They were trying to show that Brendan was a special man.
Teacher	And what sort of special?
Lenny	Well, sort of, holy.

By the seventh grade, many students should be trying to use their understanding of the world in which people lived and the beliefs and values of the people they are studying to *explain* the things these people did, not just dismiss them.

Teacher	What does the story tell us about the person who actually wrote it? Is there anything we can work out?
Trudi	I think the person who wrote this down believed in God quite strongly, because all the time he's referring things back to God, and that may be from mistakes, or what he'd heard, or been told, but I think if they didn't believe it then they wouldn't have written it down quite so much; it seems very likely they were very strong believers in God.
Haley	I think he probably wanted them to think, "Wasn't God great," probably, or something like that, or saying like, "God's really good, look what he's done, they've reached America," and stuff like that. I think he wanted the audience to think about God.
Trudi	He wanted the readers to realize that if you're good and you worship God, then he's going to be there for you, and he'll look after you, but if you don't, then he won't take care of you, because it seems very certain that they thought that and the reason why he found all these places or visited all these places was because God was looking after him.
Jane	I think that, it seems like the sort of story that was meant for, maybe like, village people who were at church or something, instead of having a Bible reading, maybe having this, getting the message across to them that religion was very

> important and they should believe in that,
> rather than just for maybe like a child reading
> it for a bedtime story or someone reading it as
> a book.

It is important, however, not to assume that only older students can think like this. After his group had worked through the material with his teacher, Don, a third grader, expressed the understanding he had achieved:

Teacher	So if the story's written like that, for that sort of reason, does that mean it can tell us more, or tell us less, or what?
Jilly	Probably about the same.
Don	It probably makes it like more, because without God doing miracles, people who weren't saints, they would say, Brendan ain't a saint, 'cos God didn't do miracles for him, so without God, being a saint, I reckon it'd be less, but if Brendan's a saint and God does stuff for him, I reckon that story must be *more* [believable].

We are now dealing with matters that are difficult for most fourth graders, so we can give them some help in the form of some possibilities to talk about. "What sort of story are we dealing with here? Have a look at these suggestions, and decide which you agree with and which you don't: (a) It is just a religious story about what a holy man St. Brendan was, showing what wonderful things he did to find the Land of Promise that was special to God. (b) It is a story about a real voyage that St. Brendan made to America. (c) It is a story based on real events, but meant as a religious story about how holy St. Brendan was. (d) It is an 'imram'—just an exciting made-up voyage story." We have to be careful here about the grounds on which students are making their choice. Some fourth graders choose (a) because the sentence gives details of what is in the story, even when they are thinking something more like (c). But once the alternatives have been clarified, students can make some penetrating points. Helen, a fifth grader, wrote:

> I think it is (c) because he wasn't all that holy [not enough, presumably, for (a)] and for (b) it wasn't all real like the talking birds, but you could make sense out of that. He wasn't being real holy and I just think that it is based on real events and he misinterpreted some things and he thought some things were supernatural sort of things instead of natural things.

Andy, an eighth grader, chose (c) and explained: "Because I think that this story *could* have happened (the geography at least), but I think that religious influence was then added to show the power of God/St. Brendan."

The task can be ended here with a return to the big question: "Did an Irish monk land in America about 1000 years before Columbus?" But a further step is possible if there is time and the students are sufficiently engaged in the problem.

Possible clues as to whether Brendan reached America—what's been found in Iceland.
Historians know that:

- *Long after Brendan's time (about 870) the Vikings started to settle in Iceland. They found Irish monks there.*

Possible clues as to whether Brendan reached America—what's been found in Greenland.
Historians know that:

- *When the Vikings first reached Greenland in about 982, they found the remains of a skin-covered boat and some stone huts.*
- *The Inuit used skin-covered boats.*
- *The Inuit usually dug homes out of the ground, and didn't use stones to build them.*
- *At the time the Vikings arrived, the Inuit may not have reached southern Greenland.*

Possible clues as to whether Brendan reached America—what's been found in Vinland.
Historians know that:

- *The Vikings reached Vinland (their name for the northeast coast of what we call Canada and America) between 986 and 1000. They met people who told them about strange men who wore white clothes and walked in a procession carrying poles with white cloths fixed to them, yelling loudly. The Vikings assumed they meant Irishmen.*
- *The Vikings called part of Vinland "White Man's Land," and another part "Greater Ireland."*
- *Later one Viking met people speaking a language he didn't understand. He thought it was like Irish.*
- *Carvings have been found on a rock in West Virginia that look similar to ancient Irish writing. One expert in old languages thinks they are ancient Irish writing. He thinks they say, "At the*

time of sunrise the sun's rays just reach the notch on the left side, when it is Christmas Day." (A "notch" in the rock is a line cut in the rock.)

Which clues fit with which?

Timeline Key

Things about Brendan—words underneath line

Things that were also happening—words above line

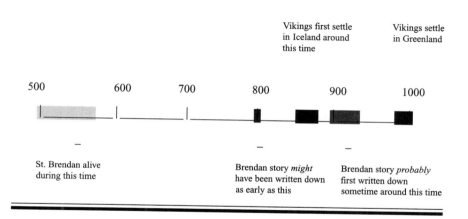

Having made some progress in deciding what kind of story St. Brendan's voyage is, we can go back to looking at other things we know might help in answering our big question. The clues include some quite shaky evidence (we do not have to use all the clues in the example here), and students tell us a great deal about their assumptions as they decide what the evidence shows (see Box 3-10). Students' ideas about the strength of this broader evidence are not easy to predict. They depend on understandings and assumptions about how people behave, how long physical objects survive, the rates at which languages change, and what importance the students attach to "usually" or the views of one "expert." But these are precisely the things we need to bring out at this stage.

A common fourth-grade response is to focus on the content and maintain that the new evidence does not help "because it's all about the Vikings." Insistence on looking carefully at the timeline and thinking about what the

BOX 3-10 The Shrinking Past

Keith Barton's work with young students in history suggests that they shrink the scale of human activities and reduce long-term processes to events or individual actions.[16] The spatial shrinkage is evident in the following example from the Brendan task:

Sonny	I would like, go on a search underwater to look for [Brendan's] boat, it might've sunk.
Charlene	I'd do what Sonny did, but I wouldn't go in a boat, I'd go in a submarine, 'cos you wouldn't sink and die. [third grade]

This is a frequent kind of strategy for finding remains, and despite Charlene's practical solution, the scale of the Atlantic and the task is hugely underestimated.

Teaching the Brendan material also produces signs of temporal shrinkage, even with older students, and sometimes a tendency to reduce a series of events to single occurrences. Some cases are very clear. "I didn't know there were people a thousand years before Columbus," said one eighth grader, "I thought there were just dinosaurs." Some are more subtle:

Anna	Seeing this other evidence I think that they *did* get to America, because the Vikings found Irish monks in Iceland, and they might have stayed on the way to America, they might have stopped and some people stayed there . . . . [seventh grade]

Vikings found can shift students' positions here. But although they can see relevant issues, they do not always find it easy to produce explanations.

Bill	Maybe Brendan got to America on Christmas Day, because it's saying at the time of sunrise a ray grazes the notch on the left side on Christmas Day.
Teacher	Who could have carved it?
Bill	They [the Native Americans] weren't really Christmas Day sort of religious people.
Teacher	How else could it have got carved there then?

It is difficult to see why Anna should think these are Brendan's monks. Why should it be the same group of monks? Is it not more likely that there has been more than one voyage? A teacher using the material comments that (after looking at what the Vikings found in Iceland) her eighth-grade students thought in a similar way with a diametrically opposite conclusion. They "wondered how Irish monks could be at an island 300 years later. They pointed out that there were no women on the island, so how could the community of monks have been continuous since St. Brendan."

Jane (seventh grade) may be making similar—past shrinking—assumptions:

Jane	It says that the Inuit usually dug homes under the ground and didn't use stones to build them, and when Vikings first reached Greenland in 982 they found the remains of a skin-covered boat and some stone huts, and this probably suggests that it could have been the monks that were there, and the stone huts would have probably survived.

Bill	Maybe somebody got there before Brendan.
Teacher	What do we need to know?
Bill	We need to know it's definitely Irish writing and it definitely does say that, not . . .
Teacher	And we need to know one other thing as well . . . Think about what you said right at the beginning, that made you suspicious of the story, when you saw the timeline.
Bill	Oh! What time it was.

Seventh graders are usually more skeptical about the Vikings' supposed recognition of the Irish language, often making comments such as "It may not necessarily have been Irish. It could've been any other language." But although they can come up with explanations for the rock carving, they can still find it difficult to envisage alternatives.

Haley	There's some carvings been found on a rock, in erm, Ancient Irish writing, I think that might have something to do with it, if Irishmen were writing on stones then it probably was the monks, who were there, I don't know who else it could be really.
Jane	I agree with Haley, I don't think somebody's going to go to a stone now and write Ancient Irish on it.

The inferences here are fine, provided we rule out more recent fraud or the possibility of simple overinterpretation of marks by people who, like many of the fourth graders, want St. Brendan to have made it to America. If such overinterpretation is a fault, however, it is not one that betrays conceptual weaknesses in connection with understanding evidence, but perhaps an understandable degree of optimism and excitement.

As a final step, we can ask some questions designed to see what more *general* ideas the students are using by the end of the task. "What would you say to someone who said: (a) We can't say anything about this. (b) We weren't there, so anyone can say what they want. (c) We either have to believe the Brendan story or we have to trash it." For fourth graders, we are likely to be quite satisfied if we get responses suggesting that we have had some impact on their everyday ideas. If we can effect a shift such as that evident in the responses of these fourth graders between the beginning of the task and the end, our students will have made valuable progress.

Ideas at the beginning of the topic:

David	You can't get it right because none of us know.
Teacher	Why do none of us know?
David	Well, like everyone's guessed.
Teacher	And why are we guessing?
David	Because we don't know what he really did.
Teacher	And why don't we know?
Jeff	Because we weren't there at that time.

Ideas toward the end of the topic:

Jeff	[If we interpret it naturally] half of it makes sense.
Teacher	So if we can't say, "It's impossible that Brendan reached America," what can we safely say?
Jeff	Inconclusive.
Teacher	Supposing someone said, "If no one left us the true story, we can't know?" Do you agree with that, or disagree with it?
David	Disagree.
Jeff	No, 'cos there's lots of evidence.

(Note that Jeff had not used "inconclusive" before this point, and the word had not been taught.) In response to the final questions, the students take a similar position, and Jeff's last comment in this excerpt could almost sum up our teaching goals for the whole unit:

Teacher	What would you say now, after working through this, to someone who said, "We can't say anything about this?"
Carly	We *could* find out about it.
Teacher	OK, what about the second thing, "We weren't there, so anyone can say what they want?"
David	Nonsense! 'Cos there's evidence, so you can, say . . .
Teacher	So you can't say just what you want? You have to say . . .
David	The truth, what you found out.
Teacher	Has the evidence shown you the *truth*, or . . .?
David	It *helps* you.
Teacher	OK, what about the last one, "We either have to believe the Brendan story or we have to trash it?" What about that one? Is that right or not?
David	No.
Jeff	In the story, there are some things that make sense, you don't have to trash it, you just have to make sense.

Research and experience suggest that understandings such as those displayed by students in the fourth-grade study of St. Brendan's voyage are likely to transfer to higher grades and to different topics.[17] Students who have such learning experiences will be better prepared for the study of the Pilgrims in a later grade. Developing students understanding of core, second-order concepts in history will be more effective if that development is planned across the years. In fact, our most important conclusion is that successfully achieving an effective integration of conceptual (second-order) understanding and content coverage, as emphasized in *How People Learn*, can best be achieved with planning of history teaching across grades 4 through 12. Individual teachers can achieve important shifts in student thinking, as we see in the lessons described above. But student progress and teacher effectiveness will be far greater if those who determine the agenda for history teaching across the school years do so with careful attention to the progression in student understanding of both second-order concepts and content coverage. An illustration of how such planning might be accomplished is provided in Appendix 3A.

APPENDIX 3A
IMPLICATIONS FOR PLANNING

Student learning in history will best be supported if instructional planning across the school years includes both second-order concepts and content coverage. Planning for progression in students' mastery of the two, however, differs in several critical respects. The sequence of substantive topics that we plan to address may be ordered by reference to chronology, theme, and scale. We offer an example across 4 years for illustrative purposes:

Grade 4:	The First Americans: Origins and Achievements
	Worlds Apart: Europe, Africa, and Asia before the Voyages of Exploration
Grade 5:	The Great Civilizations of Pre-Columbian America
	The Voyages of Exploration: First Contacts among Native Americans, Europeans, and Africans
Grade 6:	Spanish and Portuguese Conquests
	Early English Colonization: The Pilgrim Fathers
Grade 7:	Government and Liberty in the Early American Colonies
	The American Revolution

Such a plan dictates *what* is to be addressed; *when* the teacher is to do so; and, within limits, *how long* it should take. A topic such as the Pilgrim Fathers, for example, will be taught once and once only at the elementary level or in junior high school. It is likely to be taught to all students in a given grade. And, after a given period of time, all students will move on to a new topic without reference to how much they have or have not learned about the Pilgrim Fathers.

Planning for progression in second-order concepts is different. It is informed not by our selection of particular passages of the past for study, but by models of progression based on systematic research and on classroom experience of the kind illustrated in the discussion of the Pilgrim Fathers and St. Brendan's topics. These models are hierarchical and describe significant stages in the development of students' thinking over time. A model of progression for the second-order concept of *evidence* is given in Box 3A-1.

We should remember that what is presented in Box 3A-1 is *a* model and not *the* model. There is no such thing as a definitive model for evidence or for any other second-order concept, although all research-based models are—or should be—compatible. They may vary, however, in the number of levels they include and in the emphasis given to different aspects of students' thinking. Nor do these models prescribe or describe the ways in which the ideas of any individual student should or will develop. They are generalizations applicable to the majority of students that appear to be sustainable across generations and nationalities. They may be compared with footpaths across a mountainside: these footpaths exist because most walkers have elected to follow a given route across the mountainside; not all walkers will have done so, and more than one trail may lead to the desired destination.

A teacher who leads a school party may *plan* to take students along a chosen path rather than to allow each to find his or her own way across the mountain. Most would find this to be a wise decision even if some students are disposed to seek out the more boggy areas and others to head for sheer rock faces. This analogy breaks down in one crucial respect, however: while it is possible to march students along a mountain trail in reasonably good order, students will move through the levels of a model of progression at very different speeds. For example, they may jump one level altogether, moving straight from level 3 to level 5. Indeed, by tenth grade some students will have moved beyond level 6 of the model in Box 3A-1, while others will remain at level 2. It follows that levels of conceptual understanding cannot be attached to grades or to topics, and that some students will have to repeat work at quite similar levels of conceptual challenge when they change topics, while others will be able to move on to tackle new and more demanding conceptual problems.

This point is illustrated by a comparison of the responses of the sixth-grade (Pilgrim Fathers) and fourth-grade (St. Brendan) students presented

BOX 3A-1 Model of Progression in Ideas About Evidence

1. **Pictures of the past**

   The past is treated as if it is the present; students treat potential evidence as if it offers direct access to the past. Questions about the basis for statements about the past do not arise. Stories are just stories.

2. **Information**

   The past is treated as fixed and known by some authority; students treat potential evidence as information. Given statements to test against evidence, students match information or count sources to solve the problem. Questions arise about whether the information offered is correct or incorrect, but no methodology is attributed to the study of history for answering such questions beyond an appeal to books, diaries, or what has been dug up. These sources, although sometimes seen as being connected with the past, provide transparent information that is either correct or incorrect.

3. **Testimony**

   The past is reported to us either well or badly, by people living at the time. Questions regarding how we know about the past are regarded as sensible; students begin to understand that history has a methodology for testing statements about the past. Conflicts in potential evidence are thought appropriately to be settled by deciding which report is best. Notions of bias, exaggeration, and loss of information in transmission supplement the simple dichotomy between truth telling and lies. Reports are often treated as if the authors are more or less direct eyewitnesses—the more direct, the better.

above. On the whole, the sixth-grade students operate at a higher conceptual level than those in the fourth grade, but the conceptual understanding of *some* fourth-grade students is more advanced (relative to the model of progression in Box 3A-1) than that of *some* sixth-grade students. This observation may appear to argue against the wisdom, or even the practicability, of planning for the progression of understanding with respect to second-order

4. Cut and paste

The past can be probed even if no individual reporter has told us truthfully or accurately what happened. We can piece together a version by picking out the true statements from different reports and combining them. In one student's words, "You take the true bits out of this one, and the best bits out of that one, and when you've got it up, you've got a picture." Notions of bias or lies are supplemented by questions about whether the reporter is in a position to know.

5. Evidence in isolation

Statements about the past can be inferred from pieces of evidence. We can ask questions of sources that they were not designed to answer, so that evidence will bear questions for which it could not be testimony. There are many sources of evidence that are not reports of anything (nineteenth-century rail timetables, for example, were not constructed for the benefit of historians). This means historians may be able to work out historical facts even if no testimony has survived. Evidence may be defective without involving bias or lies. Reliability is not a fixed property of a source, and the weight we can place on any piece of evidence depends on what questions we ask of it.

6. Evidence in context

Evidence can be used successfully only if it is understood in its historical context: we must know what it was intended to be and how it relates to the society that produced it. Making this determination involves the suspension of certain lines of questioning and a provisional acceptance of much historical work as established fact (a known context). We cannot question everything at once. Contexts vary with place and time (a sense of period begins to be important).

concepts. If students cannot be kept together, why not allow them to make their own way across the conceptual mountainside?

There are several answers to this question. First, all students may be expected to make more rapid progress if we plan to take them along a given trail rather than leaving them to find their own way. Second, if trails are made explicit, students may grasp (and, it may be hoped, become metacognitively aware) that they are expected to walk across the mountains rather than play in the foothills and watch the clouds drift by. After all, this is what paths are for—for walking from here to there. If we plan to achieve progress in students' ideas about evidence, change, and so on, students may become aware that their understandings must develop irrespective of changes in the factual scenery as one topic succeeds another. Third, if we plan to achieve progress in students' conceptual understanding in particular ways, it is easier to anticipate the preconceptions and misconceptions that students may bring to any topic. Doing so makes it easier for us to identify, to exploit, and to remediate the ideas students use to make sense of the work at hand. To return to the previous analogy, if we notice that we have lost a few students, that they are no longer with us, it is easier to check back on or near the trail along which we planned to take them than to scour the entire mountain.

If these arguments are accepted, it remains to illustrate what planning in conformity with the second key finding of *How People Learn* might look like. Although planning should address the totality of history education from fourth to twelfth grade and *all* relevant second-order concepts, a more modest illustration may suffice.

As already indicated, history teaching at the fourth-grade level may cover such topics as The First Americans: Origins and Achievements and Worlds Apart: The Americas, Africa, Asia, and Europe before the Voyages of Exploration. These topics are likely to be broken down into a number of units of work intended to occupy 4-8 hours of teaching. The Worlds Apart topic, for instance, might include the following units:

Unit 1: Filling the World with People
Unit 2: People Go Their Separate Ways
Unit 3: First Contacts: Did St. Brendan Sail from Ireland to America?
Unit 4: First Contacts: Why Didn't the Norse Stay in America?

The topic aims to develop students' understanding of a particular period in history, that of the Voyages of Discovery. Students may be relied upon to forget much of what they are taught; thus it is necessary to identify the dates—usually for the key generalizations and understandings, rather than for the details—that we wish them to retain. Teaching tasks and assessments can then be focused on the transmission and development of these key generalizations and understandings. What these are or should be is negotiable. The Worlds Apart topic may focus narrowly, for example, on the independent evolution of new and old world civilizations to provide the students with descriptions and explanations of cultural misunderstandings and clashes in the sixteenth and seventeenth centuries. An alternative approach would aim to give students an understanding of the "one world" revolution that began with the exploration, colonization, and commercial exploration of the Americas and elsewhere, which may be seen as the start of the process we now call "globalization."

What may be less familiar is a stage of planning that goes beyond the identification of key generalizations and, in accordance with the second principle of *How People Learn*, also identifies key ideas about the second-order concepts associated with *evidence* and *accounts, change* and *development*, and *empathetic* and *causal explanation* that students use to make sense of the those generalizations. For the units of work listed under the Worlds Apart topic, teaching what we want students to learn with respect to generalizations about the past may be combined with developing their understanding of second-order concepts along the following lines.

Unit 1: Filling the World with People

Target Generalizations About the Past

- Long ago there were only a few people in the whole world. They all lived in a small part of East Africa. The rest of the world was empty—no people.
- Very slowly these East Africans increased their numbers and spread all over the world—to the rest of Africa, Asia, Australia, Europe, and the Americas.
- We may look different and speak different languages, but we are all descended from the same small groups of East Africans.
- *Some* Native Americans are descended from the first groups of people to reach North and then South America.

Target Ideas About Change

- Things were not always as they are now—they were different in the past.
- All bits of the past were not the same. Some bits of the past were more different from each other than from the present.
- Not all differences matter, and some are far more important than others.
- When there are significant differences between two bits of the past, we say that things have *changed*.
- When things are different in ways that don't matter much, we say that there is *continuity with the past*.

It should be noted, first, that attempts to refine students' understanding of change, as of any other second-order concept, should not displace teaching about the past, but will certainly affect the ways in which such teaching takes place. The discussion of the Pilgrim Fathers' and Voyage of St. Brendan tasks illustrates the nature of this impact. It is not practical to address all second-order concepts within a single unit of work. For this reason, the conceptual focus of a set of units is likely to vary, as indicated below.

Unit 2: People Go Their Separate Ways

Target Generalizations About the Past

- People forgot where their ancestors had come from and knew only about other groups of people who lived nearby. People who lived in Africa, Asia, and Europe knew nothing about the first Americans. People who lived in America knew nothing about those living in Africa, Asia, and Europe. They also knew nothing about most other groups of Americans.
- Most groups of people had little contact with each other, so languages and ways of life became more and more different.
- Over long periods of time, great but very different civilizations developed in Africa, Asia, the Americas, and Europe.

Target Ideas About Empathetic Explanation

- People in the past saw things differently from the way we see them today. (For example, their maps of the world do not look like ours.)
- People in the past had to be very clever to achieve what they did. (For example, we would find it very difficult to make such good maps and charts using the same tools as our predecessors.)
- People in the past thought and behaved differently from us because they had to solve different problems. (For example, a Portolan chart was of more use to a medieval sailor in the Mediterranean than a modern atlas would have been.)

**Unit 3: First Contacts:
Did St. Brendan Sail from Ireland to America?**

Target Generalizations About the Past

- In the past, many stories were told about people sailing to what could have been America. One of these stories is about an Irish monk, St. Brendan.
- We cannot be sure whether St. Brendan really did sail to America.
- We *do* know that even if St. Brendan did sail to America, no one followed him or knew how to repeat his voyage.

Target Ideas About Evidence and Accounts

- We can work out what happened in the past from what is left.
- Some things left from the past weren't meant to tell us anything, but we can still use them to find things out.
- The weight we can put on the evidence depends on the questions we ask.
- Often we can't be certain about the past, but we can produce stronger or weaker arguments about what it makes most sense to say.

The target ideas in these units are informed by the model of progression for evidence outlined earlier and, as previously argued, cover the range of learning outcomes accessible to the majority of fourth-grade students. Some students will still struggle to master these ideas in seventh and eighth grades, whereas the understanding of others will have moved far beyond even the most difficult of these ideas.

A final set of examples deals with the concept of causal explanation—provided in Unit 4 on page 172.

In the examples given for the Worlds Apart topic, each second-order concept is addressed once and once only. If two topics are taught at each grade, it follows that each second-order concept will be revisited at least once each year and that planning for systematic progression across grades is possible.

The examples provided here are, of course, only an illustration of the start of the planning process. Detailed planning with reference to content, materials, and activities must flesh out the key generalizations and ideas exemplified above. At the same time, our planning should also take account of the other key findings of *How People Learn*. The planning grid presented in Box 3A-2 shows how all three key findings might figure in planning to develop students' understanding of the concept of evidence, using the St. Brendan and Pilgrims' tasks as examples.

Unit 4: First Contacts: Why Didn't the Norse Colonists Stay in America?

Target Generalizations About the Past

- The first *definite* contacts between Native Americans and non-American peoples occurred when Norse sailors and colonists landed and attempted to settle in North America.
- The Norse were trying to do what they had done before—to find and to settle in empty land.
- But America was *not* empty. It was already full of people about whom the Norse knew nothing. The Native Americans fought the Norse and threw them out of the country.

Target Ideas About Causal Explanation

- Some things happen because people want and have the power to make them happen (e.g., the colonization of Iceland and Greenland).
- Other things happen that people don't want and try to prevent (e.g., the Norse eviction from North America and the later destruction of the Greenland colonies).
- Explanations of why people do things are not always the same as explanations of why things happen.
- To explain why things happen, we sometimes refer to causes that people can't or don't know how to control (e.g., climate changes, differences in population size and density).

The first column in the planning grid shows the content to be covered and the key questions that organize that content. The key questions are designed to allow us to bring together the content and the relevant second-order understandings. Although there are two different topics—St. Brendan and the Pilgrims—the questions for both the fourth- and sixth-grade work are concerned with the same key question: "How do we know?" Teaching will therefore need to focus on the concept of historical evidence. But decisions will need to be made to ensure that the teaching is appropriate for the age and ability of the students.

Before more precise teaching goals can be written into plans of this kind, some consideration must be given to the first key finding of *How People Learn*—that "students come to the classroom with preconceptions." In accordance with this finding, the planning examples for fourth and sixth grades include in the second column of the grid likely *preconceptions to be checked out*. These are planning reminders of the preconceptions about evidence that research suggests students are likely to hold. At the same time, we must keep in mind the range of ideas we are likely to encounter at any age. The point is not that all students will think the same things, but that we might expect to find ideas such as these among most fourth- or sixth-grade students, depending on what has been taught before. So if our sixth graders have already done the St. Brendan task, as well as similar work designed to develop their understanding of evidence in the context of other topics, we would expect that many of them already understand the preconceptions listed as needing to be considered in the Pilgrim Fathers' task. If the students have done no such work, we would be safer to anticipate their still holding some of the preconceptions listed under the Brendan task when the time comes to tackle the Pilgrims' task.

The preconceptions listed in Box 3A-2 for both grade 4 (ideas about sources as information or as testimony) and grade 6 (ideas about sources as evidence in isolation) relate to the progression model for evidence (Box 3A-1). That model also provides a framework for thinking about teaching targets; in Box 3A-2, the third column for both grades 4 and 6 sets forth the key conceptual understandings to be taught, in line with the second finding of *How People Learn*. These understandings build the preconceptions listed in the previous column, and are intended to ensure that our teaching enables students to consolidate or extend their previous learning. Thus, whereas the St. Brendan task targets some rather broad principles about the use of evidence that make history possible, the Pilgrims' task concentrates on important ideas about how inferences can be drawn from testimony, ideas that allow students to consolidate their understanding of evidence. The Pilgrims' task also sets a planning target for extending students' understanding by introducing ideas about situating evidence in the broader context of the society from which it comes.

If the St. Brendan grid and the Pilgrims' grid are examined together, the relationship between the preconceptions to be checked out and the key conceptual understandings to be taught becomes evident. It is this relationship that is crucial for ensuring that progression in students' understanding takes place. The evidence progression model (Box 3A-1) provides an aid to planning here. For example, it is important for a sixth-grade teacher to know not just what content has been taught to students in previous grades, but also what conceptual understandings have been gained. If colleagues are guided by common planning, such knowledge of students' understanding is likely to be a more realistic goal.

The key point here is that when students move from one topic to another, they should also be given the opportunity to move forward conceptually. It is important for teachers to have a sense of the possible progression for students. In addition to supporting the kind of planning that ensures students are given work appropriate to their abilities, this kind of knowledge can help in dealing with the range of abilities that are likely to exist within

BOX 3A-2 Planning for Progression in Ideas About Evidence

Key questions and content	Key Finding #1 Preconceptions to be checked out	Key Finding #2 Key conceptual understandings to be taught	Key Finding #3 Metacognitive questions
Grade 4 (St. Brendan task)			
How do we know? St. Brendan: Did an Irish monk reach America 1000 years before Columbus? **Substantive content** • Irish voyages • Viking voyages	**Sources as information** • The past is given. • We can't know about the past because we weren't there. **Sources as testimony** • We can find out something about the past from reports that have survived. • If no one told the truth about what happened, we can't find anything out.	**Sources as evidence in isolation** • We can work out what happened in the past from what is left. • Some things left from the past weren't meant to tell us anything, but we can still use them to find things out. • The weight we can put on the evidence depends on the questions we ask. • Often we can't be certain about the past, but we can produce stronger or weaker arguments as to what it makes most sense to say.	• Am I clear what question I'm asking? • Do I know what kind of thing this is? • Do I know what the writer is trying to do? • Does my argument work for the hard bits as well as the easy bits?

Grade 6 (Pilgrim Fathers' task)

How do we know?

How do we know about the arrival of the Pilgrims in America?

Substantive content
- Separatism
- Early English colonization
- The Pilgrim Fathers
- The Plymouth Settlement
- The Wampanoags

Sources as evidence in isolation
- We can work out what happened in the past from what is left.
- Some things left from the past weren't meant to tell us anything, but we can still use them to find things out.
- The weight we can put on the evidence depends on the questions we ask.
- Often we can't be certain about the past, but we can produce stronger or weaker arguments as to what it makes most sense to say.

Sources as evidence in isolation
- To use testimony as evidence, we need to take into account the circumstances in which it was produced.
- Testimony can unintentionally reflect the ideas and beliefs of those who produced it and still be valuable as evidence for historians.
- People can produce representations of past events that are not necessarily intended as reconstructions.

Sources as evidence in context
- Inferences from sources must take account of their cultural assumptions.

- Are my questions the same as other people's?
- How do the differences in our questions affect the way the sources can be used?
- Can the sources answer my questions? What other kinds of sources will I need?
- Do I know the circumstances in which this source was produced?
- Do I understand what beliefs or values might make the writer see things in the way he or she does?
- How do those beliefs and values affect the way I can use this as evidence?

any one class. If the fourth-grade teacher understands the learning plans of the sixth-grade teacher, it becomes possible to introduce some ideas earlier for students who may benefit. It may also be important for the sixth-grade teacher to be able to reinforce understandings that have been taught earlier but are shaky for some students.

The third key finding of *How People Learn*—that "a metacognitive approach to instruction can help students learn to take control of their own learning by defining learning goals and monitoring their progress in achieving them"—is also an important aspect of the planning process. The last column on the planning grids in Box 3A-2 lists the metacognitive questions adopted for these units of work. It is clear that these questions are closely related to the kinds of understandings we are trying to develop in students and can help raise their consciousness of what is at issue when using evidence. Questions of this kind increase students' awareness of the knowledge and understanding they have, and enable them to see that some answers to questions actually solve problems while other answers do not. This kind of awareness helps students recognize that answers provided by other students are relevant to the problems they themselves faced in their attempts at answers. Planning of the kind exemplified here that links questions to key second-order concepts can help teachers develop these questions into full-fledged metacognitive strategies. Moreover, metacognitive questions have additional advantages. Students' use of such questions allows their teachers to gain insight into their understanding and their misconceptions and thereby take advantage of learning opportunities that arise in the classroom, and to think about the kinds of adjustments that will be necessary in day-to-day planning to support individual learning needs, as well as longer-term goals.

The planning principles discussed here for fourth and sixth grades with respect to evidence would, of course, need to be extended to other second-order concepts and to other grades to enable the formulation of a long-term plan for a school history curriculum. These principles provide a structure for systematically revisiting ideas that inform all the history we want our students to learn, regardless of the topic. Such ideas are at the heart of history. They introduce students to the possibility of treating accounts of particular passages of the past as better or worse, more or less valid, in a rational way. History such as this does not succumb to vicious relativism on the one hand or to fundamentalism on the other. Rather, it exemplifies the central values of an open society.

NOTES

1. Examples of research in history education confirming this principle include Shemilt (1980) and Lee and Ashby (2000, 2001). Experience with a series of curriculum changes (the Schools History Project, the Cambridge History Project, and, more recently, the National Curriculum for History) and public assessment of students' work in the United Kingdom have provided additional confirmatory evidence.
2. We would like to thank the students and teachers in schools in Essex and Kent in England, and in Oakland (California) in the United States who took part in trials of the two tasks presented in this chapter. All names in the text are pseudonyms, and U.K. "year groups" have been converted into U.S. "grade" equivalents; for example, U.K. year 7 pupils are given as grade 6. While this is only an approximate equivalence, research (e.g. Barton, 1996; VanSledright, 2002, pp. 59-66) offers examples of ideas very similar to those found in the United Kingdom, and responses to the second task in the two countries suggest that differences between education systems do not invalidate the approximation.
3. Lee and Ashby, 2000.
4. For research on student ideas about evidence, see Shemilt (1980, 1987) and Lee et al. (1996).
5. Todd and Curtis, 1982.
6. Jordan et al., 1985.
7. Wineburg, 2001.
8. Dickinson and Lee, 1984; Ashby and Lee, 1987.
9. Shemilt, 1978.
10. Shemilt, 1980, 1987; Lee et al., 1996.
11. VanSledright, 2002.
12. Leinhardt, 1994.
13. The teaching material was inspired by and is indebted to Tim Severin's book describing his "Brendan Voyage."
14. Leinhardt, 1994.
15. Seixas, 1993, 1994.
16. Barton, 1996.
17. Shemilt, 1980.

REFERENCES

Ashby, R, and Lee, P.J. (1987). Children's concepts of empathy and understanding in history. In C. Portal (Ed.), *The history curriculum for teachers* (pp. 62-88). London, England: Falmer Press.

Barton, K.C. (1996). Narrative simplifications in elementary students' historical thinking. In J. Brophy (Ed.), *Advances in research on teaching vol. 6: Teaching and learning history* (p. 67). Greenwich, CT: JAI Press.

Dickinson, A.K., and Lee, P.J. (1984). Making sense of history. In A.K. Dickinson, P.J. Lee, and P.J. Rogers (Eds.), *Learning history* (pp. 117-153). London, England: Heinemann.

Jordan, W.D., Greenblatt, M., and Bowes, J.S. (1985). *The Americans: The history of a people and a nation.* Evanston, IL: McDougal, Littell.

Lee, P.J., and Ashby, R. (2000). Progression in historical understanding among students ages 7 to 14. In P. Seixas, P. Stearns, and S. Wineburg (Eds.), *Knowing, teaching and learning history: National and international perspectives* (pp. 192-222). New York: University Press.

Lee, P.J., and Ashby, R. (2001). Empathy, perspective taking and rational understanding. In O.L. Davis Jr., S. Foster, and E. Yaeger (Eds.), *Historical empathy and perspective taking in the social studies.* Boulder, CO: Rowman and Littlefield.

Lee, P.J., Ashby, R., and Dickinson, A.R. (1996). Progression in children's ideas about history. In M. Hughes (Ed.), *Progression in learning.* Bristol, PA: Multilingual Matters.

Leinhardt, G. (1994). History: A time to be mindful. In G. Leinhardt, I.L. Beck, and C. Stainton (Eds.), *Teaching and learning in history.* Mahwah, NJ: Lawrence Erlbaum Associates.

Seixas, P. (1993). Popular film and young people's understanding of the history of native-white relations. *The History Teacher, 26,* 3.

Seixas, P. (1994). Confronting the moral frames of popular film: Young people respond to historical revisionism. *American Journal of Education,* 102.

Severin, T. (1996). *The Brendan voyage.* London, England: Abacus.

Shemilt, D. (1978). *History 13-16 evaluation study.* Unpublished evaluation report submitted to the Schools Council, London, England.

Shemilt, D. (1980). *History 13-16 evaluation study.* Edinburgh, Scotland: Holmes McDougall.

Shemilt, D. (1987). Adolescent ideas about evidence and methodology in history. In C. Portal (Ed.), *The history curriculum for teachers.* London, England: Falmer Press.

Todd, L.P., and Curtis, M.(1982). *The rise of the American nation.* Orlando FL: Harcourt Brace Jovanovitch.

VanSledright, B. (2002). *In search of America's past* (pp. 59-66). New York: Teachers College Press.

Wineburg, S. (2001). *Historical thinking and other unnatural acts.* Philadelphia, PA: Temple University Press.

4

"They Thought the World Was Flat?" Applying the Principles of *How People Learn* in Teaching High School History

Robert B. Bain

For at least a century, educational critics and school reformers have pointed to high school history teaching as the model for poor and ineffective pedagogy. Consider, for example, the introduction to a series of nineteenth-century books on teaching written by psychologist G. Stanley Hall:

> History was chosen for the subject of the first volume of this educational library because, after much observation in the schoolrooms of many of the larger cities in the eastern part of our country, the editor . . . is convinced that no subject so widely taught is, on the whole, taught so poorly, almost sure to create a distaste for historical study—perhaps forever.[1]

History education, Hall observed, involved generally unprepared teachers who used ineffective methods to turn history into the driest of school subjects. "The high educational value of history is too great," Hall explained, "to be left to teachers who merely hear recitations, keeping the finger on the place in the text-book, and only asking the questions conveniently printed for them in the margin or the back of the book."[2] In a call to instructional arms, Hall and other late-nineteenth-century reformers urged teachers to move beyond lecture, recitation, and textbooks, asking them to "saturate" history teaching with more active historical pedagogy.

Most subsequent educational critics have shared Hall's concerns about the quality of history instruction and embraced the recommendation that teachers reform history teaching to make it more effective and engaging. However, critics have disagreed vigorously about the goals and features of an improved pedagogy. The language of reform reflects these disagreements, often urging history teachers to choose either student-centered or teacher-centered pedagogies, an emphasis on facts or concepts, hands-on learning or lecture, textbooks or primary sources, depth or breadth, inquiry or direct instruction.

History teachers know that the choices are neither so dichotomous nor so simple. Framing the instructional situation as a set of either-or choices, such as abandoning textbooks in favor of primary sources or substituting student inquiry projects for teachers' lectures, ignores the perennial challenges that history students and, consequently, history teachers face in trying to learn history and develop historical understanding. History is a vast and constantly expanding storehouse of information about people and events in the past. For students, learning history leads to encounters with thousands of unfamiliar and distant names, dates, people, places, events, and stories. Working with such content is a complex enterprise not easily reduced to choices between learning facts and mastering historical thinking processes. Indeed, attention to one is necessary to foster the other. As *How People Learn* suggests, storing information in memory in a way that allows it to be retrieved effectively depends on the thoughtful organization of content, while core historical concepts "such as stability and change" require familiarity with the sequence of events to give them meaning. Moreover, learning history entails teaching students to think quite differently than their "natural" inclinations. As Wineburg[3] suggests, historical thinking may often be an "unnatural" act, requiring us to think outside familiar and comfortable assumptions and world views. Such work, then, requires both substantial knowledge and skill on the part of the teacher to help students learn historical content while expanding their capacities to use evidence, assess interpretations, and analyze change over time.

This chapter addresses the challenges high school history teachers confront every day when, facing large classes, predefined course goals, and the required use of textbooks, they try to engage students in the intellectual work of learning and "doing" history. Given the demands on history teachers and the intellectual challenges students face while learning history, how might high school history teachers use the ideas found in *How People Learn* to construct history-specific instructional environments that support students as they work toward deeper historical understanding? As a veteran high school history teacher with over 25 years of experience, I begin by showing how I cast traditional history topics and curricular objectives as historical problems for my students to study. Reformers have long argued that historical inquiry ought to be part of history teaching, but often teachers see it as something either on the margins of instruction or as a replacement for traditional teaching. This chapter takes a different approach by building upon traditional curricular mandates and pedagogy to place inquiry at the heart of instruction. Using a case study developed around my students' studies of Columbus, exploration, and the concept of the "flat earth," I focus on ways teachers can restructure familiar curricular objectives into historiographic problems that engage students in historical thinking. Formulating such historical problems is a critical first step in history teaching.

But it is not sufficient simply to add problem formulation to the extant history curriculum and pedagogy. This chapter goes beyond problem formulation to suggest ways teachers might design history-specific "tools" to help students do history throughout the curriculum. These modest cognitive tools—"mindtools" as David Jonassen[4] calls them—provide useful ways to help students grapple with sophisticated historical content while performing complex historical thinking and acquiring substantive knowledge. Again drawing on my experiences with my students, this chapter makes a case for transforming lectures and textbooks from mere accounts of events into supports that help students grapple with historical problems as they learn historical content and construct historical meaning.

WHERE TO BEGIN?
TRANSFORMING TOPICS AND OBJECTIVES INTO HISTORICAL PROBLEMS

History begins with—and often ends with—questions, problems, puzzles, curiosities, and mysteries. Historians frame and build their historical research around problems emerging from a complex mix of personal and professional interests, unexamined and underexamined questions, gaps in established literature and knowledge, and recurring puzzles and issues. Like detectives working intently on solving the mystery at hand, historians face questions and puzzles that direct their scholarship, giving it meaning and providing coherence.[5] Seeking the answers to perplexing questions does more than simply make history an engaging activity for historians; working with problems also helps historians select, organize, and structure their historical facts. It is no surprise, therefore, that most attempts to reform history education urge teachers to begin with "big" questions. If historians are driven to learn content by their questions, so, too, might students find history engaging, relevant, and meaningful if they understood the fundamental puzzles involved. Students, like historians, can use historical problems to organize data and direct their inquiries and studies. Therefore, creating and using good questions is as crucial for the teacher as it is for the researcher.

However, much as high school history teachers might wish to frame their instruction around the historical problems arising from compelling interests, gaps, puzzles, or mysteries, they must deal with a different set of constraints from those faced by historians. History teachers are charged with teaching their students a history that others have already written; thus they typically begin with course outcomes in hand, determined by curricular mandates (i.e., district or state) or the imperatives of external testing (i.e., state exams, Advanced Placement or International Baccalaureate tests). Using the normative discourse of curriculum and standards documents, history is cast into discrete behavioral objectives and measurable student outcomes, readily used by the bureaucracies of schooling, such as testing and textbooks. Although the authors of those outcomes often started with compelling questions, central ideas, and enduring problems, the bigger issues gradually fall away as the curricula are written, reshaped, vetted, voted upon, and adopted. History, then, arrives at the classroom door as lists of things students must learn and, thus, teachers must teach—missing the problems and questions that make the content coherent, significant, and even fascinating.

Of course, beginning with measurable outcomes helps teachers establish targets for teaching and learning. However, curricular objectives rarely connect outcomes to their intellectual roots, that is, to the historical problems and questions that generated such understanding in the first place. Whatever their value for conducting assessments, lists of curricular objectives do not (nor are they intended to) provide the disciplinary connections, patterns, or relationships that enable teachers and students to construct coherent pictures of the history they study. Lists of instructional outcomes rarely frame history as an unfinished mystery that invites students to join the investigation or points teachers toward historiographic questions that might begin and sustain instruction. Nor do curricular lists help teachers anticipate students' preinstructional understandings, develop a reasonable and educationally sound trajectory of lessons, or build connections across content objectives. Yet the knowledge base summarized in *How People Learn* suggests that these are critical to effective teaching and learning. Given the form of most standards documents, history teachers must offer the intellectual and historical context necessary to provide meaning and coherence across discrete objectives.

One way teachers can build instructional cohesion, as suggested in *How People Learn,* is to organize the curriculum around history's key concepts, big ideas, and central questions.[6] Teachers can provide instructional substance by grounding the abstractions found in standards and curriculum documents in meaningful historical problems. But how do we move from lists of loosely connected objectives to central historiographic questions? How do we transform inert historical topics into historical problems?

In a sense, history teachers in the United States must play a form of instructional *Jeopardy* by inventing the big questions to fit the curricular answers. Like historians working backward from given events to the questions that precipitated them,[7] history teachers work backward from given objectives to the big historical questions. Unlike historians, however, who work only along historical lines of thinking, teachers must be bifocal by pursuing both *historical* and *instructional* lines of thinking. History teachers must go beyond merely doing history or thinking historically themselves;

they must be able to help others learn history and learn to think historically. Therefore, history teachers have to employ an instructional as well as historical logic when designing history problems, moving beyond historiographic issues to consider their students and the context within which their students learn history.

What does this mean in practice? First, teachers should try to design historiographic problems that provide links across objectives to connect the multiple scales of instructional time that teachers and students share: activities, lessons, units, and courses. Ideally, each scale is clearly nested within and connected to others, so students can see how activities become lessons forming coherent units that combine for unified courses. Unfortunately, students rarely experience such coherence in their history courses, as reflected in their belief that history comprises lists of facts, packaged in chronological containers—such as textbook chapters—that have little discernable connection to each other. Unifying problems, if well designed and historically interesting, can provide a larger frame to help students develop meaningful connections across activities, lessons, units, and courses.

Second, in creating instructional problems, teachers also must pay attention to the multiple facets of historical knowledge—history's facts, concepts, and disciplinary patterns of thinking. Aiming for instructional coherence does not mean that teachers will sacrifice the substance and rigor of the discipline in crafting problems to study. Good problems look to both the contours and details of historical stories, asking, for example, "How has democracy in the United States changed over time? What explains differences in mobility or technology over time?" Working with such problems requires students to grapple with important historical details while extending their understanding of and skill in using key historical concepts, such as significance, cause and effect, change and continuity, evidence, and historical accounts.

Further, in creating instructional problems, teachers must carefully consider the hidden challenges their students face when studying history and employing historical thinking. For example, extraordinary knowledge and skill are required to "put oneself in another's shoes," for the world views of previous generations of people were profoundly different from our own. Ninth graders can "imagine" what it felt like to be a European explorer or Native American, but their natural inclination will be to presume more similarity than difference across time. Students find it difficult to imagine a world not yet shaped by science or the Industrial Revolution, a world in which there were no social services and running water, a world in which U.S. citizens did not take democracy for granted. Students' historical present— recognized or not—shapes their understanding of the past—another dimension for teachers to consider in designing historical problems for students to study.[8]

Thus, in constructing problems or questions, high school history teachers must work on multiple instructional and historiographic levels, crafting historical problems that are transportable across scales of instructional time—activities, lessons, units, and courses—while capturing the factual, conceptual, and cognitive processes central to generating historical understanding and challenging students' assumptions. In framing these problems, history teachers must ask, "What historical questions will connect the course activities and provoke my students to learn content as they extend their capacity for historical thinking?" The following case study embodies this question by first describing the complex historical problems I used to organize my high school course and then creating a related problem for a unit within that course.

"Problematizing" Historical Accounts to Raise Year-Long Historical Questions

Creating central questions or problems challenges teachers to work at the intersection of two separate junctures—what is historically significant and what is instructive for and interesting to students. In my high school history courses, I often met this challenge by "problematizing" historical accounts—history's stories, interpretations, narratives, and representations. Focusing on historical accounts gave me material to create a robust set of problems that stimulated, organized, and guided instruction over an entire course.

What do I mean by problematizing historical accounts? At the unit level—instruction ranging from about a week to a month—it means raising questions about particular historical stories, narratives, or interpretations. At the level of the whole course, however, it means raising questions that are fundamental to historical understanding:

What is the difference between historical accounts and the "past"? How do events that occurred in the past and the accounts that people create about the past differ? If the past is fleeting, happening only once and then disappearing, how is it possible for people living in the present to create accounts of the past? How do historians move from evidence of the past to construct historical explanations and interpretations? How do historians use evidence, determine significance, structure turning points, and explain continuity and change within their accounts? Are some historical accounts "better" than others? Why? By what standards do historians assess historical accounts? Why do accounts of the same event differ and change

over time? Does it make a difference which version of the past we accept?

Such questions touch upon every facet of the discipline of history, constituting the foundational problems historians confront when doing history.

Though it might appear obvious, focusing on historical accounts would already represent a major break from traditional history instruction. The accounts that historians write and adults read—such as the currently popular biography of John Adams or the groundbreaking *Cheese and the Worms*[9]—are typically too rich and deep, too complex and time-consuming, to find their way into textbooks. Students do not read about John Adams' life, his relationship with his wife, his travels to Europe, his passions and enthusiasms, but rather read that he was President, that he held certain positions, and that he died on the same day as Thomas Jefferson. Only these discrete bits of information, the traces of historical accounts, make their way into textbooks or into curricular objectives.

Raising questions about accounts helps students see the water in which they are swimming. Historical accounts—or rather, the vestigial remains of historical accounts—are ubiquitous in high school history courses. Textbooks, media, handouts, lectures, classroom materials, technology, and teachers surround history students with fragments of historical narratives and interpretations, yet rarely do students see the nature and structure of these interpretations. Much of high school history finds students exploring vast evidenceless and authorless expanses of curriculum that promote, as historian David Lowenthal[10] asserts, a "credulous allegiance" to some version of the past:

> Historical faith is instilled in school. "Youngsters have been taught history as they were taught math as a finite subject with definite right or wrong answers," frets a museum director. Most history texts are "written as if their authors did not exist. . . ." High marks depend on giving the "correct" gloss to regurgitated facts. Textbook certitude makes it hard for teachers to deal with doubt and controversy; saying "I don't know" violates the authoritative norm and threatens classroom control.

Problematizing historical accounts, then, makes visible what is obscured, hidden, or simply absent in many history classrooms. It helps move school history beyond reproducing others' conclusions to understanding how people produced those conclusions, while considering the limitations and strengths of various interpretations. By making historical accounts our essential historical problem, we can help students develop familiarity with historical writing; identify ways in which people have interpreted past events; recognize, compare, and analyze different and competing interpretations of events; examine reasons for shifts in interpretations over time; study the ways people use evidence to reason historically; and consider interpretations in relationship to various historical periods. Indeed, all of the familiar features of history classrooms—textbooks, lectures, primary sources, maps, time lines, and even worksheets—take on new meaning for students when viewed as historical accounts.

This approach does not preclude using themes, such as changes in migration, ideas, or political culture, but rather forces teachers to anchor their themes in the issues of historical representation and interpretation. Nor does a focus on interpretation favor process at the expense of facts. In looking carefully at historical accounts, we must teach historical facts; more important however, we must also raise questions about why we should (or whether we should) consider particular sets of facts important. The study of interpretations demands that students look carefully at the ways people use facts to form and support historical accounts. Indeed, factual understanding becomes even more significant as students grapple with how people use facts in representing the past.

Moreover, a focus on multiple, shifting accounts does not mean students will hold all accounts to be equally compelling or plausible; rather, like historians, students must develop tools to evaluate and access competing stories of the past, considering evidence and argument while learning to judge what constitutes sound historical reasoning. In systematically questioning historical interpretations over the course of a school year, we can help students understand that accounts differ, and that those differences lie in the questions authors ask, the criteria they use to select evidence, and the spatial and temporal backdrop people use to tell their stories.

Therefore, I placed the fundamental questions about historical understanding cited earlier at the heart of our study for the year.

> In creating historical stories or interpretations, what questions were the historians trying to answer? How did the historians, typically not present at the events they were studying, use evidence from the past to answer their questions and construct explanations or interpretations? Within their accounts, how did the historians determine significance, structure turning points, and explain continuity/change over time? Why do accounts of the same events differ, shift in interpretation, or come into and out of fashion? Are some historical accounts "better" than others? Why? By what standards are we assessing historical accounts? Does it make a difference which version of the past we accept?

Teachers will need to explicitly introduce and help students frame central problems and concepts at the outset of a course and use them regularly, even before the students fully understand them. That is what I did, using the distinctions between "the past" and "history" to introduce students to the problems involved in creating and using historical accounts. On the surface, the difference between the past and history appears to be an easy one for students to perceive and understand. But high school teachers know how long it takes for students to fully understand and employ such distinctions in their thinking.

There are many ways to introduce these ideas, but a particularly powerful one is to have students write a short history of an event they all shared and then compare their respective histories. For example, an activity I often used was to have students write a history of the first day of school that they would read aloud on the second day. The great variance in students' choice of facts, details, stories, and perspectives revealed differences between the event under study (i.e., the first day of school) and the accounts of that event. This simple activity helped reveal the distinctions between events and historical accounts because students experienced the differences when writing about and comparing their shared pasts.

The most significant instructional goal and feature of the activity involved our naming these distinctions by creating two new and key terms—"H(ev)" and "H(ac)"—standing for "history-as-event" and "history-as-account." Why make up such new historical terms? Students typically enter history class with established conceptions and assumptions about history. They use the word "history" in two very different ways: (1) history as a past occurrence ("Well, that happened in history.") or (2) history as an account of a past occurrence ("I wrote that in my history.") Their everyday and common-sense uses of the word "history" blur the distinction between the past and accounts of the past and reinforce typical conceptions that history is but a mirror of the past. A crucial instructional move, therefore, involves creating a language to help students break out of their ordinary, customary use of "history" to make fundamental disciplinary distinctions.

Once defined, the phrases "history-as-event" and "history-as-account" or the invented terms H(ev) and H(ac) were used almost daily by students to name and frame materials commonly encountered, including textbooks, films, and class lectures. This simple linguistic device helped them situate accounts, regardless of how authoritative, in relationship to the events described by those accounts. This, in turn, heightened students' sensitivity to and awareness of when we were discussing an interpretation and when we were discussing an event. In exploring the distinction between history-as-event and history-as-account, students generated questions they used to consider the relationship between events and the accounts that describe them. For example, one class produced these questions:

How do accounts relate to the event they describe? Do the accounts capture the full event? Is it possible for accounts to fully capture events? How and why do accounts of the same event differ? Do they use different facts? Different sources? Different pictures? Different language? Do the accounts identify different turning points or significant events in the game?

Are the accounts connected to each together? Are there other possible accounts of the event? Do accounts serve different purposes? What explains the fact that people studying the same event create differing accounts? Can one account be better than another? How can we assess competing truth claims? Does it matter which version of an event we accept as true? What makes one account more compelling than another? How does an account use evidence to make its claims?

These questions, initially discussed in relationship to students' history of the first day of class, formed a valuable backdrop for each successive unit. Initial distinctions, introduced and then used regularly, helped students demystify historical accounts by constantly reminding them that historical texts are products of human thought involving investigation, selection, evaluation, and interpretation.

Establishing these initial distinctions provided students with the beginnings of a new conceptual map for the discipline of history, a map we used regularly to locate their position in historical territory. "So, were we just now working with events or accounts of those events? Who constructed the account? What evidence did they use in building the narrative or interpretation?"

No one should think that merely pointing out conceptual distinctions through a classroom activity equips students to make consistent, regular, and independent use of these distinctions. Established habits of thinking that history and the past are the same do not disappear overnight. Merely generating questions about historical accounts did not mean that my students developed the knowledge and skill needed to answer those questions, or even to raise those questions on their own. In making conceptual distinctions between the past and accounts of the past, it did not follow automatically that students developed the intellectual skills to analyze, evaluate, or construct historical accounts. Indeed, students did not even fully grasp the distinctions represented in the new linguistic conventions they were using, such as history-as-event/H(ev) and history-as-account/H(ac). Still, while not lulled into thinking that introducing concepts meant students had mastered those concepts, I expected students to use these terms regularly. In subsequent activities, the terms served as intellectual "mindtools" to guide student thinking, helping and, at times, forcing students to analyze their everyday uses of the word "history." Thus in building on students' nascent historical thinking, I tried to push them to develop more refined and nuanced historical knowledge and skill while framing a historical problem large enough to inform our entire course.

Accounting for the "Flat Earth": Building a Unit-Level Problem

How might we create a problem for a unit of study that would engage students, assist in posing the larger disciplinary questions about accounts noted above, and meet curricular objectives such as those that characterize the traditional topic of European exploration of the Americas? Early in the school year, I asked a class of ninth-grade history students, "What do you know about Columbus sailing the ocean blue in 1492? And what do you know about the people of Europe on the eve of Columbus' voyages? What were they like? What did they believe and think?"

Ben	Well, people of Europe didn't know anything about the United States or Canada, because people had not been there yet. They wanted to get to China to trade, but most people were scared to sail across the Atlantic.
Teacher	Why? What were their fears?
Ben	The world was flat and you could fall off it . . .
Amanda	People would not give him money for his ships because they figured he would fail. But Columbus proved them wrong. . . .
Ellen	Not really. Columbus never really went all the way around the earth.
Teacher	So?
Ellen	Well, people could still believe the earth was flat, just that there was another land before you got to the end of the earth.
Teacher	Oh, then, people would have to really wait until someone sailed all the way around the world before they changed their ideas?
Ellen	Yeah.
Teacher	Well, for how long did this idea exist?
Bill	All the way back to earliest times. Everyone always thought the world was flat.
Ellen	Except some scientists, right?

With some gentle questioning on my part, the students collectively told the standard and widely accepted story of Columbus, an Italian sailor who received funds from the king and queen of Spain to go to the east by sailing west. Europeans thought this was "crazy" because people had thought—forever—that the world was flat. Columbus, motivated by his search for gold, did land in the New World, but thought he had arrived in China and the Indies, which is why he named the people there "Indians" before conquering them.

For about 10 to 15 minutes, I probed students' ideas about Columbus and fifteenth-century Europe, capturing key points of agreement and disagreement on the chalkboard. I then encouraged students to think about the source of their understanding, expanding our discussion by asking, "How do you know that the flat-earth story is true? Where did you learn about it? What evidence do you have?" After a few minutes of comments ranging from "everyone knows" to "our elementary teacher told us," it was clear that students could not point to a specific account that supported their understanding of the event.

Because historical accounts were the focus for both the course and the unit, I gave the students several excerpts from the writing of nineteenth-century historians, excerpts I selected to substantiate the common view that Europeans at the time of Columbus typically believed the earth was flat (see Box 4-1). I used these nineteenth-century historical accounts simply to support students' preinstructional thinking about the flat earth, intending to return to analyze the accounts later in the unit.[11] I asked the students to read the accounts and to look for places where the accounts supported, extended, or contested their thinking about Columbus and Europeans.

In general, these accounts typify the story about Europe and Columbus that emerged in historical writing in the nineteenth century, a story that, as the students' discussion revealed, continues to hold sway with most students (and adults). The excerpts tell of Columbus' attempt to sail west to China and the challenges posed by other Europeans and their beliefs about the flat world. They reveal how the irrational beliefs of European sailors, clergy, and nobility hindered Columbus, who knew, heroically, that the world was round. They show how, in trying to achieve his dream, Columbus encountered European sailors who were afraid he and his crew would fall off the edge of the earth, clergy who were horrified by his heretical neglect of the Church and the Scripture, and elites who were shocked by Columbus' disregard for established geographic knowledge. According to these accounts, Columbus was different from other Europeans of his age: daring, courageous, and blessed with the humanist's faith that people were capable of great things if they learned enough and tried hard enough.

By design, little in these accounts surprised the students, confirming much of what they knew already about Columbus and the era in which he lived.

Carlos	He [Columbus] proved everyone wrong because he guessed the world was round.
Ellen	I think I knew that others wouldn't fund him

	because they thought the world was flat and he would fall off the edge. How could that be a good investment?
Jim	Well, he didn't know much geography because he thought he was going to India, that's why he called people Indians, right?

The only hint of surprise for students was that no account mentioned the "discovery" of a people and a new land. Mark brought up this point, telling us, "Columbus thought he discovered America, but there were natives living there." Concerning the story of the flat earth, students were confident that the flat-earth belief was a real obstacle to Columbus and other explorers.

However, most contemporary historians no longer regard this to be the case. This story of the pre-Columbian belief in the flat earth therefore provides a wonderful opportunity to explore both the details of life in fifteenth-century Europe and larger issues concerning the relationship between historical accounts and the events they attempt to represent. Columbus, most historians today argue, was hardly alone in believing the world was round; indeed, according to recent historical accounts, most educated or even partially educated Europeans believed the world was round.[12] The elite, for example, did not resist Columbus because they thought he would fall off the earth's edge; rather, they thought he had underestimated the size of the earth and would never be able to sail so far in open water (a quite reasonable concern had there not been an unanticipated land mass upon which Columbus could stumble).

Yet my students believed with unquestioning certitude that people prior to Columbus thought the earth was flat. Schooled by their culture and entering the history classroom filled with specific stories about historical events we were studying, they were hardly historical blank slates. The flat-earth story is a part of the national, collective memory. Adults regularly use it as metaphor to describe the ignorance or superstitions of the masses. "Belief in the flat earth" is shorthand for any idea that blinds people to seeking and seeing the truth. My high school students understood and could use this flat-earth metaphor. And like most people, they did not see that this story of the fifteenth-century belief in a flat earth was simply an account of the past and not the past itself. For them, the flat-earth belief was an undisputed feature of the event. Whatever distinctions students had made in our earlier lessons between events and accounts, they had not yet realized that those distinctions were relevant to their own beliefs about the flat-earth story. When faced with a story of the past that they themselves held, students returned to their presumptions that the past is a given, an unwavering set of facts that historians unearth, dust off, and then display.

BOX 4-1 Accounts of Columbian Voyages

1. "Columbus was one of the comparatively few people who at that time believed the earth to be round. The general belief was that it was flat, and that if one should sail too far west on the ocean, he would come to the edge of the world, and fall off."
SOURCE: Eggleston (1904, p. 12).

2. "'But, if the world is round,' said Columbus, 'it is not hell that lies beyond the stormy sea. Over there *must* lie the eastern strand of Asia, the Cathay of Marco Polo, the land of the Kubla Khan, and Cipango, the great island beyond it.' 'Nonsense!' said the neighbors; 'the world isn't round—can't you *see* it is flat? And Cosmas Indicopleustes [a famous geographer] who lived hundreds of years before you were born, says it is flat; and he got it from the Bible. . .'"
SOURCE: Russell (1997, pp. 5-6).

3. "Columbus met with members of the Clergy and Spanish elite at Salamanca, who told him: 'You think the earth is round, and inhabited on the other side? Are you not aware that the holy fathers of the church have condemned this belief? . . . Will you contradict the fathers? The Holy Scriptures, too, tell us expressly that the heavens are spread out like a tent, and how can that be true if the earth is not flat like the ground the tent stands on? This theory of yours looks heretical.'"
SOURCE: Russell (1997, pp. 5-6).

4. "Many a bold navigator, who was quite ready to brave pirates and tempests, trembled at the thought of tumbling with his ship into one of the openings into hell which a widespread belief placed in the Atlantic at some unknown distance from Europe. This terror among sailors was one of the main obstacles in the great voyage of Columbus."
SOURCE: White (1896, p. 97).

Two critical features of teaching history are displayed here. The first involves probing students' thinking about the historical problem they are studying and making their thinking visible for all to see. History education entails helping students learn to think historically. Students' thinking resides at the instructional center; therefore, teachers must regularly take stock of it

5. "At Council of Salamanca, one of the 'learned' men asked Columbus: 'Is there any one so foolish . . . as to believe that there are antipodes with their feet opposite to ours: people who walk with their heels upward, and their heads hanging down? That there is a part of the world in which all things are topsy-turvy; where the trees grow with their braches downward, and where it rains, hails, and snows upward? The idea of the roundness of the earth . . . was the cause of the inventing of this fable. . . .'"
SOURCE: Irving (1830, p. 63).

6. "There appeared at this time a remarkable man—Christopher Columbus. . . . He began to astonish his country men with strange notions about the world. He boldly asserted that it was round, instead of flat; that it went around the sun instead of the sun going around it; and moreover, that day and night were caused by its revolution on its axis. These doctrines the priests denounced as contrary to those of the church. When he ventured to assert that by sailing west, he could reach the East Indies, they questioned not only the soundness of his theory, but that of his intellect."
SOURCE: Patton and Lord (1903, p. 12).

7. "Now, the sailors terror-stricken, became mutinous, and clamored to return. They thought they had sinned in venturing so far from land. . . . Columbus alone was calm and hopeful; in the midst of these difficulties, he preserved the courage and noble self-control. . . . His confidence in the success of his enterprise, was not the ideal dream of a mere enthusiast; it was founded in reason, it was based on science. His courage was the courage of one, who, in the earnest pursuit of truth, loses sight of every personal consideration."
SOURCE: Patton and Lord (1903, pp. 13-14).

and make it visible. The above class discussion is an example of a formative assessment whereby I tried to probe the thinking of the whole class. I asked students to weigh in on the problem, had them spend time documenting their thinking by writing about it in their journals, and then collected their thinking on the board.

Gathering student thinking is but a first step. History teachers do not take stock of student thinking merely to stimulate interest—though it certainly can have that important effect—but also to hold it up for critical examination. This observation leads to the second key feature of history teaching demonstrated here: asking students to explain how they know what they know about the historical event. Merely asking students to retell a historical story or narrate an event is insufficient for high school history students; rather, teachers must press students to document their understanding, and to explain the evidence they are using to draw conclusions or to accept one historical account over another. Like a historian querying a text, I prodded my students by asking for evidence and support. And like a historian who uses sources to extend understanding, I asked the students how each new piece of evidence or account supported, extended, or contested their historical thinking. Here again, language used regularly—"support," "extend," or "contest"—helped novice historians analyze critically the relationship between new sources and their own understanding.

In this case, my students could not point to the specific source of their knowledge about the flat earth, and so I provided them with historical accounts to support their ideas. Then to challenge their thinking and to draw the distinction between the story they knew and the event under study, I provided students with two sources of evidence that contested their assumptions and ideas: the first, a picture of a classical statue of Atlas holding up a celestial globe, created between 150 and 73 B.C.E.; and the second, an explanation by Carl Sagan of how the classical scholar Eratosthenes determined the circumference of the world in the third century B.C.E. (see Box 4-2). In groups of three, students discussed how these sources supported, extended, and/or contested their thinking about Columbus and the flat-earth idea. We then began our class discussion by asking, "If, as you and other historians have explained, people prior to 1492 generally believed that the earth was flat, then how do we explain the classical story of Atlas holding up a round earth or of Eratosthenes figuring out the earth's circumference over 2,000 years ago?"

The pictures of Atlas resonated with stories the students knew or pictures they had seen before. The story of Eratosthenes—though not explicitly remembered from earlier courses—connected with students' ideas that some ancient "scientists" were capable of unusually progressive thinking, such as building the pyramids or planning great inventions. In other words, these stories were familiar to the students, yet they made no connection between these stories and that of the flat earth. They had compartmentalized their understandings and did not see that they possessed ideas relevant to the question at hand. Use of the pictures of Atlas or stories of pre-Columbian geographers called upon features of students' background knowledge to provoke them to reconsider the certitude with which they held the flat-earth story:

Andrew   Those other stories [accounts we read before] made it sound as if Columbus was the scientist who discovered the earth was round. But I think other scientists had figured out the world was round, like Galileo. I mean, didn't he?

Teacher   I think, I mean, wasn't Galileo born in the sixteenth century, after the Columbian voyages?

Andrew   Ok, but what I mean is that I don't really think that Columbus was the first to prove the world was round. I mean, he didn't exactly prove it. These others had thought it was round and he just proved you wouldn't fall off the edge of the earth. They thought it. He proved it.

Sarena   Now, I sort of remember that many educated people believed the earth was round. Seems odd, that everyone believed the earth was flat but Columbus, doesn't it?

As I orchestrated the class discussion, I intentionally prodded students to consider the story of the flat earth as a specific historical account that may or may not be supported by evidence and, like all historical accounts, one that emerged at a particular time and place:

So, did fifteenth-century people believe that the earth was flat? What evidence do you have? What evidence do other accounts provide? Was it possible that people at one time, say during the Classical era, had such knowledge of the world, only to forget it later? Why might the flat-earth story emerge? What purpose would it serve? Does it make a difference which version of the story people believe? Could it be that the view adopted throughout our culture is unsupported by evidence? When did it develop and become popular? Why?

The conversation in the class turned to the discrepant information students confronted, the discrepancies that resided at the juncture of their assumed ideas about the past and the presented evidence. The discussion about this specific case also began to call into question what the students generally believed about people in the past. "If people at the time of Columbus believed in a flat earth," I asked, "what might explain how people at least 1,500 years before Columbus crafted globes or created (and resolved) problems about the earth's circumference? Is it possible that at one time people had knowledge of a round earth that was 'lost'?"

BOX 4-2 Ancient Views of Earth Flat or Round?

The Atlas Farnese

In 1575, this marble figure of Atlas holding a celestial globe was found in Rome. It is called the Atlas Farnese, as Farnese was the name of the collection it entered. It was created by sculptor Crates. The exact date of the sculpture is not known. However, scholars assume that it was made sometime after 150 A.D. because of the representation of the vernal equinox on the globe, which is similar to that in Ptolemy's Almagest. To give you an idea of the size, the sphere has a diameter of about 25$\frac{1}{2}$ inches.

THE STORY OF ERATOSTHENES AND THE EARTH'S CIRCUMFERENCE

'The discovery that the Earth is a little world was made, as so many important human discoveries were, in the ancient Near East, in a time some humans call the third century BC, in the greatest metropolis of the age, the Egyptian city of Alexandria. Here there lived a man named Eratosthenes.

. . . He was an astronomer, historian, geographer, philosopher, poet, theater critic and mathematician. . . . He was also the director of the great library of Alexandria, where one day he read in a papyrus book that in the southern frontier outpost of Syene . . . at noon on June 21 vertical sticks cast no shadows. On the summer solstice, the longest day of the year, the shadows of temple columns grew shorter. At noon, they were gone. The sun was directly overhead.

It was an observation that someone else might easily have ignored. Sticks, shadows, reflections in wells, the position of the Sun—

of what possible importance could such simple everyday matters be? But Eratosthenes was a scientist, and his musings on these commonplaces changed the world; in a way, they made the world. Eratosthenes had the presence of mind to do an experiment, actually to observe whether in Alexandria vertical sticks cast shadows near noon on June 21. And, he discovered, sticks do.

Eratosthenes asked himself how, at the same moment, a stick in Syene could cast no shadow and a stick in Alexandria, far to the north, could cast a pronounced shadow. Consider a map of ancient Egypt with two vertical sticks of equal length, one stuck in Alexandria, the other in Syene. Suppose that, at a certain moment, each stick casts no shadow at all. This is perfectly easy to understand—provided the Earth is flat. The Sun would then be directly overhead. If the two sticks cast shadows of equal length, that also would make sense of a flat Earth: the Sun's rays would then be inclined at the same angle to the two sticks. But how could it be that at the same instant there was no shadow at Syene and a substantial shadow at Alexandria?

The only possible answer, he saw, was that the surface of the Earth is curved. Not only that: the greater the curvature, the greater the difference in the shadow lengths. The Sun is so far away that its rays are parallel when they reach the Earth. Sticks placed at different angles to the Sun's rays cast shadows of different lengths. For the observed difference in the shadow lengths, the distance between Alexandria and Syene had to be about seven degrees along the surface of the Earth; that is, if you imagine the sticks extending down to the center of the Earth, they would there intersect at an angle of seven degrees. Seven degrees is something like one-fiftieth of three hundred and sixty degrees, the full circumference of the Earth. Eratosthenes knew that the distance between Alexandria and Syene was approximately 800 kilometers, because he hired a man to pace it out. Eight hundred kilometers times 50 is 40,000 kilometers: so that must be the circumference of the Earth.

This is the right answer. Eratosthenes' only tools were sticks, eyes, feet and brains, plus a taste for experiment. With them he deduced the circumference of the Earth with an error of only a few percent, a remarkable achievement for 2,200 years ago. He was the first person to accurately measure the size of the planet.'

SOURCE: Sagan (1985, pp. 5-7).

To help students frame this problem more sharply—as well as to begin revealing the core historiographic debate—students read selections from the work of two contemporary scholars, Daniel Boorstin and Stephen Jay Gould (see Box 4-3). In one excerpt, Boorstin argues that the Middle Ages was a "great interruption" in the intellectual progress begun in Classical times, describing this interruption as an era when people were "more concerned with faith than facts."[13] On the other hand, Gould rejects the idea of a great interruption in European geographic knowledge, pointing to a story of continuity rather than discontinuity of ideas.

I used these excerpts strategically, for I wanted to provoke an in-class discussion and move the class toward framing an instructional/historical problem that would guide our study of European discovery: "Did people in 1492 generally believe in the flat earth? If not, when did the story of the flat earth arise? Who promoted that account? Why would people tell stories about the flat earth if the stories were not supported by evidence? What historical accounts explain European exploration of the Americas? How have historians changed those accounts over time?"

In thus problematizing the Columbian account and framing these questions, I sharpened the larger historiographic questions we were using to structure the entire course and the specific curricular objectives for the unit under study. In investigating these questions and analyzing the shifting and competing interpretations of exploration and explorers, high school history students also worked toward mastering the key content objectives for this unit of history. For example, while grappling with issues related to the nature of historical interpretation and knowledge, students had to study the context for and impact of European exploration from a number of perspectives. Historical knowledge—facts, concepts, and processes—shaped almost every feature of the unit, from the framing of the problem through the questions we employed during discussions. Students learned historical facts in the context of these large historical questions, and once they understood the questions, they saw they could not answer them without factual knowledge. The old and false distinction between facts and interpretations or between content and process collapses here. How can students learn about the accounts of the past—the growth of the flat-earth story, for example—without studying the knowledge and ideas of fourteenth- and fifteenth-century Europeans, the features of the waning Middle Ages, the emerging renaissance, tensions between the orthodoxy of the church and new scientific ideas, or the new mercantile impulses that promulgated reasonable risks in the name of profit? As students studied the development of the flat-earth story, an idea of the late eighteenth/early nineteenth century, they also worked with facts about early American national growth, conflicts with Britain and France, and Protestant concerns about Irish immigration. In trying to understand how this account of the past developed and became popular, students used specific factual detail to make their cases.

Learning historical content, though, was not the only factor that shaped the instruction. In helping students frame a historiographic problem, we publicly took stock of students' background knowledge and of their historical conceptions and misconceptions. Simply revealing students' thinking does not help them achieve higher levels of understanding. But by making visible what students thought, I was able to use their ideas to design subsequent instruction and thus encourage them to use historical evidence to question or support their ideas. The activities discussed above asked students to juxtapose their understanding against historical evidence or established historical accounts. The pedagogical moves were specifically historical; that is, in probing students' knowledge about a historical event, we went beyond just surveying what students knew or what they wanted to learn, a popular technique that begins many lessons (e.g., "Know-Want to know-Learned" charts). Rather, like historians, we used new evidence and other historical accounts to support, extend, or contest students' understanding. In establishing the unit problem, we created a place for students to consider the relationship among their own historical interpretations of the events, those of other historians, and historical evidence. Again, the three verbs I consistently asked students to use—"support," "extend," and "contest"—helped them situate historical interpretations and sources in relationship to their understanding.

Unit-level historical and instructional problems, then, emerged at the intersection of the essential course problems, the unit's specific curricular objectives, and students' understanding. Having formed historical problems and with sources now in hand, we might say that the students were doing history. However, we are cautioned by *How People Learn* and by scholarship on the challenges novices face in employing expert thinking to look beyond the trappings of the activity and consider the supports students may need to use the problems and resources effectively as they study history.

DESIGNING A "HISTORY-CONSIDERATE" LEARNING ENVIRONMENT: TOOLS FOR HISTORICAL THINKING

A central feature of learning, as *How People Learn* points out, involves students "engag[ing] in active processes as represented by the phrase 'to do.'" [14] The students in this case study were engaged in the active processes of history as they raised historiographic problems about accounts in general and the case of Columbus in particular, and in the subsequent use of historical sources to investigate those problems. In emphasizing the need to en-

BOX 4-3 Was There a Great Interruption in European Geographic Knowledge?

'Christian Europe did not carry on the work of [ancient thinkers such as] Ptolemy. Instead the leaders of orthodox Christendom built a grand barrier against the progress of knowledge about the earth. Christian geographers in the Middle Ages spent their energies embroidering a neat, theologically appealing picture of what was already known, or what was supposed to be known....

It is easier to recount what happened than to explain satisfactorily how it happened or why. After the death of Ptolemy, Christianity conquered the Roman Empire and most of Europe. Then we observe a Europe-wide phenomenon of scholarly amnesia, which afflicted the continent from A.D. 300 to at least 1400. During those centuries Christian faith and dogma suppressed the useful image of the world that had been so slowly, so painfully, and so scrupulously drawn by ancient geographers....

We have no lack of evidence of what the medieval Christian geographers thought. More than six hundred mappae mundi, maps of the world, survive from the Middle Ages....

What was surprising was the Great Interruption. All people have wanted to believe themselves at the center. But after the accumulated advances of classical geography, it required amnesiac effort to ignore the growing mass of knowledge and retreat into a world of faith and caricature....The Great Interruption of geography we are about to describe was a ...remarkable act of retreat.'

Christian geography had become a cosmic enterprise, more interested in everyplace than in anyplace, more concerned with faith than with facts. Cosmos-makers confirmed Scripture with their graphics, but these were no use to a sea captain delivering a cargo of olive oil from Naples to Alexandria....

SOURCE: Boorstin (1990, pp. 100, 102, 146).

gage students in the practices of the discipline, it is tempting to conclude that simply doing something that resembles a disciplinary activity is by itself educative and transformative. There is a danger, however, if teachers uncritically accept the historian's practices as their own and confuse doing history with doing history teaching.

History teachers, curriculum designers, and assessment architects need to be cautious when attempting to transplant activities from a community of history experts to a body of student novices. Historical tasks embedded

Dramatic to be sure, but entirely fictitious. There never was a period of "flat earth darkness" among scholars (regardless of how many uneducated people may have conceptualized our planet both then and now). Greek knowledge of sphericity never faded, and all major medieval scholars accepted the earth's roundness as an established fact of cosmology. Ferdinand and Isabella did refer Columbus's plans to a royal commission headed by Hernando de Talavera, Isabella's confessor and, following defeat of the Moors, Archbishop of Granada. This commission, composed of both clerical and lay advisers, did meet, at Salamanca among other places. They did pose some sharp intellectual objections to Columbus, but all assumed the earth's roundness. As a major critique, they argued that Columbus could not reach the Indies in his own allotted time, because the earth's circumference was too great. . . .

Virtually all major medieval scholars affirmed the earth's roundness. . . . The twelfth-century translations into Latin of many Greek and Arabic works greatly expanded general appreciation of natural sciences, particularly astronomy, among scholars, and convictions about the earth's sphericity both spread and strengthened. Roger Bacon (1220-1292) and Thomas Aquinas (1225-1274) affirmed roundness via Aristotle and his Arabic commentators, as did the greatest scientists of later medieval times, including John Buriden (1300-1358) and Nicholas Oresme (1320-1382).

SOURCE: Gould (1995, p. 42).

within an expert community draw meaning from the group's frames, scripts, and schemas. Experts differ from novices, as *How People Learn* explains, and this is an important point for history teachers to bear in mind. Students learning history do not yet share historians' assumptions. They think differently about text, sources, argument, significance, and the structure of historical knowledge.[15] The frames of meaning that sustained the disciplinary task within the community of historians will rarely exist within the classroom. Initially, students typically resist the transplanted activity, or the culture of the classroom assimilates the "authentic" activity, using it to sustain novices' naive or scholastic views. Engaging students in some legitimate disciplinary activity without restructuring the social interaction or challenging students' presuppositions will yield only ritualistic understanding. The problem for teachers is to design activities that will engage students in historical cognition without yielding to the assumption that disciplinary tasks mechanically develop students' higher functions.

As a classroom teacher, I was often caught in this paradox of trying to have my students work actively with history at the same time that I was trying to help them acquire the "unnatural" dispositions and habits of mind necessary to engage in history's intellectual work. Take, for example, the reading of primary sources—an intellectual activity that now appears to be synonymous with historical thinking in U.S. classrooms and on standardized exams. Using primary sources as historians do involves more than just finding information in sources; it requires that students pay attention to features within and outside of the text, such as who wrote the source, when was it created, in what circumstances and context, with what language, and for what reasons. Working with these questions in mind is challenging for high school students, a challenge not met merely by giving them the chance to use primary sources in grappling with a historical question.[16] Indeed, the opening activities discussed above demonstrated this point to me clearly, as only 2 of 55 asked for information about the authors in the authorless handouts I provided to frame the flat-earth problem. Though the students and I had established a good historiographic problem using competing sources, the students still needed support in doing more sophisticated reading and thinking.

The key word above is "support." As a history teacher, I wanted my students to engage in more complicated work than they could perform on their own. Believing, as Bruner [17] argues, that teachers can teach any subject to anybody at any age in some form that is honest, I found, even as a veteran history teacher, that putting historical work into honest and appropriate form for my students was an ongoing challenge. This was particularly true in classes where the learners developed history's cognitive skills at varying rates and to varying degrees—a characteristic of every class I ever taught, regardless of how small or how homogeneous. History teachers regularly face the dilemma of reducing the challenge of the historical tasks they ask students to tackle or simply moving on, leaving behind or frustrating a number of students. Instead of making such a choice, teachers can keep the intellectual work challenging for all their students by paying careful attention to the design and use of history-specific cognitive tools to help students work beyond their level of competence. The underlying idea is that with history-specific social assistance, history students can exhibit many more competencies than they could independently, and through history-specific social assistance, history's higher-order analytic approaches emerge and are subsequently internalized. Tharp and Gallimore[18] remind us that "until internalization occurs, *performance must be assisted.*" By attending to students' thinking and by embedding historians' disciplinary thinking into classroom artifacts and interactions, we can transform a class of novices into a community with shared, disciplinary expertise. Participating in such a community opens up opportunities for students to internalize the discipline's higher functions.

What do I mean by history-specific tools and social assistance? Here I refer to visual prompts, linguistic devices, discourse, and conceptual strategies that help students learn content, analyze sources, frame historical problems, corroborate evidence, determine significance, or build historical arguments. In short, these cognitive tools help students engage in sophisticated historical thinking. I demonstrated an example of a history-specific cognitive tool earlier in this chapter in my discussion of opening activities that helped students distinguish between history-as-event and history-as-account. In framing these distinctions as they emerged from students' experiences, we transcended these experiences by creating linguistic devices—H(ev) and H(ac)—that students used to explore the historical landscape. With guidance, students' experiences in the first few days of school produced a set of tools in the form of terms that they subsequently used to analyze historical events and sources. Later work on the flat-earth question revealed that students did not fully understand and were not regularly applying these distinctions on their own. In other words, they had not internalized these differences. However, the linguistic supports and my repeated reminders continued to help students use these distinctions in their studies. The special terms helped sharpen students' thinking in ways that the common use of the word "history" did not. With continued use, students began to employ the differences between the past and stories about the past more effectively and without prompting. Eventually, our need to refer to the constructed terms, H(ev) and H(ac), declined. Typically by the end of the first semester, though still regularly using the ideas behind the terms, we were using the terms only occasionally.

Reading of primary sources was another area in which specially created history-specific tools helped students engage in more sophisticated thinking. Here I established a group reading procedure to assist students in analyzing, contextualizing, sourcing, and corroborating historical material.[19] To create history-specific metacognitive tools, I tried to embed such thinking within our classroom interactions around reading primary and secondary sources. By modifying reciprocal teaching procedures[20] to reflect the strategies historians use when reading primary sources, I established reading procedures that enabled a group of students to read and question sources together in ways they did not on their own.[21]

The key here was a discipline-specific division of labor whereby I assigned each student or pair of students to "become" a particular type of historical question or questioner. For example, some students were assigned to ask "What other sources support or contest this source?" and thus became "corroborators"; others were assigned to ask about the creator of a source and thus became "sourcers." Within specific roles, students questioned classmates about the documents we were reading together, and so the discussion unfolded. Some students posed questions reflected in general reading strategies and asked classmates to identify confusing language, define difficult words, or summarize key points. However, the remaining roles/questions—e.g., corroborator, sourcer, contextualizer—were specific to the discipline of history, encouraging students to pose questions expert historians might ask. Using historians' strategies—such as corroborating, contextualizing, and sourcing—students asked their classmates questions about who created the source, its intended audience, the story line, what else they knew that supported what was in the source, and what else they knew that challenged what was in the source.

Thus, having equipped each student with a particular set of questions to ask classmates, we reread the accounts of Columbus and the flat earth (Box 4-1):

Teacher	Does anyone have any questions for their classmates about these sources? Let's begin with maybe a question about vocabulary or summaries, ok? Who wants to begin?
Chris	I guess I will. How would you summarize these stories?
Teacher	Do you want someone to summarize all the stories, all the excerpts? Or, maybe an aspect of the stories?
Chris	Ok, I guess just an aspect. What do you think these say about Columbus? Ellen?
Ellen	He is smart.
Chris	Anything else?
Ellen	Brave?
Aeysha	Chris' question has got me thinking about my questions. What do all of these stories say about the kind of person Columbus was? Do they have [some] agreement . . . with each other about him?
Teacher	Let's stop and think about this question and use our journals to write a "2-minute" essay

about what these tell us about the kind of
person Columbus was.

The journal writing gave students time to work out an answer informally
on paper before publicly talking about their ideas. After a few minutes of
writing time, the students had worked out more-detailed pictures of Columbus as represented in the accounts. For example, Ellen wrote:

*In these stories, Columbus appears to be smart. He is a real
individual and pretty brave. Everyone else was just following the ideas of the day and he was a protester, a rebel
against everyone else. These glorify him.*

After reading a few students' journal entries aloud, I asked whether
anyone else had some questions to ask classmates about the sources:

Sarena	I do. Does anyone notice the years that these were written? About how old are these accounts? Andrew?
Andrew	They were written in 1889 and 1836. So some of them are about 112 years old and others are about 165 years old.
Teacher	Why did you ask, Sarena?
Sarena	I'm supposed to ask questions about when the source was written and who wrote it. So, I'm just doing my job.
Andrew	Actually, I was wondering if something was happening then that made Columbus and this story popular. Did historians discover something new about Columbus in the 1800s?
Rita	How do you know they were historians who wrote these?
Andrew	Because the title says "Historian's Accounts."
Rita	Yeah, but Washington Irving wrote about the headless horseman. Was he a historian? And he wrote stories for kids. Were these taken from books for young kids? Maybe that is why they tell such stories about Columbus, like he was some big hero?

As they asked questions, classmates returned to the documents, made journal entries, and discussed their answers. Thus, in this structured manner, the
class raised multiple questions that guided everyone's reading and discussion of text. And students raised a number of questions that could not be

answered from the sources in front of them. They offered conjectures and speculations that we would explore through later resources, including primary sources, secondary sources, textbooks, and lectures.

This reading activity was initially awkward and time-consuming with its role assignments, complex questioning, journaling, and discussion. It differed from cooperative activities whereby a group divides a historical topic, such as European exploration, and then researches a particular component of the topic, such as Spanish explorers or English explorers or natives' responses to exploration, before reporting to classmates what they have learned about their piece of the content. In this example, the division of labor occurred along the lines of thinking needed to read and analyze a historical text. The facets of the complex historical thinking—not merely the topical features—then defined and divided the students' intellectual work. By using these roles to read and then question each other, the students avoided their habit of treating historical text as they would other text, merely as a place to find "authoritative" information.

I used this structured reading and discussion activity because I did not initially expect individual students to be capable of performing a complete, complex historical analysis of a document or a document set. Paradoxically, however, from the beginning students needed to do such analysis to work on the historical and instructional tasks I assigned. Rather than lower disciplinary standards or allow novices merely to mimic experts, we used this reading strategy to enable students—as a group—to participate in this complex, disciplinary activity. Initially, the designed cognitive tools (e.g., group reading procedure) and the teacher carried most of the intellectual load that enabled students to participate in the activity.[22]

As *How People Learn* explains, history teachers need to design student-, content-, and assessment-centered learning environments to support students' historical study. In a sense, teachers work to build a history-specific culture that, through its patterns of interactions, instructional tasks, and artifacts, assists students in thinking historically (for more examples see Bain, 2000). In designing this environment, teachers try to make the key features of expert historical thought accessible for students to use as needed—during class discussion or while working in groups, at home, or on exams. "You're giving your students crutches," some teachers have told me, "and you should not let students use crutches." However, I like the analogy because I know few people who will use crutches unless they need them. Once able to get around without them, people cast the crutches aside. So it has been with the history-specific tools in my classroom. Once students have internalized the distinctions between "past" and "history" or the multiple strategies designed to help them read sources with more power, they find that our classroom supports slow them down or get in their way. When that happens, students stop using them. On the other hand, the supports remain available when students need assistance.

In such an environment, the lecture and textbook acquire new meaning. Given our focus on historical accounts, students start to use and see lectures and textbooks as examples of historical accounts. Students can apply the same sets of questions to the textbook and to my lectures that they do to other historical accounts and sources. For example, "How does this lecture support, expand, or contest what I already understand? What else corroborates this account? What shaped it?"

Also, we can reconsider texts and lectures as possible suports—history-specific cognitive tools—to help students think historically, and not just as vehicles to transmit information. Teachers can design and use lectures and textbooks strategically to help students frame or reframe historiographic problems; situate their work in larger contexts; see interpretations that might support, extend, or contest their emerging views; work more efficiently with contradictions within and among sources; and encounter explanations and sources that, because of time, availability, or skill, students would not be able to use. With help, students can learn to actively "read" lectures and textbooks, and then use both critically and effectively in their historical study.

For example, consider again the problem my students confronted once they began to allow the possibility that fifteenth-century Europeans might not have thought the earth was flat or that people had not always told that historical story. The students raised deep, rich, and complex historical questions:

Have the stories about Columbus changed since 1492? If so, in what ways did they change? What factors explain the shifting views about Columbus? Why did the story change? Does it matter which view or interpretation people hold about the story?

The pride and excitement I derived from their questions was tempered by a recognition of how limited were our time and resources. Realistically, where would my students go to flesh out the contours of this historical problem and find the details to give it meaning? Would their textbook give the evidence needed to move forward? Had the primary sources I provided given students the material necessary to paint the larger historical picture, resolve their confusions, or answer their questions? The students needed help organizing their ideas, putting sources and evidence within a larger temporal context, understanding discrepant sources, and expanding both the facts and interpretations at hand. If my students were going to do more than ask powerful questions, they needed some assistance. In the midst of their historical inquiries appeared to be a perfect "time for telling."[23]

Therefore, I designed a lecture specifically to help students consider temporal shifts in the way people have regarded the Columbian story, questions that emerged after students had encountered discrepant accounts of the story. I saw this as a chance to revisit the unit's central problem and bring forward facts, concepts, ideas, and interpretations that might help students further their inquiries and develop their explanations. I began the lecture by asking students to write five dates in their journals—1592, 1692, 1792, 1892, and 1992—and then to predict how people living in the colonies and later in the United States marked the 100th, 200th, 300th, 400th, and 500th anniversary of the Columbian voyages. After the students had written their predictions in their journals and spent a few minutes talking about what they expected and why, I provided them with historical information about the changing and shifting nature of the Columbian story over the past 500 years.

For example, in 1592 and 1692, the European colonists and Native Americans made almost no acknowledgment of the centennial and bicentennial of the Columbian voyages. Indeed, there was little acknowledgment of Columbus as the "founder" of America. By 1792, however, the situation had changed, and a growing Columbian "sect" had emerged among former colonists and new citizens of the United States. People in the United States began to celebrate Columbus as the man who had "discovered" the new world. Columbia as a symbol took shape during this era, and people across the continent used one form of Columbus or another to name new cities and capitals. By 1892, the celebration of Columbianism was in full swing. King's College had changed its name to Columbia, and the U.S. Congress had funded the Columbian Exposition for the 1892 World's Fair. It was in the period between the third and fourth centennials that the flat earth became a key feature of the story, popularized in no small part by Washington Irving's 1830 biography of Columbus.[24]

Things had changed quite significantly by 1992. For example, in its exhibition to remember ("celebrate" and "commemorate" were contested words by 1992) the 500th anniversary of the Columbian voyages, the Smithsonian museum made no mention of "discovery," preferring to call its exhibit the "Columbian Exchange." Moreover, Columbus no longer held sway as an unquestioned hero, and many communities chose to focus on conquest and invasion in marking October 12, 1992. For example, the city council in Cleveland, Ohio, changed the name of Columbus Day to Indigenous People's Day. In crafting this lecture, I also selected supporting documents and texts as handouts. For example, I gave students longer sections from Washington Irving's *The Life and Voyages of Christopher Columbus*[25] or Kirkpatrick Sales' critical *Conquest of Paradise*[26] as examples of the different perspectives historians took in the nineteenth and twentieth centuries.

We treated the lecture as a secondary source, as a historical account constructed by the history teacher that other historians—i.e., history students—could use to investigate a historical problem. Consequently, at key points during the lecture, we stopped to employ our tools for thinking about historical accounts, asking, for example, "What are you hearing that supports, contests, or expands your thinking abut this issue?" The lecture did not answer exhaustively the larger questions concerning why certain accounts came into and out of fashion or why historians "changed their minds." But going well beyond the standard view of the lecture as a way to transmit information, this lecture provided needed intellectual support at a critical juncture to help students extend their historical understanding.

CONCLUSION

When my high school students began to study history, they tended to view the subject as a fixed entity, a body of facts that historians retrieved and placed in textbooks (or in the minds of history teachers) for students to memorize. The purpose of history, if it had one, was to somehow inoculate students from repeating past errors. The process of learning history was straightforward and, while not always exciting, relatively simple. Ironically, when I first entered a school to become a history teacher over 30 years ago, I held a similar view, often supported by my education and history courses—that teaching history was relatively straightforward and, while not always exciting, relatively simple. I no longer hold such innocent and naive views of learning or teaching history, and I try to disabuse my students of these views as well. Indeed, our experiences in my history classrooms have taught us that, to paraphrase Yogi Berra, it's not what we don't know that's the issue, it's what we know for sure that just isn't so. As this chapter has shown, learning and teaching history demands complex thinking by both teachers and students. It centers around interesting, generative, and organizing problems; critical weighing of evidence and accounts; suspension of our views to understand those of others; use of facts, concepts, and interpretations to make judgments; development of warrants for those judgments; and later, if the evidence persuades, changes in our views and judgments.

Helping students develop such historical literacy requires that history teachers expand their understanding of history learning, a task supported by the ideas found in *How People Learn* and the emerging scholarship on historical thinking. Such research paints a complex picture of learning that helps teachers rethink the connections among students' preinstructional ideas, curricular content, historical expertise, and pedagogy. This view of learning avoids the false dichotomies that have defined and hindered so many past attempts to improve history instruction. It helps teachers go beyond facile either–or choices to show that traditional methods, such as lectures, can be vital and engaging ways of helping students use historical facts and ideas and that, despite the enthusiasm hands-on activities generate, they do not automatically foster historical thinking. More important, this scholarship suggests ways teachers may transform both traditional and newer pedagogical methods to help deepen students' historical understanding. To borrow language from my case study, *How People Learn* expands and challenges our thinking about learning history, and thus assists teachers in marshaling the effort and understanding needed to enact a more sophisticated and effective historical pedagogy.

We should harbor no illusions about the challenges awaiting teachers and students engaged in such history instruction. Teaching the stories of the past while also teaching students how to read, criticize, and evaluate these stories is a complex task. It is difficult to help students recognize that all historical accounts, including those we hold, have a history. While encouraging students to recognize that all history involves interpretation, teachers must simultaneously challenge the easy conclusion that all interpretations are therefore equally compelling. Rather, historical literacy demands that students learn to evaluate arguments and decide which positions, given the evidence, are more or less plausible, better or worse. Historical study asks students to consider what they know, how they know it, and how confidently or tentatively they are "entitled" to hold their views.

It is equally important to remember the pleasures that such historical study can provide both teachers and students. Through history, teachers can fill the class with enduring human dramas and dilemmas, fascinating mysteries, and an amazing cast of historical characters involved in events that exemplify the best and worst of human experience. In what other field of study can students experience such a range of possibilities and get to know so many people and places? Where else would my students have the chance to encounter fifteenth-century Europeans and Native Americans, people from Christopher Columbus to Montezuma, and life in so many different societies and cultures?

Even this brief description of the difficulties and joys involved in learning history reveals why the study of history is so crucial and, therefore, worth our efforts. "History," historian Peter Stearns has written, "should be studied because it is essential to individuals and to society, and because it harbors beauty".[27] A disciplined study of history promotes exactly the type of reasoned thought our students deserve to have and democratic societies so desperately need.

ACKNOWLEDGMENTS

I want to thank Suzanne Wilson, Sam Wineburg, Jeff Mirel, Suzanne Donovan, John Bransford, and Kieran Egan for their thoughtful reading of this chapter. I benefited greatly from their generous support and valuable comments. Suzanne Wilson, in particular, provided me with timely and important criticism throughout the project. Greg Deegan and Bonnie Morosi also provided important help at an early stage in this work.

NOTES

1. Hall, 1883, p. vii.
2. Ibid, p. viii.
3. Wineburg, 2001.
4. Jonassen, 2000. Jonassen uses the word "mindtools" in relationship to computers and technological learning environments, seeing these as "intellectual partners with the learner in order to engage and facilitate critical thinking and higher learning." The tools I discuss in this chapter, while not electronic, serve as supports to help students engage in historical thinking, and thus fit the spirit of Jonassen's description.
5. Winks, 1969.
6. National Research Council, 1999, pp. 29-30; Levstik and Barton, 1997.
7. Collingwood, 1944.
8. Wineburg, 2001; Davis et al., 2001; Lowenthal, 1985; Shemilt, 1984.
9. McCullough, 2001; Ginzburg et al., 1980.
10. Lowenthal 1996, p. 116.
11. Initially, I gave these accounts to students without references to reinforce the need for attention to the content presented in the source. If no student asked for reference information, I provided it later. However, if a student requested this information, I gave that student the fully referenced handout shown in Box 4-1. When I taught this lesson recently, only 2 of 55 students asked about who had produced the accounts.
12. Bushman, 1992; Crosby, 1987; Russell, 1991; Sales, 1990; Schlereth, 1992.
13. Boorstin, 1990, p. 146.
14. National Research Council, 1999, p. 120.
15. Wineburg, 2001; Lee and Ashby, 2000; Leinhardt, 2000; Levstik, 2000; Barton, 1997; Seixas, 1994.
16. Wineburg, 2001.
17. Bruner, 1977.
18. Tharp and Gallimore, 1998, p. 20.
19. Wineburg, 2001.
20. Palinscar and Brown, 1984.
21. National Research Council, 1999, p. 55; Wineburg, 2001; Bain, 2000.
22. Cole, 1996.
23. Schwartz and Bransford, 1998.
24. Bushman, 1992; Crosby, 1987; Russell, 1991; Schlereth, 1992.
25. Irving, 1830.
26. Sales, 1990.
27. Stearns, 1998.

REFERENCES

Bain, R.B. (2000). Into the breach: Using research and theory to shape history instruction. In P. Seixas, P. Stearns, and S. Wineburg (Eds.), *Knowing, teaching and learning history: National and international perspectives* (pp. 331-353). New York: University Press.

Barton, K. (1997). "I just kinda know": Elementary students' ideas about historical evidence. *Theory and Research in Social Education, 25*(4), 407-430.

Boorstin, D.J. (1990). *The discoverers: A history of man's search to know his world and himself.* Birmingham, AL: Gryphon Editions.

Bruner, J. (1977). *The process of education.* Cambridge, MA: Harvard University Press.

Bushman, C.L. (1992). *America discovers Columbus: How an Italian explorer became an American hero.* Hanover, NH: University Press of New England.

Cole, M. (1996). *Cultural psychology: A once and future discipline.* Cambridge, MA: Belknap Press of Harvard University Press.

Collingwood, R.G. (1944). *An autobiography.* New York: Penguin Books.

Crosby, A.W. (1987). *The Columbian voyages, the Columbian exchange and their historians.* Washington, DC: American Historical Association.

Davis, O.L., Yeager, E.A. and Foster, S.J. (Eds.). (2001). *Historical empathy and perspective: Taking in the social studies.* Lanham, MD: Rowman & Littlefield.

Eggleston, E. (1904). *The new century history of the United States.* New York: American Book.

Ginzburg, C., Tedeschi, J.A., and Tedeschi, A. (1980). *The cheese and the worms: The cosmos of a sixteenth-century miller.* Baltimore: Johns Hopkins University Press.

Gould, S.J. (1995). *Dinosaur in a haystack: Reflections in natural history.* New York: Harmony Books.

Hall, G.S. (1883). Introduction. In G.S. Hall (Ed.), *Methods of teaching history* (pp. v-xii). Boston, MA: D.C. Heath.

Irving, W. (1830). *The life and voyages of Christopher Columbus.* New York: Burt.

Jonassen, D.H. (2000). *Computers as mindtools for schools: Engaging critical thinking,* 2nd ed. Upper Saddle River, NJ: Merrill.

Lee, P.J., and Ashby, R. (2000). Progression in historical understanding among students ages 7-14. In P. Seixas, P. Stearns, and S. Wineburg (Eds.), *Knowing, teaching and learning history: National and international perspectives* (pp. 199-222). New York: University Press.

Leinhardt, G. (2000). Lessons on teaching and learning history from Paul's pen. In P. Seixas, P. Stearns, and S. Wineburg (Eds.), *Knowing, teaching and learning history: National and international perspectives* (pp. 223-245). New York: University Press.

Levstik, L.S. (2000). Articulating the silences: Teachers' and adolescents' conceptions of historical significance. In P. Seixas, P. Stearns, and S. Wineburg (Eds.), *Knowing, teaching and learning history: National and international perspectives.* (pp. 284-305). New York: University Press.

Levstik, L.S., and Barton, K.C. (1997). *Doing history: Investigating with children in elementary and middle schools.* Mahwah, NJ: Lawrence Erlbaum Associates.

Lowenthal, D. (1985). *The past is a foreign country.* Cambridge, England: Cambridge University Press.

Lowenthal, D. (1996). *Possessed by the past: The heritage crusade and the spoils of history.* New York: Free Press.

McCullough, D.G. (2001). *John Adams.* New York: Simon and Schuster.

National Center for History in the Schools. (1996). *National standards for history.* C.A. Crabtree and G.B. Nash (Eds.). Los Angeles, CA: Author, University of California.

National Research Council. (1999). *How people learn: Brain, mind, experience, and school.* Committee on Developments in the Science of Learning. J.D. Bransford, A.L. Brown, and R.R. Cocking (Eds.). Commission on Behavioral and Social Sciences and Education. Washington, DC: National Academy Press.

Palinscar, A.S., and Brown, A.L. (1984). Reciprocal teaching of comprehension monitoring activities. *Cognition and Instruction, 1,* 117-175.

Patton, J.H., and Lord, J. (1903). The history and government of the United States. New York: The University Society.

Russell, J.B. (1997). *Inventing the flat earth: Columbus and modern historians.* New York: Praeger. (Original work in J. Johonnot [1887]. *Ten great events in history* [pp. 123-130]. New York: Appleton.)

Sagan, C. (1985). *Cosmos.* New York: Ballantine Books.

Sales, K. (1990). *The conquest of paradise: Christopher Columbus and the Columbian legacy.* New York: Knopf.

Schlereth, T.J. (1992). Columbia, Columbus, and Columbianism. *Journal of American History, 79*(3), 937-968.

Schwartz, D.L., and Bransford, J.D. (1998). A time for telling. *Cognition and Instruction, 16*(4), 475-522.

Seixas, P. (1994). Students' understanding of historical significance. *Theory and Research in Social Education, 22,* 281-304.

Shemilt, D. (1984). Beauty and the philosopher: Empathy in history and classroom. In A.K. Dickinson, P.J. Lee, and P.J. Rogers (Eds.), *Learning history* (pp. 39-84). London, England: Heinemann.

Stearns, P.N. (1998). *Why study history?* Available: http://www.theaha.org/pubs/stearns.htm [Accessed February 3, 2003].

Stearns, P.N., Seixas, P., and Wineburg, S. (Eds.). (2000). *Knowing, teaching and learning history: National and international perspectives.* New York: University Press.

Tharp, R.G., and Gallimore, R. (1998). *Rousing minds to life: Teaching, learning, and schooling in social context.* Cambridge, England: Cambridge University Press.

White, A.D. (1896). *A history of the warfare of science with theology in Christendom.* New York: Appleton.

Wineburg, S.S. (2001). *Historical thinking and other unnatural acts: Charting the future of teaching the past.* Philadelphia: Temple University Press.

Winks, R.W. (1969). *The historian as detective: Essays on evidence.* New York: Harper & Row.

Part II

MATHEMATICS

5

Mathematical Understanding: An Introduction

Karen C. Fuson, Mindy Kalchman, and John D. Bransford

For many people, free association with the word "mathematics" would produce strong, negative images. Gary Larson published a cartoon entitled "Hell's Library" that consisted of nothing but book after book of math word problems. Many students—and teachers—resonate strongly with this cartoon's message. It is not just funny to them; it is true.

Why are associations with mathematics so negative for so many people? If we look through the lens of *How People Learn,* we see a subject that is rarely taught in a way that makes use of the three principles that are the focus of this volume. Instead of connecting with, building on, and refining the mathematical understandings, intuitions, and resourcefulness that students bring to the classroom (Principle 1), mathematics instruction often overrides students' reasoning processes, replacing them with a set of rules and procedures that disconnects problem solving from meaning making. Instead of organizing the skills and competences required to do mathematics fluently around a set of core mathematical concepts (Principle 2), those skills and competencies are often themselves the center, and sometimes the whole, of instruction. And precisely because the acquisition of procedural knowledge is often divorced from meaning making, students do not use metacognitive strategies (Principle 3) when they engage in solving mathematics problems. Box 5-1 provides a vignette involving a student who gives an answer to a problem that is quite obviously impossible. When quizzed, he can see that his answer does not make sense, but he does not consider it wrong because he believes he followed the rule. Not only did he neglect to use metacognitive strategies to monitor whether his answer made sense, but he believes that sense making is irrelevant.

BOX 5-1 Computation Without Comprehension: An Observation by John Holt

One boy, quite a good student, was working on the problem, "If you have 6 jugs, and you want to put 2/3 of a pint of lemonade into each jug, how much lemonade will you need?" His answer was 18 pints. I said, "How much in each jug?" "Two-thirds of a pint." I said, "Is that more or less that a pint?" "Less." I said, "How many jugs are there?" "Six." I said, "But that [the answer of 18 pints] doesn't make any sense." He shrugged his shoulders and said, "Well, that's the way the system worked out." Holt argues: "He has long since quit expecting school to make sense. They tell you these facts and rules, and your job is to put them down on paper the way they tell you. Never mind whether they mean anything or not."[1]

A recent report of the National Research Council,[2] *Adding It Up,* reviews a broad research base on the teaching and learning of elementary school mathematics. The report argues for an instructional goal of "mathematical proficiency," a much broader outcome than mastery of procedures. The report argues that five intertwining strands constitute mathematical proficiency:

1. *Conceptual understanding*—comprehension of mathematical concepts, operations, and relations

2. *Procedural fluency*—skill in carrying out procedures flexibly, accurately, efficiently, and appropriately

3. *Strategic competence*—ability to formulate, represent, and solve mathematical problems

4. *Adaptive reasoning*—capacity for logical thought, reflection, explanation, and justification

5. *Productive disposition*—habitual inclination to see mathematics as sensible, useful, and worthwhile, coupled with a belief in diligence and one's own efficacy

These strands map directly to the principles of *How People Learn.* Principle 2 argues for a foundation of factual knowledge (procedural fluency), tied to a conceptual framework (conceptual understanding), and organized in a way to facilitate retrieval and problem solving (strategic competence). Metacognition and adaptive reasoning both describe the phenomenon of ongoing sense making, reflection, and explanation to oneself and others. And, as we argue below, the preconceptions students bring to the study of mathematics affect more than their understanding and problem solving; those preconceptions also play a major role in whether students have a productive disposition toward mathematics, as do, of course, their experiences in learning mathematics.

The chapters that follow on whole number, rational number, and functions look at the principles of *How People Learn* as they apply to those specific domains. In this introduction, we explore how those principles apply to the subject of mathematics more generally. We draw on examples from the Children's Math World project, a decade-long research project in urban and suburban English-speaking and Spanish-speaking classrooms.[3]

PRINCIPLE #1: TEACHERS MUST ENGAGE STUDENTS' PRECONCEPTIONS

At a very early age, children begin to demonstrate an awareness of number.[4] As with language, that awareness appears to be universal in normally developing children, though the rate of development varies at least in part because of environmental influences.[5]

But it is not only the awareness of quantity that develops without formal training. Both children and adults engage in mathematical problem solving, developing untrained strategies to do so successfully when formal experiences are not provided. For example, it was found that Brazilian street children could perform mathematics when making sales in the street, but were unable to answer similar problems presented in a school context.[6] Likewise, a study of housewives in California uncovered an ability to solve mathematical problems when comparison shopping, even though the women could not solve problems presented abstractly in a classroom that required the same mathematics.[7] A similar result was found in a study of a group of Weight Watchers, who used strategies for solving mathematical measurement problems related to dieting that they could not solve when the problems were presented more abstractly.[8] And men who successfully handicapped horse races could not apply the same skill to securities in the stock market.[9]

These examples suggest that people possess resources in the form of informal strategy development and mathematical reasoning that can serve as a foundation for learning more abstract mathematics. But they also suggest that the link is not automatic. If there is no bridge between informal and formal mathematics, the two often remain disconnected.

The first principle of *How People Learn* emphasizes both the need to build on existing knowledge and the need to engage students' preconceptions—particularly when they interfere with learning. In mathematics, certain preconceptions that are often fostered early on in school settings are in fact counterproductive. Students who believe them can easily conclude that the study of mathematics is "not for them" and should be avoided if at all possible. We discuss these preconceptions below.

Some Common Preconceptions About Mathematics

Preconception #1: Mathematics is about learning to compute.

Many of us who attended school in the United States had mathematics instruction that focused primarily on computation, with little attention to learning with understanding. To illustrate, try to answer the following question:

What, approximately, is the sum of 8/9 plus 12/13?

Many people immediately try to find the lowest common denominator for the two sets of fractions and then add them because that is the procedure they learned in school. Finding the lowest common denominator is not easy in this instance, and the problem seems difficult. A few people take a conceptual rather than a procedural (computational) approach and realize that 8/9 is almost 1, and so is 12/13, so the approximate answer is a little less than 2.

The point of this example is not that computation should not be taught or is unimportant; indeed, it is very often critical to efficient problem solving. But if one believes that mathematics is about problem solving and that computation is a tool for use to that end when it is helpful, then the above problem is viewed not as a "request for a computation," but as a problem to be solved that may or may not require computation—and in this case, it does not.

If one needs to find the exact answer to the above problem, computation is the way to go. But even in this case, conceptual understanding of the nature of the problem remains central, providing a way to estimate the correctness of a computation. If an answer is computed that is more than 2 or less than 1, it is obvious that some aspect of problem solving has gone awry. If one believes that mathematics is about computation, however, then sense making may never take place.

Preconception #2: Mathematics is about "following rules" to guarantee correct answers.

Related to the conception of mathematics as computation is that of mathematics as a cut-and-dried discipline that specifies rules for finding the right answers. Rule following is more general than performing specific computations. When students learn procedures for keeping track of and canceling units, for example, or learn algebraic procedures for solving equations, many view use of these procedures only as following the rules. But the "rules" should not be confused with the game itself.

The authors of the chapters in this part of the book provide important suggestions about the much broader nature of mathematical proficiency and about ways to make the involving nature of mathematical inquiry visible to students. Groups such as the National Council of Teachers of Mathematics[10] and the National Research Council[11] have provided important guidelines for the kinds of mathematics instruction that accord with what is currently known about the principles of *How People Learn*. The authors of the following chapters have paid careful attention to this work and illustrate some of its important aspects.

In reality, mathematics is a constantly evolving field that is far from cut and dried. It involves systematic pattern finding and continuing invention. As a simple example, consider the selection of units that are relevant to quantify an idea such as the fuel efficiency of a vehicle. If we choose miles per gallon, a two-seater sports car will be more efficient than a large bus. If we choose passenger miles per gallon, the bus will be more fuel efficient (assuming it carries large numbers of passengers). Many disciplines make progress by inventing new units and metrics that provide insights into previously invisible relationships.

Attention to the history of mathematics illustrates that what is taught at one point in time as a set of procedures really was a set of clever inventions designed to solve pervasive problems of everyday life. In Europe in the Middle Ages, for example, people used calculating cloths marked with vertical columns and carried out procedures with counters to perform calculations. Other cultures fastened their counters on a rod to make an abacus. Both of these physical means were at least partially replaced by written methods of calculating with numerals and more recently by methods that involve pushing buttons on a calculator. If mathematics procedures are understood as inventions designed to make common problems more easily solvable, and to facilitate communications involving quantity, those procedures take on a new meaning. Different procedures can be compared for their advantages and disadvantages. Such discussions in the classroom can deepen students' understanding and skill.

Preconception #3: Some people have the ability to "do math" and some don't.

This is a serious preconception that is widespread in the United States, but not necessarily in other countries. It can easily become a self-fulfilling prophesy. In many countries, the ability to "do math" is assumed to be attributable to the amount of effort people put into learning it.[12] Of course, some people in these countries do progress further than others, and some appear to have an easier time learning mathematics than others. But effort is still considered to be the key variable in success. In contrast, in the United States we are more likely to assume that ability is much more important than effort, and it is socially acceptable, and often even desirable, not to put forth effort in learning mathematics. This difference is also related to cultural differences in the value attributed to struggle. Teachers in some countries believe it is desirable for students to struggle for a while with problems, whereas teachers in the United States simplify things so that students need not struggle at all.[13]

This preconception likely shares a common root with the others. If mathematics learning is not grounded in an understanding of the nature of the problem to be solved and does not build on a student's own reasoning and strategy development, then solving problems successfully will depend on the ability to recall memorized rules. If a student has not reviewed those rules recently (as is the case when a summer has passed), they can easily be forgotten. Without a conceptual understanding of the nature of problems and strategies for solving them, failure to retrieve learned procedures can leave a student completely at a loss.

Yet students can feel lost not only when they have forgotten, but also when they fail to "get it" from the start. Many of the conventions of mathematics have been adopted for the convenience of communicating efficiently in a shared language. If students learn to memorize procedures but do not understand that the procedures are full of such conventions adopted for efficiency, they can be baffled by things that are left unexplained. If students never understand that x and y have no intrinsic meaning, but are conventional notations for labeling unknowns, they will be baffled when a z appears. When an m precedes an x in the equation of a line, students may wonder, Why m? Why not s for slope? If there is no m, then is there no slope? To someone with a secure mathematics understanding, the missing m is simply an unstated m = 1. But to a student who does not understand that the point is to write the equation efficiently, the missing m can be baffling. Unlike language learning, in which new expressions can often be figured out because they are couched in meaningful contexts, there are few clues to help a student who is lost in mathematics. Providing a secure conceptual understanding of the mathematics enterprise that is linked to students' sense-making capacities is critical so that students can puzzle productively over new material, identify the source of their confusion, and ask questions when they do not understand.

Engaging Students' Preconceptions and Building on Existing Knowledge

Engaging and building on student preconceptions, then, poses two instructional challenges. First, how can we teach mathematics so students come to appreciate that it is not about computation and following rules, but about solving important and relevant quantitative problems? This perspective includes an understanding that the rules for computation and solution are a set of clever human inventions that in many cases allow us to solve complex problems more easily, and to communicate about those problems with each other effectively and efficiently. Second, how can we link formal mathematics training with students' informal knowledge and problem-solving capacities?

Many recent research and curriculum development efforts, including those of the authors of the chapters that follow, have addressed these questions. While there is surely no single best instructional approach, it is possible to identify certain features of instruction that support the above goals:

- Allowing students to use their own informal problem-solving strategies, at least initially, and then guiding their mathematical thinking toward more effective strategies and advanced understandings.

- Encouraging math talk so that students can clarify their strategies to themselves and others, and compare the benefits and limitations of alternate approaches.

- Designing instructional activities that can effectively bridge commonly held conceptions and targeted mathematical understandings.

Allowing Multiple Strategies

To illustrate how instruction can be connected to students' existing knowledge, consider three subtraction methods encountered frequently in urban second-grade classrooms involved in the Children's Math Worlds Project (see Box 5-2). Maria, Peter, and Manuel's teacher has invited them to share their methods for solving a problem, and each of them has displayed a different method. Two of the methods are correct, and one is mostly correct but has one error. What the teacher does depends on her conception of what mathematics is.

One approach is to show the students the "right" way to subtract and have them and everyone else practice that procedure. A very different approach is to help students explore their methods and see what is easy and difficult about each. If students are taught that for each kind of math situation or problem, there is one correct method that needs to be taught and learned, the seeds of the disconnection between their reasoning and strategy development and "doing math" are sown. An answer is either wrong or

BOX 5-2 **Three Subtraction Methods**

Maria's add-equal-quantities method	Peter's ungrouping method	Manuel's mixed method

$$
\begin{array}{r}
1\,2\,{}^{1}4 \\
-\,{}^{1}5\ 6 \\
\hline
6\ 8
\end{array}
$$

$$
\begin{array}{r}
+\ {}^{11}2\ {}^{14}4 \\
-\ 5\ 6 \\
\hline
6\ 8
\end{array}
$$

$$
\begin{array}{r}
+\ {}^{11}2\ {}^{14}4 \\
-\,{}^{1}5\ 6 \\
\hline
5\quad 8
\end{array}
$$

right, and one does not need to look at wrong answers more deeply—one needs to look at how to get the right answer. The problem is not that students will fail to solve the problem accurately with this instructional approach; indeed, they may solve it more accurately. But when the nature of the problem changes slightly, or students have not used the taught approach for a while, they may feel completely lost when confronting a novel problem because the approach of developing strategies to grapple with a problem situation has been short-circuited.

If, on the other hand, students believe that for each kind of math situation or problem there can be several correct methods, their engagement in strategy development is kept alive. This does not mean that all strategies are equally good. But students can learn to evaluate different strategies for their advantages and disadvantages. What is more, a wrong answer is usually partially correct and reflects some understanding; finding the part that is wrong and understanding why it is wrong can be a powerful aid to understanding and promotes metacognitive competencies. A vignette of students engaged in the kind of mathematical reasoning that supports active strategy development and evaluation appears in Box 5-3.

It can be initially unsettling for a teacher to open up the classroom to calculation methods that are new to the teacher. But a teacher does not have to understand a new method immediately or alone, as indicated in the description in the vignette of how the class together figured out over time how Maria's method worked (this method is commonly taught in Latin America and Europe). Understanding a new method can be a worthwhile mathematical project for the class, and others can be involved in trying to figure out why a method works. This illustrates one way in which a classroom community can function. If one relates a calculation method to the quantities involved, one can usually puzzle out what the method is and why it works. This also demonstrates that not all mathematical issues are solved or understood immediately; sometimes sustained work is necessary.

BOX 5-3 Engaging Students' Problem-Solving Strategies

The following example of a classroom discussion shows how second-grade students can explain their methods rather than simply performing steps in a memorized procedure. It also shows how to make student thinking visible. After several months of teaching and learning, the students reached the point illustrated below. The students' methods are shown in Box 5-2.

Teacher	Maria, can you please explain to your friends in the class how you solved the problem?
Maria	Six is bigger than 4, so I can't subtract here [pointing] in the ones.
	So I have to get more ones. But I have to be fair when I get more ones, so I add ten to both my numbers. I add a ten here in the top of the ones place [pointing] to change the 4 to a 14, and I add a ten here in the bottom in the tens place, so I write another ten by my 5.
	So now I count up from 6 to 14, and I get 8 ones [demonstrating by counting "6, 7, 8, 9, 10, 11, 12, 13, 14" while raising a finger for each word from 7 to 14]. And I know my doubles, so 6 plus 6 is 12, so I have 6 tens left. [She thought, "1 + 5 = 6 tens and 6 + ? = 12 tens. Oh, I know 6 + 6 = 12, so my answer is 6 tens."]
Jorge	I don't see the other 6 in your tens. I only see one 6 in your answer.
Maria	The other 6 is from adding my 1 ten to the 5 tens to get 6 tens. I didn't write it down.
Andy	But you're changing the problem. How do you get the right answer?
Maria	If I make both numbers bigger by the same amount, the difference will stay the same. Remember we looked at that on drawings last week and on the meter stick.
Michelle	Why did you count up?
Maria	Counting down is too hard, and my mother taught me to count up to subtract in first grade.

BOX 5-3 Continued

Teacher	How many of you remember how confused we were when we first saw Maria's method last week? Some of us could not figure out what she was doing even though Elena and Juan and Elba did it the same way. What did we do?
Rafael	We made drawings with our ten-sticks and dots to see what those numbers meant. And we figured out they were both tens. Even though the 5 looked like a 15, it was really just 6. And we went home to see if any of our parents could explain it to us, but we had to figure it out ourselves and it took us 2 days.
Teacher	Yes, I was asking other teachers, too. We worked on other methods too, but we kept trying to understand what this method was and why it worked. And Elena and Juan decided it was clearer if they crossed out the 5 and wrote a 6, but Elba and Maria liked to do it the way they learned at home. Any other questions or comments for Maria? No? Ok, Peter, can you explain your method?
Peter	Yes, I like to ungroup my top number when I don't have enough to subtract everywhere. So here I ungrouped 1 ten and gave it to the 4 ones to make 14 ones, so I had 1 ten left here. So 6 up to 10 is 4 and 4 more up to 14 is 8, so 14 minus 6 is 8 ones. And 5 tens up to 11 tens is 6 tens. So my answer is 68.
Carmen	How did you know it was 11 tens?
Peter	Because it is 1 hundred and 1 ten and that is 11 tens.
Carmen	I don't get it.
Peter	Because 1 hundred is 10 tens.
Carmen	Oh, so why didn't you cross out the 1 hundred and put it with the tens to make 11 tens like Manuel?
Peter	I don't need to. I just know it is 11 tens by looking at it.
Teacher	Manuel, don't erase your problem. I know you think it is probably wrong because you got a different answer, but remember how making a mistake helps everyone learn—because other

	students make that same mistake and you helped us talk about it. Do you want to draw a picture and think about your method while we do the next problem, or do you want someone to help you?
Manuel	Can Rafael help me?
Teacher	Yes, but what kind of helping should Rafael do?
Manuel	He should just help me with what I need help on and not do it for me.
Teacher	Ok, Rafael, go up and help Manuel that way while we go on to the next problem. I think it would help you to draw quick-tens and ones to see what your numbers mean. [These drawings are explained later.] But leave your first solution so we can all see where the problem is. That helps us all get good at debugging— finding our mistakes. Do we all make mistakes?
Class	Yes.
Teacher	Can we all get help from each other?
Class	Yes.
Teacher	So mistakes are just a part of learning. We learn from our mistakes. Manuel is going to be brave and share his mistake with us so we can all learn from it.

Manuel's method combined Maria's add-equal-quantities method, which he had learned at home, and Peter's ungrouping method, which he had learned at school. It increases the ones once and decreases the tens twice by subtracting a ten from the top number and adding a ten to the bottom subtracted number. In the Children's Math Worlds Project, we rarely found children forming such a meaningless combination of methods if they understood tens and ones and had a method of drawing them so they could think about the quantities in a problem (a point discussed more later). Students who transferred into our classes did sometimes initially use Manuel's mixed approach. But students were eventually helped to understand both the strengths and weaknesses of their existing methods and to find ways of improving their approaches.

SOURCE: Karen Fuson, Children's Math Worlds Project.

Encouraging Math Talk

One important way to make students' thinking visible is through math talk—talking about mathematical thinking. This technique may appear obvious, but it is quite different from simply giving lectures or assigning textbook readings and then having students work in isolation on problem sets or homework problems. Instead, students and teachers actively discuss how they approached various problems and why. Such communication about mathematical thinking can help everyone in the classroom understand a given concept or method because it elucidates contrasting approaches, some of which are wrong—but often for interesting reasons. Furthermore, communicating about one's thinking is an important goal in itself that also facilitates other sorts of learning. In the lower grades, for example, such math talk can provide initial experiences with mathematical justification that culminate in later grades with more formal kinds of mathematical proof.

An emphasis on math talk is also important for helping teachers become more learner focused and make stronger connections with each of their students. When teachers adopt the role of learners who try to understand their students' methods (rather than just marking the students' procedures and answers as correct or incorrect), they frequently discover thinking that can provide a springboard for further instruction, enabling them to extend thinking more deeply or understand and correct errors. Note that, when beginning to make student thinking visible, teachers must focus on the community-centered aspects of their instruction. Students need to feel comfortable expressing their ideas and revising their thinking when feedback suggests the need to do so.

Math talk allows teachers to draw out and work with the preconceptions students bring with them to the classroom and then helps students learn how to do this sort of work for themselves and for others. We have found that it is also helpful for students to make math drawings of their thinking to help themselves in problem solving and to make their thinking more visible (see Figure 5-1). Such drawings also support the classroom math talk because they are a common visual referent for all participants. Students need an effective bridge between their developing understandings and formal mathematics. Teachers need to use carefully designed visual, linguistic, and situational conceptual supports to help students connect their experiences to formal mathematical words, notations, and methods.

The idea of conceptual support for math talk can be further clarified by considering the language students used in the vignette in Box 5-3 when they explained their different multidigit methods. For these explanations to become meaningful in the classroom, it was crucially important that the students explain their multidigit adding or subtracting methods using the meaningful words in the middle pedagogical triangle of Figure 5-2 (e.g., "three

Drawings for Jackie's and
Juan's Addition Methods

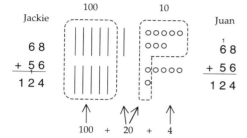

Drawing for "Show All Totals" Method

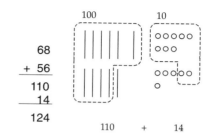

Peter's Ungrouping Method

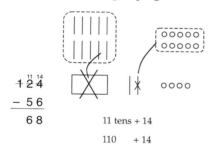

Maria's Add-Equal-Quantities Method

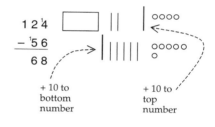

FIGURE 5-1

tens six ones"), as well as the usual math words (e.g., "thirty-six"). It is through such extended connected explanations and use of the quantity words "tens" and "ones" that the students in the Children's Math Worlds Project came to explain their methods. Their explanations did not begin that way, and the students did not spontaneously use the meaningful language when describing their methods. The teacher needed to model the language and help students use it in their descriptions. More-advanced students also helped less-advanced students learn by modeling, asking questions, and helping others form more complete descriptions.

Initially in the Children's Math Worlds Project, all students made conceptual support drawings such as those in Figure 5-1. They explicitly linked these drawings to their written methods during explanations. Such drawings linked to the numerical methods facilitated understanding, accuracy, communication, and helping. Students stopped making drawings when they were no longer needed (this varied across students by months). Eventually, most students applied numerical methods without drawings, but these numerical

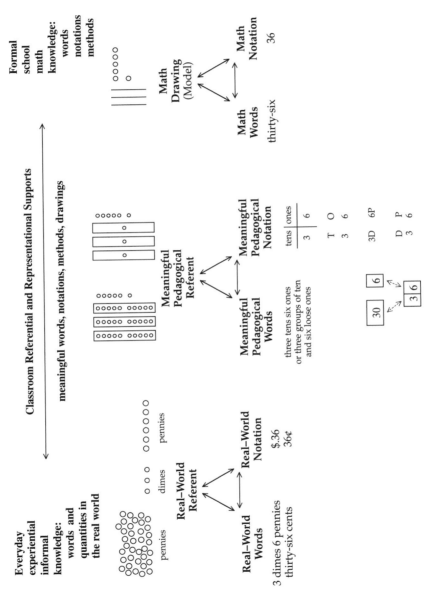

FIGURE 5-2

methods then carried for the members of the classroom the meanings from the conceptual support drawings. If errors crept in, students were asked to think about (or make) a drawing and most errors were then self-corrected.

Designing Bridging Instructional Activities

The first two features of instruction discussed above provide opportunities for students to use their own strategies and to make their thinking visible so it can be built on, revised, and made more formal. This third strategy is more proactive. Research has uncovered common student preconceptions and points of difficulty with learning new mathematical concepts that can be addressed preemptively with carefully designed instructional activities.

This kind of bridging activity is used in the Children's Math Worlds curriculum to help students relate their everyday, experiential, informal understanding of money to the formal school concepts of multidigit numbers. Real-world money is confusing for many students (e.g., dimes are smaller than pennies but are worth 10 times as much). Also, the formal school math number words and notations are abstract and potentially misleading (e.g., 36 looks like a 3 and a 6, not like 30 and 6) and need to be linked to visual quantities of tens and ones to become meaningful. Fuson designed conceptual "supports" into the curriculum to bridge the two. The middle portion of Figure 5-2 shows an example of the supports that were used to help students build meaning. A teacher or curriculum designer can make a framework like that of Figure 5-2 for any math domain by selecting those conceptual supports that will help students make links among the math words, written notations, and quantities in that domain.

Identifying real-world contexts whose features help direct students' attention and thinking in mathematically productive ways is particularly helpful in building conceptual bridges between students' informal experiences and the new formal mathematics they are learning. Examples of such bridging contexts are a key feature of each of the three chapters that follow.

PRINCIPLE #2: UNDERSTANDING REQUIRES FACTUAL KNOWLEDGE AND CONCEPTUAL FRAMEWORKS

The second principle of *How People Learn* suggests the importance of both conceptual understanding and procedural fluency, as well as an effective organization of knowledge—in this case one that facilitates strategy development and adaptive reasoning. It would be difficult to name a discipline in which the approach to achieving this goal is more hotly debated than mathematics. Recognition of the weakness in the conceptual understanding of students in the United States has resulted in increasing attention to the problems involved in teaching mathematics as a set of procedural competences.[14] At the same time, students with too little knowledge of procedures do not become competent and efficient problem solvers. When instruction places too little emphasis on factual and procedural knowledge, the problem is not solved; it is only changed. Both are clearly critical.

Equally important, procedural knowledge and conceptual understandings must be closely linked. As the mathematics confronted by students becomes more complex through the school years, new knowledge and competencies require that those already mastered be brought to bear. Box 1-6 in Chapter 1, for example, describes a set of links in procedural and conceptual knowledge required to support the ability to do multidigit subtraction with regrouping—a topic encountered relatively early in elementary school. By the time a student begins algebra years later, the network of knowledge must include many new concepts and procedures (including those for rational number) that must be effectively linked and available to support new algebraic understandings. The teacher's challenge, then, is to help students build and consolidate prerequisite competencies, understand new concepts in depth, and organize both concepts and competencies in a network of knowledge. Furthermore, teachers must provide sustained and then increasingly spaced opportunities to consolidate new understandings and procedures.

In mathematics, such networks of knowledge often are organized as learning paths from informal concrete methods to abbreviated, more general, and more abstract methods. Discussing multiple methods in the classroom—drawing attention to why different methods work and to the relative efficiency and reliability of each—can help provide a conceptual ladder that helps students move in a connected way from where they are to a more efficient and abstract approach. Students also can adopt or adapt an intermediate method with which they might feel more comfortable. Teachers can help students move at least to intermediate "good-enough" methods that can be understood and explained. Box 5-4 describes such a learning path for single-digit addition and subtraction that is seen worldwide. Teachers in some countries support students in moving through this learning path.

Developing Mathematical Proficiency

Developing mathematical proficiency requires that students master both the concepts and procedural skills needed to reason and solve problems effectively in a particular domain. Deciding which advanced methods all students should learn to attain proficiency is a policy matter involving judgments about how to use scarce instructional time. For example, the level 2 counting-on methods in Box 5-4 may be considered "good-enough" methods; they are general, rapid, and sufficiently accurate that valuable school time might better be spent on topics other than mastery of the whole network of knowledge required for carrying out the level 3 methods. Decisions about which methods to teach must also take into account that some methods are clearer conceptually and procedurally than the multidigit methods usually taught in the United States (see Box 5-5). The National Research Council's *Adding It Up* reviews these and other accessible algorithms in other domains.

This view of mathematics as involving different methods does not imply that a teacher or curriculum must teach multiple methods for every domain. However, alternative methods will frequently arise in a classroom, either because students bring them from home (e.g., Maria's add-equal-quantities subtraction method, widely taught in other countries) or because students think differently about many mathematical problems. Frequently there are viable alternative methods for solving a problem, and discussing the advantages and disadvantages of each can facilitate flexibility and deep understanding of the mathematics involved. In some countries, teachers emphasize multiple solution methods and purposely give students problems that are conducive to such solutions, and students solve a problem in more than one way.

However, the less-advanced students in a classroom also need to be considered. It can be helpful for either a curriculum or teacher or such less-advanced students to select an accessible method that can be understood and is efficient enough for the future, and for these students to concentrate on learning that method and being able to explain it. Teachers in some countries do this while also facilitating problem solving with alternative methods.

Overall, knowing about student learning paths and knowledge networks helps teachers direct math talk along productive lines toward valued knowledge networks. Research in mathematics learning has uncovered important information on a number of typical learning paths and knowledge networks involved in acquiring knowledge about a variety of concepts in mathematics (see the next three chapters for examples).

Instruction to Support Mathematical Proficiency

To teach in a way that supports both conceptual understanding and procedural fluency requires that the primary concepts underlying an area of mathematics be clear to the teacher or become clear during the process of teaching for mathematical proficiency. Because mathematics has traditionally been taught with an emphasis on procedure, adults who were taught this way may initially have difficulty identifying or using the core conceptual understandings in a mathematics domain.

BOX 5-4 A Learning Path from Children's Math Worlds for Single-Digit Addition and Subtraction

Children around the world pass through three levels of increasing sophistication in methods of single-digit addition and subtraction. The first level is direct modeling by counting all of the objects at each step (counting all or taking away). Students can be helped to move rapidly from this first level to counting on, in which counting begins with one addend. For example, 8 + 6 is not solved by counting from 1 to 14 (counting all), but by counting on 6 from 8: counting 8, 9, 10, 11, 12, 13, 14 while keeping track of the 6 counted on.

For subtraction, Children's Math Worlds does what is common in many countries: it helps students see subtraction as involving a mystery addend. Students then solve a subtraction problem by counting on from the known addend to the known total. Earlier we saw how Maria solved 14 - 6 by counting up from 6 to 14, raising 8 fingers while doing so to find that 6 plus 8 more is 14. Many students in the United States instead follow a learning path that moves from drawing little sticks or circles for all of the objects and crossing some out (e.g., drawing 14 sticks, crossing out 6, and counting the rest) to counting down (14, 13, 12, 11, 10, 9, 8, 7, 6). But counting down is difficult and error prone. When first or second graders are helped to move to a different learning path that solves subtraction problems by forward methods, such as counting on or adding on over 10 (see below), subtraction becomes as easy as addition. For many students, this is very empowering.

The third level of single-digit addition and subtraction is exemplified by Peter in the vignette in Box 5-2. At this level, students can chunk

---

The approaches in the three chapters that follow identify the central conceptual structures in several areas of mathematics. The areas of focus—whole number, rational number, and functions—were identified by Case and his colleagues as requiring major conceptual shifts. In the first, students are required to master the concept of *quantity*; in the second, the concept of *proportion* and relative number; and in the third, the concept of *dependence* in quantitative relationships. Each of these understandings requires that a supporting set of concepts and procedural abilities be put in place. The extensive research done by Griffin and Case on whole number, by Case and Moss on rational number, and by Case and Kalchman on functions provides a strong foundation for identifying the major conceptual challenges students

numbers and relate these chunks. The chunking enables them to carry out make-a-ten methods: they give part of one number to the other number to make a ten. These methods are taught in many countries. They are very helpful in multidigit addition and subtraction because a number found in this way is already thought of as 1 ten and some ones. For example, for 8 + 6, 6 gives 2 to 8 to make 10, leaving 4 in the 6, so 10 + 4 = 14. Solving 14 − 8 is done similarly: with 8, how many make 10 (2), plus the 4 in 14, so the answer is 6. These make-a-ten methods demonstrate the learning paths and network of knowledge required for advanced solution methods. Children may also use a "doubles" strategy for some problems— e.g., 7 + 6 = 6 + 6 + 1= 12 + 1 = 13—because the doubles (for example, 6 + 6 or 8 + 8) are easy to learn.

The make-a-ten methods illustrate the importance of a network of knowledge. Students must master three kinds of knowledge to be able to carry out a make-a-ten method fluently: they must (1) for each number below 10, know how much more makes 10; (2) break up any number below 10 into all possible pairs of parts (because 9 + 6 requires knowing 6 = 1 + 5, but 8 + 6 requires knowing 6 = 2 + 4, etc.); and (3) know 10 + 1 = 11, 10 + 2 = 12, 10 + 3 = 13, etc., rapidly without counting.

Note that particular methods may be more or less easy for learners from different backgrounds. For example, the make-a-ten methods are easier for East Asian students, whose language says, "Ten plus one is ten one, ten plus two is ten two," than for English-speaking students, whose language says, "Ten plus one is eleven, ten plus two is twelve, etc."

face in mastering these areas. This research program traced developmental/ experiential changes in children's thinking as they engaged with innovative curriculum. In each area of focus, instructional approaches were developed that enable teachers to help children move through learning paths in productive ways. In doing so, teachers often find that they also build a more extensive knowledge network.

As teachers guide a class through learning paths, a balance must be maintained between learner-centered and knowledge-centered needs. The learning path of the class must also continually relate to individual learner knowledge. Box 5-6 outlines two frameworks that can facilitate such balance.

BOX 5-5 Accessible Algorithms

In over a decade of working with a range of urban and suburban classrooms in the Children's Math Worlds Project, we found that one multidigit addition method and one multidigit subtraction method were accessible to all students. The students easily learned, understood, and remembered these methods and learned to draw quantities for and explain them. Both methods are modifications of the usual U.S. methods. The addition method is the write-new-groups-below method, in which the new 1 ten or 1 hundred, etc., is written below the column on the line rather than above the column (see Jackie's method in Figure 5-1). In the subtraction fix-everything-first method, every column in the top number that needs ungrouping is ungrouped (in any order), and then the subtracting in every column is done (in any order). Because this method can be done from either direction and is only a minor modification of the common U.S. methods, learning-disabled and special-needs students find it especially accessible. Both of these methods stimulate productive discussions in class because they are easily related to the usual U.S. methods that are likely to be brought to class by other students.

PRINCIPLE #3: A METACOGNITIVE APPROACH ENABLES STUDENT SELF-MONITORING

Learning about oneself as a learner, thinker, and problem solver is an important aspect of metacognition (see Chapter 1). In the area of mathematics, as noted earlier, many people who take mathematics courses "learn" that "they are not mathematical." This is an unintended, highly unfortunate, consequence of some approaches to teaching mathematics. It is a consequence that can influence people for a lifetime because they continue to avoid anything mathematical, which in turn ensures that their belief about being "nonmathematical" is true.[15]

An article written in 1940 by Charles Gragg, entitled "Because Wisdom Can't be Told," is relevant to issues of metacognition and mathematics learning. Gragg begins with the following quotation from Balzac:

> So he had grown rich at last, and thought to transmit to his only son all the cut-and-dried experience which he himself had purchased at the price of his lost illusions; a noble last illusion of age.

Except for the part about growing rich, Balzac's ideas fit many peoples' experiences quite well. In our roles as parents, friends, supervisors, and professional educators, we frequently attempt to prepare people for the future by imparting the wisdom gleaned from our own experiences. Some-

BOX 5-6 Supporting Student and Teacher Learning Through a Classroom Discourse Community

Eliciting and then building on and using students' mathematical thinking can be challenging. Yet recent research indicates that teachers can move their students through increasingly productive levels of classroom discourse. Hufferd-Ackles and colleagues[16] describe four levels of a "math-talk learning community," beginning with a traditional, teacher-directed format in which the teacher asks short-answer questions, and student responses are directed to the teacher. At the next level, "getting started," the teacher begins to pursue and assess students' mathematical thinking, focusing less on answers alone. In response, students provide brief descriptions of their thinking. The third level is called "building." At this point the teacher elicits and students respond with fuller descriptions of their thinking, and multiple methods are volunteered. The teacher also facilitates student-to-student talk about mathematics. The final level is "math-talk." Here students share responsibility for discourse with the teacher, justifying their own ideas and asking questions of and helping other students.

Key shifts in teacher practice that support a class moving through these levels include asking questions that focus on mathematical thinking rather than just on answers, probing extensively for student thinking, modeling and expanding on explanations when necessary, fading physically from the center of the classroom discourse (e.g., moving to the back of the classroom), and coaching students in their participatory roles in the discourse ("Everyone have a thinker question ready.").

Related research indicates that when building a successful classroom discourse community, it is important to balance the *process* of discourse, that is, the ways in which student ideas are elicited, with the *content* of discourse, the substance of the ideas that are discussed. In other words, how does a teacher ensure both that class discussions provide sufficient space for students to share their ideas and that discussions are mathematically productive? Sherin[17] describes one model for doing so whereby class discussions begin with a focus on "idea generation," in which many student ideas are solicited. Next, discussion moves into a "comparison and evaluation" phase, in which the class looks more closely at the ideas that have been raised, but no new ideas are raised.

The teacher then "filters" ideas for the class, highlighting a subset of ideas for further pursuit. In this way, student ideas are valued throughout discussion, but the teacher also plays a role in determining the extent to which specific mathematical ideas are considered in detail. A class may proceed through several cycles of these three phases in a single discussion.

times our efforts are rewarded, but we are often less successful than we would like to be, and we need to understand why.

The idea that "wisdom can't be told" helps educators rethink the strategy of simply telling students that some topic (e.g., mathematics) is important, and they can master it if they try. There are important differences between simply being told something and being able to experience it for oneself. Students' experiences have strong effects on their beliefs about themselves, as well as their abilities to remember information and use it spontaneously to solve new problems.[18] If their experiences in mathematics classes involve primarily frustration and failure, simply telling them, "trust me, this will be relevant someday" or "believe me, you have the ability to understand this" is a weak intervention. On the other hand, helping students experience their own abilities to find patterns and problems, invent solutions (even if they are not quite as good as expert solutions), and contribute to and learn from discussions with others provides the kinds of experiences that can help them learn with understanding, as well as change their views about the subject matter and themselves.[19]

However, research on metacognition suggests that an additional instructional step is needed for optimal learning—one that involves helping students reflect on their experiences and begin to see their ideas as instances of larger categories of ideas. For example, students might begin to see their way of showing more ones when subtracting as one of several ways to demonstrate this same important mathematical idea.

One other aspect of metacognition that is nicely illustrated in the context of mathematics involves the claim made in Chapter 1 that metacognition is not simply a knowledge-free ability, but requires relevant knowledge of the topics at hand. At the beginning of this chapter, we noted that many students approach problems such as adding fractions as purely computational (e.g., "What is the approximate sum of 8/9 plus 11/13?"). Ideally, we also want students to monitor the accuracy of their problem solving, just as we want them to monitor their understanding when reading about science, history, or literature.

One way to monitor the accuracy of one's computation is to go back and recheck each of the steps. Another way is to estimate the answer and see whether there is a discrepancy between one's computations and the estimate. However, the ability to estimate requires the kind of knowledge that might be called "number sense." For the above fraction problem, for example, a person with number sense who computes an answer and sees that it is greater than 2 knows that the computation is obviously wrong. But it is "obvious" only if the person has learned ways to think about number that go beyond the ability merely to count and compute.

Instruction That Supports Metacognition

Much of what we have discussed with regard to making student thinking visible can be thought of as ongoing assessment of students. Such assessment can include students so they become involved in thinking about their own mathematical progress and that of their classmates. Such ongoing assessment can then become internalized as metacognitive self-monitoring. Classroom communication about students' mathematical thinking greatly facilitates both teacher and student assessment of learning. Teachers and students can see difficulties particular students are having and can help those students by providing explanations. Teachers can discern primitive solution methods that need to be advanced to more effective methods. They also can see how students are advancing in their helping and explaining abilities and plan how to foster continued learning in those areas.

Students can also learn some general problem-solving strategies, such as "make a drawing of the situation" or "ask yourself questions" that apply to many different kinds of problems. Drawings and questions are a means of self-monitoring. They also can offer teachers windows into students' thinking and thus provide information about how better to help students along a learning path to efficient problem-solving methods.

An Emphasis on Debugging

Metacognitive functioning is also facilitated by shifting from a focus on answers as just right or wrong to a more detailed focus on "debugging" a wrong answer, that is, finding where the error is, why it is an error, and correcting it. Of course, good teachers have always done this, but there are now two special reasons for doing so. One is the usefulness of this approach in complex problem solving, such as debugging computer programs. Technological advances mean that more adults will need to do more complex problem solving and error identification throughout their lives, so debugging—locating the source of an error—is a good general skill that can be learned in the math classroom.

The second reason is based on considerable amount of research in the past 30 years concerning student errors. Figure 5-3 illustrates two such typical kinds of errors in early and late school topics. The partial student knowledge reflected in each error is described in the figure. One can also see how a focus on understanding can help students debug their own errors. For example, asking how much the little "1's" really represent can help students start to see their error in the top example and thus modify the parts of the method that are wrong.

Early Partial Knowledge

```
  268
+ 156
─────
  514
```

This error reflects a wrong generalization from 2-digit problems: where the little 1 is put above the left-most column. Left-most and next-left are confused in this solution. Trying to understand the meanings of the 1s as 1 ten and as 1 hundred can debug this error. The student does know to add ones, to add tens, and to add hundreds and does this correctly.

Later Partial Knowledge

1. What shape would the graph of the function $y = x^2 + 1$ have? Draw it below.

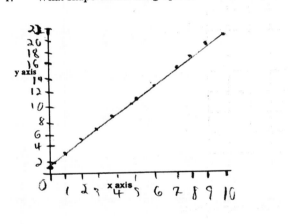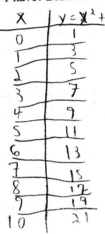

A common error among middle school students is to treat an exponent as a coefficient or multiplier. Here, Graham has generated a table of values for the function $y = 2x + 1$ rather than $y = x^2 + 1$. This type of error has broad implications. For example, it will be difficult for students to develop a good conceptual understanding for functions and the ways in which their representations are interconnected because the graph of $y = 2x + 1$ is a straight line rather than the parabolic curve of $y = x^2 + 1$. He does know, however, how to make a table of values and to graph resulting pairs of values. He also knows how to solve for y in an equation given x.

FIGURE 5-3

Internal and External Dialogue as Support for Metacognition

The research summarized in *How People Learn* and *Adding It Up* and the professional experience summarized in the standards of the National Council of Teachers of Mathematics all emphasize how important it is for students to communicate about mathematics and for teachers to help them learn to do so. Students can learn to reflect on and describe their mathematical thinking. They can learn to compare methods of solving a problem and identify the advantages and disadvantages of each. Peers can learn to ask thoughtful questions about other students' thinking or help edit such statements to clarify them. Students can learn to help each other, sometimes in informal, spontaneous ways and sometimes in more organized, coaching-partner situations. The vignette in Box 5-3 illustrates such communication about mathematical thinking after it has been developed in a classroom. Experience in the Children's Math Worlds Project indicates that students from all backgrounds can learn to think critically and ask thoughtful questions, reflect on and evaluate their own achievement, justify their points of view, and understand the perspectives of others. Even first-grade students can learn to interact in these ways.

Of course, teachers must help students learn to interact fruitfully. To this end, teachers can model clear descriptions and supportive questioning or helping techniques. In a classroom situation, some students may solve problems at the board while others solve them at their seats. Students can make drawings or use notations to indicate how they thought about or solved a problem. Selected students can then describe their solution methods, and peers can ask questions to clarify and to give listeners a role. Sometimes, pairs of students may explain their solutions, with the less-advanced partner explaining first and the other partner then expanding and clarifying. Students usually attend better if only two or three of their fellow students explain their solution method for a given problem. More students can solve at the board, but the teacher can select the methods or the students for the class to hear at that time. It is useful to vary the verbal level of such explainers. Doing so assists all students in becoming better explainers by hearing and helping classmates expand upon a range of explanations. The goal in all of this discussion is to advance everyone's thinking and monitoring of their own understanding and that of other students rather than to conduct simple turn taking, though of course over time, all students can have opportunities to explain.

Seeking and Giving Help

Students must have enough confidence not only to engage with problems and try to solve them, but also to seek help when they are stuck. The dialogue that occurs in pair or class situations can help generate self-regulating speech that a student can produce while problem solving. Such helping can also increase the metacognitive awareness of the helper as he or she takes into consideration the thinking of the student being helped.

The Framework of *How People Learn*: Seeking a Balanced Classroom Environment

The framework of *How People Learn* suggests that classroom environments should at the same time be learner-centered, knowledge-centered, assessment-centered, and community-centered (see Chapter 1). These features map easily to the preceding discussion of the three principles, as well as to the chapters that follow. The instruction described is learner-centered in that it draws out and builds on student thinking. It is also knowledge-centered in that it focuses simultaneously on the conceptual understanding and the procedural knowledge of a topic, which students must master to be proficient, and the learning paths that can lead from existing to more advanced understanding. It is assessment-centered in that there are frequent opportunities for students to reveal their thinking on a topic so the teacher can shape instruction in response to their learning, and students can be made aware of their own progress. And it is community-centered in that the norms of the classroom community value student ideas, encourage productive interchange, and promote collaborative thinking.

Effective teaching and learning depend, however, on balance among these features of the classroom environment. There must be continual connections between the learner-centered focus on student knowledge and the more formal knowledge networks that are the goals of teaching in a domain. Traditional teaching has tended to emphasize the knowledge networks and pay insufficient attention to conceptual supports and the need to build on learner knowledge. Many students learn rote knowledge that cannot be used adequately in solving problems. On the other hand, an overemphasis on learner-centered teaching results in insufficient attention to connections with valued knowledge networks, the crucially important guiding roles of teachers and of learning accessible student methods, and the need to consolidate knowledge. Four such excesses are briefly discussed here.

First, some suggest that students must invent all their mathematical ideas and that we should wait until they do so rather than teach ideas. This view, of course, ignores the fact that all inventions are made within a supportive culture and that providing appropriate supports can speed such inventions. Too much focus on student-invented methods per se can hold students back; those who use time-consuming methods that are not easily generalized need to be helped to move on to more rapid and generalizable "good-enough" methods. A focus on sense making and understanding of the methods that are used is the balanced focus, rather than an emphasis on whether the method was invented by the student using it.

Second, classroom discussions may not be sufficiently guided by the teacher through the learning path. Students may talk on and on, meandering without much focus. Descriptions of student thinking may have a turn-taking, "every method is equally wonderful" flavor so that other students do not listen carefully or ask questions, but passively await their turn to talk. Different student methods may be described, but their advantages and disadvantages, or at least their similar and different features, are not discussed. There may be no building toward student-to-student talk, but everything said may be directed toward the teacher.

Third, the use of real-world situations and conceptual supports may consist more of a series of activities in which the mathematical ideas are not sufficiently salient and not connected enough to the standard math notations and vocabulary. The result may be a scattershot approach involving many different activities rather than careful choices of core representations or bridging contexts that might guide students through a coherent learning path.

Fourth, learning may not be consolidated enough because of an excessive focus on the initial learning activities. Time for consolidation of learning, with feedback loops should errors arise, is vital for mathematical fluency.

The recent Third International Mathematics and Science Study showed that teaching in the United States is still overwhelmingly traditional. However, the above caveats need to be kept in mind as teachers move forward in implementing the principles of *How People Learn.*

NEXT STEPS

There are some curricula that implement, at least partially, the principles of *How People Learn.* Even without extensive curricular support, however, teachers can substantially improve their practice by understanding and using these principles. This is particularly true if they can examine their own teaching practices, supported by a teaching–learning community of like-minded colleagues. Such a community can help teachers create learning paths for themselves that can move them from their present teaching practices to practices that conform more fully to the principles of *How People Learn* and thereby create more effective classrooms. Two such teacher communities, involving video clubs and lesson study, respectively, are summarized in Boxes 5-7 and 5-8. A third approach to a teacher learning community is to organize teacher discussions around issues that arise from teaching a curriculum that supports conceptual approaches. Box 5-9 describes research summarizing one productive focus for such discussions—the use of openings in the curriculum where teachers can focus on student questions or misunderstandings.

BOX 5-7 Learning to Use Student Thinking in Teacher Video Clubs

Research indicates that teachers can develop their ability to attend to and interpret student thinking not only in the midst of class discussions, but also outside of class as they reflect on students' ideas. One model for doing so is the use of video clubs in which teachers meet together to watch and discuss video excerpts from their classrooms.[20] By providing teachers opportunities to examine student thinking without the pressure of having to respond immediately, video clubs can help prompt the development of new techniques for analyzing student thinking among teachers—techniques that teachers can then bring back to their classrooms.

BOX 5-8 Lesson Study: Learning Together How to Build on Student Knowledge

Lesson study is "a cycle in which teachers work together to consider their long-term goals for students, bring those goals to life in actual 'research lessons,' and collaboratively observe, discuss, and refine the lessons."[21] Lesson study has been a major form of teacher professional development in Japan for many decades, and in recent years has attracted the attention of U.S. teachers, school administrators, and educational researchers.[22] It is a simple idea. Teachers collaboratively plan a lesson that is taught by one group member while others observe and carefully collect data on student learning and behavior. The student data are then used to reflect on the lesson and revise it as needed. Lesson study is a teacher-led process in which teachers collaboratively identify a concept that is persistently difficult for students, study the best available curriculum materials in order to rethink their teaching of this topic, and plan and teach one or more "research lessons" that enable them to see student reactions to their redesigned unit. Ideally, a lesson study group allows teachers to share their expertise and knowledge, as well as questions related to both teaching and subject matter. Lesson study groups may also draw on knowledgeable outsiders as resources for content knowledge, group facilitation, and so on.

NOTE: Resources, including a handbook, videotapes, listserve, and protocols for teachers who wish to engage in lesson study, can be found at the websites of the Lesson Study Research Group at Teachers College, Columbia University: (http://www.tc.columbia.edu/lessonstudy/) and the Mills College Lesson Study Group (www.lessonresearch.net). See also Lewis (2002).

BOX 5-9 Teachers as Curriculum Designers: Using Openings in the Curriculum to Determine Learning Paths

Even when using a prepared curriculum, teachers have an important role as curriculum designers. In a study of two elementary teachers using a new textbook, Remillard[23] found that teachers made regular decisions about what parts of the teacher's guide to read, which suggestions to follow and to what ends, how to structure students' mathematical activities, and how to respond to students' questions and ideas. The decisions teachers made had a substantial impact on the curriculum experienced by students. In other words, written curriculum alone does not determine students' experiences in the classroom; this is the role of the teacher.

Remillard and Geist[24] use the term "openings in the curriculum" to denote those instances during instruction in which things do not go as described in the preset curriculum. These openings are often prompted by students' questions or teachers' observations about student understanding or misunderstanding. The authors argue that teachers must navigate these openings by (1) carefully analyzing student work and thinking, (2) weighing possible options for proceeding against one's goals for student learning, and (3) taking responsive action that is open to ongoing examination and adjustment. They suggest that teaching with curriculum guides can be improved as teachers recognize and embrace their role while navigating openings in the curriculum to determine learning paths for students.

Similarly, Remillard[25] found that teachers came to reflect on their beliefs and understandings related to their teaching and its content while involved in the very work of deciding what to do next by interpreting students' understanding with respect to their goals for the students and particular instructional tasks. Thus, some of the most fruitful opportunities for teacher learning when using a new curriculum occurred when teachers were engaged in the work of navigating openings in the curriculum.

It will take work by teachers, administrators, researchers, parents, and politicians to bring these new principles and goals to life in classrooms and to create the circumstances in which this can happen. Nonetheless, there are enough examples of the principles in action to offer a vision of the new kinds of learning that can be accessible to all students and to all teachers. Some materials to support teachers in these efforts do exist, and more are being developed. Helpful examples of the three principles in action are given in the chapters that follow. It is important to note, once again, that other projects have generated examples that implement the principles of *How People Learn*. Some of these examples can be found in the authors' references to that research and in the suggested teacher reading list. All of this work indicates that we have begun the crucial journey into mathematical proficiency for all and that the principles of *How People Learn* can guide us on this journey.

NOTES

1. Holt, 1964, pp. 143-144.
2. National Research Council, 2001.
3. See Fuson, 1986a, 1986b, 1990; Fuson and Briars, 1990; Fuson and Burghardt, 1993, 1997; Fuson et al., 1994, 2000; Fuson and Smith, 1997; Fuson, Smith, and Lott, 1977; Fuson, Wearne et al., 1997; Fuson, Lo Cicero et al., 1997; Lo Cicero et al., 1999; Fuson et al., 2000; Ron, 1998.
4. Carey, 2001; Gelman, 1990; Starkey et al., 1990; Wynn, 1996; Canfield and Smith, 1996.
5. Case et al., 1999; Ginsburg, 1984; Saxe, 1982.
6. Carraher, 1986; Carraher et al., 1985.
7. Lave, 1988; Sternberg, 1999.
8. De la Rocha, 1986.
9. Ceci and Liker, 1986; Ceci, 1996.
10. National Council of Teachers of Mathematics, 2000.
11. National Research Council, 2001.
12. See, e.g., Hatano and Inagaki, 1996; Resnick, 1987; Stigler and Heibert, 1997.
13. Stigler and Heibert, 1999.
14. National Research Council, 2004.
15. See, e.g., Tobias, 1978.
16. Hufferd-Ackles et al., 2004.
17. Sherin, 2000a, 2002.
18. See, e.g., Bransford et al., 1989.
19. See, e.g., Schwartz and Moore, 1998.
20. Sherin, 2000b, 2001.
21. Lewis, 2002, p. 1.
22. Fernandez, 2002; Lewis, 2002; Stigler and Heibert, 1999.
23. Remillard, 1999, 2000.
24. Remillard and Geist, 2002.
25. Remillard, 2000.

REFERENCES

Anghileri, J. (1989). An investigation of young children's understanding of multiplication. *Educational Studies in Mathematics, 20*, 367-385.

Ashlock, R.B. (1998). *Error patterns in computation.* Upper Saddle River, NJ: Prentice-Hall.

Baek, J.-M. (1998). Children's invented algorithms for multidigit multiplication problems. In L.J. Morrow and M.J. Kenney (Eds.), *The teaching and learning of algorithms in school mathematics.* Reston, VA: National Council of Teachers of Mathematics.

Baroody, A.J., and Coslick, R.T. (1998). *Fostering children's mathematical power: An investigative approach to k-8 mathematics instruction.* Mahwah, NJ: Lawrence Erlbaum Associates.

Baroody, A.J., and Ginsburg, H.P. (1986). The relationship between initial meaningful and mechanical knowledge of arithmetic. In J. Hiebert (Ed.), *Conceptual and procedural knowledge: The case of mathematics* (pp. 75-112). Mahwah, NJ: Lawrence Erlbaum Associates.

Beishuizen, M. (1993). Mental strategies and materials or models for addition and subtraction up to 100 in Dutch second grades. *Journal for Research in Mathematics Education, 24,* 294-323.

Beishuizen, M., Gravemeijer, K.P.E., and van Lieshout, E.C.D.M. (Eds.). (1997). *The role of contexts and models in the development of mathematical strategies and procedures.* Utretch, The Netherlands: CD-B Press/The Freudenthal Institute.

Bergeron, J.C., and Herscovics, N. (1990). Psychological aspects of learning early arithmetic. In P. Nesher and J. Kilpatrick (Eds.), *Mathematics and cognition: A research synthesis by the International Group for the Psychology of Mathematics Education.* Cambridge, England: Cambridge University Press.

Bransford, J.D., Franks, J.J., Vye, N.J., and Sherwood, R.D. (1989). New approaches to instruction: Because wisdom can't be told. In S. Vasniadou and A. Ortony (Eds.), *Similarity and analogical reasoning* (pp. 470-497). New York: Cambridge University Press.

Brophy, J. (1997). Effective instruction. In H.J. Walberg and G.D. Haertel (Eds.), *Psychology and educational practice* (pp. 212-232). Berkeley, CA: McCutchan.

Brownell, W.A. (1987). AT Classic: Meaning and skill—maintaining the balance. *Arithmetic Teacher, 34*(8), 18-25.

Canfield, R.L., and Smith, E.G. (1996). Number-based expectations and sequential enumeration by 5-month-old infants. *Developmental Psychology, 32,* 269-279.

Carey, S. (2001). Evolutionary and ontogenetic foundations of arithmetic. *Mind and Language, 16*(1), 37-55.

Carpenter, T.P., and Moser, J.M. (1984). The acquisition of addition and subtraction concepts in grades one through three. *Journal for Research in Mathematics Education, 15*(3), 179-202.

Carpenter, T.P., Fennema, E., Peterson, P.L., Chiang, C.P., and Loef, M. (1989). Using knowledge of children's mathematics thinking in classroom teaching: An experimental study. *American Educational Research Journal, 26*(4), 499-531.

Carpenter, T.P., Franke, M.L., Jacobs, V., and Fennema, E. (1998). A longitudinal study of invention and understanding in children's multidigit addition and subtraction. *Journal for Research in Mathematics Education, 29,* 3-20.

Carraher, T.N. (1986). From drawings to buildings: Mathematical scales at work. *International Journal of Behavioural Development, 9,* 527-544.

Carraher, T.N., Carraher, D.W., and Schliemann, A.D. (1985). Mathematics in the streets and in schools. *British Journal of Developmental Psychology, 3,* 21-29.

Carroll, W.M. (2001). *A longitudinal study of children using the reform curriculum everyday mathematics.* Available: http://everydaymath.uchicago.edu/educators/references.shtml [accessed September 2004].

Carroll, W.M., and Fuson, K.C. (1999). *Achievement results for fourth graders using the standards-based curriculum everyday mathematics.* Unpublished document, University of Chicago, Illinois.

Carroll, W.M., and Porter, D. (1998). Alternative algorithms for whole-number operations. In L.J. Morrow and M.J. Kenney (Eds.), *The teaching and learning of algorithms in school mathematics* (pp. 106-114). Reston, VA: National Council of Teachers of Mathematics.

Case, R. (1985). *Intellectual development: Birth to adulthood.* New York: Academic Press.

Case, R. (1992). *The mind's staircase: Exploring the conceptual underpinnings of children's thought and knowledge.* Mahwah, NJ: Lawrence Erlbaum Associates.

Case, R. (1998). *A psychological model of number sense and its development.* Paper presented at the annual meeting of the American Educational Research Association, April, San Diego, CA.

Case, R., and Sandieson, R. (1988). A developmental approach to the identification and teaching of central conceptual structures in mathematics and science in the middle grades. In M. Behr and J. Hiebert (Eds.), *Research agenda in mathematics education: Number concepts and in the middle grades* (pp. 136-270). Mahwah, NJ: Lawrence Erlbaum Associates.

Case, R., Griffin, S., and Kelly, W.M. (1999). Socioeconomic gradients in mathematical ability and their responsiveness to intervention during early childhood. In D.P. Keating and C. Hertzman (Eds.), *Developmental health and the wealth of nations: Social, biological, and educational dynamics* (pp. 125-149). New York: Guilford Press.

Ceci, S.J. (1996). *On intelligence: A bioecological treatise on intellectual development.* Cambridge, MA: Harvard University Press.

Ceci, S.J., and Liker, J.K. (1986). A day at the races: A study of IQ, expertise, and cognitive complexity. *Journal of Experimental Psychology, 115*(3), 255-266.

Cotton, K. (1995). *Effective schooling practices: A research synthesis.* Portland, OR: Northwest Regional Lab.

Davis, R.B. (1984). *Learning mathematics: The cognitive science approach to mathematics education.* Norwood, NJ: Ablex.

De la Rocha, O.L. (1986). The reorganization of arithmetic practice in the kitchen. *Anthropology and Education Quarterly, 16*(3), 193-198.

Dixon, R.C., Carnine, S.W., Kameenui, E.J., Simmons, D.C., Lee, D.S., Wallin, J., and Chard, D. (1998). *Executive summary. Report to the California State Board of Education, review of high-quality experimental research.* Eugene, OR: National Center to Improve the Tools of Educators.

Dossey, J.A., Swafford, J.O., Parmantie, M., and Dossey, A.E. (Eds.). (2003). Multidigit addition and subtraction methods invented in small groups and teacher support of problem solving and reflection. In A. Baroody and A. Dowker (Eds.), *The development of arithmetic concepts and skills: Constructing adaptive expertise.* Mahwah, NJ: Lawrence Erlbaum Associates.

Fernandez, C. (2002). Learning from Japanese approaches to professional development. The case of lesson study. *Journal of Teacher Education, 53*(5), 393-405.

Fraivillig, J.L., Murphy, L.A., and Fuson, K.C. (1999). Advancing children's mathematical thinking in everyday mathematics reform classrooms. *Journal for Research in Mathematics Education, 30*, 148-170.

Fuson, K.C. (1986a). Roles of representation and verbalization in the teaching of multidigit addition and subtraction. *European Journal of Psychology of Education, 1*, 35-56.

Fuson, K.C. (1986b). Teaching children to subtract by counting up. *Journal for Research in Mathematics Education, 17*, 172-189.

Fuson, K.C. (1990). Conceptual structures for multiunit numbers: Implications for learning and teaching multidigit addition, subtraction, and place value. *Cognition and Instruction, 7*, 343-403.

Fuson, K.C. (1992a). Research on learning and teaching addition and subtraction of whole numbers. In G. Leinhardt, R.T. Putnam, and R.A. Hattrup (Eds.), *The analysis of arithmetic for mathematics teaching* (pp. 53-187). Mahwah, NJ: Lawrence Erlbaum Associates.

Fuson, K.C. (1992b). Research on whole number addition and subtraction. In D. Grouws (Ed.), *Handbook of research on mathematics teaching and learning* (pp. 243-275). New York: Macmillan.

Fuson, K.C. (2003). Developing mathematical power in whole number operations. In J. Kilpatrick, W.G. Martin, and D. Schifter (Eds.), *A research companion to principles and standards for school mathematics* (pp. 68-94). Reston, VA: National Council of Teachers of Mathematics.

Fuson, K.C., and Briars, D.J. (1990). Base-ten blocks as a first- and second-grade learning/teaching approach for multidigit addition and subtraction and place-value concepts. *Journal for Research in Mathematics Education, 21*, 180-206.

Fuson, K.C., and Burghardt, B.H. (1993). Group case studies of second graders inventing multidigit addition procedures for base-ten blocks and written marks. In J.R. Becker and B.J. Pence (Eds.), *Proceedings of the fifteenth annual meeting of the North American chapter of the international group for the psychology of mathematics education* (pp. 240-246). San Jose, CA: The Center for Mathematics and Computer Science Education, San Jose State University.

Fuson, K.C., and Burghardt, B.H. (1997). Group case studies of second graders inventing multidigit subtraction methods. In *Proceedings of the 19th annual meeting of the North American chapter of the international group for the psychology of mathematics education* (pp. 291-298). San Jose, CA: The Center for Mathematics and Computer Science Education, San Jose State University.

Fuson, K.C., and Fuson, A.M. (1992). Instruction to support children's counting on for addition and counting up for subtraction. *Journal for Research in Mathematics Education, 23*, 72-78.

Fuson, K.C., and Kwon, Y. (1992). Korean children's understanding of multidigit addition and subtraction. *Child Development, 63*(2), 491-506.

Fuson, K.C., and Secada, W.G. (1986). Teaching children to add by counting with finger patterns. *Cognition and Instruction, 3*, 229-260.

Fuson, K.C., and Smith, T. (1997). Supporting multiple 2-digit conceptual structures and calculation methods in the classroom: Issues of conceptual supports, instructional design, and language. In M. Beishuizen, K.P.E. Gravemeijer, and E.C.D.M. van Lieshout (Eds.), *The role of contexts and models in the development of mathematical strategies and procedures* (pp. 163-198). Utrecht, The Netherlands: CD-B Press/The Freudenthal Institute.

Fuson, K.C., Stigler, J., and Bartsch, K. (1988). Grade placement of addition and subtraction topics in Japan, mainland China, the Soviet Union, Taiwan, and the United States. *Journal for Research in Mathematics Education, 19*(5), 449-456.

Fuson, K.C., Perry, T., and Kwon, Y. (1994). Latino, Anglo, and Korean children's finger addition methods. In J.E.H. van Luit (Ed.), *Research on learning and instruction of mathematics in kindergarten and primary school,* (pp. 220-228). Doetinchem/Rapallo, The Netherlands: Graviant.

Fuson, K.C., Perry, T., and Ron, P. (1996). Developmental levels in culturally different finger methods: Anglo and Latino children's finger methods of addition. In E. Jakubowski, D. Watkins, and H. Biske (Eds.), *Proceedings of the 18th annual meeting of the North American chapter for the psychology of mathematics education* (2nd edition, pp. 347-352). Columbus, OH: ERIC Clearinghouse for Science, Mathematics, and Environmental Education.

Fuson, K.C., Lo Cicero, A., Hudson, K., and Smith, S.T. (1997). Snapshots across two years in the life of an urban Latino classroom. In J. Hiebert, T. Carpenter, E. Fennema, K.C. Fuson, D. Wearne, H. Murray, A. Olivier, and P. Human (Eds.), *Making sense: Teaching and learning mathematics with understanding* (pp. 129-159). Portsmouth, NH: Heinemann.

Fuson, K.C., Smith, T., and Lo Cicero, A. (1997). Supporting Latino first graders' ten-structured thinking in urban classrooms. *Journal for Research in Mathematics Education, 28,* 738-760.

Fuson, K.C., Wearne, D., Hiebert, J., Murray, H., Human, P., Olivier, A., Carpenter, T., and Fennema, E. (1997). Children's conceptual structures for multidigit numbers and methods of multidigit addition and subtraction. *Journal for Research in Mathematics Education, 28,* 130-162.

Fuson, K.C., De La Cruz, Y., Smith, S., Lo Cicero, A., Hudson, K., Ron, P., and Steeby, R. (2000). Blending the best of the 20th century to achieve a mathematics equity pedagogy in the 21st century. In M.J. Burke and F.R. Curcio (Eds.), *Learning mathematics for a new century* (pp. 197-212). Reston, VA: National Council of Teachers of Mathematics.

Geary, D.C. (1994). *Children's mathematical development: Research and practical applications.* Washington, DC: American Psychological Association.

Gelman, R. (1990). First principles organize attention to and learning about relevant data: Number and the animate-inanimate distinction as examples. *Cognitive Science, 14,* 79-106.

Ginsburg, H.P. (1984). *Children's arithmetic: The learning process.* New York: Van Nostrand.

Ginsburg, H.P., and Allardice, B.S. (1984). Children's difficulties with school mathematics. In B. Rogoff and J. Lave (Eds.), *Everyday cognition: Its development in social contexts* (pp. 194-219). Cambridge, MA: Harvard University Press.

Ginsburg, H.P., and Russell, R.L. (1981). Social class and racial influences on early mathematical thinking. *Monographs of the Society for Research in Child Development* 44(6, serial #193). Malden, MA: Blackwell.

Goldman, S.R., Pellegrino, J.W., and Mertz, D.L. (1988). Extended practice of basic addition facts: Strategy changes in learning-disabled students. *Cognition and Instruction, 5*(3), 223-265.

Goldman, S.R., Hasselbring, T.S., and the Cognition and Technology Group at Vanderbilt (1997). Achieving meaningful mathematics literacy for students with learning disabilities. *Journal of Learning Disabilities, March 1*(2), 198-208.

Greer, B. (1992). Multiplication and division as models of situation. In D. Grouws (Ed.), *Handbook of research on mathematics teaching and learning* (pp. 276-295). New York: Macmillan.

Griffin, S., and Case, R. (1997). Re-thinking the primary school math curriculum: An approach based on cognitive science. *Issues in Education, 3*(1), 1-49.

Griffin, S., Case, R., and Siegler, R.S. (1994). Rightstart: Providing the central conceptual structures for children at risk of school failure. In K. McGilly (Ed.), *Classroom lessons: Integrating cognitive theory and classroom practice* (pp. 13-48). Mahwah, NJ: Lawrence Erlbaum Associates.

Grouws, D. (1992). *Handbook of research on mathematics teaching and learning.* New York: Teachers College Press.

Hamann, M.S., and Ashcraft, M.H. (1986). Textbook presentations of the basic addition facts. *Cognition and Instruction, 3*, 173-192.

Hart, K.M. (1987). Practical work and formalisation, too great a gap. In J.C. Bergeron, N. Hersovics, and C. Kieren (Eds.), *Proceedings from the eleventh international conference for the psychology of mathematics education* (vol. 2, pp. 408-415). Montreal, Canada: University of Montreal.

Hatano, G., and Inagaki, K. (1996). *Cultural contexts of schooling revisited. A review of the learning gap from a cultural psychology perspective.* Paper presented at the Conference on Global Prospects for Education: Development, Culture, and Schooling, University of Michigan.

Hiebert, J. (1986). *Conceptual and procedural knowledge: The case of mathematics.* Mahwah, NJ: Lawrence Erlbaum Associates.

Hiebert, J. (1992). Mathematical, cognitive, and instructional analyses of decimal fractions. In G. Leinhardt, R. Putnam, and R.A. Hattrup (Eds.), *The analysis of arithmetic for mathematics teaching* (pp. 283-322). Mahwah, NJ: Lawrence Erlbaum Associates.

Hiebert, J., and Carpenter, T.P. (1992). Learning and teaching with understanding. In D. Grouws (Ed.), *Handbook of research on mathematics teaching and learning* (pp. 65-97). New York: Macmillan.

Hiebert, J., and Wearne, D. (1986). Procedures over concepts: The acquisition of decimal number knowledge. In J. Hiebert (Ed.), *Conceptual and procedural knowledge: The case of mathematics* (pp. 199-223). Mahwah, NJ: Lawrence Erlbaum Associates.

Hiebert, J., Carpenter, T., Fennema, E., Fuson, K.C., Murray, H., Olivier, A., Human, P., and Wearne, D. (1996). Problem solving as a basis for reform in curriculum and instruction: The case of mathematics. *Educational Researcher, 25*(4), 12-21.

Hiebert, J., Carpenter, T., Fennema, E., Fuson, K.C., Wearne, D., Murray, H., Olivier, A., and Human, P. (1997). *Making sense: Teaching and learning mathematics with understanding*. Portsmouth, NH: Heinemann.

Holt, J. (1964). *How children fail*. New York: Dell.

Hufferd-Ackles, K., Fuson, K., and Sherin, M.G. (2004). Describing levels and components of a math-talk community. *Journal for Research in Mathematics Education, 35*(2), 81-116.

Isaacs, A.C., and Carroll, W.M. (1999). Strategies for basic-facts instruction. *Teaching Children Mathematics, 5*(9), 508-515.

Kalchman, M., and Case, R. (1999). Diversifying the curriculum in a mathematics classroom streamed for high-ability learners: A necessity unassumed. *School Science and Mathematics, 99*(6), 320-329.

Kameenui, E.J., and Carnine, D.W. (Eds.). (1998). *Effective teaching strategies that accommodate diverse learners*. Upper Saddle River, NJ: Prentice-Hall.

Kerkman, D.D., and Siegler, R.S. (1993). Individual differences and adaptive flexibility in lower-income children's strategy choices. *Learning and Individual Differences, 5*(2), 113-136.

Kilpatrick, J., Martin, W.G., and Schifter, D. (Eds.). (2003). *A research companion to principles and standards for school mathematics*. Reston, VA: National Council of Teachers of Mathematics.

Knapp, M.S. (1995). *Teaching for meaning in high-poverty classrooms*. New York: Teachers College Press.

Lampert, M. (1986). Knowing, doing, and teaching multiplication. *Cognition and Instruction, 3*, 305-342.

Lampert, M. (1992). Teaching and learning long division for understanding in school. In G. Leinhardt, R.T. Putnam, and R.A. Hattrup (Eds.), *The analysis of arithmetic for mathematics teaching* (pp. 221-282). Mahwah, NJ: Lawrence Erlbaum Associates.

Lave, J. (1988). *Cognition in practice: Mind, mathematics and culture in everyday life*. London, England: Cambridge University Press.

LeFevre, J., and Liu, J. (1997). The role of experience in numerical skill: Multiplication performance in adults from Canada and China. *Mathematical Cognition, 3*(1), 31-62.

LeFevre, J., Kulak, A.G., and Bisanz, J. (1991). Individual differences and developmental change in the associative relations among numbers. *Journal of Experimental Child Psychology, 52*, 256-274.

Leinhardt, G., Putnam, R.T., and Hattrup, R.A. (Eds.). (1992). The *analysis of arithmetic for mathematics teaching*. Mahwah, NJ: Lawrence Erlbaum Associates.

Lemaire, P., and Siegler, R.S. (1995). Four aspects of strategic change: Contributions to children's learning of multiplication. *Journal of Experimental Psychology: General, 124*(1), 83-97.

Lemaire, P., Barrett, S.E., Fayol, M., and Abdi, H. (1994). Automatic activation of addition and multiplication facts in elementary school children. *Journal of Experimental Child Psychology, 57*, 224-258.

Lewis, C. (2002). *Lesson study: A handbook of teacher-led instructional change*. Philadelphia, PA: Research for Better Schools.

Lo Cicero, A., Fuson, K.C., and Allexaht-Snider, M. (1999). Making a difference in Latino children's math learning: Listening to children, mathematizing their stories, and supporting parents to help children. In L. Ortiz-Franco, N.G. Hernendez, and Y. De La Cruz (Eds.), *Changing the faces of mathematics: Perspectives on Latinos* (pp. 59-70). Reston, VA: National Council of Teachers of Mathematics.

McClain, K., Cobb, P., and Bowers, J. (1998). A contextual investigation of three-digit addition and subtraction. In L. Morrow (Ed.), *Teaching and learning of algorithms in school mathematics* (pp. 141-150). Reston, VA: National Council of Teachers of Mathematics.

McKnight, C.C., and Schmidt, W.H. (1998). Facing facts in U.S. science and mathematics education: Where we stand, where we want to go. *Journal of Science Education and Technology, 7*(1), 57-76.

McKnight, C.C., Crosswhite, F.J., Dossey, J.A., Kifer, E., Swafford, J.O., Travers, K.T., and Cooney, T.J. (1989). *The underachieving curriculum: Assessing U.S. school mathematics from an international perspective.* Champaign, IL: Stipes.

Miller, K.F., and Paredes, D.R. (1990). Starting to add worse: Effects of learning to multiply on children's addition. *Cognition, 37*, 213-242.

Moss, J., and Case, R. (1999). Developing children's understanding of rational numbers: A new model and experimental curriculum. *Journal for Research in Mathematics Education, 30*(2), 122-147.

Mulligan, J., and Mitchelmore, M. (1997). Young children's intuitive models of multiplication and division. *Journal for Research in Mathematics Education, 28*(3), 309-330.

National Council of Teachers of Mathematics. (1989). *Curriculum and evaluation standards for school mathematics.* Reston, VA: National Council of Teachers of Mathematics.

National Council of Teachers of Mathematics. (1991). *Professional standards for teaching mathematics.* Reston, VA: National Council of Teachers of Mathematics.

National Council of Teachers of Mathematics. (2000). *Principles and standards for school mathematics.* Reston, VA: National Council of Teachers of Mathematics.

National Research Council. (2001). *Adding it up: Helping children learn mathematics.* Mathematics Learning Study Committee, J. Kilpatrick, J. Swafford, and B. Findell (Eds.). Center for Education, Division of Behavioral and Social Sciences and Education. Washington, DC: National Academy Press.

National Research Council. (2002). *Helping children learn mathematics.* Mathematics Learning Study Committee, J. Kilpatrick, J. Swafford, and B. Findell (Eds.). Center for Education, Division of Behavioral and Social Sciences and Education. Washington, DC: The National Academies Press.

National Research Council. (2004). *Learning and instruction: A SERP research agenda.* Panel on Learning and Instruction. M.S. Donovan and J.W. Pellegrino (Eds.). Division of Behavioral and Social Sciences and Education. Washington, DC: The National Academies Press.

Nesh, P., and Kilpatrick, J. (Eds.). (1990). Mathematics *and cognition: A research synthesis by the International Group for the Psychology of Mathematics Education.* Cambridge, MA: Cambridge University Press.

Nesher, P. (1992). Solving multiplication word problems. In G. Leinhardt, R.T. Putnam, and R.A. Hattrup (Eds.), *The analysis of arithmetic for mathematics teaching* (pp. 189-220). Mahwah, NJ: Lawrence Erlbaum Associates.

Peak, L. (1996). *Pursuing excellence: A study of the U.S. eighth-grade mathematics and science teaching, learning, curriculum, and achievement in an international context*. Washington, DC: National Center for Education Statistics.

Remillard, J.T. (1999). Curriculum materials in mathematics education reform: A framework for examining teachers' curriculum development. *Curriculum Inquiry, 29*(3), 315-342.

Remillard, J.T. (2000). Can curriculum materials support teachers' learning? *Elementary School Journal, 100*(4), 331-350.

Remillard, J.T., and Geist, P. (2002). Supporting teachers' professional learning though navigating openings in the curriculum. *Journal of Mathematics Teacher Education, 5*(1), 7-34.

Resnick, L.B. (1987). *Education and learning to think*. Committee on Mathematics, Science, and Technology Education, Commission on Behavioral and Social Sciences and Education. Washington, DC: National Academy Press.

Resnick, L.B. (1992). From protoquantities to operators: Building mathematical competence on a foundation of everyday knowledge. In G. Leinhardt, R.T. Putnam, and R.A. Hattrup (Eds.), *The analysis of arithmetic for mathematics teaching* (pp. 373-429). Mahwah, NJ: Lawrence Erlbaum Associates.

Resnick, L.B., and Omanson, S.F. (1987). Learning to understand arithmetic. In R. Glaser (Ed.), *Advances in instructional psychology* (vol. 3, pp. 41-95). Mahwah, NJ: Lawrence Erlbaum Associates.

Resnick, L.B., Nesher, P., Leonard, F., Magone, M., Omanson, S., and Peled, I. (1989). Conceptual bases of arithmetic errors: The case of decimal fractions. *Journal for Research in Mathematics Education, 20*(1), 8-27.

Ron, P. (1998). My family taught me this way. In L.J. Morrow and M.J. Kenney (Eds.), *The teaching and learning of algorithms in school mathematics* (pp. 115-119). Reston, VA: National Council of Teachers of Mathematics.

Saxe, G.B. (1982). Culture and the development of numerical cognition: Studies among the Oksapmin of Papua New Guinea. In C.J. Brainerd (Ed.), *Progress in cognitive development research: Children's logical and mathematical cognition* (vol. 1, pp. 157- 176). New York: Springer-Verlag.

Schmidt, W., McKnight, C.C., and Raizen, S.A. (1997). *A splintered vision: An investigation of U.S. science and mathematics education*. Dordrecht, The Netherlands: Kluwer.

Schwartz, D.L., and Moore, J.L. (1998). The role of mathematics in explaining the material world: Mental models for proportional reasoning. *Cognitive Science, 22*, 471-516.

Secada, W.G. (1992). Race, ethnicity, social class, language, and achievement in mathematics. In D. Grouws (Ed.), *Handbook of research on mathematics teaching and learning* (pp. 623-660). New York: Macmillan.

Sherin, M.G. (2000a). Facilitating meaningful discussions about mathematics. *Mathematics Teaching in the Middle School, 6*(2), 186-190.

Sherin, M.G. (2000b). Taking a fresh look at teaching through video clubs. *Educational Leadership, 57*(8), 36-38.

Sherin, M.G. (2001). Developing a professional vision of classroom events. In T. Wood, B.S. Nelson, and J. Warfield (Eds.), *Beyond classical pedagogy: Teaching elementary school mathematics* (pp. 75-93). Mahwah, NJ: Lawrence Erlbaum Associates.

Sherin, M.G. (2002). A balancing act: Developing a discourse community in a mathematics classroom. *Journal of Mathematics Teacher Education, 5*, 205-233.

Shuell, T.J. (2001). Teaching and learning in a classroom context. In N.J. Smelser and P.B. Baltes (Eds.), *International encyclopedia of the social and behavioral sciences* (pp. 15468-15472). Amsterdam: Elsevier.

Siegler, R.S. (1988). Individual differences in strategy choices: Good students, not-so-good students, and perfectionists. *Child Development, 59*(4), 833-851.

Siegler, R.S. (2003). Implications of cognitive science research for mathematics education. In J. Kilpatrick, W.G. Martin, and D.E. Schifter (Eds.), *A research companion to principles and standards for school mathematics* (pp. 1289-1303). Reston, VA: National Council of Teachers of Mathematics.

Simon, M.A. (1995). Reconstructing mathematics pedagogy from a constructivist perspective. *Journal for Research in Mathematics Education, 26*, 114-145.

Starkey, P., Spelke, E.S., and Gelman, R. (1990). Numerical abstraction by human infants. *Cognition, 36*, 97-127.

Steffe, L.P. (1994). Children's multiplying schemes. In G. Harel and J. Confrey (Eds.), *The development of multiplicative reasoning in the learning of mathematics* (pp. 3-39). New York: State University of New York Press.

Steffe, L.P., Cobb, P., and Von Glasersfeld, E. (1988). *Construction of arithmetical meanings and strategies*. New York: Springer-Verlag.

Sternberg, R.J. (1999). The theory of successful intelligence. *Review of General Psychology, 3*(4), 292-316.

Stigler, J.W., and Hiebert, J. (1999). *Teaching gap*. New York: Free Press.

Stigler, J.W., Fuson, K.C., Ham, M., and Kim, M.S. (1986). An analysis of addition and subtraction word problems in American and Soviet elementary mathematics textbooks. *Cognition and Instruction, 3*(3), 153-171.

Stipek, D., Salmon, J.M., Givvin, K.B., Kazemi, E., Saxe, G., and MacGyvers, V.L. (1998). The value (and convergence) of practices suggested by motivation research and promoted by mathematics education reformers. *Journal for Research in Mathematics Education, 29*, 465-488.

Thornton, C.A. (1978). Emphasizing thinking in basic fact instruction. *Journal for Research in Mathematics Education, 9*, 214-227.

Thornton, C.A., Jones, G.A., and Toohey, M.A. (1983). A multisensory approach to thinking strategies for remedial instruction in basic addition facts. *Journal for Research in Mathematics Education, 14*(3), 198-203.

Tobias, S. (1978). *Overcoming math anxiety*. New York: W.W. Norton.

Van de Walle, J.A. (1998). *Elementary and middle school mathematics: Teaching developmentally, third edition*. New York: Longman.

Van de Walle, J.A. (2000). *Elementary school mathematics: Teaching developmentally, fourth edition*. New York: Longman.

Wynn, K. (1996). Infants' individuation and enumeration of actions. *Psychological Science, 7*, 164-169.

Zucker, A.A. (1995). Emphasizing conceptual understanding and breadth of study in mathematics instruction. In M.S. Knapp (Ed.), *Teaching for meaning in high-poverty classrooms*. New York: Teachers College Press.

SUGGESTED READING LIST FOR TEACHERS

Carpenter, T.P. Fennema, E., Franke, M.L., Empson, S.B., and Levi, L.W. (1999). *Children's mathematics: Cognitively guided instruction*. Portsmouth, NH: Heinemann.

Fuson, K.C. (1988). Subtracting by counting up with finger patterns. (Invited paper for the Research into Practice Series.) *Arithmetic Teacher, 35*(5), 29-31.

Hiebert, J., Carpenter, T., Fennema, E., Fuson, K.C., Wearne, D., Murray, H., Olivier, A., and Human, P. (1997). *Making sense: Teaching and learning mathematics with understanding*. Portsmouth, NH: Heinemann.

Jensen, R.J. (Ed.). (1993). *Research ideas for the classroom: Early childhood mathematics*. New York: Macmillan.

Knapp, M.S. (1995). *Teaching for meaning in high-poverty classrooms*. New York: Teachers College Press.

Leinhardt, G., Putnam, R.T., and Hattrup, R.A. (Eds.). (1992). *The analysis of arithmetic for mathematics teaching*. Mahwah, NJ: Lawrence Erlbaum Associates.

Lo Cicero, A., De La Cruz, Y., and Fuson, K.C. (1999). Teaching and learning creatively with the Children's Math Worlds Curriculum: Using children's narratives and explanations to co-create understandings. *Teaching Children Mathematics, 5*(9), 544-547.

Owens, D.T. (Ed.). (1993). *Research ideas for the classroom: Middle grades mathematics*. New York: Macmillan.

Schifter, D. (Ed.). (1996). *What's happening in math class? Envisioning new practices through teacher narratives*. New York: Teachers College Press.

Wagner, S. (Ed.). (1993). *Research ideas for the classroom: High school mathematics*. New York: Macmillan.

6

Fostering the Development of Whole-Number Sense: Teaching Mathematics in the Primary Grades

Sharon Griffin

After 15 years of inquiry into children's understanding and learning of whole numbers, I can sum up what I have learned very simply. To teach math, you need to know three things. You need to know where you are now (in terms of the knowledge children in your classroom have available to build upon). You need to know where you want to go (in terms of the knowledge you want all children in your classroom to acquire during the school year). Finally, you need to know what is the best way to get there (in terms of the learning opportunities you will provide to enable all children in your class to achieve your stated objectives). Although this sounds simple, each of these points is just the tip of a large iceberg. Each raises a question (e.g., Where are we now?) that I have come to believe is crucial for the design of effective mathematics instruction. Each also points to a body of knowledge (the iceberg) to which teachers must have access in order to answer that question. In this chapter, I explore each of these icebergs in turn in the context of helping children in the primary grades learn more about whole numbers.

Readers will recognize that the three things I believe teachers need to know to teach mathematics effectively are similar in many respects to the knowledge teachers need to implement the three *How People Learn* principles (see Chapter 1) in their classrooms. This overlap should not be surprising. Because teaching and learning are two sides of the same coin and because effective teaching is defined primarily in terms of the learning it supports, we cannot talk about one without talking about the other. Thus when I address each of the three questions raised above, I will at the same time offer preschool and elementary mathematics teachers a set of resources they can use to implement the three principles of *How People Learn* in their classrooms and, in so doing, create classrooms that are student-centered, knowledge-centered, community-centered, and assessment-centered.

Addressing the three principles of *How People Learn* while exploring each question occurs quite naturally because the bodies of knowledge that underlie effective mathematics teaching provide a rich set of resources that teachers can use to implement these principles in their classrooms. Thus, when I explore question 1 (Where are we now?) and describe the number knowledge children typically have available to build upon at several specific age levels, I provide a tool (the Number Knowledge test) and a set of examples of age-level thinking that teachers can use to enact Principle 1—*eliciting, building upon, and connecting student knowledge*—in their classrooms. When I explore question 2 (Where do I want to go?) and describe the knowledge networks that appear to be central to children's mathematics learning and achievement and the ways these networks are built in the normal course of development, I provide a framework that teachers can use to enact Principle 2—*building learning paths and networks of knowledge*—in their classrooms. Finally, when I explore question 3 (What is the best way to get there?) and describe elements of a mathematics program that has been effective in helping children acquire whole-number sense, I provide a set of learning tools, design principles, and examples of classroom practice that teachers can use to enact Principle 3—*building resourceful, self-regulating mathematical thinkers and problem solvers*—in their classrooms. Because the questions I have raised are interrelated, as are the principles themselves, teaching practices that may be effective in answering each question and in promoting each principle are not limited to specific sections of this chapter, but are noted throughout.

I have chosen to highlight the questions themselves in my introduction to this chapter because it was this set of questions that motivated my inquiry into children's knowledge and learning in the first place. By asking this set of questions every time I sat down to design a math lesson for young children, I was able to push my thinking further and, over time, construct better answers and better lessons. If each math teacher asks this set of questions on a regular basis, each will be able to construct his or her own set of answers for the questions, enrich our knowledge base, and improve mathematics teaching and learning for at least one group of children. By doing so, each teacher will also embody the essence of what it means to be a resourceful, self-regulating mathematics teacher. The questions themselves are thus more important than the answers. But the reverse is also true:

although good questions can generate good answers, rich answers can also generate new and better questions.

I now turn to the answers I have found useful in my own work with young children. By addressing question 2 (Where do I want to go?) first, I hope to give readers a sense of the general direction in which we are heading before I turn to question 1 (Where are we now?) and provide a detailed description of the knowledge children generally have available to build upon at each age level between 4 and 8. While individual children differ a great deal in the rate at which they acquire number knowledge, teachers are charged with teaching a class of students grouped by age. It is therefore helpful in planning instruction to focus on the knowledge typical among children of a particular age, with the understanding that there will be considerable variation. In a subsequent section, I use what we have learned about children's typical age-level understandings to return to the issue of the knowledge to be taught and to provide a more specific answer for question 2.

DECIDING WHAT KNOWLEDGE TO TEACH

All teachers are faced with a dizzying array of mathematics concepts and skills they are expected to teach to groups of students who come to their classrooms with differing levels of preparedness for learning. This is true even at the preschool level. For each grade level, the knowledge to be taught is prescribed in several documents—the national standards of the National Council of Teachers of Mathematics (NCTM), state and district frameworks, curriculum guides—that are not always or even often consistent. Deciding what knowledge to teach to a class as a whole or to any individual child in the class is no easy matter.

Many primary school teachers resolve this dilemma by selecting number sense as the one set of understandings they want all students in their classrooms to acquire. This makes sense in many respects. In the NCTM standards, number sense is the major learning objective in the standard (numbers and operations) to which primary school teachers are expected to devote the greatest amount of attention. Teachers also recognize that children's ability to handle problems in other areas (e.g., algebra, geometry, measurement, and statistics) and to master the objectives listed for these standards is highly dependent on number sense. Moreover, number sense is given a privileged position on the report cards used in many schools, and teachers are regularly required to evaluate the extent to which their students "demonstrate number sense." In one major respect, however, the choice of number sense as an instructional objective is problematic. Although most teachers and lay people alike can easily recognize number sense when they see it, defining what it is and how it can be taught is much more difficult.

Consider the responses two kindergarten children provide when asked the following question from the Number Knowledge test (described in full later in this chapter): "If you had four chocolates and someone gave you three more, how many would you have altogether?"

Alex responds by scrunching up his brow momentarily and saying, "seven." When asked how he figured it out, he says, "Well, 'four' and 'four' is 'eight' [displaying four fingers on one hand and four on the other hand to demonstrate]. But we only need three more [taking away one finger from one hand to demonstrate]. So I went—'seven,' 'eight.' Seven is one less than eight. So the answer is seven."

Sean responds by putting up four fingers on one hand and saying (under his breath), "Four. Then three more—'five, six, seven.'" In a normal tone of voice, Sean says "seven." When asked how he figured it out, Sean is able to articulate his strategy, saying, "I started at four and counted—'five, six, seven'" (tapping the table three times as he counts up, to indicate the quantity added to the initial set).

It will be obvious to all kindergarten teachers that the responses of both children provide evidence of good number sense. The knowledge that lies behind that sense may be much less apparent, however. What knowledge do these children have that enables them to come up with the answer in the first place and to demonstrate number sense in the process? Scholars have studied children's mathematical thinking and problem solving, tracing the typical progression of understanding or developmental pathway for acquiring number knowledge.[1] This research suggests that the following understandings lie at the heart of the number sense that 5-year-olds such as Alex and Sean are able to demonstrate on this problem: (1) they know the counting sequence from "one" to "ten" and the position of each number word in the sequence (e.g., that "five" comes after "four" and "seven" comes before "eight"); (2) they know that "four" refers to a set of a particular size (e.g., it has one fewer than a set of five and one more than a set of 3), and thus there is no need to count up from "one" to get a sense of the size of this set; (3) they know that the word "more" in the problem means that the set of four chocolates will be increased by the precise amount (three chocolates) given in the problem; (4) they know that each counting number up in the counting sequence corresponds precisely to an increase of one unit in the size of a set; and (5) it therefore makes sense to count on from "four" and to say the next three numbers up in the sequence to figure out the answer (or, in Alex's case, to retrieve the sum of four plus four from memory, arrive at "eight," and move one number back in the sequence). This complex knowledge network—called a *central conceptual structure for whole number*—is described in greater detail in a subsequent section.

The knowledge that Alex and Sean demonstrate is not limited to the understandings enumerated above. It includes computational fluency (e.g., ease and proficiency in counting) and awareness of the language of quantity (e.g., that "altogether" indicates the joining of two sets), which were acquired earlier and provided a base on which the children's current knowledge was constructed. Sean and Alex also demonstrate impressive metacognitive skills (e.g., an ability to reflect on their own reasoning and to communicate it clearly in words) that not only provide evidence of number sense, but also contributed to its development.

Finally, children who demonstrate this set of competencies also show an ability to answer questions about the joining of two sets when the contexts vary considerably, as in the following problems: "If you take four steps and then you take three more, how far have you gone?" and "If you wait four hours and then you wait three more, how long have you waited?" In both of these problems, the quantities are represented in very different ways (as steps along a path, as positions on a dial), and the language used to describe the sum ("How far?" "How long?") differs from that used to describe the sum of two groups of objects ("How many?"). The ability to apply number knowledge in a flexible fashion is another hallmark of number sense.

Each of the components of number sense mentioned thus far is described in greater detail in a subsequent section of this chapter. For now it is sufficient to point out that the network of knowledge the components represent—the central conceptual structure for whole number—has been found to be central to children's mathematics learning and achievement in at least two ways. First, as mentioned above, it enables children to make sense of a broad range of quantitative problems in a variety of contexts (see Box 6-1 for a discussion of research that supports this claim). Second, it provides the base—the building block—on which children's learning of more complex number concepts, such as those involving double-digit numbers, is built (see Box 6-2 for research support for this claim). Consequently, this network of knowledge is an important set of understandings that should be taught. In choosing number sense as a major learning goal, teachers demonstrate an intuitive understanding of the essential role of this knowledge network and the importance of teaching a core set of ideas that lie at the heart of learning and competency in the discipline (learning principle 2). Having a more explicit understanding of the factual, procedural, and conceptual understandings that are implicated and intertwined in this network will help teachers realize this goal for more children in their classrooms.

Once children have consolidated the set of understandings just described for the oral counting sequence from "one" to "ten," they are ready to make sense of written numbers (i.e., numerals). Now, when they are exposed to

BOX 6-1 **The Central Conceptual Structure Hypothesis: Support for the First Claim**

A central conceptual structure is a powerful organizing knowledge network that is extremely broad in its range of application and that plays a central role in enabling individuals to master the problems that the domain presents. The word "central" implies (1) that the structure is vital to successful performance on a range of tasks, ones that often transcend individual disciplinary boundaries; and (2) that future learning in these tasks is dependent on the structure, which often forms the initial core around which all subsequent learning is organized.

To test the first of these claims, Griffin and Case selected two groups of kindergarten children who were at an age when children typically have acquired the central conceptual structure for whole number, but had not yet done so.[2] All the children were attending schools in low-income, inner-city communities. In the first part of the kindergarten year, all the children were given a battery of developmental tests to assess their central conceptual understanding of whole number (Number Knowledge test) and their ability to solve problems in a range of other areas that incorporate number knowledge, including scientific reasoning (Balance Beam test), social reasoning (Birthday Party task), moral reasoning (Distributive Justice task), time telling (Time test), and money knowledge (Money test). On this test administration, no child in either group passed the Number Knowledge test, and fewer than 20 percent of the children passed any of the remaining tests.

One group of children (the treatment group) was exposed to a mathematics program called Number Worlds that had been specifically designed to teach the central conceptual structure for whole number. The second group of children (a matched control group) received a variety of other forms of mathematics instruction for the same time period (about 10 weeks). The performance of these two groups on the second administra-

the symbols that correspond to each number name and given opportunities to connect name to symbol, they will bring all the knowledge of what that name means with them, and it will accrue to the symbol. They will thus be able to read and write number symbols with meaning. To build a learning path that matches children's observed progression of understanding, this would be a reasonable next step for teachers to take. Finally, with experience in using this knowledge network, children eventually become capable

tion of the same tests at the end of the kindergarten year is presented in the following table. The treatment group—those exposed to the Number Worlds curriculum—improved substantially in all test areas, far surpassing the performance of the control group. Because no child in the treatment group had received any training in any of the areas tested in this battery besides number knowledge, the strong post-training performance of the treatment group on these tasks can be attributed to the construction of the central conceptual structure for whole number, as demonstrated in the children's (post-training) performance on the Number Knowledge test. Other factors that might have accounted for these findings, such as more individual attention and/or instructional time given to the treatment group, were carefully controlled in this study.

Percentages of Children Passing the Second Administration of the Number Knowledge Test and Five Numerical Transfer Tests

Test[a]	Control Group (N = 24)	Treatment Group (N = 23)
Number Knowledge (5/6)	25	87
Balance Beam (2/2)	42	96
Birthday Party (2/2)	42	96
Distributive Justice (2/2)	37	87
Time Telling (4/5)	21	83
Money Knowledge (4/6)	17	43

[a]Number of items out of total used as the criterion for passing the test are given in parentheses.

of applying their central conceptual understandings to two distinct quantitative variables (e.g., tens and ones, hours and minutes, dollars and cents) and of handling two quantitative variables in a coordinated fashion. This ability permits them to solve problems involving double-digit numbers and place value, for example, and introducing these concepts at this point in time (sometime around grade 2) would be a reasonable next step for teachers to

BOX 6-2 The Central Conceptual Structure Hypothesis: Support for the Second Claim

To test the second centrality claim—that future learning is dependent on the acquisition of the central conceptual structure for whole number—Griffin and Case conducted a follow-up study using the same sample of children as that in Box 6-1.[3] Children in both the treatment and control groups had graduated to a variety of first-grade classrooms in a number of different schools. Those who had remained in the general geographic area were located 1 year later and given a range of assessments to obtain measures of their mathematics learning and achievement in grade 1. Their teachers, who were blind to the children's status in the study, were also asked to rate each child in their classroom on a number of variables.

The results, displayed in the following table, present an interesting portrait of the importance of the central conceptual structure (assessed by performance at the 6-year-old level of the Number Knowledge test) for children's learning and achievement in grade 1. Recall that 87 percent of the treatment group had passed this level of the number knowledge test at the end of kindergarten compared with 25 percent of the control group. As the table indicates, most of the children in the control group (83 percent) had acquired this knowledge by the end of grade 1, but it appears to have been too late to enable many of them to master the grade 1 arithmetic tasks that require conceptual understanding (e.g., the Oral Arithmetic test; the Word Problems; test and teacher ratings of number sense, number meanings, and number use). On all of these measures, children who had acquired the central conceptual structure before the start of the school year did significantly better.

On the more traditional measures of mathematics achievement (e.g., the Written Arithmetic test and teacher ratings of addition and subtraction) that rely more on procedural knowledge than conceptual understanding, the performance of children in the control group was stronger. It was still inferior, however, in absolute terms to the performance of children in the treatment group.

Possibly the most interesting finding of all is the difference between the two groups on tests that tap knowledge not typically taught until grade 2 (e.g., the 8-year-old level of the Number Knowledge test and the 8-year-old level of the Word Problems test). On both of these tests, a number of children in the treatment group demonstrated that they had built upon their central conceptual structure for whole number during their first-grade experience and were beginning to construct the more elaborate understandings required to mentally solve double-digit arithmetic problems. Few children in the control group demonstrated this level of learning.

**Percentages of Children Passing the Number Knowledge
Test and Measures of Arithmetic Learning and
Achievement at the End of Grade 1**

Test	Control Group (N = 12)	Treatment Group (N= 11)	Significance of difference[a]
Number Knowledge Test			
6-year-old level	83	100	ns
8-year-old level	0	18	[a]
Oral Arithmetic Test	33	82	[a]
Written Arithmetic Test	75	91	ns
Word Problems Test			
6-year-old level	54	96	[a]
8-year-old level	13	46	[a]
Teacher Rating			
Number sense	24	100	[a]
Number meaning	42	88	[a]
Number use	42	88	[a]
Addition	66	100	ns
Subtraction	66	100	ns

ns= not significant; [a] = significant at the .01 level or better.

take in building learning paths that are finely attuned to children's observed development of number knowledge.

In this brief example, several developmental principles that should be considered in building learning paths and networks of knowledge (learning principle 2) for the domain of whole numbers have come to light. They can be summarized as follows:

- Build upon children's current knowledge. This developmental principle is so important that it was selected as the basis for one of the three primary learning principles (principle 1) of *How People Learn.*
- Follow the natural developmental progression when selecting new knowledge to be taught. By selecting learning objectives that are a natural next step for children (as documented in cognitive developmental research and described in subsequent sections of this chapter), the teacher will be creating a learning path that is developmentally appropriate for children, one that fits the progression of understanding as identified by researchers. This in turn will make it easier for children to construct the knowledge network that is expected for their age level and, subsequently, to construct the higher-level knowledge networks that are typically built upon this base.
- Make sure children consolidate one level of understanding before moving on to the next. For example, give them many opportunities to solve oral problems with real quantities before expecting them to use formal symbols.
- Give children many opportunities to use number concepts in a broad range of contexts and to learn the language that is used in these contexts to describe quantity.

I turn now to question 1 and, in describing the knowledge children typically have available at several successive age levels, paint a portrait of the knowledge construction process uncovered by research—the step-by-step manner in which children construct knowledge of whole numbers between the ages of 4 and 8 and the ways individual children navigate this process as a result of their individual talent and experience. Although this is the subject matter of cognitive developmental psychology, it is highly relevant to teachers of young children who want to implement the developmental principles just described in their classrooms. Because young children do not reflect on their own thinking very often or very readily and because they are not skilled in explaining their reasoning, it is difficult for a teacher of young children to obtain a picture of the knowledge and thought processes each child has available to build upon. The results of cognitive developmental research and the tools that researchers use to elicit children's understandings can thus supplement teachers' own knowledge and expertise in important ways, and help teachers create *learner-centered classrooms* that build effectively on students' current knowledge. Likewise, having a rich picture of the step-by step manner in which children typically construct knowledge of whole numbers can help teachers create *knowledge-centered classrooms* and learning pathways that fit children's spontaneous development.

BUILDING ON CHILDREN'S CURRENT UNDERSTANDINGS

What number knowledge do children have when they start preschool around the age of 4? As every preschool teacher knows, the answer varies widely from one child to the next. Although this variation does not disappear as children progress through the primary grades, teachers are still responsible for teaching a whole classroom of children, as well as every child within it, and for setting learning objectives for their grade level. It can be a great help to teachers, therefore, to have some idea of the range of understandings they can expect for children at their grade level and, equally important, to be aware of the mistakes, misunderstandings, and partial understandings that are also typical for children at this age level.

To obtain a portrait of these age-level understandings, we can consider the knowledge children typically demonstrate at each age level between ages 4 and 8 when asked the series of oral questions provided on the Number Knowledge test (see Box 6-3). The test is included here for discussion purposes, but teachers who wish to use it to determine their student's current level of understanding can do so.

Before we start, a few features of the Number Knowledge test deserve mention. First, because this instrument has been called a test in the developmental research literature, the name has been preserved in this chapter. However, this instrument differs from school tests in many ways. It is administered individually, and the questions are presented orally. Although right and wrong answers are noted, children's reasoning is equally important, and prompts to elicit this reasoning (e.g., How do you know? How did you figure that out?) are always provided on a subset of items on the test, especially when children's thinking and/or strategy use is not obvious when they are solving the problems posed. For these reasons, the "test" is better thought of as a tool or as a set of questions teachers can use to elicit children's conceptions about number and quantity and to gain a better understanding of the strategies children have available to solve number problems. When used at the beginning (and end) of the school year, it provides a good picture of children's entering (and exit) knowledge. It also provides a model for the ongoing, formative assessments that are conducted throughout the school year in *assessment-centered classrooms.*

Second, as shown in Box 6-3, the test is divided into three levels, with a preliminary (warm-up) question. The numbers associated with each level

BOX 6-3 Number Knowledge Test

Preliminary

Let's see if you can count from 1 to 10. Go ahead.

Level 0 (4-year-old level): Go to Level 1 if 3 or more correct.

1. Can you count these chips and tell me how many there are? (Place 3 counting chips in front of child in a row.)

2a. (Show stacks of chips, 5 vs. 2, same color.) Which pile has more?
2b. (Show stacks of chips, 3 vs. 7, same color.) Which pile has more?

3a. This time I'm going to ask you which pile has less.
   (Show stacks of chips, 2 vs. 6, same color.) Which pile has less?
3b. (Show stacks of chips, 8 vs. 3, same color.) Which pile has less?

4. I'm going to show you some counting chips (Show a line of 3 red and 4 yellow chips in a row, as follows: R Y R Y R Y Y). Count just the yellow chips and tell me how many there are.

5. (Pick up all chips from the previous question.) Here are some more counting chips (show mixed array [not in a row] of 7 yellow and 8 red chips.) Count just the red chips and tell me how many there are.

Level 1 (6-year-old level): Go to Level 2 if 5 or more correct.

1. If you had 4 chocolates and someone gave you 3 more, how many chocolates would you have altogether?

2. What number comes right after 7?

3. What number comes two numbers after 7?

4a. Which is bigger: 5 or 4?
4b. Which is bigger: 7 or 9?

5a. This time, I'm going to ask you about smaller numbers.
   Which is smaller: 8 or 6?
5b. Which is smaller: 5 or 7?

6a. Which number is closer to 5: 6 or 2? (Show visual array after asking the question.)

6b. Which number is closer to 7: 4 or 9? (Show visual array after asking the question.)

7. How much is 2 + 4? (OK to use fingers for counting.)

8. How much is 8 take away 6? (OK to use fingers for counting.)

9a. (Show visual array 8 5 2 6. Ask child to point to and name each numeral.) When you are counting, which of these numbers do you say first?

9b. When you are counting, which of these numbers do you say last?

Level 2 (8-year-old level): Go to Level 3 if 5 or more correct.

1. What number comes 5 numbers after 49?

2. What number comes 4 numbers before 60?

3a. Which is bigger: 69 or 71?

3b. Which is bigger: 32 or 28?

4a. This time I'm going to ask you about smaller numbers. Which is smaller: 27 or 32?

4b. Which is smaller: 51 or 39?

5a. Which number is closer to 21: 25 or 18? (Show visual array after asking the question.)

5b. Which number is closer to 28: 31 or 24? (Show visual array after asking the question.)

6. How many numbers are there in between 2 and 6? (Accept either 3 or 4.)

7. How many numbers are there in between 7 and 9? (Accept either 1 or 2.)

8. (Show visual array 12 54.) How much is 12 + 54?

9. (Show visual array 47 21.) How much is 47 take away 21?

(0, 1, 2) are drawn from the cognitive developmental tradition and are meant to suggest that the knowledge demonstrated at Level 0 is foundational for the knowledge demonstrated at Level 1, which represents a new, higher-order knowledge structure and a major reorganization of children's thought. The knowledge demonstrated at Level 2 represents an even more sophisticated version of this knowledge structure. The ages associated with each level of the test represent the midpoint in the 2-year age period during which this knowledge is typically constructed and demonstrated. Thus, the 4-year-old level captures children's thinking between the ages of 3 and 5 years, and the 6-year-old level captures children's thinking between the ages of 5 and 7 years. Finally, the age norms given in the test are the age ranges within which children in developed societies (drawn primarily from middle-income homes) typically pass that level of the test. But even when the norm is accurate for a group of children, it is important to remember that the knowledge possessed by individual children can differ by as much as 2 years (e.g., from knowledge typical of a 3- and a 5-year-old among the group at age 4). The test thus provides a set of broad developmental milestones for the majority of U.S. children, although the extent to which these levels hold true for children from vastly different sociocultural groups remains to be determined. (Directions for administering and scoring the test are provided in Box 6-4.)

Understandings of 4-Year-Olds

By the age of 4 to 5, most children can accurately count a set of three chips that are placed in front of them (Level 0, #1) and tell how many there are. They typically do so by touching the chips in a systematic fashion, usually proceeding from left to right; by saying "one," "two," "three" as they do so; and by giving the last number said, "three," as the answer. Fewer children (but still the majority) can also solve the more challenging counting problems at this level. They can count a set of four yellow chips that are intermixed with three red chips in a row (Level 0, #4) by counting just the yellow chips in the row or by physically moving the yellow chips into a separate space to make counting easier, and tell you how many there are. They can also count a set of eight red chips that are intermixed with seven white chips in a randomly distributed array (Level 0, #5), using one of the strategies just mentioned. Children who are successful with these items have learned to isolate the partial set to be counted, either mentally or physically, and to count items in this set in a systematic fashion, making sure that they know which chip they counted first and that they touch each chip only once when counting.

Children who are unsuccessful often fail to count systematically. They say the counting words and touch the chips, but these strategies are not

BOX 6-4 Directions for Administering and Scoring the Number Knowledge Test

Administration: The Number Knowledge test is an oral test. It is administered individually, and it requires an oral response. Paper and pencil are not permitted. Use of a follow-up question — "How did you figure that out?"— for Questions 1, 3, and 7 at Level 1 and Questions 1, 2, and 8 at Level 2 provides additional insight into children's reasoning and strategy use.

Scoring: One point is assigned for each item passed at Levels 0, 1, and 2. For all two-part items, both (a) and (b) must be passed to earn a point.

Props Needed: For Level 0: 12 red and 8 yellow counting chips, at least 1/8" thick (other contrasting colors can be substituted). For Levels 1 and 2: visual displays (see samples below). Each image should be at least twice the size of the samples shown here.

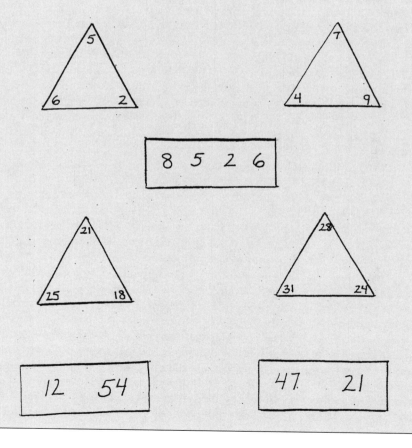

aligned, so they say more words than chips touched or skip some chips while counting, or (particularly on item #5) forget which chip they started with and count one or more chips twice. Children who make these errors are demonstrating some knowledge of counting. They are typically able to say the string of counting words in the correct sequence, and they know what must be done to figure out the answer to the question (e.g., touch the objects present while saying the words). What they do not yet understand is that the chips must be touched in a certain order and manner to coincide precisely with their recitation of the counting words. An even less sophisticated response is given by children who have not yet learned to say the counting words in the correct sequence and who may count the four red chips in item #4 by saying, "one," "two," "five," seven."

By the age of 4, most children can also compare two stacks of chips that differ in height in obvious, perceptually salient ways (Level 0, #2 and #3) and tell which pile has more or less. Children who can do this can solve the same problem when the question is phrased "Which pile is bigger (or smaller)?" and can solve similar problems involving comparisons of length (when the chips are aligned along a table) and of weight (when the chips are placed on a balance scale), provided the differences between the sets are visually obvious. Children who fail these items often look genuinely puzzled by the question, and either sit quietly waiting for further instruction or start to play with the chips by taking the stacks apart and moving the chips about. It appears that the words "more–less" (or "bigger–smaller," "longer–shorter," "heavier–lighter") and the comparison process that underlies them have no meaning for these children, and they are uncertain how to respond.

Although most children of this age can handle these quantity comparisons easily, they fail to achieve more than a chance rate of success when the differences between the sets are not visually obvious, and counting is required to determine which set has more or less. Although 4-year-olds have acquired some fairly sophisticated counting skills (as suggested above), they tend not to use counting to make quantity judgments, instead relying almost exclusively on visual cues in answering this sort of question.

If 4-year-olds can do these things, what might that suggest about what they know? Using this test and other performance assessments, researchers have constructed hypotheses about children's knowledge, which can be summarized as follows. By the age of 4, most children have constructed an initial *counting schema* (i.e., a well-organized knowledge network) that enables them to count verbally from one to five, use the one-to-one correspondence rule, and use the cardinality rule.[4] By the same age, most have also constructed an initial *quantity schema* that gives them an intuitive understanding of relative amount (they can compare two groups of objects that differ in size and tell which has a lot or a little) and of the transformations that change this amount (they know that one group will get bigger or smaller if objects are added to it or taken away). Most preschoolers can also use words to talk about these quantity relations and transformations.[5] As suggested earlier, however, most preschoolers do not use these schemas in a coordinated or integrated fashion.[6] It is as if they were stored in separate files in children's minds.

Understandings of 5-Year-Olds

A major change takes place for children when they can begin to solve problems involving small (single-digit) numbers and quantities without having real objects available to count. For the typical child this happens some time during the kindergarten year, between ages 5 and 6. With this change, children behave as if they are using a "mental counting line" inside their heads and/or their fingers to keep track of how many items they have counted. When asked how many chocolates they would have if they had four and someone gave them three more (Level 1, #1), the majority of children aged 5 to 6 can figure out the answer. The most advanced children will say that they just knew the answer was seven because four and three makes seven. More typically, children in this age range will use their fingers and one of three counting strategies to solve the problem. They may use the count-on strategy (the most sophisticated counting strategy) by starting their count at "four," often holding up four fingers to represent the first set, and then counting on "five," "six," "seven," often putting up three additional fingers to represent the second set. Alternatively, they may use the less sophisticated count-up-from-one strategy by starting their count at "one," putting up four fingers in sequence as they count up to four (to mark off the first set), and then continuing to count up to seven as they raise three additional fingers (to mark off the second set). Children who are unsure of this strategy will use it to put up seven fingers, counting as they do so, and will then use their noses or nods of their heads to count the fingers they have raised and thus determine that the answer to the question is seven.

Although it may take children 1 or 2 years to move from the least to the most sophisticated of these strategies, children using these approaches are in all cases demonstrating their awareness that the counting numbers refer to real-world quantities and can be used, in the absence of countable objects, to solve simple addition problems involving the joining of two sets. Children who respond to the same question by saying "I don't know" or by taking a wild guess and saying "one hundred" appear to lack this awareness. In between these two extremes are children who make a common error and say the answer is "five," thus demonstrating *some* understanding of addition (i.e., that the answer must be larger than four) but an incomplete understanding of how to use counting numbers to find the answer.

Kindergarten children use the same range of strategies to figure out what number comes two numbers after seven (Level 1, #3). Some use the count-on strategy to solve this problem and say, "seven [pause], eight, nine. The answer is nine." Others count up from one to get the same answer. Two common errors that children make on this problem shed light on what successful children appear to know about the number sequence. The first error involves starting at seven, saying two counting words—"seven, eight"—and explaining that eight is the answer. The second error is to say that the answer is "eight and nine" and to repeat this answer when prompted with the question, "Well, which is it—eight or nine?" Both of these answers show an understanding of the *order* of counting words but a weak (or incomplete) understanding of the position of each word in the number sequence and what position entails in terms of quantity. Finally, children who say "I don't know" to this question appear to lack either sufficient knowledge of the counting sequence or sufficient understanding of the term "after" to even attempt the problem.

At this age level, children are also able to tell which of two single-digit *numbers* is bigger or smaller (Level 1, #4 and #5). This is a large leap from the previous (4-year-old) level, at which children could compare quantities that were physically present as long as the differences between them were visible to the naked eye. This new competence implies the presence of a sophisticated set of understandings. Children who are successful with these items appear to know (1) that numbers indicate quantity and therefore (2) that numbers themselves have magnitude, (3) that the word "bigger" or "more" is sensible in this context, (4) that the numbers seven and nine occupy fixed positions in the counting sequence, (5) that seven comes before nine when one is counting up, (6) that numbers that come later in the sequence—are higher up—indicate larger quantities, and (7) that nine is therefore bigger (or more) than seven. Children who lack these understandings typically guess hesitantly. (Note that because children can get the right answer to these questions 50 percent of the time by guessing, they must pass both parts of each question to receive credit for these items on the test.)

Understandings of 6-Year-Olds

The last three items on Level 1 of the test are typically not passed until children are 6 years old, in first grade, and have had the benefit of some formal schooling. The addition problem "How much is two plus four?" and the subtraction problem "How much is eight take away six?" are particularly challenging because they are stated formally, in a decontextualized fashion, and because the quantity to be added or subtracted is larger than three, making it difficult for children to easily count up or back a few numbers to figure out the answer. The most sophisticated response children provide to the addition question is to count on from the largest addend (intuitively using the commutative principle) and to say "four [pause], five, six." Although many children use this strategy, many others start with the first addend in the stated problem (two); they then have the cumbersome job of counting on four more, making sure they count correctly at the same time they are keeping track of how many they have counted. It is not surprising that this strategy results in more errors in counting than does the first strategy.

Although some children make wild guesses in response to these questions, two other examples of a partial understanding are provided more frequently when children say, after pausing to think, that the answer is "five." Although five appears to be a favorite number for many children, regardless of the context, it is also a reasonable answer for both of these questions. If it reflects an awareness that the answer to the addition problem must be bigger than four (the largest addend), and the answer to the subtraction problem must be smaller than eight (the first subtrahend), it suggests a partial understanding of addition and subtraction.

The final item at Level 1 (#9) presents children with a conflicting cue (i.e., four numerals presented in a random order—8, 5, 6, 2) and gives them a chance to show just how solid their understanding of the counting sequence is: "When you're counting, which of these numbers do you say first (and last)?" Children can easily solve this problem if their experience with counting is extensive and their knowledge solid. If this is not the case, they are easily confused and give the first (or last) numeral listed in the display as their answer. As with all other items at this level of the test, the majority (about 60 percent) of children in developed societies acquire the knowledge needed for success sometime between the ages of 5 and 7.

Again we can ask what knowledge undergirds these performances. Scholars hypothesize that, around the age of 5 to 6, as children's knowledge of counting and quantity becomes more elaborate and differentiated it also gradually becomes more integrated, eventually merging in a single knowledge network termed here as a *central conceptual structure for whole number,* or a *mental counting line structure.*[7] This structure is illustrated in Figure 6-1. The figure can be thought of as a blueprint showing the important pieces of knowledge children have acquired (depicted by words or pictures in the figure) and the ways these pieces of knowledge are interrelated (depicted by arrows in the figure).

The top row of the figure illustrates children's knowledge of the counting words and suggests that they can not only say those words in sequence, but also understand the position of each word in the sequence and tell what number comes next, after, or before any number from one to ten. The second row shows that children know they touch each object once and only once when counting. The third row shows that children know the precise

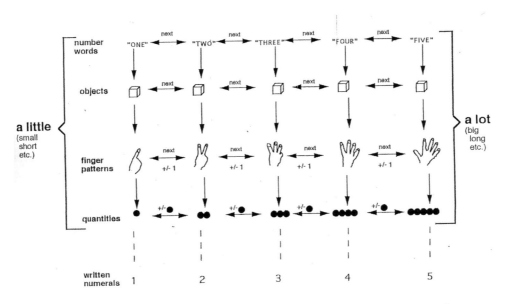

FIGURE 6-1 Mental counting line structure—a blueprint showing the important pieces of knowledge children have acquired (words or pictures) and the ways these pieces are interrelated (arrows).

finger patterns associated with each counting word; as indicated by the horizontal and vertical arrows that connect finger displays to each other and to the counting words, they also know that the finger display contains one more finger each time they count up by one and contains one less finger each time they count down by one. The fourth row suggests that children have acquired similar understandings with respect to objects (and other real-world quantities). The fifth row is connected to all the others with dotted lines to show that children acquire knowledge of the numerals that are associated with each counting word somewhat later, and this knowledge is not a vital component of the central conceptual structure. What is vital, however, are the brackets that contain the first four rows and connect the knowledge indicated within them (i.e., knowledge of counting) to several words used to make quantity judgments. These connectors show that children at this age can use their knowledge of counting to make precise judgments about relative amount.

With this higher-order knowledge structure, children come to realize that a question about addition or subtraction can be answered, in the absence of any concrete set of objects, simply by counting forward or backward along the counting string. They also come to realize that a simple verbal statement about a transformation, such as "I have four things, and then I get three more," has an automatic entailment with regard to quantity. One does not even need to see the objects involved or know anything else about them. These simple understandings actually mark a major revolution in children's understanding, which changes the world of formal mathematics from something that can occur only "out there" to something that can occur inside their own heads and under their own control. As this change takes place, children begin to use their counting skills in a wide range of other contexts. In effect, children realize that counting is something one can do to determine the relative value of two objects on a wide variety of dimensions (e.g., width, height, weight, musical tonality).[8]

Around age 6 to 7, supported by their entry into formal schooling, children typically learn the written numerals (though this is taught to some children earlier). When this new understanding is linked to their central conceptual understanding of number, children understand that the numerals are symbols for number words, both as ordered "counting tags" and as indicators of set size (i.e., numerical cardinality).

Understandings of 7-Year-Olds

Around the age of 7 to 8, in grade 2, children are able to solve the same sorts of problems they could solve previously for single-digit numbers, but for double-digits numbers. When asked what number comes five numbers after forty-nine (Level 2, #1) or four numbers before sixty (Level 2, #2), the majority of second graders can figure out the answer. They do so by counting up from forty-nine (or down from sixty), often subvocally and, less frequently than at the previous stage, using their fingers to keep track of how many they have counted up (or down). When children make errors on these problems, they demonstrate the same sorts of partial understandings that were described earlier. That is, they may show a strong partial understanding of double-digit numbers by making a counting error (e.g., counting the number from which they start as the first number added or subtracted), or a weak understanding by saying, "I don't know. That's a big number. I haven't learned them yet." Between these two extremes are children who know intuitively that the answer to each problem must be in the fifties but are unsure how to count up or down.

At this age level, children can also tell which of two double-digit numbers is bigger or smaller (Level 2, #3 and #4). To do so, they must recognize that numbers in the tens place of each problem (e.g., sixty-nine versus seventy-one) have a much greater value than numbers in the ones place, and thus outweigh the value of even big numbers such as nine that occur in the units position. In short, children who succeed on these items recognize that any number in the seventies is automatically bigger than any number in the sixties "because you have to go through all the numbers in the sixties before you even hit seventy." A common error children make—which reveals an absence of this awareness—is to choose consistently on the basis of the value of the unit digits and to say, for example, that sixty-nine is bigger than seventy-one because nine is larger than one.

Finally, typically toward the end of this age period, children are able to figure out how many whole numbers are in between two and six (Level 2, #7) and in between seven and nine (Level 2, #8). These are complex single-digit problems that require the use of two mental counting lines, one with the numbers involved in the problem and one with the numbers involved in the solution. Children who are successful with the first item often start the solution process by looking fixedly ahead and saying "two" [pause] "six," as if they were looking at an imaginary counting line and marking the numbers two and six on this line. They then proceed to count the numbers in between by nodding their heads; saying "three," "four," "five" (sometimes using their fingers to keep track of the second number line, in which "three" is one, "four" is two, and "five" is three); and providing "three" as the answer. This behavior suggests they are using one mental counting line as an operator to count the numbers on a second mental number line that shows the beginning and end points of the count. By contrast, children who are unsuccessful with this item often give "five" as the answer and explain this answer by saying that five is in between two and six. Although this answer demonstrates an understanding of the order of numbers in the counting sequence, it completely ignores the part of the question that asks, "How many numbers are there in between?" Other children look stunned when this question is posed, as if it is not a meaningful thing to ask, and respond "I don't know," suggesting that they have not yet come to understand that numbers have a fixed position in the counting sequence and can themselves be counted.

Understandings of 8-Year-Olds

The last two items at Level 2 are more complex than the previous items, and they are frequently not solved until children are 8 years old. Children succeed on the problem "How much is 12 plus 54?" most easily by reducing one of these numbers to a benchmark value, carrying the amount that was taken away in their heads, adding the new values, and then adding on the amount that was carried (e.g., "ten and fifty-four is sixty-four; add two; the answer is sixty-six"). Use of this strategy implies a good understanding of the additive composition of double-digit numbers and of the value of using benchmark numbers to make addition and subtraction easier.

Other children solve these problems more laboriously, with less sophisticated strategies. Some count on from fifty-four by ones until they have marked twelve fingers, essentially ignoring the base-ten value of these numbers and treating them as units. Others try to line the numbers up in their heads into the typical vertical format used on worksheets in the classroom. They then add the numbers in the ones column—"two and four is six"—and the numbers in the tens column—"five and one is six"—and, with much mental effort, say that the answer is sixty-six. Children using this solution strategy are essentially performing two single-digit addition operations in succession and are not demonstrating a good understanding of the base-ten features of double-digit numbers. As with all the other test problems, there are always some children who take a wild guess and produce an answer that is not even in the ballpark or who look puzzled and say, more or less forlornly, "I don't know. I haven't learned that yet."

Again we can ask what knowledge underlies these performances. Researchers have suggested that, around the age of 7 to 8 years, children's central conceptual understandings become more elaborate and more differentiated, permitting them to represent two distinct quantitative dimensions, such as tens and ones, in a coordinated fashion. With this new structure, called a *bidimensional central conceptual structure for number,* children are able to understand place value (e.g., represent the tens dimension and the ones dimension in the base-ten number system and work with these dimensions in a coordinated fashion). They are also able to solve problems involving two quantitative dimensions across multiple contexts, including time (hours and minutes), money (dollars and cents), and math class (tens and ones).[9]

ACKNOWLEDGING TEACHERS' CONCEPTIONS AND PARTIAL UNDERSTANDINGS

As illustrated in the foregoing discussion, the questions included on the Number Knowledge test can provide a rich picture of the number understandings, partial understandings, and problem-solving strategies that children in several age groups bring to instruction.

The test can serve another function as well, however, which is worth discussing in the present context: it can provide an opportunity for teachers to examine their own mathematical knowledge and to consider whether any of the partial understandings children demonstrate are ones they share as well. My own understanding of number has grown considerably over the past several years as a result of using this test with hundreds of children, listening to what they say, and examining how their explanations and understandings change as they grow older. Three insights in particular have influenced my teaching.

Insight #1: Math Is Not About Numbers, but About Quantity

It is easy to endorse the myth that math is about numbers because numbers, after all, are everywhere in math. What my work with children has taught me is that math is about quantity, and numbers express those quantities. As the age-level descriptions of children's understandings suggest, numbers acquire meaning for children when they recognize that each number refers to a particular quantity (which may be represented in a variety of different ways) and when they realize that numbers provide a means of describing quantity and quantity transformations more precisely than is possible using everyday language such as "lots," "little," or "more." This realization—that numbers are tools that can be used to describe, predict, and explain real-world quantities and quantity transactions—gives children a tremendous boost in mastering and using the number system. To help children construct this understanding, therefore, it is crucial to introduce numbers to children in the context of the quantities (e.g., objects, pictures of objects) and quantity representations (e.g., dot set patterns, number lines, thermometers, bar graphs, dials) that will give these numbers meaning as quantities.

Insight #2: Counting Words Is the Crucial Link Between the World of Quantity and the World of Formal Symbols

Numbers are expressed in our culture in two quite different ways: orally, as a set of counting words, and graphically, as a set of formal symbols. Because children start using the counting words so early—learning to say "one–two–three" almost as soon as they learn to talk—it may be tempting to think that they should abandon this early form of expression when they start their formal schooling and learn to use the graphic symbol system instead. But children have spent most of their preschool years using the counting words in the context of their real-world exploration and ever so slowly building up a network of meaning for each word. Why should they be deprived of this rich conceptual network when they start their school-based math instruction and be required, instead, to deal with a set of symbols that have no inherent meaning? Mathematics instruction that takes advantage of this prior knowledge and experience—rather than denying it or presenting math as distinct from these everyday experiences—is bound to be more accessible to children.

In my own work, I have found that the key to helping children acquire meanings for symbols is providing opportunities for them to connect the symbol system to the (more familiar) counting words. This is best accomplished when children have previously acquired a solid set of connections between the counting words themselves and the quantities to which they refer. Many third graders are still constructing this latter understanding (e.g., acquiring an awareness of the links between double-digit counting numbers and the quantities to which they refer). Thus, to enable children to use their current understandings to build new ones, it is crucial that they have ample opportunities to use the oral language system to make sense of quantitative problems and that they be introduced to the graphic equivalents of that system in this familiar context.

Insight #3: Acquiring an Understanding of Number Is a Lengthy, Step-by-Step Process

I used to think (or at least I liked to believe) that if I designed an especially elegant lesson that made the concept I was attempting to teach transparent for children, I could produce an "aha" experience and enable the children to grasp a connection that was previously unavailable to them. I now realize that this goal (or wish) is not only unrealistic, but also unobtainable if the concept to be learned is not within reach of the child's current level of understanding. As the earlier age-level descriptions of children's understanding suggest, the acquisition of number knowledge is, by its very nature, a step-by-step process, with each new understanding building systematically and incrementally on previous understandings. Although I still believe in the value of carefully designed, elegant lessons, my goals, while still ambitious, are more limited. Now, I hope that a lesson or series of lessons will enable a child to move up one level at a time in his or her understanding, to deepen and consolidate each new understanding before moving on to the next, and to gradually construct a set of understandings that are more sophisticated and "higher-level" than the ones available at the start. I now recognize that such a process takes time and that each child may move through the process at his or her own pace.

REVISITING QUESTION 2: DEFINING THE KNOWLEDGE THAT SHOULD BE TAUGHT

Now that we have a better idea of the knowledge children have available to work with at several age levels and the manner in which this knowledge is constructed, it is possible to paint a more specific portrait of the knowledge that should be taught in school, at each grade level from preschool through second grade, to ensure that each child acquires a well-developed whole-number sense. As suggested previously, the knowledge taught to each child should be based, at least in part, on his or her existing understandings (Principle 1). However, because teachers are required to teach whole classrooms of children (as well as individuals), they need a set of general learning objectives for each grade level that will be appropriate for the range of children involved. Two sets of objectives are paramount for this purpose. The first is to ensure that all children in the class attain the developmental milestones—the central conceptual structures for whole number—described earlier; the second is to ensure that all children become familiar with the major ways in which number and quantity are represented and talked about so they can recognize and make sense of number problems they encounter across contexts.

The framework presented in the previous section leads to a clear set of learning goals for each grade level from prekindergarten through grade 2 that are within reach of the majority of children at that level and that teachers can use to "teach" the developmental milestones (i.e., to ensure that children who have not yet acquired these central conceptual understandings have an opportunity to do so). Using this framework, it can be suggested that a major goal for the preschool year is to ensure that children acquire a well-developed counting schema and a well-developed quantity schema. A major goal for the kindergarten year is to ensure that children acquire a well-consolidated central conceptual structure for single-digit numbers. A major goal for first grade is to help children link this structure to the formal symbol system and to construct the more elaborated knowledge network this entails. Finally, a major goal for second grade is to help children acquire the bidimensional central conceptual structure for double-digit numbers that underlies a solid understanding of the base-ten system.

These grade-level goals (see Box 6-5) not only specify knowledge networks to be taught at specific grade levels to foster the development of whole-number sense, but also form a "number sense" learning pathway—a sequence of learning objectives teachers can use to individualize instruction for children who are progressing at a rate that is faster or slower than that of the rest of the class. The second body of knowledge to be taught—knowledge of the major ways number and quantity are represented and talked about—can be defined most clearly in the context of the tools developed to teach it, as discussed in the following section.

HOW CAN THIS KNOWLEDGE BE TAUGHT?: THE CASE OF NUMBER WORLDS

During the past two decades, several innovative programs and approaches to mathematics teaching have been developed to teach whole-number concepts and to put the principles of *How People Learn* into curricular action.[10] The program described here—Number Worlds—was designed specifically to teach the knowledge described above. It is also the one with which I am most familiar. As codeveloper of this program, I was involved in its inception in 1988 under the name Rightstart. In the ensuing years, I have continued to participate in the program's development, revising it annually to achieve a better fit with teachers' needs and learning goals, conducting program evaluations to assess its effects on children's learning and achievement, and ultimately producing the expanded set of prekindergarten–grade 2 programs now called Number Worlds.[11] Like the other programs and approaches referred to above, Number Worlds was designed specifically to (1) build on children's existing understandings (learning principle 1), (2) help children construct new knowledge, both factual and conceptual, that is organized so as to facilitate retrieval and application (learning principle 2), and (3) require and teach metacognitive strategies (learning principle 3). Like each of the other programs and approaches referred to above, Number Worlds provides a distinctive way of thinking about mathematics and mathematics teaching.

To maximize opportunities for all children to achieve the knowledge objectives of the Number Worlds program, a set of design principles drawn from the *How People Learn* research base was adopted and used to create each of the more than 200 activities included in the program. The principles that are most relevant to the present discussion are listed below. In the ensuing discussion, each design principle is described more fully and illustrated with one or more activities from the Number Worlds program:

1. Activities should expose children to the major ways number is represented and talked about in developed societies.

2. Activities should provide opportunities to link the "world of quantity" with the "world of counting numbers" and the "world of formal symbols."

3. Activities should provide visual and spatial analogs of number representations that children can actively explore in a hands-on fashion.

4. Activities should be affectively engaging and capture children's imagination so knowledge constructed is embedded not only in their minds, but also in their hopes, fears, and passions.

5. Activities should provide opportunities for children to acquire computational fluency as well as conceptual understanding.

6. Activities should encourage or require the use of metacognitive processes (e.g., problem solving, communication, reasoning) that will facilitate knowledge construction.

Design Principle 1: Exposing Children to Major Forms of Number Representation

Number is represented in our culture in five major ways: through objects, dot set patterns, segments on a line, segments on a scale (or bar graph),

BOX 6-5 Learning Goals for Prekindergarten Through Grade 2

Grade Level	Knowledge Networks That All Children Should Acquire	Examples of Specific Competencies within Each Network[a]
Prekindergarten	Initial counting schema	Can count verbally from one to five (or ten). Can use the one-to one correspondence rule. Knows the cardinal value of each number.
	Initial quantity schema	Understands relative amount (a lot–a little). Knows that an amount gets bigger if objects added and smaller if objects taken away.
Kindergarten	Central conceptual structure for single-digit numbers	Knows the relative value of numbers. Knows that set size increases by one with each counting number up in the sequence.

and segments or points on a dial. Children who are familiar with these forms of representation and the language used to talk about number in these contexts have a much easier time making sense of the number problems they encounter inside and outside of school. The Number Worlds program provides one example of how these forms of representation can be taught. In so doing, it illustrates what a *knowledge-centered classroom* might look like in the area of elementary mathematics.

At each grade level in this program, children explore five different lands. Learning activities developed for each land share a particular form of number representation while simultaneously addressing specific knowledge goals (i.e., the developmental milestones) for each grade level. The five forms of representation and the lands in which they appear are illustrated in Figure 6-2. As the figure suggests, the first land to which children are exposed is Object Land, where numbers are represented by the bundling of several

		Can use the counting numbers alone to solve addition and subtraction problems.
Grade 1	Central conceptual structure linked to formal symbol system	Knows the symbols associated with each number word and the names and symbols for addition, subtraction, and equality.
Grade 2	Central conceptual structure for double-digit numbers	Understands place value (e.g., a two in the ones place means two and a two in the tens place means 20); can solve double-digit addition and subtraction problems mentally.

a Additional, more concrete, examples of the sorts of problems children can solve when they have acquired each knowledge network can be found in the Number Knowledge Test (Box 6-1). See the 4-year-old level items for the prekindergarten network; the 6-year-old level items (1 through 6) for the kindergarten network; the remaining 6-year-old level items for the grade 1 network; and the 8-year-old level items for the grade 2 network.

objects, such as pennies or fingers, into groups. This is the first way in which numbers were represented historically and the first that children learn naturally.[12] In Object Land, children first work with real objects (e.g., "How many crackers will you have left after you eat one? After you eat one more?") and then move on to working with pictures of objects (e.g., "Are there enough hats so that each clown will have one? How many more do you need? How do you know?").

The second land to which children are introduced is Picture Land, where numbers are represented as stylized, semiabstract dot set patterns that are equivalent to mathematical sets. These patterns provide a link between the world of movable objects and the world of abstract symbols. Unlike the real objects they represent, dot set pictures cannot be placed physically in one-to-one correspondence for easier comparison. Instead, a child must make a mental correspondence between two sets, for example by noticing that the

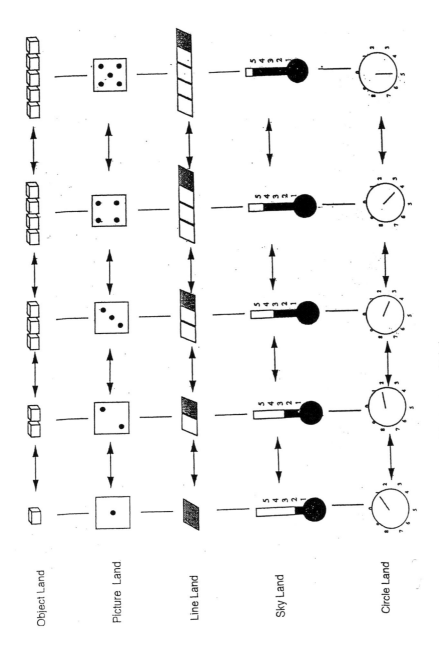

Object Land

Picture Land

Line Land

Sky Land

Circle Land

FIGURE 6-2 The five forms of representation and the lands in which they appear.

pattern for five is the same as that for four, except that the five pattern has one extra dot in the center. As children engage in Picture Land activities (e.g., by playing an assortment of card and dice games similar in format to War, Fish, and Concentration), they gradually come to think of these patterns as forming the same sort of ordered series as do the number words themselves. Numerals, another way of representing numbers, are also part of Picture Land, and are used extensively in the activity props that are provided at all grade levels and, by the children themselves, in the upper levels of the program. Tally marks are used as well in this land to record and compare quantities.

A third way to represent numbers is as segments along a line—for example, the lines that are found on board games such as Chutes and Ladders. The language that is used for numbers in this context is the language of distance. In Line Land, children come to understand (by playing games on a Human Game Mat and on an assortment of smaller number line game boards) that a number such as "four" can refer not only to a particular place on a line, but also to a number of moves *along* the line. One can talk about going four numbers forward from the number four on one's fourth turn. Perhaps the most important transition that children must make as they move from the world of small countable objects to that of abstract numbers and numerical operations is to treat the physical addition or subtraction of objects as equivalent to movement forward or backward along a line. All children eventually make this correspondence; until they do, however, they are unable to move from physical to mental operations with any insight.

Yet another way to represent numbers is with bar graphs and scales, such as thermometers. In Sky Land (a name chosen as a child-friendly substitute for the word "scale," as in "reach for the sky"), this sort of representation is always used in a vertical direction, such that bigger numbers are higher up. These forms of representation make a convenient context for introducing children to the use of numbers as a measure, as a way to keep track of continuous quantity in standard units. Systems for measuring continuous quantity have the same long history as do systems for enumerating discrete objects, and it is important to develop children's intuitions for the properties of the former systems from the outset.[13]

Dials are the final representation of number included in Number Worlds. Sundials and clocks are more sophisticated ways of representing numbers since they incorporate the cyclic quality—a path that repeats itself—possessed by certain real-world dimensions, such as time and the natural rhythm of the seasons. In Circle Land, children develop spatial intuitions (e.g., by playing games on a skating rink configuration that requires them to chart progress within and across revolutions to determine a winner) that become the foundation for understanding many concepts in mathematics dealing with circular motion (e.g., pie charts, time, and number bases).

Although the five forms of number representation have been introduced in a fixed order here, from easiest to most difficult, an important goal of the Number Worlds program is to help children appreciate the equivalence of these forms of representation and of the language used to talk about number in these contexts. To this end, children are encouraged to explore all lands and all number representations early in the school year by beginning with activities in each land that target lower-level knowledge objectives (labeled Level 1 activities) and by proceeding throughout the year to activities in each land that target higher-level knowledge objectives (labeled Level 3 activities). By moving back and forth across lands throughout the year, children gradually come to appreciate, for example, that "nine" is bigger than "seven" by a precise amount and that this difference holds whether these numbers are represented as groups of objects, as positions along a path, or as points on a scale. They also come to appreciate that this difference is the same whether it is talked about as "more" in one context, as "farther along" in another, or as "higher up" in a third. For adults, these various manifestations of the whole-number counting system are easily seen to be equivalent. To very young children, they are quite different, so different that they might appear to be from different "worlds." Helping children construct an organized knowledge network in which these ideas are interconnected (learning principle 2) is thus a major goal of Number Worlds.

Design Principle 2: Providing Opportunities to Link the "World of Quantity" with the "World of Counting Numbers" and the "World of Formal Symbols"

Although every activity created for the Number Worlds program provides opportunities to link the "world of quantity" with the "world of counting numbers" and the "world of formal symbols"—or to link two of these worlds—the three activities described in this section illustrate this principle nicely, at the simplest level. Readers should note that the remaining design principles are also illustrated in these examples, but to preserve the focus are not highlighted in this section.

Plus Pup

Plus Pup is an Object Land activity that is used in both the preschool and kindergarten programs to provide opportunities for children to (1) count a set of objects and identify how many there are, and (2) recognize that when one object is added, the size of the set is increased by one (see Figure 6-3). To play this game, the teacher and children put a certain number of cookies into a lunch bag to bring to school, carefully counting the cookies as they do so, and being sure they remember how many cookies they placed

FIGURE 6-3 Plus Pup—an Object Land activity used to provide opportunities for children to understand addition problems.

inside the bag. Next, the teacher (or a child volunteer) takes a little walk (as if going to school) and encounters Plus Pup along the way (by picking up the Plus Pup card). As the icon on the card suggests, Plus Pup gives the cookie carrier one more cookie. The bag is opened up slightly to receive a real cookie and is then promptly closed. The challenge children confront is this: How many cookies are in the bag now? How can we figure this out?

If the teacher is patient and allows children to explore these questions as genuine problems, a range of solution strategies are often provided as children play and replay the game with different quantities of cookies. The first and most obvious solution children suggest (and implement) is to open the bag, take the cookies out, and count them. This provides opportunities for the teacher to draw children's attention to the quantity transaction that has occurred to produce this amount. For example, the teacher may say, "We have five cookies now. How do we know how many Plus Pup gave us? How can we figure this out?" If no answers are forthcoming, the teacher can prompt the children by asking, "Does anyone remember how many cookies we had at the start?"—thus leading them to make sense of the quantity transaction that has occurred (i.e., the initial amount, the amount added, the end total) by describing the entire process in their own words.

As children replay this game, they gradually come to realize that they can use the counting numbers themselves, with or without their fingers, to solve this sort of problem, and that dumping the cookies out of the bag to count them is unnecessary. When children begin to offer this solution strategy, the teacher can shift the focus of her questions to ask, "Who can predict how many cookies are in the bag now? How do you know?" After predictions and explanations (or proofs) have been offered, the children can be allowed to examine the contents of the bag "to confirm or verify their predictions." Although preschoolers are often unfamiliar with these scientific terms when first introduced, it is not long before they understand the meaning of the terms in this context and use these words themselves, feeling very pleased with the air of sophistication this language bestows on their own mathematical activity. By encouraging problem solving and communication, this activity, like all activities in the program, makes children's thinking visible, and in so doing provides the basis for ongoing assessment that is the hallmark of *assessment-centered classrooms*.

The rationale that was created for this activity is as follows: "In this activity, a giving pup icon is used to give children a meaningful mental image of the addition operation. This image will serve as a conceptual bridge and help children build strong connections between an increase in quantity in the real world and the +1 symbol that describes this increase in the world of formal mathematics" (Object Land: Lesson #7). Although children are not expected to make explicit use of the +1 symbol in either the preschool or kindergarten program, it is available for those who are ready to take advantage of it. To our delight, children who have been exposed to this activity in their preschool or kindergarten year spontaneously remember Plus Pup when they encounter more complex addition problems later on, providing evidence they have indeed internalized the set of connections (among name, icon, and formal symbol) to which they were exposed earlier and are able to use this knowledge network to help them make sense of novel addition problems.

Minus Mouse

Once children have become familiar with Plus Pup and what Plus Pup does, they are introduced to Minus Mouse (see Figure 6-4). The format of

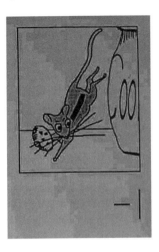

FIGURE 6-4 Minus Mouse—an Object Land activity used to provide opportunities for children to understand subtraction problems.

this activity is identical to that of the former except, of course, that whereas Plus Pup will add one cookie to the bag, Minus Mouse will take one away. The challenge children are asked to deal with in this activity is this: "How many cookies will we have left?" How can we figure this out? The similarly in format between these two activities and the repetition that results proves not to be the deterrent to children that adults might expect. Most young children prefer the comfort of the familiar to the excitement of the novel. Indeed, they appear to thrive on the opportunities this similarity provides for them to anticipate what might happen and, with confidence, make predictions about those outcomes.

Plus Pup Meets Minus Mouse

Once children have become familiar with Minus Mouse and reasonably adept at solving the problems this activity presents for a range of single-digit quantities, the teacher makes the problem more complex by including both Plus Pup and Minus Mouse in the same activity. This time, when the cookie carrier walks to school, he or she draws a card from a face-down pack and either Plus Pup or Minus Mouse will surface. The challenge this time is to interpret the icon with its associated symbol, to determine the action that should be performed (adding one more cookie to the bag or taking one away), and to figure out how to solve the problem of how many cookies are in the bag now and how we can figure this out. Children who have become reasonably competent at counting on (from the initial amount) to solve Plus Pup problems and counting back (from the initial amount) to solve Minus Mouse problems will now have to employ these strategies in a much more flexible fashion. They will also have to pay much closer attention to the meaning of the icon and its associated symbol and what this entails in terms of the quantity transaction to be performed. Both of these challenges pose bigger problems for children than adults might expect; thus, by providing opportunities for children to confront and resolve these challenges, this activity scaffolds the development of whole-number sense.

All three of the above activities can provide multiple opportunities for teachers to assess each child's current level of understanding as reflected in the solutions constructed (or not constructed) for each of the problems posed, the explanations provided, and the strategies employed (e.g., emptying the cookies out of the bag to determine how many or using the counting numbers instead, with or without fingers, to solve the problem). These informal assessments, in turn, can help teachers determine the quantity of cookies that would provide an appropriate starting place for the next round of each activity and the sorts of questions that should be posed to individual children to help them advance their knowledge. By using assessment in this formative fashion—to create learning opportunities that are finely attuned to children's current understandings and that help them construct new knowledge at the next level up—teachers are creating classrooms that are, at one and the same time, *learner-centered*, *knowledge-centered*, and *assessment-centered*.

Design Principle 3: Providing Visual and Spatial Analogs of Number Representations That Children Can Actively Explore in a Hands-On Fashion

Because the central conceptual understandings that the program was designed to teach involve the coordination of spatial and numeric concepts, it was deemed important to provide several opportunities for children to explore the number system in a variety of spatial contexts, to scaffold this coordination. The spatial contexts that were created for the Number Worlds program often take the form of game boards on which number is depicted as a position on a line, scale, or dial and on which quantity is depicted as segments on these line, scale, and dial representations. By using a pawn to represent "self" as player and by moving through these contexts to solve problems posed by the game, children gain a vivid sense of the relationship between movement along a line, scale, or dial and increases and decreases in quantity. This experience is illustrated in the following activities.

The Skating Party Game

This game is played in Circle Land at the kindergarten level. It was designed to help children realize that a dial (or a circular path) is another device for representing quantity, and that the same relationships that apply between numbers and movement on a number line apply also to numbers and movement in this context (see Figure 6-5). In this game, a dial is represented as a circular path. By including 10 segments on this path, numbered 0 to 9, this prop provides opportunities for children to acquire an intuitive understanding of the cyclical nature of the base-ten number system. This understanding is explicitly fostered and built upon in activities children encounter later on, at higher levels of the program. The explicit learning objectives that were developed for the Skating Party game are as follows: (1) identify or compute set size, and associate set size with a position on a dial (i.e., a circular path); (2) associate increasing a quantity with moving around a dial; and (3) compare positions on a dial to identify which have more, less, or the same amount, and use this knowledge to solve a problem.

These objectives are achieved as children engage in game play and respond to questions that are posed by the teacher (or by a child serving as group leader). With four children sharing one game board, children start

FIGURE 6-5 Skating Party game board—a Circle Land activity used to provide a hands-on representation for children to explore the relationship between movement and increases and decreases in quantity.

game play by placing their pawns at the starting gate. They then take turns rolling a die, counting the dots, and moving their pawns that many spaces around the dial. Each time they complete a revolution around the dial, they collect an Award card. At the end of the game, children count and compare their Award cards, and the child with the most cards is the first winner, followed by the child with the second most, who is the second winner, and so on. In one variation of this game, the Award cards collected by each group of four children are computed and compared, and a group winner is declared.

Questions are posed at several points in game play, and the sorts of questions that are put to individual children are most productive if they are finely tuned to each child's current level of understanding (learning principle 1). For example, when all children have their pawns on the board, they can be asked, "Who is farther around? Who has gone the least distance? How much farther do you need to go to win an Award card?" These questions are always followed by "How do you know?" or "How did you figure that out?" Plenty of time needs to be allowed for children to come up with answers that make sense to them and for them to share their answers with each other. When children are counting their Award cards, they can be asked, "How many times did you go around the rink? Who has the most Award cards? How come that child went around the rink more times than this child if everyone had the same number of turns?" The last question is the most challenging of this set, and beginning players often attribute going around the rink more times to skating faster (rather than to rolling a lot of high numbers).

Eventually children will make this connection, and they can be encouraged to do so by being asked to pay close attention to movement around the rink the next time they play. For example, the teacher might say, "Did that child really skate faster? Let's watch next time we play and see." In encouraging children to construct their own answers to the question by reflecting on their own activity, teachers are encouraging the use of metacognitive processes and allowing children to take charge of their own learning (learning principle 3).

In a follow-up activity, the teacher adds another level of complexity to this game by providing an illustrated set of skating cards that show either "+1, You skate well"; "–1, You stumbled"; or "0," blank symbol and image (see Figures 6-6a and 6-6b). In this version of the game, children play as before, but in addition, they draw a skating card from the face-down deck after every turn and follow the instructions on the card to move one space forward or backward around the rink, or to stay where they are. This version of the game provides opportunities for children to meet an additional learning objective—identifying how many there will be if a set is increased or decreased by one (or by two in a challenge activity). This objective, in turn, is met most easily if the teacher scaffolds children's learning by providing opportunities for them to talk about the quantity transactions they are performing. For example, when a child draws a card, the teacher can ask, "Where are you now? What does that card tell you to do? How far around the rink will you be after you do that? Is that closer to the finish line

FIGURE 6-6 An illustrated set of skating cards used in the Circle Land Skating Party game.

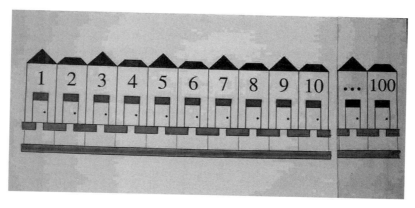

FIGURE 6-7 Neighborhood Number Line game board—used to help children understand the base-ten number system.

or farther away from it? How do you know?" By answering and discussing these questions and by confirming or disconfirming their thoughts and predictions with real actions, children gradually build up a solid intuitive understanding of the links among the world of quantity (in spatial contexts), the world of counting numbers, and the world of formal symbols.

Rosemary's Magic Shoes

This game provides an illustration of a spatial context developed for Line Land in the second-grade program to help children build an understanding of the base-ten number system. The prop itself—the Neighborhood Number Line—comprises 10 blocks of houses, each containing 10 houses that attach with Velcro to create a linear neighborhood of 100 houses that is 15 feet long when fully assembled (see Figure 6-7). This prop is used extensively in the first-grade program as well, to teach several concepts implicit in the 1–100 number sequence. The character created for this game, a professional monster-tracker called Rosemary, has a pair of magic shoes that allows her to leap over 10 houses in a single bound. For Rosemary's shoes to work, however, she first must tell them how many times to jump 10 houses and how many times to walk past 1 house.

To play this game, children take turns picking a number tile that indicates a house where the presence of a monster has been suspected. Using Rosemary's magic shoes, they then move to the house as quickly and efficiently as possible; check for monsters (by drawing a card from a face-down deck that indicates the monsters' presence or absence); and, if indicated, place a sticker on the house to show that it is a "monster-free zone." In later versions of this game, children are required to keep a written record of Rosemary's movements, using the formal symbol system to do so. In all versions of this game, they are required to watch each player carefully to see if the oral directions given (e.g., "Magic shoes, jump over 5 blocks and walk to the eighth house") were followed precisely, to consider whether other ways of getting to the same house (#58) might have been more efficient, and to share their thinking with the class.

With exposure to this game, children gradually come to realize that they can leap over 10 houses (i.e., count up or down by tens) from any number in the sequence, not just from the decade markers (e.g., 10, 20, 30). They also come to realize that they need not always move in a forward direction (e.g., count up) to reach a particular number, that it might be more efficient to move to the closest tens marker and go back a few steps (e.g., jump over 6 blocks and walk back two steps to get to house #58). With these realizations and opportunities to put them into practice, children gain fluency in computing the distance between any two numbers in the 1-100 sequence and in moving fluently from one location (or number) to the next, using benchmark values to do so. They also gain an appreciation of the relative value of numbers in this sequence (e.g., that 92 is a long way away from 9) and can recognize immediately that the sum of 9 + 2 could not possibly be 92, an error that is not uncommon for this age group. The knowledge gains that have just been described—the acquisition of procedural fluency, factual knowledge, and conceptual understanding—appear to be greatly facilitated by the provision of spatial analogs of the number system that children can actively explore in a hands-on fashion (design principle 3 as set forth in this chapter), coupled with opportunities to explain their thinking, to communicate with their peers, and to reflect on their own activity (learning principle 3).

Design Principle 4: Engaging Children's Emotions and Capturing Their Imagination So Knowledge Constructed Is Embedded Not Only in Their Minds, but Also in Their Hopes, Fears, and Passions

Each of the activities described thus far has been engaging for children and has captured their imagination. The one described in this section possibly achieves this purpose to a greater extent than most others. It also provides an example of how the Number Worlds program addresses a major learning goal for first grade: helping children link their central conceptual structure for whole number to the formal symbol system.

FIGURE 6-8 Dragon Quest game board—a Picture Land activity that uses numerals and operation signs to achieve the game's goals.

Dragon Quest

Dragon Quest was developed for Picture Land in the first-grade program (see Figure 6-8). Although the game is played on a line and children can use objects to solve the problems posed by the game, the major representation of number that children must work with in this game to achieve the game's goals are numerals and operation signs. For this reason, this game is classified as a Picture Land activity. Children are introduced to Phase 1 of this activity by being told a story about a fire-breathing dragon that has been terrorizing the village where the children live. The children playing the game are heroes who have been chosen to seek out the dragon and put out his fire. To extinguish this dragon's fire (as opposed to that of other, more powerful dragons they will encounter in later phases), a hero will need at least 10 pails of water. If a hero enters the dragon's area with less than 10 pails of water, he or she will become the dragon's prisoner and can be rescued only by one of the other players.

To play the game, children take turns rolling a die and moving their playing piece along the colored game board. If they land on a well pile (indicated by a star), they can pick a card from the face-down deck of cards that illustrate, with images and symbols (e.g., + 4), a certain number of pails of water. Children are encouraged to add up their pails of water as they receive them and are allowed to use a variety of strategies to do so, ranging from mental math (which is encouraged) to the use of tokens to keep track of the quantity accumulated. The first child to reach the dragon's lair with at least 10 pails of water can put out the dragon's fire and free any teammates who have become prisoners.

Needless to say, this game is successful in capturing children's imagination and inducing them to engage in the increasing series of challenges posed by later versions. As they do so, most children acquire increasingly sophisticated number competencies. For example, they become capable of performing a series of successive addition and subtraction operations in their heads when spill cards (e.g., – 4) are added to the set of cards in the well pile. When they encounter more-powerful dragons whose fire can be extinguished only with 20 buckets of water, they become capable of performing these operations with larger sets of numbers and with higher numbers. When they are required to submit formal proof to the mayor of the village that they have amassed sufficient pails of water to put out the dragon's fire before they are allowed to do so, they become capable of writing a series of formal expressions to record the number of pails received and spilled over the course of the game. In such contexts, children have ample opportunity to use the formal symbol system in increasingly efficient ways to make sense of quantitative problems they encounter in the course of their own activity.

Design Principle 5: Providing Opportunities for Children to Acquire Computational Fluency As Well As Conceptual Understanding

Although opportunities to acquire computational fluency as well as conceptual understanding are built into every Number Worlds activity, computational fluency is given special attention in the activities developed for the Warm-Up period of each lesson. In the prekindergarten and kindergarten programs, these activities typically take the form of count-up and count-down games that are played in each land, with a prop appropriate for that land. This makes it possible for children to acquire fluency in counting and, at the same time, to acquire a conceptual understanding of the changes in quantity that are associated with each successive number up (or down) in the counting sequence. This is illustrated in an activity, developed for Sky Land, that is always introduced after children have become reasonably fluent in the count-up activity that uses the same prop.

Sky Land Blastoff

In this activity, children view a large, specially designed thermometer with a moveable red ribbon that is set to 5 (or 10, 15, or 20, depending on children's competence) (see Figure 6-9). Children pretend to be on a rocket ship and count down while the teacher (or a child volunteer) moves the red ribbon on the thermometer to correspond with each number counted. When the counting reaches "1," all the children jump up and call "Blastoff!" The sequence of counting is repeated if a counting mistake is made or if anyone jumps up too soon or too late. The rationale that motivated this activity is as follows: "Seeing the level of red liquid in a thermometer drop while counting down will give children a good foundation for subtraction by allowing

FIGURE 6-9 *A specially designed thermometer for the Sky Land Blastoff activity—to provide an understanding of the changes in quantity associated with each successive number (up) or down in the counting sequence.*

them to see that a quantity decreases in scale height with each successive number down in the sequence. This will also lay a foundation for measurement" (Sky Land: Activity #2).

This activity is repeated frequently over the course of the school year, with the starting point being adjusted over time to accommodate children's growing ability. Children benefit immensely from opportunities to perform (or lead) the count-down themselves and/or to move the thermometer ribbon while another child (or the rest of the class) does the counting. When children become reasonably fluent in basic counting and in serial counting (i.e., children take turns saying the next number down), the teacher adds a level of complexity by asking them to predict where the ribbon will be if it is on 12, for example, and they count down (or up) two numbers, or if it is on 12 and the temperature drops (or rises) by 2 degrees. Another form of complexity is added over the course of the school year when children are asked to demonstrate another way (e.g., finger displays, position on a human game mat) to represent the quantity depicted on the thermometer and the way this quantity changes as they count down. By systematically increasing the complexity of these activities, teachers expose children to a learning path that is finely attuned to their growing understanding (learning principle 1) and that allows them to gradually construct an important network of conceptual and procedural knowledge (learning principle 2).

In the programs for first and second grade, higher-level computation skills (e.g., fluent use of strategies and procedures to solve mental arithmetic problems) are fostered in the Warm-Up activities. In Guess My Number, for example, the teacher or a child picks a number card and, keeping it hidden, generates two clues that the rest of the class can use to guess the number (e.g., it is bigger than 25 and smaller than 29). Guessers are allowed to ask one question, if needed, to refine their prediction (e.g., "Is it an odd number?" "Is it closer to 25 or to 29?").

Generating good clues is, of course, more difficult than solving the problem because doing so requires a refined sense of the neighborhood of numbers surrounding the target number, as well as their relationship to this number. In spite of the challenges involved, children derive sufficient enjoyment from this activity to persevere through the early stages and to acquire a more refined number sense, as well as greater computational fluency, in the process. In one lovely example, a first-grade student provided the following clues for the number he had drawn: "It is bigger than 8 and it is 1 more than 90 smaller than 100." The children in the class were stymied by these clues until the teacher unwittingly exclaimed, "Oh, I see, you're using the neighborhood number line," at which point all children followed suit, counted down 9 blocks of houses, and arrived at a correct prediction, "9."

Design Principle 6: Encouraging the Use of Metacognitive Processes (e.g., Problem Solving, Communication, Reasoning) That Will Facilitate Knowledge Construction

In addition to opportunities for problem solving, communication, and reasoning that are built into the activities themselves (as illustrated in the examples provided in this chapter), three additional supports for these processes are included in the Number Worlds program. The first is a set of question cards developed for specific stages of each small-group game. The questions (e.g., "How many buckets of water do you have now?") were designed to draw children's attention to the quantity displays they create during game play (e.g., buckets of water collected and spilled) and the changes in quantity they enact (e.g., collecting four more buckets), and to prompt them to think about these quantities and describe them, performing any computations necessary to answer the question. Follow-up questions that are also included (e.g., "How did you figure that out?") prompt children to reflect on their own reasoning and to put it into words, using the language of mathematics to do so. Although the question cards are typically used by the teacher (or a teacher's aide) at first, children can gradually take over this function and, in the process, take greater control over their own learning (learning principle 3). This transition is facilitated by giving one child in the group the official role of Question Poser each time the game is played. By giving children important roles in the learning process (e.g., Question-Poser, Facilitator, Discussion Leader, Reporter) and by allowing them to be teachers as well as learners, teachers can create the sort of *community-centered classroom* that is described in Chapters 1 and 5.

The second support is a set of dialogue prompts included in the teacher's guide, which provides a more general set of questions (e.g., "Who has gone the farthest? How do you know?") than those provided with the game. Although both sets of questions are highly useful in prompting children to use metacognitive processes to make mathematical sense of their own activity, they provide no guidance on how a teacher should respond to the answers children provide. Scaffolding good math talk is still a significant challenge for most primary and elementary teachers. Having a better understanding of the sorts of answers children give at different age levels, as well as increased opportunities to listen to children explain their thinking, can be helpful in building the expertise and experience needed for the exceedingly difficult task of constructing follow-up questions for children's answers that will push their mathematical thinking to higher levels.

The third support for metacognitive processes that is built into the Number Worlds program is a Wrap-Up period that is provided at the end of each lesson. In Wrap-Up, the child who has been assigned the role of Reporter for the small-group problem-solving portion of the lesson (e.g., game play) describes the mathematical activity his or her group did that day and what they learned. The Reporter then takes questions from the rest of the class, and any member of the Reporter's team can assist in providing answers. It is during this portion of the lesson that the most significant learning occurs because children have an opportunity to reflect on aspects of the number system they may have noticed during game play, explain these concepts to their peers, and acquire a more explicit understanding of the concepts in the process. Over time, Wrap-Up comes to occupy as much time in the math lesson as all the preceding activities (i.e., the Warm-Up activities and small-group problem-solving activities) put together.

With practice in using this format, teachers become increasingly skilled at asking good questions to get the conversation going and, immediately thereafter, at taking a back seat in the discussion so that children have ample opportunity to provide the richest answers they are capable of generating at that point in time. (Some wonderful examples of skilled teachers asking good questions in elementary mathematics classrooms are available in the video and CD-ROM products of the Institute for Learning [www.institutefor learning.org].) This takes patience, a willingness to turn control of the discussion over to the children, and faith that they have something important to say. Even at the kindergarten level, children appear to be better equipped to rise to this challenge than many teachers, who, having been taught that they should assume the leadership role in the class, often feel that they should dominate the discussion. Teachers who can rise to this challenge have found that their faith is amply rewarded by the sophistication of the explanations children provide, even at the kindergarten level; by the opportunities this occasion provides for assessing children's growth and current understandings; and by the learning and achievement gains children demonstrate on standard measures.

WHAT SORTS OF LEARNING DOES THIS APPROACH MAKE POSSIBLE?

The Number Worlds program was developed to address three major learning goals: to enable children to acquire (1) conceptual knowledge of number as well as procedural knowledge (e.g., computational fluency); (2) number sense (e.g., an ability to use benchmark values, an ability to solve problems in a range of contexts); and (3) an interest in and positive attitude toward mathematics. Program evaluation for the most part has focused on assessing the extent to which children who have been exposed to the program have been able to demonstrate gains on any of these fronts. The results of several evaluation studies are summarized below.

The Number Worlds program has now been tried in several different communities in Canada and in the United States. For research purposes, the groups of students followed have always been drawn from schools serving low-income, predominantly inner-city communities. This decision was based on the assumption that if the program works for children known to be at risk for school failure, there is a good chance that it will work as well, or even better, for those from more affluent communities. Several different forms of evaluation have been conducted.

In the first form of evaluation, children who had participated in the kindergarten level of the program (formerly called Rightstart) were compared with matched controls who had taken part in a math readiness program of a different sort. On tests of mathematical knowledge, on a set of more general developmental measures, and on a set of experimental measures of learning potential, children who had participated in the Number Worlds program consistently outperformed those in the control groups (see Box 6-1 for findings from one of these studies).[14] In a second type of evaluation, children who had taken part in the kindergarten level of the program (and who had graduated into a variety of more traditional first-grade classrooms) were followed up 1 year later and evaluated on an assortment of mathematical and scientific tests, using a double-blind procedure. Once again, those who had participated in the Number Worlds program in kindergarten were found to be superior on virtually all measures, including teacher evaluations of "general number sense" (see Box 6-2).[15]

The expansion of the Number Worlds program to include curricula for first and second grades permitted a third form of evaluation—a longitudinal study in which children were tracked over a 3-year period. At the beginning of the study and the end of each year, children who had participated in the Number Worlds program were compared with two other groups: (1) a second low-socioeconomic-status group that had originally been tested as having superior achievement in mathematics, and (2) a mixed-socioeconomic-status (largely middle-class) group that had also demonstrated a higher level of performance at the outset and attended an acclaimed magnet school with a special mathematics coordinator and an enriched mathematics program. These three groups are represented in the figure of Box 6-6, and the differences between the magnet school students and the students in the low-socioeconomic-status groups can be seen in the different start positions of the lines on the graph. Over the course of this study, which extended from the beginning of kindergarten to the end of second grade, children who had taken part in the Number Worlds program caught up with, and gradually outstripped, the magnet school group on the major measure used throughout this study—the Number Knowledge test (see Box 6-6). On this measure, as well as on a variety of other mathematics tests (e.g., measures of number sense), the Number Worlds group outperformed the second low-socioeconomic-status group from the end of kindergarten onward. On tests of procedural knowledge administered at the end of first grade, they also compared very favorably with groups from China and Japan that were tested on the same measures.[16]

These findings provide clear evidence that a program based on the principles of *How People Learn* (i.e., the Number Worlds program) works for the population of children most in need of effective school-based instruction—those living in poverty. In a variety of studies, the program enabled children from diverse cultural backgrounds to start their formal learning of arithmetic on an equal footing with their more-advantaged peers. It also enabled them to keep pace with their more-advantaged peers (and even outperform them on some measures) as they progressed through the first few years of formal schooling and to acquire the higher-level mathematics concepts that are central for continued progress in this area. In addition to the mathematics learning and achievement demonstrated in these studies, two other findings are worthy of note: both teachers and children who have used the Number Worlds program consistently report a positive attitude toward the teaching and learning of math. For teachers, this often represents a dramatic change in attitude. Math is now seen as fun, as well as useful, and both teachers and children are eager to do more of it.

BOX 6-6 Comparing Number Worlds and Control Group Outcomes

As the figure below shows, the magnet school group began kindergarten with substantially higher scores on the Number Knowledge test than those of children in the Number Worlds and control groups. The gap indicated a developmental lag that exceeded one year, and for many children in the Number Worlds group was closer to 2 years. By the end of the kindergarten year, however, the Number Worlds children had narrowed this gap to a small fraction of its initial size. By the end of the second grade, the Number Worlds children actually outperformed the magnet school group. In contrast, the initial gap between the control group and the magnet school group did not narrow over time. The control group children did make steady progress over the 3 years; however, they were never able to catch up.

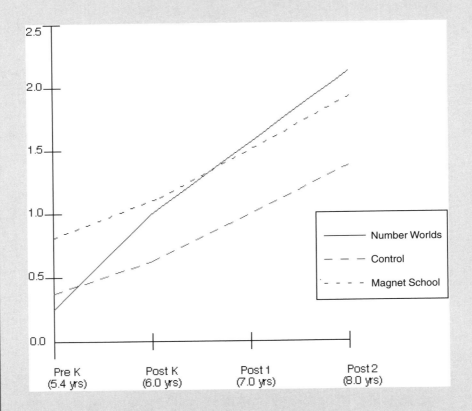

Mean developmental level scores on Number Knowledge test at four time periods.

SUMMARY AND CONCLUSION

It was suggested at the beginning of this chapter that the teaching of whole-number concepts could be improved if each math teacher asked three questions on a regular basis: (1) Where am I now? (in terms of the knowledge children in their classrooms have available to build upon); (2) Where do I want to go? (in terms of the knowledge they want all children in their classrooms to acquire during the school year); and (3) What is the best way to get there? (in terms of the learning opportunities they will provide to enable all children in their class to reach the chosen objectives). The challenges these questions pose for primary and elementary teachers who have not been exposed in their professional training to the knowledge base needed to construct good answers were also acknowledged. Exposing teachers to this knowledge base is a major goal of the present volume. In this chapter, I have attempted to show how the three learning principles that lie at the heart of this knowledge base—and that are closely linked to the three questions posed above—can be used to improve the teaching and learning of whole numbers.

To illustrate learning Principle 1 (eliciting and building upon student knowledge), I have drawn from the cognitive developmental literature and described the number knowledge children typically demonstrate at each age level between ages 4 and 8 when asked a series of questions on an assessment tool—the Number Knowledge Test—that was created to elicit this knowledge. To address learning Principle 2 (building learning paths and networks of knowledge), I have again used the cognitive developmental literature to identify knowledge networks that lie at the heart of number sense (and that should be taught) and to suggest learning paths that are consistent with the goals for mathematics education provided in the NCTM standards.[17] To illustrate learning Principle 3 (building resourceful, self-regulating mathematics thinkers and problem solvers), I have drawn from a mathematics program called Number Worlds that was specifically developed to teach the knowledge networks identified for Principle 2 and that relied heavily on the findings of *How People Learn* to achieve this goal. Other programs that have also been developed to teach number sense and to put the principles of *How People Learn* into action have been noted in this chapter, and teachers are encouraged to explore these resources to obtain a richer picture of how Principle 3 can be realized in mathematics classrooms.

In closing, I would like to acknowledge that it is not an easy task to develop a practice that embodies the three learning principles outlined herein. Doing so requires continuous effort over a long period of time, and even when this task has been accomplished, teaching in the manner described in this chapter is hard work. Teachers can take comfort in the fact the these efforts will pay off in terms of children's mathematics learning and achievement; in the positive attitude toward mathematics that students will acquire and carry with them throughout their lives; and in the sense of accomplishment a teacher can derive from the fruits of these efforts. The well-deserved professional pride that this can engender, as well as the accomplishments of children themselves, will provide ample rewards for these efforts.

ACKNOWLEDGMENTS

The development of the Number Worlds program and the research that is described in this chapter were made possible by the generous support of the James S. McDonnell Foundation. The author gratefully acknowledges this support, as well as the contributions of all the teachers and children who have used the program in various stages of development, and who have helped shape its final form.

NOTES

1. Referenced in Griffin and Case, 1997.
2. Griffin and Case, 1996a.
3. Ibid.
4. Gelman, 1978.
5. Starkey, 1992.
6. Siegler and Robinson, 1982.
7. Case and Griffin, 1990; Griffin et al., 1994.
8. Griffin et al., 1995.
9. Griffin et al., 1992.
10. Ball, 1993; Carpenter and Fennema, 1992; Cobb et al., 1988; Fuson, 1997; Hiebert, 1997; Lampert, 1986; Schifter and Fosnot, 1993.
11. Griffin and Case, 1996b; Griffin, 1997, 1998, 2000.
12. Schmandt-Basserat, 1978.
13. Damerow et al., 1995.
14. Griffin et al., 1994, 1995.
15. Also see Griffin et al., 1994; Griffin and Case, 1996a.
16. Griffin and Case, 1997.
17. National Council of Teachers of Mathematics, 2000.

REFERENCES

Ball, D.L. (1993). With an eye on the mathematical horizon: Dilemmas of teaching elementary school mathematics. *Elementary School Journal, 93*(4), 373-397.
Carpenter, T., and Fennema, E. (1992). Cognitively guided instruction: Building on the knowledge of students and teachers. *International Journal of Research in Education, 17*(5), 457-470.

Case, R., and Griffin, S. (1990). Child cognitive development: The role of central conceptual structures in the development of scientific and social thought. In E.A. Hauert (Ed.), *Developmental psychology: Cognitive, perceptuo-motor, and neurological perspectives* (pp. 193-230). North-Holland, The Netherlands: Elsevier.

Cobb, P., Yackel, E., and Wood, T. (1988). A constructivist approach to second grade mathematics. In E. von Glasserfeld (Ed.), *Constructivism in mathematics education.* Dordecht, The Netherlands: D. Reidel.

Dehaene, S., and Cohen, L. (1995). Towards an anatomical and functional model of number processing. *Mathematical Cognition, 1,* 83-120.

Damerow, P., Englund, R.K., and Nissen, H.J. (1995). The first representations of number and the development of the number concept. In R. Damerow (Ed.), *Abstraction and representation: Essays on the cultural evolution of thinking* (pp. 275-297). Book Series: Boston studies in the philosophy of science, vol. 175. Dordrecht, The Netherlands: Kluwer Academic.

Fuson, K. (1997). Snapshots across two years in the life of an urban Latino classroom. In J. Hiebert (Ed.), *Making sense: Teaching and learning mathematics with understanding.* Portsmouth, NH: Heinemann.

Gelman, R. (1978). Children's counting: What does and does not develop. In R.S. Siegler (Ed.), *Children's thinking: What develops* (pp. 213-242). Mahwah, NJ: Lawrence Erlbaum Associates.

Griffin, S. (1997). *Number worlds: Grade one level.* Durham, NH: Number Worlds Alliance.

Griffin, S. (1998). *Number worlds: Grade two level.* Durham, NH: Number Worlds Alliance.

Griffin, S. (2000). *Number worlds: Preschool level.* Durham, NH: Number Worlds Alliance.

Griffin, S. (in press). Evaluation of a program to teach number sense to children at risk for school failure. *Journal for Research in Mathematics Education.*

Griffin, S., and Case, R. (1996a). Evaluating the breadth and depth of training effects when central conceptual structures are taught. *Society for Research in Child Development Monographs, 59,* 90-113.

Griffin, S., and Case, R. (1996b). *Number worlds: Kindergarten level.* Durham, NH: Number Worlds Alliance.

Griffin, S., and Case, R. (1997). Re-thinking the primary school math curriculum: An approach based on cognitive science. *Issues in Education, 3*(1), 1-49.

Griffin, S., Case, R., and Sandieson, R. (1992). Synchrony and asynchrony in the acquisition of children's everyday mathematical knowledge. In R. Case (Ed.), *The mind's staircase: Exploring the conceptual underpinnings of children's thought and knowledge* (pp. 75-97). Mahwah, NJ: Lawrence Erlbaum Associates.

Griffin, S., Case, R., and Siegler, R. (1994). Rightstart: Providing the central conceptual prerequisites for first formal learning of arithmetic to students at-risk for school failure. In K. McGilly (Ed.), *Classroom lessons: Integrating cognitive theory and classroom practice* (pp. 24-49). Cambridge, MA: Bradford Books MIT Press.

Griffin, S., Case, R., and Capodilupo, A. (1995). Teaching for understanding: The importance of central conceptual structures in the elementary mathematics curriculum. In A. McKeough, I. Lupert, and A. Marini (Eds.), *Teaching for transfer: Fostering generalization in learning* (pp. 121-151). Mahwah, NJ: Lawrence Erlbaum Associates.

Hiebert, J, (1997). *Making sense: Teaching and learning mathematics with understanding.* Portsmouth, NH: Heinemann.

Lampert, M. (1986). Knowing, doing, and teaching multiplication. *Cognition and Instruction 3*(4), 305-342.

National Council of Teachers of Mathematics. (2000). *Principles and standards for school mathematics.* Reston, VA: National Council of Teachers of Mathematics.

Schifter, D., and Fosnot, C. (1993). *Reconstructing mathematics education.* New York: Teachers College Press.

Schmandt-Basserat, D. (1978). The earliest precursor of writing. *Scientific American, 238*(June), 40-49.

Siegler, R.S., and Robinson, M. (1982). The development of numerical understanding. In H.W. Reese and R. Kail (Eds.), *Advances in child development and behavior.* New York: Academic Press.

Starkey, P. (1992). The early development of numerical reasoning. *Cognition and Instruction, 43,* 93-126.

7

Pipes, Tubes, and Beakers: New Approaches to Teaching the Rational-Number System

Joan Moss

© 1977 United Features Syndicate, Inc.

PEANUTS reprinted by permission of United Feature Syndicate, Inc.

Poor Sally. Her anger and frustration with fractions are palpable. And they no doubt reflect the feelings and experiences of many students. As mathematics education researchers and teachers can attest, students are often vocal in their expression of dislike of fractions and other representations of rational numbers (percents and decimals). In fact, the rational-number system poses problems not only for youngsters, but for many adults as well.[1] In a recent study, masters students enrolled in an elementary teacher-training program were interviewed to determine their knowledge and understanding of basic rational-number concepts. While some students were confident and produced correct answers and explanations, the majority had difficulty with the topic. On attempting to perform an operation involving fractions, one student, whose sentiments were echoed by many, remarked, "Oh fractions! I know there are lots of rules but I can't remember any of them and I never understood them to start with."[2]

We know from extensive research that many people—adults, students, even teachers—find the rational-number system to be very difficult.[3] Introduced in early elementary school, this number system requires that students reformulate their concept of number in a major way. They must go beyond whole-number ideas, in which a number expresses a fixed quantity, to understand numbers that are expressed in relationship to other numbers. These new proportional relationships are grounded in multiplicative reasoning that is quite different from the additive reasoning that characterizes whole numbers (see Box 7-1).[4] While some students make the transition smoothly, the majority, like Sally, become frustrated and disenchanted with mathematics.[5] Why is this transition so problematic?

A cursory look at some typical student misunderstandings illuminates the kinds of problems students have with rational numbers. The culprit appears to be the continued use of whole-number reasoning in situations where it does not apply. When asked which number is larger, 0.059 or 0.2, a majority of middle school students assert that 0.059 is bigger, arguing that the number 59 is bigger than the number 2.[6] Similarly, faulty whole-number reasoning causes students to maintain, for example, that the fraction 1/8 is larger than 1/6 because, as they say, "8 is a bigger number than 6."[7] Not surprisingly, students struggle with calculations as well. When asked to find the sum of 1/2 and 1/3, the majority of fourth and sixth graders give the answer 2/5. Even after a number of years working with fractions, some eighth graders make the same error, illustrating that they still mistakenly count the numerator and denominator as separate numbers to find a sum.[8] Clearly whole-number reasoning is very resilient.

Decimal operations are also challenging.[9] In a recent survey, researchers found that 68 percent of sixth graders and 51 percent of fifth and seventh graders asserted that the answer to the addition problem 4 + .3 was .7.[10] This example also illustrates that students often treat decimal numbers as whole numbers and, as in this case, do not recognize that the sum they propose as a solution to the problem is smaller than one of the addends.

The introduction of rational numbers constitutes a major stumbling block in children's mathematical development.[11] It marks the time when many students face the new and disheartening realization that they no longer understand what is going on in their mathematics classes.[12] This failure is a cause for concern. Rational-number concepts underpin many topics in advanced mathematics and carry significant academic consequences.[13] Students cannot succeed in algebra if they do not understand rational numbers. But rational numbers also pervade our daily lives.[14] We need to be able to understand them to follow recipes, calculate discounts and miles per gallon, exchange money, assess the most economical size of products, read maps, interpret scale drawings, prepare budgets, invest our savings, read financial statements, and examine campaign promises. Thus we need to be able to

BOX 7-1 Additive and Multiplicative Reasoning

Lamon,[15] whose work on proportional reasoning and rational number has made a great contribution to our understanding of students' learning, elucidates the distinction between relative and absolute reasoning. She asks the learner to consider the growth of two fictitious snakes: String Bean, who is 4 feet long when the story begins, and Slim, who is 5 feet long. She tells us that after 5 years, both snakes have grown. String Bean has grown from 4 to 7 feet, and Slim has grown from 5 to 8 feet (see the figure below). She asks us to compare the growth of these two snakes and to answer the question, "Who grew more?"

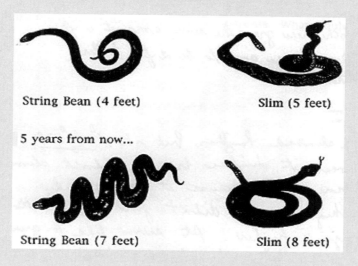

String Bean (4 feet)   Slim (5 feet)

5 years from now...

String Bean (7 feet)   Slim (8 feet)

Lamon suggests that there are two answers. First, if we consider absolute growth, both snakes grew 3 feet, so both grew the same amount. The second answer deals with relative growth; from this perspective, String Bean grew the most because he grew 3/4 of his length, while Slim grew only 3/5 of his length. If we compare the two fractions, 3/4 is greater than 3/5, and so we conclude that String Bean has grown proportionally more than Slim.

Lamon asks us to note that while the first answer, about the *absolute* difference, involves addition, the second answer, about the *relative* difference, is solved through multiplication. In this way she shows that absolute thinking is *additive*, while relative thinking is *multiplicative*.

understand rational numbers not only for academic success, but also in our lives as family members, workers, and citizens.

Do the principles of learning highlighted in this book help illuminate the widespread problems observed as students grapple with rational number? Can they point to more effective approaches to teaching rational number? We believe the answer to both these questions is "yes." In the first section below we consider each of the three principles of *How Students Learn*, beginning with principle 2—the organization of a knowledge network that emphasizes core concepts, procedural knowledge, and their connections. We then turn to principle 1—engaging student preconceptions and building on existing understandings. Finally we consider metacognitive instruction as emphasized in principle 3.

The second section focuses on instruction in rational number. It begins with a description of frequently used instructional approaches and the ways in which they diverge from the above three principles. We then describe an experimental approach to teaching rational number that has proven to be successful in helping students in fourth, fifth, and sixth grades understand the interconnections of the number system and become adept at moving among and operating with the various representations of rational number. Through a description of lessons in which the students engaged and protocols taken from the research classrooms, we set out the salient features of the instructional approach that played a role in shaping a learning-centered classroom environment. We illustrate how in this environment, a focus on the interconnections among decimals, fractions, and percents fosters students' ability to make informed decisions on how to operate effectively with rational numbers. We also provide emerging evidence of the effectiveness of the instructional approach. The intent is not to promote our particular curriculum, but rather to illustrate the ways in which it incorporates the principles of *How People Learn*, and the observed changes in student understanding and competence with rational numbers that result.

RATIONAL-NUMBER LEARNING AND THE PRINCIPLES OF *HOW PEOPLE LEARN*

The Knowledge Network: New Concepts of Numbers and New Applications (Principle 2)

What are the core ideas that define the domain of rational numbers? What are the new understandings that students will have to construct? How does a beginning student come to understand rational numbers?

Let us look through the eyes of a young student who is just beginning to learn about rational number. Until this point, all of her formal instruction in arithmetic has centered on learning the whole-number system. If her learning has gone well, she can solve arithmetic problems competently and easily makes connections between the mathematics she is learning and experiences of her daily life. But in this next phase of her learning, the introduction of rational number, there will be many new and intertwined concepts, new facts, new symbols that she will have to learn and understand—a new knowledge network, if you will. Because much of this new learning is based on multiplicative instead of whole-number relations, acquiring an understanding of this new knowledge network may be challenging, despite her success thus far in mathematics. As with whole-number arithmetic, this domain connects to everyday life. But unlike whole numbers, in which the operations for the most part appear straightforward, the operations involved in the learning of rational numbers may appear to be less intuitive, at odds with earlier understandings (e.g., that multiplication always makes things bigger), and hence more difficult to learn.

New Symbols, New Meanings, New Representations

One of the first challenges facing our young student is that a particular rational number can take many forms. Until now her experience with symbols and their referents has been much simpler. A number—for example, four—is represented exclusively by one numeral, 4. Now the student will need to learn that a rational number can be expressed in different ways—as a decimal, fraction, and percent. To further complicate matters, she will have to learn that a rational-number quantity can be represented by an infinite number of equivalent common and decimal fractions. Thus a rational number such as one-fourth can be written as 1/4, 2/8, 3/12, 4/16, 0.25, 0.250, and so on.

Not only does the learning of rational number entail the mastery of these forms and of the new symbol systems that are implied, but the learner is also required to move among these various forms flexibly and efficiently.[16] Unfortunately, this flow between representations does not come easily.[17] In fact, even mature students are often challenged when they try to understand the relations among the representations.[18] To illustrate how difficult translating between fractions and decimals can be, I offer two examples taken from our research.

In a recent series of studies, we interviewed fourth, sixth, and eighth graders on a number of items that probed for rational-number understanding. One of the questions we asked was how the students would express the quantity 1/8 as a decimal. This question proved to be very challenging for many, and although the students' ability increased with age and experience, more than half of the sixth and eighth graders we surveyed asserted that as a decimal, 1/8 would be 0.8 (rather than the correct answer, 0.125).

In the next example, an excerpt taken from an interview conducted as part of a pretest, Wyatt, a traditionally trained fifth-grade student, discussed ordering a series of rational numbers presented to him in mixed representations.

Interviewer   Here are 3 numbers: 2/3, 0.5, and 3/4. Could you please put these numbers in order from smallest to largest?

Wyatt   Well, to start with, I think that the decimal 0.5 is bigger than the fractions because it's a decimal, so it's just bigger, because fractions are really small things.

The response that 1/8 would equal 0.8 should be familiar to many who have taught decimals and fractions. As research points out, students have a difficult time understanding the quantities involved in rational number and thus do not appear to realize the unreasonableness of their assertion.[19] As for Wyatt's assertion in the excerpt above that decimals and fractions cannot be compared, this answer is representative of the reasoning of the majority of the students in this class before instruction. Moreover, it reflects more general research findings.[20] Since most traditional instruction in rational number presents decimals, fractions, and percents separately and often as distinct topics, it is not surprising that students find this task confusing. Indeed, the notion that a single quantity can have many representations is a major departure from students' previous experience with whole numbers; it is a difficult set of understandings for them to acquire and problem-laden for many.[21]

But this is not the only divergence from the familiar one-to-one correspondence of symbol to referent that our new learner will encounter. Another new and difficult idea that challenges the relatively simple referent-to-symbol relation is that in the domain of rational number, a single rational number can have several conceptually distinct meanings, referred to as "subconstructs." Now our young student may well become completely confused.

The Subconstructs or the Many Personalities of Rational Number

What is meant by conceptually distinct meanings? As an illustration, consider the simple fraction 3/4. One meaning of this fraction is as a *part–whole* relation in which 3/4 describes 3 of 4 equal-size shares. A second interpretation of the fraction 3/4 is one that is referred to as the *quotient* interpretation. Here the fraction implies division, as in 4 children sharing 3 pies. As a ratio, 3/4 might mean there are, for example, 3 red cars for every 4 green cars (this is not to be confused with the part–whole interpretation that 3/7 of the cars are red). Rational numbers can also indicate a *measure*. Here rational number is a fixed quantity, most frequently accompanied by a number line, that identifies a situation in which the fraction 1/4 is used repeatedly to determine a distance (e.g., 3/4 of an inch = 1/4, 1/4, 1/4). Finally, there is the interpretation of rational number as a *multiplicative operator*, behaving as an operation that reduces or enlarges the size of another quantity (e.g., the page has been reduced to 3/4 its original size).

The necessity of coordinating these different interpretations requires a deep understanding of the concepts and interrelationships among them. On the one hand, a student must think of rational numbers as a division of two whole numbers (quotient interpretation); on the other, she must also come to know these two numbers as an entity, a single quantity (measure), often to be used in another operation. These different interpretations, generally referred to as the "subconstructs" of rational number, have been analyzed extensively[22] and are a very important part of the knowledge network that the learner will construct for rational number.

Reconceptualizing the Unit and Operations

While acquiring a knowledge network for rational-number understanding means that new forms of representation must be learned (e.g., decimals, fractions) and different interpretations coordinated, the learner will encounter many other new ideas—ideas that also depart from whole numbers. She will have to come to understand that rational numbers are "dense"—meaning that between any two rationals we can find an infinity of other numbers. In the whole-number domain, number is discrete rather than continuous, and the main operation is counting. This is a very big change indeed.[23]

Another difficult new set of understandings concerns the fundamental change that students will encounter in the nature of the unit. In whole numbers, the unit is always explicit (6 refers to 6 units). In rational numbers, on the other hand, the unit is often implied. But it is the unstated unit that gives meaning to the represented quantities, operations, and the solutions. Consider the student trying to interpret what is meant by the task of multiplying, for example, 1/2 times 1/8. If the student recognizes that the "1/8" in the problem refers to 1/8 of one whole, she may reason correctly that half of the quantity 1/8 is 1/16. However since the 1 is not stated but implied, our young student may err and, thinking the unit is 8, consider the answer to be 1/4 (since 4 is one-half of 8)—a response given by 75 percent of traditionally instructed fourth and sixth graders students in our research projects.

New Conceptualizations: Understanding Numbers As Multiplicative Relations

Clearly the transition to learning rational numbers is challenging. Fundamentally, students must construct new meanings for numbers and operations. Development of the network of understandings for rational numbers requires a core conceptual shift: numbers must be understood in multiplicative relationship.

As a final illustration, I offer one more example of this basic shift. Again, consider the quantity 3/4 from our new learner's perspective. All of our student's prior learning will lead her to conclude that the 3 and 4 in 3/4 are two separate numbers that define separate quantities. Her knowledge of whole numbers will provide an additive understanding. Thus she will know that 3 and 4 are contiguous on the number line and have a difference of 1. But to interpret 3/4 as a rational number instead of considering these two numbers to be independent, as many students mistakenly continue to do,[24] our student must come to understand this fraction as a new kind of quantity that is defined multiplicatively by the relative amount conveyed by the symbols. Suddenly numbers are no longer simple. When placed in the context of a fraction, 3 and 4 become a quantity between 0 and 1. Obvious to adults, this numerical metamorphosis can be confusing to children.

How can children learn to make the transition to the complex world of rational numbers in which the numbers 3 and 4 exist in a relationship and are less than 1? Clearly, instruction will need to support a major conceptual change. Looking at students' prior conceptions and relevant understandings can provide footholds to support that conceptual change.[25]

Students' Errors and Misconceptions Based on Previous Learning (Principle 1)

As the above examples suggest, students come to the classroom with conceptions of numbers grounded in their whole-number learning that lead them astray in the world of rational numbers. If instruction is to change those conceptions, it is important to understand thoroughly how students reason as they puzzle through rational-number problems. Below I present verbatim interviews that are representative of faulty understandings held by many students.

In the following excerpt, we return to our fifth grader, Wyatt. His task was to order a series of rational numbers in mixed representations. Recall his earlier comments that these representations could not be compared. Now as the interview continues, he is trying to compare the fractions 2/3 and 3/4. The interview proceeds:

Interviewer	What about 2/3 and 3/4? Which of those is bigger?
Wyatt	Well, I guess that they are both the same size because they both have one piece missing.
Interviewer	I am not sure I understand what you mean when you say that there is one piece missing.
Wyatt	I'll show you. [Wyatt draws two uneven circles, roughly partitions the first in four parts, and then proceeds to shade three parts. Next he divides the second circle into three parts and shades two of them (see Figure 7-1). O.K., here is 3/4 and 2/3. You see they both have one part missing. [He points to the unshaded sections in both circular regions.] You see one part is left out, so they are both the same.

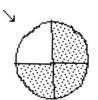 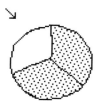

FIGURE 7-1

Wyatt's response is typical in asserting that 2/3 and 3/4 must be the same size. Clearly he has not grasped the multiplicative relations involved in rational numbers, but makes his comparisons based on operations from his whole-number knowledge. When he asserts that 2/3 and 3/4 are the same size because there is "one piece missing," Wyatt is considering the difference of 1 in additive terms rather than considering the multiplicative relations that underlie these numbers.

Additive reasoning is also at the basis of students' incorrect answers on many other kinds of rational-number tasks. Mark, a sixth grader, is working on a scaling problem in which he is attempting to figure out how the length and width of an enlarged rectangle are related to the measurements of a smaller, original rectangle. His challenge is to come up with a proportional relation and, in effect, solve a "missing-term problem" with the following relations: 8 is to 6 as 12 is to what number?

Interviewer	I have two pictures of rectangles here (see Figure 7-2). They are exactly the same shape, but one of them is bigger than the other. I

made this second one bigger by taking a picture of the first one and then enlarging it just a bit. As you can see, the length of the first rectangle is 8 cm and the width is 6 cm. Unfortunately, we know only the length of the second one. That is 12 cm. Can you please tell me what you think the width is?

Mark   Well, if the first one (rectangle) is 8 cm and 6 cm, then the next one is 12 cm and 10 cm. Because in the 8 and 6 one (rectangle) you subtract 2 from the 8 (to get the difference of the width and the length). So in the bigger rectangle you have to subtract 2 from the 12. So that's 10. So the width of the big rectangle is 10.

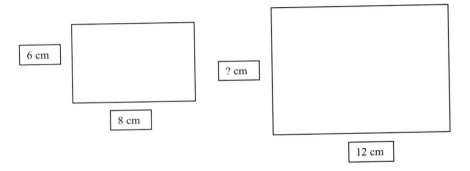

FIGURE 7-2

Mark's error in choosing 10 instead of the correct answer of 9 is certainly representative of students in his age group—in fact, many adults use the same kind of faulty reasoning.[26] Mark clearly attempts to assess the relations, but he uses an additive strategy to come up with a difference of 2. To answer this problem correctly, Mark must consider the multiplicative relations involved (the rectangle was enlarged so that the proportional relationship between the dimensions remains constant)—a challenge that eludes many.

It is this multiplicative perspective that is difficult for students to adopt in working with rational numbers. The misconception that Mark, the sixth grader, displays in asserting that the height of the newly sized rectangle is 10 cm instead of the correct answer of 9 cm shows this failure clearly. Wyatt certainly was not able to look at the relative amount in trying to distinguish between the quantities 2/3 and 3/4. Rather, he reasoned in absolute terms about the circles, that ". . . both have one piece missing."

Metacognition and Rational Number (Principle 3)

A metacognitive approach to instruction helps students monitor their understanding and take control of their own learning.[27] The complexity of rational number—the different meanings and representations, the challenges of comparing quantities across the very different representations, the unstated unit—all mean that students must be actively engaged in sense making to solve problems competently.[28] We know, however, that most middle school children do not create appropriate meanings for fractions, decimals, and percents; rather, they rely on memorized rules for symbol manipulation.

The student errors cited at the beginning of this chapter indicate not only the students' lack of understanding of rational number, but also their failure to monitor their operations and judge the reasonableness of their responses.[29] If classroom teaching does not support students in developing metacognitive skills—for example, by encouraging them to explain their reasoning to their classmates and to compare interpretations, strategies, and solutions—the consequences can be serious. Student can stop expecting math to make sense. Indeed for many students, rational number marks the point at which they draw this conclusion.

INSTRUCTION IN RATIONAL NUMBER

Why does instruction so often fail to change students' whole-number conceptions? Analyses of commonly used textbooks suggest that the principles of *How People Learn* are routinely violated. First, it has been noted that—in contrast to units on whole-number learning—topics in rational number are typically covered quickly and superficially. Yet the major conceptual shift required will take time for students to master thoroughly. Within the allotted time, too little is devoted to teaching the conceptual meaning of rational number, while procedures for manipulating rational numbers receive greater emphasis.[30] While procedural competence is certainly important, it must be anchored by conceptual understanding. For a great many students, it is not.

Other aspects of the knowledge network are shortchanged as well, including the presentation and teaching of the notation system for decimals, fractions, and percents. Textbooks typically treat the notation system as something that is obvious and transparent and can simply be given by definition at a lesson's outset. Further, operations tend to be taught in isolation and divorced from meaning. Virtually no time is spent in relating the various representations—decimals, fractions, percents—to each other.[31]

While these are all significant problems and oversights, however, there are more basic problems with traditional instruction. The central problem with most textbook instruction, many researchers agree,[32] is the failure of textbooks to provide a grounding for the major conceptual shift to multiplicative reasoning that is essential to mastering rational number. To support this claim, let us look at how rational number is typically introduced in traditional practice.

Pie Charts and a Part–Whole Interpretation of Rational Numbers

Most of us learned fractions with the model of a pie chart, and for many people, fractions remain inextricably linked to a picture of a partly shaded shape. Instruction traditionally begins with the presentation of pictures of circles (pies) and rectangles (cakes) that are partitioned and partially shaded. First, students are asked to count the number of parts in the whole shape and then the number of parts shaded. They then use these counts as the basis for naming and symbolically representing fractions. They learn that the top number, the numerator, always indicates how many pieces are shaded and that the bottom number, the denominator, always tells how many pieces there are in all. Next, using these same sorts of pictures (see Figure 7-3), instruction continues with simple addition and subtraction operations: "Two shaded 1/4 pieces (the bottom half of the circle) + 1 shaded 1/4 piece (the top left piece of the circle) = 3 shaded 1/4 pieces or 3/4."

From a psychological perspective, this introduction is sound because it is based on students' present knowledge and aligned with their experiences both in and out of school. We know that students' formal mathematics programs have been based on counting, and that from everyday experience, students know about cutting equal pieces of pies and cakes. Thus, the act of assessing partitioned regions is well within their experience.

From a mathematical point of view, the rationale for this introduction is

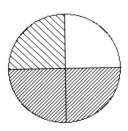

FIGURE 7-3

2⁄4 + 1⁄4 = 3⁄4

also clear. Mathematically, this approach promotes an understanding of one particular aspect of rational number—the way rational numbers indicate parts of a whole. This part–whole subconstruct is one of the basic interpretations of rational numbers.

However, this introduction is grounded in *additive* thinking. It reinforces the very concept that students must change to master rational number. Children tend to treat the individual parts that result from a partition as discrete objects. The four pieces into which a pie is cut are just four pieces. Although the representation does have the potential to bring out the multiplicative relations inherent in the numbers—considering the shaded parts in relation to the whole—this is not what students naturally extract from the situations presented given their strong preconceptions regarding additive relationships.[33]

Recall that Wyatt, the fifth grader, asserted that 2/3 and 3/4 were the "same sized" number, supporting his erroneous claim with reference to pie charts. He explained that the picture showed they were both missing one piece. His lack of focus on the different relations that are implied in these two fractions is evident from his interpretation.

Alternative Instructional Approaches: Ratio and Sharing

For some time now, researchers have wondered whether alternative instructional approaches can help students overcome this misunderstanding. As Kieren[34] points out, ". . . rather than relying on children's well developed additive instincts we must find the intuitions and schemes that go beyond those that support counting. Whole number understandings are carefully built over a number of years; now we must consider how rational number understanding develops and is fostered."

But what would such instruction look like? Over the last several years, a number of innovative approaches have been developed that highlight the multiplicative relations involved, a few of which are highlighted here. Kieren[35] has developed a program for teaching fractions that is based on the multiplicative operations of splitting. As part of his approach he used paper folding rather than pie charts as its primary problem situation. In this approach, both the operator and measure subconstructs are highlighted. Confrey's[36] 3-year developmental curriculum uses a number of contexts for ratio, including cooking, shadows, gears, and ramps.[37] Streefland's[38] approach to teaching fractions is also driven by an emphasis on ratio. His basic image is of equal shares and quotients. In his procedure for teaching fractions, children are presented with realistic situations in which they are asked to share a quantity of something, such as chocolate bars or pancakes (e.g., five children sharing two bars). To represent these situations, children use a notation system that they devise themselves, which emphasizes proportional rather than additive relations. Mack's[39] approach is to engage the students in part–whole activities as a starting point, and to ground these concepts in realistic situations in which students are pressed to consider the multiplicative relations. Finally, Lamon[40] has devised programs that address each of the subconstructs separately. All of these programs and others developed by the Rational Number Project have demonstrated a significant impact on the participating students.

Below I present a different approach to teaching rational number that I developed with my colleague Robbie Case. Our approach, shown through controlled experimental trials to be effective in helping students in the fourth, fifth, and sixth grades[41] gain a strong initial grounding in the number system, also highlights multiplicative understanding, with an additional focus on the interrelations among fractions, decimals, and percents.[42] While there is no one best method or best set of learning activities for rational number,[43] our approach provides an opportunity to describe how instruction in rational number can be built around the principles of *How People Learn* that are the theme of this volume.

First, as will be elaborated, our curriculum is based on our analyses of students' prior understandings (Principle 1). Our instructional strategy is to help students to further develop these informal understandings and then integrate them into a developmentally sequenced set of activities designed to help them develop a network of concepts and relations for rational numbers (Principle 2). Finally, as will be illustrated throughout our accounts of the lessons, a central feature of this program is the fostering of a metacognitive approach to rational number (Principle 3). By providing students with an understanding of the interconnections among decimals, fractions, and percents, our curriculum helps them develop the ability to make informed decisions on how best to operate with rational numbers.

Pipes, Tubes, and Beakers: A New Approach to Rational-Number Learning

Percents as a Starting Point

In our curriculum, rather than teaching fractions and decimals first, we introduce percents—which we believe to be a "privileged" proportion in that it only involves fractions of the base 100.[44] We do this through students' everyday understandings. We situate the initial learning of percent in linear measurement contexts, in which students are challenged to consider the relative lengths of different quantities. As will be shown below, our initial activities direct students' attention to ideas of relative amount and proportion from the very beginning of their learning of rational number. For example, we use beakers of water: "If I fill this beaker 50 percent full, approximately where will the line be? Now fill this bigger beaker 50 percent full. Do you notice that although they are both 50 percent full, there is more water in this bigger one?" These ideas of percents and proportion serve as an anchoring concept for the subsequent learning of decimals and fractions, and then for an overall understanding of the number system as a whole.

Starting Point: Visual Proportional Estimation and Halving and Doubling

Our starting point in developing our curriculum was to consider students' informal knowledge and the intuitions they have developed that could serve as a foundation. (As has been shown many times in this chapter, students have previous understandings and knowledge of mathematics that are not productive for rational-number understanding.) To this end, we highlighted two kinds of understandings that students have generally developed by this age. One is an ability to estimate proportions visually such as halves;[45] the other is an ability to work with successive halving[46] (see Box 7-2).

BOX 7-2 Students' Informal Knowledge

Proportional Understandings

While we know that formal proportional reasoning is slow to develop[47] it has nonetheless been shown that children from a very early age have a strong propensity for making proportional evaluations that are nonnumerical and based on perceptual cues. For example, young children have little difficulty perceiving narrow, upright containers in proportional terms. Although they can see which of two such containers has more liquid in it in absolute terms, they can also see which has more in proportional terms. That is to say, they can see which one is fuller.[48]

Halving and Doubling

The ability to do repeated halving is evident is students' reasoning at this age. As Confrey and Kieren[49] point out, halving and doubling have their roots in a primitive scheme that they call *splitting*. Splitting, they assert, is based on actions that are purely multiplicative in nature and are separate from those of additive structures and counting. Whereas in counting the actions are joining, annexing, and removing, in splitting the primitive action is creating simultaneous multiple versions of an original by dividing symmetrically, growing, magnifying, and folding.

Although one of these sets of understandings—proportional estimation—is primarily visual and nonnumerical, while the other, halving and doubling, is numeric, both have their grounding in multiplicative operations. It was our proposal that if we could help students merge these separate kinds of multiplicative understandings, we would allow them to construct a core conceptual grounding for rational numbers.[50]

Our strategy from the beginning was to develop what we called a "bridging context"[51] to help students first access and then integrate their knowledge of visual proportions and their flexibility in working with halving numbers. The context we chose was to have students work with percents and linear measurement. As will be elaborated below, students were engaged from the start of the instructional sequence in estimating proportional relations based on length and in using their knowledge of halving to compute simple percent quantities. In our view, the percent and measurement context allowed students to access these initial kinds of understandings and then integrate them in a natural fashion. We regarded the integration of initial intuitions and knowledge as a foundation for rational-number learning.

Why Percent As a Starting Point?

While we found that starting with percent was useful for highlighting proportionally, we also recognized that it was a significant departure from traditional practice. Percent, known as the most difficult representation for students, is usually introduced only after fractions and decimals. Several considerations, however, led to this decision. First, with percents students are always working with the denominator of 100. We therefore postpone the problems that arise when students must compare or manipulate ratios with different denominators. This allows students to concentrate on developing their own procedures for comparison and calculation rather than requiring them to struggle to master a complex set of algorithms or procedures for working with different denominators.

Second, a further simplification at this beginning stage of learning is that all percentages have a corresponding decimal or fractional equivalent that can be relatively easy to determine (e.g., 40 percent = 0.40 or 0.4 = 40/100 or 4/10 or 2/5). By introducing percents first, we allow children to make their preliminary conversions among the different rational-number representations in a direct and intuitive fashion while developing a general understanding of how the three representations are related.

Finally, children know a good deal about percents from their everyday experiences.[52] By beginning with percents rather than fractions or decimals, we are able to capitalize on children's preexisting knowledge of the meanings of these numbers and the contexts in which they are important.[53]

Curriculum Overview

The curriculum is divided into roughly three parts. First the students are introduced to a single form of rational number—percent—using concrete props that highlight linear measurement. After students have spent time working with percents in many contexts, we present our next form of rational number, the two-place decimal. We do this in the context of percent, illustrating that a two-place decimal number is like the percent of the way between two whole numbers. Finally, our focus turns to activities that promote comparing and ordering rational numbers and moving among decimals and percents. Fractions are also taught at this stage in relation to percents and decimals.[54] The sections that follow provide details of many of the activities we devised and include accounts of how fourth, fifth, and sixth graders from our research classrooms worked through these activities. These lessons are described in a fair amount of detail so that interested teachers can try some of these activities with their own students. I also include these details to illustrate the strategies that were used to foster students' pride and investment in and willingness to monitor their work.

Lessons Part 1: Introduction to Percents

Percents in Everyday Life

Imagine a typical fourth-, fifth-, or sixth-grade class, in which the students have received no formal instruction in percent. Thus each time we implemented our curriculum, we began the lessons with discussions that probed the students' everyday knowledge of this topic. These questions generated a great number of responses in each of our research classrooms. Not only were the students able to volunteer a number of different contexts in which percents appear (e.g., siblings' school marks, price reductions in stores, and taxes on restaurant bills), but they also had a strong qualitative understanding of what different numerical values "mean." For example, students commented that 100 percent means "everything," 99 percent means "almost everything," 50 percent means "exactly half," and 1 percent means "almost nothing." As one student remarked, "You know if you are on a diet you should drink 1 percent milk instead of 4 percent milk."

Pipes and Tubes: A Representation for Fullness

To further explore students' intuitions and informal understandings, we presented them with a set of props specifically designed for the lessons. The set included a series of black drainage pipes (of varying heights) with white venting tubes[55] on the outside that could be raised or lowered, simulating the action of water filling them to different levels (see Figures 7-4a and 7-4b). To discover more about the students' understanding of percents and proportion, we asked them to consider how they would use these props to teach percent to a younger child. Again the students were full of ideas, many of which are central to the knowledge network for rational number.

First students demonstrated their understanding of the unit whole, as mentioned earlier, a concept that is often elusive in traditional instruction: "Each of these pipes is 100 percent." They also demonstrated understanding of the part–whole construct: "If you raise the tube up here [pointing to three-quarters of the length of the pipe], then the part that is covered is 75 percent, and the part that is left over is 25 percent." Students also naturally displayed their sense of rational number as operator: "This is 50 percent of the tube, and if we cut it in half again it is 25 percent." In addition, students demonstrated insights for proportions: "50 percent on this bigger pipe is bigger than 50 percent on this little pipe, but they're both still 50 percent." The idea of rational number as a measure was also embedded in the students' reasoning! "I know this is about 75 percent covered, because this first bit is 25 percent, and if you move the 25 percent piece along the tube three times, you get 75 percent." Clearly, they had strong intuitions about the general properties and interpretations of rational numbers in their informal understandings of percent.

We also were interested to see whether the use of these props could generate ideas about another difficult concept—the elusive idea of percents greater than 100.[56] Sam, an eager student, attempted to demonstrate this to his classmates. He first held up a tall pipe (80 cm): "We know that this whole pipe is 100 percent." Next, he picked up a second, shorter pipe (20 cm) and stood it beside the taller one, estimating that it was about 25 percent of the taller pipe. To confirm this conjecture, he moved the smaller pipe along the taller one, noting that it fit exactly four times. "Okay," he declared, "this is definitely 25 percent of the longer pipe. So, if you join the two [pipes] together like this [laying both pipes on the ground and placing the shorter one end to end with the larger], this new pipe is 125 percent of the first one."

Percents on Number Lines: More Estimation

In addition to drainage pipes, we included activities with laminated, meter-long number lines calibrated in centimeters to provide students with another way of visualizing percent (see Figures 7-5a and 7-5b). For example, we incorporated exercises in which children went on "percent walks." Here the number lines, which came to be known as "sidewalks," were lined up end to end on the classroom floor with small gaps between them. Students challenged each other to walk a given distance (e.g., "Can you please walk 70 percent of the first sidewalk? Now, how about 3 whole sidewalks and 65

FIGURE 7-4a

FIGURE 7-4b

FIGURE 7-5a

FIGURE 7-5b

percent of the fourth?"). The number-line activities were used to consolidate percent understandings and to extend the linear measurement context.

Computing with Percent

Next we introduced beakers of water with varying degrees of fullness (see Figures 7-6a and 7-6b). In keeping with the previous lessons, the students used percent terminology to estimate the "fullness" of these containers: "Approximately what percent of this beaker do you think is full?" or "How high will the liquid rise when it is 25 percent full?" As it turned out, the children's natural tendency when confronted with fullness problems was to use a repeated halving strategy. That is, they determined where a line representing 50 percent would go on the cylinder, then 25 percent, then 12 1/2 percent, and so on. These activities with fullness estimates led naturally to a focus on computation and measurement. For example, if it was discovered on measuring a beaker that it was 8 cm tall, then 4 cm from the bottom was the 50 percent point, and 2 cm was the 25 percent point. The halving strategies exemplified in these calculations became the basis for the computations the students tackled next.

Invented Procedures

Despite the move to calculating, the children were not given any standard rules to perform these operations, and so they naturally employed a series of strategies of their own invention using halves, quarters, and eighths as benchmarks to guide their calculations. For example, to calculate 75 percent of the length of a 60 cm desktop, the students typically considered this task in a series of steps: Step 1, find half, and then build up as necessary (50 percent of 60 = 30); Step 2, use a halving strategy to find 25 percent of 60, and if 50 percent of 60 = 30, then 25 percent of 60 = 15); and Step 3, sum the parts (30 + 15 = 45).

String Challenges: Guessing Mystery Objects

String measurement activities also proved to be an excellent way of considering percent quantities and calculating percentages using benchmarks. A string challenge that became a regular feature of classroom life was what we called "The Mystery Object Challenge." In this activity, which often started the lessons, the teacher held up a piece of string that was cut to the percent of the length of a certain object in the room. The routine went something like this:

FIGURE 7-6a

FIGURE 7-6b

Teacher	I have here a length of string that is 25 percent of the height of a mystery object in the class-room. Any ideas as to what the mystery object might be?
Student	I think that it is the desktop or maybe the poster on the wall.
Teacher	How did you figure that out?
Student	Well, I just imagined moving the string along the desk four times and I think it works. [The student, then, carefully moving the string along the desk, was able to confirm her assertion.]

Since these kinds of challenges were so popular with the children, we went on to invite pairs of students to find their own mystery object to challenge their classmates. Students went around the room, measured their chosen object, and then cut a piece of string to a percent of the total. As a culminating activity, the students made what they called "percent families" of strings using the length of their mystery object as a base. Each pair of children was given a large piece of cardboard on which they pasted lengths of string to represent the benchmarks of 100 percent, 50 percent, 25 percent, 75 percent, and 12 1/2 percent of the height of the object. These activities provided opportunities for calculating percents (e.g., if the object was 70 cm long, students would have to calculate and then measure and cut strings of 50 percent lengths, or 35 cm; of 25 percent lengths, or 17.5 cm; of 75 percent lengths, or 52.5 cm; etc.). Furthermore, the visual displays thus produced proved helpful in reinforcing the idea of proportion for the students. As students often remarked, "Our string lengths are different even though all of our percents are the same."

Summary of Lessons Part 1

The first phase of the lessons began with estimations and then calculations of percent quantities. These initial activities were all presented in the context of linear measurement of our specially designed pipes and tubes, beakers of water, string, and number lines. Students were not given formal instruction in specific calculating procedures; rather, they naturally employed procedures of their own that involved percent benchmarks and repeated halving. While percent was the only form of rational number that we officially introduced at this point, students often referred to fractions when working on these initial activities. At the beginning, all of the children naturally used the term "one-half" interchangeably with "fifty percent," and most knew that 25 percent (the next split) could be expressed as "one-quarter."

We also told them that the 12 1/2 percent split was called "one-eighth" and showed them the fraction symbol 1/8.

Although the props were enjoyable to the students, they also served an important function. The activities consistently helped students integrate their sense of visual proportion with their ability to do repeated halving. Our goal in all of these initial activities was to create situations in which these two kinds of informal understandings could become linked and serve as a foundation for the students' further learning of this number system.

Lessons Part 2: Introduction of Decimals

While the first phase of the lessons was designed to extend and elaborate students' knowledge of percent, the next phase moved the students to a new developmental level. At this point in our instructional program, we introduced students to a new form of rational number—the two-place decimal. The initial decimal lessons also had a strong focus on measurement and proportion.

Research has confirmed that a solid conceptual grounding in decimal numbers is difficult for students to achieve.[57] The similarities between the symbol systems for decimals and whole numbers lead to a number of misconceptions and error types.[58] Grasping the proportional nature of decimals is particularly challenging. In our program, we made a direct link from percents—which by now the students thought of in proportional terms—to decimals. In fact, we told the students that since they were now "percent experts," they could become "decimal experts." What we did with the students at this point was show that a two-place decimal number represents a percentage of the way between two adjacent whole numbers. In this way of thinking, a decimal represents an intermediate *distance* between two numbers (e.g., 5.25 is a distance that is 25 percent of the way between 5 and 6).

Decimals and Stopwatches

To begin the lessons in decimals, the students were given LCD stopwatches with screens that displayed seconds and hundredths of seconds (the latter indicated by two small digits to the right of the numbers; see Figure 7-7). The students were asked to consider what the two "small numbers" might mean and how these small numbers related to the bigger numbers to the left (seconds). After experimenting with the stopwatches, the children noted that there were 100 of these small time units in 1 second. With this observation, they made the connection to percents: "It's like they are percents of a second." After considerable discussion of what to name these small time intervals (e.g., some suggested that they were milliseconds), the students came to refer to these hundredths of seconds as

08 01 2004   15:10

FIGURE 7-7

"centiseconds," a quantity they understood to be the percentage of time that had passed between any 2 whole seconds. We continued our work with decimals and stopwatches, with a focus on ordering numbers.

Magnitude and Order in Decimal Numbers

To illuminate the difficult concepts of magnitude and order (recall Wyatt's assertion that 2/3 = 3/4 and others' comments that 0.2 is smaller than 0.059), we devised many activities to help the students work with ordering decimals. The first of these activities was the "Stop-Start Challenge." In this exercise, students attempted to start and stop the watch as quickly as possible, several times in succession. After discussion, they learned to record their times as decimals. So, for example, 20 centiseconds was written as .20, 9 centiseconds as 0.09, and so on. Next, the students compared their personal quickest reaction time with that of their classmates, then ordered the times from quickest to slowest. In this exercise, the students could learn from their experience of trying to get the quickest time that, for example, 0.09 is a smaller number than .10 and eventually realize that .09 is smaller than .1. Another stopwatch game designed to actively engage students in issues of magnitude was "Stop the Watch Between": "Can you stop the watch between 0.45 and 0.50?" We also explored decimals through the laminated number lines, whereby students were asked to indicate parts of 100 using decimal representations: "Please put a mark where 0.09 is on this number line."

Summary of Lessons Part 2

In this second level of the instructional program, the students were introduced to decimals for the first time. Students worked on many activities that helped them first understand how decimals and percents are related and then learn how to represent decimals symbolically. As the decimal lessons proceeded, we moved on to activities designed to help students to consider and reflect on magnitude. Thus the final activities included situations in which students engaged in comparing and ordering decimals. This level of the program was the first step in students' learning to translate among the representations of rational number and gain fluency with different kinds of operations.

Lessons Part 3: Fractions and Mixed Representations of Rational Numbers

Fractions First: Equivalencies

As noted earlier, although the curriculum began with percents as the initial representation of rational numbers, we found that the students made many references to fractions. Now, at this final level of the program, our goal was to give students a chance to work with fractions more formally and then provide them with opportunities to translate flexibly among fractions, decimals, and percents. In a first series of activities, students worked on tasks in which they were asked to represent a fraction in as many ways as they could. Thus, for example, if their assignment was to show 3/4, students typically responded by presenting fraction equivalencies, such as 6/8 and 75/100. Students were also asked to compose "word problems" that incorporated fractions and were in turn given to their classmates to solve. Another activity that students enjoyed a great deal was challenging others to find the answers to equations of their own invention with questions such as "How much more to make one whole? (for example, 1/8 + 1/2 + 1/16 + 1/4 + ? = 1)," or "Is the following equation true or false? (1/4 + 1/8 + 5/10 + 1/8 = 1)." The reasoning of a fifth grader as he attempted to answer this question is typical of the reasoning of many of his classmates: "Well, 5/10 is 1/2. If you add 1/4 that makes three-quarters, so you need another quarter to make a whole and you have two-eighths, so it does equal one whole and so it is true!"

While students initially used fractions in these equations, they soon incorporated the other representations in challenges they composed. For example, one student posed the following question: "Here is my equation: 1/8 + 12.5 percent + 1/4 + .25 percent + ? = 1. How much more to make one whole?" To discover the missing quantity, the students' reasoning (anchored in percents and decimals) sounded something like this: "Well 12 1/2 (1/8) and 12 1/2 is 25 percent and another 25 percent (1/4) makes 50 percent and another .25 makes 75 percent so you would need another 25 percent to make a whole."

Crack the Code

The students carried out further work on conversions with the LCD stopwatches used earlier in the program. In a favorite game called "Crack the Code," students moved between representations of rational numbers as they were challenged to stop the watch at the decimal equivalent of different fractions and percents. For example, given a relatively simple secret code, e.g., 2/5, students stopped the watch at close to 40 centiseconds or 0.40 seconds as possible. Similarly with slightly more complex secret codes, such as "1/4 + 10 percent," students had to stop the watch at .35 seconds. This allowed them to increase their understanding of the possibility of fluid movement between representations.

Card Games

In one set of lessons, I gave the students a set of specially designed cards depicting various representations of fractions, decimals, and percents (e.g., there was a 3/8 card, a card with .375, and a card that read 37 1/2 percent). The students used the cards to design games that challenged their classmates to make comparisons among and between representations.

In the first game, the leader dealt the cards to the students, who in turn placed one card from their hand face up on the classroom floor. The challenge was to place the cards in order of increasing quantity. Students who disagreed with the placement of a particular card challenged the student who had gone before. This led to a great deal of debate. Sarah, for instance, had a card on which was written 5/9. This was a fraction that the students had not previously encountered in their lessons, and Sarah was not sure where to place it. Finally, she put the 5/9 card before a card on which was 50 percent, thus revealing that she thought that 5/9 was less than 50 percent. "That can't be right," asserted Jules. "In order to get 1/2 (50 percent) you would have to have 4 point 5 ninths and that is less than 5/9 so, 5/9 is larger than 1/2." The game ended when the children reached consensus and the teacher confirmed that all of the cards had been ordered correctly. The cards took up the entire length of the classroom by the time every student had placed his or her cards on the floor!

A second card game employing the same deck of cards, invented by a pair of students, had as its goal not only the comparison of decimals, fractions, and percents in mixed representations, but also the addition and subtraction of the differences between these numbers. This game again used the LCD stopwatches introduced earlier in the lessons. The two students who invented the game, Claire and Maggie, based it on the popular card game War. The students dealt the whole deck into two "hands," then simultaneously turned over the top card. The winner's score is increased by the difference in value of the two cards. In one turn, for example, Maggie's card had .20 written on it and Clare's had 1/8. What happened next is transcribed from the videotape of their play:

Claire	OK, now we have to figure out who has more.
Maggie	I do. 'Cause *you* only have 12$\frac{1}{2}$ percent [one-eighth] but *I* have 20 percent. So *mine* is more.
Claire	Yeah, you're right; Ok I have to write down your score. . . . Hum . . .
	So that's 20 percent take away 12$\frac{1}{2}$ percent so that's 7 1/2 [percent]. [Claire then took a pencil, and finding Maggie's place in the score column, wrote .075.]

At this point in the lessons, most of the students were comfortable thinking about percents, decimals, and fractions together. In fact, they assumed a shorthand way of speaking about quantities as they translated from fraction to percent. To illustrate this, I present a short excerpt from a conversation held by a visiting teacher who had watched the game the two girls had started and asked them to explain their reasoning.

Teacher	I was interested to know how you figured out which of the numbers is more, .20 or one-eighth. First of all, how did you know that one-eighth is equal to 12 1/2 percent?
Maggie	Ok, it is like this. One-eighth is half of one-fourth, and one-fourth is 25 percent. So, half of that is 12 1/2 percent.
Teacher	Well, you certainly know percents very well. But what about decimals? Do you know what 12 1/2 percent is as a decimal?

| Claire: | You see, 12 1/2 percent is like point 12 and a half and that's the same as point 12 point 5, because the point five is like half. |
| Maggie: | Yeah, but in decimals you have to say it's really point 125. |

Summary of Lessons Part 3

In the third part of the curriculum, we focused primarily on students' uses of mixed representations. We began with some formal activities with fractions and equivalencies, including tasks in which students had to work with and devise lengthy equations. We also had the students make up their own games and challenges to help them gain more practice in this kind of flexible movement from one operation to another. One of our primary goals here was to provide students with habits of mind regarding multiple representations that will be with them throughout their learning and lay the foundations for their ability to solve mathematical problems.

Results from Our Studies

To date, variations of our curriculum have been implemented and assessed in four experimental classrooms. From the very first lessons, students demonstrated and used their everyday knowledge of percents and worked successfully with percents in situations that called on their understanding of proportion. Our particular format also allowed students to express their informal knowledge of other concepts and meanings that are central to rational number understanding. Recall that when working with the pipes and tubes and the beakers of water, students successfully incorporated ideas of the rational-number subconstructs of measure, operator, and ratio. What was also evident was that they had a strong understanding of the unit whole and its transformations. Similarly, when decimals were introduced in the context of stopwatches, the students readily made sense of this new representation and were able to perform a variety of computations. Finally, by the end of the experimental sessions, the students had learned a flexible approach to translating among the representations of rational numbers using familiar benchmarks and halving and doubling as a vehicle of movement.

While the class as a whole appeared to be engaged and motivated by the lessons, we needed to look at the improvement made by individual students at the end of the experimental intervention. We were also interested to see how the performance of students in the experimental group compared with that of students who had traditional classroom instruction. To these ends, we assessed the experimental students on a variety of tasks before and after the course of instruction and administered these same tasks to students from classrooms in which textbook instruction had been pro-vided.[59]

Briefly, we found that students in the experimental group had improved significantly.[60] Further, the scores that they obtained after instruction were often higher than those of children who had received instruction in conventional classrooms and who were many years older. Not only were students in the experimental classrooms able to answer more questions than did the "textbook" students, but the quality of their answers was better. Specifically, the experimental group made more frequent reference to proportional concepts in justifying their answers than did the students in the nonexperimental group. What follows are some examples of changes in students' reasoning following participation in the experimental program, consisting of selections from interviews that were conducted following the conclusion of the experimental classes.

Children's Thinking After Instruction

Let us return to the question posed to Wyatt at the start of the program (and excerpted at the beginning of this chapter) and look at the responses of two students, Julie and Andy, whose reasoning was typical of that of the other students at the end of the program.

Interviewer	Here are three numbers: 2/3, 0.5, and 3/4. Could you please put these numbers in order from smallest to largest?
Julie	Well, let's see. Point 5 is the smallest because 3/4 is 75 percent. I am not exactly sure what 2/3 is as a percent *but* it is definitely more than a half. Can I use this paper to try it out? [Julie took two pieces of paper. Holding them horizontally, she first folded one in four equal parts and then pointed to three sections, remarking that this was 3/4. Next she folded the second sheet in three pieces and then lined the two pages up together to compare the differences between the 2/3 and 3/4]. So 3/4 is the biggest.

Andy responded to this same question differently.

Andy	It's easy: .5 is 50 percent and 2/3 is 66 percent, and so it goes first .5 then 2/3 and then 3/4 cause that's 75 percent.

As can be seen, both Andy and Julie correctly ordered the numbers using their knowledge of percent as a basis for their reasoning. Andy, a high-achieving student, simply converted these quantities to percents. Julie, identified as a lower achiever, used paper folding as a way of finding the bigger fraction. Both used multiplicative solutions, one concrete and one abstract.

Another example taken from posttest interviews illustrates not only the students' understanding of order and magnitude, but also their understanding of the density property of rational numbers—that there is an infinite number of numbers between any two rational numbers.

Interviewer	Can any fractions fit between one-fourth and two-fourths? And if so, can you name one?
Maggie	Well, I know that one-quarter is 25 percent and so two quarters is a half, so that's 50 percent. So, there's tons of numbers between them like 40 percent. So that would be 40/100.
Jed	One-quarter is the same as 2/8 and 2/4 is the same as 4/8, so the answer is three-eighths.

The above answers are in sharp contrast to those of children before our instruction or those from traditional classrooms, the majority of whom claimed no numbers could come between 1/4 and 2/4.

In a final example, students were asked to compute a percent of a given quantity—65 percent of 160. Although this type of computation was performed regularly in our classrooms, 65 percent of 160 was a significantly more difficult calculation than those the students had typically encountered in their lessons. Furthermore, this item required that students work with 10 percent as well as with the familiar benchmarks (25 percent, 50 percent, 75 percent, and 12 1/2 percent) that served as a basis for most of their classroom work. Despite these differences, students found ways to solve this difficult problem.

Interviewer	What is 65 percent of 160?
Sascha	Okay, 50 percent of 160 is 80. Half of 80 is 40, so that is 25 percent. So if you add 80 and 40 you get 120. But that (120) is too much because that's 75 percent. So you need to minus 10 percent (of 160) and that's 16. So, 120 take away 16 is 104.
Neelam	The answer is 104. First I did 50 percent, which was 80.

> Then I did 10 percent of 160, which is 16. Then
> I did 5 percent, which was 8. I added them [16
> + 8] to get 24, and added that to 80 to get 104.

For anyone who has seen a colleague pause when asked to compute a percentage, as one must, say, to calculate a tip, the ease with which these students worked through these problems is striking.

Knowledge Network

These are only a few examples from the posttest interviews that illustrate the kinds of new understandings and interconnections students had been able to develop through their participation in the curriculum. Overall, our analyses of the children's thinking revealed that students had gained (1) an overall understanding of the number system, as illustrated by their ability to use the representations of decimals, fractions, and percents interchangeably; (2) an appreciation of the magnitude of rational numbers, as seen in their ability to compare and order numbers within this system; (3) an understanding of the proportional- and ratio-based constructs of this domain, which underpins their facility with equivalencies; (4) an understanding of percent as an operator, as is evident in their ability to invent a variety of solution strategies for calculating with these numbers; and (5) general confidence and fluency in their ability to think about the domain using the benchmark values they had learned, which is a hallmark of number sense.

Our research is still in an early stage. We will continue to pursue many questions, including the potential limitations of successive halving as a way of operating with rational numbers, downplaying of the important understandings associated with the quotient subconstruct, as well as a limited view of fractions. Furthermore, we need to learn more about how students who have been introduced to rational numbers in this way will proceed with their ongoing learning of mathematics.

While we acknowledge that these questions have not yet been answered, we believe certain elements of our program contributed to the students' learning, elements that may have implications for other rational-number curricula. First, our program began with percents, thus permitting children to take advantage of their qualitative understanding of proportions and combine that understanding with their knowledge of the numbers from 1 to 100, while avoiding (or at least postponing) the problems presented by fractions. Second, we used linear measurement as a way of promoting the multiplicative ideas of relative quantities and fullness. Finally, our program emphasized benchmark values—of halves, quarters, eighths, etc.—for moving among equivalencies of percents, decimals, and fractions, which allowed students to be flexible and develop confidence in relying on their own procedures for problem solving.

CONCLUSION: HOW STUDENTS LEARN RATIONAL NUMBER

Principle #1: Prior Understandings

For years mathematics researchers have focused their attention on understanding the complexities of this number system and how to facilitate students' learning of the system. One well-established insight is that rational-number teaching focused on pie charts and part–whole understandings reinforces the primary problem students confront in learning rational number: the dominance of whole-number reasoning. One response is to place the multiplicative ideas of relative quantity, ratio, and proportion at the center of instruction.

However, our curriculum also builds on our theory and research findings pointing to the knowledge students typically bring to the study of rational number that can serve as a foundation for conceptual change. Two separate kinds of understandings that 10-year-olds typically possess have a multiplicative orientation. One of these is visual proportional estimation; for children, this understanding usually functions independently of numbers, at least initially. The second important kind of understanding is the numerical procedure for repeated halving. By strengthening and merging these two understandings, students can build a solid foundation for working flexibly with rational numbers.

Our initial instructional activities are designed to elicit these informal understandings and to provide instructional contexts that bring them together. We believe this coordination produces a new interlinked structure that serves both as foundation for the initial learning of rational number and subsequently as the basis on which to build a networked understanding of this domain.

Principle #2: Network of Concepts

At the beginning of this chapter, I outlined the complex set of core concepts, representations, and operations students need to acquire to gain an initial grounding in the rational-number system. As indicated above, the central conceptual challenge for students is to master proportion, a concept grounded in multiplicative reasoning. Our instructional strategy was to design a learning sequence that allowed students to first work with percents and proportion in linear measurement and next work with decimals and fractions. Extensive practice is incorporated to assure that students become fluent in translating between different forms of rational number. Our intention was to create a percent measurement structure that would become a central network to which all subsequent mathematical learning could be linked. This design is significantly different from traditional instruction in rational number, in which topics are taught separately.

Principle #3: Metacognition

In this chapter, I have not made detailed reference to students' developing metacognition. Yet the fostering of metacognition is in fact central to our curriculum. First, as the reader may have noted, we regularly engaged the students in whole-group discussions in which they were asked to explain their reasoning and share invented procedures with their classmates. We also designed the lessons so that students worked in small groups to collaborate in solving problems and constructing materials; we thereby provided students with a forum to express and refine their developing understandings. There were also many opportunities for students to consider how they would teach rational number to others, either younger students or their own classmates, by designing their own games and producing teaching plans for how these new concepts could be taught. In all these ways, we allowed students to reflect on their own learning and to consider what it meant for them and others to develop an understanding of rational number. Finally, we fostered metacognition in our program through the overall design and goals of the experimental curriculum, with its focus on interconnections and multiple representations. This focus, I believe, provided students with an overview of the number system as a whole and thus allowed them to make informed decisions on how best to operate with rational numbers.

Final Words

I conclude this chapter with an interchange, recorded verbatim, between a fourth-grade student and a researcher. Zach, the fourth grader, was being interviewed by the researcher as part of a posttest assessment. The conversation began when Zach had completed two pages of the six-page posttest and remarked to the interviewer, "I have just done 1/3 of the test;...that is 33.3 percent." When he finished the third page, he noted, "Now I have finished 1/2 or 50 percent of the test." On completing the fourth page he remarked, "Okay, so I have now done 2/3 of the test, which is the same as 66 percent." When he had completed the penultimate page, he wondered out loud what the equivalent percentage was for 5/6: "Okay, let's see; it has got to be over 66.6 percent and it is also more than 75 percent. I'd say that it is about 80 percent....No, wait; it can't be 80 percent because that is 4/5 and this [5/6] is more than 4/5. It is 1/2 plus 1/3...so it is 50 percent plus 33.3 percent, 83.3 percent. So I am 83.3 percent finished."

This exchange illustrates the kind of metacognitive capability that our curriculum is intended to develop. First, Zach posed his own questions, unprompted. Further, he did not expect that the question had to be answered by the teacher. Rather, he was confident that he had the tools, ideas, and concepts that would help him navigate his way to the answer. We also see that Zach rigorously assessed the reasonableness of his answers and that he used his knowledge of translating among the various representations to help him solve the problem. I conclude with this charming vignette as an illustration of the potential support our curriculum appears to offer to students beginning their learning of rational number.

Students then go on to learn algorithms that allow them to calculate a number like 83.3 percent from $^5/_6$ efficiently. But the foundation in mathematical reasoning that students like Zach possess allow them to use those algorithms with understanding to solve problems when an algorithm has been forgotten and to double check their answers using multiple methods. The confidence created when a student's mathematical reasoning is secure bodes well for future mathematics learning.

NOTES

1. Armstrong and Bezuk, 1995; Ball, 1990; Post et al., 1991.
2. Moss, 2000.
3. Carpenter et al., 1980.
4. Ball, 1993; Hiebert and Behr, 1988; Kieren, 1993.
5. Lamon, 1999.
6. Hiebert and Wearne, 1986; Wearne and Hiebert, 1988.
7. Hiebert and Behr, 1988.
8. Kerslake, 1986.
9. Heibert, 1992.
10. National Research Council, 2001.
11. Carpenter et al., 1993.
12. Lamon, 1999.
13. Lesh et al., 1988.
14. Baroody, 1999.
15. Lamon, 1999.
16. National Council of Teachers of Mathematics, 1989, 2000.
17. Markovits and Sowder, 1991, 1994; Sowder, 1995.
18. Cramer et al., 1989.
19. Sowder, 1995.
20. Sowder, 1992.
21. Hiebert and Behr, 1988.
22. Behr et al., 1983, 1984, 1992, 1993; Kieren, 1994, 1995; Ohlsson, 1988.
23. Hiebert and Behr, 1988.
24. Kerslake, 1986.
25. Behr et al., 1984; Case, 1998; Hiebert and Behr, 1988; Lamon, 1995; Mack, 1990, 1993, 1995; Resnick and Singer, 1993.

26. Hart, 1988; Karplus and Peterson, 1970; Karplus et al., 1981, 1983; Cramer et al., 1993; Noelting, 1980a, 1980b.

27. National Council of Teachers of Mathematics, 1989, 2000; National Research Council, 2001.

28. Ball, 1993.

29. Sowder, 1988.

30. Baroody, 1999; Heibert, 1992; Hiebert and Wearne, 1986; Moss and Case, 1999; Post et al., 1993.

31. Armstrong and Bezuk, 1995; Ball, 1993; Hiebert and Wearne, 1986; Mack, 1990, 1993; Markovits and Sowder, 1991, 1994; Sowder, 1995.

32. Confrey, 1994, 1995; Kieren, 1994, 1995; Post et al., 1993; Streefland, 1991, 1993.

33. Kieren, 1994, 1995; Mack, 1993, 1995; Sowder, 1995; Streefland, 1993.

34. Kieren, 1994, p. 389.

35. Kieren, 1992, 1995.

36. Confrey, 1995.

37. Lachance and Confrey, 1995.

38. Streefland, 1991, 1993.

39. Mack, 1990, 1993.

40. Lamon, 1993, 1994, 1999.

41. As of this writing, this curriculum is being implemented with students of low socioeconomic status in a grade 7 and 8 class. Preliminary analyses have shown that it is highly effective in helping struggling students relearn this number system and gain a stronger conceptual understanding.

42. Kalchman et al., 2000; Moss, 1997, 2000, 2001, 2003; Moss and Case, 1999.

43. National Research Council, 2001.

44. Parker and Leinhardt, 1995.

45. Case, 1985; Noelting, 1980a; Nunes and Bryant, 1996; Spinillo and Bryant, 1991.

46. Confrey, 1994; Kieren, 1994.

47. Resnick and Singer, 1993.

48. Case, 1985.

49. Confrey, 1994; Kieren, 1993.

50. Case and Okomoto, 1996.

51. Case, 1998; Kalchman et al., 2000.

52. Parker and Leinhardt, 1995.

53. Lembke and Reys, 1994.

54. While the activities and lessons we designed are organized in three phases, the actual order of the lessons and the pacing of the teaching, as well as the particular content of the activities described below, varied in different classrooms depending on the needs, capabilities, and interests of the participating students.

55. These materials are available at any building supply store.

56. Parker and Leinhardt, 1995.

57. Hiebert et al., 1991.

58. Resnick et al., 1989.

59. Kalchman et al., 2000; Moss, 1997, 2000, 2001; Moss and Case, 1999.
60. From pre- to posttest, achieving effect sizes between and 1 and 2 standard deviations.

REFERENCES

Armstrong, B.E., and Bezuk, N. (1995). Multiplication and division of fractions: The search for meaning. In J.T. Sowder and B.P. Schappelle (Eds.), *Providing a foundation for teaching mathematics in the middle grades* (pp. 85-120). Albany, NY: State University of New York Press.

Ball, D.L. (1990). The mathematics understanding that prospective teachers bring to teacher education elementary school. *Journal, 90*, 449-466.

Ball, D.L. (1993). Halves, pieces and twoths: Constructing and using representational contexts in teaching fractions. In T.P. Carpenter, E. Fennema, and T.A. Romberg (Eds.), *Rational numbers: An integration of research* (pp. 157-196). Mahwah, NJ: Lawrence Erlbaum Associates.

Baroody, A.J. (1999). *Fostering children's mathematical power: An investigative approach to K-8 mathematics instruction.* Mahwah, NJ: Lawrence Erlbaum Associates.

Behr, M.J., Lesh, R., Post, T.R., and Silver, E.A. (1983). Rational-number concepts. In R. Lesh and M. Landau (Eds.), *Acquisition of mathematics concepts and processes* (pp. 91-126). New York: Academic Press.

Behr, M.J., Wachsmuth, I., Post, T.R., and Lesh, T. (1984). Order and equivalence of rational numbers: A clinical teaching experiment. *Journal for Research in Mathematics Education, 15*(4), 323-341.

Behr, M.J., Harel, G., Post, T.R, and Lesh, R. (1992). Rational number, ratio, and proportion. In D.A. Grouws (Ed.), *Handbook of research on mathematics teaching and learning* (pp. 296-333). New York: Macmillan.

Behr, M.J., Harel, G., Post, T.R, and Lesh, R. (1993). Rational numbers: Towards a semantic analysis: Emphasis on the operator construct. In T.P. Carpenter, E. Fennema, and T.A. Romberg (Eds.), *Rational numbers: An integration of research* (pp. 13-48). Mahwah, NJ: Lawrence Erlbaum Associates.

Carpenter, T.P., Kepner, H., Corbitt, M.K., Lindquist, M.M., and Reys, R.E. (1980). Results of the NAEP mathematics assessment: Elementary school. *Arithmetic Teacher, 27*, 10-12, 44-47.

Carpenter, T.P., Fennema, E., and Romberg, T.A. (1993). Toward a unified discipline of scientific inquiry. In T. Carpenter, E. Fennema, and T.A. Romberg (Eds.), *Rational numbers: An integration of research* (pp. 1-12). Mahwah, NJ: Lawrence Erlbaum Associates.

Case, R. (1985). *Intellectual development: Birth to adulthood.* New York: Academic Press.

Case, R. (1998, April). *A psychological model of number sense and its development.* Paper presented at the annual meeting of the American Educational Research Association, San Diego, CA.

Case, R., and Okamoto, Y. (1996). The role of central conceptual structures in the development of children's thought. *Monographs of the Society for Research in Child Development, 246*(61), 1-2. Chicago, IL: University of Chicago Press.

Confrey, J. (1994). Splitting, similarity, and the rate of change: A new approach to multiplication and exponential functions. In G. Harel and J. Confrey (Eds.), *The development of multiplicative reasoning in the learning of mathematics* (pp. 293-332). Albany, NY: State University of New York Press.

Confrey, J. (1995). Student voice in examining "splitting" as an approach to ratio, proportions and fractions. In L. Meira and D. Carraher (Eds.), *Proceedings of the 19th international conference for the Psychology of Mathematics Education* (vol. 1, pp. 3-29). Recife, Brazil: Universidade Federal de Pernambuco.

Cramer, K., Post, T., and Behr, M. (1989). Cognitive restructuring ability, teacher guidance and perceptual distractor tasks: An aptitude treatment interaction study. *Journal for Research in Mathematics Education, 20*(1), 103-110.

Cramer, K., Post, T., and Currier, D. (1993). Learning and teaching ratio and proportion: Research implications. In D. Owens (Ed.), *Research ideas for the classroom: Middle grade mathematics* (pp. 159-179). New York: Macmillan.

Hart, K. (1988). Ratio and proportion. In J. Hiebert and M. Behr (Eds.), *Number concepts and operations in the middle grades* (pp. 198-220). Mahwah, NJ: Lawrence Erlbaum Associates.

Hiebert, J. (1992). Mathematical, cognitive, and instructional analyses of decimal fractions. In G. Leinhardt, R. Putnam, and R.A. Hattrup (Eds.), *Analysis of arithmetic for mathematics teaching* (pp. 283-322). Mahwah, NJ: Lawrence Erlbaum Associates.

Hiebert, J., and Behr, J.M. (1988). Capturing the major themes. In J. Hiebert and M. Behr (Eds.), *Number concepts and operations in the middle grades* (vol. 2, pp. 1-18). Mahwah, NJ: Lawrence Erlbaum Associates.

Hiebert, J., and Wearne, D. (1986). Procedures over concepts: The acquisition of decimal number knowledge. In J. Hiebert (Ed.), *Conceptual and procedural knowledge: The case of mathematics* (pp. 199-244). Mahwah, NJ: Lawrence Erlbaum Associates.

Hiebert, J., Wearne, D., and Taber, S. (1991). Fourth graders' gradual construction of decimal fractions during instruction using different physical representations. *Elementary School Journal, 91,* 321-341.

Kalchman, M., Moss, J., and Case, R. (2000). Psychological models for the development of mathematical understanding: Rational numbers and functions. In S. Carver and D. Klahr (Eds.), *Cognition and Instruction: 25 years of progress.* Mahwah, NJ: Lawrence Erlbaum Associates.

Karplus, R., and Peterson, R.W. (1970). Intellectual development beyond elementary school II: Ratio, a survey. *School Science and Mathematics, 70*(9), 813-820.

Karplus, R., Pulos, S., and Stage, E.K. (1981). *Proportional reasoning of early adolescents.* Berkeley, CA: University of California, Lawrence Hall of Science.

Karplus, R., Pulos, S., and Stage, E.K. (1983). Proportional reasoning of early adolescents. In R. Lesh and M. Landau (Eds.), *Acquisition of mathematics concepts and processes* (pp. 45-90). Orlando, FL: Academic.

Kerslake, D. (1986). *Fractions: Children's strategies and errors.* Windsor, UK: NFER Nelson.

Kieren, T.E. (1992). Rational and fractional numbers as mathematical and personal knowledge. In G. Leinhardt, R. Putnam, and R.A. Hattrup (Eds.), *Analysis of arithmetic for mathematics teaching* (pp. 323-372). Mahwah, NJ: Lawrence Erlbaum Associates.

Kieren, T.E. (1993). Rational and fractional numbers: From quotient fields to recursive understanding. In T. Carpenter, E. Fennema, and T.A. Romberg (Eds.), *Rational numbers: An integration of research* (pp. 49-84). Mahwah, NJ: Lawrence Erlbaum Associates.

Kieren, T.E. (1994). Multiple views of multiplicative structure. In G. Harel and J. Confrey (Eds.), *The development of multiplicative reasoning in the learning of mathematics* (pp. 387-397). Albany, NY: State University of New York Press.

Kieren, T.E. (1995). Creating spaces for learning fractions. In J.T. Sowder and B.P. Schappelle (Eds.), *Providing a foundation for teaching mathematics in the middle grades*. Albany, NY: State University of New York Press.

Lachance, A., and Confrey, J. (1995). Introducing fifth graders to decimal notation through ratio and proportion. In D.T. Owens, M.K. Reed, and G.M. Millsaps (Eds.), *Proceedings of the seventeenth annual meeting of the North American chapter of the International Group for the Psychology of Mathematics Education* (vol. 1, pp. 395-400). Columbus, OH: ERIC Clearinghouse for Science, Mathematics and Environmental Education.

Lamon, S.J. (1993). Ratio and proportion: Children's cognitive and metacognitive processes. In T.P. Carpenter, E. Fennema, and T.A. Romberg, (Eds.), *Rational numbers: An integration of research* (pp. 131-156). Mahwah, NJ: Lawrence Erlbaum Associates.

Lamon S.J. (1994). Ratio and proportion: Cognitive foundations in unitizing and norming. In G. Harel and J. Confrey (Eds.), *The development of multiplicative reasoning in the learning of mathematics* (pp. 89-122). Albany, NY: State University of New York Press.

Lamon, S.J. (1995). Ratio and proportion: Elementary didactical phenomenology. In J.T. Sowder and B.P. Schappelle (Eds.), *Providing a foundation for teaching mathematics in the middle grades*. Albany, NY: State University of New York Press.

Lamon, S.J. (1999). *Teaching fractions and ratios for understanding: Essential content knowledge and instructional strategies for teachers*. Mahwah, NJ: Lawrence Erlbaum Associates.

Lembke, L.O., and Reys, B.J. (1994). The development of, and interaction between, intuitive and school-taught ideas about percent. *Journal for Research in Mathematics Education, 25*(3), 237-259.

Lesh, R., Post, T., and Behr, M. (1988). Proportional reasoning. In M. Behr and J. Hiebert (Eds.), *Number concepts and operations in the middle grades* (pp. 93-118). Mahwah, NJ: Lawrence Erlbaum Associates.

Mack, N.K. (1990). Learning fractions with understanding: Building on informal knowledge. *Journal for Research in Mathematics Education, 21*, 16-32.

Mack, N.K. (1993). Learning rational numbers with understanding: The case of informal knowledge. In T.P. Carpenter, E. Fennema, and T.A. Romberg (Eds.), *Rational numbers: An integration of research* (pp. 85-105). Mahwah, NJ: Lawrence Erlbaum Associates.

Mack, N.K. (1995). Confounding whole-number and fraction concepts when building on informal knowledge. *Journal for Research in Mathematics Education, 26*(5), 422-441.

Markovits, Z., and Sowder, J.T. (1991). Students' understanding of the relationship between fractions and decimals. *Focus on Learning Problems in Mathematics, 13*(1), 3-11.

Markovits, Z., and Sowder, J.T. (1994). Developing number sense: An intervention study in grade 7. *Journal for Research in Mathematics Education, 25*(1), 4-29, 113.

Moss, J. (1997). *Developing children's rational number sense: A new approach and an experimental program.* Unpublished master's thesis, University of Toronto, Toronto, Ontario, Canada.

Moss, J. (2000). *Deepening children's understanding of rational numbers.* Dissertation Abstracts.

Moss, J. (2001). Percents and proportion at the center: Altering the teaching sequence for rational number. In B. Littweiller (Ed.), *Making sense of fractions, ratios, and proportions. The NCTM 2002 Yearbook* (pp. 109-120). Reston, VA: National Council of Teachers of Mathematics.

Moss, J. (2003). On the way to computational fluency: Beginning with percents as a way of developing understanding of the operations in rational numbers. In *Teaching children mathematics* (pp. 334-339). Reston, VA: National Council of Teachers of Mathematics.

Moss, J., and Case, R. (1999). Developing children's understanding of rational numbers: A new model and experimental curriculum. *Journal for Research in Mathematics Education, 30*(2), 119, 122-147.

National Council of Teachers of Mathematics. (1989). *Curriculum and evaluation standards for school mathematics.* Reston, VA: National Council of Teachers of Mathematics.

National Council of Teachers of Mathematics. (2000). *Curriculum and evaluation standards for school mathematics.* Reston, VA: National Council of Teachers of Mathematics.

National Research Council. (2001). *Adding it up: Helping children learn mathematics.* Mathematics Learning Study Committee, J. Kilpatrick, J., Swafford, J., and B. Findell (Eds.). Center for Education. Division of Behavioral and Social Sciences and Education. Washington, DC: National Academy Press.

Noelting, G. (1980a). The development of proportional reasoning and the ratio concept. Part I: Differentiation of stages. *Educational Studies in Mathematics, 11,* 217-253.

Noelting, G. (1980b). The development of proportional reasoning and the ratio concept. Part II: Problem-structure at successive stages: Problem-solving strategies and the mechanism of adaptive restructuring. *Educational Studies in Mathematics, 11,* 331-363.

Nunes, T., and Bryant, P. (1996). *Children doing mathematics.* Cambridge, MA: Blackwell.

Ohlsson, S. (1988). Mathematical meaning and applicational meaning in the semantics of fractions and related concepts. In J. Hiebert and M. Behr (Eds.), *Number concepts and operations in the middle grades* (vol. 2, pp. 53-92). Mahwah, NJ: Lawrence Erlbaum Associates.

Parker, M., and Leinhardt, G. (1995). Percent: A privileged proportion. *Review of Educational Research, 65*(4), 421-481.

Post, T., Harel, G., Behr, M., and Lesh, R. (1991). Intermediate teachers' knowledge of rational number concepts. In E. Fennema, T. Carpenter, and S. Lamon (Eds.), *Integrating research on teaching and learning mathematics* (pp. 177-198). Albany, NY: State University of New York Press.

Post, T.R., Cramer, K.A., Behr, M., Lesh, R., and Harel, G. (1993). Curriculum implications of research on the learning, teaching and assessing of rational number concepts. In T.P. Carpenter, E. Fennema, and T.A. Romberg (Eds.), *Rational numbers: An integration of research* (pp. 327-362). Mahwah, NJ: Lawrence Erlbaum Associates.

Resnick, L.B., and Singer, J.A. (1993). Protoquantitative origins of ratio reasoning. In T.P. Carpenter, E. Fennema, and T.A. Romberg (Eds.), *Rational numbers: An integration of research* (pp. 107-130). Mahwah, NJ: Lawrence Erlbaum Associates.

Resnick, L.B., Nesher, P., Leonard, F., Magone, M., Omanson, S., and Peled I. (1989). Conceptual bases of arithmetic errors: The case of decimal fractions. *Journal for Research in Mathematics Education, 20*(1), 8-27.

Sowder, J.T. (1988). Mental computation and number comparison: Their roles in the development of number sense and computational estimation. In J. Hiebert and M. Behr (Eds.), *Number concepts and operations in the middle grades* (vol. 2, pp. 182-198). Mahwah, NJ: Lawrence Erlbaum Associates.

Sowder, J.T. (1992). Making sense of numbers in school mathematics. In G. Leinhardt, R. Putnam, and R. Hattrup, (Eds.), *Analysis of arithmetic for mathematics* (pp. 1-51). Mahwah, NJ: Lawrence Erlbaum Associates.

Sowder, J.T. (1995). Instructing for rational number sense. In J.T. Sowder and B.P. Schappelle (Eds.), *Providing a foundation for teaching mathematics in the middle grades*. Albany, NY: State University of New York Press.

Spinillo, A.G., and Bryant, P. (1991). Children's proportional judgements: The importance of "half." *Child Development, 62,* 427-440.

Streefland, L. (1991). Fractions: An integrated perspective. In L. Streefland (Ed.), *Realistic mathematics education in primary school* (pp. 93-118). Utrecht, The Netherlands: Freudenthal Institute.

Streefland, L. (1993). Fractions: A realistic approach. In T.P. Carpenter, E. Fennema, and T.A. Romberg (Eds.), *Rational numbers: An integration of research* (pp. 289-327). Mahwah, NJ: Lawrence Erlbaum Associates.

Wearne, D., and Hiebert, J. (1988). Constructing and using meaning for mathematical symbols: The case of decimal fractions. In J. Hiebert and M. Behr (Eds.), *Number concepts and operations in the middle grades* (vol. 2, pp. 220-235). Mahwah, NJ: Lawrence Erlbaum Associates.

Teaching and Learning Functions

Mindy Kalchman and Kenneth R. Koedinger

This chapter focuses on teaching and learning mathematical functions.[1] Functions are all around us, though students do not always realize this. For example, a functional relationship between quantities is at play when we are paying for gasoline by the gallon or fruit by the pound. We need functions for financial plans so we can calculate such things as accrued income and interest. Functions are important as well to interpretations of local and world demographics and population growth, which are critical for economic planning and development. Functions are even found in such familiar settings as baseball statistics and metric conversions.

Algebraic tools allow us to express these functional relationships very efficiently; find the value of one thing (such as the gas price) when we know the value of the other (the number of gallons); and display a relationship visually in a way that allows us to quickly grasp the direction, magnitude, and rate of change in one variable over a range of values of the other. For simple problems such as determining gas prices, students' existing knowledge of multiplication will usually allow them to calculate the cost for a specific amount of gas once they know the price per gallon (say, $2) with no problem. Students know that 2 gallons cost $4, 3 gallons cost $6, 4 gallons cost $8, and so on. While we can list each set of values, it is very efficient to say that for all values in gallons (which we call x by convention), the total cost (which we call y by convention), is equal to 2x. Writing y = 2x is a simple way of saying a great deal.

As functional relationships become more complex, as in the growth of a population or the accumulation of interest over time, solutions are not so easily calculated because the base changes each period. In these situations, algebraic tools allow highly complex problems to be solved and displayed in a way that provides a powerful image of change over time.

Many students would be more than a little surprised at this description. Few students view algebra as a powerful toolkit that allows them to solve complex problems much more easily. Rather, they regard the algebra itself as the problem, and the toolkit as hopelessly complex. This result is not surprising given that algebra is often taught in ways that violate all three principles of learning set forth in *How People Learn* and highlighted in this volume.

The first principle suggests the importance of building new knowledge on the foundation of students' existing knowledge and understanding. Because students have many encounters with functional relationships in their everyday lives, they bring a great deal of relevant knowledge to the classroom. That knowledge can help students reason carefully through algebra problems. Box 8-1 suggests that a problem described in its everyday manifestation can be solved by many more students than the same problem presented only as a mathematical equation. Yet if the existing mathematics understandings students bring to the classroom are not linked to formal algebra learning, they will not be available to support new learning.

The second principle of *How People Learn* argues that students need a strong conceptual understanding of function as well as procedural fluency. The new and very central concept introduced with functions is that of a *dependent relationship:* the value of one thing depends on, is determined by, or is a function of another. The kinds of problems we are dealing with no longer are focused on determining a specific value (the cost of 5 gallons of gas). They are now focused on the *rule* or expression that tells us how one thing (cost) is related to another (amount of gas). A "function" is formally defined in mathematics as "a set of ordered pairs of numbers (x, y) such that to each value of the first variable (x) there corresponds a unique value of the second variable (y)."[2] Such a definition, while true, does not signal to students that they are beginning to learn about a new class of problems in which the value of one thing is determined by the value of another, and the rule that tells them how they are related.

Within mathematics education, function has come to have a broader interpretation that refers not only to the formal definition, but also to the multiple ways in which functions can be written and described.[3] Common ways of describing functions include tables, graphs, algebraic symbols, words, and problem situations. Each of these representations describes how the value of one variable is determined by the value of another. For instance, in a verbal problem situation such as "you get two dollars for every kilometer you walk in a walkathon," the dollars earned depend on, are determined by, or are a function of the distance walked. Conceptually, students need to understand that these are different ways of describing the same relationship.

Good instruction is not just about developing students' facility with performing various procedures, such as finding the value of y given x or creating a graph given an equation. Instruction should also help students develop a conceptual understanding of function, the ability to represent a function in a variety of ways, and fluency in moving among multiple representations of functions. The slope of the line as represented in an equation, for example, should have a "meaning" in the verbal description of the relationship between two variables, as well as a visual representation on a graph.

The third principle of *How People Learn* suggests the importance of students' engaging in metacognitive processes, monitoring their understanding as they go. Because mathematical relationships are generalized in algebra, students must operate at a higher level of abstraction than is typical of the mathematics they have generally encountered previously. At all levels of mathematics, students need to be engaged in monitoring their problem solving and reflecting on their solutions and strategies. But the metacognitive engagement is particularly important as mathematics becomes more abstract, because students will have few clues even when a solution has gone terribly awry if they are not actively engaged in sense making.

When students' conceptual understanding and metacognitive monitoring are weak, their efforts to solve even fairly simple algebra problems can, and often do, fail. Consider the problem in Figure 8-1a. How might students approach and respond to this problem? What graph-reading and table-building skills are required? Are such skills sufficient for a correct solution? If students lack a conceptual understanding of linear function, what errors might they make? Figure 8-1b shows an example student solution.

What skills does this student exhibit? What does this student understand and not understand about functions? This student has shown that he knows how to construct a table of values and knows how to record in that table coordinate points he has determined to be on the graph. He also clearly recalls that an algorithm for finding the slope of the function is dividing the change in $y(\Delta y)$ by the change in $x(\Delta x)$. There are, however, significant problems with this solution that reveal this student's weak conceptual understanding of functions.

Problem: Make a table of values that would produce the function seen on page 356.

First, and most superficially, the student (likely carelessly) mislabeled the coordinate for the y-intercept $(0, 3)$ rather than $(0, -3)$. This led him to make an error in calculating Δy by subtracting 0 from 3 rather than from -3. In so doing, he arrived at a value for the slope of the function that was negative—an impossible solution given that the graph is of an increasing linear function. This slip, by itself, is of less concern than the fact that the

BOX 8-1 Linking Formal Mathematical Understanding to Informal Reasoning

Which of these problems is most difficult for a beginning algebra student?

Story Problem

When Ted got home from his waiter job, he multiplied his hourly wage by the 6 hours he worked that day. Then he added the $66 he made in tips and found he had earned $81.90. How much does Ted make per hour?

Word Problem

Starting with some number, if I multiply it by 6 and then add 66, I get 81.9. What number did I start with?

Equation

Solve for x:
x * 6 + 66 = 81.90

Most teachers and researchers predict that students will have more difficulty correctly solving the story or word problem than the equation.[4] They might explain this expectation by saying that a student needs to read the verbal problems (story and word) and then translate them into the equation. In fact, research investigating urban high school students' performance on such problems found that on average, they scored 66 percent on the story problem, 62 percent on the word problem, and only 43 percent on the equation.[5] In other words, students were more likely to solve the verbal problems correctly than the equation. Investigating students' written work helps explain why.

Students often solved the verbal problems without using the equation. For instance, some students used a generate-and-test strategy: They estimated a value for the hourly rate (e.g., $4/hour), computed the corresponding pay (e.g., $90), compared it against the given value ($81.90), and repeated as needed. Other students used a more efficient unwind or working backwards strategy. They started with the final value of 81.9 and subtracted 66 to undo the last step of adding 66. Then they took the resulting 15.9 and divided by 6 to undo the first step of multiplying by 6. These strategies made the verbal problems easier than expected. But why were the equations difficult for students? Although experts in algebra may believe no reading is involved in equation solving, students do in fact need to learn how to read equations. The majority of student errors on equations can be attributed to difficulties in correctly comprehending the meaning of the equation.[6] In the above equation, for example, many students added 6 and 66, but no student did so on the verbal problems.

Besides providing some insight into how students think about algebraic problem solving, these studies illustrate how experts in an area such as algebra may have an "expert blind spot" for learning challenges beginners may experience. An expert blind spot occurs when someone skilled in an area overestimates the ease of learning its formalisms or jargon and underestimates learners' informal understanding of its key ideas. As a result, too little attention is paid to linking formal mathematical understanding to informal reasoning. Looking closely at students' work, the strategies they employ, and the errors they make, and even comparing their performance on similar kinds of problems, are some of the ways we can get past such blind spots and our natural tendency to think students think as we do.

Such studies of student thinking contributed to the creation of a technology-enhanced algebra course, originally Pump Algebra Tutor and now Cognitive Tutor Algebra.[7] That course includes an intelligent tutor that provides students with individualized assistance as they use multiple representations (words, tables, graphs, and equations) to analyze real-world problem situations. Numerous classroom studies have shown that this course significantly improves student achievement relative to alternative algebra courses (see www.carnegielearning.com/research). The course, which was based on basic research on learning science, is now in use in over 1,500 schools.

a

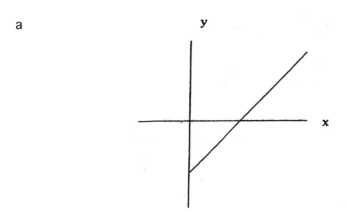

b

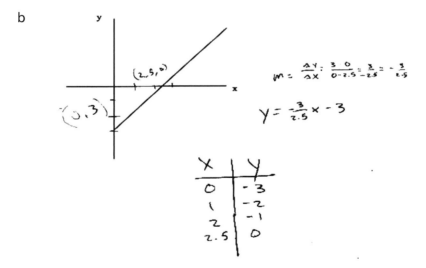

FIGURE 8-1

student did not recognize the inconsistency between the positive slope of the line and the negative slope in the equation. Even good mathematicians could make such a mistake, but they would likely monitor their work as they went along or reflect on the plausibility of the answer and detect the inconsistency. This student could have caught and corrected his error had he acquired both fluency in interpreting the slope of a function from its equation (i.e., to see that it represents a decreasing function) and a reflective strategy for comparing features of different representations.

A second, more fundamental error in the student's solution was that the table of values does not represent a linear function. That is, there is not a constant change in y for every unit change in x. The first three coordinates in the student's table were linear, but he then recorded (2.5, 0) as the fourth coordinate pair rather than (3, 0), which would have made the function linear. He appears to have estimated and recorded coordinate points by visually reading them off the graph without regard for whether the final table embodied linearity. Furthermore, the student did not realize that the equation he produced, $y = \dfrac{-3}{2.5}x - 3$, translates not only into a decreasing line, but also into a table of numbers that decreases by $\dfrac{-3}{2.5}$ for every positive unit change in x.

At a surface level, this student's solution reflects some weaknesses in procedural knowledge, namely, getting the sign wrong on the y-intercept and imprecisely reading x-y coordinates off the graph. More important, however, these surface errors reflect a deeper weakness in the student's conceptual understanding of function. The student either did not have or did not apply knowledge for interpreting key features (e.g., increasing or decreasing) of different function representations (e.g., graph, equation, table) and for using strategies for checking the consistency of these interpretations (e.g., all should be increasing). In general, the student's work on this problem reflects an incomplete conceptual framework for linear functions, one that does not provide a solid foundation for fluid and flexible movement among a function's representations.

This student's work is representative of the difficulties many secondary-level students have with such a problem after completing a traditional textbook unit on functions. In a study of learning and teaching functions, about 25 percent of students taking ninth- and eleventh-grade advanced mathematics courses made errors of this type—that is, providing a table of values that does not reflect a constant slope—following instruction on functions.[8] This performance contrasts with that of ninth- and eleventh-grade mathematics students who solved this same problem after receiving instruction based on the curriculum described in this chapter. This group of students had an 88 percent success rate on the problem. Because these students had developed a deeper understanding of the concept of function, they knew that the y-values in a table must change by the same amount for every unit change in x for the function to be linear. The example in Figure 8-1c shows such thinking.

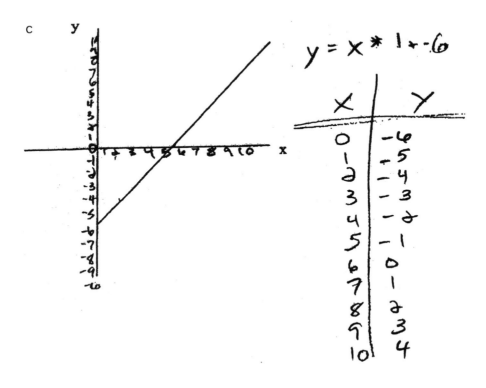

FIGURE 8-1

Problem: Make a table of values that would produce the function seen above.

This student identified a possible y-intercept based on a reasonable scale for the y-axis. She then labeled the x- and y-axes, from which she determined coordinate pairs from the graph and recorded them in a table of values. She determined and recorded values that show a constant increase in y for every positive unit change in x. She also derived an equation for the function that not only corresponds to both the graph and the table, but also represents a linear relationship between x and y.

How might one teach to achieve this kind of understanding? The goal of this chapter is to illustrate approaches to teaching functions that foster deep understanding and mathematical fluency. We emphasize the importance of designing thoughtful instructional approaches and curricula that reflect the principles of *How People Learn* (as outlined in Chapter 1), as well as recent research on what it means to learn and understand functions in particular. We first describe our approach to addressing each of the three principles. We then provide three sample lessons that emphasize those principles in sequence. We hope that these examples provide interesting activities to try with students. More important, these activities incorporate important discoveries about student learning that teachers can use to design other instructional activities to achieve the same goals.

ADDRESSING THE THREE PRINCIPLES

Principle #1: Building on Prior Knowledge

Principle 1 emphasizes the importance of students and teachers continually making links between students' experiences outside the mathematics classroom and their school learning experiences. The understandings students bring to the classroom can be viewed in two ways: as their everyday, informal, experiential, out-of-school knowledge, and as their school-based or "instructional" knowledge. In the instructional approach illustrated here, students are introduced to function and its multiple representations by having their prior experiences and knowledge engaged in the context of a walkathon. This particular context was chosen because (1) students are familiar with money and distance as variable quantities, (2) they understand the contingency relationship between the variables, and (3) they are interested in and motivated by the rate at which money is earned.

The use of a powerful instructional context, which we call a "bridging context," is crucial here. We use this term because the context serves to bridge students' numeric (equations) and spatial (graphic) understandings and to link their everyday experiences to lessons in the mathematics classroom. Following is an example of a classroom interaction that occurred during students' first lesson on functions, showing how use of the walkathon context as an introduction to functions in multiple forms—real-world situation (walkathon), table, graph, verbal ("$1.00 for each kilometer"), situation-specific symbols ($ = 1 * km), and generic symbolic (y = x * 1)—accomplishes these bridging goals. Figures 8-2a through 8-2c show changes in the whiteboard as the lesson proceeded.

| Teacher | What we're looking at is, we're looking at what we do to numbers, to one set of numbers, to get other numbers. . . . So how many of you have done something like a walkathon? A readathon? A swimathon? A bikeathon? |

	[Students raise their hands or nod.] So most of you...So I would say "Hi Tom [talking to a student in class], I'm going to raise money for such and such a charity and I'm going to walk ten kilometers."
Tom	OK.
Teacher	Say you're gonna sponsor me one dollar for every kilometer that I walk. So that's sort of the first way that we can think about a function. It's a rule. One dollar *for* every kilometer walked. So you have one dollar for each kilometer [writing "$1.00 for each kilometer" on the board while saying it]. So then what I do is I need to calculate how much money I'm gonna earn. And I have to start somewhere. So at zero kilometers how much money do I have Tom? How much are you gonna pay me if I collapse at the starting line? [Fills in the number 0 in the left-hand column of a table labeled "km"; the right-hand column is labeled "$".]
Tom	None.
Teacher	So Tom, I managed to walk one kilometer [putting a "1" in the "km" column of the table of values below the "0"]. . . .
Tom	One dollar.
Teacher	One dollar [moving to the graph]. So I'm going to go over one kilometer and up one dollar [see Figure 8-2a].

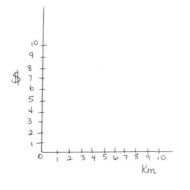 

FIGURE 8-2a Graphing a point from the table: "Over by one kilometer and up by one dollar." The teacher uses everyday English ("up by") and maintains connection with the situation by incorporating the units "kilometer" and "dollar."

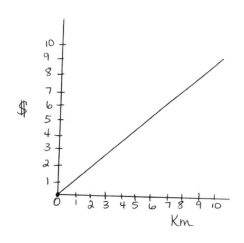

Km	$
0	0
1	1
2	2
3	3
4	4
5	5
6	6

FIGURE 8-2b The teacher and students construct the table and graph point by point, and a line is then drawn.

[Students continue to provide the dollar amounts for each of the successive kilometer values. Simple as it is, students are encouraged to describe the computation—"I multiply two kilometers by one to get two dollars." The teacher fills in the table and graphs each coordinate pair. [The board is now as shown in Figure 8-2b.]

Teacher   Now, what I want you to try and do, first I want you to look at this [pointing to the table that goes from x = 0 to x = 10 for y = x] and tell me what's happening here.

Melissa   You, like, earn one dollar every time you go up. Like it gets bigger by one every time.

Teacher   So every time you walk one kilometer you get one more dollar, right? [Makes "> 1" marks between successive "$" values in the table—see Figure 8-2c.] And if you look on the graph, every time I walk one kilometer I get one more dollar. [Makes "step" marks on the graph.] So now I want to come up with an equation, I want to come up with some way of using this symbol [pointing to the "km" header in the left-hand column of the table] and this symbol [pointing to the "$" header in the right-hand column of the table] to say the same thing, that for every kilometer I walk, let's put it this way, the money I earn is gonna be equal to one times the number of kilometers I walk. Someone want to try that?

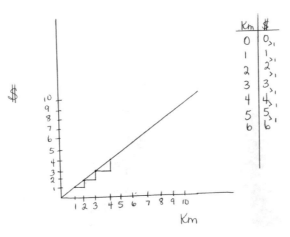

FIGURE 8-2c The teacher highlights the "up by" amount in the table (">1" marks), graph (over and up "step" marks), and symbolic equation (pointing at "*1").

| Alana | Um, kilometers times one equals money. [The teacher writes "km x 1 = $" and "y = x * 1"; see Figure 8-2c.] |
| Teacher | So this equation, this table, and this graph are all the same function. They all mean the same thing. They all mean that you're multiplying each of these numbers (pointing to the values along the x-axis of the graph) by one to get new numbers. |

Another way of building on students' prior knowledge is to engage everyday experiential knowledge. Students frequently know things through experience that they have not been taught explicitly. They can often solve problems in ways we do not teach them or expect if, and this is an important qualification, the problems are described using words, drawings, or notations they understand. For example, the topic of slope is typically reserved for ninth-grade mathematics, and is a part of students' introduction to relations and functions in general and to linear functions in particular. It is generally defined as the ratio of vertical distance to horizontal distance, or "rise to run." The rise is the change in the vertical distance, and the run is the change in the horizontal distance so that $slope = \dfrac{rise}{run}$. Once the equation for a straight line, $y = mx + b$, has been introduced, m is defined as the slope of that line and is calculated using the formula $m = \dfrac{y_2 - y_1}{x_2 - x_1}$.

For students to understand slope in these definitional and symbolic ways, they must already have in place a great deal of formal knowledge, including the meaning of ratio, coordinate graphing, variables, and subscripts, and such skills as solving equations in two variables and combining arithmetic operations. Knowing algorithms for finding the slope of a function, however, does not ensure that the general *meaning* of slope will be understood. As illustrated in Figure 8-1a, a student can know the algorithm for finding the slope, but not understand that the slope of a line characterizes its relative steepness on a graph and tells something about the rate of change in covarying, dependent quantities.

We have found that younger students have intuitive and experiential understandings of slope that can be used to underpin the formal learning that involves conventional notations, algorithms, and definitions. To illustrate, we gave a class of fifth and sixth graders the following situation:

> Jane is in a walkathon. A rule or "function" tells us how much Jane will earn depending on how many kilometers she walks. We don't know what the function is. It is a mystery. We do know that if Jane walks 1 kilometer she will earn 4 dollars and if she walks 3 kilometers she will earn 8 dollars.

Students were asked to figure out the slope of the function that tells how much Jane will earn. Half of the students were provided with the formal rise-over-run ratio definition of slope; the other half were given a definition of slope that reflected more familiar, student language, being told that the slope of a function is the amount by which the answer goes up for every change of one in the start value.

We found that many of these younger students were able to describe informally the slope of the function given in the story problem by figuring out how much Jane's earnings go up by for every kilometer she walks. They noticed that when Jane walks three kilometers instead of one, she earns four more dollars; thus she earns two more dollars for every extra kilometer she walks. In this way, these prealgebra students identified the slope of the mystery function as 2 without receiving instruction on formal definitions or procedures. In contrast, students who were given the textbook definition of slope were not able to determine the slope in this example.

Our point is not that all problems should be phrased in "student language." It is important for students to learn formal mathematics terminology and abstract algebraic symbolism. Our point, instead, is that using student language is one way of first assessing what knowledge students are bringing to a particular topic at hand, and then linking to and building on what they already know to guide them toward a deeper understanding of formal mathematical terms, algorithms, and symbols.

In sum, students' prior knowledge acts as a building block for the development of more sophisticated ways of thinking mathematically. In some cases, we may underestimate the knowledge and skills students bring to the learning of functions. Topics and activities we presume to be challenging and difficult for students may in fact have intuitive or experiential underpinnings, and it is important to discover these and use them for formalizing students' thinking.

Principle #2: Building Conceptual Understanding, Procedural Fluency, and Connected Knowledge

The focus of Principle 2 is on simultaneously developing conceptual understanding and procedural fluency, and helping students connect and organize knowledge in its various forms. Students can develop surface facility with the notations, words, and methods of a domain of study (e.g., functions) without having a foundation of understanding. For students to understand such mathematical formalisms, we must help them connect these formalisms with other forms of knowledge, including everyday experience, concrete examples, and visual representations. Such connections form a conceptual framework that holds mathematical knowledge together and facilitates its retrieval and application.

As described previously, we want students to understand the core concept of a fuctional relationship: that the value of one variable is dependent on the value of another. And we want them to understand that the relationship between two variables can be expressed in a variety of ways—in words, equations, graphs, tables—all of which have the same meaning or use the same "rule" for the relationship. Ultimately, we want students' conceptual understanding to be sufficiently secure, and their facility with representing functions in a variety of ways and solving for unknown variables sufficiently fluid, that they can tackle sophisticated problems with confidence. To this end, we need an instructional plan that deliberately builds and secures that knowledge. Good teaching requires not only a solid understanding of the content domain, but also specific knowledge of student development of these conceptual understandings and procedural competencies. The developmental model of function learning that provides the foundation for our instructional approach encompasses four levels—0 to 3—as summarized in Table 8-1. Each level describes what students can typically do at a given developmental stage. The instructional program is then designed to build those competences.

Level 0

Level 0 characterizes the kinds of numeric/symbolic and spatial understandings students typically bring to learning functions. Initially, the numeric and spatial understandings are separate. The initial numeric understanding is one whereby students can iteratively compute *within* a single string of whole numbers. That is, given a string of positive, whole numbers such as 0,

TABLE 8-1 A Developmental Model for Learning Functions

Level	General Description	Example Tasks and Understandings
0	Students have separate numeric and spatial understandings.	
	• Initial numeric understanding: students iteratively compute (e.g., "add 4") *within* a string of positive whole numbers.	Extend the pattern 3, 7, 11, 15, ___, ____, ____.
	• Initial spatial understanding: students represent the relative sizes of quantities as bars on a graph and perceive patterns of qualitative changes in amount by a left-to-right visual scan of the graph, but cannot quantify those changes.	Notice in a bar graph of yearly population figures that each bar is taller than the previous bar.
1	Spatial and numeric understandings are elaborated and integrated, forming a central conceptual structure.	
	• Elaboration of numeric understanding: — Iteratively apply a single operation to, rather than within, a string of numbers to generate a second string of numbers. — Construct an algebraic expression for this repeated operation.	Multiply each number in the sequence 0, 1, 2, ... by 2 to get a set of pairs: 0-0, 1-2, 2-4, ... Generalize the pattern and express it as $y = 2x$.
	• Elaboration of spatial understanding: — Use continuous quantities along the horizontal axis. — Perceive emergent properties, such as linear or increasing, in the shape of the line drawn between points.	Notice that a graph of daily plant growth must leave spaces for unmeasured Saturday and Sunday values.
	• Integration of elaborated understandings:	For every 1 km, a constant "up by" $2 in both the y-column of a table and the y-axis in a graph generates a linear pattern (spatial) with a slope of 2 (numeric). $y = 2x$ can be read

Continued

TABLE 8-1 Continued

Level	General Description	Example Tasks and Understandings
	— See the relationship between the differences in the y-column in a table and the size of the step from one point to the next in the associated graph. • Interpret algebraic representations both numerically and spatially.	from, or produced in, both a table and a graph.
2	• Elaborate initial integrated numeric and spatial understandings to create more sophisticated variations. • Integrate understanding of $y = x$ and $y = x + b$ to form a mental structure for linear functions. • Integrate rational numbers and negative integers. • Form mental structures for other families of functions, such as $y = x^n + b$.	Look at the function below. Could it represent $y = x - 10$? Why or why not? If you think it could not, sketch what you think it looks like.
3	• Integrate variant (e.g., linear and nonlinear) structures developed at level 2 to create higher-order structures for understanding more-complex functions, such as polynomials and exponential and reciprocal functions. • Elaborate understanding of graphs and negative integers to differentiate the four quadrants of the Cartesian plane. • Understand the relationship of these quadrants to each other.	At what points would the function $y = 10x - x^2$ cross the x axis? Please show all of your work.

2, 4, 6, 8, ..., students are able to see the pattern of adding 2 to each successive number. The initial spatial understanding is one whereby students can represent the relative sizes of quantities as bars on a graph. Students can easily see differences in the sizes of bars (how tall they are) and can use this spatial information to draw inferences about associated quantities. Students can read bar graphs that, for instance, show daily measurements of the growth of a plant in the classroom. They can see that each bar is taller than the previous one, that the plant is taller on Friday than on Thursday, but cannot easily quantify those changes.

Level 1

At level 1, students begin to elaborate and integrate their initial numeric and spatial understandings of functions. They elaborate their numeric understanding in two steps. First, whereas students at level 0 can extend a single sequence of numbers such as 0, 2, 4, 6, ..., at level 1 they can operate on one sequence of numbers to produce a second sequence. For example, students can multiply each number in the sequence 0, 1, 2, 3, ... by 2 and form the resulting pairs of values: 0-0, 1-2, 2-4, 3-6, ... Students learn to record these pairs of values in a table and to construct an algebraic equation for this repeated operation by generalizing the pattern into an equation such as $y = 2x$.

Students' spatial understanding is also improving. They come to understand that maintaining equal distances between values on the x-axis is critical to having a meaningful graph of a function. They also progress from understanding graphs with verbal or categorical values along the x-axis, such as cities (with their populations on the y-axis), to understanding graphs with quantitative values along the x-axis, such as time quantified as days (with the height of a plant on each successive day on the y-axis). The example of graphing plant growth is an interesting one because it is an activity at the cusp of this transition. Students initially view values on the x-axis as categorical, not sequenced (so that Thursday, Friday, Monday is okay). Later they come to view these values as quantitative, in a sequence with a fixed distance between the values (such that Thursday, Friday, Monday is not okay because Saturday and Sunday must be accounted for).

Without being able to view the x-axis as quantitative, students cannot see graphs as representing the relationship between two changing quantities. Drawing a line to join the points provides a visual representation of the relationship between the quantities. The line offers a way of packaging key properties of the function or pattern of change that can be perceived quickly and easily. For example, students can see how much earnings change per kilometer by looking at the steepness of the line.

As their initial numeric and spatial understandings are elaborated, students at level 1 also begin to connect, or integrate, these understandings. They make connections between tables and graphs of x-y pairs, using one representation to generate inferences that can be checked by the other. The overall pattern of a function can be understood both in the size of the increments in the y-column of the table and in the steepness of the line moving from one point to another in the graph. The constant "up-by" 1 seen, for example, in Figure 8-2c in the right-hand column of a table is the same as the constant "up-by" 1 in a line of a graph (see the same figure). As these views become integrated, students develop a deeper and more flexible understanding of functions, in this case, a linear pattern with a rise of 1. With this new integrated mental structure for functions, students can support numeric and spatial understandings of algebraic representations such as $y = 1x$.

Grasping why and how the line on a graph maps onto the relationship described in a word problem or an equation is a core conceptual understanding. If students' understanding is only procedural, they will not be well prepared for the next level (see Box 8-2). To ensure that students master the concepts at this level, complex content is avoided. Students are not required to operate with negative or rational numbers or carry out more than one operation in a single function (such as multiplying x by any value and adding or subtracting a constant, as in the general $y = mx + b$ form). Such limiting of these complicating factors is intended to minimize loads on processing and working memory, thus enabling students to focus on the essence of the integration of numeric and spatial understandings of function. Students learn more complex content during levels 2 and 3.

Level 2

As students progress to level 2, they begin to elaborate their initial integrated numeric and spatial understandings. In doing so, they begin to combine operations and develop fluency with functions in the form $y = mx + b$, where m and b can be positive or negative rational numbers. They also work with $y = x^n + b$, where n is a positive whole number, and b is any positive or negative rational number. For a full elaboration to occur, it is necessary for students to understand integers and rational numbers and have facility in computing with both of these number systems. Finally, students differentiate families of functions to see differences in the shapes and characteristics of linear, quadratic, and cubic functions.

Level 3

At level 3, students learn how linear and nonlinear terms can be related and understand the properties and behaviors of the resulting entities by analyzing these relations. To achieve this understanding, students must have well-constructed and differentiated models of different sorts of functions, such as quadratics in the form $y = ax^2 + bx + c$ or $y = a(x - p)^2 + q$; polynomials; and reciprocal, exponential, and growth functions. They must also have the necessary facility with computational, algebraic, and graphing operations to interrelate the numeric/symbolic and spatial representations of these complex functions. Furthermore, students must elaborate their understanding of graphs so they differentiate the four quadrants of the Cartesian plane, understand the relationship of these quadrants to each other, and relate these quadrants to negative numbers.

Recall Figure 8-1a and the difficulties the student had in producing a table of values for an increasing linear function with a negative y-intercept. This student did not recognize, or at least did not acknowledge, why it is impossible for the given function to have a negative slope and to have a table of values without a constant rate of change. These are the sorts of problems that occur when students experience instruction that fails to promote the development of a sound conceptual framework for functions. Now consider the solution to the problem in Box 8-3, in which a student introduces a table (without prompting) to help solve a problem about interpreting a graph in terms of an equation.

This student exhibited an integrated concept of function. He generated a response that showed consistency between the spatial (graph) and numeric (table and equation) representations of the function. He explained why the function has a slope of –2 as per its numeric (tabular) and spatial (graphic) representations and correctly symbolized that rationale in the equation.

Such integration can be supported in the classroom. For example, throughout the walkathon classroom exchange reported earlier, the teacher is moving fluidly and rapidly between numeric and spatial representations of a function (the table and equation and the graph, respectively). Such movement helps students simultaneously build understandings of each of these representations in isolation, and of the integrated nature of the representations in particular and the concept in general. This integration helps students begin to understand and organize their knowledge in ways that facilitate the retrieval and application of relevant mathematical concepts and procedures.

If students' numeric and spatial understandings are not integrated, they may not notice when a conclusion drawn from one understanding is inconsistent with a conclusion drawn from another. The inconsistencies found in the student's work in Figure 8-1a illustrate such a lack of reflective recognition.

BOX 8-2 **The Devil's in the Details: The 3-Slot Schema for Graphing a Line**

What students glean from instruction is often very different from what we as teachers intend. This observation is nicely illustrated by the research of Schoenfeld and colleagues.[9] They detail the surprising misunderstandings of a 16-year old advanced algebra student who is grappling with conceptual questions about equations and graphs of linear functions.

Most standard algebra instruction is intended to guide students toward developing what Schoenfeld and colleagues[10] call the "2-slot schema" for understanding and graphing an equation for a line. This schema says that knowing the slope of a line and its y-intercept enables one to obtain a complete description of the line, both graphically and algebraically. Call the line L; let its slope be m and its y-intercept b. Algebraically, the line L has equation $y = mx + b$ if and only if the line has slope m and y-intercept b. Graphically, the line L passes through the point (0, b) and rises m units vertically for each unit it traverses horizontally.

The student in Schoenfeld's study, called IN, was relatively sophisticated in understanding aspects of the above schema. However, IN's knowledge was not fully integrated, and she exhibited a surprising misunderstanding. She initially believed that three quantities must be known to graph an equation of a line: (1) slope, (2) y-intercept, and (3) x-intercept. After having solved the equation $2 = 4x + 1$ to get $x = 1/4$, she was asked to the graph the function $4x + 1$ on the right side of this equation. She responded as follows: "the slope, which is 4, . . . the y-intercept, which is 1,…and…the x-intercept, which is 1/4, so we've found everything." Note that IN said that to find "everything," she needed the slope, y-intercept, *and* x-intercept. In other words, she appeared to have a 3-slot schema for understanding and graphing a linear equation instead of the 2-slot schema described above.

Clearly this student had received extensive instruction in linear functions. For instance, in an earlier exchange, when asked for an equation of

Principle #3: Building Resourceful, Self-Regulating Problem Solvers

As discussed above, teaching aimed at developing robust and fluent mathematical knowledge of functions should build on students' existing real-world and school knowledge (Principle 1) and should integrate procedural

a straight line, she immediately said, "y = mx + b." However, IN lacked a well-integrated understanding of the relationships between the features of the equation and graphical forms of a line. Schoenfeld and colleagues[11] explain:

> When a person knowledgeable about the domain determines that the slope of a particular line is some value (say, 1. . .) and that its intercept is some other value (say, 3), then the job is done. The equation of the line must be y = (1)x + 3. IN had no such procedure. Although she believed that the slope, x-intercept, and y-intercept were all important (and she could read the values of the slope and y-intercept off equations of the form y = mx + b), she did not have a stable procedure for determining the values of those entities from a graph and did not know what to do with the values when she had them.

> As other researchers have shown,[12] learners often struggle to tell the difference between the surface features of a subject, which are easy to see but can be misleading, and the deep features, which are difficult to see but are needed for understanding and accurate performance. In this case, three "entities" or aspects of the graph of a line stood out when IN looked at a graph: namely, where it crossed the x-axis, where it crossed the y-axis, and the steepness of the line. All three are important, but IN had the surface understanding that all three are *necessary*. She appeared to lack the deeper understanding that only two of these three are needed to draw a line. She did not understand how using the y-intercept and slope, in particular, facilitate an efficient graphing strategy because they can be read immediately off the standard form of an equation.

Schoenfeld and colleagues' fine-grained analysis of learning nicely illustrates how subtle and easily overlooked misconceptions can be—even among our best students.[13]

skill and conceptual understanding (Principle 2). However, instruction should assist students not only in thinking *with* mathematical procedures and concepts, but also in thinking *about* procedures and concepts and in reflecting on and articulating their own thinking and learning. This kind of thinking about thinking, or metacognition, is the focus of Principle 3. Encouraging students to reflect on and communicate their ideas about functions supports

BOX 8-3 An Integrated Understanding of Functions

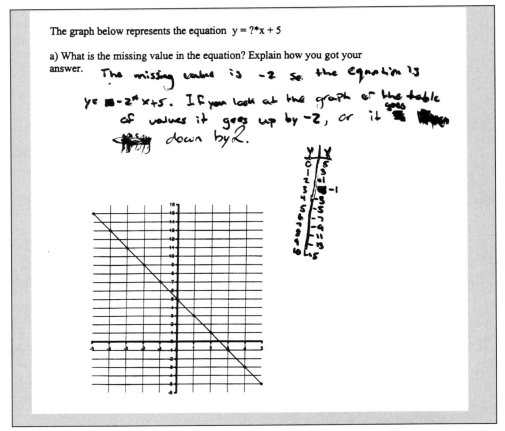

The graph below represents the equation $y = ?*x + 5$

a) What is the missing value in the equation? Explain how you got your answer.

The missing value is -2 so the equation is $y = \blacksquare -2^* x + 5$. If you look at the graph or the table of values it goes up by -2, or it goes down by 2.

them in making the connections among representations that are necessary for flexible, fluent, and reliable performance.

A particularly important type of metacognitive thinking in mathematics is coordinating conclusions drawn from alternative mathematical representations or strategies. Teachers will recognize one form of such coordination in the well-known recommendation that students solve problems in more than one way (e.g., add up and add down) to check whether the same answer is found. A more subtle form of such coordination was exemplified in the earlier discussion of desired student performance on the assessment item shown in Figure 8-1a. In this example, good metacognitive thinking was not about checking the consistency of *numeric answers* obtained using different *strategies*, but about checking the consistency of *verbal interpretations* (e.g., increasing vs. decreasing) of different *representations*. In other words, we want to encourage students to think about problems not only in multiple ways (strategies), but also with multiple tools (representations), and to draw conclusions that are not only quantitative (numeric answers), but also qualitative (verbal interpretations).

Supporting metacognitive thinking and attitudes goes beyond reflection and coordination of alternative mathematical representations and strategies. It includes creating a classroom atmosphere in which students feel comfortable to explore, experiment, and take risks in problem solving and learning. It also includes helping students develop a tolerance for the difficulties mathematics sometimes presents and a will to persevere when, for example, they are unable to detect the pattern in the table of values that identifies the relationship between x and y in a particular function. Yet another type of instructional support for metacognitive thinking involves helping students become better help seekers. Students need to learn to recognize when they have reached the limits of their understanding and to know how to obtain the support they need, including asking the teacher or a fellow student; consulting reference materials; and using such tools as computer software, the Internet, or a graphing calculator.

TEACHING FUNCTIONS FOR UNDERSTANDING

Good teaching requires more than knowledge of the content to be taught and of a developmental model for how students acquire an understanding of that content. It also requires a set of instructional strategies for moving students along that developmental pathway and for addressing the obstacles and opportunities that appear most frequently along the way. Below we describe a unit of instruction, based on the developmental model described above, that has been shown experimentally to be more effective than traditional instruction in increasing understanding of functions for eighth and tenth graders.[14] In fact, sixth-grade students taught with this instructional approach were more successful on a functions test than eighth and tenth graders who had learned functions through conventional instruction. At the secondary level, tenth graders learning with this approach demonstrated a deeper understanding of complex nonlinear functions. For instance, they performed significantly better on a test item requiring them to draw a "qualitative" graph (no scale on the axes) of the function $y = x^3$ in relation to a given graph of $y = x^4$.

Curriculum for Moving Students Through the Model

This section summarizes the key features and activities of a curriculum that was developed for moving students through the four-level learning sequence described above. We believe such theory-based instruction encourages students (1) to build on and apply their prior knowledge (Principle 1),

(2) to construct an integrated conceptual framework for understanding functions (principle 2), and (3) to apply metacognitive skills to their learning (principle 3). An overview of this curriculum is presented in Table 8-2, followed by a more detailed description. Example lessons are provided in the next section.

The curricular sequence we suggest has been used effectively with students in sixth, eighth, tenth, and eleventh grades. Because timetables and scheduling vary from school to school and from grade to grade, the amount of material per lesson will also vary depending on the available class time. This unit requires approximately 650 minutes of class time to complete. We recommend that it be taught as a whole and in the sequence suggested, even if students are in an upper secondary-level grade and require the more advanced level 3 material. We emphasize implementing the full sequence of topics because the concepts addressed in the level 3 material are supported by a deep and flexible understanding of the ideas found in the level 1 and 2 material, an understanding that is often insufficiently developed in earlier grades. Students in the senior grades will likely move more quickly through the beginning part of the unit than will junior students, and the extra time allotted for the unit can then be used for working through more-advanced ideas that are likely beyond younger students' capabilities.

The instructional approach we are suggesting is different from some more traditional approaches in many ways. First, the latter approaches often use different contexts or situations for introducing the individual topics within the domain, rather than the single bridging context of the walkathon we use. Within one curriculum, for example, the gradient of a hill may be used for introducing slope, and fixed cost in production may be used for introducing y-intercept. Mixing contexts can make understanding $y = mx + b$ as an integrated concept more difficult than is the case if slope and y-intercept are introduced within the same context.

The use of multiple representations is another significant feature of the suggested curriculum, one that again distinguishes it from more traditional approaches. In many traditional approaches, instruction may be focused on a single representation (e.g., equation or graph) for weeks before multiple representations are related. In our curricular approach, tables, graphs, equations, and verbal rules are copresented within seconds, and students are encouraged to see them as equivalent representations of the same mathematical relationship. Emphasis is placed on moving among these representations and on working to understand how they relate to each other.

Our approach also engages students in the construction of functional notation, and thus helps them build notations and meanings for such constructs as slope and y-intercept into equations. This approach contrasts with many existing curricula, which give students the formal notation and then focus on introducing them to procedures for finding, for example, the slope of a linear function or the vertex of a quadratic function. Over the course of our instruction, students progressively formalize their own initial notations until those notations correspond with conventional general equations, such as $y = mx + b$ or $y = ax^2 + bx + c$.

Finally, the kinds of follow-up activities we suggest may differ from those of more traditional approaches. We suggest activities that allow students to remain situated in the context of instruction for the first part of the unit (that is, related to a walkathon) until they are confident and competent with the concepts on a more abstract basis. Then, when students move to the computer environment, they engage in activities in which no new concepts are introduced at first. Rather, students have time to consolidate the individual concepts addressed in the first part of the unit, and then move on to more challenging activities that advance their thinking and understanding in the domain. These more challenging activities involve the addition of new features to familiar structures. For example, the left-hand quadrants of the Cartesian plane are eventually included in activities, and linear terms are added to $y = x^2 + b$ to generate equations in the form $y = ax^2 + bx + c$. Students also give presentations on a particular kind of function (e.g., linear, quadratic, reciprocal, cubic) to their classmates. In these presentations, students share their understanding of and expertise in key characteristics and behaviors of these functions.

Example Lessons

In the following sections, we elaborate on three specific lessons that highlight the role of the three principles of *How People Learn* in the curriculum described in Table 8-2. Although we do not provide a complete description of these lessons, the example activities should be sufficient to suggest how the lessons might be used in other classrooms. The three lessons and their companion activities illustrate the principles of *How People Learn* in three key topic areas: slope, y-intercept, and quadratic functions. Example lesson 1, "Learning Slope," illustrates principle 1, building on students' prior knowledge. Example lesson 2, "Learning y-intercept," illustrates principle 2, connecting students' factual/procedural and conceptual knowledge. Example lesson 3, "Operating on $y = x^2$," illustrates principle 3, fostering reflective thinking or metacognition in students. Although each of the selected lessons is used to highlight one of the principles in particular, the reader should keep in mind that all three principles interact simultaneously throughout each lesson.

TABLE 8-2 Suggested Curricular Sequence

Topic	Description	Activities
Level 1 Introduction	The walkathon bridging context is introduced. Students record in tables the money earned for each kilometer walked and plot each pair of values for a variety of rules. Using kilometers and dollars, an equation is constructed based on the rule of sponsorship.	Student partners each invent at least two of their own sponsorship arrangements, for which their partner constructs tables, graphs, and equations.
Slope	Slope is introduced as the constant numeric up-by (or down-by) amount between successive dollar values in a table or a graph. It is a relative measure of the steepness of a function. It is the amount by which each kilometer (x – value) is multiplied.	Students are asked to find the slope of several different functions expressed in tables, graphs, and equations.
y-Intercept	y-Intercept is introduced as the "starter offer," that is, a fixed starting bonus students receive before the walkathon begins. It affects only the vertical starting point of the numeric sequence and graph. It does not affect the steepness or shape of the line.	Students invent two linear functions that allow them to earn exactly $153.00 after walking 10 kilometers. Students record the slope and y-intercept of each function and explain how the y-intercept of each function can be found in its table, graph, and equation.
Curving functions	Nonlinear functions are introduced as those having up-by amounts that increase (or decrease) after each kilometer walked. They are	Students are asked to decide which of four functions expressed in tables are nonlinear and to explain their reasoning. They are also

TABLE 8-2 Continued

Topic	Description	Activities
	derived by multiplying the kilometers (x) by itself at least . once The more times x is multiplied by itself, the greater is the difference between dollar values and thus the steeper the curve.	asked to write an equation for and to sketch and label the graph of each function. Students are asked to come up with a curved-line function for earning $153.00 over 10 kilometers.
Levels 2 and 3 Computer activities	Level 2 students use spreadsheet technology and prepared files and activity sheets to consolidate and extend the understandings they constructed about slope, y-intercept, and linearity in the first part of the curriculum. Level 3 extensions include working in all four quadrants to transform quadratic and cubic functions and to explore the properties, behaviors, and characteristics of exponential, reciprocal, and other polynomial functions.	Students change the steepness, y-intercept, and direction of $y = x$ and $y = x^2$ to make the function go through preplotted points. They record the numeric, algebraic, and graphic effects of their changes. They also invent functions with specific attributes, such as parallel to $y = 4x$ and a y-intercept below the x-axis, or an inverted parabola that is compressed and in the lower left-hand quadrant.
Presentations	Groups of students investigate and then prepare a presentation about a particular type of function. Presentations stimulate discussion and summarizing of key concepts and serve as a partial teacher assessment for evaluating students' post-instruction understanding about functions.	Groups of students use computer-generated output of graphs, equations, and tables to illustrate a particular type of function's general properties and behaviors. Students give presentations about their function and share their expertise with classmates.

Example Lesson 1: Learning Slope

The classroom interaction recounted below took place during students' first lesson on slope. The students had already worked through the construction of representations for the introductory rule of the walkathon—earning one dollar for every kilometer walked. In this interaction we can see how Katya quickly grasps the idea of slope as relative steepness, as defined by the variable relationship between two quantities (distance walked and money earned in this case):

Teacher	I want to think of a way, let's see, Katya, how might you sponsor me that would make a line that is steeper than this [y = x is already drawn on graph, as in Figure 8-2b]?
Katya	Steeper? Alright . . . every kilometer you walk you get two dollars.
Teacher	Two dollars. So let's try that. So at zero kilometers how much am I going to have?
Katya	At zero kilometers you'll have zero.
Teacher	At one?
Katya	You'll have two.
Teacher	And what happens at ten?
Katya	At ten you'll have twenty.
Teacher	So Katya, what have you done each time?
Katya:	I've just multiplied by two.
Teacher	You've multiplied each one of these [pointing to the numbers in the left column of the table] by two, right? Zero times two, one times two [moving finger back and forth between columns]. If I graph that, where's it going to start, Katya?
Katya	It's going to start at zero.
Teacher	So at zero kilometers, zero money. At one?
Katya	At one it's going to go to two.
Teacher	At two it's going to go to?
Katya	Four.
Teacher	Over two up to four. At three?
Katya	It's going to go to six.
Teacher	What do you see on the graph? What do you see happening?

Katya	It's going higher. It's steeper than the other one.
Teacher	So it's steeper and it's going up by how much?
Katya	Two.
Teacher	So Katya, since this is your function, what would the equation for this function be?
Katya	Kilometers times two equals money.
Teacher	That's absolutely right. And what do you notice about these values [pointing to dollar values in the table and making ">" marks between successive values]?
Katya	They're going up by 2.

The Lesson. The lesson on slope is the second lesson suggested in the overall sequence of instruction, after the walkathon has been introduced. It requires about two class periods, or 90 minutes. We introduce slope as the constant numeric up-by amount that is found between successive y-values for every unit change in x. This up-by amount can be seen in a function's table or its graph. The up-by terminology was invented by students who were asked to describe the meaning of slope using their own words. When introducing this up-by idea to students, we suggest beginning with the graph and the table for the rule of earning one dollar for every kilometer walked ($ = 1 x km) and having students see that in each of these representations, the dollar amount goes up by one for each kilometer walked. To show this on the graph, the teacher may draw a staircase-like path from point to point that goes over one and then up one (see Figure 8-2c). In the table, a third column may be created to show the constant up-by difference between successive y-values, as also illustrated in Figure 8-2c. We then suggest drawing students' attention to the facts that this up-by amount corresponds to the mathematical concept of slope and that slope is a relative measure of a function's steepness. That is, the greater the up-by amount, the steeper is the function. From this point on, y = x (y = 1 • x with a slope of 1) may be employed as a landmark function for students to use in qualitative reasoning, by comparison, about the slopes (and later the y-intercepts) of other functions. Conceptual landmarks are crucial tools to support learners in making sense of, catching, and correcting their own and others' errors.

After having created tables and graphs for the one dollar per kilometer context, we challenge students such as Katya to provide sponsorship rules (or functions) having slopes that are steeper and less steep than y = x. To facilitate the comparison of graphs of functions with different slopes, we encourage students to plot functions on the same set of axes. Before each rule is graphed, we ask the students to predict the steepness of the line relative to y = x. We also have them invent other rules and make tables and graphs for those rules. These explorations in multiple contexts and representations develop students' deeper understanding of slope. After all, the essence of understanding is being able to apply a concept flexibly in different contexts and with different representations. After having worked with functions having varying degrees of steepness, we ask the students to summarize their findings about slope and to explain that steeper lines are the result of functions having bigger up-by amounts.

In our instruction, we do not provide students at the outset with an algorithm for finding the slope of a function. However, we do suggest that students be asked for their ideas about how the steepness, or slope, of a function can be quantified—that is, represented as a number—and how they can obtain that number from any of the representations of a function they have seen. This is illustrated by the following teacher–student exchange from a ninth-grade class:

Teacher	This line [pointing to a graph of y = x] has a certain steepness to it. . . . If you had to give a number to this steepness, what would you give it? Look at these numbers (pointing to the corresponding table of values).
Aaron	One.
Teacher	Why one?
Aaron	'Cause they all go up by one.

Introducing and working with functions having negative slopes is also important to show that the way the students have been constructing slope as the up-by amount is applicable to all straight-line functions, whether they increase or decrease. We generally introduce negative values along the y-axis by asking students to think about how the negative values along the y-axis can be used. One situation we employ is from the perspective of the donor or sponsor, who loses money as the participant walks. In our experience, students generally recognize that these lines have a down-by amount when a fixed amount of money is given away for each kilometer walked.

Summary of Principle #1 in the Context of Learning Slope. We have used a lesson on slope to illustrate how students' initial knowledge of a topic can be used for building formal or conventional mathematical knowledge and notation structures. In this case, we draw on three sorts of prior knowledge. First, students' prior knowledge of familiar situations such as earning money in a walkathon can be used to elicit and extend the students' informal, intuitive ideas about a difficult topic such as slope. Second, students' prior knowledge of natural language, such as "up-by," can be used to build a sound foundation of understanding for explaining and working with more formal concepts and procedures, such as finding slope from a graph. Third, prior knowledge with respect to initial numeric and spatial understandings can be integrated through instruction to help students construct a conceptual understanding of slope within a broader framework for understanding functions in general.

Example Lesson 2: Learning y-Intercept

This example lesson focuses on learning and teaching y-intercept. It illustrates the effect of theory-based instructional design in connecting students' factual/procedural and conceptual knowledge (principle 2).

A commonly taught procedure for finding the y-intercept of a function is to substitute x = 0 into the function's equation, with the result being the y-intercept. Instead of starting by formally introducing this method, this lesson begins by having students explore situations in which a nonzero starting amount is used. This approach appears to do a better job of helping students learn the formal procedure in the context of a robust conceptual understanding.

The Lesson. The lesson on y-intercept follows that on slope in the overall curricular sequence. Two class periods of about 90 minutes are suggested for working with y-intercept. We introduce the y-intercept by suggesting the idea of a starting bonus or an initial amount of money that may be contributed before the walkathon even begins. Students have termed this starting amount the "starter offer" or "starter upper." These phrases have repeatedly been shown to be simple for students to understand first in the walkathon context and then in more abstract situations.

We again begin this lesson with a sponsorship arrangement of earning one dollar for every kilometer walked. We then have students graph this function, construct a table of values, and write a symbolic representation for the function. We then tell students they will be given a five-dollar starter offer just for participating in the walkathon. That is, before they have walked at all, they will already have earned five dollars. In addition to this starting bonus, they will still be earning one dollar for every kilometer walked. Students are then asked to construct a table for this function and to calculate how much money they will have earned at zero kilometers, one kilometer, two kilometers, and so on. After the table has been constructed, students are asked to graph the function and to make an equation for it. Having students verbally describe the relationship between the kilometers and dollars helps them formulate an equation. For example, a student might say, "I think it would be five plus the kilometers equals money." That description could then be translated into the situation-specific symbolic expression 5 + km = $, and that expression, in turn, formalized into the general expression, y = x + 5.

As the lesson proceeds, we suggest other rules whereby students earn one dollar per kilometer but have different starter offer amounts, such as two dollars, ten dollars, and three and a half dollars. We ask the students first to predict where on a graph each new function will be relative to the first example given (y = x + 5) and then to construct tables, graphs, and equations for each new function. Students are asked to describe any patterns or salient characteristics they see in this group of functions. What we want students to see, both literally and figuratively, is that all of the functions are parallel, with a slope of 1, but their starting point on the graph changes in accordance with the starting bonus offered. Furthermore, the distance between points on any two graphs is equal to the difference in starting bonuses. For example, the functions 5 + km = $ and 10 + km = $ are five units apart at every point along the line of each function. Likewise, in examining the tables for each of the functions, we want students to see that all of the functions go up by one (accounting for the parallel lines), but the first value in the dollar column of each of the tables is equal to the starting bonus. We then connect the "starting points" of the graphs and tables with the structure of the equations to show that the starting bonus is indeed added to each x-value.

Emphasizing that the only effect of changing the starter offer is a vertical shift in a function is crucial because a number of researchers have found that students regularly confuse the values for slope and y-intercept in equations. That is, in an equation such as y = 2x + 7, many students are unsure of which "number" is the y-intercept and which is the slope. Initially, students of all ages and grades in our program often predict that changing the starter offer will also change the steepness (slope) of a function. However, working through many examples for which the amount earned per kilometer (the slope) is held constant will help students see, in context, that changing the starting bonus does not affect the amount being earned per kilometer, which is how the steepness or slope of the function is determined. Ultimately, by establishing the meaning of y-intercept in the context of the walkathon and by applying that meaning to the different representations of a function, the confusion of slope and y-intercept is significantly minimized for students.

Negative y-intercepts are introduced using the idea of debt. In this case, students have to pay off a starter offer amount. For example, a student in one of our studies suggested that if she owed ten dollars on her credit card and paid off one dollar every time she walked a kilometer, she would have to start at minus ten dollars. Then after one kilometer, she would pay off one dollar and still be nine dollars in debt, then eight, then seven, etc. Students can construct tables, graphs, and equations for such situations that they invent and perhaps share with a partner or the class. The writing of the equations for these functions may take different forms at first. Many students choose to adhere to the notion that the starter offer is "added" in the equation. Thus an equation for a function such as that described above would look like $ = 1 • km + –10. While students are consolidating the concept of y-intercept and distinguishing it from slope, we recommend that they be allowed to write equations in this way. An alternative, more conventional format may be suggested by repeating the function and writing it in conventional notation alongside the student-constructed expression. Again, we stress the importance of students' developing a conceptual framework for these difficult concepts, which can be formalized over time once the ideas are firmly in place.

Following is a short classroom exchange between a teacher and a student. The context of earning five dollars per day for a paper route had already been developed by the teacher for an earlier teaching example. The teacher continued with this context in introducing linear functions with negative y-intercepts and positive slopes.

Teacher	We owe 90 dollars, so think of it as a negative amount we have and over time we're coming up toward zero. We're coming toward breaking even; towards no longer being in debt. So every day that goes 5 dollars toward zero [referring to and constructing both a graph and a table]. So up by 5, up by 5, up by 5, and so on. What are these differences [referring to the y values in the table]?
Justin	Positive 5.
Teacher	Ya, we're going up by 5 so as we go across 1 we go up by 5.

In the lessons on nonlinear functions, the starter offer idea is also applied. Generally, students quickly see that including the starter offer in a curved-line function has the same effect as it does on straight-line functions. That is, the steepness of the line (or curve) is not altered by changing the starter offer, only the place at which the function meets the vertical axis in a graph. The result is that each point on the curve is shifted up (or down) by the starter offer amount.

A suggested follow-up activity that addresses both slope and y-intercept is to have students, either individually or in pairs, invent two functions that will allow them to earn exactly $153 upon completing a ten-kilometer walkathon. Both strategies must produce straight lines. We ask students to construct tables, graphs, and equations to show their work, and also ask them to identify the slope and y-intercept of each function. Individuals or pairs of students then show their functions to the whole group. Samples of student work are shown in Box 8-4. We also challenge students to work "backwards," that is, to find what the starter offer would have to be if the slope were 10, or what the slope would have to be if the starter offer were 20.

Summary of Principle #2 in the Context of Learning y-Intercept. We have used a lesson on y-intercept to illustrate how students connect their factual/procedural and conceptual knowledge within the instructional bridging context of a walkathon. The walkathon context is intended to help students relate their new and existing knowledge within an organized conceptual framework in ways that facilitate efficient retrieval of that knowledge. The idea of a "starter offer" gives students a reasonably familiar situation that provides a context for learning y-intercept—ordinarily a relatively abstract and difficult mathematical topic that is often confused with slope in students' understanding of linear function. In our approach, students still learn the notations, symbols, words, and methods necessary for identifying the y-intercept of a function (linear or nonlinear). However, they acquire that knowledge in context and initially without algorithms, and with a depth of understanding and attribution of meaning that minimize the procedural and conceptual difficulties many students experience with the topic.

Example Lesson 3: Operating on $y = x^2$

After the first four lessons, which take place in the classroom, students move to a computer environment where they work with spreadsheet technology to consolidate and apply the concepts introduced in the classroom instruction and to extend their understandings to new situations. The particular lesson we use for illustrating principle 3, developing metacognitive skills, is the fourth in the series of computer activities.

The Lesson. Pairs of students use prepared spreadsheet files to work with a computer screen such as that seen in Figure 8-3. Students are asked to change specific parameters in the function $y = ax^2 + b$ to move the graph through preplotted colored points. The file is designed so the students can change the value of just the exponent, the coefficient of x^2, the y-intercept, or any combination of these. With each change, the graph and table of values change instantly and automatically to reflect the numeric (tabular) and graphic (spatial) implications of that change. For example, students are asked to describe and record what happens to the graph and the "Y" column of the table of values when the exponent in $y = x^2$ is changed to 3, to 4, and then more generally to any number greater than 2. Students are then asked to describe and record what happens to the curve when x^2 is multiplied by

BOX 8-4 Two Different Student Solutions to an Open-Ended Problem

Think of a straight-line function that would allow you to earn exactly that amount in a 10 km walkathon. Consider that you might be given an initial donation ("starter offer") from the school.

a. Make a table of values for your function.

Student 1

x	Y
0	133
1	135
2	137
3	139
4	141
5	143
6	145
7	147
8	149
9	151
10	153

Student 2

Km	$
0	3
1	18
2	33
3	48
4	63
5	78

km	$
6	93
7	108
8	123
9	138
10	153

b. **Sketch** the graph of your function.

Student 1

Student 2

	Student 1	Student 2
Write the equation for your function:	$y = 2 * x + 133$	$km * 15 + 3 = $ $
What is the slope of your function?	2	15
Where is the y-intercept of your function?	$133	3

a value larger than 1, smaller than 1 but greater than 0, and less than 0. They are then asked to compare the tables and graphs for $y = x^2$, $y = 2 * x^2$, $y = 3 * x^2$, $y = 4 * x^2$, etc. and to describe in words what patterns they find. Finally, students are asked to compare the table of values for $y = 2 * x^2$ and $y = -2 * x^2$ and describe what they notice.

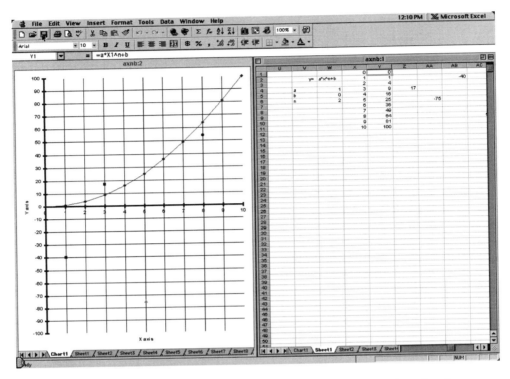

FIGURE 8-3 Sample computer screen. In this configuration, students can change the value of a, n, or b to effect immediate and automatic changes in the graph and the table. For example, if students change the value of b, just the y-intercept of the curve will change. If students change a or n to a positive value other than 1, the degree of steepness of the curve will change. If students change the value of a to a negative value, the curve will come down. All graphic patterns will be reflected in the table of values.

Students must employ effective metacognitive strategies to negotiate and complete these computer activities. Opportunities for exploring, persevering, and knowing when and how to obtain help are abundant. Metacognitive activity is illustrated in the following situation, which has occurred among students from middle school through high school who have worked through these activities.

When students are asked to change the parameters of $y = x^2$ to make it curve down and go through a colored point that is in the lower right quadrant, their first intuition is often to make the exponent rather than the coefficient negative. When they make that change, they are surprised to find that the graph changes shape entirely and that a negative exponent will not satisfy their needs. By trying a number of other possible alterations (persevering), some students discover that they need to change the coefficient of x^2 rather than the exponent to a negative number to make the function curve down. It is then a matter of further exploration and discovery to find the correct value that will make the graph pass through the point in question. Some students, however, require support to discover this solution. Some try to subtract a value from x^2 but are then reminded by the result they see on the computer screen that subtracting an amount from x^2 causes a downward vertical shift of the graph. Drawing students' attention to earlier exercises in which they multiplied the x in y = x by a negative number to make the numeric pattern and the graph go down encourages them to apply that same notion to $y = x^2$. To follow up, we suggest emphasizing for students the numeric pattern in the tables of values for decreasing curves to show how the number pattern decreases with a negative coefficient but not with a negative exponent.

Following is a typical exchange between the circulating teacher and a pair of students struggling with flipping the function $y = x^2$ (i.e., reflecting it in the x-axis). This exchange illustrates the use of metacognitive prompting to help students supervise their own learning by suggesting the coordination of conclusions drawn from one representation (e.g., slope in linear functions) with those drawn from another (e.g., slope in power functions).

Teacher	How did you make a straight line come down or change direction?
John	We used minus.
Teacher	How did you use "minus"?
Pete	Oh yeah, we times it by minus something.
Teacher	So . . . how about here [pointing at the x^2]?
John	We could times it by minus 2 [typing in $x^2 \cdot -2$]. There! It worked.

Without metacognitive awareness and skills, students are at risk of missing important inconsistencies in their work and will not be in a position to self-correct or to move on to more advanced problem solving. The example shown earlier in Figure 8-1a involves a student not reflecting on the inconsistency between a negative slope in his equation and a positive slope in his graph. Another sort of difficulty may arise when students attempt to apply "rules" or algorithms they have been taught for simplifying a solution to a situation that in fact does not warrant such simplification or efficiency.

For example, many high school mathematics students are taught that "you only really need two points to graph a straight line" or "if you know it's a straight line, you only need two points." The key phrase here is "if you know it's a straight line." In our research, we have found students applying

What shape would the graph of the function $y = x^2 + 1$ have? Draw it below.

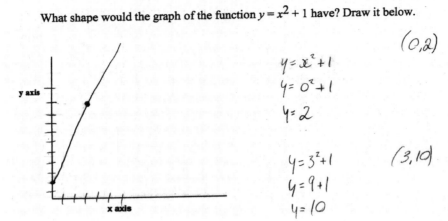

$(0,2)$

$y = x^2 + 1$
$y = 0^2 + 1$
$y = 2$

$y = 3^2 + 1$ $(3,10)$
$y = 9 + 1$
$y = 10$

FIGURE 8-4

that two-point rule for graphing straight lines to the graphing of curved-line functions. In the example shown in Figure 8-4, an eleventh-grade advanced mathematics student who had been learning functions primarily from a textbook unit decided to calculate and plot only two points of the function $y = x^2 + 1$ and then to join them incorrectly with a straight line. This student had just finished a unit that included transformations of quadratic functions and thus presumably *knew* that $y = x^2$ makes a parabola rather than a straight line. What this student did not know to perform, or at least exercise, was a metacognitive analysis of the problem that would have ruled out the application of the two-points rule for graphing this particular function.

Summary of Principle #3 in the Context of Operating on $y = x^2$. The general metacognitive opportunities for the computer activities in our curriculum are extensive. Students must develop and engage their skills involving prediction, error detection, and correction, as well as strategies for scientific inquiry such as hypothesis generating and testing. For instance, because there are innumerable combinations of y-intercept, coefficient, and exponent that will move $y = x^2$ through each of the colored points, students must recognize and acknowledge alternative solution paths. Some students may fixate on the steepness of the curve and get as close to the colored points as possible by adjusting just the steepness of the curve (by changing either the exponent or the coefficient of x^2) and then changing the y-intercept. Others may begin by selecting a manageable y-intercept and then adjust the steepness of the curve by changing the exponent or the coefficient. Others may use both strategies equally. Furthermore, students must constantly be predicting the shapes and behaviors of the functions with which they are working and adjusting and readjusting their expectations with respect to the mathematical properties and characteristics of linear and nonlinear functions.

SUMMARY

Sometimes mathematics instruction can lead to what we refer to as "ungrounded competence." A student with ungrounded competence will display elements of sophisticated procedural or quantitative skills in some contexts, but in other contexts will make errors indicating a lack of conceptual or qualitative understanding underpinning these skills. The student solution shown earlier in Figure 8-1a illustrates such ungrounded competence. On the one hand, the student displays elements of sophisticated skills, including the slope formula and negative and fractional coefficients. On the other hand, the student displays a lack of coordinated conceptual understanding of linear functions and how they appear in graphical, tabular, and symbolic representations. In particular, he does not appear to be able to extract qualitative features such as linearity and the sign of the slope and to check that all three representations share these qualitative features.

The curricular approach described in this chapter is based on cognitive principles and a detailed developmental model of student learning. It was designed to produce grounded competence whereby students can reason with and about multiple representations of mathematical functions flexibly and fluently. Experimental studies have shown that this curriculum is effective in improving student learning beyond that achieved by the same teachers using a more traditional curriculum. We hope that teachers will find the principles, developmental model, and instructional examples provided here useful in guiding their curriculum and teaching choices.

We have presented three example lessons that were designed within one possible unifying context. Other lessons and contexts are possible and desirable, but these three examples illustrate some key points. For instance, students may learn more effectively when given a gradual introduction to ideas. Our curriculum employs three strategies for creating such a gradual introduction to ideas:

- Starting with a familiar context: Contexts that are familiar to students, such as the walkathon, allow them to draw on prior knowledge to think through a mathematical process or idea using a concrete example.
- Starting with simple content: To get at the essence of the idea while avoiding other, distracting difficulties, our curriculum starts with mathematical content that is as simple as possible—the function "you get one dollar for every kilometer you walk" ($y = x$).

- Focusing on having students express concepts in their own language before learning and using conventional terminology: To the extent that a curriculum initially illustrates an idea in an unfamiliar context or with more-complex content, students may be less likely to be able to construct or invent their own language for the idea. Students may better understand and explain new ideas when they progress from thinking about those ideas using their own invented or natural language to thinking about them using formal conventional terms.

A risk of simplicity and familiarity is that students may not acquire the full generality of relevant ideas and concepts. Our curriculum helps students acquire correct generalizations by constructing multiple representations for the same idea for the same problem at the same time. Students make comparisons and contrasts across representations. For example, they may compare the functions $y = .5x$, $y = 2x$, and $y = 10x$ in different representations and consider how the change in slope looks in the graph and how the table and symbolic formula change from function to function. We also emphasize the use of multiple representations because it facilitates the necessary bridging between the spatial and numerical aspects of functions. Each representation has both spatial and numerical components, and students need experience with identifying and constructing how they are linked.

As illustrated earlier in Figure 8-1a, a curriculum that does not take this multiple-representation approach can lead students to acquire shallow ideas about functions, slope, and linearity. The student whose response is shown in that figure had a superficial understanding of how tables and graphs are linked: he could read off points from the graph, but he lacked a deep understanding of the relationship between tables and graphs and the underlying idea of linearity. He did not see or "encode" the fact that because the graph is linear, equal changes in x must yield equal changes in y, and the values in the table must represent this critical characteristic of linearity.

The curriculum presented in this chapter attempts to focus limited instructional time on core conceptual understanding by using multiple representations and generalizing from variations on just a few familiar contexts. The goal is to develop robust, generalizable knowledge, and there may be multiple pathways to this end. Because instructional time is limited, we decided to experiment with a primary emphasis on a single simple, real-world context for introducing function concepts instead of using multiple contexts or a single complex context. This is not to say that students would not benefit from a greater variety of contexts and some experience with rich, complex, real-world contexts. Other contexts that are relevant to students' *current* real-world experience could help them build further on prior knowledge. Moreover, contexts that are relevant to students' *future* real-world experiences, such as fixed and variable costs of production, could help them in their later work life. Since our lessons can be accomplished in anywhere from 3 to 6 weeks (650 minutes), there is sufficient time for other activities to supplement and extend students' experience.

In addition to providing a gradual introduction to complex ideas, a key point illustrated by our lessons is that curriculum should be mathematically sound and targeted toward high standards. Although the lessons described here start gradually, they quickly progress to the point at which students work with and learn about sophisticated mathematical functions at or beyond what is typical for their grade level. For instance, students progress from functions such as $y = x$ to $y = 10 - .4x$ in their study of linear functions across lessons 1 to 3, and from $y = x^2$ to $y = (x - 2)^2 + 4$ in their study of nonlinear functions across lessons 4 to 8.

We do not mean to suggest that this is the only curriculum that promotes a deep conceptual understanding of functions or that illustrates the principles of *How People Learn*. Indeed, it has important similarities, as well as differences, with other successful innovations in algebra instruction, such as the Jasper Woodbury series and Cognitive Tutor Algebra (previously called PUMP), both described in *How People Learn*. All of these programs build on students' prior knowledge by using problem situations and making connections among multiple representations of function. However, whereas the Jasper Woodbury series emphasizes rich, complex, real-world contexts, the approach described in this chapter keeps the context simple to help students perceive and understand the richness and complexity of the underlying mathematical functions. And whereas Cognitive Tutor Algebra uses a wide variety of real-world contexts and provides intelligent computer tutor support, the approach described here uses spreadsheet technology and focuses on a single context within which a wide variety of content is illustrated.

All of these curricula, however, stand in contrast to more traditional textbook-based curricula, which have focused on developing the numeric/symbolic and spatial aspects of functions in isolation and without particular attention to the out-of-school knowledge that students bring to the classroom. Furthermore, these traditional approaches do not endeavor to connect the two sorts of understandings, which we have tried to show is an essential part of building a conceptual framework that underpins students' learning of functions and ultimately their learning in related areas.

ACKNOWLEDGMENTS

Thanks to Ryan Baker, Brad Stephens, and Eric Knuth for helpful comments. Thanks to the McDonnell Foundation for funding.

NOTES

1. The study of functions, as we define it here, overlaps substantially with the topic of "algebra" traditionally taught in the United States in ninth grade, though national and many state standards now recommend that aspects of algebra be addressed in earlier grades (as is done in most other countries). Although functions are a critical piece of algebra, other aspects of algebra, such as equation solving, are not addressed in this chapter.
2. Thomas, 1972, p. 17.
3. Goldenberg, 1995; Leinhardt et al., 1990; Romberg et al., 1993.
4. Nathan and Koedinger, 2000.
5. Koedinger and Nathan, 2004.
6. Koedinger and Nathan, 2004.
7. Koedinger et al., 1997.
8. Kalchman, 2001.
9. Schoenfeld et al., 1993.
10. Schoenfeld et al., 1987.
11. Schoenfeld et al., 1998, p. 81.
12. Chi et al., 1981.
13. Chi et al., 1981; Schoenfeld et al., 1993.
14. Kalchman, 2001.

REFERENCES

Chi, M.T.H., Feltovich, P.J., and Glaser, R. (1981). Categorization and representation of physics problems by experts and novices. *Cognitive Science, 5,* 121-152.

Goldenberg, E.P. (1995). Multiple representations: A vehicle for understanding. In D. Perkins, J. Schwartz, M. West, and M. Wiske (Eds.), *Software goes to school: Teaching for understanding with new technologies* (pp. 155-171). New York: Oxford University Press.

Kalchman, M. (2001). *Using a neo-Piagetian framework for learning and teaching mathematical functions.* Doctoral Dissertation, Toronto, Ontario, University of Toronto.

Koedinger, K.R., and Nathan, M.J. (2004). The real story behind story problems: Effects of representations on quantitative reasoning. *Journal of the Learning Sciences, 13*(2).

Koedinger, K.R., Anderson, J.R., Hadley, W.H., and Mark, M.A. (1997). Intelligent tutoring goes to school in the big city. *International Journal of Artificial Intelligence in Education, 8,* 30-43.

Leinhardt, G., Zaslavsky, O., and Stein, M. (1990). Functions, graphs, and graphing: Tasks, learning, and teaching. *Review of Educational Research, 60*(1), 1-64.

Nathan, M.J., and Koedinger, K.R. (2000). Teachers' and researchers' beliefs of early algebra development. *Journal for Research in Mathematics Education, 31*(2), 168-190.

Romberg, T., Fennema, E., and Carpenter, T.P. (1993). *Integrating research on the graphical representation of functions.* Mahwah, NJ: Lawrence Erlbaum Associates.

Schoenfeld, A.H. (1987). *Cognitive science and mathematics education.* Mahwah, NJ: Lawrence Erlbaum Associates.

Schoenfeld, A.H. (1998). Reflections on a course in mathematical problem solving. In A.H. Schoenfeld, J. Kaput, and E. Dubinsky (Eds.), *CBMS issues in mathematics education* (vol. 7, pp. 81-99.) Washington, DC: Conference Board of the Mathematical Sciences.

Schoenfeld, A.H., Smith J., and Arcavi A. (1993). Learning: The microgenetic analysis of one student's evolving understanding of a complex subject matter. In R. Glaser (Ed.), *Advances in Instructional Psychology* (vol. 4, pp. 55-175). Mahwah, NJ: Lawrence Erlbaum Associates.

Thomas, G.B. (1972). *Calculus and analytic geometry.* Reading, MA: Addison-Wesley.

OTHER RELEVANT READINGS

Bednarz, N., Kieran, C., and Lee, L. (1996). *Approaches to algebra. Perspectives for research and teaching.* Dordrecht, The Netherlands: Kluwer Academic Press.

Confrey, J., and Smith, E. (1995). Splitting, co-variation, and their role in the development of exponential functions. *Journal for Research in Mathematics Education, 26*(1), 66-86.

Janvier, C. (1987). *Problems of representation in the teaching and learning of mathematics.* Mahwah, NJ: Lawrence Erlbaum Associates.

Kaput, J.J. (1989). Linking representations in the symbol systems of algebra. In S. Wagner and C. Kieran (Eds.), *Research issues in the learning and teaching of algebra* (pp. 167-181). Reston, VA: National Council of Teachers of Mathematics.

Part III

SCIENCE

9

Scientific Inquiry and
How People Learn

John D. Bransford and M. Suzanne Donovan

Many of us learned science in school by studying textbooks that re-ported the conclusions of what scientists have learned over the decades. To know science meant to know the definitions of scientific terms and impor-tant discoveries of the past. We learned that an insect has three body parts and six legs, for example, and that water (H_2O) is a molecule composed of two hydrogen atoms and one oxygen atom. We learned that the planets in our solar system revolve around the sun and that gravity holds us to the earth. To be good at science meant to reproduce such information as accu-rately and completely as possible. The focus of this kind of instruction was on *what* scientists know.

Of course, many of us were also introduced to "the scientific method." This typically involved some variation on steps such as "formulate a hypoth-esis, devise a way to test the hypothesis, conduct your test, form conclusions based on your findings, and communicate what you have found." Often information about the scientific method was simply one more set of facts to be memorized. But some of us were given opportunities to use the scientific method to perform hands-on experiments. We might have tested whether wet or dry paper towels could hold the most weight; whether potential insulators such as aluminum foil, paper, or wool were the best ways to keep a potato hot; and so forth. This emphasis on the scientific method was designed to provide insights into *how* scientists know. Much of this science instruction—both the "what" and the "how"—was inconsistent with the prin-ciples highlighted in *How People Learn* (see Chapter 1).

Two major national efforts conducted during the last decade have pro-vided new guidelines and standards for creating more effective science education. The new guidelines include an emphasis on helping students develop (1) familiarity with a discipline's concepts, theories, and models; (2) an understanding of how knowledge is generated and justified; and (3) an ability to use these understandings to engage in new inquiry.[1] At first glance, the traditional science instruction described above appears to fit these guidelines quite well. The first (emphasis on familiarity with a discipline's concepts, theories, models) appears to focus on what scientists know; the second (emphasis on understanding how knowledge is generated and justified) *how* they know. If we let students engage in experimentation, this appears to comport with the third guideline (emphasis on an ability to engage in new inquiry). Like Lionni's fish (see Chapter 1), we can graft the new guidelines onto our existing experience.

But both the new guidelines and the principles of *How People Learn* suggest a very different approach to teaching. Simply telling students what scientists have discovered, for example, is not sufficient to support change in their existing preconceptions about important scientific phenomena.[2] Similarly, simply asking students to follow the steps of "the scientific method" is not sufficient to help them develop the knowledge, skills, and attitudes that will enable them to understand what it means to "do science" and participate in a larger scientific community. And the general absence of metacognitive instruction in most of the science curricula we experienced meant that we were not helped in learning how to learn, or made capable of inquiry on our own and in groups. Often, moreover, we were not supported in adopting as our own the questioning stance and search for both supporting and conflicting evidence that are the hallmarks of the scientific enterprise.

The three chapters that follow provide examples of science instruction that are different from what most of us experienced. They are also consistent with the intent of the guidelines of the National Research Council[3] and the American Association for the Advancement of Science,[4] as well as the principles of *How People Learn*. The authors of these chapters do indeed want to help students learn *what* scientists know and *how* they know, but they go about it in ways that are quite different from more traditional science instruction.

The three chapters focus, respectively, on light (elementary school), physical forces such as gravity (middle school), and genetics and evolution (high school). They approach these topics in ways that support students' abilities to (1) learn new concepts and theories with understanding; (2) experience the processes of inquiry (including hypothesis generation, modeling, tool use, and social collaboration) that are key elements of the culture of science; and (3) reflect metacognitively on their own thinking and participation in scientific inquiry. Important principles of learning and instruction are discussed below.

PRINCIPLE #1: ADDRESSING PRECONCEPTIONS

It is often claimed that "experience is the best teacher." While this is arguably true in many contexts, what we learn from our experience varies considerably in terms of its generality and usefulness. With respect to science, everyday experiences often reinforce the very conceptions of phenomena that scientists have shown to be limited or false, and everyday modes of reasoning are often contrary to scientific reasoning.

Everyday Concepts of Scientific Phenomena

Students bring conceptions of everyday phenomena to the classroom that are quite sensible, but scientifically limited or incorrect. For example, properties are generally believed to belong to objects rather than to emerge from interactions.[5] Force, for instance, is seen as a property of bodies that are forceful rather than an interaction between bodies.[6] As described in Chapter 10, students believe objects to "be" a certain color, and light can either allow us to see the color or not. The notion that white light is composed of a spectrum of colors and that the specific colors absorbed and reflected by a particular object give the object the appearance of a particular color is not at all apparent in everyday experience. Scientific tools (prisms) can break white light into colors. But without tools, students see only white light and objects that appear in different colors (rainbows are an exception, but for the untrained they are a magnificent mystery).

Students enter the study of science with a vast array of such preconceptions based on their everyday experiences. Teachers will need to engage those ideas if students are to understand science. The instructional challenge of working with students' preconceptions varies because some conceptions are more firmly rooted than others. Magnusson and Palincsar (Chapter 10) note that some elementary students in their classrooms believe that shadows are "objects," but this preconception is easily dispelled with fairly simple challenges. Other preconceptions, such as the idea that only shiny objects reflect light, require much more time and effort to help students change their ideas.

It is important to remember that most preconceptions are reasonable based on students' everyday experiences. In the area of astronomy, for example, there is a widespread belief that the earth's seasons are caused by the distance of the earth from the sun rather than by the angle of the earth's axis with respect to the sun, and it is very difficult for students to change these preconceptions.[7] Many experiences support the idea that distance from a heat source affects temperature. The closer we stand to radiators, stoves, fireplaces, and other heat sources, the greater is the heat.

Interestingly, there are also experiences in which we can manipulate the intensity of heat by changing the angle of a heat source—by pointing a hair dryer on one's head at different angles, for example. But without the ability to carefully control distance from the head or the tools to measure small changes in temperature (and without some guidance that helps people think to do this experiment in the first place), the relationship between heat and angle with respect to the heat source can easily be missed.

Everyday Concepts of Scientific Methods, Argumentation, and Reasoning

Students bring ideas to the classroom not only about scientific phenomena, but also about what it means to "do science." Research on student thinking about science reveals a progression of ideas about scientific knowledge and how it is justified.[8] The developmental sequence is strikingly similar to that described in Chapter 2 regarding student reasoning about historical knowledge. Scientific knowledge is initially perceived as right or wrong. Later, discrepant ideas and evidence are characterized as "mere opinion," and eventually as "informed" and supported with evidence.[9] As in history, the sequence in science is more predictable than the timing. Indeed, many students may not complete the sequence without instructional support. In several studies, a large proportion of today's high school students have been shown to be at the first stage (right or wrong) when thinking about various phenomena.[10]

Research has also explored students' reasoning regarding scientific experimentation, modeling, the interpretation of data, and scientific argumentation. Examples of conceptions that pose challenges for understanding the scientific enterprise are summarized in Box 9-1. While research findings have been helpful in identifying problematic conceptions, less is known regarding the pace at which students are capable of moving along the developmental trajectory, or undergoing conceptual change, with effective instructional experiences. The chapters that follow provide many compelling examples demonstrating the kinds of changes in student thinking that carefully designed instructional experiences can support.

Conceptual Change

How People Learn emphasizes that instruction in any subject matter that does not explicitly address students' everyday conceptions typically fails to help them refine or replace these conceptions with others that are scientifically more accurate. In fact, the pioneering research that signaled the tenacity of everyday experience and the challenge of conceptual change was done in the area of science, especially physics.[11] One of the pioneers was

Jim Minstrell, a high school physics teacher and author—along with Pamela Kraus—of Chapter 11. That chapter begins with Minstrell describing an experience in his classroom that prompted him to rethink how he taught physics. He was teaching about universal gravitation and forces at a distance. He found that his students did reasonably well when asked to compute force based on "what if" questions involving a change in the distance of an object from a planet. He found, however, that when asked to think qualitatively about the situation, most of his students were basing their thinking on ideas that were reasonable from their everyday perspective, yet widely discrepant from the ways physicists have learned to think about these situations. For example, when Minstrell asked students to assume that there was no air or friction affecting an object pulling a weight, a number of the students offered that everything would just float away since that is how things work in outer space.

Minstrell notes that this experience raised fundamental questions in his mind, such as what good it is to have students know the quantitative relation or equation for gravitational force if they lack a qualitative understanding of force and concepts related to the nature of gravity and its effects. It became clear that simply teaching students about abstract principles of physics provided no bridge for changing their preconceptions. Minstrell and Kraus discuss ways of teaching physics that are designed to remedy this problem. A study suggesting the advantages of assessing student preconceptions and designing instruction to respond to those preconceptions is summarized in Box 9-2.

The authors of all three of the following chapters pay close attention to the preconceptions that students hold about subject matter. For example, the elementary school students discussed by Magnusson and Palincsar (Chapter 10) had had many years of experience with light, darkness, and shadows—and they brought powerful preconceptions to the classroom. The high school students discussed by Stewart, Cartier, and Passmore (Chapter 12) came with many beliefs about genetics and evolution that are widespread among the adult population, including the beliefs that acquired characteristics can be passed on to offspring, and that evolution is purposeful and proceeds toward a specific goal.

The authors of each chapter focus on issues of conceptual change as a major goal for their instruction. This view of learning is quite different from the more traditional view that learning simply involves the addition of new facts and skills to an existing knowledge base. Understanding scientific knowledge often requires a change in—not just an addition to—what people notice and understand about everyday phenomena.[12]

The chapters that follow focus specifically on creating conditions that allow students to undergo important changes in their thinking and noticing. Everything from the choice of topics to be explored to the procedures for

BOX 9-1 Student Conceptions of Knowledge Generation and Justification in Science

Research into students' thinking about scientific knowledge and processes reveals some common misconceptions and limited understandings (summarized by AAAS[13]):

- **Experimentation:** Upper elementary- and middle-school students may not understand experimentation as a method of testing ideas, but rather as a method of trying things out or producing a desired outcome.[14] With adequate instruction, it is possible to have middle school students understand that experimentation is guided by particular ideas and questions and that experiments are tests of ideas. . . . Students of all ages may overlook the need to hold all but one variable constant, although elementary students already understand the notion of fair comparisons, a precursor to the idea of "controlled experiments"[15]. . . . Students tend to look for or accept evidence that is consistent with their prior beliefs and either distort or fail to generate evidence that is inconsistent with these beliefs. These deficiencies tend to mitigate over time and with experience.[16]

- **Models:** Middle school and high-school students typically think of models as physical copies of reality, not as conceptual representations.[17] They lack the notion that the usefulness of a model can be tested by comparing its implications to actual observations. Students know models can

hypothesis testing and discussion contributes to the successful achievement of this goal. For example, Magnusson and Palincsar note that the study of light allows children to see the world differently and challenge their preconceptions. The examples discussed in the chapters on physics and genetics also illustrate many rich opportunities for students to experience and understand phenomena from new perspectives. Such opportunities for students to experience changes in their own noticing, thinking, and understanding are made possible because of another feature of the programs discussed in these chapters: they all integrate content learning with inquiry processes rather than teaching the two separately. This point is elaborated below.

be changed but changing a model for them means (typical of high-school students) adding new information or (typical of middle-school students) replaing a part that was made wrong (p. 26).

- **Interpretation of Data:** Students of all ages show a tendency to uncritically infer cause from correlations.[18] Some students think even a single co-occurance of antecedent and outcome is always sufficient to infer causality. Rarely do middle-school students realize the indeterminacy of single instances, although high-school students may readily realize it. Despite that, as covariant data accumulate, even high-school students will infer a causal relation based on correlations. Further, students of all ages will make a causal inference even when no variation occurs in one of the variables. For example, if students are told that light-colored balls are used successfully in a game, they seem willing to infer that the color of the balls will make some difference in the outcome even without any evidence about dark-colored balls.

- **Inadequacies in Arguments:** Most high-school students will accept arguments based on inadequate sample size, accept causality from contiguous events, and accept conclusions based on statistically insignificant differences.[19] More students can recognize these inadequacies in arguments after prompting (for example, after being told that the conclusions drawn from the data were invalid and asked to state why).[20]

PRINCIPLE #2: KNOWLEDGE OF WHAT IT MEANS TO "DO SCIENCE"

Feynman characterized the scientific method in three words: observation, reason, and experiment.[21] Einstein emphasized the importance of imagination to scientific advancement, making it possible for the reasoning that follows observation to go beyond current understanding. This view of science extolled by some of its greatest minds is often not recognizable in classroom efforts to teach students how to do science.

We have noted that in the past, teaching the processes, not just the outcomes, of science often involved no more than memorizing and reproducing the steps of an experiment. However, even when science instruction

BOX 9-2 Diagnosing Preconceptions in Physics

A computer-based DIAGNOSER program was designed to help teachers elicit and work with student preconceptions in physics.[22] The program assesses students' beliefs about various physical phenomena and provides recommended activities that help students reinterpret phenomena from a physicist's perspective. The teacher uses the feedback from DIAGNOSER to guide instruction.

Data were collected for students of three teachers at Mercer Island School who used the program and were compared with data for students in a comparable school where the program was not used in physics instruction. Data were collected on Miller Analogies Test math scores for students from both schools, so that individual students were compared with others who had the same level of mathematics achievement. In the figure below, the math scores for both groups on the same mechanics final exam are plotted. The results suggest that students' understanding of important concepts in physics was substantially better in the Mercer Island school, and this result was true for students at all mathematics achievement levels.

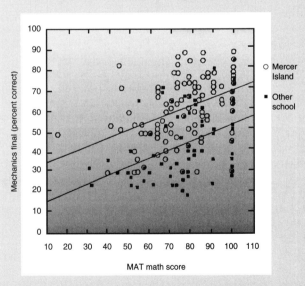

Scores of students from Mercer Island and a comparable school on mechanics final.

is shifted in the direction of engaging in scientific inquiry (as is happening more frequently in today's classrooms), it can be easy to emphasize giving students "recipes for experiments"—hands-on activities that students engage in step by step, carefully following instructions, using measurement tools, and collecting data. These lockstep approaches shortchange observation, imagination, and reasoning. Experimenting may mean that students are asked to conduct a careful sequence of activities in which the number of quarters a wet and dry paper towel can hold is compared in multiple trials, and data are carefully collected and averaged. Yet the question that needs investigation is often unclear, and the reasoning that would lead one to think that either a wet or a dry paper towel would be stronger can remain a mystery to students. As in specific content areas in science, information about the enterprise of science can be passed along to students without an opportunity for them to understand conceptually what that enterprise is about. Indeed, many students believe that everything they learn in science classes is factual; they make no distinction between observation and theory.[23]

The science programs discussed in the following chapters represent a very different approach to scientific inquiry. They do not involve simply setting aside "inquiry time" during which students conduct experiments that are related in some way to the content they are learning. Instead, students learn the content by actively engaging in processes of scientific inquiry. Students may still learn what others have discovered about a phenomenon (see Magnusson and Palincsar's discussions of helping students learn from "second-hand knowledge"). But this is different from typical textbook exercises because the value of reading about others' discoveries is clear to students—it helps them clarify issues that arise in their own inquiry. Reading to answer a question of interest is more motivating than simply reading because someone assigned it. It also changes how people process what they read.[24]

Opportunities to learn science as a process of inquiry (rather than simply having "inquiry times" that are appended to an existing curriculum) has important advantages. It involves observation, imagination, and reasoning about the phenomena under study. It includes the use of tools and procedures, but in the context of authentic inquiry, these become devices that allow students to extend their everyday experiences of the world and help them organize data in ways that provide new insights into phenomena.[25] Crucial questions that are not addressed by lockstep experimental exercises include the following: Where do ideas for relevant observations and experiments come from in the first place? How do we decide what count as relevant comparison groups? How can sciences (e.g., astronomy, paleontology) be rigorously empirical even though they are not primarily experimental? Definitions of what counts as "good science" change as a function of what is being studied and current theorizing about the ideas being investigated. A simple but informative example of how definitions of good scientific methods depend on knowledge of the conceptual issues one is studying is provided in Box 9-3.

One of the most important aspects of science—yet perhaps one of the least emphasized in instruction—is that science involves processes of imagination. If students are not helped to experience this for themselves, science can seem dry and highly mechanical. Indeed, research on students' perceptions of science indicates that "they see scientific work as dull and rarely rewarding, and scientists as bearded, balding, working alone in the laboratory, isolated and lonely.[26] Few scientists we know would remain in the field of science if it were as boring as many students believe.

Generating hypotheses worth investigating was for Einstein an extremely important part of science, where the "imagination of the possible" played a major role. Nobel Laureate Sir Peter Medawar also emphasizes the role of imagining the possible:

> *Like other exploratory processes, [the scientific method] can be resolved into a dialogue between fact and fancy, the actual and the possible; between what could be true and what is in fact the case. The purpose of scientific enquiry is not to compile an inventory of factual information, nor to build up a totalitarian world picture of Natural Laws in which every event that is not compulsory is forbidden. We should think of it rather as a logically particular structure of justifiable beliefs about a Possible World—a story which we invent and criticize and modify as we go along, so that it ends by being, as nearly as we can make it, a story about real life.[27]*

The importance of creative processes in the conduct of science can also be understood by exploring the types of reasoning and investigative choices that have made some scientific investigations particularly productive and feasible. For example, Mendel's critical insight about the discrete nature of heredity was a consequence of his selecting peas for his experiment (see Box 9-4). Other major advances in understanding heredity were equally dependent on scientists finding an approach to investigation that would allow the complexity of the world to be sufficiently simplified to uncover fundamental relationships.[28] This very engaging dimension of the scientific enterprise is hidden when students' inquiry experience is limited to the execution of step-by-step experiments.

The chapters that follow present a variety of ways to help students experience the excitement of doing science in a way that does justice to all stages of the process. The authors describe experiences that allow students to see everyday phenomena with new eyes. They provide opportunities for both inventing and testing models of invisible processes, adopting and sometimes adapting tools to make the invisible visible. Students reason about relationships between theory and data. Furthermore, they do so by creating classroom communities that simulate the important roles of scientific communities in actual scientific practice.[29] This involves paying careful attention to the arguments of others, as well as learning the benefits of group interaction for advancing one's own thinking.

PRINCIPLE #3: METACOGNITION

The third principle of *How People Learn* emphasizes the importance of taking a metacognitive approach to instruction. Much of the research on metacognition focused on the comprehension of text (see Chapter 1) clearly applies to science, where texts can be quite complex and difficult for many students to comprehend. However, more recent research targeted specifically to the monitoring of and reflection on scientific reasoning has also shown promising effects.

A striking example is the work of White and Frederiksen (see Box 9-5), who designed a physics inquiry curriculum called ThinkerTools. The curriculum uses inquiry instruction to engage students in investigations that allow them to confront their misconceptions and develop a scientific understanding of force and motion. Students taught with the ThinkerTools curriculum displayed a deeper conceptual understanding than students taught with a traditional curriculum. This advantage remained even when the ThinkerTools students were in inner-city schools and were compared with students in suburban schools, and when the ThinkerTools students were several years younger. White and Frederiksen later extended the curriculum to include a metacognitive component—what they refer to as "reflective assessment." Students taught with the curriculum including this metacognitive component outperformed those taught with the original curriculum. Gains were particularly striking for lower-achieving students.

Another study, by Lin and Lehman,[30] demonstrates that metacognitive instruction can be effective for college students. In their experiments, students learned about strategies for controlling variables in a complex science experiment that was simulated via computer. As they studied, some received periodic questions that asked them to reflect on—and briefly explain—what they were doing and why; others did not receive these questions. On tests of the extent to which students' knowledge transferred to new problems, those in the metacognitive group outperformed those in the comparison groups.

The authors of the following chapters do not necessarily label their relevant instructional moves as "metacognitive," but they emphasize helping students reflect on their role in inquiry and on the monitoring and critiquing of one's own claims, as well as those of others. They also emphasize that

BOX 9-3 Evaluating the Methods Used in an Experiment

Imagine being asked to evaluate the following experiment and conclusions:

A group of biologists compare data from across the world and note that frogs seem to be disappearing in an alarming number of places. This deeply concerns them, because the frogs may well be an indicator species for environmental changes that could hurt us all. The biologists consider a number of hypotheses about the frogs' disappearance. One is that too much ultraviolet light is getting through the ozone layer.

One group of researchers decides to test the ultraviolet light hypothesis. They use five different species of frogs—an equal number of male and female. Half of the frogs receive constant doses of ultraviolet light for a period of 4 months; this is the experimental group. The other half of the frogs—the control group—are protected so they receive no ultraviolet light.

At the end of the 4 months, the biologists find that there is no difference in death rates between the frogs in the experimental and control groups. This finding suggests that ultraviolet light is probably not the cause of the frogs' demise.

What do you think about the biologists' experiments and conclusions? Are there questions you would want to ask before accepting their conclusions? Are there new experiments that you would want to propose?

This problem has been addressed by hundreds of individuals in classes and workshops.[31] Many of these individuals know a considerable amount about experimental design and typically note a number of strengths and weaknesses about the experiment. Strengths include the fact that it had an experimental/control design that involved several different species of frogs, used stratified random sampling, and so forth. Weaknesses include such concerns as the possibility that the doses of ultra-violet light that were used were too weak; that the light was provided for too short a time (i.e., only 4 months); or that the experimenters did not wait long enough to see the effects of the ultraviolet light, so maybe they should have looked at differences in illness between the two groups rather than comparing the death rates.

Such concerns are valid and relatively sophisticated, but they reflect a lack of knowledge about general principles of biology—principles that raise serious questions about the preceding experiment. In particular, very few people question the fact that only adult frogs were used in the experiment (multimedia materials viewed by participants showed clearly that the frogs were all adults). To understand potential environmental effects on a species, one must look at the life cycle of the species and attempt to identify points in that cycle where the species might be the most vulnerable. For example, when DDT endangered eagles, it did so not by killing the adults but by making the egg shells so brittle that they broke before the offspring could hatch. Overall, what counts as an adequate experimental or empirical design is strongly affected by the current state of knowledge of a particular field. Learning about "the scientific method" in the abstract fails to help students grasp this important idea.

An interesting side note is that people who have participated in the preceding demonstration have been asked whether they ever studied life cycles in school. Almost all have said "yes"; however, they learned about life cycles as isolated exercises (e.g., they were asked to memorize the stages of the life cycle of a fly or mosquito) and never connected this information to larger questions, such as the survival of a species. As a consequence, the idea of life cycles had never occurred to them in the context of attempting to solve the above problem.

In Chapter 1, Bruner's ideas[32] about curriculum organization are discussed; those ideas are highly relevant in this context. For example, he cautions against teaching specific topics or skills without clarifying their context in the broader fundamental structure of the field; rather, students need to attain an understanding of fundamental principles and ideas. Those presented with the frog problem may have learned about life cycles, but their teachers and texts did not explain the importance of this information in the broader structure of the field of knowledge. To paraphrase Whitehead,[33] knowledge that was potentially important for exploring the frog problem remained "inert."

BOX 9-4 **The Proof Was in the Peas**

Gregor Mendel's major contribution to the field of genetics rested on his choice of peas. Many famous men at the time were conducting experiments in plant breeding, but no general principles had emerged from these experiments. Typically they involved plant organisms that differed on a variety of dimensions, and the offspring were found to be intermediate or, in rare cases, more like one parent plant than the other.

Mendel chose peas for certain critical features: they have both male and female structures and are generally self-fertilizing, but their structure makes it possible to prevent self-fertilization (by removing the anthers before they mature). Numerous varieties of peas were available that differed on certain discrete dimensions; Mendel chose varieties with seeds that were green or yellow, smooth or wrinkled, etc. When the peas were cross-fertilized, they consistently showed one of the two characteristics. When plants with smooth and wrinkled seeds were crossed, they consistently had offspring with smooth seeds. This result suggested that one characteristic is, in Mendel's term, dominant. But when these offspring were self-fertilized and produced their own offspring, characteristics of each of the original parent plants appeared in members of the new generation. The stunning conclusion—that offspring carry genetic information that is recessive but can nonetheless be passed along to future generations—represented a major advance.

To appreciate Mendel's contribution is not just to know the terms he used and the experimental procedures he followed, or even the outcome of his work. It is to understand as well the important role played by his experimental design, as well as the reasoning that led him to design a productive experiment.

being metacognitive about science is different from simply asking whether we comprehend what we read or hear; it requires taking up the particular critical lens through which scientists view the world.

Magnusson and Palincsar provide excellent examples of how metacognitive habits of mind for science require different kinds of questions than people typically ask about everyday phenomena. For example, they note that for young children and for many adults, the assumption that things are as they appear seems self-evident. But science is about questioning the obvious. When we do this, unexpected discoveries often come to light. For example, a scientific mindset suggests that the observation that shiny things reflect light needs to be explained, and this requires explaining why dull objects do not reflect light. As these issues are investigated, it becomes clear that the initial assumption was wrong and that dull objects do indeed reflect light—but at a level that is not always obvious in our everyday experiences. As Magnusson and Palincsar note:

> *Engaging children in science, then, means engaging them in a whole new approach to questioning. Indeed, it means asking them to question. . . . It means questioning the typical assurance we feel from evidence that confirms our prior beliefs, and asking in what ways the evidence is incomplete and may be countered by additional evidence.*

The authors of Chapters 11 and 12 also place a great deal of emphasis on helping students become aware of ways in which scientific inquiry goes beyond peoples' everyday ways of interacting with their environment. The authors attempt to help students compare their personal "ways of knowing" with those developed through centuries of scientific inquiry. Helping students understand the tendency of us all to attempt to confirm rather than rigorously test (and possibly refute) our current assumptions is one example of a metacognitive approach to science instruction. The approach is deepened when we help students learn why and how to create models of phenomena (especially the invisible aspects of phenomena) that can then be put to an empirical test.

The following chapters emphasize another aspect of metacognition as well: helping students learn about themselves as learners. The authors describe classroom activities and discussion that encourage students to reflect on the degree to which they contribute to or detract from group processes, and on the degree to which efforts to communicate findings (e.g., in writing) uncover "holes" in one's thinking that otherwise might remain invisible.

The authors' decisions about the topics they discuss (light, force and gravity, genetics and evolution) were guided in part by the opportunities these topics provide to help students think differently not only about the subject matter, but also about how they "know," and how their everyday approaches to knowing compare with those scientists have developed over the last few centuries.

THE *HOW PEOPLE LEARN* FRAMEWORK

As noted in Chapter 1, authors of the chapters in this volume were not asked to tie their discussion explicitly to the framework of *How People Learn* that suggests classrooms should be learner-centered, knowledge-centered, assessment-centered, and community-centered. Nevertheless, it can be useful to see how this framework applies to their work.

BOX 9-5 Reflective Assessment in ThinkerTools

ThinkerTools is an inquiry-based curriculum that allows students to explore the physics of motion. The curriculum is designed to engage students' conceptions, to provide a carefully structured and highly supported computer environment for testing those conceptions, and to steep students in the processes of scientific inquiry. The curriculum has demonstrated impressive gains in students' conceptual understanding and the ability to transfer knowledge to novel problems.

White and Frederiksen[34] designed and tested a "reflective assessment" component that provided students with a framework for evaluating the quality of an inquiry—their own and that of others. The assessment categories included understanding the main ideas, understanding the inquiry process, being inventive, being systematic, reasoning carefully, applying the tools of research, using teamwork, and communicating well. Students who were engaged in reflective assessment were compared with matched control students who were taught with ThinkerTools, but were asked to comment on what they did and did not like about the curriculum without a guiding framework. Each teacher's classes were evenly divided between the two treatments. There were no significant differences in students' initial average standardized test scores (the Comprehensive Test of Basic Skills was used as a measure of prior achievement) between the classes assigned (randomly) to the different treatments.

Students in the reflective assessment classes showed higher gains both in understanding the process of scientific inquiry and in understanding the physics content. For example, one of the outcome measures was a written inquiry assessment that was given both before and after the ThinkerTools inquiry curriculum was administered. This was a written test in which students were asked to explain how they would investigate a specific research question: "What is the relationship between the weight of an object and the effect that sliding friction has on its motion?"[35] Students were instructed to propose competing hypotheses, design an experiment (on paper) to test the hypotheses, and pretend to carry out the experiment, making up data. They were then asked to use the data they generated to reason and draw conclusions about their initial hypotheses.

Presented below are the gain scores on this challenging assessment for both low- and high-achieving students and for students in the reflective assessment and control classes. Note first that students in the reflective assessment classes gained more on this inquiry assessment. Note also that this was particularly true for the low-achieving students. This is evidence that the metacognitive reflective assessment process is beneficial, particularly for academically disadvantaged students.

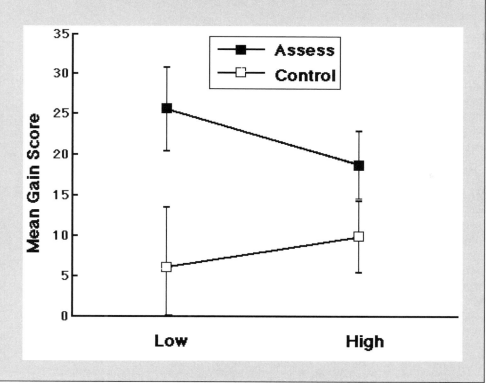

Learner-Centered

All three of the following chapters place a great deal of emphasis on the ideas and understandings that students bring to the classroom. Each begins by engaging students in activities or discussions that draw out what they know or how they know, rather than beginning with new content. Students are viewed as active processors of information who have acquired concepts, skills, and attitudes that affect their thinking about the content being taught, as well as about what it means to do science. Like Lionni's fish (see Chapter 1), students bring preconceptions to class that can shape (or misshape) learning if not addressed. These chapters engage students' ideas so that they can be reexamined, reshaped, and built upon.

Knowledge-Centered

Issues of what should be taught play a fundamental role in each of the chapters that follow. While engaging in inquiry involves a great deal of activity that is under students' control, the authors are quite clear about the knowledge that students need to acquire to understand the topic, and they guide students' inquiry to ensure that the necessary concepts and information (including the terminology) are learned. The chapters emphasize both what scientists know and how they know. But the authors' approaches to instruction make these more than lists of information to be learned and steps to be followed.

Of particular importance, opportunities for inquiry are not simply tacked on to the content of a course; rather, they are the method for learning the content. This sets the stage for a number of important changes in science instruction. Simply having students follow "the scientific method" probably introduces more misconceptions about science than it dispels. First, different areas of science use different methods. Second, as discussed above, lockstep approaches to conducting science experiments exclude the aspects of science that are probably the most gratifying and motivating to scientists—generating good questions and ways to explore them; learning by being surprised (at disconfirmations); seeing how the collective intelligence of the group can supersede the insights of people working solely as individuals; learning to "work smart" by adopting, adapting, and sometimes inventing tools and models; and experiencing the excitement of actually discovering—and sharing with friends—something that provides a new way of looking at the world.

Assessment-Centered

The word "assessment" rarely appears in the three chapters that follow, but in fact the chapters are rich in assessment opportunities. Students are helped to assess the quality of their hypotheses and models, the adequacy of their methods and conclusions, and the effectiveness of their efforts as learners and collaborators. These assessments are extremely important for students, but also help teachers see the degree to which students are making progress toward the course goals and use this information in deciding what to do next. It is noteworthy that these are formative assessments, complete with opportunities for students (and teachers) to use feedback to revise their thinking; they are not merely summative assessments that give students a grade on one task (e.g., a presentation about an experiment) and then go on to the next task.

Community-Centered

The dialogue and discussion in each of the following chapters indicate that the teachers have developed a culture of respect, questioning, and risk taking. Disconfirmation is seen as an exciting discovery, not a failure. A diverse array of thoughts about issues and phenomena is treated as a resource for stimulating conversations and new discoveries—not as a failure to converge immediately on "the right answer." Discussions in class help support the idea of a "learning community" as involving people who can argue with grace, rather than people who all agree with one another (though, as Magnusson and Palincsar suggest, this can take some time and effort to develop).

CONCLUSION

While each of the three chapters that follow has much to offer in demonstrating instructional approaches designed to incorporate important lessons from research on learning, we remind the reader that these chapters are intended to be illustrative. As noted earlier, there are many ways to build a bridge that are consistent with the principles of physics, and this is also true of relationships between course design and general principles of learning. It is the intention of the following chapters to provide approaches and ideas for instruction that other teachers may find useful in their own teaching. Indeed, the approaches are ones that require of teachers a great deal of responsiveness to their students' ideas and thinking. Such approaches to teaching will most likely succeed if teachers understand the principles that drive instruction and incorporate them into their own thinking and teaching, rather than making an effort to replicate what is described in the chapters that follow.

NOTES

1. American Association for the Advancement of Science, 1993; National Research Council, 1996.
2. Carey, 2000.
3. National Research Council, 1996.
4. American Association for the Advancement of Science, 1993.
5. Brosnan, 1990.
6. Driver et al., 1985.
7. Schneps and Sadler, 1987.
8. Benchmarks Online Available: http://www.project2061.org/tools/benchol/bolintro.htm [October 2004].
9. Kitchener, 1983; Perry, 1970.
10. Kitchener, 1983; Kitchener and King, 1981.
11. Clement, 1993; Driver et al., 1985; Pfundt and Duit, 1991.
12. Carey, 2000; Hanson, 1970; National Research Council, 2000.
13. American Association for the Advancement of Science, 1993.
14. Carey et al., 1989; Schauble et al., 1991; Solomon, 1992.
15. Wollman, 1997a, 1997b; Wollman and Lawson, 1977.
16. Schauble, 1990, p. 2.
17. Grosslight et al., 1991.
18. Kuhn et al., 1988.
19. Jungwirth, 1987; Jungwirth and Dreyfus, 1990, 1992.
20. Jungwirth, 1987; Jungwirth and Dreyfus, 1992.
21. Feynman, 1995.
22. Hunt and Minstrell, 1994.
23. Brook et al., 1983.
24. Biswas et al., 2002; Palincsar and Brown, 1984.
25. Petrosino et al., 2003.
26. American Association for the Advancement of Science, 1993.
27. Medawar, 1982.
28. Moore, 1972, Chapter 4.
29. Kuhn, 1989.
30. Lin and Lehman, 1999.
31. Bransford, 2003.
32. Bruner, 1960.
33. Whitehead, 1929.
34. White and Frederiksen, 1998.
35. White and Frederiksen, 2000, p. 2.

REFERENCES

American Association for the Advancement of Science. (1993). *Benchmarks for science literacy*. New York: Oxford University Press.

Biswas, G., Schwartz, D., Bransford, J., and the Teachable Agent Group at Vanderbilt. (2002). Technology support for complex problem solving: From SAD environments to AI. In K.D. Forbus and P.J. Feltovich (Eds.), *Smart machines in education: The coming revolution in educational technology* (pp. 71-97). Menlo Park, CA: AAAI/MIT Press.

Bransford, J.D. (2003). *Frog problem*. Paper presented at the American Physiological Society as the Claude Bernard Distinguished Lecturer of the Teaching of Physiology, San Diego, CA.

Brook, A., Briggs, H., and Bell, B. (1983). *Secondary students' ideas about particles*. Leeds, England: The University of Leeds, Centre for Studies in Science and Mathematics Education.

Brosnan, T. (1990). Categorizing macro and micro explanations of material change. In P.L. Lijnse, P. Licht, W. de Vos, and A.J. Waarlo (Eds.), *Relating macroscopic phenomena to microscopic particles* (pp. 198-211). Utrecht, The Netherlands: CD-p Press.

Bruner, J. (1960). *The process of education*. Cambridge, MA: Harvard University Press.

Carey, S. (2000). Science education as conceptual change. *Journal of Applied Developmental Psychology, 21*(1), 13-19.

Carey, S., Evans, R., Honda, M., Jay, E., and Unger, C. (1989). An experiment is when you try it and see if it works: A study of grade 7 students' understanding of the construction of scientific knowledge. *International Journal of Science Education, 11*, 514-529.

Clement, J. (1993). Using bridging analogies and anchoring institutions to deal with students' preconceptions in physics. *Journal of Research in Science Teaching, 30*(10), 1241-1257.

Driver, R., Guesne, E., and Tiberghien, A. (1985). Some features of children's ideas and their implications for teaching. In R. Driver, E. Guesne, and A. Tiberghien (Eds.), *Children's ideas in science* (pp. 193-201). Berkshire, England: Open University Press.

Feynman, R.P. (1995). *Six easy pieces: Essentials of physics explained by its most brilliant teacher*. Reading, MA: Perseus Books.

Grosslight, L., Unger, C., Jay, E., and Smith, C. (1991). Understanding models and their use in science: Conceptions of middle and high school students and experts. *International Journal of Science Education, 17*(16), 59-74.

Hanson, N.R. (1970). A picture theory of theory meaning. In R.G. Colodny (Ed.), *The nature and function of scientific theories* (pp. 233-274). Pittsburgh, PA: University of Pittsburgh Press.

Hunt, E., and Minstrell, J. (1994). A cognitive approach to the teaching of physics. In K. McGilly (Ed.), *Classroom lessons: Integrating cognitive theory and classroom practice* (pp. 51-74). Cambridge, MA: MIT Press.

Jungwirth, E. (1987). Avoidance of logical fallacies: A neglected aspect of science education and science-teacher education. *Research in Science and Technological Education, 5*, 43-58.

Jungwirth, E., and Dreyfus, A. (1990). Identification and acceptance of a posteriori casual assertions invalidated by faulty enquiry methodology: An international study of curricular expectations and reality. In D. Herget (Ed.), *More history and philosophy of science in science teaching* (pp. 202-211). Tallahassee, FL: Florida State University.

Jungwirth, E., and Dreyfus, A. (1992). After this, therefore because of this: One way of jumping to conclusions. *Journal of Biological Education, 26,* 139-142.

Kitchener, K. (1983). Educational goals and reflective thinking. *The Educational Forum,* 75-95.

Kitchener, K., and King, P. (1981). Reflective judgment: Concepts of justification and their relationship to age and education. *Journal of Applied Developmental Psychology, 2,* 89-116.

Kuhn, D. (1989). Children and adults as intuitive scientists. *Psychological Review, 96,* 674-689.

Kuhn, D., Amsel, E., and O'Loughlin, M. (1988). *The development of scientific thinking skills.* San Diego, CA: Academic Press.

Lin, X.D., and Lehman, J. (1999). Supporting learning of variable control in a computer-based biology environment: Effects of prompting college students to reflect on their own thinking. *Journal of Research in Science Teaching, 36*(7), 837-858.

Medawar, P. (1982*). Plato's republic.* Oxford, England: Oxford University Press.

Moore, J.A. (1972). *Heredity and development* (second edition). Oxford, England: Oxford University Press.

National Research Council. (1996). *National science education standards.* National Committee on Science Education Standards and Assessment, Center for Science, Mathematics, and Engineering Education. Washington, DC: National Academy Press.

National Research Council. (2000). *How people learn: Brain, mind, experience, and school.* Committee on Developments in the Science of Learning and Committee on Learning Research and Educational Practice, Commission on Behavioral and Social Sciences and Education. Washington, DC: National Academy Press.

Palinscar, A.S., and Brown, A.L. (1984). Reciprocal teaching of comprehension-fostering and comprehension monitoring activities. *Cognition and Instruction, 1*(2),117-175.

Perry, W.G., Jr. (1970). *Forms of intellectual and ethical development in the college years.* Fort Worth, TX: HBJ College Publishers.

Petrosino, A., Lehrer, R., and Shauble, L. (2003). Structuring error and experimental variation as distribution in the fourth grade. *Mathematical Thinking and Learning, 5*(2 and 3),131-156.

Pfundt, H., and Duit, R. (1991). *Bibliography: Students' alternative frameworks and science education* (third edition). Kiel, Germany: Institute for Science Education at the University of Kiel.

Schauble, L. (1990). Belief revision in children: The role of prior knowledge and strategies for generating evidence. *Journal of Experimental Child Psychology, 49,* 31-57.

Schauble, L., Klopfer, L.E., and Raghavan, K. (1991). Students' transition from an engineering model to a science model of experimentation. *Journal of Research in Science Teaching, 28,* 859-882.

Schneps, M.H., and Sadler, P.M. (1987). *A private universe* (Video). Cambridge, MA: Harvard Smithsonian Center for Astrophysics.

Solomon, J., Duveen, J., Scot, L., and McCarthy, S. (1992). Teaching about the nature of science through history: Action research in the classroom. *Journal of Research in Science Teaching, 29,* 409-421.

White, B.C., and Frederiksen, J.R. (1998). Inquiry, modeling, and metacognition: Making science accessible to all students. *Cognition and Instruction.* 16(1), 3-117.

White, B.C., and Frederiksen, J.R. (2000). Technological tools and instructional approaches for making scientific inquiry accessible to all. In M.J. Jacobson and R.B. Kozma (Eds.), *Innovations in science and mathematics education* (pp. 321-359). Mahwah, NJ: Lawrence Erlbaum Associates.

Whitehead, A.N. (1929). *The aims of education.* New York: Macmillan.

Wollman, W. (1977a). Controlling variables: Assessing levels of understanding. *Science Education, 61,* 371-383.

Wollman, W. (1977b). Controlling variables: A neo-Piagetian developmental sequence. *Science Education, 61,* 385-391.

Wollman, W., and Lawson, A. (1977). Teaching the procedure of controlled experimentation: A Piagetian approach. *Science Education, 61,* 57-70.

10

Teaching to Promote the Development of Scientific Knowledge and Reasoning About Light at the Elementary School Level

Shirley J. Magnusson and Annemarie Sullivan Palincsar

Children at play outside or with unfamiliar materials look as though they might be answering such questions as: What does this do? How does this work? What does this feel like? What can I do with it? Why did that happen? This natural curiosity and exploration of the world around them have led some people to refer to children as "natural" scientists. Certainly these are the very types of questions that scientists pursue. Yet children are not scientists. Curiosity about how the world works makes engaging children in science relatively easy, and their proclivity to observe and reason (see Chapter 1, Box 1-1) is a powerful tool that children bring to the science classroom. But there is a great deal of difference between the casual observation and reasoning children engage in and the more disciplined efforts of scientists.

How do we help students develop scientific ideas and ways of knowing?[1] Introducing children to the culture of science—its types of reasoning, tools of observation and measurement, and standards of evidence, as well as the values and beliefs underlying the production of scientific knowledge—is a major instructional challenge. Yet our work and that of others suggest that children are able to take on these learning challenges successfully even in the earliest elementary grades.[2]

THE STUDY OF LIGHT

Unlike mathematics, in which topics such as whole-number arithmetic are foundational for the study of rational number, and both are foundational for the study of functions, there is currently little agreement on the selection and sequencing of specific topics in science, particularly at the elementary level.[3] What clearly is foundational for later science study, however, is learning what it means to engage in scientific inquiry—learning the difference between casual and scientific investigations. That learning can be accomplished in the context of many different specific topics.

In this chapter, we choose light as our topic of focus because it affords several benefits. The first is practical: the topic involves relatively simple concepts that children can understand from investigating with relatively simple materials. For example, our bodies and the sun make shadows that can be studied, and similar studies can occur with common flashlights and classroom materials. Pencil and paper, and perhaps some means of measuring distance, are all that is needed for data collection. Children can also study light using simple light boxes (Elementary Science Study's *Optics* unit[4]) in which light bulbs are placed in cardboard boxes containing openings covered with construction paper masks that control the amount of light emanating from the box. Thin slits in the masks make the thin beams of light necessary for studies of reflection and refraction. Multiple wider openings covered with different colored cellophane filters enable investigations mixing colors of light. And again, pencil and paper are all that are needed for data collection showing the paths of light.

In addition, developing scientific knowledge of light challenges us to conceptualize aspects of the world that we do not directly experience—a critical element of much scientific study. For example, light travels, yet we do not see it do so; we infer its travel when we turn on a flashlight in the dark and see a lighted spot across the room.

Developing scientific knowledge often requires conceptual change[5] in which we come to view the physical world in new ways.[6] Students must learn that things are not always what they seem—itself a major conceptual leap. The study of light gives children an accessible opportunity to see the world differently and to challenge their existing conceptions. We see the world around us because light reflects from objects to our eyes, and yet we do not sense that what we see is the result of reflected light.

Some children, moreover, view shadows as objects instead of understanding that shadows are created when light is blocked. Conceptual development is required if they are to understand the relationship among a light source, an object, and the shadow cast by that object. Working with flashlights can provide children an opportunity to challenge directly everyday conceptions about shadows, providing them with a powerful early experience of scientific ways of knowing. Because casual observation of the behavior of light can be misleading, but a relatively accessible investigation of light can be illuminating, the study of light demonstrates the contrast between casual observation and experimentation. For all these reasons, then, the study of light supports children's understanding that relationships in the physical world are not self-evident and that constructing scientific knowledge from observation of the world is different from their everyday reasoning.

Three major instructional challenges parallel the principles of *How People Learn* as they apply to the study of light: (1) providing students with opportunities to develop deep conceptual understanding of targeted aspects of light, and of standards and norms in science for investigating and drawing conclusions (both about light and more generally); (2) supporting students in building or bridging from prior knowledge and experience to scientific concepts; and (3) encouraging children to engage in the kind of metacognitive questioning of their own thinking that is requisite to scientific practice.

Conceptual Understanding

How People Learn suggests that learning for understanding requires the organization of knowledge around core concepts. Thus while light can be studied with tools that are easy to use and opportunities to observe the behavior of light abound, if the classroom activity described in this chapter were simply a set of experiences and observations, it would leave students with little deep knowledge. Experiencing many individual activities (e.g., seeing that light reflects from wood as well as mirrors) does not ensure that students understand the overarching concepts about light outlined below that allow them to predict how light will behave in a wide variety of circumstances. As a result, a major focus in this chapter is on the role of the teacher in guiding students' observations, reasoning, and understanding so that core concepts are grasped.

What conceptual understandings do we consider to be core? As suggested above, grasping the differences between everyday observations and reasoning and those of science is not only core in our approach to teaching about light, but also paramount in providing a foundation for further science study. Salient concepts include the following:

- Standards of the scientific community for understanding and communicating ideas and explanations about how the world works are different from everyday standards. Science requires careful observations that are recorded accurately and precisely, and organized so that patterns can be observed in the data.
- Patterns in observations are stated as knowledge claims.

- Claims are judged on the quality of the evidence supporting or disconfirming them.
- Hypotheses take on the status of claims only after they have been tested.
- Claims are subject to challenge and not considered new scientific knowledge until the scientific community accepts them.

These understandings are foundational for all future study of science.

There are also core concepts regarding the topic of light that we want students to master. These will vary somewhat, however, according to the grade level and the amount of time that will be devoted to the topic. These concepts include the following:

- All objects (experienced in our everyday lives) reflect and absorb light, and some objects also transmit light.
  - Dark or black objects mainly absorb light; light or white objects mainly reflect light.
  - There is an inverse relationship between light reflected from and absorbed by an object: more reflected light means less absorbed light.
- Light reflects from objects in a particular way: the angle of incoming light equals the angle of reflected light.
- What we see is light reflected from objects.
  - There must be a source of light for us to see an object.
  - Sources of illumination can produce light (e.g., the sun) or reflect light (e.g., the moon).
- When an object blocks a source of light, a shadow is formed. Shadows are dark because there is no light reaching them to be reflected to our eyes. The distance of an object from a source of light it blocks determines the size of the object's shadow. The shape of an object's shadow depends on the angle of the object to the light, so the shadow of an object may have more than one shape.
- The color of an object is the color of light reflected from the object.
  - The colors of light come from white light, which can be separated into many colors.
  - The color of an object depends on the extent to which particular colors of light in white light are reflected and absorbed.

Other concepts—such as the nature of light as both a wave and a particle—are beyond what elementary students need to understand. But teachers need to know these core concepts to deal effectively with questions that may arise, as we discuss later in this chapter.

Prior Knowledge

Students bring many prior conceptions about light to the classroom. Some of these are influenced relatively easily. For example, some students believe a shadow is an object, but this conception is not deeply held, and simple experiments with light can provide convincing evidence to the contrary. Other scientifically inaccurate conceptions are not so easily changed by simple experiments.

A very common belief is that light reflects only from shiny objects, such as a mirror or shiny metals. This is hardly surprising; reflections from shiny objects are strikingly obvious, while observing reflection from objects with no apparent shine requires a tool (e.g., a simple device such as a piece of paper strategically placed to show reflected light, or a more sophisticated device such as an electronic meter that measures light energy). In fact, the nature of light has puzzled scientists for centuries.[7] Part of the challenge to our understanding is that the behaviors and effects of light are not easily determined by our senses. Light travels too fast for us to see it traveling, and our observation of light that has traveled great distances, such as light from the sun and other stars, provides no direct evidence of the time it has taken to reach us. Scientists have determined that light exerts pressure, but this is not something we can feel. We see because light is reflected to our eyes, but we have no way of experiencing that directly. We commonly think of color as an intrinsic characteristic of an object because we do not experience what actually occurs: that the color we see is the color of light reflected from the object. Furthermore, grasping this notion requires understanding that white light is made up of colors of light that are differentially absorbed and reflected by objects. If none are reflected, we see black, and if all are reflected, we see white, and this is counter to our experience with colored pigments that make a dark color when mixed together. Finally, perhaps the strongest testimony to the complex nature of light is the fact that scientists use two very different models to characterize light: a particle and a wave.

Because daily experience reinforces ideas that may be quite different from scientific understanding, fostering conceptual change requires supporting students in paying close attention to how they reason from what they observe. For this reason, the approach to teaching we suggest in this chapter provides students with a great many opportunities to make and test knowledge claims, and to examine the adequacy of their own and others' reasoning in doing so. Once again, however, the role of the teacher is critical. As we will see, the prior conceptions with which students work may lead them to simply not notice, quickly dismiss, or not believe what they do not expect to see.

Metacognition

Young children, and indeed many adults, assume that things are as they appear, and no further questioning is required. That light reflects off objects only if they are shiny may appear to be true and in no need of further questioning. Science, however, is about questioning—even when something seems obvious—because explanation is at the heart of scientific activity. Thus the search for an explanation for why shiny objects reflect light must include an answer to the question of why nonshiny objects do not. Such a search, of course, would lead to evidence refuting the notion that only shiny objects reflect light. Engaging children in science, then, means engaging them in a whole new approach to questioning. Indeed, it means asking them to question in ways most of us do not in daily life. It means questioning the typical assurance we feel from evidence that confirms our prior beliefs, and asking in what ways the evidence is incomplete and may be countered by additional evidence. To develop thinking in this way is a major instructional challenge for science teaching.

THE STUDY OF LIGHT THROUGH INQUIRY

With the above principles in mind, we turn now to the learning of science through investigative activity in the classroom, or inquiry-based instruction.[8] Investigations in which students directly observe phenomena, we believe, serve several critical functions. First, when students experiment with light and observe phenomena they do not expect, these discrepant experiences can directly challenge their inaccurate or partially developed conceptions. Students will need many opportunities to observe and discuss the behavior of light that behaves in unexpected ways if they are to develop scientific conceptions of light. Inquiry that is designed to occur over weeks and allows students to work with many different materials can provide that experience. The opportunity for repeated cycles of investigation allows students to ask the same questions in new contexts and new questions in increasingly understood contexts as they work to bring their understanding of the world in line with what scientists think. Equally important, participation in well-designed guided-inquiry instruction provides students with a first-hand experience of the norms of conducting scientific investigation.

But inquiry is a time- and resource-intensive activity, and student investigations do not always lead to observations and experiences that support the targeted knowledge. Therefore, we combine first-hand investigations with second-hand investigations in which students work with the notebook of a fictitious scientist to see where her inquiry, supported by more sophisticated tools, led. This second-hand inquiry provides a common investigative experience that allows the teacher to direct attention to steps in the reasoning process pursued by the scientist that led to the development of core concepts. Moreover, it allows students to see that while scientists engage in a similar type of inquiry, more sophisticated tools, more control over conditions, and larger sample sizes are critical to drawing conclusions that can be generalized with some confidence.

A Heuristic for Teaching and Learning Science Through Guided Inquiry

To aid our discussion of the unfolding of instruction, we present a heuristic—a thinking tool—to support planning, enacting, and evaluating guided-inquiry instruction with elementary school teachers.[9] This heuristic (see Figure 10-1[10]), which shares many features with other researched-based approaches to teaching elementary science through investigation,[11] represents instruction in terms of cycles with phases. The words in all capital letters in Figure 10-1 indicate the phases, and the lines with arrows show the progression from one phase to the next. *Reporting* is a key phase in this conception of instruction; it is the occasion when groups of students report the results of their investigations to their classmates. Students are expected to report on knowledge claims they feel confident in making and providing evidence for those claims from the data they collected during investigation. This expectation lends accountability to students' investigative activity that is often absent when they are simply expected to observe phenomena. To make a claim, students will need precise and accurate data, and to have a

FIGURE 10-1 A cycle of investigation in guided-inquiry science.

claim that is meaningful to the class, they will need to understand the relationship between the question that prompted investigation and the way in which their investigation has enabled them to come up with an answer.

Multiple lines leading from one phase to another indicate the two basic emphases of investigative activity in science: generating knowledge that describes how the world works (outer loop), and generating and testing theories to explain those relationships (inner loop). The reporting phase always marks the end of a cycle of inquiry, at which point a decision is made about whether to engage in another cycle with the same question and investigative context, or to re-engage with a novel investigative context or a new question. Cycles focused on developing knowledge claims about empirical relationships generally precede cycles in the same topic area focused on developing explanations for those relationships. Thinking and discussing explanations may occur in other cycles, but the focus of the cycle represented by the inner loop is on testing explanations.

Each phase in the heuristic presents different learning opportunities and teaching challenges. Each also provides opportunities to focus on ideas describing the physical world (concepts and theories or *content*) as well as the means by which we systematically explore the nature of the physical world (methods and reasoning or *process*).

Each phase requires different types of thinking and activity on the part of the students and the teacher; hence, each has a unique role to play in supporting the development of scientific knowledge and ways of knowing. The following illustrations of teacher and student activity in each phase of instruction are drawn from our work in elementary school classrooms.[12]

The Engage Phase

Description. Each unit of study begins with an engagement phase, which orients thinking and learning in a particular direction. In the elementary classroom, a version of the classic KWL (i.e., what do I Know, what do I Want to learn, what have I Learned) can be a fine way to initiate engagement. In contrast to the typical use of KWL in the language arts, however, to maximize the value of having students identify what they know, teachers should invite students to identify *how* they have come to know the topic area. Doing so can develop students' awareness that "knowing" can mean different things. Does their knowledge arise from something they actually observed? If so, where and when did that occur, and under what circumstances? Or did others observe it and report it to them? If so, how confident were they in what was reported and why? If a student reports knowledge from something written in a book, what other information was provided? Were any data provided to substantiate the claim? How extensive was the information provided regarding what the student reports knowing? This discussion can provide the grist for later comparisons of ways of knowing in everyday life versus in science, history, or the language arts. It also affords teachers an opportunity to draw out and learn about students' prior knowledge, metacognitive awareness, and reasoning abilities. For example, in a class beginning to investigate how light interacts with matter, one student stated that he already knew the answer because he knew that objects were opaque, transparent, or translucent. This statement indicated to the teacher that the student might assume light interacts with an object in only one way, which could limit what he observed. Knowing of this possibility, the teacher would want to monitor for it, and possibly raise questions about the thoroughness of students' observations.

The scientific community defines for itself what knowing in particular ways means. For example, in each discipline (e.g., physics, chemistry, biology), the community defines what are acceptable methods for data collection and what constitutes precise and accurate observation. The community also dictates what constitutes a valuable contribution to the knowledge base. The relative value of a contribution is a function of the extent to which it extends, refines, or challenges particular theories of how the world works. In our everyday world, we do not have a community determining the validity of our thinking or experiences. Thus, the initial conversation when beginning a new area of study provides an important opportunity for the teacher to ascertain children's awareness of the roots of their knowledge, as well as the expectations of the scientific community. For example, when students describe knowing something about the physical world but indicate that their knowledge did not arise from observation or direct experience, the teacher might ask them to think about what they have observed that might be the kind of evidence scientists would expect to have. When students do provide evidence, the teacher might ask them questions about that evidence such as those above, reflecting the norm that systematic study under controlled conditions is a hallmark of the practice of science, and that evidence not obtained under those conditions would lead scientific thinkers to be skeptical about the knowledge claim.

The next step in engagement is to begin to focus the conversation about the topic of study in ways that are likely to support the learning goals. For example, showing students the kinds of materials and equipment available for investigating can lead to a productive conversation about phenomena they can explore. Focusing on ideas that were generated during the KWL activity, the children can be encouraged to suggest ways they might investigate to determine whether those ideas are scientifically accurate (meaning that the claims can be backed by evidence from investigation). Students can also be encouraged to identify what cannot easily be studied within the classroom (because of the nature of the phenomenon or a lack of resources or time) and might be better studied in a second-hand way (i.e., through reading or hearing about what others have studied and concluded from first-hand investigation). For example, we observed a group of third graders studying light who had numerous questions about black holes, the speed of light, and light sources on different planets, all of which they decided were best pursued through second-hand investigation.

At the end of engagement, the students should have a sense of a general question they are trying to answer (e.g., How does light interact with matter?), and should have identified a particular question or questions to be the focus of the first cycle of investigation. To this end, a teacher might (1) focus the class on a particular phenomenon to study and have them suggest specific questions, (2) draw upon conflicting ideas that were identified in the KWL activity and have the class frame a question for study that can inform the conflict, or (3) draw on a question that was identified during the discussion that is a profitable beginning for investigation.

Illustration. What does this kind of beginning look like in a classroom? In a kindergarten classroom,[13] after a brief opportunity for the children to state what they thought they knew about light and how it behaved, the teacher, Ms. Kingsley, arranged for pairs of students to take turns using flashlights in an area of the classroom that had been darkened. This activity provided children an opportunity to become familiar with investigative materials and phenomena that Ms. Kingsley knew would be the focus of later investigation. The children responded to this activity in a variety of ways, from initially becoming focused on finding spiders to dwelling later on the effects they could create with flashlights. For example, one student commented on the colors she saw as she shone the flashlight on the wall in the darkened area: "There's color. When it shines on a color, then it's the color, green, or white, or red, or black. And then you put the light on the ceiling, it's gone." In the following interaction, the children "discover" reflection:

> [Anisha walks forward under the loft, holding the flashlight with her left hand at an angle to the mirror that she holds flat in front of her.]
>
> Anisha   Oh Deanna, look, I can bounce the light.
>
> [Deanna holds the mirror so light is bouncing directly behind her.]
>
> Deanna [excitedly] If you look back, maybe you can see the light.

A third student focused on what he saw while holding objects in the beam of light. The following interchange occurred when the students explored with large cardboard cutouts of letters of the alphabet.

| Jeremy | [working with a letter] Ooo, this makes a shadow. A different shadow [than the one he just saw]. [He picks up the letter G and hands it to his partner.] See if the G makes a shadow. |
| Hazel | It does make a shadow. See, look at this. |

When the children described their observations to the class, Ms. Kingsley was able to use those observations to elicit the children's current ideas about light and shadows and how they might investigate those ideas.

In a fourth-grade classroom,[14] the teacher, Ms. Lacey, introduced her students to the study of light by asking them what they wondered about light. The children identified over 100 "wonderings," including questions about how we see, why we see rainbows of color from some glass objects or jewelry, what makes light from the plastic sticks you bend to make them "glow" in the dark, what are black holes, and how fast is the speed of light. The next day, students were given a written assessment about light, presented as an opportunity for them to identify their current thinking about the nature and behavior of light. After reviewing students' responses, Ms. Lacey wrote statements on the board (see Table 10-1) indicating the variety of ideas the class held about light. The variation in views of light exhibited by the students provided a reason to investigate to determine the accuracy of the ideas and the relationships among them.

TABLE 10-1 Fourth Graders' Initial Ideas About Light

Light travels.	Light can be blocked by materials.
Light travels in a curved path.	Light can shine through materials.
Light travels in a straight line.	Light can go into materials.
Light travels in all directions.	Light can bounce off of materials.

Later in the unit on light, Ms. Lacey turned to other wonderings the students had about color and light. In the following excerpt, she ascertains whether students' questions came from what they had been told, read, or observed, and she prompted one student to hypothesize about color from what had previously been learned about the behavior of light.

| Ms. Lacey | I know you guys had a few questions about color, so I'm wondering what you know or would like to know about color? What is it you think you want to learn? Levon? |
| Levon | When I said that my shirt's a light blue, you said how do we know it? And you said we might be able to tell. |

Ms. Lacey	Mm-hmm. You want to know how you know it's blue?
Levon	And you said we might be able to tell how.
Ms. Lacey	Well, I think you want to know why when you see a blue shirt, you—it's blue. Okay. We might be able to figure that out. Tom? What is it you want to know?
Tommy	How you change color with light. I know it's real, cause I seen it.
Ms. Lacey	What did you see?
Tommy	Light makes your shirt be a different color. I want to know how to do that.
Ms. Lacey	Hmm. Jared?
Jared	I'm wondering how light can make color.
Ms. Lacey	How light can make color? You think it does?
Jared	Yeah.
Ms. Lacey	Oh. Marcus?
Marcus	I think light is color.
Ms. Lacey	You think light is color. Hmm. So, is that a hypothesis or is that something you really think?
Marcus	Hypothesis. It's something I heard.
Ms. Lacey	Okay. So we'll see if that's right or not.
Marcus	How does light blend, blend.
Ms. Lacey	How does it . . .
Marcus	Different colors of light blend. Like, in the first-hand, the white light blends with . . .
Ms. Lacey	Do you mean bend? Okay.
Michael	I don't really have a question about color, but I have a question about light. Why do they call light, light?
Ms. Lacey	Ah! Good question.
Marcus	Cause it's, cause it's light, like a light color. You can't even see it.
Michael	And why did they call it that? Why did they call it?
Ms. Lacey	What do you think they should call it?
Michael	Something 'cause it's so light, you can't see it.
Chris	How does color make white?
Ms. Lacey	How does color make white? It does?
Chris	Mm-hmm.

Ms. Lacey	You think so?
Chris	Yeah. I saw it in a book.
Ms. Lacey	So, that is your hypothesis.
Ronny	How does color interact with light?
Jared	How does light, how does light form color?
Ms. Lacey	How does light make color? You think it does?
Jared	How does light form color and make color?
Ms. Lacey	Do you think there's a difference between the word form and make? Or do you think it's the same thing?
Jared	It's kinda the same. Forms like light, or something.
Ms. Lacey	Do you think light forms color?
Jason	Yeah.
Ms. Lacey	What makes you think that it might do that?
Jason	Cause light does.
Ms. Lacey	You just think that? That's a hypothesis you're thinking. Okay.
Andrew	It's not a, I don't have a question, but it's sort of a thought. I read in this book that when colored light reflects off, like, the same color, that it'll reflect off that.
Ms. Lacey	I don't understand what you mean.
Andrew	Okay. If, if there's red light and it reflected off somebody's red shirt . . .
Ms. Lacey	Reflected like off like Jared's shirt?
Andrew	Red, yeah, red shirt.
Ms. Lacey	Okay.
Andrew	And then, to another red shirt and off.
Ms. Lacey	So you think this red light can bounce only if it's on red stuff? Is that what you're thinking?
Andrew	Yeah. Or if it reflects on like green, red light can't reflect on a green object.
Ms. Lacey	Red light can't reflect on a green object? What would happen to it if it wouldn't reflect?
Andrew	It'd stay in. It'll absorb.
Ms. Lacey	You think it might absorb? Could it do anything else?
Andrew	[pause] Transmit?
Ms. Lacey	You think it might transmit? Oh. Jamal? We've got some good ideas here. . . .

A common strategy for engagement not illustrated here is the use of a discrepant event—a phenomenon whose behavior or result is unexpected. For example, if one shines a bright, thin beam of light at an angle into a rectangular block of clear, colorless glass with a frosted surface, one can see that the light interacts with the block in multiple ways. Because the object is transparent, students are not surprised to see light through it, but they may be surprised that the light goes through at an angle (refraction), and they are surprised that light also reflects off the block where it enters and where the refracted light exits the block. We can then ask the question: If light behaves in all these ways with this material, does it do the same with other materials?

While it may be easy to engage children with unfamiliar phenomena or new aspects of familiar phenomena, it is more challenging to support them in developing scientific understanding of the world because scientists often "see" the world differently from what our senses tell us. So using the engagement phase to gain knowledge about the conceptual resources students bring to instruction is just the first step. As the knowledge-building process unfolds in subsequent phases, paying attention to how students use those ideas, promoting the use of particular ideas over others, and introducing new ideas are key. In the next phase, the primary focus shifts from eliciting students' thinking about what the physical world is like to preparing them to investigate it in scientific ways.

The Prepare-to-Investigate Phase

Description. Preparing to investigate is an opportunity for teachers to support children in learning how scientific knowledge is produced. While inquiry often begins with a general question, investigation must be guided by very specific questions. Thus, an important goal of this phase of instruction is to establish the specific question that will be the subject of the subsequent investigation.[15] The question must be specific enough to guide investigation, amenable to investigation by children, and central to the unit of study so that students can construct the desired knowledge of scientific concepts, procedures, and ways of knowing. If the teacher presents a question, it is important that this be done in a way that involves the children in discussion about why the question is important and relevant to understanding the broader topic of inquiry. This discussion provides an opportunity to signal the role of questions in scientific investigation and prompts the metacognitive activity that is the hallmark of any good reasoning. If students suggest a question, or the teacher and students together generate the question, it is still important to check the students' understanding about how the question is relevant to the topic of study.[16]

Once a question has been specified, attention can turn to determining how the question will be investigated. This is a critical issue for scientists, and is no less important for children's developing understanding. The teacher may provide information about procedures to use, students may invent or design procedures, or the teacher and students may work together to determine how investigation should be carried out. Increasingly, there is evidence that children can think meaningfully about issues of methodology in investigation.[17] Nevertheless, it is always important for the teacher to check students' understandings about *why* particular approaches and procedures are useful to answering the question. To this end, the teacher might ask students to describe the advantage of using particular materials or tools over others, or to tell why particular steps or tools are necessary. Then, during the actual investigation, the teacher should periodically reassess students' understanding of what they are doing to ascertain whether accurate understanding was sustained in the face of their actual encounter with phenomena. In addition, the teacher can ask students to evaluate the effectiveness and accuracy of their tools or procedures. These actions support students' metacognitive awareness regarding the question–investigation relationship.

We think of investigation in classrooms as addressing how students should interact with materials, as well as with one another (when investigation is carried out by groups of students). A critical aspect of preparing to investigate is determining with students what they will document and how during their investigation. This may take the form of discussing the extent to which procedures need to be documented (only to a small degree when students are all investigating in the same way, but in detail when groups of students investigate differently), and promoting and illustrating the use of drawings to show investigative setups.

If the amount of data collection has been left undefined, the students will need to consider how they will know when they have collected enough data. The fact that students will have to make and report claims and evidence to their classmates lends greater significance to this issue. Students may find they need to collect more data to have sufficient amounts to convince their classmates of their claim in comparison with what they might have found convincing. Finally, it will be important to have students discuss how to document observations so they are accurate, precise, and informative.

When students are working in groups, assigning them roles can be helpful in supporting them in working together effectively. There are various types of roles that students can adopt during investigation. Possible roles to support effective *management* of the students' activity are Equipment Manager, Timekeeper,[18] and Recorder. These roles are not unique to scientific inquiry, but other roles are. For example, having the required materials does not mean that students will use them effectively; it is necessary to monitor that the correct procedures are being carried out and with care.

In addition, a number of responsibilities attend data collection, such as ensuring that enough data will be collected to fulfill the norms of scientific investigation, determining the level of precision with which observations are to be made (e.g., whether length should be recorded to the centimeter, tenth of a centimeter, or hundredth of a centimeter).[19] These sorts of issues form the basis for *intellectual* roles that students can adopt, in contrast to the management roles discussed above.[20] These roles, rather than being named for a task, are named for the conceptual focus maintained during investigation. For example, one student in a group can assume primary responsibility for pressing the group to evaluate how well procedures are working and being carried out in order to answer the question. Another student can be given primary responsibility for evaluating the extent to which the data being collected are relevant to the question. Finally, another student can be given primary responsibility for checking whether the group has enough data to make a claim in answer to the question.

If the practice of adopting roles is utilized, the prepare-to-investigate phase is used to set this up. Modeling and role-playing are helpful to support students in adopting roles that are new to them. In addition, the formal assignment of roles may change over time because while management roles may always be needed, intellectual roles represent ways of thinking that we want all students to adopt. Thus, the need to formalize such roles should decrease over time as students appropriate them as a matter of course when engaging in scientific investigation.

Finally, it is useful to give some attention to the issue of how data will be recorded. At times it may be best to provide a table and simply have students discuss how they will use it and why it is a useful way to organize their data. At other times it may be best to have the class generate a list of possible means for recording data. Sometimes it may be sufficient to indicate that students should be sure to record their observations in their notebooks, and have the students in their groups decide what approach is best for recording their observations.

Illustration. In the unit on light and shadows, Ms. Kingsley posed to her kindergarteners the question of whether an object's shadow can be more than one shape, following the opportunity they had to explore with flashlights prior to beginning any formal investigation. She knew that not all the children had made shadows during their exploration, so she used part of the discussion in this phase to ascertain students' understanding of how to put objects in the light to make shadows. She showed the class how the materials would be set up, with a light source placed a couple of feet from a wall and a piece of poster paper taped on the wall to allow them to draw the shadows they observed.

During her fourth graders' investigation of the interaction of light and matter, Ms. Lacey bridged from the children's wonderings to a question she introduced: How does light interact with solid objects? She began the preparing-to-investigate phase by ascertaining students' understanding of the question. One boy asked what "interacts" means. She responded that she was interacting with the students, and then asked them to interpret the question without using the word "interact." The students responded with such questions as: "What would it do"? "How does it act"? "How does it behave"? "How do they act together (but not like in a movie)"? Ms. Lacey then solicited questions about other words in the investigation question, and a boy asked, "What is a solid?" Students responded with statements such as: "A solid is not like water."" It's filled in." "It's hard, maybe." "It doesn't bend." At this point, Ms. Lacey picked up a bendable solid, bent it, and asked the students whether it was a solid. Students were divided on whether it was. Ms. Lacey proceeded to review states of matter with the students, discussing properties and examples. She then returned to the preparation for investigating light.

The materials on which the students would shine a flashlight were simple, but there were many of them (more than 20 items), and describing each in order to identify it would have been cumbersome (e.g., blue plastic sheet, colorless plastic sheet, plastic sheet with gold coating on one side). So Ms. Lacey prepared a poster with each type of material mounted on it and numbered. She used the poster to show children the materials with which they would be working, and they discussed the use of the numbers to facilitate documenting their observations.

Ms. Lacey also introduced a new tool to the students: a small rectangular piece of white construction paper, which she called a "light catcher." This tool functioned as a screen to look for reflected or transmitted light. Figure 10-2 shows the setup Ms. Lacey showed the students, with the letters A and B indicating the places where the students expected they might see light.

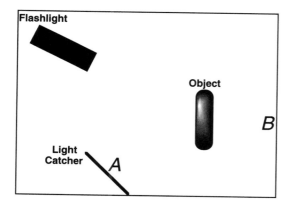

FIGURE 10-2 Investigative setup for studying how light interacts with solid objects.

In addition, the class talked about categorizing objects in terms of how light behaved. Ms. Lacey asked the students what they thought the light might do, and they discussed categorizing the objects based on whether light bounced off, went through, became trapped, or did something else (the students were not sure what this might be, but they wanted to have a category for other possibilities).[21] In the course of that conversation, Ms. Lacey introduced the terms "reflected," "transmitted," and "absorbed," which she stated were terms used by scientists to name the behaviors they had described. There was some discussion about what it meant when an object blocked light: Did that mean light had been absorbed, or was it simply stopped by the material? Ms. Lacey suggested that the class leave that question open, to be discussed again after they had investigated and had the opportunity to observe the light.

Ms. Lacey chose to focus students' recording of their observations by preparing a simple table for them to complete: a column for the number/name of the material and a column each for indicating whether light reflected, transmitted (went through), or was absorbed (trapped by) the material. The use of the table seemed straightforward, so there was little discussion. Ms. Lacey later noticed that most students used the table as though their task was to determine which single column to check for each object. She realized that the students needed guidance to check for each object whether light was reflected, transmitted, or absorbed. The next time Ms. Lacey taught this topic, she made two changes in this phase. First, she was careful to raise the question of whether light could behave in more than one way with a material. Students were divided on whether they thought this was possible, which gave them a reason to investigate and supported them in realizing the need to be thorough in observing light with each object. Second, she asked students how they might provide evidence that light did not interact in particular ways with an object. This discussion led students to realize that they would have information to record in each column of the table, and that what does not happen can be as informative as what does happen.

The Investigate Phase

Description. In this phase, students interact with the physical world, document their observations, and think about what these observations mean about the physical world. The teacher's role is to monitor students' use of materials and interactions with others (e.g., in small groups), as well as attend to the conceptual ideas with which students are working and the ways in which their thinking is similar and different from that of their classmates.

Investigating involves the interaction of content and process. It may appear to students to be more about process because what we observe is a function of when, how, and with what tools we choose to observe. At the same time, what we observe is also a function of what we expect to observe, and how we interpret our observations is clearly influenced by what we already know and believe about the physical world. For example, we have experienced children describing only one type of interaction when shining light on objects because they expected that light could interact in only one way. Thus they described light as only "going through" a piece of clear, colorless plastic wrap even though we could see bright spots of light on the front of the wrap indicating reflected light. Furthermore, students described light as only "being blocked" from a piece of cardboard even though a disc of light the size of the flashlight beam could be seen on the back of the piece of cardboard, indicating that light was going through it.[22]

The teacher determines whether and when to prompt students' awareness of the ways in which their prior knowledge may be influencing their observations. With respect to students' interactions with *materials*, it is important to monitor whether students are using them appropriately. Students invariably use materials in unexpected ways; hence, the teacher needs to observe student activity closely. When students use materials incorrectly, the teacher needs to determine whether to provide corrective feedback. Since it is important for the development of metacognition that students be in the "driver's seat" and not simply follow the teacher's directions, determining whether, when, and how to provide feedback is critical. If the teacher judges that the students' activity is so off the mark that the targeted learning goals will be sacrificed, it is critical to provide prompt corrective feedback. An example in the study of light would be if students measuring angles of the path of light coming into and reflecting off of a mirror were using the protractor incorrectly.

Other cases, however, provide opportunities for students to become aware of gaps in their thinking. An example of this occurred when the teacher in the kindergarten class studying light and shadows noticed that some students were tracing the object directly on their recording paper rather than tracing the object's shadow. When the teacher saw this happening, she joined the group as they were working and began to ask them about their data. In the course of the conversation, she asked them to show her how they had made the shadows, which led them to indicate that some were tracings of the objects themselves, not the shadows. She then asked them, "If our question is about shadows, which drawings show shadows?" The students were able to point to their drawings that were shadows. She then asked, "How could you mark your drawings so that you can tell which ones are shadows, so that when we look for patterns, you'll know which drawings to look at?" They devised a scheme—to draw dots around the drawings that were shadows—and the teacher moved on to another group. Later, when the former group reported, the rest of the class learned about their strategy and how they had dealt with the "mixed" nature of their observations.

Another important category of feedback is when the teacher brings out the norms and conventions of scientific investigation (e.g., holding conditions the same when trials are conducted, measuring from the same reference point, and changing only one variable at a time). Attention to such issues can be prompted by asking students about the decisions they are making about how to investigate. For example, in the fourth-grade investigation of the interaction of light and matter, one group's response to Ms. Lacey's question about what they had found out revealed a lack of attention to the transmission of light. Ms. Lacey handled this in the following way:

Ms. Lacey	When we were preparing to investigate, we said that light might also be transmitted, but I didn't hear you say anything about that. Did you check for that?
Student	No, but we already know light doesn't go through these materials; they block it.
Ms. Lacey	But remember that scientists believe it is important to test out such ideas, and as scientific thinkers, your classmates will be encouraged to look for such evidence. How will you convince them that these materials don't transmit light?

Here Ms. Lacey gave students an important message about the need to rule out possibilities instead of relying on assumptions.

With small-group investigation, in addition to general monitoring to support student collaboration, the teacher needs to be attentive to whether differences in students' ideas create difficulties. In the excerpt below, two kindergarten children in Ms. Kingsley's class are investigating reflection from a mirror. Their initial conflict is due to Brian's interest in placing the mirror so that its back faces the light source. Amanda objects because her exploration during the engage phase revealed that reflection is best from the front of the mirror. She is very interested in seeing the reflection because the class is examining a claim she made from her exploration activity, which was that you can use a mirror to make light "go wherever you want it to."

Amanda	[tracing line to mirror] This goes to here. The light has to hit the mirror. Then . . .

Brian	I want it to go that way. [referring to placement of the mirror with its back to the light source]
Amanda	No, the mirror has to face the light source.
Amanda	[turns mirror to face the light source] Lookey! Light, see.
Brian	[turns mirror back around] Lookey, no light, see.
Amanda	But that's because it's not facing that way. [turns mirror to face the light]
Brian	You said you could move it wherever you wanted it to go. So your plan has failed. . . .
Amanda	The light has to do the—okay. This is the light source, right? [*points to source*] This light has to hit the mirror . . . And then, look, look, see . . . Now you think my plan works, see? Watch, see . . .
Brian	[takes hold of mirror] I can't make it go this way! [referring to making the light go behind the mirror] If I take this off [removes mirror from where it rests on their drawing paper], it's going my way. But [puts mirror back onto paper], it's not going my way.
Amanda	The mirror has to face . . . The light has to hit the mirror. [taps mirror with hand] And look: light, light, light. [points to reflected beams of light]
Brian	But you said it could go anywhere. You said it could go anywhere you wanted it to go and I wanted it to go backwards, like this. [referring to making the light go behind the mirror]
Amanda	But the mirror [forcefully places the mirror on their drawing paper] has to face the light source [forceful gesture toward light source], face the light source, and THEN you can move it. [referring to the reflected beam of light]

The interaction of content and process that occurs during investigation means that teachers must be mindful of children's cognitive activity as they undergo and interpret their experiences with the physical world. Teachers should ask students what they are observing and what they think their observations mean about the question under investigation. Sometimes it is useful to ask students *why* they think what they are doing will help them answer the question. In addition, the teacher needs to observe what students observe so students can be prompted to notice important phenomena they might otherwise ignore or be encouraged to pursue observations the teacher believes useful to the knowledge-building process.

When investigative procedures are simple, students are able to focus more of their attention on what the data are and what these data suggest about the question being investigated. When procedures are more complex, students need more time to focus on the meaning of the data apart from the actual investigation. When students design the investigation themselves, they may need to give more attention during the investigation to evaluating how well their plans are working so they can make adjustments. Thus, teachers need to monitor how well children are handling the complexity of the investigation so that sufficient time is allocated to support the knowledge-building process.[23]

Once the data have been collected, students need to analyze them. Identifying patterns is a deductive analytic process in which students work from specific datasets to identify general relationships. From this step, students make knowledge claims, just as scientists would. That is, they make claims about the physical world, using the patterns they identified to generate those claims. We consider this aspect of investigation to be a different instructional phase because the nature of the cognitive activity for the teacher and students has changed. This aspect is discussed as part of the preparing-to-report phase.

Illustration

To illustrate the investigation phase, we draw upon an event that occurred in Ms. Kingsley's kindergarten class during their investigation of light and shadows. Amanda and Rochelle were working together, with Amanda basically directing Rochelle. When Ms. Kingsley checked on them and asked questions to determine their thinking about what they were finding out, it became clear to her that Amanda was quite certain that the shadow from an object could be only one shape, and Rochelle appeared to go along with whatever Amanda thought. While Amanda's thinking was incorrect, Ms. Kingsley chose not to intervene, recognizing that during reporting, the children would have the opportunity to see a wider range of data and possibly reconsider their thinking (see the illustration of the reporting phase).

The following excerpt is from Ms. Lacey's fourth-grade class. This interchange occurred early in the investigation, and Ms. Lacey was checking on a group of three girls that she knew from previous experience had found investigative activity challenging. She began by asking which materials the students had used in their investigation and what they had found out. She learned that one student in the group had been working independently instead of with the other two, and they had not been discussing their results.

Ms. Lacey encouraged them to work together, especially since it would be helpful to have one person holding the flashlight and material, and another person using the light catcher.

Ms. Lacey	[picks up a blue styrofoam object and shines the flashlight on it] What's it doing?
Mandy	Some goes through.
Ms. Lacey	How do you know?
Mandy	Some blue light is on the wall.
Ms. Lacey	Does it do anything else? [Ms. Lacey directs the student to use the light catcher to check other possibilities.]
Mandy	Some is reflected.
Ms. Lacey	Write that down.

Perhaps the most important question asked by the teacher in this excerpt is "How do you know?" This question is at the core of distinguishing systematic research from our everyday sense making. It also sent the message that the students were accountable for their observations, and allowed Ms. Lacey to indicate the need to check for multiple ways in which light might behave with the object.

The Prepare-to-Report Phase

Description

As the activity shifts to a focus on the public sharing of one's findings from investigation (reporting phase), the role of the class as a community of scientific thinkers takes on new meaning. In scientific practice, this phase marks a shift in emphasis from divergent to convergent thinking, and from operating with the values, beliefs, norms, and conventions of the scientific community in the background to operating with them in the foreground.[24] Now it matters a great deal what fellow classmates will think and not just what the investigating group thinks.

In this phase, just as scientists use their laboratory documents to prepare papers for public presentation to the larger scientific community, students use the information and observations in their notebooks to prepare materials for public presentation to their classmates. The public nature of sharing one's claims and evidence means that students need to determine the claim(s) for which there is enough evidence to warrant public scrutiny, and what data they should feature as the compelling evidence backing their own claim(s) and supporting or refuting the claims of others.

Students can use poster-size paper as the medium for reporting, thus allowing the information to be large enough for everyone in the class to see. Posters are expected to include a statement of the group's knowledge claim(s), as well as data backing the claim(s); if groups investigated different questions, the poster should include the question as well. Data may be presented in written, tabular, or graphical form (including figures or graphs), and students may decide to include a diagram of the investigative setup to provide a context for the data. (This is to be expected when students investigated in different ways.) As each group prepares its poster, students should be thinking about how to present their findings to best enable others to understand them, *and* be convinced of the group's claim. Decisions about how to state a claim and what data to include in presenting one's claim provide important learning opportunities.

A major aspect of the teacher's role in this phase is to reflect the norms of the scientific community regarding the development and evaluation of knowledge claims. In the scientific community, for example, there is an expectation that relationships will be stated precisely and backed by unambiguous and reliable data. It should also be recognized that claims can be stated in the negative, thus indicating a relationship that is claimed to be inaccurate—for example, the brightness of the light source does not affect whether light reflects from an object. Such claims help the community narrow its consideration of possible relationships.

Another role of the teacher is to help students attend to issues that may affect the quality of their public presentation. For example, teachers can encourage students to draw as well as write out their ideas to communicate them more effectively. Furthermore, teachers can prompt students to evaluate their poster for its effectiveness in communicating findings. For example: Is it readable? Are things clearly stated? Is there enough information for others to evaluate the claim or be convinced of its validity?

Finally, a key role for the teacher is to monitor the types of claims students are generating and the nature of the evidence they are selecting. The teacher determines whether and to what extent to prompt students' awareness of the role played by process in determining what they observed (e.g., ascertaining students' awareness of imprecise or inaccurate data). With respect to content, the teacher determines whether and when to focus students on particular strategies for interpreting or analyzing their data or to provide additional information to support students in writing claims. It may be necessary for the teacher to help groups reorganize their data to find patterns. For example, Table 10-2 shows two tables. The top table shows the data as they were originally recorded. The order of the columns matches the order of places that students looked to check for light from the flashlight. The order of objects in the first column is simply the order students selected to observe them. The bottom table shows the same data in a similar form,

TABLE 10-2 Data Tables from Initial Recording and with Revisions for Analysis Purposes

Original Data Table and Observations:

Object	On Light Catcher in Front of Object (reflected)	On Back of Object (transmitted)	On Light Catcher Behind Object (absorbed)
Clear glass	dim light	bright light	light shadow
Purple glass	dim purple light	bright purple light	dark purple shadow
Silver wrap	bright light	no light	dark shadow
White plastic sheet	dim light	medium light	medium shadow
White typing paper	bright light	dim light	medium shadow
Black felt	no light	no light	very dark shadow
Orange cardboard	dim orange light	dim reddish light	dark shadow

Reorganized Data Table and Simplified Observations:

Object	On Light Catcher in Front of Object (reflected)	On Back of Object (transmitted)	On Light Catcher Behind Object (absorbed)
Black felt	no light	very dark shadow	no light
Orange cardboard	dim light	dark shadow	dim light
Purple glass	dim light	dark shadow	bright light
White plastic sheet	dim light	medium shadow	medium light
Clear glass	dim light	light shadow	bright light
Silver wrap	bright light	dark shadow	no light
White typing paper	bright light	medium shadow	dim light

but to facilitate looking for patterns, the columns and rows have been reordered, and the data have been simplified (information about color has been removed). This type of reorganization and simplification of data is common for scientists, and may be necessary for students to find patterns from which to make a claim.

Often, the teacher's support is at the level of helping groups figure out how best to state the claim(s) they want to make from their data. It does not include evaluating whether their data support the claim; that is part of the reporting phase and should be shared by the class.

On the other hand, the teacher may choose to support students in making additional claims based on the data they have, particularly in instances where the group has unique data to make a claim that the teacher believes would promote desired knowledge-building for the class. In Ms. Lacey's fourth-grade class, for example, despite students' assumptions that light would behave in only one way with an object, a group had evidence that light behaved in more than one way. Given that this was the only group in the class making such a claim from that body of evidence, Ms. Lacey supported the group to ensure that they would include the claim in their poster so it would be introduced to the whole class.

An alternative approach involves the teacher's questioning students during the prepare-to-investigate phase to lead them to consider the possibility that light may behave in more than one way. The emphasis in this case may be on ruling out the possibility of disconfirming evidence. With this approach, the teacher monitors during the investigation phase whether students are checking for multiple possibilities, and will know whether the students observe light interacting with objects in more than one way.

Illustration. The following excerpt from an investigation of light by third graders shows a typical teacher–student interaction as students attempted to generate knowledge claims.[25] The students were working with light boxes producing narrow beams of light and had been given latitude regarding which questions—identified during the engagement phase—they would like to study. As a result, different groups of students investigated with different types of materials. In the transcript, note that the students did most of the talking. The teacher primarily asked questions to determine the nature of the students' thinking. Note also that the teacher reflected an important norm of scientific activity by asking the students how they planned to represent the observations supporting their claim.

Ms. Sutton	What claim are you working on right now?
Don	We had to change it because we thought that the speed of light would be a [second-hand investigation].
Ms. Sutton	Mm hmm.
Kevin	So, light can reflect off a mirror. Any other object that's not a mirror, like a piece of paper. Let me demonstrate. [Ms. Sutton: Okay.] This is a piece of paper. You see, when the light hits the paper, it disappears. But before it disap-

	pears, it hits the paper, it goes through the paper. It disappears.
Ms. Sutton	Hmm. Does *all* the light disappear through the paper?
Kevin	No. Okay, you see all the light that's coming through, from this hole?
Ms. Sutton	Yeah.
Kevin	It goes *to* the piece of paper. It disappears when it hits that piece—that object.
Ms. Sutton	Where do you think it goes?
Don	Through the paper. There's a little light over here. And it stops here because it doesn't have enough power to go anymore.
Ms. Sutton	Okay. Hang on a second. So, you're saying a little bit of light goes through the paper. And you think the rest of the light just disappears?
Kevin	No. The rest of the light that hits the paper disappears from the light—from the object, cause it's not a mirror. But if it hits the mirror it can reflect off of it.
Ms. Sutton	So if it's a mirror, the light goes in another direction, or reflects off. If it's something besides a mirror . . .
Kevin	It doesn't get reflected.
Ms. Sutton	It just disappears, it doesn't reflect?
Kevin	Yep.
Ms. Sutton	Okay. Are you going to try to prove that some way to the group? You have to show some data.
Don	Well, it's not exactly data. We sort of . . .
Kevin	I drew a picture out here.
Ms. Sutton	How could you show that? We could get another piece of paper. Save what you've got so far. How could you show on another piece of paper how the light is different with differ-ent—with the mirror and with the paper? How could you show it? What you just said—so you could show it to the rest of the group?
Kevin	We can draw the top and just say that the light is coming through—put light right here. And then the light through—going out of the box. And then we can put, make like a little part of it

	like this, like the target. And put the paper right here.
Ms. Sutton	So, Kevin is saying, when the light hits the mirror, it looks one way. When the light hits a piece of paper, it looks another way. How could you *show* how it looks those two ways on a piece of paper?
Don	And, another thing is, I sort of drew this thing. That's the light that's over here that goes there. And then when it hits these, it stays there and it doesn't come back.
Ms. Sutton	That's interesting, too. But you guys need to stick to one claim and deal with that. When you think you have evidence for that, if you want to explore something else and have some time, you could do that.

The Report Phase

Description. A critical feature of inquiry-based instruction is the point at which students' findings are publicly shared and discussed. This phase has two parts (see Figure 10-1). First, groups of students who have been investigating together present their claims and evidence, which are discussed by the class in terms of their own merits and in light of the findings presented by previous groups. Second, the class discusses the commonalities and differences among the claims and evidence presented, noting claims that can be rejected, developing a class list of community-accepted claims, and determining claims or questions that need further investigation. In addition to providing occasions for discussing important issues related to the investigative process (e.g., possible errors, missed observations), public reports require students to make and defend statements about their understandings, and provide occasions for examining their own thinking and sense making as well as that of others.[26] In addition, when students publicly share their results, the need for vocabulary and a common language to communicate ideas becomes salient. Thus, there is an important opportunity for the teacher to support and guide students in the use of scientific terms to facilitate their communication.

When students first experience this activity, the teacher plays a pivotal role in communicating and modeling expectations for audience members. This includes establishing and maintaining conversational norms. Despite the fact that children may need to challenge the ideas or work of their classmates, the teacher is key in setting the tone so that this is done with the understanding that the students are all thinking together so they can collectively determine how to understand the aspect of the physical world under investigation. The primary expectations for audience members are to determine whether there is a clearly stated claim that is related to the question under investigation, whether there is evidence backing that claim, and whether the evidence is unambiguous in supporting the claim. The issue of unambiguous support concerns whether there is any evidence—either from other groups or from within the presenting group's data—that would counter the claim. With teacher modeling and practice with the teacher's feedback, students become able to sustain substantive conversations regarding the knowledge they are developing about the physical world.

The reporting phase is particularly complex and rich with opportunities for the teacher to engage in supporting children's thinking and actions. As each group shares its claim(s) and describes the relationship between these claims and their data, the teacher assumes multiple roles: monitoring for understanding, working with the students to clarify ambiguous or incomplete ideas, seeding the conversation with potentially helpful language or ideas, and serving as the collective memory of prior conversations (both in the whole-class context and in the small-group investigation contexts). The challenge in this phase of instruction is to promote the group's advancement toward deeper understanding of the phenomenon under investigation, as well as the nature of scientific ways of knowing, using the fruits of the investigation activity and the collective thinking of the classroom community.

The reporting phase culminates with the whole class discussing the claims that have been shared to determine which if any have sufficiently convincing evidence (and a lack of contradictory evidence) to elevate them to the status of "class claim"—indicating that there is class consensus about the validity of the claim. This discussion of claims typically results in identifying where there is disagreement among claims or contradictory evidence related to particular claims (e.g., when the data presented by one group can also be used to contradict the claim of another), which provides the motivation for the next cycle of investigation.

Illustration. Excerpts from classroom instruction illustrate various aspects of teacher and student activity during this phase. The following transcript is from the beginning of the reporting phase in Ms. Lacey's fourth-grade class. Ms. Lacey introduces students to the class claim chart, on which the class will track the claims that have been introduced and the classroom community's reaction to them. She also forewarns students that they have conflicting views, anticipating the need to prepare the students to hear things from their classmates with which they will not agree.

| Ms. Lacey | And we're going to start making a list of claims. Or we might have a list of—we don't know whether we believe that or not. . . . Some of our claims may end up being "think abouts." We need to think about them some more. . . . |
| | You know what? You guys don't all agree. I've been to every group . . . so you better pay attention. They may not convince you, but you might think to yourself, "aha! I'm gonna try that." Or, "I might need to check that out." |

Ms. Lacey's introduction of the class claim chart sends an important message about the dynamic nature of the inquiry process: reporting is not a culminating activity; it is part of an ongoing activity, the next phase of which will be shaped by what has just transpired. Her decision to alert students to the presence of conflicting ideas provides an authentic purpose for paying attention to one another during the reporting phase and stimulated metacognition.

In the next excerpt, a student questions one of the claims made by the reporting group. The group made a claim that "light can't be trapped" and cited as evidence that "you can't roll it up and throw it." The students' interaction presents the teacher with many issues to which she could react to support the students' development of scientific knowledge and ways of knowing.

Bobby	When you said that you believe that light can't be trapped because it's a gas, you can't roll it up and throw it. What do you mean?
Megan	We mean we can't grab light and throw it at someone.
Heather	It's not solid.
Megan	It's not a liquid, either.
Bobby	So you're saying that light is a gas? How do you know light is a gas?
Heather	Air is a gas, and you can't feel it. Well, you can feel it only when it's blowing. But you can't feel light because it's not blowing.
Bobby	So you guys are saying that you think light is a gas because light is like air?

Ms. Lacey could have pointed out that a claim about light being a gas is unrelated to the focus of this particular investigation; she could have truncated the interaction by providing the information that light is a form of energy, not matter; she could have identified this claim as one that requires further exploration, perhaps in a second-hand way. But Ms. Lacey chose not to interject at all. While this decision has limitations with respect to developing scientific knowledge about light, it has the advantage of giving the students opportunity and responsibility to examine one another's thinking with respect to the norms and conventions of scientific practice, as illustrated by Bobby's pressing the girls to address how they know light is a gas. Such questions can provide opportunities for students particularly interested in a question to pursue it outside of class, or resources might be brought into the class (books or descriptions downloaded from the Internet) that provide information pertinent to the question.

In the next two excerpts, Ms. Lacey responds in two different ways to students' questioning of the reporting group based on her judgment of the reasons for those questions. In the first excerpt, she responds to confusion that she suspects arises from the way students are interpreting language in the phrasing of claims. The excerpt illustrates the language demands involved in both representing one's thinking in a claim and interpreting the claims of others.

Barbie	I'm confused—"we believe light does go in a path." Well, how do you know it goes in a path? It could go different ways. ["A path" appears to be interpreted as "one path."]
Megan	We tried it on the flashlight. It's just straight. ["A path" appears to have meant "a straight path."]
Barbie	Cause there's a whole bunch of light. Light can go [other ways] [shows with hand]. ["A path" appears to be interpreted as "one particular path" instead of many possible paths.]
Megan	We don't believe that.
Ms. Lacey	Can you draw a diagram on the board? [Change from an oral to a written medium may resolve issues due to language demands.]

The girls used a context from their preinstruction assessment—a tree, a person, and the sun—to show two different possibilities regarding the path of light: wavy and straight lines. They drew multiple paths from the sun and pointed to the straight lines as the representations that matched their claim. Ms. Lacey then worked with the class to modify the students' claim about the path of light so that it was consistent with the illustration:

Ms. Lacey	[*to class*] Can you think of some way they could switch that claim to make more sense to us? She's telling us one thing, and they didn't put that one word in. [*to Megan and Heather*] Cause you don't think it goes wavy, you think it goes . . .
Megan	Straight.
Ms. Lacey	How could you change your claim to say that?
Heather	We believe light goes only in a straight path.
Ms. Lacey	[*to class*] Will that make better sense to us?
Class	Yeah.

In the second excerpt, a student struggles to make sense of the claim that light reflects and goes through. Ms. Lacey suspects, because of the student's language, he has difficulty conceptualizing that light can behave in multiple ways simultaneously. As a result, she intervenes, asking a question to help achieve greater clarity regarding the student's confusion:

Megan	Yeah. Stefan?
Stefan	Reflect and go through—on the plastic tray. When you put it on reflect, it reflected off the plastic tray. And when you put it on go through, it went through the plastic tray. But I don't get it. If it reflected off, then how did it go through?
Megan	Well, we put it on an angle and shined it and it went on our screen. And when we put it straight, it went through.
Ms. Lacey	Stefan, are you having a hard time thinking that light can do two things at once? If it reflects off, why did it also go through? Did they explain?

In both of the above examples, as well as in the excerpt at the beginning of this chapter in which a second-grade student objected to a claim about light reflecting from wood, students are revealing that they lack a conception of light that allows it to behave in the ways indicated by other students. Brad does not have a way to think about light that would account for its ability to reflect from wood. Stefan does not have a way to think about light that would account for its ability to simultaneously reflect and pass through an object. How does some of the light "know" to reflect, while other light gets transmitted through the material? These are reasonable issues, and we should not be surprised that the students do not readily accept claims that speak to a reality they do not believe. It is part of the scientific culture to be skeptical about claims that do not fit existing scientific theories, as these claims clearly did not fit the students' preexisting ideas. Indeed, there are numerous examples of scientific papers that presented novel scientific claims and were rejected by top scientific journals because of their inconsistency with prevailing knowledge and beliefs, but later became highly regarded and even prize-winning.[27] Thus when such events occur, it is important for the teacher to recognize that the issue is the fit between the idea presented and the students' conceptual framework. As *How People Learn* suggests, it is precisely in these situations that students' thinking must be fully engaged if they are to develop desired scientific understanding.

There are several ways to proceed in such circumstances. Some research has demonstrated that having students observe relationships can lead them to change their initial thinking about those relationships,[28] or at least come up with alternative ideas.[29] In the case of the second grader who was skeptical about the reflection of light, this would mean setting up the materials so he could observe the reflection from wood that his classmates saw and providing opportunities to examine the reflection from other solids. Other researchers have proposed engaging students in reasoning through a series of phenomena that are closely related,[30] helping students bridge analogous circumstances. In the case of disbelief about light reflecting from wood or other nonshiny solids, this might mean starting with observing instances of reflection that students readily accept (e.g., reflection from a mirror); linking to observations of a very thick mirror, whereby the light beam can be seen traveling through to the silvered back surface of the mirror and reflecting from there; linking to reflection from a less reflective surface, such as lead (a metal, but not shiny); then linking to a similarly less reflective surface but of a different type, such as gray construction paper; and so on. The bridging could go as far as examining reflection from black felt, a material students are initially quite sure does not reflect light, but can be observed to do so if the room is dark enough.[31]

Another approach to addressing the nonacceptance of claims that contradict everyday experience is to tell students that part of learning science means developing new conceptions of reality.[32] This does not necessarily mean discarding existing ideas.[33] However, it does mean that students need to recognize that in a science context, the cultural beliefs and practices that guide knowledge production in the scientific community dictate what knowledge is valued and accepted and hence is considered scientific knowledge,[34] and that they need to operate accordingly in their knowledge-building activity during science instruction.

Despite the challenge of accepting claims that are initially counter to everyday thinking, we have regularly observed students, even very young children, developing new ideas that are counter to their initial thinking. The following example comes from Ms. Kingsley's kindergarten class during their study of light and shadows. The class was discussing two claims that arose from the day's investigation and were posted on the board: (1) an object can make more than one shadow shape, and (2) an object can make only one shadow shape. When Ms. Kingsley asked the class to evaluate the claims in light of the data from students' investigations, which were also posted, Amanda, who had repeatedly stated her view that an object's shadow can be only one shape, gave the following response:

Ms. Kingsley	Okay, look at the evidence we've got here. Does it support the claim that objects make more than one shadow?
Amanda	Both.
Ms. Kingsley	You think it says both Amanda, tell me why.
Amanda	Because um [touching each of the posters with multiple shapes of shadows], all shadow, all shadow, all shadow, all shadow. [touching each of the drawings containing only one shape of shadow] One shadow, one shadow.

Here, Amanda correctly pointed out that the data did not conclusively support one claim over the other, drawing attention to the ambiguity of the results. This provided a reason to investigate further, so the teacher suggested that the class do so the next day. The next excerpt is an exchange that occurred following the next day's investigation. Again, all the groups' data were posted at the front. After examining the data from the second day, all of which showed more than one shadow, Amanda provided a different evaluation of the evidence:

Ms. Kingsley	We need to find out if the documentation supports that a shape can make one shadow or more than one shadow. Does this evidence support the claim . . . [points to the two posted claims]
JT	More!
Derek	One!
Amanda	The first one [an object can make more than one shadow] is true.
Ms. Kingsley	Why?
Amanda	Because one object can make more shadows, see? Because look at all these shadows on the papers. [runs hand along all the posters because they all show multiple shapes of shadows for an object]

Of note is that Ms. Kingsley and the other teachers featured in this section allowed the children to work with the ideas they had, but pressed them to continually reexamine those ideas in light of the results of their own and others' investigations. Amanda needed the time of several cycles of investigation to become convinced of a different idea from the one she initially held. Thus, the cycling process of investigation within the same context is an important aspect of promoting desired development of scientific knowledge and ways of knowing.

Second-Hand Investigation

Our focus thus far has been on the development of understanding through first-hand investigation. Such experiences give students repeated opportunities to articulate and test their reasoning and ideas against one another's first-hand observations, and steep them in the differences between a scientific approach to knowledge building from experience and a more casual everyday approach. However, inquiry-based science instruction can also profitably include learning from text-based resources (as suggested by the *National Science Education Standards*).[35] The study of accumulated knowledge is authentic to scientific practice[36] and involves cognitive activities that have many similarities with first-hand inquiry about the physical world.[37] Second-hand sources can also reliably focus student attention on the core concepts of interest. The question is how to engage students in such activity in a way that keeps them actively engaged intellectually relative to scientific ways of knowing and permits a skeptical stance that is common to a scientific mindset.

To achieve this goal, we developed a novel type of text for inquiry-based instruction, whose use is called a second-hand investigation. These texts are modeled after the notebook of a scientist and so are referred to as notebook texts. They consist of excerpts from the notebook of a fictitious scientist, Lesley Park, who uses her notebook to "think aloud" regarding the inquiry in which she is engaged, sharing with the reader her observations of the phenomenon she is studying, the way in which she has modeled that phenomenon, the nature of her investigation, the data collected in the course of her investigation, and the knowledge claims suggested by the data.[38]

We share excerpts from this instruction to illustrate how text can be approached in an inquiry-based fashion to support students' engagement in scientific reasoning and what role the teacher plays in such activity. The specific notebook text with which the children were working reports on an investigation with materials very similar to those used by the students in studying the interaction of light with matter, although there were several differences in Lesley's investigation, including her use of a light meter to measure the light she observed.

Of note are the various ways that the teacher, Ms. Sutton, supported the students' learning from the text. For example, she led the students in a quick overview of the text during which the students identified the features that signaled this was a scientist's notebook: a header with the scientist's name and date of activity, drawings showing investigative setups, and tables of data. During the reading of the text, a significant amount of time was devoted to examining the relationship between the information in the notebook and the students' own experiences. Ms. Sutton accomplished this by revisiting the claims list arising from the students' own first-hand investigations. The students identified those claims on which there was consensus and those that were still under consideration, but for which there was insufficient evidence. In addition, there were numerous instances in which Ms. Sutton called the students' attention to vocabulary that was introduced in the notebook text and how it compared with terms the students had been using in their own writing and discussion (e.g., Lesley's use of "absorbed" to describe the behavior students referred to as the "blocking" of light).

The following three excerpts illustrate how the text, in combination with the teacher's facilitation, supported the students' engagement in scientific reasoning. In the first excerpt, the students have encountered a table in which Lesley presents data in units she calls "candles."

Ms. Sutton	Okay, it's the readout of how many candles. And right now it's showing the flashlight all by itself has . . .?
Leo	Ten candles.
Ms. Sutton	Ten candles.
Jihad	Could it be like 10.5 or something or 10.3?
Ms. Sutton	I would imagine. Don't you think it could go up or down depending on how bright the light is?
Jihad	So, if she puts zero candles, so that means it doesn't transmit at all?
Ms. Sutton	Yes. Good observation.
Tatsuro	Are there such thing as like, um, a millicandle?

Ms. Sutton mediated the students' sense making with the table. To understand any of the other findings in this table, it was important for the students to recognize that the amount of light from the light source (the flashlight) was "ten candles." This discussion, however, led several students to wonder about this unit of measure. Transferring their knowledge about other units of measure, they inquired about the system from which this unit is derived and how that system "works" (i.e., whether it works like the metric system).

In the next excerpt, the students have encountered Lesley's claim that "all objects reflect and absorb light."

Ms. Sutton	What evidence did you see that would support that [all objects reflect and absorb] even though that wasn't your claim?
Ian	That almost all the objects did and maybe if we used a light meter, we might have found out that every single object did a little.
Ms. Sutton	How about you, Megan?
Megan	Some objects did both things—two different things, but not . . . we didn't, like, kind of find out that for all objects . . .
Ms. Sutton	If you had done more, do you think we might have?
Megan	Maybe.
Ms. Sutton	If you had tested more?
Megan	We didn't do all the objects, yet.

In this exchange, we see how Ms. Sutton related the second-hand investigation to the students' first-hand investigation by calling their attention to the differences between their claims and Lesley's claim. This led to a discussion of two issues: the role of measurement and the sample size. Lesley used a light meter to collect her data, while the children had no means of measurement; they simply described their visual observations as precisely as possible. Ian suggested that with a measuring device, the class's findings might have been consistent with Lesley's. Ms. Sutton introduced the possibility that additional investigation might have yielded a different finding, to which Megan responded that the class had not investigated with all the materials yet. Determining how much evidence is enough to make a broad claim confidently, such as "all objects reflect and absorb light," is fundamental to scientific problem solving.

In the following excerpt, the students entertain other possible explanations for the differences between their findings and Lesley's. In this instance, Lesley is reporting the data for what happens when a flashlight shines on a piece of black felt. She reports that no transmitted light was recorded by her light meter. The majority of students, however, reported having seen transmitted light. Here the class considers why there might be these different findings:

Catherine	When we stuck the lamp like, not like directly next to the black but a little bit up close to the black, it came out a maroon color on the other side.
Ms. Sutton	So we were getting some transmitted. We thought we had some transmitted light, too. She's not getting—detecting that, is she, with her light meter?
Jihad	But she would be more sure because she has a light meter and we don't.
Ms. Sutton	What might cause a difference in results from what you did and from what she did?
Student	She may have had her flashlight back farther and we had ours up very close.
Ms. Sutton	Anything else might have made a difference? Ian?
Ian	She might have either had a weaker flashlight or a thicker piece of felt or something.
Ms. Sutton	Okay, so two things there.
Student	Yeah, or maybe it was because of the light meter.
Ms. Sutton	What about the light meter? How would the light meter make it harder to detect transmitted light?
Tatsuro	Because it's in, measuring in the tens. What if it was like 0.09?
Ms. Sutton	So maybe it's not measuring to the tenth or the millicandle?
Student	Or maybe she's just rounding off.
Ms. Sutton	Maybe she's rounding it off. Maybe the little machine rounds off. Good.
Louise	Or maybe it's because like, in the diagram, it shows it had the sensor pretty far back. Maybe the transmitted light didn't go that far.

In this excerpt, the students began to identify the range of variables that might explain the differences between their outcomes and Lesley's, including differences in the setup, the materials, the strength of the light source, the device used to record the data, and the scientist's decisions regarding the reporting of the data. This exchange is significant to the extent that the students demonstrate an appreciation for the role variables play in the design of an investigation. With this understanding, they are now situated to consider the control of variables that is necessary so that only a single contrast is featured in an experiment.[39]

One final observation about the successful use of text in inquiry-based instruction is the importance of students assuming a skeptical stance rather than simply deferring to the text. The following three excerpts are illustrative. The first two are examples of instances in which students questioned the generality of Lesley's claim that "all objects reflect and absorb light." In the first instance, Kit interjects, "I think that she says 'all' too much. Like she could just say 'most' or she could test more objects because 'all' is kind of a lot because she only tested like, seven." Ms. Sutton responds, "Okay, so you're saying you don't know if she's tested enough to say 'all,' to make that kind of statement."

The second excerpt begins when one student, Katherine, expresses concern that Lesley has not provided sufficient information about the kinds of materials with which she investigated. This leads a second student, Megan, to observe that the objects with which Lesley investigated are quite similar (i.e., they are all "flat") and that Lesley should have selected objects with different characteristics if she wished to make the claim that "all objects absorb and reflect light." Ms. Sutton prompts for more specificity, to which Megan responds, "None of them are kind of like a ball or something that's 3-D. They're all, like, flat . . . because something that's 3-D . . . it gets thicker because if you had a green ball and you shine light through, it would be . . . probably be a darker color because there's two sides to a ball and not just one."

In a related criticism, Kit observes that Lesley needed to consider not only the color of the object she was investigating, but also the material of which it was made:

Kit	I don't think the claim would be as true if the white [objects] were different materials.
Ms. Sutton	Okay, so you would get a—if you had a light meter to measure like she did and you were measuring all the black objects on this list, do you think you still would get different readings? They'd absorb differently? They wouldn't all absorb the same amount?
Students	Yeah . . . yeah. . . .
Ms. Sutton	How many people agree with that, that all the black objects probably wouldn't absorb the same amount of light? Okay, so they're agreeing with you.

SUPPORTING LEARNING THROUGH CYCLES OF INVESTIGATION

Whether students' experiences with investigation are first- or second-hand, the outcome of any single cycle of investigation will not result in development of all the targeted knowledge and reasoning goals for a particular topic of study. Thus, inquiry in any topic area requires multiple cycles of investigation. Discussion of how to design curriculum units with cycles of investigation and the interplay between first- and second-hand experiences is beyond the scope of this chapter. The important point is that students need to have multiple opportunities to learn concepts (i.e., multiple cycles of investigation that provide occasions for dealing with the same concepts) and encounter those concepts in multiple contexts (e.g., reflection is studied in contexts with mirrors, as well as in contexts with other opaque objects). The purpose of this section is to discuss how teachers might think about the development of knowledge across cycles of investigation.

The classroom community determines the fate of any knowledge claim generated by a group. Within and across each cycle, knowledge claims are generated, tested, refuted, tweaked, embraced, discarded, and ignored. (Note that the teacher's guidance is critical to ensure that false claims are not embraced without further exploration and that core claims are understood.) Figure 10-3 illustrates this process. In this case, the class worked with five

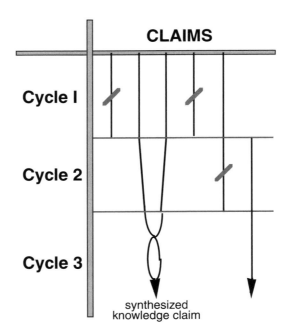

FIGURE 10-3 The development of community knowledge across cycles of investigation.

knowledge claims during Cycle 1 of its investigation. Following the reporting phase, two of these claims were abandoned: one because the child who had initially championed it no longer did so, and the other because there was significant evidence countering it. Three claims survived this first cycle of inquiry: one because there was clear and consistent data supporting it, and the other two because the data were insufficient to make a definitive judgment.

The reporting phase of Cycle 2 of the investigation led to the emergence of a new claim and the abandonment of one of the initial claims because only one of nine groups presented evidence in support of that claim, and the class expressed reservations regarding that group's data collection procedures. The two remaining claims survived, but were revised in ways that suggested they might be related.

Cycle 3 began with the class considering three extant claims. During the reporting phase, the two claims that appeared to be related became combined and synthesized into one claim. This is a significant development from a scientific perspective given the value placed on simplicity and parsimony of claims about the physical world. The final claim, while still in the running, was not accepted by the class, but neither was it rejected.

This progression of events with the community knowledge claims resulting from each cycle is like threads that when woven together create the fabric of scientific knowledge and reasoning on the topic of study. Some threads will dangle, never fully attended to; some will be abandoned; while others will be central to understanding the topic of study and may need to be blended together to create a strong weave. The fate of each thread is determined by classroom community judgments about which claims have the most evidence, account for the greatest range of data, and are simple and concise; that is, the standards for acceptance are values adhered to by scientists in the production of scientific knowledge. Although it can be difficult for teachers to stand by while students initially make scientifically inaccurate claims, the teacher's imposition of the constraints of the scientific community's cultural norms—norms that the students themselves eventually enforce—results in the final set of community claims being scientifically accurate or having indeterminate status with respect to science. Furthermore, whereas dangling threads in a fabric are problematic, they are important to the process of learning science because the reasons for rejecting or abandoning claims form part of the understanding of scientific ways of knowing.

The Development of Conceptual Frameworks

Imagine now that the students have been through several cycles of investigation. What is to prevent these cycles from being experienced as a set of disconnected experiences, resulting in isolated knowledge? How are the students to develop, elaborate, and refine conceptual frameworks from repeated inquiry experiences? We have argued[40] that the "threads that bind" take the form of explicit attention to the relationships among knowledge claims. Conclusions from *How People Learn* tell us that the formulation of a conceptual framework is a hallmark of developing deep understanding, and that a focus on the development of deep understanding is one of the principles distinguishing school reform efforts that result in increases in student achievement from those that do not.[41]

The development of *organized* knowledge is key to the formulation of conceptual frameworks. Developing organized knowledge is enabled by well-designed curriculum materials, but requires specific guidance by teachers as well. Some of that guidance needs to involve pressing students to work from the perspective of the norms for knowledge building in the scientific community. For example, scientists assume that there are regularities in how the world works. If the sky appears gray with no evidence of clouds or the sun, a scientist, who has seen the sun in the sky every other day, will assume that it is still there and infer that something must be blocking it. This perspective dictates different questions than one that does not assume such regularity.

Another area of guidance comes from pressing students to focus on the relationships among the claims they are making. Sorting out these relationships may result in multiple claims being revised into a single claim, as shown in Figure 10-3. Alternatively, revisions may need to be more extensive to fit the expectation of scientists that relationships within a topic area fit together; that is, they are coherent with one another.[42] If we claim that light reflects off the front of a mirror but does not appear to reflect off the back, or if we claim that light can go through glass but does not go through a glass mirror, what is the relationship between those ideas? It is not coherent to claim that light does and does not reflect from a mirror. Similarly, it is not coherent to say that light transmits through glass but not through a glass object (i.e., a mirror). Of course, the coherent view is that light is transmitted through glass, but in the case of a mirror, it is transmitted through the glass part but reflects from the backing that is placed on the glass to make it a mirror. To develop these kinds of perspectives, students must learn concepts in combination, with attention to the relationships among them.

Illustration: The Development of Conceptual Frameworks for Light

In this section we trace the development of student understanding about light over four cycles of investigation in Ms. Lacey's class, guided by the question of how light interacts with matter. This instruction took place over

4 weeks, with each cycle taking about a week of daily instruction. We present concept maps constructed from classroom discourse during the instruction.[43] That is, the maps represent the collective knowledge building that would be evident to the teacher and the class. Transcript excerpts accompany the maps to illustrate the nature of the conversation among the students and teacher.

During Cycle 1, students focused on the differences among objects, assuming that light interacted with each object in only one way. During reporting, they made statements such as: "Light can go through glass if it's clear enough," "Light reflects off mirrors and shiny materials, too," and "We had a solid thing here. It just stopped at the object. It didn't reflect." Students wrestled with whether claims indicating that light could "be blocked" and "stay in" meant the same thing or something different. Figure 10-4 suggests that students thought light could interact with matter in one of three ways.

The question marks in the figure indicate that some individuals or groups asserted the relationships shown, but not all the students accepted these relationships, including one group that provided evidence that light can interact with an object in two ways—a finding that could have dramatically changed the structure of the class's knowledge from what is shown in the figure. This particular group did not recognize the significance of its findings, focusing instead on the one way it should categorize objects from which it had observed multiple interactions. In the following excerpt, the teacher encourages the group to think of its results as a new claim.

| Kevin | We saw sort of a little reflection, but we, it had mostly just see-through. |
| Ms. Lacey | So you're saying that some materials could be in two different categories. |

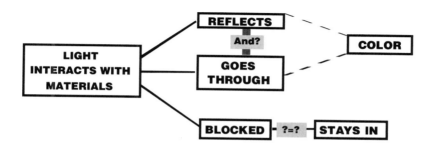

FIGURE 10-4 Community knowledge from the first cycle of investigation (first-hand).

Derek	Yes, because some were really see-through and reflection together, but we had to decide which one to put it in.
Ms. Lacey	Do you think you might have another claim here?
Kevin	Light can do two things with one object.

With the introduction of the idea that light can interact with matter in more than one way, the students embarked upon a second cycle of investigation with the same materials, with the intent of determining which if any objects exhibited the behavior claimed by Kevin and Derek. From this second round of investigation, all groups determined that multiple behaviors can occur with some objects, but there was uncertainty about whether these interactions occur with some types of materials and not others (see Figure 10-5). Nevertheless, the significance of this day's findings is that they represent a different conceptual organization from that of the first cycle (see Figure 10-4) to the extent that light is not confined to behaving in only one way. At the same time, the possibilities for the behavior of light have increased significantly, and only the case of four types of interaction has been ruled out in discussion by the community (following interaction comparing what different groups meant by "blocked" versus "absorbed").

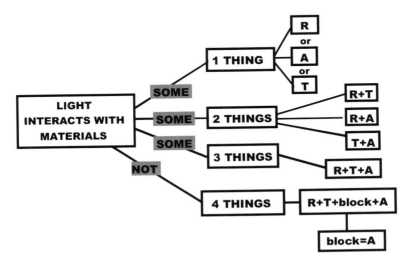

FIGURE 10-5 Community knowledge from the second cycle of investigation (first-hand). R = reflect; T = transmit; A = absorb.

In addition, some students expressed puzzlement about *how* light could interact with a material in more than one way. In response to this question, one group introduced the idea that there was a quantitative relationship among the multiple behaviors observed when light interacted with an object:

Miles	If you said that light can reflect, transmit, and absorb, absorb means to block. How can it be blocked . . . and still go through?
Corey	If just a little bit came through, then most of it was blocked.
Ms. Lacey	Would you draw him a picture, please? [Corey and Andy draw setup.]
Corey	Here's the light, a little being blocked inside, and a little of it comes out . . .
Andy	Some of it's reflecting.

During the third cycle of investigation, in which the students and the teacher interactively read a Lesley Park notebook text about light using reciprocal teaching strategies,[44] the students encountered more evidence that light can interact with matter in multiple ways (see Figure 10-6). This led to conversation concerning how general a claim might be made about the behavior of light:

Andy	Can all objects reflect, absorb, and transmit? Tommy?
Tommy	Most of them.
Andy	Corey?

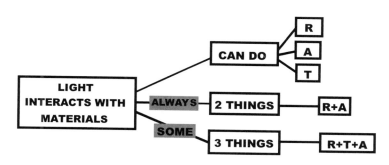

FIGURE 10-6 Community knowledge from the third cycle of investigation (second-hand).

Corey	Yes, because it says right in here, "Light can be reflected, absorbed and transmitted by the same object."
Ms. Lacey	I think we need to clarify something, because you said one thing, Corey, and Miles said something else. Andy's question was "Can *all* objects reflect, absorb, and transmit light?"
Alan	No. It just says light can be reflected, absorbed, and transmitted by the same object. It doesn't say anything about every object.
Ms. Lacey	So you say not all can. Do we have any data in our reading that tells us that not all things absorb, reflect, and transmit?
Tommy	We have evidence that all objects reflect and absorb [referring to a table in the notebook text].

The concept map representing the community's understanding about light up to this point shows greater specification of the prevalence of relationships ("always" versus "sometimes") and a narrowing of the possible relationships that can occur when light interacts with matter: light always reflects and is absorbed.

Lesley's quantitative data about the amount of reflection and transmission of light from an object as measured by a light meter supported additional conversation about the issue of quantitative relationships raised by one group in the previous cycle. However, students did not yet add those ideas to their class claims chart.

In the fourth cycle of investigation, students returned to a first-hand investigation and were now quite comfortable with the idea that light can simultaneously interact with matter in multiple ways. In addition, despite not having tools to compare the brightness of the light, they qualitatively compared the amount of light behaving in particular ways. This is represented in the map in Figure 10-7.

Do all students have the understanding represented in Figure 10-7? The excerpt below suggests that this is unlikely. In this excerpt, a student reveals that he and his partner did not think light would reflect from an object even after the class had established in the previous cycle that light always reflects:

Ms. Lacey	When you saw the blue felt, is that the claim you first thought?
Kenny	Yeah, we learned that this blue felt can do three—reflect, transmit, and absorb—at one, at this one object. And it did. It reflected a little, and transmitted some and it absorbed some.

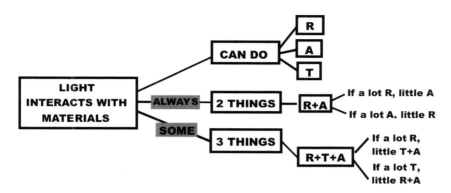

FIGURE 10-7 Community knowledge from the fourth cycle of investigation (first-hand).

Ms. Lacey	And when you started out, what did you think was going to happen?
Kenny	That it was only going to transmit and absorb. We didn't think it would reflect.
Ms. Lacey	What do we know about materials and reflecting?
Class	They always reflect and absorb.

We see the teacher checking on the student's understanding, which is scientifically accurate. But we know that for such a claim—that light reflects off all materials—many experiences may be needed for that knowledge to be robust. Relationships such as this for which we have no direct experience or that are counterintuitive (we see reflected light from objects, not the objects themselves) take time and attention, as well as recursive tacking to knowledge-building processes and the conceptual framework that is emerging from those processes. Conceptual frameworks that represent the physical world in ways we have not experienced (e.g., the electromagnetic spectrum) or are counterintuitive (light is a particle and a wave) pose even greater challenges to the development of scientific knowledge.

THE ROLE OF SUBJECT-SPECIFIC KNOWLEDGE IN EFFECTIVE SCIENCE INSTRUCTION

At the core of teacher decision making featured in this chapter is the need to mediate the learning of individual students. To do this in a way that leads to targeted scientific knowledge and ways of knowing, teachers must be confident about their knowledge of the learning goals. That is, teachers must have sufficient subject matter knowledge, including aspects of the culture of science that guide knowledge production, to fully understand the nature of the learning goals. When students say that light "disappears" into paper but reflects off of mirrors, a teacher's uncertainty about whether that claim is accurate will hamper effective decision making. When students claim an object is opaque and the question at hand is how light interacts with matter, the teacher needs to recognize that the word "opaque" describes the object and not light, and that an opaque object can reflect and absorb light and even transmit some light in certain cases (e.g., a piece of cardboard).

At the same time, having accurate subject matter knowledge is not sufficient for effective teaching. When students claim that light is a gas, it is not sufficient for the teacher to know that light is energy, not a state of matter. The teacher also needs to know what observations of light might convince students that it is not a gas, which in turn is informed by knowing how students think of gases, what their experiences of gas and light have likely been, and what it is possible to observe within a classroom context. This knowledge is part of specialized knowledge for teaching called pedagogical content knowledge because it is derived from content knowledge that is specifically employed to facilitate learning. It is the knowledge that teachers have about how to make particular subject matter comprehensible to particular students.[45]

Pedagogical content knowledge includes knowledge of the concepts that students find most difficult, as well as ways to support their understanding of those concepts. For example, it is difficult for students to understand that the color of objects is the color of light reflected from them because we are not aware of the reflection. Having students use a white screen to examine the color of light reflected from colored objects can reveal this phenomenon in a way that is convincing to them. Pedagogical content knowledge also includes knowledge of curriculum materials that are particularly effective for teaching particular topics. A still valuable resource for the study of light in the elementary grades is the *Optics* kit mentioned earlier that is part of *Elementary Science Study* curriculum materials developed in the 1960s. A teacher's knowledge of these materials and how they can be used to support knowledge building is key to employing them effectively in mediating student learning.

Finally, pedagogical content knowledge includes ways to assess student knowledge. A classic item to determine students' understanding of how we see is a diagram with the sun, a tree, and a person looking at the tree.[46] Students are asked to draw lines with arrows in the diagram to show how the person sees the tree. Arrows should be drawn from the sun to the tree to the person, but it is not uncommon for students to draw arrows from the sun to the person and the person to the tree. Use of this item at the beginning of a unit of study can provide a teacher with a wealth of information on current student thinking about how we see, as well as stimulate students to wonder about such questions.

The more teachers know and understand about how their students think about particular concepts or topics of study, how that thinking might develop and unfold during systematic study of the topic, and how they might ascertain what students' understanding of the topic is at any point in time, the better they are able to optimize knowledge building from students' varied experiences and support students in developing desired scientific knowledge and ways of knowing. When and how to employ particular strategies in the service of supporting such knowledge building is a different issue, but the topic-specific knowledge for teaching that is identified as pedagogical content knowledge is a necessary element if students are to achieve the standards we have set.

CONCLUSION

Science instruction provides a rich context for applying what we know about how people learn. A successful teacher in this context is aware that he or she is supporting students in activating prior knowledge and in building upon and continuing to organize this knowledge so it can be used flexibly to make sense of and appreciate the world around them. To do this well, the teacher must be knowledgeable about the nature of science, including both the products—the powerful ideas of science—and the values, beliefs, and practices of the scientific community that guide the generation and evaluation of these powerful ideas. Furthermore, teachers must be knowledgeable about children and the processes of engaging them in knowledge building, reflecting upon their thinking and learning new ways of thinking.

We have proposed and illustrated a heuristic for conceptualizing instruction relative to the opportunities and challenges of different aspects of inquiry-based instruction, which we have found useful in supporting teachers in effective decision making and evaluation of instruction. We have argued that the development of scientific knowledge and reasoning can be supported through both first- and second-hand investigations. Furthermore, we have proposed that the teacher draws upon a broad repertoire of practices for the purposes of establishing and maintaining the classroom as a learning community, and assessing, supporting, and extending the knowledge building of each member of that community. All of these elements are necessary for effective teaching in the twenty-first century, when our standards for learning are not just about the application of scientific knowledge, but also its evaluation and generation.

NOTES

1. Schwab, 1964.
2. Hapgood et al., in press; Lehrer et al., 2001; Magnusson et al., 1997; Metz, 2004.
3. National Research Council, 2003.
4. These materials, originally developed in the 1960s, can be purchased from Delta Education: http://www.delta-education.com/.
5. Whereas some view conceptual change as referring to a change from existing ideas to new ones, we suggest that new ideas are often developed in parallel with existing ones. The new ideas are rooted in different values and beliefs—those of the scientific community rather than those guiding our daily lives.
6. Chi, 1992.
7. Galili and Hazan, 2000.
8. Our decision to focus on instruction in which investigation is central reflects the national standard that calls for science instruction to be inquiry based.
9. We use the term "guided" inquiry to signal that the teacher plays a prominent role in shaping the inquiry experience, guiding student thinking and activity to enable desired student learning from investigation.
10. Magnusson and Palincsar, 1995.
11. Barnes, 1976; Bybee et al., 1989; Karplus, 1964; Osborne and Freyberg, 1985; Lehrer and Schauble, 2000.
12. All of the instruction featured in this chapter was conducted by teachers who were a part of GIsML Community of Practice, a multiyear professional development effort aimed at identifying effective practice for inquiry-based science teaching.
13. This discussion draws on a study focused on children's self-regulation during science instruction, which took place in a school in a relatively small district (about 4,600 students) that includes a state university. Approximately 45 percent of the students in this district pass the state standardized tests, and 52 percent are economically disadvantaged.
14. This class is in a school in a relatively small district (about 3,000 students) near a major industrial plant in a town with a state university. Approximately 38 percent of the students in this district pass the state standardized tests, and 63 percent are economically disadvantaged.
15. While we are featuring contexts in which there is a single question, teachers could choose to have a context in which children are investigating different questions related to the same phenomenon. However, it is important to recognize the substantially greater cognitive and procedural demands this approach places on the teacher, so it is not something we recommend if a teacher is inexperienced in conducting inquiry-based instruction.
16. Although it can be motivating and conceptually beneficial for students to be placed in the role of generating questions for investigation, the teacher needs to be mindful of the consequences of taking time to investigate questions that may be trivial or peripheral to the unity of study. The teacher may judge the time to be useful as students can still learn a great deal about investigation, but

the teacher also may seek to reshape the question so it is not so conceptually distant as to sidetrack the focus relative to the desired content goals.

17. Hapgood et al., in press; Lehrer et al., 2001; Metz, 2004.

18. This person monitors the time the group is taking for the investigation to support the students in examining how efficiently they are working and deciding whether it is necessary to adjust the tempo of their activity to finish in the allotted time.

19. It is very reasonable for the teacher to discuss these issues with the whole class during the preparing-to-investigate phase and to invite the class to specify procedures. Addressing these matters with the whole class gives the teacher opportunities to model thinking for the benefit of all. However, while this is enabling for students when they are quite new to investigating, it constrains students' development of the knowledge and skills needed to make these decisions independently. Thus it is important for the teacher to give students an opportunity to make these types of decisions on their own during some investigations.

20. Herrenkohl et al., 1999.

21. The students inadvertently interpreted the idea of categorizing to mean that light would behave in only one way with each object. This led many students to stop observing an object as soon as they had identified one way light behaved with it.

22. In both cases, the fact that we can see the object tells us that light is reflected. However, students had not yet established that relationship, so we refer here only to the direct evidence of light.

23. Blumenfeld and Meece, 1988.

24. Magnusson et al., in press.

25. This class is in a moderately sized district (about 16,700) students) in a town with a major university. Approximately 70 percent of the students in this district pass the state standardized tests, and 16 percent are economically disadvantaged.

26. Brown and Campione, 1994; Palincsar et al., 1993.

27. Campanario, 2002.

28. Osborne, 1983.

29. Magnusson et al., 1997.

30. Clement, 1993

31. We observed a group of children in a fourth-grade class working very hard to determine if black felt reflects light. They piled their materials in the bathroom in the classroom, taped around the door to block out any light, and studied the black felt. They were quite proud to report their evidence that it did indeed reflect light.

32. Chi, 1992.

33. Mortimer, 1995.

34. Driver et al., 1994.

35. National Research Council, 1996.

36. Crawford et al., 1996.

37. Magnusson and Palincsar, in press-b.

38. See Magnusson and Palincsar (in press-a) for discussion of the theory and principles underlying the development of these texts; Palincsar and Magnusson (2001), for a more complete description of Lesley's notebook and of research investigating the use of these notebook texts; and Magnusson and Palincsar (in press-b) for a discussion of teaching from these notebook tests.
39. Klahr et al., 2001.
40. Magnusson et al., in press; Palincsar et al., 2001.
41. Newmann et al., 1995.
42. Einstein, 1950.
43. Ford, 1999.
44. Palincsar and Brown, 1984.
45. Magnusson et al., 1999; Wilson et al., 1988.
46. Eaton et al., 1984.

REFERENCES

Barnes, D. (1976). *From communication to curriculum.* Hammondsworth, UK: Penguin Books.

Blumenfeld, P.C., and Meece, J.L. (1988). Task factors, teacher behavior, and students' involvement and use of learning strategies in science. *Elementary School Journal, 88*(3), 235-250.

Brown, A.L., and Campione, J.C. (1994). Guided discovery in a community of learners. In K. McGilly (Ed.), *Classrooms lessons: Integrating cognitive theory and classroom practice* (pp. 229-272). Cambridge, MA: MIT Press.

Bybee, R.W., Buchwald, C.E., Crissman, S., Heil, D.R., Kuerbis, P.J., Matsumoto, C., and McInerney, J.D. (1989). *Science and technology education for the elementary years: Frameworks for curriculum and instruction.* Washington, DC: National Center for Improving Science Education.

Campanario, J.M. (2002). The parallelism between scientists' and students' resistance to new scientific ideas. *International Journal of Science Education, 24*(10), 1095-1110.

Chi, M.T.H. (1992). Conceptual change within and across ontological categories: Examples from learning and discovery in science. In R. Giere (Ed.), *Cognitive models of science: Minnesota studies in the philosophy of science* (pp. 129-186). Minneapolis, MN: University of Minnesota Press.

Clement, J. (1993). Using bridging analogies and anchoring intuitions to deal with students' preconceptions in physics. *Journal of Research in Science Teaching, 30,* 1241-1257.

Crawford, S.Y., Hurd, J.M., and Weller, A.C. (1996). *From print to electronic: The transformation of scientific communication.* Medford, NJ: Information Today.

Driver, R., Asoko, H., Leach, J., Mortimer, E., and Scott, P. (1994). Constructing scientific knowledge in the classroom. *Educational Researcher, 23*(7), 5-12.

Eaton, J.F., Anderson, C.W., and Smith, E.L. (1984). Students' misconceptions interfere with science learning: Case studies of fifth-grade students. *Elementary School Journal, 84,* 365-379.

Einstein, A. (1950). *Out of my later years.* New York: Philosophical Library.

Ford, D. (1999). The role of text in supporting and extending first-hand investigations in guided inquiry science. *Dissertation Abstracts International, 60*(7), 2434.

Galili, I., and Hazan, A. (2000). Learners' knowledge in optics: Interpretation, structure and analysis. *International Journal of Science Education, 22*(1), 57-88.

Hapgood, S., Magnusson, S.J., and Palincsar, A.S. (in press). Teacher, text, and experience: A case of young children's scientific inquiry. *Journal of the Learning Sciences.*

Herrenkohl, L., Palincsar, A.S., DeWater L.S., and Kawasaki, K. (1999). Developing scientific communities in classrooms: A sociocognitive approach. *Journal of the Learning Sciences, 8*(3-4), 451-494.

Karplus, R. (1964). *Theoretical background of the science curriculum improvement study.* Berkeley, CA: Science Curriculum Improvement Study, University of California.

Klahr, D., Chen, Z., and Toth, E. (2001). Cognitive development and science education: Ships that pass in the night or beacons of mutual illumination? In S. Carver and D. Klahr (Eds.), *Cognition and instruction: Twenty-five years of progress* (pp. 75-120). Mahwah, NJ: Lawrence Erlbaum Associates.

Lehrer, R., and Schauble, L. (2000). Modeling in mathematics and science. In R. Glaser (Ed.), *Advances in instructional psychology, vol. 5: Educational design and cognitive science* (pp. 101-159). Mahwah, NJ: Lawrence Erlbaum Associates.

Lehrer, R., Schauble, L., and Petrosino, A.J. (2001). Reconsidering the role of experiment in science education. In K. Crowley, C.D. Schunn, and T. Okada (Eds.), *Designing for science: Implications from everyday, classroom, and professional settings.* Mahwah, NJ: Lawrence Erlbaum Associates.

Magnusson, S.J., and Palincsar, A.S. (1995). The learning environment as a site of science education reform. *Theory into Practice, 34*(1), 43-50.

Magnusson, S.J., and Palincsar, A.S. (in press-a). The application of theory to the design of innovative texts supporting science instruction. In M. Constas and R. Sternberg (Eds.), *Translating educational theory and research into practice.* Mahwah, NJ: Lawrence Erlbaum Associates.

Magnusson, S.J., and Palincsar, A.S. (in press-b). Learning from text designed to model scientific thinking. In W. Saul (Ed.), *Crossing borders in literacy and science instruction: Perspectives on theory and practice.* Newark, DE: International Reading Association.

Magnusson, S.J., Templin, M., and Boyle, R.A. (1997). Dynamic science assessment: A new approach for investigating conceptual change. *Journal of the Learning Sciences, 6*(1), 91-142.

Magnusson, S.J., Borko, H., and Krajcik, J.S. (1999). Nature, sources, and development of pedagogical content knowledge for science teaching. In J. Gess-Newsome and N. Lederman (Eds.), *Science teacher knowledge.* Dordrecht, The Netherlands: Kluwer Academic.

Magnusson, S.J., Palincsar, A.S., and Templin, M. (in press). Community, culture, and conversation in inquiry-based science instruction. In L. Flick and N. Lederman (Eds.), *Scientific inquiry and the nature of science: Implications for teaching, learning, and teacher education.* Dordrecht, The Netherlands: Kluwer Academic.

Metz, K.E. (2004). Children's understanding of scientific inquiry: Their conceptualization of uncertainty in investigations of their own design. *Cognition and Instruction, 22*(2), 219-290.

Mortimer, E.F. (1995). Conceptual change or conceptual profile change? *Science and Education, 4,* 267-285.

National Research Council. (1996). *National science education standards.* National Committee on Science Education Standards and Assessment, Center for Science, Mathematics, and Engineering Education. Washington, DC: National Academy Press.

National Research Council. (2003). *Learning and instruction: A SERP research agenda.* M.S. Donovan and J.W. Pellegrino (Eds.), Panel on Learning and Instruction, Strategic Education Research Partnership. Washington, DC: The National Academies Press.

Newmann, F.M., Marks, H.M., and Gamoran, A. (1995). *Authentic pedagogy: Standards that boost student performance.* (Issue Report #8, Center on Organization and Restructuring of Schools.) Madison, WI: Wisconsin Center for Educational Research, University of Wisconsin.

Osborne, R. (1983). Towards modifying children's ideas about electric current. *Research in Science & Technological Education, 1*(1), 73-82.

Osborne, R., and Freyberg, P. (1985). *Learning in science: The implications of children's science.* Portsmouth, NH: Heinemann.

Palincsar, A.S., and Brown, A.L. (1984). Reciprocal teaching of comprehension-fostering and monitoring activities. *Cognition and Instruction, 1,* 117-175.

Palincsar, A.S., and Magnusson, S.J. (2001). The interplay of first-hand and text-based investigations to model and support the development of scientific knowledge and reasoning. In S. Carver and D. Klahr (Eds.), *Cognition and instruction: Twenty-five years of progress* (pp. 151-194). Mahwah, NJ: Lawrence Erlbaum Associates.

Palincsar, A.S., Anderson, C.A., and David, Y.M. (1993). Pursuing scientific literacy in the middle grades through collaborative problem solving. *Elementary School Journal, 93*(5), 643-658.

Palincsar, A S., Magnusson, S.J., and Hapgood, S. (2001). *Trafficking ideas through the rotaries of science instruction: Teachers' discourse moves and their relationships to children's learning.* Paper presented at the annual meeting of the American Educational Research Association, Seattle, WA.

Schwab, J.J. (1964). Structure of the disciplines: Meanings and significances. In G.W. Ford and L. Pugno (Eds.), *The structure of knowledge and the curriculum* (pp. 6-30). Chicago, IL: Rand McNally.

Wilson, S.M., Shulman, L.S., and Richert, E.R. (1988). '150 different ways' of knowing: Representations of knowledge in teaching. In J. Calderhead (Ed.), *Exploring teachers' thinking.* New York: Taylor and Francis.

11

Guided Inquiry in the Science Classroom

James Minstrell and Pamela Kraus

The story of the development of this piece of curriculum and instruction starts in the classroom of the first author more than 25 years ago. I had supposedly taught my classes about universal gravitation and the related inverse square force law. The students had performed reasonably well on questions of the sort that asked, "What would happen to the force if we increased the distance from the planet?" They supposedly understood something about gravitational forces, resistive forces of air resistance and friction, and the idea of force in general. Then came a rude awakening.

I don't remember why, but we happened to be talking about a cart being pulled across a table by a string attached to a weight over a pulley. The students were becoming confused by the complexity of the situation. So, in an attempt to simplify the context, I suggested, "Suppose there is no friction to worry about, no rubbing, and no friction." Still the students were confused and suggested, "Then there would be so much wind resistance." I waved that notion away as well: "Suppose there were no friction at all and no air resistance in this situation. Suppose there were no air in the room. Now what would be the forces acting on this cart as it was moving across the table?"

I was not prepared for what I heard. Several voices around the room were saying, in effect, "Then things would just drift off the table. The weight and string and cart would all just float away." I was tempted to say, "No, don't think like that." I suppressed that urge and instead asked in a nonevaluative tone, "Okay, so you say things would just float away. How do you know that?" They suggested, "You know, like in space. There is no air, and things just drift around. They aren't held down, because there is no air to hold them down." The students said they knew this because they had heard from the media that in space things are weightless. Indeed, they had seen pictures of astronauts just "floating" around. They had also been told that there is no air in space, and they put the two (no air and weightless) together. But they had no first-hand experiences to relate to what they knew from these external "authorities."

If we really want to know what students are thinking, we need to ask them and then be quiet and listen respectfully to what they say. If we are genuinely interested and do not evaluate, we can learn from our students.

What good is having my students know the quantitative relation or equation for gravitational force if they lack a qualitative understanding of force and the concepts related to the nature of gravity and its effects? They should be able to separate the effects of gravity from the effects of the surrounding air. Later, they should be able to explain the phenomena of falling bodies, which requires that they separate the effects of gravity from those of air. While many physical science books focus on the constancy of gravitational acceleration, most students know that all things do not fall with the same acceleration. They know that a rock reaches the floor before a flat sheet of paper, for example. Not addressing the more common situation of objects falling differently denies the students' common experiences and is part of the reason "school science" may not seem relevant to them. So, we need to separate the effects of air from those of gravity.

Learning is an active process. We need to acknowledge students' attempts to make sense of their experiences and help them confront inconsistencies in their sense making.

Even more fundamental, I want my students to understand and be able to apply the concept of force as an interaction between objects in real-life situations. They should have first-hand experiences that will lead to the reasonable conclusion that force can be exerted by anything touching an object, and also that forces can exist as "actions at a distance" (i.e., without touching the object, forces might be exerted through the mechanisms of gravity, electrostatic force, and magnetic force).

I also want my students to understand the nature of scientific practice. They should be able to interpret or explain common phenomena and design simple experiments to test their ideas. In short, I want them to have the skills necessary to inquire about the world around them, to ask and answer their own questions, and to know what questions they need to ask themselves in the process of thinking about a problematic situation.

Teachers' questions can model the sorts of questions students might ask themselves when conducting personal inquiry.

Research and best practice suggest that, if we are really clever and careful, students will come more naturally to the conceptual ideas and processes we want them to learn. Being clever means incorporating what we have come to understand about how students learn. This chapter describes a series of activities from which the experience of teachers and researchers demonstrates students do learn about the meaning of force and about the nature and processes of science. It also explains how the specific activities and teaching strategies delineated here relate to what we know from research on how people learn, as reflected in the three guiding principles set forth in Chapter 1 with regard to students' prior knowledge, the need to develop deep understanding, and the development of metacognitive awareness. We attempt to give the reader a sense of what it means to implement curriculum that supports these principles. It is our hope that researchers will see that we have built upon their work in designing these activities and creating the learning environment. We want teachers to get a sense of what it means to teach in such an environment. We also want readers to get an idea of what it is like to be a learner.

The following unit could come before one on forces to explain motion (i.e., Newton's Laws). By the end of this unit, students should have arrived at a qualitative understanding of force as applied in contexts involving buoyancy, gravitation, magnetics, and electrostatics. The activities involved are designed to motivate and develop a sense of the interrelationships between ideas and events. The expected outcome includes qualitative understanding of ideas, not necessarily formulas.

THE UNIT: THE NATURE OF GRAVITY AND ITS EFFECTS

Part A: What Gravity Is Not

Getting the Unit Started: Finding Out About Students' Initial Ideas

Teachers need to unconditionally respect students' capacities for learning complex ideas, and students need to learn to respect the teacher as an instructional leader. Teachers will need to earn that respect through their actions as a respectful guide to learning.

For students to understand the following lessons, we need to establish some prerequisite knowledge and dispositions during earlier lessons. Students will need to understand that measurements of a single quantity may vary depending on three factors: the object being measured, the instrument being used, and the person using the instrument. The teacher needs to have enough experience with the class so that the students are confident that the class will achieve resolution over time. Thus, this unit comes about a month or so into the school year. Students need to persevere in learning and trusting that the teacher will help guide them to the big ideas. This should probably not be the students' first experience with guided inquiry. While the set of experiences in Part A below takes a week or more to resolve, prior initial experiences with guided inquiry may take a class period or two, depending on the students' tolerance for ambiguity.

Identifying Preconceptions: What Would Happen If . . . ?

> Teachers need to know students' initial and developing conceptions. Students need to have their initial ideas brought to a conscious level.

One way to find out about students' preconceptions for a particular unit is to ask them to give, in writing, their best answers to one or more questions related to the unit. At the beginning of this unit on the nature of gravity and its effects, the teacher poses the following situation and questions associated with Figure 11-1.

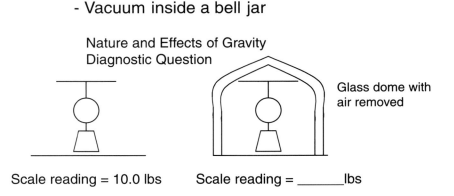

FIGURE 11-1 A diagnostic question to use at the beginning of this unit.

Nature and Effects of Gravity, Diagnostic Question 1: Predict the scale reading under the glass dome with air removed.

> *In the diagram with question 1, we have a large frame and a big spring scale, similar to what you might see at the local market. Suppose we put something on the scale and the scale reading is 10.0 lb. Now suppose we put a large glass dome over the scale, frame and all, and seal all the way around the base of the dome. Then, we take a large vacuum pump and evacuate all the air out from under the dome. We allow all the air to escape through the pump, so there is no air left under the glass dome.*
>
> *What would happen to the scale reading with no air under the dome? You may not be able to give a really precise answer, but say what you think would happen to the scale reading, whether it would increase, decrease, or stay exactly the same and if you think there will be a change, about how much? And briefly explain how you decided.*
>
> *I will not grade you on whether your answer is correct. I just want to know your ideas about this situation at this time. We are just at the beginning of the unit. What I care most about is that you give a good honest best attempt to answer at this point in time. I know that some of you may be tempted to say "I don't know," but just give your best answer at this time. I'm pretty sure most all of you can come up with an answer and, most importantly, some rationale to support that answer. Just give me your best answer and reasoning at this point in time. We will be working to investigate this question over the next few days.*

When asked, more than half of students cite answers that suggest they believe air only presses down. Half of those suggest that the scale reading would go to zero in the vacuous environment. About a third of introductory students believe that the surrounding air has absolutely no effect on the scale reading regardless of the precision of the scale. Most of the rest believe that air only pushes up on the object and that it does so with a strong force. Typically, only about one student in a class will suggest that the air pushes up and down but with slightly greater force in the upward direction, the result being a very slight increase in the scale reading for the vacuous environment—a "best answer" at this time.

This question may be more about understanding buoyancy than understanding gravity. However, part of understanding the effects of gravity is learning what effects are *not* due to gravity.

Students need opportunities to explore the relationships among ideas.

Gravitational force is an interaction between any two objects that have mass. In this case, the gravitational force is an interaction between the object on the scale and the earth as the other object. Many students believe gravity is an interaction between the object and the surrounding air. Thus, this has become a first preconception to address in instruction. If teachers fail to address this idea, we know from experience that students will likely not change their basic conceptual understanding, and teachers will obtain the poor results described earlier.

In contrast with the above question, we have seen curricula that attempt to identify students' preconceptions simply by asking students to write down what they know about X. In our experience, this question is so generic that students tend not to pay much attention to it and simply "do the assignment" by writing anything. Instead, preinstruction questions should be more specific to a context, but open up the issues of the discipline as related to that context. These sorts of questions are not easy to create and typically evolve out of several iterations of teaching a unit and finding out through discussions what situations elicit the more interesting responses with respect to the content at hand.

A Benchmark Lesson[1]: Weighing in a Vacuum

In discussion following the posing of this question, I encourage students to share their answers and rationales. Because I am interested in getting students' thinking out in the open, I ask that other students not comment or offer counter arguments at this point, but just listen to the speaker's argument. I, in turn, listen carefully to the sorts of thinking exhibited by the students. I know this will faciliate my helping the class move forward later.

With encouragement and support on my part, some students volunteer to share their answers. Some suggest the scale will go to zero "with no air to hold the object down." Others suggest, "The scale reading will not go to zero but will go down some because gravity is still down and the weight of the air pushes down too, but since air doesn't weigh very much, the downward air won't be down much and the scale reading won't go down much." Some students suggest that the scale reading will increase (slightly or substantially) "because there is no air to hold the object up. It's about buoyancy. The air is like water. Water pushes up and so does air. No air, there is no buoyancy." Still others suggest that the scale reading should stay the same "because air doesn't do anything. The weight is by gravity not by air pressure." And others agree that the scale reading will not change, "but air is pushing on the object. It pushes up and down equally on the object, so there shouldn't be any change." By now several students have usually chimed in to say that one or another of the ideas made sense to them. The ideas are now "owned" by several class members, so we can discuss and even criticize the ideas without criticizing a particular person. It is important to be supportive of free expression of ideas while at the same time being critical of ideas.

> *Students are more likely to share their thinking in a climate where others express genuine interest in what they have to say. Waiting until one student has completely expressed his or her idea fosters deeper thinking on that speaker's part. Asking speakers critical questions to clarify what they are saying or to help them give more complete answers and explanations fosters their own engagement and learning.*

With most of their initial thinking having been expressed, I encourage students to share potentially contradictory arguments in light of the candidate explanations. Students might suggest, "When they vacuum pack peanuts, they take the air away and the weight doesn't go to zero"; or "The weight of the column of air above an object pushes down on the object"; or "Air acts like water and when you lift a rock in water it seems lighter than lifting it out of water, so air would help hold the object up"; or "But, I read where being on the bottom of the ocean is like having an elephant standing on your head, so air must push down if it acts like water"; or "Air is just around things. It doesn't push on things at all, unless there is a wind." Some students begin to say they are getting more confused, for many of these observations and arguments sound good and reasonable.

Once arguments pro and con for most of the ideas have been expressed, it is time to begin resolving issues. Thus far, we have been freely expressing ideas, but I want students to know that science is not based simply on opinion. We can achieve some resolution by appealing to nature; indeed, our inferences should be consistent with our observations of nature. I ask, "Sounds like a lot of good arguments and experiences suggested here, so how can we get an answer? Should we just vote on which should be the right answer and explanation?" Typically, several of the students suggest, "No, we can try it and see what happens. Do you have one of those vacuum things? Can we do the experiment?"

I just happen to have a bell jar and vacuum pump set up in the back room. First, I briefly demonstrate what happens when a slightly inflated balloon (about 2 inches in diameter) is placed under the bell jar and the pump is turned on: the balloon gets larger. I ask the students to explain this result. The students (high school age at least) usually are able to articulate that I did not add air to the balloon, but the air outside the balloon (within the bell jar) was evacuated, so the air in the balloon was freer to expand the balloon.

> *Attention is extremely important to learning.*

We hang a weight on the spring scale, put it under the jar, and seal the edges, and I ask students to "place their bets." This keeps students motivated and engaged. "How many think the scale reading will increase?" Hands go up. "Decrease?" Many hands go up. "Decrease to zero?" A few hands go up. "Stay exactly the same?" Several hands go up. I start the pump.

> *It is important to give students opportunities to apply (without being told, if possible) ideas learned earlier.*

The result surprises many students. The scale reading does not appear to change at all. Some students give a high five. I ask, "What can we conclude about the effects of air on the scale reading?" Some students suggest, "Air doesn't do anything." Sometimes to get past this response, I need to prime the discussion of implications of the results by asking, "Do we know air has absolutely no effect?" A few students are quick to say, "We don't know that it has absolutely no effect. We just know it doesn't have enough effect to make a difference." I ask, "Why do you say that?" They respond, "Remember about measurements, there is always some plus or minus to it. It could be a tiny bit more than it was. It could be a tiny bit less, or it might be exactly the same. We can't tell for sure. Maybe if we had a really, really accurate scale we could tell."

I also want the students to see that conclusions are different from results, so I often guide them carefully to discuss each. "First, what were the actual results of the experiment? What did happen? What did we observe?" Students agree that there was no observable change in the scale reading. "Those were the results. We observed no apparent change in the scale reading."

> *Students should be provided opportunities to differentiate between summarizing observable results and the conclusions generalized from those results.*

Because I want students to understand the role of experimentation in science, I press them for a conclusion: "So, what do we know from this experiment? Did we learn anything?" Although a few students suggest, "We didn't learn anything," others are quick to point out, "There can't be any big changes. We know that the air doesn't have a big effect." At this point, it appears students have had sufficient experience talking about the ideas, so I may try to clarify the distinction between results and conclusions: "Conclusions are different from results. Conclusions are about the meaning of the results, about making sense of what we observed. So, what can we conclude? What do these results tell us about the effects of the air?" With some additional discussion among the students, and possibly some additional clarification of the difference between results and conclusions, most students are ready to believe the following summary of their comments: "If the air has any effect on the scale reading, it is not very large. And apparently gravity is not caused by air pressure pressing things down."

Activity A1

Activity A1 is a simple worksheet asking students to review their answers to questions about their initial ideas, other ideas that have come out in discussion, and the results and conclusions from the preceding benchmark lesson. Typically, I hand this summary sheet out as homework and collect it at the beginning of the next class. By reviewing what students have written, I can identify related issues that need to be discussed further with certain students. Alternatively, I may ask students to check and discuss their answers with each other in groups and to add a page of corrections to their own answers before handing in their original responses. One purpose of this activity is to encourage students to monitor their own learning.

> *Students need opportunities to learn to monitor their own learning.*

Progressing from the preinstruction question through the benchmark discussion takes about one class period. In showing that gravity is not caused by air pressure, we have generated questions about the effects of the surrounding air. Students now want to know the answer to the original question. I used to end the investigations of the surrounding air at this point and move on to investigating factors affecting gravity, but I discovered that students slipped back to believing that air pressed only down or only up. Therefore, we redesigned the curriculum activities to include more time for investigation into the effects of surrounding fluids. Doing so also allows us to incorporate some critical introductory experiences with qualitative ideas about forces on objects. This experience helps lay the groundwork for the later unit on forces, when we will revisit these ideas and experiences. To deepen students' understanding of the effects of surrounding fluids then, we now engage in several elaboration activities wherein students have opportunities to test various hypotheses that came up in the benchmark discussion.

> *Revisiting ideas in new contexts helps organize them in a rich conceptual framework and facilitates application across contexts.*

Opportunities for Students to Suggest and Test Related Hypotheses

In the benchmark lesson, several ideas were raised that need further testing. Some students suggested air only pushed up, others that air only pushed down, still others that air pushed equally or did not push at all. Some suggested that air was like water; others contested that idea. Each of the following activities is intended to give students opportunities to test these ideas in several contexts, recognizable from their everyday world. That is, each activity could easily be repeated at home; in fact, some students may have already done them. One goal of my class is for students to leave seeing the world differently. Groups of three or four students each are assigned to "major" in one of the elaboration activities and then to get around also to investigating each of the other activities more briefly. In every case, they are asked to keep the original bell jar experiment in mind: "How does this activity help us understand the bell jar situation?" With respect to the activity in which they are majoring, they will also be expected to present their results and conclusions to the class.

Elaboration Activity A2: The Inverted Glass of Water. This activity was derived from a trick sometimes done at parties. A glass of water with a plastic card over the opening is inverted. If this is done carefully, the water stays in the glass. Students are asked to do the activity and see what they can learn about the directions in which air and water can push. They are also given the opportunity to explore the system and see what else they can learn.

> *Allowing students freedom to explore may give teachers opportunities to learn. Teachers need to allow themselves to learn.*

My purpose here is to help students see that air can apparently push upward (on the card) sufficiently to support the card and the water. That is usually one conclusion reached by some students. Early in my use of the activity, however, I was surprised by a student who emptied the water and placed the card over the open end of the inverted glass and concluded, "It's the stickiness of water that holds the card to the glass." For a moment I was taken aback, but fortunately other students came to my rescue. They said, "At first we thought it might be because the card just stuck to the wet glass, but then we loaded the card with pennies to see how many pennies the card would hold to the empty glass. We found it would only hold about three pennies before the card would drop off. The water we had in the glass weighs a lot more than three pennies. Stickiness might help, but it is not the main reason the card stays on. The main reason must be the air below the card."

This was such a nice example of suggesting and testing alternative explanations that I now bring up the possibility of the stickiness being all that is needed if this idea does not come up in the group presentation. More recently, other students have tested the stickiness hypothesis by using a rigid plastic glass with a tiny (~1 mm) hole in the bottom. When they fill the glass, put on the card, and invert the glass, they put their finger over the hole. When they move their finger off the hole, the water and card fall. They conclude that the air rushing in the hole pushes down on the water and that the air pushing from under the card is not providing sufficient support. I now make sure I have plastic cups available in case I need to "seed" the discussion.

After making these observations, students are ready to draw the tentative conclusion that the upward push by the air on the card must be what is supporting most of the weight of the water on the card. They note the water must push down on the card, and since the stickiness of the water is not enough to hold the card, there must be a big push up by the air. This conclusion is reached more easily by more mature students than by middle-level students. The latter need help making sense of this argument. Most are willing to say tentatively that it makes sense that the air pushes up and are more convinced after they see the various directions in which air pushes in the other activities.

Elaboration Activity A3: Inverted Cylinder in a Cylinder of Water. This activity was derived from some students describing observations they had made while hand-washing dishes. They had observed what happened when an inverted glass was submerged in a dishpan of water. In activity A3, a narrow cylinder (e.g., 100 ml graduated cylinder) is inverted and floated in a larger cylinder (e.g., 500 ml graduated cylinder) of water. Again, students are asked to see what they can learn about the directions that air and water can push.

I want students to see that air and water can push up and down, and that the deeper one goes in a fluid, the greater is the push in any direction. While doing this activity, students observe that the farther down one pushes the floating cylinder, the more difficult it is to push. Thus, they conclude that the water is pushing upward on the air in the small cylinder, and the push is greater the deeper one goes. Typically, some students cite as additional evidence the observation that the water level in the small cylinder rises within that cylinder the farther down one pushes the small cylinder, thus compressing the air. I commend these students for their careful observation and suggest that other students observe what happens to the level of the water in the inner cylinder. The more the air is compressed, the harder the water must be pushing upward on the air to compress it, and the more the compressed air must be pushing upward on the inside of the small cylinder.

The students appear to have reached the conclusions I hoped for. Although I primed them with relevant questions, they made the observations and reached the conclusions.

Elaboration Activity A4: Leaky Bottle. This activity, like the others, came from experiences students had suggested helped them with their thinking about fluids. A 2-liter plastic soda bottle with three holes in it at three different heights is filled to the top with water and allowed to leak into a basin. Again, students are asked to see what they can learn about the directions in which air and water can push.

> By listening to students' arguments, the teacher can learn what related experiences make sense to them.

Here I want students to learn that air and water can push sideways as well as up and down and again, that the push of air and water is greater the deeper one goes. "Suppose there is a tiny drop of water at this opening. In what direction would the air push on it? In what direction would the water in the container push on the droplet?" With some guidance to think about the directions in which air and water push on a tiny droplet right in the opening of one of the holes, the students conclude that the inside water must be pushing outward (sideways) on the droplet, since the droplet comes out. They also observe that the water comes out with different trajectories at the three different-elevation holes. They again see this as evidence that the deeper one goes, the greater is the push by the fluid, in this case sideways. I see some students capping the bottle and observing air going in (bubbles rising) the top hole while water is coming out the lower holes. They conclude that at the top hole, the outside air must push the hypothetical droplet into the water since that is the direction the air goes. Thus, they see that air and water can push sideways and that pressure is greater with depth.

Elaboration Activity A5: Water and Air in a Straw. I think most parents have been embarrassed by their children doing something like this activity while out to dinner. Students place a straw a few centimeters into a container of water and put a finger over the upper end of the straw before withdrawing the straw from the water. Typically, this results in a bit of air in the upper part of the straw and a few milliliters of water staying in the bottom part of the straw. Students are invited to explain.

> In science, we strive for the simplest hypothesis necessary to explain the phenomenon.

Observing that the water stays in the straw, some students conclude that the air below the straw helps support the water. Other students may suggest that the air or vacuum above the water may be "sucking" the water up, an alternative hypothesis. This latter hypothesis is probably cued by the situation because virtually all of these students have experienced sucking on a straw to get liquid to rise. Other students counter by turning the straw over while keeping their finger over the one end, now the bottom end. This leaves the water in what is now the top of the straw, with air in the straw below the water. One student suggests, "The air in the straw is now holding up the water. But, see how the water at the end of the straw now goes down a bit into the straw. That means the weight of the water is causing the air in the straw to be compressed slightly, and if we take our finger away, the air in the straw goes out and the water falls because it is not supported." Other students chime in with their experiment of making two bits of water in the straw with a bit of air between them. They have a bubble of air in the bottom of the straw with a bit of water next, then a bubble of air, and finally more water in the top of the straw. These students argue that the middle bubble of air is both pushing up on the bit of water above and pushing down on the bit of water below. The sucking hypothesis, although not completely eradicated, seems less necessary. Thus, most students come to the conclusion that air can push up and down at the same time.

The first time I tried these activities, I had planned them as a "circus lab." After about 10 minutes, I told students to move on to the next station. Most students stayed where they were. It was 40 minutes before I could get the three girls at the straw station to give it up. I now allow students to major in one activity and visit the others. They get engaged in these simple, common activities, and challenged, they need time to come up with and test explanatory ideas. So I now plan for students to have two class periods in which to complete their major activity, briefly visit each of the other activities, and prepare to present their findings to the class. Toward the end of the second period, we may begin class presentations.

On a third day, we finish the presentations and have a class discussion about what we learned. We summarize the similarities and differences in the properties of air and water. Virtually all students now agree that air and water can push up and down and sideways, that is, can push in all directions. Virtually all agree that the deeper one goes in water, the greater is the push in all directions. There is not quite the same strength of agreement that the push by air is greater the deeper one goes. But usually some students will note that the higher one goes up a mountain, the lower is the air pressure. Other students agree with this observation and add their own, such as that this is why airplanes are pressurized. So, they argue, air and water have many similar properties. Students now have sufficient background for me to introduce the technical term "fluid" properties. Both air and water are fluids.

They can exert pressures in all directions, and they appear to have this increase in pressure with depth.

> *After students have had experiences and come up with ideas to summarize those experiences, it makes sense to introduce a technical term for ease of communication.*

What are the differences? With some guidance, students suggest that air is "squishable" and water is not. They know that water is denser, heavier for the same volume, for we studied density earlier in the year. Students also may talk about the stickiness of water to itself and to other things, like the containers it is in. Since the students have summarized the ideas, I can now introduce the technical terms "cohesion" and "adhesion." Now they are ready for another elaboration activity that more closely approximates the initial benchmark activity.

Elaboration Activity A6: "Weighing" an Object in a Fluid Medium. In this activity, I weigh a solid cylinder suspended by a string and ask, "What will happen to the scale reading if I attempt to weigh this object while it is under water?" Virtually all students suggest the scale reading will be lower than when the object is weighed out of the water. They are given an opportunity to test their predictions and are then encouraged to explain the results.

> *When complex explanations involving several factors are needed for their reasoning, students need more time to put the pieces together.*

The scale reading is lower. Some students conclude that the water is pushing up by an amount that is the difference between what the object weighed when out of the water and when in the water. Note, however, that this is going back to the conclusion that water pushes up, with no mention of any downward push. Many textbooks let students off the hook at this point: "This upward force by the water is called the buoyant force." But this prevents a deeper, more useful understanding involving the resolution of the up and down forces, so I press for more: "Tell me about the pushes by the water on this solid, metal cylinder." Several students jump in with claims based on their previous experiences. They introduce their earlier conclusion that the water is pushing on the top and sides as well as on the bottom. I probe for more: "In what directions are those pushes?" Now students are even more eager to apply the ideas that have emerged in the last few days.

A few students say, "The water on top pushes down." Several others add, "The water below pushes up. The water on the sides pushes sideways."

I now ask, "So, how do we explain the observation that the scale reading is less?" Several students are now constructing an explanation. I give them a few minutes to work on their explanations in small groups and then ask them to share their conclusions: "The water pushes up and the water pushes down. But the push up is greater than the push down, 'cuz it is deeper." Some students have it, but others are still struggling. If students do not volunteer consideration of the comparison between the pushes, I may ask the question, "Why should the push from below be larger? Why does that make sense?" Several students respond, "Because the deeper we go the bigger the push."

At this point, several students have represented the application of our recently derived ideas with words. In the interest of deepening the understanding for all students, I suggest they represent the situation with pictures, using arrows to show the directions of the forces and varying the lengths of the arrows to show the magnitude (size) of the forces. I ask each group to take white board and a marking pen and draw such a picture of the submerged metal cylinder. After a few minutes, we compare diagrams and have members of each group describe their drawings and explain the situation. By now, nearly all the groups have drawn the cylinder with a larger arrow up than down. Each of these arrows, they say, represents the size and direction of the push by the water on that part of the cylinder.

Building an Analogy to Understand the Benchmark Experience

Now that it appears the students understand the weighing-in-water situation, I direct them back to the weighing-in-a-vacuum situation. "So, what does all of this tell us about the situation of weighing under the bell jar? If we had a really accurate instrument, what do you think would have happened to the scale reading and why?" A few students begin to construct an analogy: "Weighing in air would be like the weighing in water." I ask, "How so?" One student responds, "The air around the world is kind of like an ocean of air. Down here is like being deep in the ocean of air. On a mountain air doesn't press as hard." Another adds, "Air can push in all directions, just like water. So if water can push up and down on the cylinder, so can air." "But air doesn't push as much [hard], so you don't get as big a difference," says another. With some guidance from me, the students build an analogy: "Weighing in the water is to weighing out of the water (in air) as weighing in the ocean of air is to weighing out of the air, that is in a vacuum." I ask, "So what would happen to the scale reading in the vacuum if we had a very accurate instrument?" One student responds, "The scale reading would be more."

Another adds, "Just like the scale is more when we take the thing out of the water."

> *Building an analogy from a situation students understand to one they do not can build understanding of the new situation.*

Consensus Discussion and Summary of Learning

There are expectations for what students should have learned from the curricular activities performed thus far. Up to this point, I have been attempting to identify students' understandings about the pushes of the surrounding fluid (water or air). In the class, I now guide a discussion aimed at achieving consensus on what we can conclude about water and air from our observations. On the topical content side, learners should know the following:

- Water and air have some similar properties.
  — Fluids (at least water and air) can push in all directions, up, down, sideways.
  — The deeper one goes in the fluid, the greater is the push in any direction.
- Water and air have some different properties.
  —Since water is denser than air, the effects of the pushes by water are greater.
  —Water can stick to itself (cohesion).
  —Water can stick to other materials and things (adhesion).
  —Air is more squishable (compressable) than water.

The learners should have evidence (results) from the class experiences that they can use to support each of these conclusions.

> *Students need opportunities to reflect on and summarize what they have learned.*

Learners also have had an opportunity to practice some habits of mind that are consistent with learning and reasoning in science:

- Inferences come from observations (evidence-based reasoning).
- Controlled experiments can be used to test most of our ideas.

- Dialogue in science means questioning for clarity of observations, ideas, and explanations.
- Dialogue in science means being supportive and encouraging to elicit the ideas of others while at the same time asking critical questions, such as "How do you know?"
- If we persevere, we will likely be able to understand complex situations.

Students need opportunities to monitor their own learning.

If habits of reasoning and action are also among our learning goals, we need to make them as explicit as we make our content goals.

Diagnostic Assessment

At some point after the benchmark lesson and the more focused elaboration lessons, and after the class has begun to develop tentative resolutions for some of the issues raised, it is useful to give students the opportunity to check their understanding and reasoning individually. Although I sometimes administer these questions on paper in large-group format, I prefer to allow the students to quiz themselves when they feel ready to do so. They think they understand, but they need opportunities to check and tune their understanding. To address this need for ongoing formative assessment, I use a computerized tool[2] that assists the teacher in individualizing the assessment and keeping records on student progress. When students feel they are ready, they are encouraged to work through computer-presented questions and problem appropriate to the unit being studied.

Typical questions related to the key ideas of the preceding activities might juxtapose three situations involving weighing a solid object—the solid object in air, in water, and in a vacuum—each object suspended from a string attached to a spring scale. A first question checks on the students' recall of the specific results obtained and asks them to put the expected scale readings in order assuming the scale has the precision needed. A second question checks on the students' reasoning: "What reasoning best justifies the answer you chose?" For this question, I look for responses that suggest "the water pushes up," "the air pushes down," or "air has no effect on scale readings." Have the students fallen back into their preconceptions, or have they made the desired progress?

Other questions extend the students' application of the ideas to new contexts: "Using the ideas of pushes by air and water, explain how the squeezable plant watering container (with the long curved 'straw' on top) works." Another question suggests a special room wherein the air pressure can be increased from normal to much higher: "What would happen to the scale reading and why?" Another asks students to predict what would happen to a scale reading if we attempted to weigh the solid object in alcohol, which is less dense than water but more dense than air.

Assessment should help the teacher monitor whether students are still operating on the basis of preconceptions, as well as whether they have attained the learning goal(s).

For all these questions, I look for evidence to determine whether the students' ideas have changed or they are still showing evidence of believing their original idea that fluids only push up or down or that the weight is proportional to air pressure. Thus, I aim to move students' understanding across the gap from their preconceptions to a more scientific understanding. The assessment allows them to monitor their learning. If there is trouble, they get feedback suggesting they rethink their answer and/or reasoning in light of the class experiences. I thus obtain a report of what sort of problematic thinking students have exhibited and what experiences might help them move farther across the learning gap.

Part B: What Is Gravitational Attraction?

Exploring Similarities and Differences Between Actions at a Distance

In the previous subunit (Part A) the class separated the effects of the surrounding medium from the effects of gravity on static objects. We appear to have taken a bit of a detour into understanding more about the effects of air and water and other fluids on objects submerged in the fluid. Later we will need to return to looking at the effects of the surrounding fluid when we explore falling bodies (Parts C and D). First, however, we explore the concept of "action at a distance," a key notion in understanding gravity.

Students should be able to see science as involving many questions as yet unanswered.

Although there are still many unanswered questions about gravity, the students do know a great deal about what it does and about the variables on which the strength of the gravity force depends. In Part B, now that the students know about some effects that are not due to gravity, we explore some of the effects that are. Because many effects of gravity are so subtle and pervasive (we live and deal with them every day), the students need to explore gravity by comparing and contrasting its effects with some similar effects and causes they can investigate first-hand.

Research has shown that many students do not separate gravitational effects from magnetic or electrostatic effects. But the effects are similar in that they are all "actions at a distance"; that is, one object can affect another without touching it. Actions at a distance can act through materials and even across empty space. The first activity (B1) in this subunit is to construct analogies among the various actions at a distance. The goal is for students to see that the situations are similar, but the properties of the objects or materials on which the influencing objects act are different.

Benchmark Lesson: Making a Torsion Bar Do the Twist

In the classroom, several meter sticks are hanging from their center points from strings attached to the ceiling. They should be hanging so that each meter stick is horizontal and free to rotate horizontally. On the two ends of one meter stick are hanging two identical brass spheres. From the ends of another hang two aluminum spheres, from another two wooden spheres, from another two steel spheres, and from another two foam spheres. Each system should hang fairly still with the meter stick horizontal (though this is sometimes difficult with students moving around the room). Each is arranged to be what is called a "torsion balance" or "torsion bar." The word "torsion" comes from "torque," which means twist. So, we are going to see whether these bars can be made to twist by bringing something near the objects hanging from the ends without touching the objects (see Figure 11-2). Care must be taken not to bump or even touch the bars except to adjust them to remain still at first. Note that, depending on the maturity and coordination of the students, it will likely be necessary to set up and run the experiment as a demonstration after students have made their predictions individually. Some teachers have found that it helps keep the torsion bars still if movement of students around the room is limited, and even the

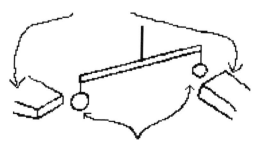

FIGURE 11-2 Torsion bar, spheres, and influencing material.

heating/cooling fan for the room is turned off and windows and doors closed. Even quick hand motions near these delicate balances will cause them to move—possible air effects again. Now the problem:

> *Suppose one end of a magnet is very slowly brought near (but not touching) a sphere on one end of each torsion bar. (Notice that there is a similar situation on the other end of the torsion bar. We will be discussing mainly what happens at one end of the bar, but because of symmetry we can generalize the effect to both ends.)*
>
> *1. Predict what the torsion bar will do in each case. If you think the bar will twist, tell whether it will go toward or away from the magnet.*
> *When brought near the brass sphere the bar will*
> _____.
>
> *When brought near the aluminum sphere the bar will*
> _____.
>
> *When brought near the wooden sphere the bar will*
> _____.
>
> *When brought near the steel sphere the bar will*
> _____.
>
> *When brought near the foam sphere the bar will*
> _____.
>
> *2. Briefly explain how you decided which will twist and in what direction.*
>
> *If any will not twist, tell why you think they will not.*

> *To keep students thinking, teachers should not give answers but present opportunities for students to test their answers.*

While students are answering the questions individually, I circulate around the room, making sure that they understand the questions and that I am getting a feeling for the sorts of answers and thinking I will hear during the discussion. When it appears most students have finished answering and explaining, I ask them to share their predictions and explanations with others. One student suggests, "I think all the metal ones will move because metal is attracted to magnets." I ask whether that makes sense to others, and most of the class appears to agree. Another student says he has tried this before and only "silverish" metal things get attracted, not things like gold rings. Another says, "Not all silver things are attracted, 'cuz I've tried to pick up money, and magnets don't pick up quarters, nickels, or dimes." A few others agree. After only a few minutes of this discussion, students are ready to see what happens. So I carefully and slowly bring the magnet near one of the spheres in first one situation and then another until we have tried them all. While doing this, I suggest that the students write down the results of each situation. The results are that only the steel sphere is attracted to the magnet, and none of the others are affected.

In this case, because the students typically know little about various kinds of metals and their properties and because I do not want to lose the focus on actions at a distance, I elect to tell the students about the metals that are attracted to magnets. I suggest that, while most materials have some magnetic properties, only metals containing iron readily show the effects with magnets such as those we are using.

Preinstruction assessment should check for specific preconceptions.

Next I bring out a styrofoam cup that I have been careful to leave in my desk for several days, so it likely will not be electrostatically charged. I ask the students to predict whether the cup will affect any of the spheres on the torsion balances. There are no clear patterns of prediction. Most students appear to be just trying to guess. I immediately show them what happens: the foam cup does not affect any of the objects (unless the spheres themselves happen to have become charged electrically).

In guided inquiry, the teacher needs to monitor class ideas as they exist initially and as they develop.

Then I rub the cup across my hair a couple of times and ask the students what they expect will happen now. Some students say they think the cup will attract the steel "because you magnetized the cup." Others say no, that the cup now has "electrical charge," so it will attract all the metal pieces because "metal conducts electricity." Still others say, "Because the metals conduct the charge away, they won't be affected." Again, given the confusion and, in some cases, lack of experience with the phenomena, it is time to move quickly to doing the experiments. So I bring the charged cup near each sphere. The results are that every sphere is attracted to the cup. One student facetiously suggests, "That's static cling." For now we conclude that all materials are attracted to an object that has been electrostatically charged. In later investigations of electrostatics, I want students to see that there are two kinds of electrostatic charge and the neutral condition, but I elect not to encourage that investigation at this time so we can keep building the action-at-a-distance story.

Next, I "cuddle" the cup in my hands. By gently putting my hands all over the cup and breathing warm, moist air on it, I am discharging it. When I am pretty sure it has been discharged, when I see that it will not pick up a tiny scrap of paper, I go through the test of bringing the cup near but not touching each sphere again, and we find that there is no effect on any of the spheres. (Note that this part of the lesson is tricky, and it takes practice to make sure the cup is no longer charged.) So I cuddle the magnet as well, but it still attracts the steel sphere and no others. I rub the magnet across my hair and test it, again with no effect except with the steel sphere.

> *Students need opportunities to summarize the big ideas that have been developed by the class.*

It is now time to have students summarize and build consensus. Magnets attract steel pieces without touching them, but do not affect any other materials that we can readily see. And the magnet effect cannot be cuddled off. Static-charged foam cups (and other things such as plastic rulers and inflated latex balloons) attract all kinds of materials without touching them, but the charge can be cuddled off. Thus magnets and static-charged objects are similar in that they both influence other things without touching them, and I suggest this is called "action at a distance." I continue to point out that the two phenomena are apparently different kinds of action at a distance, since they affect different kinds of material. Magnets affect materials that contain iron, but static-charged things can affect almost anything made out of almost any material. Finally, the electrical charge can be cuddled off, but the magnetic effect cannot.

> *Technical media can be used to enhance or extend the students' experience.*

What about gravity? It also acts without touching. The students have heard slogans about gravity making things fall here on earth, holding the moon in orbit, and holding the planets in orbit around the sun, but how can I make that abstraction real for them? What does gravity affect? Can it be cuddled away?

> *Thinking needs to be challenged whenever passive media are used.*

I show a piece of film that demonstrates a torsion balance experiment similar to what we have been observing during the first half of the class period. In the film, a meter stick is again used as the torsion bar. In this case,

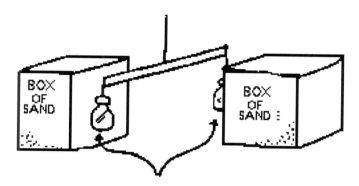

FIGURE 11-3 Experiment illustrating gravitational torsion balance.

quart milk bottles are hung from each end of the bar and adjusted until the bar is horizontal and remaining still. Then a large cardboard box of sand is pulled close (but not touching) to one side of one bottle, and another box of sand is pulled to the other side of the balance but near the other bottle of water (see Figure 11-3). To help students understand the film, I stop it and simulate the situation in one corner of the classroom with bottles and boxes. Then the students watch the film as the bar slowly twists such that the bottles get closer to the boxes. Because the effect is so unbelievable to students and because an indirect measure of the movement of the bar is used in the film, I talk the students through the procedure, the results, and the final conclusion:

Teacher	Do you understand the procedure? How is it like the procedure we used for the magnet situation and the electric charge situation?
Student 1	There are things hanging from the stick in all of 'em.
Student 2	The stick could turn if something made it turn, like a magnet or rubbed foam cup.
Teacher	What is brought into this situation like the magnet or the charged cup?
Student 3	A box of sand?
Student 4	Two boxes of sand.
Teacher	So is there an effect here?
Student 3	No, it is not like the magnet, a box of sand can't cause the bottle to move.

Teachers can foster students' thinking by asking questions, by reflecting students' comments back to them, and by avoiding expressing judgments about whether those comments are right or wrong.

[Partly because students do not believe there should be an effect, and partly because the film uses a subtle way of detecting the movement, most students fail to see the movement at first. I tape a small piece of mirror to the middle of the meter stick with the bottles and shine a flashlight on the mirror. This is also done in the film. A spot of reflected light hits the wall over my shoulder.]

One goal of inquiry-based teaching is to get students to be the ones asking the questions and challenging or bringing up apparently conflicting observations.

Teacher	What would happen to the spot of light if the meter stick twisted?
Student 5	The spot would move. It's like when the light hits my watch and makes a spot and then I move my wrist and make the spot hit somebody in the face. [some laughter]
Teacher	Yes, good example, although it might be distracting, so please don't do it in class. In the film they were shining a light on the mirror in the center of the meter stick. What happened to the light?
Student 5	It moved.
Student 6	Yeah. The light went first one way, then the other.
Student 2	But that would mean that something like a magnet made the stick turn.
Student 4	The box of sand pulled on the bottle of water and made the stick turn.
Student 7	No way, Jose! [laughter] Sand can't pull on water.
Student 3	Yeah maybe they had a magnet or foam cup or something to do it.
Teacher	Good question, lets see how they address that in the film.

[I run the film through the part where they show the effect is not an electrical one, and the voice of the physicist on the film concludes that the bottles moved because of the gravitational attraction between the sand-filled boxes and the bottles of water.]

Student 3   But, how come we can't see that [gravitational attraction] here with our stuff?

Teacher   Another good question. The gravitational effect of a box of sand on a bottle of water is so weak that it requires a very delicate setup. Although Sir Isaac Newton, in 1687, suggested every object in the universe pulled on every other object in the universe, it really wasn't until about a hundred years later that another scientist named Henry Cavendish built a very sensitive torsion balance and was able to see evidence of gravitational attraction happening with ordinary things in a laboratory.

Providing some information from the history of science can help give students perspective on human involvement in the development of ideas.

[When I was at the university I had a chance to repeat Cavendish's experiment. The equipment was so delicate that when a truck went by the building I was in, we had to start the experiment over again. It made the equipment shake, even though we could not even feel or hear the truck. Note that in the film, the experiment is conducted in a mostly vacant building, and the torsion bar is hung from the rafters.]

Teacher   OK, so this was about the best I could do to show you that any thing that has mass will pull on any and every other thing that has mass. This is part of Newton's law of universal gravitation. Even ordinary things like boxes of sand and bottles of water exert a gravitational pull on each other, and they do it without touching each other. Gravity is also an action at a distance. Can we rub it off? No, not unless we could get rid of the mass. But, then we would have nothing, because everything has

Teacher | mass. Let's summarize in a table [which I write on the board and encourage them to record in their notes for the day].

So remember these three different sets of

Three different kinds of action at a distance:

Magnetism	Acts at a distance	Acts mostly on iron things	Can't be cuddled away easily
Static electricity	Acts at a distance	Acts on anything (charged or neutral)	Can be cuddled away
Gravity	Acts at a distance	Acts on anything (with mass)	Can't be cuddled away at all

circumstances associated with three different forces that can all act at a distance, even across empty space. We conclude that they all three are "actions at a distance," but they act on different materials. Some we can make come and go under certain circumstances (e.g., cuddling, and I will end class with changing a magnet). So far we have no way of making the gravity go away. And we have some evidence that you might encounter in later classes that gravity is the force that holds planets in their orbits and makes dust and gases in the universe come together to form stars.

If students have had sufficient first-hand experience, short lectures can make sense even to young students.

Mainly for fun and motivation, I show the students that if I beat on an iron bar with a hammer while holding the bar parallel to the earth's magnetic field, I can cause the bar to become a magnet. For fun, I have them chant as I beat on the bar: [bang bang] "uwa," [bang bang] "tafu," [bang bang] "yiyam." As I beat the pairs of hits faster and faster, the chant begins to sound more and more like "ohwhat afool Iam." The bell rings, and the students leave laughing and agreeing with the chant. That concludes the main lesson showing the various types of actions at a distance.

Humor can enliven the learning experience and help build positive relationships between students and teachers.

Factors on Which the Magnitude (Size) of Gravitational Force Depends

The purpose of the next series of lessons is to build a case for students to believe that the magnitude (size) of the gravitational force grows as each of the two interacting masses becomes larger, and that the greater the separation distance between the two masses, the smaller is the gravitational force that each exerts on the other. High school physics students and more mathematically capable middle school students may be able to conclude with analogous experiences from magnetism and electrostatics that the dependence on distance of separation is an inverse square law. For middle school students, teachers can be more successful building cases that yield qualitative relationships as opposed to yielding mathematical relations and especially equations. The following activities include first-hand observations, reasoning from results to formulate conclusions, and analogical reasoning from concrete situations to abstractions not readily accessible through classroom experiences. From these more qualitative experiences, later algebraic formulation of the gravitational force law can make more sense to students.

We saw early in this unit that gravity does not depend on air pressure pressing down on an object. From other prior experiences, students know that we can measure the weight of something fairly precisely using a spring scale (see Figure 11-4). The heavier the object, the greater the spring scale

FIGURE 11-4 *Common experiences using a spring scale to weigh objects.*

reading will be. But what is the cause of that reading if it is not air pressing down? I could just wave my hands and suggest "gravity," but I want students to have a deeper understanding of gravity by at least understanding the factors on which it depends. I build the case for factors affecting gravity by determining factors that affect magnetic force, and then arguing by analogy about factors affecting gravity.

Students generally love playing with magnets, especially strong ones. I recommend having at least one strong magnet available for each physical science classroom. Among other experiences set up for students' investigations with magnets, one station has a spring scale firmly attached to a heavy brick on a table. A string is tied to the hook on the spring scale. The other end of the string has a loop on which to hang one or more identical paper clips (see Figure 11-5). Set up properly, the magnet attracts the paper clips and the string pulls on the spring scale, registering a reading even without the magnet touching the paper clips. The teacher might ask, "How can the magnet do that?" Most students from the earlier lesson see that the magnet is exerting a force at a distance.

> *Answering such questions as "How do you know?" or "Why do you believe?" helps students build understanding of how knowledge in the discipline is constructed.*

Teacher	What kind of action at a distance is the magnet exerting, and what kind of material does it affect?
Student 1	Magnetic.
Student 2	Magnetism.
Teacher	How do you know?
Student 3	'Cuz the paper clips are made of iron.
Teacher	Did any other action at a distance affect iron?
Student 3	Yeah. Electric force.

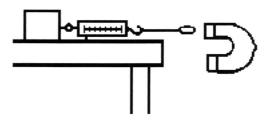

FIGURE 11-5 Apparatus for testing factors that affect magnetic force.

Student 4	And gravity because the paper clips have a little mass.
Student 1	But, I know in this case it's magnetic because there is a magnet.
Student 2	Also, when we set it up we touched the paper clips a lot and that's like cuddling, so there shouldn't be any electric force.
Teacher	Very good. So, we're pretty sure it is magnetic and not electric force. And we are pretty sure it is not gravitational because gravity force is so weak.
Student 3	Yeah, we know all that without even talking about it.
Student 2	So, what's the point?

I see now that I am losing their attention, so I elect to demonstrate the apparatus initially myself. I set it up so there are four paper clips being pulled by but not touching the magnet, and I ask one student to read the spring scale reading and record the reading on the board. I ask another student to carefully measure the distance between the paper clips and the magnet. (Note we are just measuring the separation distance here. With more mature students, we could get into concerns about measuring center-to-center distance as necessary for the force equation.)

I then ask what we might do to make the scale reading lower. Upper elementary and middle school students' intuition suggests that using a weaker magnet would make the scale reading lower. Some also suggest that if we had fewer paper clips, that might do it, too. Other students suggest we might need more paper clips to lessen the force. Since no one has mentioned the separation distance, I ask how it might make the scale reading lower. I ask the students to answer the question for themselves first without saying their answers out loud, so everyone has a chance to do the thinking. Most students suggest moving the magnet farther away will decrease the force and the scale reading.

Quiet can allow each student time to do his or her own thinking.

It appears that the students are now ready to test their predictions and hypotheses. We try a weaker magnet and fewer paper clips, but I allow the distance to get smaller as well. The scale reading rises. Although this is confusing, I want to give students an opportunity to notice and suggest the need to control variables without my having to tell them to do so.

> *Sometimes, there are emergent goals that need to be addressed before returning to the primary instructional goal. For example, teaching about the content may need to move to the background of the instruction while teaching about the processes of science are brought to the foreground, even though both are always present.*

Student 2	See, it's what I thought, less paper clips makes it stronger.
Student 3	No it's what I said. Smaller distance makes it bigger.
Student 4	We got too many things happening.
Student 1	I'm getting lost.
Student 3	It's like we studied before about making fair tests. This isn't a fair test.
Student 4	Oh yeah.
Teacher	OK. Why not, Chris? Why isn't it a fair test? Hang in there Tommy [Student 1]. I think we are about to clear this up. I will have you decide when the argument and results of the experiments make sense to you. The rest of you need to talk to Tommy to convince him of what you are saying. Chris, you were saying?
Student 3	You gotta keep things constant. Like change only one thing and keep other things constant.
Student 4	Oh yeah, like we did before, make a fair test. OK, Tommy?
Student 1	No, I don't remember anything about a fair test.
Student 4	It's like when we said we have to keep all the things [a few students are saying "variables"]. Yeah, we have to keep all the variables the same except one.
Teacher	But, does that help you, Tommy?
Student 1	Not really. What's it got to do with this experiment? That was something we did before when we were studying other stuff.
Student 3	In this experiment we have to keep the number of paper clips the same and the strong magnet the same and change the distance. Only change the distance, if we want to see whether

the distance changes the scale reading. Otherwise, if we change other things too, we will not know whether it is distance or something else that made it bigger.

> *To become learners, independent of authority, students need opportunities to make sense of experiences and formulate rational arguments.*

Student 1	OK. So, what happened?
Student 3	Well, we didn't keep the other things, variables, the same. So, we need to do that to find out what happens.
Teacher	Good, to find out whether that one variable, for example the distance, affects how big the magnetic force is. [At this point, because the apparatus is difficult to control, I demonstrate what does happen when we keep the big magnet and the number of paper clips the same and just decrease the distance between the magnet and paper clips. The scale reading rises.] Now can we tell if varying the distance affects the force?
Student 2	Yeah. It does.
Teacher	How does distance affect force, Tommy? Which way does it go? The smaller the distance . . .
Student 1	The smaller the distance, the bigger the force. Does it get smaller if the distance gets bigger?
Teacher	Good question. Let's try it. [I increase the distance, and the scale reading is lower.] So, what can we conclude now?
Student 1	The bigger the distance the smaller the scale, and the smaller the distance, the bigger the force scale.
Teacher	Good. Now, what do we need to do to test whether the number of paper clips makes a difference in the force?
Student 1	Would we change the paper clips or keep them the same?
Student 2	If you want to test the paper clips, you change the number of paper clips and see if that changes the force.

Student 1   Is that right? Oh! Oh! I get it. So to see if one thing affects the other thing, you change the one thing and see what happens to the other.

The teacher's questions to clarify students' statements help the students become clearer about what they know.

Teacher   That's sounding like you've got the idea of fair test or what is sometimes called "controlling variables," but could you say it again and say what you mean by the word "thing," which you used several times.

Student 1   OK. To see if paper clips affect the scale, the force, you change the number of paper clips and see if the force changes. Right?

Teacher   Yes, good. Now suppose you wanted to see if the strength of the magnet affected the force. What would you do?

Student 1   Change the magnet and see if the force changed.

Teacher   What would you do about the other variables?

Student 2   I'd keep . . . [At this point I interrupt to let Tommy (Student 1) continue his thinking. Meanwhile, other students are getting restless, so I let them go ahead with the apparatus and see what they can find out, which I charge them with demonstrating later for the rest of us. Meanwhile, I continue with Tommy and anyone else who admits to needing some help here.]

All students can learn, but some need more assistance than others, and some need more challenge than others.

Teacher   So, Tommy. What are the factors that we want to investigate here?

Student 1   See if bigger magnets have a bigger force.

Teacher   OK. Anything else?

Student 1   See if more paper clips makes the force reading bigger.

Student 5	And see if distance makes the force bigger or smaller.
Student 1	We already saw that one.
Teacher	If we changed the number of paper clips and we changed the magnet, would we know whether one of these affected the force?
Student 6	Not if we changed both. If we changed both, one or both might be changing the force.
Teacher	So, what do we need to do, Tommy?
Student 1	Oh, do we need to only change one thing, like change the strength of magnet we use and don't change the paper clips?
Student 6	And we'd need to keep the distance the same too right, else that might be changing the force too?
Teacher	Good. So, we think that strength of magnet, the number of paper clips, and the distance might all change the magnetic force. So we just change one of those variables at a time and keep the others constant and see if the force changes and in what direction.

Assuming all the students are familiar with the equipment, sometimes it is more important to help some students focus on the argument while others wrestle with the details of manipulating the equipment.

In a while, I bring the whole class together. I help the students summarize the ideas they have developed and how the controlled experiments helped test those ideas. The group that had the challenge to test factors demonstrates the apparatus and the procedures they used to obtain the following results:

* The more paper clips, the higher the scale reading (keeping magnet and distance constant).
* The stronger the magnet, the higher the scale reading (keeping number of paper clips and distance of separation constant).
* The greater the distance of separation, the lower the scale reading (keeping number of paper clips and strength of the magnet constant).

Students need assistance in differentiating between results and conclusions. Results are specific to the experiment, while conclusions generalize across situations.

From these results we conclude that the magnetic force grows larger with more magnetic "stuff" (paper clips containing iron), with a stronger magnet, or with closer distance of separation between the big magnet and the iron pieces.

Building a Bridge from Understanding Magnetic Action at a Distance to Understanding Gravitational Action at a Distance

Analogies can help bridge from the known to the unknown and from the concrete to the abstract.

I now illustrate two situations on the front board. One is something like the situation we have just investigated, with a large magnet pulling on an iron object and stretching a spring scale. Since this diagram is a bit different from the previous one, I ask students to discuss the similarities and differences. When they appear to see that the situations just seem to be different representations of the same conclusions we drew, I move on to the second diagram. It looks like the first, except that a large sphere represents the earth, and the object is anything that has mass (see Figure 11-6). The spring scale is the same. I ask students how this situation is similar and different from the weighing of a fish depicted in Figure 11-4.

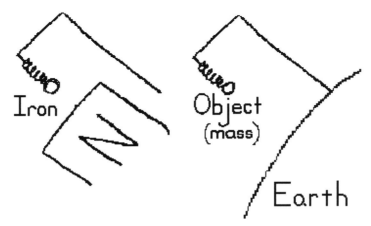

FIGURE 11-6 Diagramming an analogy between magnetism and gravity.

Student 5	Oh, it's like, the earth pulls on the object like the magnet pulls on the piece of iron.
Student 7	They are both actions at a distance.
Student 4	So what. We already knew that.

[So the students appear to recognize the analogous situations. Now comes the difficult part.]

Teacher	From our previous experiments you know on what factors the magnetic force depends. Right?

[There is a chorus of "yes," but I don't trust it because we now have a different diagram, and I want to know if the students are transferring what they know about the previous situation. Students recite the list: "how much iron," "how big (strong) the magnet is," "how far apart they are." Now reasonably assured, I move on.]

Teacher	What are some possible factors on which gravitational force might depend, if it acts similarly to magnetism?
Student 2	Oh. Maybe it depends on the separation distance?
Student 8	Maybe on the mass of the thing, 'cuz that would be like the number of paper clips.
Student 1	Maybe on the strength of the magnet.
Student 3	No, there is no magnet in the gravity situation.
Teacher	OK. Hang on. Tommy [Student 1], there is no magnet in this situation [pointing to the gravitational case], but what might be similar to the strength of the magnet?
Student 1	The strength of the earth?

To build deep understanding of ideas, students need opportunities to transfer the ideas across contexts. Teachers need to check on this transfer of knowledge to new situations.

Teacher	It is kind of like the strength of the earth isn't it. Just like the magnetic force depends on how big and strong the magnet is, the gravitational force might depend on how big, how much mass there is in the earth. Just like the more magnet we have, the bigger the force; the more mass the earth has, the bigger the force. I cannot easily show you, with experiments, on what factors the gravity force depends. But by what is called an "analogy," we can make a good guess at the factors gravity depends on. If gravity action at a distance acts like magnetic action at a distance, it should depend on how much there is of each of the two objects interacting and on how big the separation distance is. By careful experiments with sensitive apparatus like the Cavendish torsion balance we saw before, scientists have verified that the guesses we just made work out in experiments. That is, the gravity force, evidenced by the spring scale reading, would be smaller if the mass of the earth were smaller, if the mass of the ball being held near the earth were of less mass, or if the ball were placed farther away from the earth.

Parts C and D: What Are the Effects of Gravity?

Explaining Falling Bodies

Part A was about "what gravity is not." That is, the effects of the surrounding fluid are not the cause of weight or gravity. But we ended up seeing that fluids such as air and water can have an effect on scale readings when we attempt to weigh objects. Part B was about the nature of gravitational force being one of the actions at a distance. And by analogy we concluded that the magnitude of the gravitational force depends on the masses of the two interacting objects and on the separation distance between them. Investigations into the nature of forces could stop here or could continue and focus on gaining a better understanding of the effects of gravity.

Subsequent investigations in my classes involve explaining the phenomena of falling bodies. Part of a rich understanding of falling bodies is to understand the effects of air (or fluid) resistance as well those of gravity.

Activities in these subunits are more consistent with what is presently suggested in curricula, so they are not described here. But students' preconceptions, such as "heavier falls faster," need to be addressed. More mature students can also quantify the acceleration of freely falling bodies and arrive at equations describing the motion in free fall. But younger students can gain a qualitative understanding of free fall as speeding up uniformly, and they can gain some understanding of factors affecting air resistance.

Explaining Motion of Projectiles

Next investigations, especially for older students, can involve understanding the motion of projectiles. Preconceptions, including "horizontal motion slows the vertical fall," will need to be addressed. Understanding the independence of horizontal and vertical motions is a learning goal. Again those activities are not discussed in detail here. Suffice it to say that additional investigations into the nature and effects of gravity will build a stronger relationship between ideas and increase the likelihood that what is learned will be understood and remembered.

SUMMARY

In this chapter, we have tried to make real the principles of *How People Learn* by writing from our experience and the experience of other teachers, researchers, and curriculum developers. The sequence of activities described is not the only one that could foster learning of the main ideas that have been the focus here. Likewise, the dialogues presented are just examples of the many conversations that might take place. Teaching and learning are complex activities that spawn multiple problems suggesting multiple solutions. What we have discussed here is just one set of solutions to exemplify one set of generalizations about how students learn.

That having been said, the activities described are ones that real teachers are using. But this chapter has not been just about activities that teachers can take away and use next week. Our main purpose is to give teachers and curriculum developers an idea of what it looks like when assessment, curriculum, and teaching act as a system consistent with the principles of *How People Learn*. We have tried to give the reader the flavor of what it means to teach in a way that is student-centered, knowledge-centered, and assessment-centered. By looking at the teacher's decision making, we have attempted to provide a glimpse of what it is like to be a teacher or a learner in a learning community that is respectful of members of the community while at the same time being critical of the ideas they voice. Students are encouraged to question each other by asking, "What do you mean by that?" "How do you know?" But they are also guided to listen and allow others in the community to speak and complete their thoughts.

Students' preconceptions are identified and addressed, and subsequent learning is monitored. This means assessment is used primarily for formative learning purposes, when learning is the purpose of the activities in the classroom. By listening to their students, teachers can discern the sorts of experiences that are familiar and helpful in fostering the learning of other students.

Learning experiences need to develop from first-hand, concrete experiences to the more distant or abstract. Ideas develop from experiences, and technical terms develop from the ideas and operations that are rooted in those experiences. When terms come first, students just tend to memorize so much technical jargon that it sloughs off in a short while. Students need opportunities to see where ideas come from, and they need to be held responsible for knowing and communicating the origins of their knowledge. The teacher should also allow critical questions to open the Pandora's box of issues that are critical to the content being taught. The better questions are those that raise issues about the big ideas important to deep understanding of the discipline. Some of the best questions are those that come from students as they interact with phenomena.

Students need opportunities to learn to inquire in the discipline. Teachers can model the sorts of questions that the students will later ask themselves. Free inquiry is desirable, but sometimes (e.g., when understanding requires careful attention and logical development) inquiry is best guided, especially when the teacher is responsible for the learning of 30 or more students. But the teacher does not need to tell students the answers; doing so often short-circuits their thinking. Instead, teachers can guide their students with questions—not just factual questions, such as "What did you see?", but the more important questions that foster student thinking, such as those that ask students to provide explanations or make sense of the phenomena observed. By listening respectfully and critically to their students, teachers can model appropriate actions in a learning community. Through questions, teachers can assist learners in monitoring their own learning. Finally, teachers also need the freedom to learn in their classrooms—to learn about both learning and about teaching.

NOTES

1. We use the term "benchmark lesson" to mean a memorable lesson that initiates students' thinking about the key content issues in the next set of activities.

2. The computer-based Diagnoser assessment system described is available on the web through www.FACETInnovations.com. Thus, it is accessible to teachers and students anytime from a computer with web access and appropriate browser. The concept and program were developed by the authors, Minstrell and Kraus, Earl Hunt, and colleagues at the University of Washington, FACET Innovations, Talaria Inc., and surrounding school districts. It includes sets of questions for students, reports for teachers, and suggested lessons to address problematic facets of thinking.

12

Developing Understanding Through Model-Based Inquiry

James Stewart, Jennifer L. Cartier, and
Cynthia M. Passmore

A classroom of students need only look at each other to see remarkable variation in height, hair color and texture, skin tone, and eye color, as well as in behaviors. Some differences, such as gender, are discrete: students are male or female. Others, such as hair color or height, vary continuously within a certain range. Some characteristics—10 fingers, 10 toes, and one head—do not vary at all except in the rarest of cases. There are easily observed similarities between children and their parents or among siblings, yet there are many differences as well. How can we understand the patterns we observe?

Students need only look through the classroom window to take these questions a next step. Birds have feathers and wings—characteristics on which they vary somewhat from each other but on which they are completely distinct from humans. Dogs, cats, and squirrels have four legs. Why do we have only two? As with much of science, students can begin the study of genetics and evolution by questioning the familiar. The questions mark a port of entry into more than a century of fascinating discovery that has changed our understanding of our similarities, our differences, and our diseases and how to cure them. That inquiry has never been more vital than it is today.

It is likely that people observed and wondered about similarities of offspring and their parents, and about how species of animals are similar and distinct, long before the tools to record those musings were available. But major progress in understanding these phenomena has come only relatively recently through scientific inquiry. At the heart of that inquiry is the careful collection of data, the observation of patterns in the data, and the generation of causal models to construct and test explanations for those patterns. Our goal in teaching genetics and evolution is to introduce students to the conceptual models and the wealth of knowledge that have been generated by that scientific enterprise. Equally important, however, we want to build students' understanding of scientific modeling processes more generally—how scientific knowledge is generated and justified. We want to foster students' abilities not only to understand, but also to use such understandings to engage in inquiry.

For nearly two decades, we have developed science curricula in which the student learning outcomes comprise both disciplinary knowledge and knowledge about the nature of science. Such learning outcomes are realized in classrooms where students learn by "doing science" in ways that are similar to the work scientists do in their intellectual communities. We have created classrooms in which students are engaged in discipline-specific inquiry as they learn and employ the causal models and reasoning patterns of the discipline. The topics of genetics and evolution illustrate two different discipline-specific approaches to inquiry. While causal models are central in both disciplines, different reasoning patterns are involved in the use or construction of such models. The major difference is that the reconstruction of past events, a primary activity in the practice of evolutionary biology, is not common in the practice of genetics. The first section of this chapter focuses on genetics and the second on evolution. The third describes our approach to designing classroom environments, with reference to both units.

Our approach to curriculum development emerged as a result of collaborative work with high school teachers and their students (our collaborative group is known as MUSE, or Modeling for Understanding in Science Education).[1] As part of that collaboration, we have conducted research on student learning, problem solving, and reasoning. This research has led to refinements to the instruction, which in turn have led to improved student understanding.

GENETICS

An important step in course design is to clarify what we want students to know and be able to do.[2] Our goal for the course in genetics is for students to come away with a meaningful understanding of the concepts introduced above—that they will become adept at identifying patterns in the variations and similarities in observable traits (phenotypes) found within family lines. We expect students will do this using realistic data that they generate themselves or, in some cases, that is provided. However, while simply being familiar with data patterns may allow students to predict the outcomes of future genetic crosses, it provides a very incomplete understanding of genetics because it does not have explanatory power. Explanatory power comes from understanding that there is a physical basis for those patterns in the transmission of genetic material (i.e., that there are genes, and those genes are "carried" on chromosomes from mother and father to offspring as a result of the highly specialized process of cell division known as meiosis) and as a result of fertilization.

To achieve this understanding, students must learn to explain the patterns they see in their data using several models in a consistent fashion. Genetics models (or inheritance pattern models) explain how genes interact to produce variations in traits. These models include Mendel's simple dominance model, codominance, and multiple alleles. But to understand how the observed pairings of genes (the genotype) came about in the first place, students must also understand models of chromosome behavior, particularly the process of segregation and independent assortment during meiosis (the meiotic model).

We have one additional learning outcome for students—that they will couple their understanding of the transmission of the genetic material and their rudimentary understanding of how alleles interact to influence phenotype with an understanding of the relationship of DNA to genes and the role played by DNA products (proteins) in the formation of an organism's phenotype (biomolecular models). DNA provides the key to understanding why there are different models of gene interaction and introduces students to the frontier of genetic inquiry today.

These three models (genetic, meiotic, and biomolecular) and the relationships among them form the basic conceptual framework for understanding genetics. We have designed our instruction to support students in putting this complex framework in place.

Attending to Students' Existing Knowledge

While knowledge of the discipline of genetics has shaped our instructional goals, students' knowledge—the preconceptions they bring to the classroom and the difficulties they encounter in understanding the new material—have played a major role in our instructional design as well.

The genetics course is centered around a set of scientific models. However, in our study of student learning we have found, as have others,[3] that students have misunderstandings about the origin, the function, and the very nature of causal models (see Box 12-1). They view models in a "naïve realistic" manner rather than as conceptual structures that scientists use to explain data and ask questions about the natural world.[4]

Following our study of student thinking about models, we altered the instruction in the genetics unit to take into consideration students' prior knowledge about models and particular vocabulary for describing model attributes. Most important, we recognized the powerful prior ideas students had brought with them about models as representational entities and explic-

BOX 12-1 Student Conceptions of Models

One early study of student learning in the genetics unit focused on identifying the criteria students used when assessing their models for inheritance phenomena.[5] The study was predicated on a commitment to developing with students early in the course the idea of consistency as a basis for model assessment. Students read a mystery scenario involving a car accident and evaluated several explanations of the cause of the accident. Each explanation was problematic because it was either (1) inconsistent with some of the information the students had been given, (2) inconsistent with their prior knowledge about the world, or (3) unable to account for all of the information mentioned in the original scenario. Students discussed these explanations and their shortcomings, and the teacher provided the language for talking about model assessment criteria: she instructed them to seek explanatory power, predictive power (which was discussed but not applied to the accident scenario), internal consistency (among elements within the model), and external consistency (between a model and one's prior knowledge or other models).

Throughout the genetics unit, students were prompted to use these criteria to evaluate their own inheritance models. Despite the explicit emphasis on consistency as a criterion for model assessment, however, we found that very few students actually judged their models this way. Instead, students valued explanatory adequacy, visual simplicity, and "understandability" more strongly. A closer look at the work of students in this study showed that most of them viewed models not as conceptual structures but as physical replicas, instructional tools, or visual representations. In fact, the common use of the term to describe small replicas—as in model airplanes—sometimes interferes with students' grasp of a causal model as a representation of a set of relationships. Similarly, when attempting to apply model assessment criteria to their explanations for data patterns in liquid poured from a box, several students treated "internal consistency" and "external consistency" literally: they evaluated the box's proposed internal components and the external phenomena (observations) separately. This confusion stemmed from students' prior understanding of concepts associated with the vocabulary we provided: clearly "internal" and "external" were already meaningful to the students, and their prior knowledge took precedence over the new meanings with which we attempted to imbue these terms. Given this misunderstanding of models, it was not surprising that our genetics students neither applied nor discussed the criterion of conceptual consistency within and among models.

itly addressed these ideas at the outset of the unit. In the genetics unit, teachers employ tasks early on that solicit students' ideas about scientific models and explicitly define the term "model" as it will be used in the science unit. Frequently, teachers present sample models that purport to explain the phenomena at hand and ask students to evaluate these models. Teachers create models that have particular shortcomings in order to prompt discussion by students. Most commonly, students will describe the need for a model to explain all the data, predict new experimental outcomes, and be realistic (their term for conceptual consistency). Throughout the course, teachers return to these assessment criteria in each discussion about students' own inheritance models.

A subsequent study has shown that these instructional modifications (along with other curricular changes in the genetics unit) help students understand the conceptual nature of scientific models and learn how to evaluate them for consistency with other ideas.[6] We now provide an example of an initial instructional activity—the black box—designed to focus students' attention on scientific modeling.

As Chapter 1 suggests, children begin at a very young age to develop informal models of how things work in the world around them. Scientific modeling, however, is more demanding. Students must articulate their model as a set of propositions and consider how those propositions can be confirmed or disconfirmed. Because this more disciplined modeling is different from what students do in their daily lives, we begin the course with an activity that focuses only on the process of modeling. No new scientific content is introduced. The complexity of the task itself is controlled to focus students on the "modeling game" and introduce them to scientific norms of argumentation concerning data, explanations, causal models, and their relationships. This initial activity prepares students for similar modeling pursuits in the context of sophisticated disciplinary content.

During the first few days of the genetics course, the teacher presents the students with a black box—either an actual box or a diagram and description of a hypothetical box—and demonstrates or describes the phenomenon associated with it. For example, one box is a cardboard detergent container that dispenses a set amount of detergent each time it is tipped, while another is a large wooden box with a funnel on top and an outlet tube at the bottom that dispenses water in varying amounts, shown in Figure 12-1. Once the students have had an opportunity to establish the data pattern associated with the particular box in question, the teacher explains that the students' task is to determine what mechanisms might give rise to this observable pattern. During this activity (which can take anywhere from 3 to 11 class periods, depending on the black box that is used and the extent to which students can collect their own data), the students work in small teams. At the conclusion of the task, each team creates a poster representing its explana-

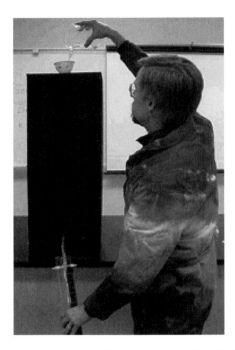

Black Box

A typical pattern of data would be:

Water In (ml)	Water Out (ml)
400	0
400	400
400	600
400	400
400	0
400	1000
400	0
400	400

and so forth.

FIGURE 12-1 One black box used in the MUSE science curriculum and typical data patterns associated with the box.

tion for the box mechanism and presents it to the class. Classmates offer criticism and seek clarification during these presentations.

As the dialogue below suggests, the exercise begins with students engaged in a central activity of scientists—making observations.

Teacher	Making observations is important in science. I want you to observe this carton. Just call out what you notice and I will write it on the board.

The students respond with a variety of observations:

Ian	The box is white with blue lettering.
Delia	The contents slosh around and it looks like liquid soap when we pour it.
Sarah	Hey, it stopped coming out! Try to pour it again so we can see what happens.
Owen	It always pours about the same amount then stops.

After several minutes of listening to the students, the teacher stops them and invites them to take a closer look at the carton, prompting them to identify patterns associated with their observations. Their reflection on these patterns leads the students to propose manipulations of the container, which in turn produce more observations. The teacher now interrupts them to guide their attention, saying:

> Teacher   Okay, you've made some wonderful observations, ones that you are going to be using in just a few minutes. But, there is more to science than making observations. Scientists also develop ideas of what is not visible in order to explain that which is. These ideas are called models.

She goes on to challenge them:

> Teacher   Imagine an invisible "world" inside the container that, if it existed in the way that you imagine, could be used to explain your observations. I want you to make drawings of your imagined world and maybe some groups will have time to develop a three-dimensional representation too. And, one last thing, I want each group to develop at least one test of your model. Ask yourself, "If the world inside the carton is as I imagine it and I do X to the carton, what result would I expect?"

Over the next two class periods, the students work in animated groups to develop models that can be used to explain their observations. They describe, draw, and create three-dimensional representations of what they think is in the carton. They argue. They negotiate. They revise. Then they share drawings of their models with one another.

> Sarah   Hey Scott, you have a different idea than ours. How does that flap work?
>
> Scott   The flap is what stops the detergent from gushing out all at once when you tip it.
>
> Delia   Yeah, I get that, but does your design allow the same amount of detergent to come out every time? Because we tried a flap, too, but we couldn't figure out how to get the amount to be the same.

The students also propose tests of their models:

Sarah	Well, Scott is saying that the flap is like a trapdoor and it closes to keep the detergent in. But I think that if there is a trapdoor-like thing in there, then we should be able to hear it close if we listen with a stethoscope, right?
Delia	Hey, Mrs. S., can we get a stethoscope?

A visitor to the classroom would notice that Mrs. S. listens attentively to the descriptions that each group gives of its model and the observations the model is designed to explain. She pays special attention to the group's interactions with other groups and is skillful in how she converses with the students during their presentations. Through her comments she demonstrates how to question the models of others and how to present a scientific argument. To one group she says, "I think I follow your model, but I am not sure how it explains why you get 90 milliliters of liquid each time you tip the box." To another she comments, "You say that you have used something similar to a toilet bowl valve. But I don't understand how your valve allows soap to flow in both directions." And to a third group she asks, "Do you think that Ian's model explains the data? What question would you ask his group at this point?" By the end of the multiday activity, the students are explicit about how their prior knowledge and experiences influence their observations and their models. They also ask others to explain how a proposed model is consistent with the data and challenge them when a component of a model, designed to explain patterns in observations, does not appear to work as described.

This activity creates many opportunities to introduce and reinforce foundational ideas about the nature of scientific inquiry and how one judges scientific models and related explanations. As the class shares early ideas, the teacher leads discussion about the criteria they are using to decide whether and how to modify these initial explanations. Together, the class establishes that causal models must be able to explain the data at hand, accurately predict the results of future experiments, and be consistent with prior knowledge (or be "realistic") (see the example in Box 12-2). Through discussion and a short reading about scientific inquiry and model assessment, the teacher helps students connect their own work on the black boxes with that of scientists attempting to understand how the natural world works. This framework for thinking about scientific inquiry and determining the validity of knowledge claims is revisited repeatedly throughout the genetics unit.

Other modeling problems might serve just as well as the one we introduce here. What is key is for the problem to be complex enough so that students have experiences that allow them to understand the rigors of scien-

BOX 12-2 Assessing Knowledge Claims in Genetics

While working to revise Mendel's simple dominance model to account for an inheritance pattern in which there are five variations (rather than two), many students propose models in which each individual in the population has three alleles at the locus in question. However, such a model fails to hold up when evaluated according to the criteria established during the black box activity because it is inconsistent with the students' prior knowledge about meiosis and equal segregation of parental information during gamete formation:

Teacher	I'm confused. I'm just curious. I'm a newcomer to this research lab and I see you using two alleles in some areas and three in other areas.
David	We got rid of the three allele model.
Michelle	Cross that out. It didn't work.
David	We didn't know how two parents who each had three alleles could make kids with three alleles.
Michelle	When we tried to do the Punnett square and look at what was happening in meiosis, it didn't make sense.
Chee	Right. We thought maybe one parent would give the kid two alleles and the other parent would just give one. But we didn't like that.
David	We had to stick with only two alleles, so we just made it three different kinds of alleles in the population.
Chee	But now every person has only two alleles inside their cells. Right?
Teacher	In other words, you didn't like this first, three allele, model because it is inconsistent with meiosis?

tific modeling. In particular, the activity is designed to give students an opportunity to do the following:

• *Use prior knowledge to pose problems and generate data.* When science teaching emphasizes results rather than the process of scientific inquiry, students can easily think about science as truths to be memorized, rather than as understandings that grow out of a creative process of observing, imagining, and reasoning by making connections with what one already knows. This latter view is critical not only because it offers a view of science that is more engaging and inviting, but also because it allows students to grasp that what we understand today can be changed, sometimes radically, by tomorrow's new observations, insights, and tools. By carrying out a modeling activity they see as separate from the academic content they are studying in the unit, students are more likely to engage in understanding how models are generated rather than in learning about a particular model.

- *Search for patterns in data.* Often the point of departure between science and everyday observation and reasoning is the collection of data and close attention to its patterns. To appreciate this, students must take part in a modeling activity that produces data showing an interesting pattern in need of explanation.

- *Develop causal models to account for patterns.*[7] The data produced by the activity need to be difficult enough so that the students see the modeling activity as posing a challenge. If an obvious model is apparent, the desired discourse regarding model testing and consideration of the features of alternative models will not be realized.

- *Use patterns in data and models to make predictions.* A model that is adequate to explain a pattern in data provides relatively little power if it cannot also be used for predictive purposes. The activity is used to call students' attention to predictive power as a critical feature of a model.

- *Make ideas public, and revise initial models in light of anomalous data and in response to critiques of others.* Much of the schoolwork in which students engage ends with a completed assignment that is graded by a teacher. Progress in science is supported by a culture in which even the best work is scrutinized by others, in which one's observations are complemented by those of others, and in which one's reasoning is continually critiqued. For some students, making ideas public and open to critique is highly uncomfortable. A low-stakes activity like this introductory modeling exercise can create a relatively comfortable setting for familiarizing students with the culture of science and its expectations. A teacher might both acknowledge the discomfort of public exposure and the benefits of the discussion and the revised thinking that results in progress in the modeling effort. Students have ample opportunity to see that scientific ideas, even those that are at the root of our most profound advances, are initially critiqued harshly and often rejected for a period before they are embraced.

Learning Genetics Content

Having provided this initial exposure to a modeling exercise, we turn to instruction focused specifically on genetics. While the core set of causal models, assumptions, and argument structures generated the content and learning outcomes for our genetics unit, our study of student understanding and reasoning influenced both the design and the sequencing of instructional activities. For example, many high school students do not understand the interrelationships among genetic, meiotic, and biomolecular models, relationships that are key to a deep understanding of inheritance phenomena.[8] To deal with this problem, we identified learning outcomes that address the conceptual connections among these families of models, and the models are introduced in a sequence that emphasizes their relatedness. Initially, for example, we introduced genetic models, beginning with Mendel's model of simple dominance, first. This is typical of many genetics courses. In our early studies (as well as in similar studies on problem solving in genetics[9]), students often did not examine their inheritance models to see whether they were consistent with meiosis. In fact, students proposed models whereby offspring received unequal amounts of genetic information from their two parents or had fewer alleles at a particular locus than did their parents.[10] Because of their struggles and the fact that meiosis is central to any model of inheritance, we placed this model first in the revised curricular sequence. Students now begin their exploration of Mendelian inheritance with a firm understanding of a basic meiotic model and continue to refer to this model as they examine increasingly complex inheritance patterns.

A solid integration of the models does not come easily, however. In early versions of the course, it became apparent that students were solving problems, even sophisticated ones, without adequately drawing on an integrated understanding of meiotic and genetic models.[11] In response, we designed a set of data analysis activities and related homework that required students to integrate across models (cytology, genetics, and molecular biology) when conducting their genetic investigations and when presenting model-based explanations to account for patterns in their data. By providing tasks that require students to attend to knowledge across domains and by structuring classrooms so that students must make their thinking about such integration public, we have seen improvements in their understanding of genetics.[12]

We then focus on inheritance models, beginning with Mendel's model of simple dominance. Mendel, a nineteenth-century monk, grew generation after generation of pea plants in an attempt to understand how traits were passed from parent plants to their offspring. As Chapter 9 indicates, Mendel's work represented a major breakthrough in understanding inheritance, achieved in large part by selecting a subject for study—peas—that had discontinuous trait variations. The peas were yellow or green, smooth or wrinkled. Peas can be self-fertilized, allowing Mendel to observe that some offspring from a single genetic source have the same phenotype as the parent plants and some have a different phenotype. Mendel's work confirmed that individuals can carry alleles that are recessive—not expressed in the phenotype. By performing many such crosses, Mendel was able to deduce that the distribution of alleles follows the laws of probability when the pairing of alleles is random. These insights are fundamental to all the work in classical transmission genetics since Mendel. Students need ample opportunity to work with Mendel's model if they are to make these fundamental insights their own.

The development of modern genetic theory from its classical Mendelian origins has been the subject of much historical and philosophical analysis. Darden[13] draws on historical evidence to identify a set of strategies used by scientists to generate and test ideas while conducting early inquiries into the phenomenon of inheritance. She traces the development of a number of inheritance models that were seen at least originally to be at odds with those underlying a Mendelian (i.e., simple dominance) explanation of inheritance. Among these models are those based on the notions of linkage and multiple forms (alleles) of a single gene. In short, Darden provides a philosophical analysis of the history of model-based inquiry into the phenomenon of inheritance from a classical genetics perspective. Drawing on Darden's work and our own experiences as teachers and researchers, we made a primary feature of the course engaging students in building and revising Mendel's simple dominance model. Students thereby have rich opportunities to learn important genetics concepts, as well as key ideas about the practice of genetics.

Inheritance is considerably more complex than Mendel's simple dominance model suggests. Mendel was not wrong. However, simple dominance applies to only a subset of heritable traits. Just as geneticists have done, students need opportunities to observe cases that cannot be explained by a simple dominance model. We provide such opportunities and thus allow students to conclude that Mendel's model is not adequate to explain the data. Students propose alternatives, such as the codominance model, to explain these more complex patterns.

Once students have come to understand that there are multiple models of allele interaction, they are primed for an explanation of why we observe these different inheritance patterns. How can a recessive allele sometimes have an influence and sometimes not? With that question in mind, we introduce DNA and its role in protein production. What drives the instructional experience throughout is students' active engagement in inquiry, which we turn to in the next section.

Student Inquiry in Genetics

Early instruction in the genetics class includes a few days during which students learn about the meiotic model[14] and the phenomena this model can explain. In an introductory activity, students look at sets of pictures and are asked to determine which individuals are members of the same families. The bases for their decisions include physical similarities between parents and children and between siblings. Thus, instruction about meiosis focuses on how the meiotic model can account for these patterns: children resemble their parents because they receive information from both of them, and siblings resemble each other but are not exactly alike because of the random assortment of parental information during meiosis.

After students have developed some understanding of meiosis, they create, with guidance from the teacher, a representation of Mendel's model of simple dominance (see Figures 12-2a and 12-b) in an attempt to further explain why offspring look like parents. First, "Mendel" (a teacher dressed in a monk's habit) pays the class a visit and tells them he would like to share some phenomena and one important model from his own research with them. In character, "Mendel" passes out three packets of peas representing a parental generation and the F1 and F2 generations (the first and second filial generations, respectively). He asks the students to characterize the peas according to color and shape. For example, the parental generation includes round green peas and wrinkled yellow peas. The F1 generation contains only round yellow peas. Finally, the F2 generation contains a mix of round yellow, wrinkled yellow, round green, and wrinkled green peas in a ratio of approximately 9:3:3:1. Using what they already know about meiosis—particularly the fact that offspring receive information from both parents—the students reconstruct Mendel's model of simple dominance to explain these patterns (see Figures 12-2a and 12-b).

While Darden's work (discussed above) aides in the identification of important inheritance models and strategies used by scientists to judge those models, it is the work of Kitcher[15] that places the simple dominance model developed by students into context with comparable models of geneticists. According to Kitcher,[16] genetic models provide the following information:

> *(a) Specification of the number of relevant loci and the number of alleles at each locus; (b) Specification of the relationships between genotypes and phenotypes; (c) Specification of the relations between genes and chromosomes, of facts about the transmission of chromosomes to gametes (for example, resolution of the question whether there is disruption of normal segregation) and about the details of zygote formation; (d) Assignment of genotypes to individuals in the pedigree.*

Moreover, Kitcher[17] describes how such models might be used in inquiry:

> *. . . after showing that the genetic hypothesis is consistent with the data and constraints of the problem, the principles of cytology and the laws of probability are used to compute expected distributions of phenotypes from crosses. The expected distributions are then compared with those assigned in part (d) of the genetic hypothesis.*

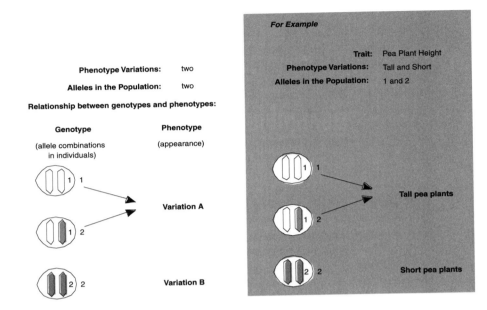

FIGURE 12-2 Mendel's model of simple dominance.

(a) Students' representation of Mendel's simple dominance model. This model accounts for the inheritance of discrete traits for which there are two variants (designated A and B). Each individual in the population possesses two alleles (designated 1 and 2) for the trait; one allele (here, allele 1) is completely dominant over the other. For plant height, for example, there are two phenotypic variants: short and tall. There are only two different alleles in the population. Plants with a genetic makeup of (1,1) or (1,2) will be tall, whereas plants with a genetic makeup of (2,2) will be short.

(b) Meiotic processes governing inheritance. The underlying processes governing simple dominance are Mendel's law of segregation (the meiotic process of sex cell formation during which half of all parental genetic information is packaged into sperm or egg cells) and fertilization (during which genetic information from both parents combines in the offspring).

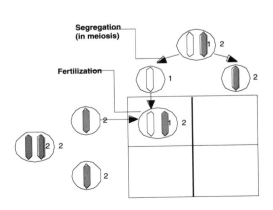

With their teacher's guidance, students represent Mendel's simple dominance model in a manner consistent with Kitcher's description of the models of geneticists. They pay particular attention to (b) and (d) above: specifying the relationships between genotypes and phenotypes and identifying the genotypes of individuals in their experimental populations. Because our unit does not address multigene traits, one locus per trait is assumed (thus part of criterion (a) above is not applicable in this case), and students focus on determining the number of alleles at that locus. Finally, the students' prior understanding of meiosis—developed earlier in the unit—enables them to specify chromosomal transmission of genes for each particular case (item (c) above). The vignette below portrays students engaged in this type of inquiry.

Genetic Inquiry in the Classroom: A Vignette

Nineteen students are sitting at lab tables in a small and cluttered high school biology classroom. The demonstration desk at the front of the room is barely visible under the stacks of papers and replicas of mitotic cells. A human skeleton wearing a lab coat and a sign reading "Mr. Stempe" stands in a corner at the front of the room, and the countertops are stacked with books, dissecting trays, and cages holding snakes and gerbils.

During the previous few days, the students in this class have studied the work of Mendel. Years of work resulted in his publication of *Experiments on Plant Hybridization*,[18] a paper in which he presented his model explaining the inheritance of discontinuous traits in plants.[19] The students have read an edited version of this paper and refer to Mendel's idea as the "simple dominance model" because it explains the inheritance of traits derived from two alleles (or pieces of genetic information) when one of the alleles is completely dominant over the other (see Figures 12-2a and 12-2b).

During class on this day, the students' attention is drawn to the cabinet doors along the length of the room. These doors are covered with students' drawings of family pedigrees labeled "Summers: Marfan" (see Figure 12-3a), "Healey: Blood Types," "Jacques: Osteogenesis Imperfecta," and "Cohen: Achondroplasia." The teacher is standing at the side of the room facilitating a discussion about these family pedigrees.

Teacher	Now that we've learned about Mendel's model, can we use it to explain any of the patterns in our pedigrees?
Kelly	Well, I think Marfan is dominant.
Teacher	Okay. Since we are using 1's and 2's to show alleles in the Mendel model, can you put some numbers up there so we can see what you're talking about?

Kelly walks to one of the cabinets at the side of the room and begins to label each of the circles and squares on the pedigree with two alleles: some are assigned the genotype 1,2 (heterozygous or possessing two different alleles) and others 2,2 (homozygous recessive or possessing two recessive alleles) (see Figures 12-3a and 12-3b, respectively).

Teacher	Kelly thinks that the allele that causes Marfan syndrome is dominant and she's put some genotypes up there to help us see her idea. What do you all think about that?
Chee	Yeah, that's OK. That works.
Jamie	Yeah, because all the filled in ones, the ones who have Marfan, are all 1,2's, so it's dominant.
Curtis	Well, but we started off by saying that it's dominant. I mean, we made that assumption. If we say that the Marfan allele is recessive and switch all the affected genotypes to 2,2's then that would work too. Do you know what I'm saying?
Teacher	Wow! That's quite an idea. I think we need help thinking about that, Curtis, so can you write your genotypes next to Kelly's in a different color?

Curtis proceeds to label the same pedigree consistently with his idea that the Marfan allele is actually recessive (see Figure 12-3c).

Teacher	Well, that's very interesting.
David	I don't get it. Both of them work.
Teacher	You think they both work. Marfan could be dominant or recessive.
Lucy	Well, we can't tell right now.
Sarah	But if we could take two people with Marfan, like the grandmother and the son, and find out what kind of kids they'd have, then we could tell for sure.
Sam	That's sick, man!
Teacher	Wait a minute. Wait a minute. What's Sarah saying here?
Sarah	That if you got children from two affected people . . .

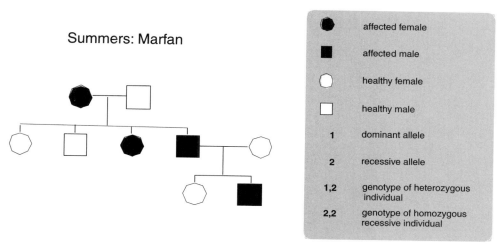

FIGURE 12-3 Pedigrees representing inheritance of Marfan symdrome in the Summers family. (a) The original pedigree, representing the inheritance pattern within the Summers family without specifying individual genotypes.

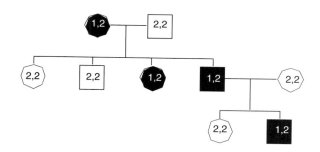

FIGURE 12-3 (b) Kelly's genotype assignments, assuming that Marfan syndrome is inherited as a dominant trait.

Curtis	. . . that you could tell if it was recessive or dominant.
Teacher	What would you see?
Sarah	Well, if it's recessive, then all the kids would be Marfan, too. But if it's dominant, then some of the kids might not be Marfan 'cause they could get like a 2 from both parents.

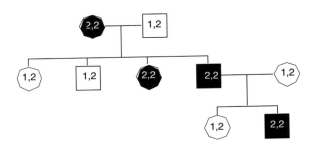

FIGURE 12-3 (c) Curtis' genotype assignments, assuming that Marfan syndrome is inherited as a recessive trait.

Teacher	Do you all see that? Sarah is saying that if the parents had what genotype?
Sam	They'd have to be a 1,2, right?
Teacher	A 1,2. Then if these parents had kids, their kids could be what?
Kelly	1,2 or 1,1 or 2,2.
Teacher	Right. So Sarah is actually proposing an experiment that we could do to find out more [see Box 12-3].
Teacher	Now what about the Healey pedigree? Can Mendel explain that one?
Chee	I don't think so.
Chris	Why not?
Chee	Because there's four things. And Mendel only saw two.
Teacher	Four things?
Sarah	Yeah. Like phenotypes or traits or whatever.
David	There's people who have type A and people who have B and some who have AB or O.
Tanya	But isn't AB the most dominant or something?
Teacher	What do you mean by "most dominant," Tanya?
Tanya	I don't know. It's just like . . .
Chee	. . . like it's better or stronger or something.
Tanya	Like you're gonna see that showing up more.
Lee	Well even if that's true, you still can't really explain why there're A's and B's, too. It's not just AB is dominant to O, right? You still have

BOX 12-3 Sarah's Thought Experiment

In Sarah's thought experiment, two individuals with Marfan's syndrome would produce sex cells, and those sex cells would recombine during fertilization (see Figure 12-3). Looking at the children from such a mating would enable the students to determine whether Marfan's syndrome is inherited as a dominant or recessive trait because the only situation in which one would expect to see both unaffected and affected children would be if Marfan's is inherited as a dominant trait (see below).

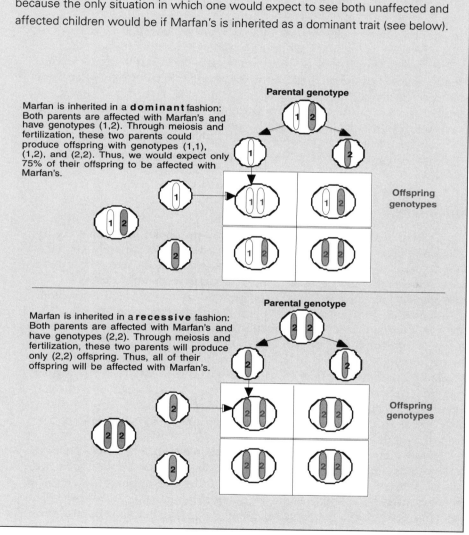

Marfan is inherited in a **dominant** fashion: Both parents are affected with Marfan's and have genotypes (1,2). Through meiosis and fertilization, these two parents could produce offspring with genotypes (1,1), (1,2), and (2,2). Thus, we would expect only 75% of their offspring to be affected with Marfan's.

Marfan is inherited in a **recessive** fashion: Both parents are affected with Marfan's and have genotypes (2,2). Through meiosis and fertilization, these two parents will produce only (2,2) offspring. Thus, all of their offspring will be affected with Marfan's.

	four different things to explain and Mendel didn't see that.
Teacher	OK, so Mendel's model of simple dominance isn't going to be enough to explain this pattern is it?
Chris	Nope.

The students in this high school biology class are engaged in genetic inquiry: they are examining data and identifying patterns of inheritance for various traits. They are also attempting to use a powerful causal model, Mendel's model of simple dominance, to explain the patterns they see. And just as scientists do, they recognize the limitations of their model when it simply cannot explain certain data patterns. These students are poised to continue their inquiry in genetics by revising Mendel's model such that the resulting models will be able to explain a variety of inheritance patterns, including the multiple allele/codominance pattern within the Healey pedigree.

Multiple Examples in Different Contexts

Chapter 1 argues that learning new concepts with understanding requires multiple opportunities to use those concepts in different contexts. Our course is designed to provide those opportunities. Once the students have represented and used the simple dominance model to explain phenomena such as the inheritance of characteristics in peas and disease traits in humans, they use the model to explain data they generate using the software program Genetics Construction Kit or GCK.[20] This program enables students to manipulate populations of virtual organisms (usually fruit flies) by performing matings (or crosses) on any individuals selected. Each cross produces a new generation of organisms whose variations for particular traits (e.g., eye color, wing shape) are described. Thus, the students develop expertise using the simple dominance model to explain new data, and they also design and perform crosses to test their initial genotype-to-phenotype mappings within these populations.

The beginning of this process is illustrated in Figure 12-4, which shows an excerpt from one student's work with GCK and the simple dominance model. After the student's model is discussed, the teacher presents or revisits phenomena that the simple dominance model cannot explain. For example, students realize when applying the model to explain their human pedigrees that it is inadequate in some cases: it cannot account for the inheritance of human blood types or achondroplasia. The next step for the class is to study these "anomalous" inheritance patterns using GCK. They begin with achondroplasia, a trait for which there are three variations rather than two. Students revise the simple dominance model to account for the codominant

Field Population

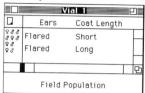

So we can only tell that there is one variation for ears but two for coat length. Another variation for ears might show up.

F1: Cross a female Flared Short with a male Flared Long from the Field Population

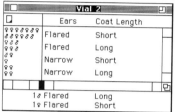

Since a Flared was crossed with another Flared, and the result was both Flared and Narrow, Flared must be dominant since it carried alleles for both variations. Both Flared parents must have been (1,2) for both variations to show. I can't tell if Long or Short is dominant but one of them must be recessive, a (2,2), and the other parent must have been a (1,2) in order to get a mix of both Long and Short in the kids.

F2: Cross two Narrow Short individuals from F1

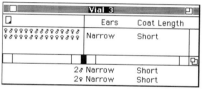

Both Narrow and Short must be recessive. I already determined that Flared was dominant, so crossing two Narrow and getting all Narrows confirms that their parents were (2,2) because if Short was dominant the parents would have been both (1,2)'s, given their heritage. So the only way to get all Short would be to cross 2 (2,2)'s.

F2: Cross two Flared Long individuals from F1

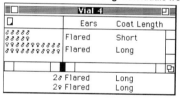

The parent Flareds must have been either both (1,1)'s or a (1,1) and a (1,2) in order to get all Flareds. The Short is a (2,2) and the Long must have been a (1,1) in order to get all Longs. The children Longs must be all (1,2)'s.

F3: Cross a Flared Short male with a Flared Long female from F2

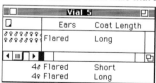

Again, the Flareds must have been both (1,1)'s or (1,1) and (1,2) in order to get all Flareds. The Short is a (2,2), and the Long must have been a (1,1) in order to get all Longs. The children Longs must be all (1,2)'s.

What might the offspring phenotypes be if you were to cross a Flared-eared, Long-coat individual from Vial 5 with a Flared-eared, Short-coat individual from Vial 2? Describe the genetic reasoning behind your answer.

The offspring will either be all Flared, if the parents are (1,1) and (1,1) or (1,2) and (1,1) or there will be a mix Flared and Narrow if the parents are (1,2) and (1,2). Since the Longs in Vial 5 are all (1,2), when they are crossed with a Short, the offspring will be both Long and Short.

FIGURE 12-4 Example of student work on a GCK homework assignment. Students were asked to infer as much as possible from each successive cross within this population. The student's work is shown to the right of each cross.

inheritance pattern observed for this trait. While solving GCK problems such as this, students propose models that specify some or all of the information (a through d) noted above and then test their models for fit with existing data, as well as for the ability to predict the results of new experiments accurately.

Since most students ultimately explain the inheritance of achondroplasia using a codominant model (whereby each possible genotype maps to a distinct phenotype), they must also revise their understanding of dominance and recessiveness. Up to this point, most students tend to associate recessiveness with either (1) a phenotype, (2) any genotype that contains a recessive allele (designated with the number 2), or (3) both. It is quite common for students to conclude that the phenotypes associated with (1,1) and (1,2) genotypes are both "recessive."[21] However, this conclusion is inconsistent with the students' prior concept of recessiveness as it was developed under the simple dominance model. Thus, it is at this point in the unit that we emphasize the need for models to be consistent with other knowledge in a scientific discipline. In other words, geneticists must assess a new inheritance model in part on the basis of how well it fits within an existing family of related models, such as those for meiosis (including cytological data) and molecular biology (which specifies the relationships between DNA and proteins, as well as protein actions in cells). After explicit instruction about DNA transcription, translation, and protein function, students attempt to reconcile their codominance models with this new model of protein action in cells. In the case of codominance, doing so requires them to conceptualize recessiveness at the level of alleles and their relationships to one another, rather than at the level of phenotypes or genotypes.[22] In the process, students construct meanings for dominance and recessiveness that are consistent across various inheritance models (e.g., simple dominance, codominance, multiple alleles, etc.), as well as models of meiosis and molecular biology.

For the final GCK inquiry, the students are organized into two research teams, each of which consists of four small research groups. Each team is assigned a population of virtual fruit flies and told to explain the inheritance of four traits within this population (see Figure 12-5). The work is divided such that each research group studies two of the traits. Consequently, there is some overlap of trait assignments among the groups within a team. The teams hold research meetings periodically, and a minimal structure for those meetings is imposed: two groups present some data and tentative explanations of the data, one group moderates the meeting, and one group records the proceedings. The roles of individual groups alternate in successive meetings.

Each of the fly populations in this last problem contains traits that exhibit the following inheritance patterns: (1) Mendelian simple dominance; (2) codominance; (3) multiple alleles (specifically, three different alleles with varying dominant/codominant relationships between pairs of alleles); and

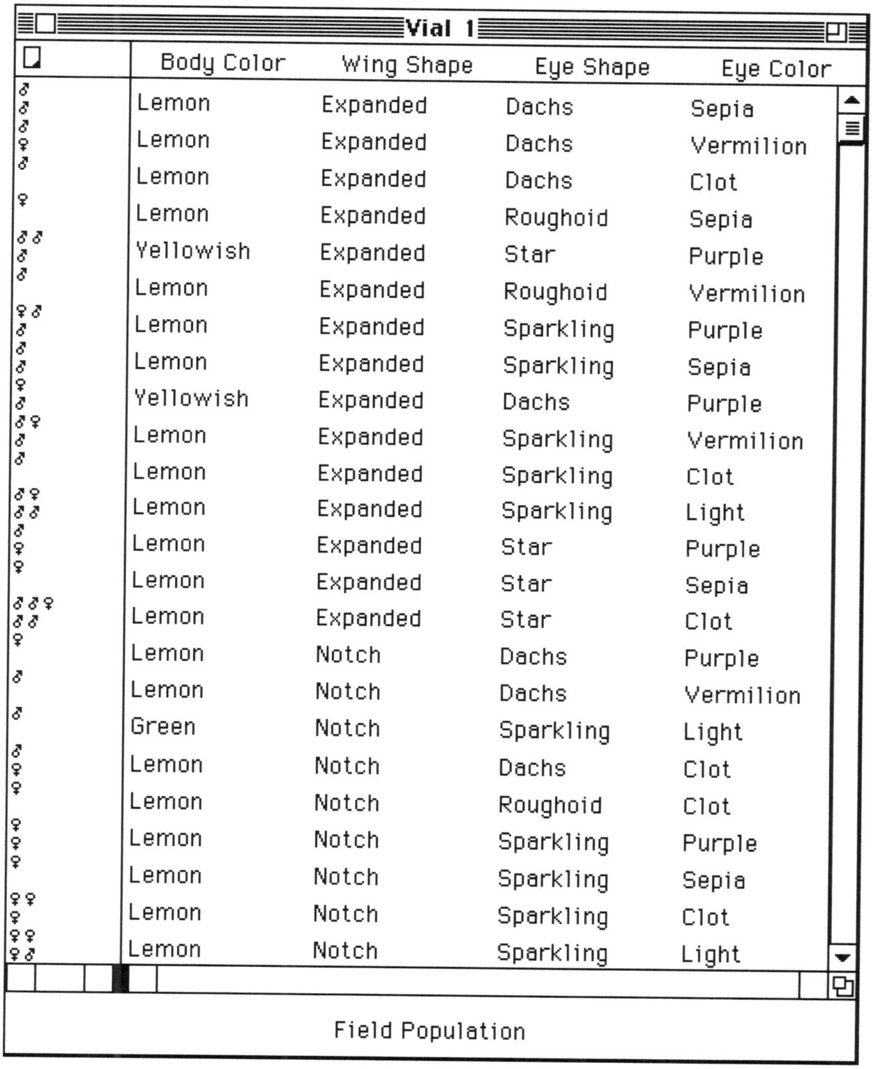

☐	Body Color	Wing Shape	Eye Shape	Eye Color
♂♂♂♀♂	Lemon	Expanded	Dachs	Sepia
	Lemon	Expanded	Dachs	Vermilion
	Lemon	Expanded	Dachs	Clot
♀	Lemon	Expanded	Roughoid	Sepia
♂♂♂♂	Yellowish	Expanded	Star	Purple
	Lemon	Expanded	Roughoid	Vermilion
♀♂♂♂♀♂♀♂♂	Lemon	Expanded	Sparkling	Purple
	Lemon	Expanded	Sparkling	Sepia
	Yellowish	Expanded	Dachs	Purple
	Lemon	Expanded	Sparkling	Vermilion
	Lemon	Expanded	Sparkling	Clot
♂♀♂♂♀♀	Lemon	Expanded	Sparkling	Light
	Lemon	Expanded	Star	Purple
	Lemon	Expanded	Star	Sepia
♂♂♀♂♂♀	Lemon	Expanded	Star	Clot
	Lemon	Notch	Dachs	Purple
♂	Lemon	Notch	Dachs	Vermilion
♂	Green	Notch	Sparkling	Light
♂♀♀	Lemon	Notch	Dachs	Clot
	Lemon	Notch	Roughoid	Clot
♀♀♀	Lemon	Notch	Sparkling	Purple
	Lemon	Notch	Sparkling	Sepia
♀♀♀♀♀♂	Lemon	Notch	Sparkling	Clot
	Lemon	Notch	Sparkling	Light

Field Population

FIGURE 12-5   Initial GCK population for the final GCK inquiry.

(4) x-linkage. After about a week of data collection, model testing, and team meetings, each small research group is usually able to describe a model of inheritance for at least one of the traits in its population, and most groups can describe inheritance models for both of the traits on which they chose to focus. The entire class then gathers for a final conference during which students create posters that summarize their research findings, take turns

making formal presentations of their models, and critique their classmates' models.

This high school biology curriculum is designed to give students opportunities to learn about genetic inquiry in part by providing them with realistic experiences in conducting inquiry in the discipline. As a primary goal of practicing scientists is to construct causal models to explain natural phenomena, involving students in the construction of their own models is given major emphasis in the classroom. The students work in groups structured like scientific communities to develop, revise, and defend models for inheritance phenomena. The overall instructional goals include helping students to understand mechanistic explanations for inheritance patterns in fruit flies and humans, and to appreciate the degree to which scientists rely on empirical data as well as broader conceptual knowledge to assess models.

Metacognition: Engaging Students in Reflective Scientific Practice

Ultimately, students need to learn to reflect on and judge their own work rather than relying solely on assessments from others. Several early studies of students' GCK work in our genetics unit revealed that students assessed their tentative models primarily on the basis of empirical rather than conceptual criteria.[23] Even when conceptual inconsistencies occurred between the students' proposed models and other models or biological knowledge, their primary focus was usually on how well a given model could explain the data at hand. They frequently had difficulty recognizing specific inconsistencies between their models and meiosis or other biological knowledge, such as the method of sex determination in humans. In some instances, students recognized that their models were inconsistent with other knowledge but were willing to overlook such inconsistencies when they judged their models to have adequate explanatory power. (For example, students sometimes proposed models to account for x-linkage inheritance patterns wherein a male organism simply could never be heterozygous. They gave no explanation consistent with independent assortment in meiosis for this model.) Thus, students paid more attention to empirical than conceptual issues and tended to value empirical power over conceptual consistency in models when both criteria were brought to bear.

White and Frederiksen[24] describe a middle school science curriculum designed to teach students about the nature of inquiry generally and the role of modeling in specific scientific inquiries. One aspect of the curriculum that had a measurable effect on its success was the emphasis on students' reflective (metacognitive) assessment. Following modeling activities, students were asked to rate themselves and others in various categories, including "understanding the science," "understanding the processes of inquiry," "being systematic," and "writing and communicating well." Involving the students in

BOX 12-4 Simple Dominance Homework Assignment

Students are asked to use Mendel's simple dominance model to explain a realistic data pattern. They are also asked to justify their reasoning explicitly, in a manner similar to that in which they argue in support of their ideas in regular classroom activities.

Inheritance of PKU in the Samsom Family

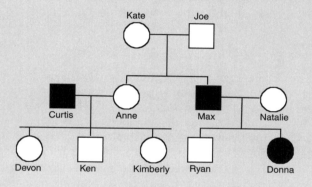

1. Use Mendel's simple dominance model to assign genotypes to the individuals in this pedigree.

2. Do the affected individuals in this pedigree show a dominant or recessive variation of the trait? Pick two family groups (a group is one set of parents and their offspring), and describe how those groups helped you make that decision.

3. Describe how you would convince another student who had no knowledge of how PKU is inherited that you understand the inheritance of this trait. As the student is not easily convinced, you must carefully show how the Mendel model can be used to support your idea.

such an explicit evaluation task helped emphasize the importance of learning about inquiry and modeling in addition to learning how to do inquiry.

Our work in developing tasks for students is also predicated on the importance of metacognitive reflection on the students' part. Influenced by our research in the genetics unit, we built into the curriculum more tasks that require students to reflect upon, write about, and discuss conceptual aspects of genetic modeling. These tasks include journal writing, written self-assessments, homework assignments that require students to explain their reasoning (see Box 12-4), and class presentations (both formal and informal). Most important, we created a complex problem involving several different inheritance patterns and asked the students to account for these new data while working in cooperative laboratory teams. As described above, the regular team interactions required students to be critical of their own thinking and that of others. Moreover, situating the study of these inheritance patterns within the context of a single population of organisms helped emphasize the need for each inheritance model to be basically consistent with other models within genetics. We have found that in this new context, students are more successful at proposing causal models and have a better understanding of the conceptual nature of such scientific models.[25]

Summary

The structure of the genetics class that we have described reflects important aspects of scientific practice: students are engaged in an extended inquiry into inheritance in which they collect data, seek patterns, and attempt to explain those patterns using causal models. The models proposed by students are also highly similar to those of practicing geneticists in that they specify allelic relationships and genotype-to-phenotype mappings for particular traits. In the next section, we describe a course in evolutionary biology that provides opportunities for students to participate in realistic inquiry within another subdiscipline of biology.

DEVELOPING DARWIN'S MODEL OF NATURAL SELECTION IN HIGH SCHOOL EVOLUTION

Hillary and Jerome are sitting next to each other in their sixth-hour science class waiting for the bell to ring.

| Jerome | What are we doing in here today? |
| Hillary | I think we will be starting the next case study. |

The bell rings, and their teacher announces that the class will start work on the last of three case studies designed to allow the students to continue to develop and use Darwin's model of natural selection. She tells the students that there are two parts to this third case. First, they will need to use their knowledge of the natural selection model to develop an explanation for the bright coloration of the male ring-necked pheasant. Second, they will have to write a research proposal that will then be considered by the rest of the students in a research grant competition.

| Teacher | Each of you has seen during the past two cases that there are aspects of your explana- |

> tion that you would like to explore further or
> confirm in some way. This is your opportunity
> to imagine how you might do that. Each group
> will need to think about their explanation and
> identify areas that could use a bit more
> evidence.

As the teacher passes out the eight pages of case materials, she asks the students to get to work. Each group receives a file folder containing the task description and information about the ring-necked pheasant. There are color pictures that show adult males, adult females, and young. Some of the pages contain information about predators, mating behavior, and mating success. Hillary, Jerome, and their third group member, Grace, begin to shuffle through the pages in the folder.

Hillary	The males look completely different from the females!
Jerome	Okay, so what are we supposed to be doing here?
Grace	It is similar to the last case. We need to come up with a Darwinian explanation for why the males look brighter than the females.
Hillary	How can this be? It seems like being bright would be a problem for the males, so how can it fit with Darwin's ideas?
Grace	Well, I guess we need to look at the rest of the stuff in the folder.

The three students spend the remainder of the period looking over and discussing various aspects of the case. By the middle of the period on Tuesday, this group is just finalizing their explanation when Casey, a member of another group, asks if she can talk to them.

Casey	What have you guys come up with? Our group was wondering if we could talk over our ideas with you.
Grace	Sure, come over and we can each read our explanations.

These two groups have very different explanations. Hillary's group is thinking that the males' bright coloration distracts predators from the nest, while Casey's group has decided that the bright coloration confers an advantage on the males by helping them attract more mates. A lively discussion ensues.

Ed	But wait, I don't understand. How can dying be a good thing?
Jerome	Well, you have to think beyond just survival of the male himself. We think that the key is the survival of the kids. If the male can protect his young and give them a better chance of surviving then he has an advantage.
Claire	Even if he dies doing it?
Grace	Yeah, because he will have already passed on his genes and stuff to his kids before he dies.
Casey	How did you come up with this? Did you see something in the packets that we didn't see?
Grace	One reason we thought of it had to do with the last case with the monarchs and viceroy.
Hillary	Yeah, we were thinking that the advantage isn't always obvious and sometimes what is good for the whole group might not seem like it is good for one bird or butterfly or whatever.
Jerome	We also looked at the data in our packets on the number of offspring fathered by brighter versus duller males. We saw that the brighter males had a longer bar.
Grace	See, look on page 5, right here.
Jerome	So they had more kids, right?
Casey	We saw that table too, but we thought that it could back up our idea that the brighter males were able to attract more females as mates.

The groups agree to disagree on their interpretation of this piece of data and continue to compare their explanations on other points.

The students in the above vignette are using Darwin's model of natural selection and realistic data to create arguments about evolution in a population of organisms. In doing so, they attend to and discuss such ideas as selective advantage and reproductive success that are core components of the Darwinian model. Early in the course, students have opportunities to *learn about* natural selection, but as the course progresses, they are required to *use* their understanding to develop explanations (as illustrated in the vignette). As was true in teaching genetics, our goals for student learning include both deep understanding of evolution and an understanding of how knowledge in evolution is generated and justified. And once again we want students to be able to use their understanding to engage in scientific inquiry—to construct their own Darwinian explanations.

There is an important difference between the two units, however, that motivated the decision to include both in this chapter. The nature of the scientific inquiry involved in the study of evolution is different from that involved in the study of genetics—or in some other scientific disciplines for that matter. The difference arises because of the important role that history plays in evolution and the inability of biologists to "replay the tape of the earth's history." Engaging students in authentic inquiry therefore presents a new set of challenges. Mayr[26] suggests that "there is probably no more original, more complex, and bolder concept in the history of ideas than Darwin's mechanistic explanation of adaptation." Our teacher/researcher collaborative took on the challenge of designing a course that would allow students to master this powerful concept and to use it in ways that are analogous to those of evolutionary biologists.

Attending to Significant Disciplinary Knowledge

The choices we make when designing curricula are determined in part by an examination of the discipline under study. In the case of evolution, it is clear that a solid understanding of natural selection provides a foundation upon which further knowledge depends—the knowledge-centered conceptual framework referred to in the principles of *How People Learn* (see Chapter 1). But that foundation is hard won and takes time to develop because the concepts that make up the natural selection model are difficult for students to understand and apply. To understand natural selection, students must understand the concept of random variation. They must understand that while some differences are insignificant, others confer an advantage or a disadvantage under certain conditions. The length of a finch's beak, for example, may give it access to a type of food that allows it to survive a drought. Survivors produce offspring, passing their genes along to the next generation. In this way, nature "selects" for particular characteristics within species.

Equally important in our instructional approach is that students understand how Darwinian explanations are generated and justified. Kitcher[27] describes a Darwinian history as a "narrative which traces the successive modifications of a lineage of organisms from generation to generation in terms of various factors, most notably that of natural selection." The use of narrative explanation is a key means of distinguishing evolutionary biology from other scientific disciplines. "Narratives fix events along a temporal dimension, so that prior events are understood to have given rise to subsequent events and thereby explain them."[28] Thus, our concept of a Darwinian explanation draws together the components of the natural selection model and a narrative structure that demands attention to historical contingency. Textbook examples of explanations for particular traits frequently take the form of "state explanations"—that is, they explain the present function of particular character states without reference to their history.[29] In contrast, what we call a Darwinian explanation attempts to explain an event or how a trait might have come into being. This type of explanation is summarized by Mayr:[30]

> When a biologist tries to answer a question about a unique occurrence such as "Why are there no hummingbirds in the Old World?" or "Where did the species Homo sapiens originate?" he cannot rely on universal laws. The biologist has to study all the known facts relating to the particular problem, infer all sorts of consequences from the reconstructed constellation of factors, and then attempt to construct a scenario that would explain the observed facts in this particular case. In other words, he constructs a historical narrative.

Providing opportunities for students to use the natural selection model to develop narrative explanations that are consistent with the view described above is a central goal of the course.

Attending to Student Knowledge

Anyone who has ever taught evolution can attest to the fact that students bring a wide range of conceptions and attitudes to the classroom. During the past two decades, researchers have documented student ideas both before and after instruction.[31] These studies have confirmed what teachers already know: students have very tenacious misconceptions about the mechanism of evolution and its assumptions.

As Mayr suggests, the scientific method employed by evolutionary biologists in some respects resembles history more than it does other natural sciences. This resemblance can be problematic. In disciplines such as history, for example, we look for motivations. While students may struggle to understand that in different times and under different circumstances, the motivations of others may be different from our motivations today, motivation itself is a legitimate subject for inquiry. But in the Darwinian model, naturally occurring, random variation within species allows some individuals to survive the forces of nature in larger numbers. The random nature of the variation, the role of natural phenomena in selecting who flourishes and who withers, and the absence of motivation or intent make Darwinian narrative antithetical to much of the literary or historical narrative that students encounter outside the science classroom.

We have found that replacing this familiar approach to constructing a narrative with the scientific approach used in evolutionary biology requires a significant period of time and multiple opportunities to try out the Darwinian model in different contexts. Many courses or units in evolutionary biology at the high school level require far shorter periods of time than the 9 weeks described here and also include additional sophisticated concepts, such as genetic drift and speciation. With a large number of concepts being covered in a short period of time, however, the likelihood that students will develop a deep understanding of any concept is diminished; a survey of content is not sufficient to support the required conceptual change.

In the next section, we highlight key instructional activities that we have developed over time to support students in acquiring an understanding of evolution and an ability to engage in evolutionary inquiry.

Instruction

The three principles of *How People Learn* are interwoven in the design of the instructional activities that make up the course in evolutionary biology. For example, the related set of concepts that we consider to be central to students' understanding (Principle 2) was expanded when we realized that students' preconceptions (about variation, for example) or weak foundational knowledge (about drawing inferences and developing arguments) served as barriers to learning. Instructional activities designed to support students' ability to draw inferences and make arguments at the same time strengthen their metacognitive abilities. All three principles are tightly woven in the instruction described below.

Laying the Groundwork

Constructing and defending Darwinian explanations involves drawing inferences and developing arguments from observed patterns in data. In early versions of the course, we found that students' ability to draw inferences was relatively weak, as was their ability to critique particular arguments. Our course has since been modified to provide opportunities for students to develop a common framework for making and critiquing arguments. As with the black box activity at the beginning of the genetics course, we use a cartoon sequencing activity that does not introduce course content, thus allowing students to focus more fully on drawing inferences and developing arguments.

Students are given a set of 13 cartoon frames (see Box 12-5) that have been placed in random order. Their task is to work with their group to reconstruct a story using the information they can glean from the images. Students are enthusiastic about this task as they imagine how the images relate to one another and how they can all be tied together in a coherent story. The whole class then assembles to compare stories and discuss how

BOX 12-5 Cartoon Sequencing Activity

Below are the differing interpretations and sequencing of the same cartoon images by two different groups of students. There are images in the complete set that the students worked with for this activity. The 13 images are given to the students in random order, and the students are asked to create narrative stories.

Group One

"We think that in this first frame little red riding hood is telling the pigs that she is going to visit her sick grandmother. In the second scene, the pigs are telling the wolf about little red riding hood and her sick grandmother and showing him which way she went. In the next frame, the pigs see that the grandmother is tied up in the woods and they feel bad that they gave the wolf the information earlier."

Group Two

"The pigs have discovered grandma tied up in the woods and they try to throw the wolf off the track by telling him that he must get away before the hunter comes. In the last frame, little red riding hood is thanking the pigs for saving the grandmother and they feel bashful."

decisions were made. The sequences presented by different groups usually vary quite a bit (see Box 12-5 for two examples). This variation provides a context for discussing how inferences are drawn.

The initial discussion centers on students' observations about the images. However, it quickly becomes apparent that each person does not place the same importance on specific observations and that even though groups may have observed the same thing, they may not have made the same decisions about the order of the cards. What ensues is a conversation about considerations that entered into the students' decision making. Students realize that they are all examining the same images (the data), but that each also brings a lifetime of experience with cartoons and stories to the table. Together the students establish that the process of drawing inferences about the order of the cards is influenced by both what they observe (the data) and their own prior knowledge and beliefs. This notion is then generalized, and students see that all inferences can be thought of as having these two bases. They discuss how scientific arguments are usually a collection of several inferences, all of which are dependent on data and prior knowledge and beliefs. The teacher supports this discussion by pointing out examples of fruitful questioning and encouraging the students to think about what it means to foster a community in which communication about important ideas is expected.

In addition to introducing general norms for classrooms in which scientific argumentation is central, the cartoon activity serves to orient students to a framework for critiquing arguments in evolution. At one level, this framework is common to all science disciplines. In this capacity, the emphasis is on the importance of being explicit about how prior knowledge and beliefs influence the inferences drawn from particular data. At this general level, the activity is linked to the common MUSE framework of models and modeling as the teacher connects the ideas concerning inferences to those concerning models. The teacher does this by explaining that a causal model is an idea that is used to create explanations for some set of phenomena and that models are based on several inferences. Students then read some material on models and as a class discuss the ways in which models can be assessed. Through examples in the reading and from their own experience, the group settles on criteria for judging models: explanatory power and consistency with other knowledge. Note that, in contrast with the genetics course, there is no mention of predictive adequacy here as a major assessment criterion because explanation is much more central than prediction in the evolution course. This is one example of the assertion we have made previously: disciplines do rely on differing methods for making and evaluating claims. The demonstrative inference that is common in the genetics course gives way to a greater reliance on nondemonstrative inference in the evolution course. This occurs as students create Darwinian explanations. Such explanations, with their characteristic narrative structure, are developed to make sense out of the diverse data (structural and behavioral characteristics of organisms, patterns in their molecular biology, patterns of distribution in both time and geography, and so on) that are characteristic of evolutionary argumentation.

A second evolution-specific function served by the cartoon activity is to introduce students to one of the more important undertakings of evolutionary biologists—the reconstruction of past events (the development of a trait, such as the vertebrate eye, or the speciation events that led to the "tree of life"). Such historical reconstructions do not have close analogues in genetic inquiry.

A second instructional component was added to the course when we observed students' difficulties in understanding the concept of variation. These difficulties have been documented in the literature,[32] and we have encountered them in our own classrooms. Because of the experiences students have with variability in most genetics instruction—in which they usually examine traits with discrete variations—the concept of continuous variation can be a significant challenge for them. We have seen that an incomplete understanding of variation in populations promotes students' ideas that adaptations are a result of a single dramatic mutation and that selection is an all-or-none event operating on one of two to three possible phenotypes. Recognition of these problems has led us to incorporate explicit instruction on variability in populations and, perhaps more important, to provide opportunities for students to examine and characterize the variability present in real organisms before they begin using the concept in constructing Darwinian explanations.

One of the activities used for this purpose is a relatively simple one, but it provides a powerful visual representation on which students can draw later when thinking about variation in populations. Typically, students do not recognize the wide range of variation that is present even in familiar organisms. To give them experience in thinking about and characterizing variation, we have them examine sunflower seeds. Their task is to count the stripes on a small sample of seeds (but even this simple direction is less than straightforward since the class must then negotiate such matters as what counts as a stripe and whether to count one side or two).

Once they have come up with common criteria and have sorted their sample into small piles, the teacher has them place their seeds into correspondingly numbered test tubes. The result, once the test tubes have been lined up in a row, is a clear visual representation of a normal distribution. The subsequent discussion centers on ways to describe distributions using such concepts as mean, median, and mode. This activity takes place before students need to draw on their understanding of variation to construct explanations using the natural selection model.

Understanding the Darwinian Model

The second major section of the course engages students in examining three historical models that account for species' adaptation and diversity. The students must draw on the framework established during the cartoon activity to accomplish this comparison. This means that as they examine each argument, they also identify the major inferences drawn and the data and prior knowledge and beliefs that formed the basis for those inferences. The three models are (1) William Paley's model of intelligent design, which asserts that all organisms were made perfectly for their function by an intelligent creator; (2) Jean Baptiste de Lamarck's model of acquired characteristics, which is based on a view that adaptations can result from the use or disuse of body parts and that changes accumulated during an organism's lifetime will be passed on to offspring; and (3) Darwin's model of natural selection. The models of Paley and Lamarck were chosen because each represents some of the common ideas students bring with them to the classroom. Specifically, it is clear that many students attribute evolutionary change to the needs of an organism and believe that extended exposure to particular environments will result in lasting morphological change. Many students are also confused about the role of supernatural forces in evolution. Darwin's model is included in the analysis so students can see how the underlying assumptions of his model compare with those of the Paley and Lamarck models.

For students to compare the prior knowledge and beliefs of the authors, however, they must first become familiar with the models. To this end, each model is examined in turn, and students are discouraged from making comparisons until each model has been fully explored. All three models are presented in the same way. Students read edited selections of the author's original writing, answer questions about the reading, and participate in a class discussion in which the proposed explanation for species diversity and adaptation is clarified and elaborated. In the following example, Claire and Casey are working with Hillary in a group during class. They are trying to analyze and understand an excerpt of original writing by Lamarck. Hillary is looking over the discussion questions:

Hillary	It seems like Lamarck did think that species changed over time, so I can see that as an underlying assumption of his, but I'm having a hard time figuring out how he thought that happened.
Casey	I agree, he is definitely different from Paley who didn't think things had changed at all.
Claire	But how did the change happen? It seems like

	Lamarck puts it on the organisms themselves, that they try to change.
Hillary	I'm not sure what you mean.
Claire	Well, he talks a lot about the usefulness of particular traits for an animal and about repeated use of a body part causing a change.

Students are also given an opportunity to explore the natural phenomena or data that served as an inspiration for each author: they examine fossils as discussed by Lamarck, dissect an eye to examine the structure/function relationships that so fascinated Paley, and are visited by a pigeon breeder who brings several of the pigeon varieties that Darwin described in his *Origin of Species*. Once students have developed an understanding of the explanation that each author proposed and some familiarity with the observations on which it was based, they examine the readings again to identify the prior knowledge and beliefs that each author may have held.

Following this discussion, the students compare the three models. First, they assess the explanatory power of the models, using each to explain phenomena other than those described in the original writings. For example, they attempt to use Paley's model to explain the presence of fossils and Lamarck's model to explain the structure of the eye. Sometimes the model can easily account for new phenomena; Lamarck's model of use inheritance, for example, is easily adapted to explaining the diversity of pigeon varieties. In other instances, the students recognize the limitations of the model; Paley's model, for instance, cannot easily account for the presence of fossils or extinct organisms. The students then compare the underlying assumptions or beliefs of the authors. Even if a model can account for diverse phenomena on its own terms, it is still necessary to examine and critique the underlying assumptions. Many students question the necessity of the supernatural force underlying Paley's model, and still more find the role of need to be a questionable assumption in Lamarck's model.

These explicit discussions of some of the major views students bring to the study of evolution lay the groundwork for the future use and extension of Darwin's model. Comparing the assumptions of the three models enables students to distinguish between those beliefs that underlie the model of natural selection and those that do not. Unlike some classroom contexts, however, in which it is the students' ideas that are laid bare and examined for inconsistencies, here we have developed a situation in which students' ideas are represented by the models of Paley and Lamarck. We have found that through this approach, students are willing to attend to the differences between ideas rather than spending their time and energy being defensive; because they do not feel that their own ideas are being criticized, the discussions are fruitful.

These two activities foster a classroom community that operates from a common set of commitments. For our purposes, the most important of these is that Darwin proposed a naturalistic mechanism of species change that acts on variation among individuals within a species and that assumptions of supernatural influence and individual need are not a part of his model. Keeping this distinction in mind while using the natural selection model later in the course enables students to avoid some common misconceptions, or at least makes identification of those misconceptions more straightforward. For example, when students use the natural selection model to explain the bright coloration of the monarch butterfly, they often challenge each other when need-based or Lamarckian language is used.

Using the Darwinian Model

During the final weeks of the course, students are engaged in creating Darwinian explanations using the components of the natural selection model to make sense of realistic data they have been given. Each scenario is presented to the students as a case study, and they are given materials that describe the natural history of the organism. Photographs, habitat and predator information, mating behavior and success, and phylogenetic data are examples of the types of information that may be included in a given case. Students then weave the information into a narrative that must take into account all of the components of a natural selection model and describe the change over time that may have occurred (see Box 12-6 for one group's Darwinian explanation). As students hone their abilities to develop and assess evolutionary arguments over three successive case studies, they are able to participate in realistic evolutionary inquiry.

In the first case study, students develop a Darwinian explanation for differences in seed coat characteristics among populations of a hypothetical plant species. The second case study involves explaining the bright, and similar, coloration of monarch and viceroy butterflies. The final case requires that students develop an explanation for how the sexual dimorphism exhibited by ring-necked pheasants might have arisen.

During each case study, the time is structured so that a group will consult with at least one other group as they develop their explanations. This task organization reinforces the nature of argumentation in evolutionary biology, as it includes the expectation that students will attend to the central feature of any Darwinian explanation—that it have a historical component. But it is not enough to just have a history. In tracing the possible historical development of a trait, students must weave a complex story that draws on available data, as well as their understanding of an array of biological models (e.g., genetic models), to explain the role of heritable variation, superfecundity, competition, and agents of selection. Within their research

BOX 12-6 Darwinian Explanation Written by a Group of Students at the End of the Monarch/Viceroy Case

Monarchs and viceroys are very similar in appearance, although this has not always been true. The brightness in both butterflies is viewed as an advantage in their environment—where a main predator is the blue jay—an advantage that may be explained by the Darwinian model.

Each butterfly lays many more eggs than can survive on the limited resources in its environment. As a result of this limit, there is a struggle among the offspring for survival. As within all species, there exists natural variation among the populations of monarchs and viceroys, including variations of color. In the past populations, some butterflies were brightly colored and others were dull. Blue jays, a main predator of the monarch, rely on movement and coloration to identify their prey when hunting. They can vomit up bad-tasting or poisonous food, and exhibit an ability to learn to avoid such food in the future.

As caterpillars, monarchs have as a source of food milkweed leaves, which contain cardenolides—poisonous or unpalatable substances. As the larva are growing, they ingest a large amount of cardenolides. When they become butterflies, these substances remain in their bodies, making them unpalatable to their predators.

When blue jays eat monarchs, they react to the cardenolides by vomiting up their prey. They learn from this experience that they should avoid the brightly colored monarchs to avoid the cardenolides. The dull monarchs, although poisonous, were still consumed by their predators more because they more closely resembled nonpoisonous prey such as moths, grasshoppers, and lacewings. The brightly colored monarchs survived more than the dull ones and were more prolific. After many generations, most monarchs were bright because of their success in the environment. Because of the blue jays' association of bright colors with bad food, the brightly colored viceroys, although not poisonous like the monarch, were also avoided, and this advantageous variation was passed on as with the monarch.

groups, meetings between research groups, and whole-class discussions, students question one another using a variety of sophisticated stances. These include ensuring that there is consistency among the data, the natural selection model, and claims; that the history of the shift in a trait is feasible (i.e., consistent with genetics); and that the proposed selection agent could have brought about the change in the trait between times 1 and 2. The students question one another to ensure that their explanations are both internally and externally consistent. In so doing, they normally propose more than a single explanation, thus recognizing that, in evolution at least, it is important to consider multiple interpretations. As they examine competing Darwinian explanations for the same phenomena, they invoke an evolution-specific argument-analysis norm—that the explanation of the history of a trait has to be consistent with the natural selection model. For example, the second case requires students to provide a Darwinian explanation for the similarity in color between the monarch and viceroy butterflies. Frequently students will say such things as "the viceroy needs to look like the monarch so that the birds won't eat it." When statements such as these are made, other students will often challenge the speaker to use Darwinian rather than Lamarckian language. The work on the cases allows students to practice using the Darwinian model in appropriate ways, and the interactive nature of all of the work in class affords them opportunities to think explicitly about and defend their own ideas.

The culminating activities for each of the three cases require public sharing of ideas in a forum where the expectation is that the presenting groups and audience members will consider thoughtfully the ideas before them. Each case has a different type of final presentation. The first case ends with a poster session, the second with a roundtable discussion, and the last with a research proposal and an oral presentation.

One particularly powerful experience students have occurs during the final case study. For the first two case studies, students use their understanding of the Darwinian model to account for the changes that may have occurred in particular populations and to explicitly tie data from the case materials to their claims. For the final case study, they must construct a Darwinian explanation for the sexual dimorphism observed between male and female ring-necked pheasants, and in addition, they must produce a research proposal to shed light on their explanation. Typically, students choose to focus their research proposal on a single aspect of their explanation. This activity requires that they think carefully about the components of their explanation and the confidence they place in each of those components. Thus in this instance they are not evaluating the entire explanation as a single entity, but are considering each part in relation to the others. Once they have decided on a research proposal, they must determine how their proposed research would strengthen their argument. Being able to examine an argument as a whole and according to its parts is an important skill that this task helps develop. This case also stimulates interesting conversations among groups. The nonpresenting groups act as a proposal review panel and interact with the presenting groups in an attempt to understand the proposal. Once all groups have presented, the students discuss the merits and shortcomings of each proposal and then decide individually which proposal should be funded.

CLASSROOM ENVIRONMENTS THAT SUPPORT LEARNING WITH UNDERSTANDING

We have found that much of what students learn in genetics and evolutionary biology units grounded in model-based inquiry depends on their active and thoughtful participation in the classroom community.[33] To learn about the process of modeling and about discipline-specific patterns of argumentation, students must be critically aware of the elements that influence their own knowledge generation and justification. The MUSE curricula are designed to facilitate this type of student thinking through explicit discussion of students' expectations for engaging in argumentation, the design of student tasks, and the use of various tools for interacting with and representing abstract concepts.

Knowledge-Centered

By the end of our courses, students are able to reason in sophisticated ways about inheritance patterns and about evolutionary phenomena. Realizing that goal, we believe, is due in large measure to careful attention to the core disciplinary knowledge, as well as persistent attention to students' preconceptions and the supports required for effective conceptual change. The instructional activities we have described highlight a classroom environment that is knowledge-centered in putting both the core concepts and scientific approaches to generating and justifying those concepts at the center of instruction.

Learner-Centered

The classrooms are also learner-centered in several respects. The curriculum was designed to address existing conceptions that we had observed were creating problems for students as they tried to master new material. We also identified weaknesses in students' knowledge base—such as their understanding of models and their ability to draw inferences and develop arguments—and designed activities to strengthen those competencies. The use of frequent dialogue in our courses allows an attentive teacher to continuously monitor students' developing thinking.

Assessment-Centered

We have attempted to embed formative and authentic assessments throughout our courses. Assessment of student understanding needs to be undertaken with an eye to the various types of prior knowledge described above (misconceptions of science concepts, ideas about what science is, and the extent to which students' knowledge is integrated). We have seen, time and again, teachers becoming aware of students' common struggles and beginning to "hear" their own students differently. Thus, an important feature of instructional activities that give students opportunities to make their thinking and knowledge public and therefore visible to teachers is that they make assessment and instruction seamless. This becomes possible when students articulate the process of arriving at a solution and not simply the solution itself.

Because students struggle with conceptual problems in the genetics unit, for example, we incorporate a number of assessments that require them to describe the relationships between models or ideas that they have learned (see Box 12-7). Whenever possible, we design formal assessments as well as written classroom tasks that reflect the structure of students' work in the classroom. Our students spend a great deal of their class time working in groups, pouring over data, and talking with one another about their ideas. Thus, assessments also require them to look at data, propose explanations, and describe the thinking that led to particular conclusions.

In the evolution course, students are required during instruction to use the natural selection model to develop Darwinian explanations that account for rich data sets. To then ask them about data or the components of natural selection in a multiple-choice format that would require them to draw on only bits and pieces of knowledge for any one question appears incomplete at best. Instead, we provide them with novel data and ask them to describe their reasoning about those data using the natural selection model—a task analogous to what they have been doing in class. An instance of this type of assessment on the final exam asks students to write a Darwinian explanation for the color of polar bear fur using information about ancestral populations. In this way, during assessment we draw on students' ideas and skills as they were developed in class rather than asking students to simply recall bits of information in contrived testing situations.

While assessments provide teachers with information about student understanding, students also benefit from assessments that give them opportunities to see how their understanding has changed during a unit of study. One method we have used is to require each student to critique her or his own early work based on what she or he knows at the conclusion of a course. Not only does this approach give teachers insights into students' knowledge, but it also allows students to glimpse how much their knowledge and their ability to critique arguments have changed. Students' consideration of their own ideas has been incorporated into the assessment tasks in both units. On several occasions and in different ways, students examine their own ideas and explicitly discuss how those ideas have changed. For example, one of the questions on the final exam in evolution requires students to read and critique a Darwinian explanation they created on the first

BOX 12-7 Sample Exam Question: Consistency Between Models

This exam question is one of several tasks designed to produce evidence of students' understandings about the need for models to be consistent with one another and with the data they purport to explain.

Below is a concept map that represents the relationships among specific models, models in general, and data. Use the map to respond to the tasks below.

a. Remember that a <u>line</u> in a concept map represents a relationship between two terms (concepts, ideas, etc.) in the map. Write <u>a few sentences</u> that describe the numbered relationships between the terms given. Be as specific as you can: use the appropriate vocabulary of genetics to make your point as clearly as possible.

b. Draw a line (not necessarily a straight one) to separate the world of ideas from that of observations on this map. Please label both sides. Justify your placement of that line.

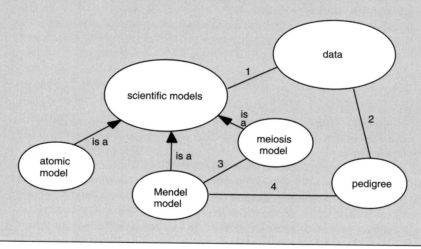

day of class (see Box 12-8). We have found this to be one of the most powerful moments for many students, as they recognize how much their own ideas have changed. Many students are critical of the need-based language that was present in their original explanation, or they find that they described evolutionary change as having happened at the individual rather than the population level.

BOX 12-8 Examples of Students' Critiques of Their Own Darwinian Explanations

On the first day of class, students were asked to explain how the carapace of Galapagos tortoises may have changed from the dome shape to the saddleback shape. As part of the final exam for the class, students were asked to critique the explanation they had given on the first day. Below are the original explanation and critique offered by one student.

Original Answer

The saddleback carapace came into being due to the need of migrating tortoises to adjust to a new environment. On Albermarle Island the domed shaped carapaces served well for shedding rain and eating ground vegetation. However, when the tortoises began to migrate to a smaller, drier island with less ground vegetation, they had to adapt in order to survive. The majority of the food was now higher up and the domed shell served as a hindrance. Over time, the saddleback carapace developed to allow the neck to extend further, thereby allowing the tortoises to reach the fleshy green parts of the prickly pear cactus. This evolutionary process created a new species of giant tortoise that could live successfully in a new environment.

Critique on Final Exam

In my original answer, I used an almost exclusive Lamarckian definition of evolution. In my introductory statement I stated that the saddleback carapace came into being due to the need of the tortoise to fit its environment. I needed to acknowledge the existence of variation within the tortoise population of the shape of the shell. My original explanation makes the evolutionary process sound like a physical change taking place during the life of the tortoise and then being passed on to the offspring. I now know that variations that are advantageous give animals a better chance of survival (survival of the fittest!) and allow them a better chance of passing on their advantageous trait to their offspring. In my original explanation I also touched on ideas of use and disuse to explain how the saddleback carapace came to be, this is a Lamarkian model of evolution which is incorrect. I did explain how the saddleback carapace was an advantage because it allowed the tortoise to eat higher vegetation. Since I didn't understand evolution through the generations, I wasn't able to describe how the species changed over time. Overall, I would say I had a basic but flawed understanding of evolution but I lacked the tools to explain evolution from a scientific and Darwinian perspective, until now.

Community-Centered

As Chapter 1 suggests, the knowledge-centered, learner-centered, and assessment-centered classrooms come together in the context of a classroom community. The culture of successful scientific communities includes both collaboration and questioning among colleagues. It involves norms for making and justifying claims. At the source of the productivity of such a community is an understanding of central causal models, the ability to use such models to conduct inquiry, and the ability to engage in the assessment of causal models and related explanations. We have found that these outcomes can be realized in classrooms where students are full participants in a scientific community.[34] Interestingly, one unexpected outcome of structuring classrooms so that students are expected to participate in the intellectual work of science has been increased involvement and achievement by students not previously identified as successful in science.

In addition to establishing expectations for class participation and a shared framework for knowledge assessment, MUSE curricula promote metacognitive reflection on the part of students by incorporating tasks that require discourse (formal and informal) at all stages of student work. While working in groups and presenting results to the class as a whole, students are required to share their ideas even when those ideas may not be fully formed. Moreover, recall that the context for idea sharing is one in which discipline-specific criteria for assessment of ideas have been established. Thus, discourse is anchored in norms of argumentation that reflect scientific practice to the extent possible.

Learning with Understanding

While the four features of classroom environments can be described individually, in practice they must interact if students are to deeply engage in learning for understanding. High school students have had more than 9 years of practice at playing the "game of school." Most have become quite adept at memorizing and reiterating information, seeking answers to questions or problems, and moving quickly from one topic to another. Typically during the game of school, students win when they present the correct answer. The process by which one determines the answer is irrelevant or, at best, undervalued. The students described here are quite typical in this regard: they enter our genetics and evolution classes anticipating that they will be called upon to provide answers and are prepared to do so. In fact, seeking an end product is so ingrained that even when we design tasks that involve multiple iterations of modeling and testing ideas, such as within the genetics course, students frequently reduce the work to seeking algorithms that have predictive power instead of engaging in the much more difficult task of evaluating models on the basis of their conceptual consistency within a family of related ideas.[35]

After studying how people solved problems in a variety of situations, Klayman and Ha[36] noted the frequent use of what they call a "positive test strategy." That is, solvers would propose a model (or solution) and test it by attempting to apply it to the situation most likely to fit the model in the first place. If the idea had explanatory or predictive power, the solver remained satisfied with it; if not, the solver would quickly test another idea. The positive test strategy was frequently applied by students in early versions of our genetics course.[37] This method of problem solving does not map well to scientific practice in most cases, however: it is the absence of disproving evidence, and not the presence of confirming evidence that is more commonly persuasive to scientists. Moreover, testing a model in limited situations in which one expects a data–model match would be considered "confirmation bias" within scientific communities. Nevertheless, Klayman and Ha point out that this positive test strategy is often quite useful in real-life situations.

Given our students' facility with the game of school and the general tendency to apply less scientific model-testing strategies when problem solving, we were forced to create tasks that not only afford the opportunity for reflection, but actually *require* students to think more deeply about the ways in which they have come to understand science concepts, as well as what is involved in scientific argumentation. We want students to realize that the models and explanations they propose are likely to be challenged and that the conflicts surrounding such challenges are the lifeblood of science. Thus, we explicitly discuss with our students the expectations for their participation in the course. Teachers state that the students' task is not simply to produce an "answer" (a model in genetics or a Darwinian explanation in evolutionary biology), but also to be able to defend and critique ideas according to the norms of a particular scientific discipline. In other words, we ask the students to abandon the game of school and begin to play the game of science.

Examination of ideas requires more than simply providing space for reflection to occur; it also involves working with students to develop systematic ways of critiquing their own ideas and those of others. This is why we begin each course with an activity whose focus is the introduction of discipline-specific ways of generating and critiquing knowledge claims. These activities do not require that students will come to understand any particular scientific concepts upon their completion. Rather, they will have learned about the *process* of constructing and evaluating arguments in genetics or evolutionary biology. Specific criteria for weighing scientific explanations are revisited throughout each course as students engage in extended inquiries within these biological disciplines.

SUMMARY

For students to develop understanding in any scientific discipline, teachers and curriculum developers must attend to a set of complex and interrelated components, including the nature of practice in particular scientific disciplines, students' prior knowledge, and the establishment of a collaborative environment that engages students in reflective scientific practice. These design components allow educators to create curricula and instructional materials that help students learn about science both *as* and *by* inquiry.

The students in the biology classrooms described in this chapter have developed sophisticated understandings of some of the most central explanatory frameworks in genetics and evolutionary biology. In addition, they have, unlike many high school students, shown great maturity in their abilities to reason about realistic biological data and phenomena using these models. Moreover, they have accomplished this in classrooms that are structured along the lines of scientific communities. This has all been made possible by a concerted collaboration involving high school teachers and their students, university science educators, and university biologists. That MUSE combined this collaboration with a research program on student learning and reasoning was essential. With the knowledge thus gained, we believe it is possible to help others realize the expectations for improving science education that are set forth in reform documents such as the *National Science Education Standards*.[38] In particular, there has been a call for curricular reforms that allow students to be "engaged in inquiry" that involves "combin[ing] processes and scientific knowledge as they use scientific reasoning and critical thinking to develop their understanding of science."[39] Recommendations for improved teaching of science are solidly rooted in a commitment to teaching both *through* and *about* inquiry. Furthermore, the *National Science Education Standards* do not simply suggest that science teachers incorporate inquiry in classrooms; rather, they demand that teachers embrace inquiry in order to:

- Plan an inquiry-based science program for their students.
- Focus and support inquiries while interacting with students.
- Create a setting for student work that is flexible and supportive of science inquiry.
- Model and emphasize the skills, attitudes, and values of scientific inquiry.

It is just these opportunities that have been described in this chapter.

NOTES

1. We encourage readers to visit our website (www.wcer.wisc.edu/ncusla/muse/). The site includes discussions of student knowledge and reasoning, intended learning outcomes, instructional activities, instructional notes, assessments, examples of student work, teachers' reflections, and connections to the *National Science Education Standards* and *Benchmarks for Science Literacy.*
2. Wiggins and McTighe, 1998, Chapter 1.
3. Grosslight et al., 1991.
4. Grosslight et al., 1991; Harrison and Treagust, 1998.
5. Cartier, 2000a.
6. Cartier, 2000b.
7. We consider a causal model to be an idea or set of ideas that can be used to explain particular natural phenomena. Models are complex constructions that consist of conceptual objects (e.g., alleles, populations) and processes (e.g., selection, independent assortment) in which the objects participate or interact.
8. Cartier, 2000a; Kindfield, 1994; Wynne et al., 2001.
9. Kindfield, 1994.
10. Cartier, 2000a.
11. Cartier, 2000a; Wynne et al., 2001.
12. Cartier, 2000b.
13. Darden, 1991.
14. Meiosis is the process by which sperm and egg cells are formed. During meiosis, chromosomal replication is followed by two rounds of cell division. Thus, one cell undergoing meiosis produces four new cells, each of which contains half the number of chromosomes of the original parent cell.
15. Kitcher, 1984, 1993.
16. Kitcher, 1984, p. 356.
17. Kitcher, 1984, p. 356.
18. Mendel, 1959.
19. Discontinuous traits are those for which two or more distinct categories of phenotypes (or variants) are identified. For example, Mendel studied the trait of height in pea plants. He noted that the pea plants were either short (18 in.) or tall (84 in.). In contrast, height is not a discontinuous trait in humans: human height is best characterized as continuously variable, or nondiscrete, because humans are not simply either 18 or 84 in. tall. Thus, the phenotype categories for height in humans are not clear-cut.
20. Calley and Jungck, 2002.
21. Achondroplasia is inherited in a codominant fashion. Individuals with two disease alleles (2,2) are severely dwarfed and seldom survive. Individuals who are heterozygous (1,2) are achondroplastic dwarfs, having disproportionately short arm and leg bones relative to their torsos. Thus while these two phenotypes differ from normal stature, they are distinct from one another.
22. In the past, our students have developed the following explanations for protein action in traits inherited in a codominant fashion:

- One allele (designated 1) codes for an active protein. The other allele codes for an inactive protein. Thus, individuals with genotype (1,1) have the greatest amount (or dose) of active protein and the associated phenotype at the organismal level. Individuals who are (2,2) have little or no measurable protein activity, and this is reflected in the phenotype. Heterozygous individuals (1,2) have an intermediate level of protein activity and a phenotype that is also intermediate. For example, in the case of achondroplasia, (1,1) individuals would have two alleles for a growth receptor and a phenotype of normal stature; (2,2) individuals would have few or no functional receptors and suffer from severe growth retardation; and heterozygotes (1,2) would have half as much growth receptor activity as the (1,1) individuals and consequently be short-statured achondroplastic dwarves without the additional health problems of the (2,2) individuals. This example of codominance is admittedly simplified, as students do not study the systemic effects of achondroplasia. However, this model is applied widely in genetics and sometimes referred to as the "dosage" model.
- Both alleles code for active proteins, giving rise to observable phenotypes at the macroscopic level. Heterozygotes display the phenotypes associated with both alleles. For example, in human blood types, individuals carrying alleles for protein A and protein B have both of these proteins on their blood cells. The phenotype is not blended or dosage dependent as in the achondroplasia example above. Instead, both proteins are detected intact in heterozygous individuals.

23. Cartier, 2000a, 2000b.
24. White and Frederiksen, 1998, p. 25.
25. Cartier 2000a, 2000b.
26. Mayr, 1982, p. 481.
27. Kitcher, 1993, pp. 20-21.
28. Richards, 1992, p. 23.
29. O'Hara, 1988.
30. Mayr, 1997, p. 64.
31. Bishop and Anderson, 1990; Demastes et al., 1992, 1995, 1996.
32. Bishop and Anderson, 1990.
33. Cartier, 2000a, 2000b; Passmore and Stewart, 2002.
34. Cartier, 2000b; Passmore and Stewart, 2000.
35. Cartier, 2000a.
36. Klayman and Ha, 1987.
37. Cartier, 2000a.
38. National Research Council, 1996.
39. National Research Council, 1996, p. 105.

REFERENCES

Bishop, B.A., and Anderson, C.W. (1990). Student conceptions of natural selection and its role in evolution. *Journal of Research in Science Teaching, 27*(5), 415-427.

Calley, J., and Jungck, J.R. (2002). *Genetics construction kit.* (The BioQUEST Library IV, version 1.1B3) [Computer software]. New York: Academic Press.

Cartier, J.L. (2000a). *Assessment of explanatory models in genetics: Insights into students' conceptions of scientific models.* Research report 98-1 for the National Center for Improving Student Learning and Achievement in Mathematics and Science. Available: http://www.wcer.wisc.edu/ncisla/publications/main. html#reports/RR98-1.pdf [accessed February 3, 2003].

Cartier, J.L. (2000b). *Using a modeling approach to explore scientific epistemology with high school biology students.* Research report 99-1 for the National Center for Improving Student Learning and Achievement in Mathematics and Science. Available: http://www.wcer.wisc.edu/ncisla/publications/reports/RR99-1.pdf [accessed February 3, 2003].

Darden, L. (1991). *Theory change in science: Strategies from Mendelian genetics.* New York: Oxford University Press.

Demastes, S., Good, R., and Peebles, P. (1995). Students' conceptual ecologies and the process of conceptual change in evolution. *Science Education, 79*(6), 637-666.

Demastes, S., Good, R., and Peebles, P. (1996). Patterns of conceptual change in evolution. *Journal of Research in Science Teaching, 33*(4), 407-431.

Demastes, S.S., Trowbridge, J.E., and Cummins, C.L. (1992). Resource paper on evolution education research. In R.G. Good, J.E. Trowbridge, S.S. Demastes, J.H. Wandersee, M.S. Hafner, and C.L. Cummins (Eds.), *Proceedings of the 1992 Evolution Education Conference,* Louisiana State University, Baton Rouge, LA.

Grosslight, L., Unger, C., Jay, E., and Smith, C.L. (1991). Understanding models and their use in science: Conceptions of middle and high school students and experts. *Journal of Research in Science Teaching, 28,* 799-822.

Harrison, A.G., and Treagust, D.F. (1998). Modeling in science lessons: Are there better ways to learn with models? *School Science and Mathematics, 98*(8), 420-429.

Kindfield, A.C.H. (1994). Understanding a basic biological process: Expert and novice models of meiosis. *Science Education, 78*(3), 255-283.

Kitcher, P. (1984). 1953 and all that: A tale of two sciences. *The Philosophical Review, 93,* 335-373.

Kitcher, P. (1993). *The advancement of science: Science without legend, objectivity without illusions.* New York: Oxford University Press.

Klayman, J., and Ha, Y. (1987). Confirmation, disconfirmation, and information in hypothesis testing. *Psychological Review, 94,* 211-228.

Mayr, E. (1982). *The growth of biological thought: Diversity, evolution, and inheritance.* Cambridge, MA: Belknap Press of Harvard University Press.

Mayr, E. (1997). *This is biology: The science of the living world.* Cambridge, MA: Belknap Press of Harvard University Press.

Mendel, G. (1959; Original publication date 1865). Experiments on plant hybridization. In J. Peters (Ed.), *Classic papers in genetics.* Upper Saddle River, NJ: Prentice Hall.

National Research Council. (1996). *National science education standards.* National Committee on Science Education Standards and Assessment, Center for Science, Mathematics, and Engineering Education. Washington, DC: National Academy Press.

O'Hara, R.J. (1988). Homage to Clio, or, toward a historical philosophy for evolutionary biology. *Systematic Zoology, 37,* 142-155.

Passmore, C.M., and Stewart, J. (2002). A modeling approach to teaching evolutionary biology in high schools. *Journal of Research in Science Teaching, 39,* 185-204.

Richards, R.J. (1992). The structure of narrative explanation in history and biology. In M.H. Nitecki and D.V. Nitecki (Eds.), *History and evolution* (pp. 19-53). Albany, NY: State University of New York Press.

White, B.Y., and Frederiksen, J.R. (1998). Inquiry, modeling, and metacogntion: Making science accessible to all students. *Cognition and Instruction, 16,* 3-118.

Wiggins, G., and McTighe, J. (1998). *Understanding by design.* Upper Saddle River, NJ: Merrill/Prentice-Hall.

Wynne, C., Stewart, J., and Passmore, C. (2001). High school students' use of meiosis when solving genetics problems. *The International Journal of Science Education, 23*(5), 501-515.

A FINAL SYNTHESIS:
REVISITING THE THREE LEARNING PRINCIPLES

13

Pulling Threads

M. Suzanne Donovan and John D. Bransford

What ties the chapters of this volume together are the three principles from *How People Learn* (set forth in Chapter 1) that each chapter takes as its point of departure. The collection of chapters in a sense serves as a demonstration of the second principle: that a solid foundation of detailed knowledge and clarity about the core concepts around which that knowledge is organized are both required to support effective learning. The three principles themselves are the core organizing concepts, and the chapter discussions that place them in information-rich contexts give those concepts greater meaning. After visiting multiple topics in history, math, and science, we are now poised to use those discussions to explore further the three principles of learning.

ENGAGING RESILIENT PRECONCEPTIONS

All of the chapters in this volume address common preconceptions that students bring to the topic of focus. Principle one from *How People Learn* suggests that those preconceptions must be engaged in the learning process, and the chapters suggest strategies for doing so. Those strategies can be grouped into three approaches that are likely to be applicable across a broad range of topics.

*1. **Draw on knowledge and experiences that students commonly bring to the classroom but are generally not activated with regard to the topic of study.***

This technique is employed by Lee, for example, in dealing with students' common conception that historical change happens as an *event*. He points out that students bring to history class the everyday experience of "nothing much happening" until an event changes things. Historians, on the other hand, generally think of change in terms of the *state of affairs*. Change in this sense may include, but is not equivalent to, the occurrence of events. Yet students have many experiences in which things change gradually—experiences in which "nothing happening" is, upon reflection, a mischaracterization. Lee suggests, as an example, students might be asked to "consider the change from a state of affairs in which a class does not trust a teacher to one in which it does. There may be no event that could be singled out as marking the change, just a long and gradual process."

There are many such experiences on which a teacher could draw, such as shifting alliances among friends or a gradual change in a sports team's status with an improvement in performance. Each of these experiences has characteristics that support the desired conception of history. Events are certainly not irrelevant. A teacher may do particular things that encourage trust, such as going to bat for a student who is in a difficult situation or postponing a quiz because students have two other tests on the same day. Similarly, there may be an incident in a group that changes the dynamic, such as a less popular member winning a valued prize or taking the blame for an incident to prevent the whole group from being punished. But in these contexts students can see, perhaps with some guided discussion, that single events are rarely the sole explanation for the state of affairs.

It is often the case that students have experiences that can support the conceptions we intend to teach, but instructional guidance is required to bring these experiences to the fore. These might be thought of as "recessive" experiences. In learning about rational number, for example, it is clear that whole-number reasoning—the subject of study in earlier grades—is dominant for most students (see Chapter 7). Yet students typically have experience with thinking about percents in the context of sale items in stores, grades in school, or loading of programs on a computer. Moss's approach to teaching rational number as described in Chapter 7 uses that knowledge of percents to which most students have easy access as an alternative path to learning rational number. She brings students' recessive understanding of proportion in the context of reasoning about percents to the fore and strengthens their knowledge and skill by creating multiple contexts in which proportional reasoning is employed (pipes and tubes, beakers, strings). As with events in history, students do later work with fractions, and that work at times presents them with problems that involve dividing a pizza or a pie into discrete parts—a problem in which whole-number reasoning often dominates. Because a facility with proportional reasoning is brought to bear, however, the division of a pie no longer leads students so easily into whole-number traps.

Moss reinforces proportional reasoning by having students play games in which fractions (such as $1/4$) must be lined up in order of size with decimals (such as .33) and percents (such as 40 percent). A theme that runs throughout the chapters of this volume, in fact, is that students need many opportunities to work with a new or recessive concept, especially when doing so requires that powerful preconceptions be overturned or modified.

Bain, for example, writes about students' tendency to see "history" and "the past" as the same thing: "No one should think that merely pointing out conceptual distinctions through a classroom activity equips students to make consistent, regular, and independent use of these distinctions. Students' habits of seeing history and the past as the same do not disappear overnight." Bain's equivalent of repeated comparisons of fractions, decimals, and percents is the ever-present question regarding descriptions and materials: is this "history-as-event"—the description of a past occurrence—or "history-as-account"—an explanation of a past occurrence. Supporting conceptual change in students requires repeated efforts to strengthen the new conception so that it becomes dominant.

2. Provide opportunities for students to experience discrepant events that allow them to come to terms with the shortcomings in their everyday models.

Relying on students' existing knowledge and experiences can be difficult in some instances because everyday experiences provide little if any opportunity to become familiar with the phenomenon of interest. This is often true in science, for example, where the subject of study may require specialized tools or controlled environmental conditions that students do not commonly encounter.

In the study of gravity, for example, students do not come to the classroom with experiences that easily support conceptual change because gravity is a constant in their world. Moreover, experiences they have with other forces often support misconceptions about gravity. For example, students can experience variation in friction because most have opportunities to walk or run an object over such surfaces as ice, polished wood, carpeting, and gravel. Likewise, movement in water or heavy winds provide experiences with resistance that many students can easily access. Minstrell found his students believed that these forces with which they had experience explained why they did not float off into space (see Chapter 11). Ideas about buoyancy and air pressure, generally not covered in units on gravity, influenced these students' thinking about gravity. Television images of astronauts floating in space reinforced for the students the idea that, without air to hold things down, they would simply float off.

Minstrell posed to his students a question that would draw out their thinking. He showed them a large frame from which a spring scale hung and placed an object on the scale that weighed 10 pounds. He then asked the students to consider a situation in which a large glass dome would be placed over the scale and all the air forced out with a vacuum pump. He asked the students to predict (imprecisely) what would happen to the scale reading. Half of Minstrell's students predicted that the scale reading would drop to zero without air; about a third thought there would be no effect at all on the scale reading; and the remainder thought there would be a small change. That students made a prediction and the predictions differed stimulated engagement. When the experiment was carried out, the ideas of many students were directly challenged by the results they observed.

In teaching evolution, Stewart and colleagues found that students' everyday observations led them to underestimate the amount of variation in common species. In such cases, student observations are not so much "wrong" as they are insufficiently refined. Scientists are more aware of variation because they engage in careful measurement and attend to differences at a level of detail not commonly noticed by the lay person. Stewart and colleagues had students count and sort sunflower seeds by their number of stripes as an easy route to a discrepant event of sorts. The students discovered there is far more variation among seeds than they had noticed. Unless students understand this point, it will be difficult for them to grasp that natural selection working on natural variation can support evolutionary change.

While discrepant events are perhaps used most commonly in science, Bain suggests they can be used productively in history as well (see Chapter 4). To dislodge the common belief that history is simply factual accounts of events, Bain asked students to predict how people living in the colonies (and later in the United States) would have marked the anniversary of Columbus's voyage 100 years after his landing in 1492 and then each hundred years after that through 1992. Students wrote their predictions in journals and were then given historical information about the changing Columbian story over the 500-year period. That information suggests that the first two anniversaries were not really marked at all, that the view of Columbus's "discovery of the new world" as important had emerged by 1792 among former colonists and new citizens of the United States, and that by 1992 the Smithsonian museum was making no mention of "discovery" but referred to its exhibit as the "Columbian Exchange." If students regard history as the reporting of facts, the question posed by Bain will lead them to think about *how* people might have celebrated Columbus's important discovery, and not *whether* people would have considered the voyage a cause for celebration at all. The discrepancy between students' expectation regarding the answer to the question and the historical accounts they are given in the classroom lecture cannot help but jar the conception that history books simply report events as they occurred in the past.

3. Provide students with narrative accounts of the discovery of (targeted) knowledge or the development of (targeted) tools.

What we teach in schools draws on our cultural heritage—a heritage of scientific discovery, mathematical invention, and historical reconstruction. Narrative accounts of how this work was done provide a window into change that can serve as a ready source of support for students who are being asked to undergo that very change themselves. How is it that the earth was discovered to be round when nothing we casually observe tells us that it is? What is place value anyway? Is it, like the round earth, a natural phenomenon that was discovered? Is it truth, like $e = mc^2$, to be unlocked? There was a time, of course, when everyday notions prevailed, or everyday problems required a solution. If students can witness major changes through narrative, they will be provided an opportunity to undergo conceptual change as well.

Stewart and colleagues describe the use of such an approach in teaching about evolution (see Chapter 12). Darwin's theory of natural selection operating on random variation can be difficult for students to grasp. The beliefs that all change represents an advance toward greater complexity and sophistication and that changes happen in response to use (the giraffe's neck stretching because it reaches for high leaves, for example) are widespread and resilient. And the scientific theory of evolution is challenged today, as it was in Darwin's time, by those who believe in intelligent design—that all organisms were made perfectly for their function by an intelligent creator. To allow students to differentiate among these views and understand why Darwin's theory is the one that is accepted scientifically, students work with three opposing theories as they were developed, supported, and argued in Darwin's day: William Paley's model of intelligent design, Jean Baptiste de Lamarck's model of acquired characteristics based on use, and Darwin's theory of natural selection. Students' own preconceptions are generally represented somewhere in the three theories. By considering in some depth the arguments made for each theory, the evidence that each theorist relied upon to support his argument, and finally the course of events that led to the scientific community's eventually embracing Darwin's theory, students have an opportunity to see their own ideas argued, challenged, and subjected to tests of evidence.

Every scientific theory has a history that can be used to the same end. And every scientific theory was formulated by particular people in particular circumstances. These people had hopes, fears, and passions that drove their work. Sometimes students can understand theories more readily if they learn about them in the context of those hopes, fears, and passions. A narrative that places theory in its human context need not sacrifice any of the technical material to be learned, but can make that material more engaging and meaningful for students.

The principle, of course, does not apply only to science and is not restricted to discovery. In mathematics, for example, while some patterns and relationships were discovered, conventions that form our system of counting were *invented*. As the mathematics chapters suggest, the use of mathematics with understanding—the engagement with problem solving and strategy use displayed by the best mathematics students—is undermined when students think of math as a rigid application of given algorithms to problems and look for surface hints as to which algorithm applies. If students can see the nature of the problems that mathematical conventions were designed to solve, their conceptions of what mathematics is can be influenced productively.

Historical accounts of the development of mathematical conventions may not always be available. For purposes of supporting conceptual change, however, fictional story telling may do just as well as history. In *Teaching as Story Telling,* Egan[1] relates a tale that can support students' understanding of place value:

A king wanted to count his army. He had five clueless counselors and one ingenious counselor. Each of the clueless five tried to work out a way of counting the soldiers, but came up with methods that were hopeless. One, for example, tried using tally sticks to make a count, but the soldiers kept moving around, and the count was confused. The ingenious counselor told the king to have the clueless counselors pick up ten pebbles each. He then had them stand behind a table that was set up where the army was to march past. In front of each clueless counselor a bowl was placed. The army then began to march past the end of the table.

As each soldier went by, the first counselor put one pebble into his bowl. Once he had put all ten pebbles into the bowl, he scooped them up and then continued to put one pebble down for each soldier marching by the table. He had a very busy afternoon, putting down his pebbles one by one and then scooping them up when all were in the bowl. Each time he scooped up the ten pebbles, the clueless counselor to his left put one pebble into her bowl [gender equity]. When her ten pebbles were in her bowl, she too scooped them out again, and continued to put one back into the bowl each time the clueless counselor to her right picked his up.

The clueless counselor to her left had to watch her through the afternoon, and he put one pebble into his bowl each time she picked bers up. And so on for the remaining counselors. At the end of the afternoon, the counselor on the far left had only one pebble in his bowl, the next counselor had two, the next had seven, the next had six and the counselor at the other end of the table, where the soldiers had marched by, had three pebbles in his bowl. So we know that the army had 12,763 soldiers. The king was delighted that his ingenious counselor had counted the whole army with just fifty pebbles.[2]

When this story is used in elementary school classrooms, Egan encourages the teacher to follow up by having the students count the class or some other, more numerous objects using this method.

The story illustrates nicely for students how the place-value system allows the complex problem of counting large numbers to be made simpler. Place value is portrayed not as a truth but as an invention. Students can then change the base from 10 to other numbers to appreciate that base 10 is not a "truth" but a "choice." This activity supports students in understanding that what they are learning is designed to make number problems raised in the course of human activity manageable.

That imaginative stories can, if effectively designed, support conceptual change as well as historical accounts is worth noting for another reason: the fact that an historical account is an *account* might be viewed as cause for excluding it from a curriculum in which the nature of the account is not the subject of study. Historical accounts of Galileo, Newton, or Darwin written for elementary and secondary students can be contested. One would hope that students who study history will come to understand these as accounts, and that they will be presented to students as such. But the purpose of the accounts, in this case, is to allow students to experience a time when ideas that they themselves may hold were challenged and changed, and that purpose can be served even if the accounts are somewhat simplified and their contested aspects not treated fully.

ORGANIZING KNOWLEDGE AROUND CORE CONCEPTS

In the *Fish Is Fish* story discussed in Chapter 1, we understand quite easily that when the description of a human generates an image of an upright fish wearing clothing, there are some key missing concepts: adaptation, warm-blooded versus cold-blooded species, and the difference in mobility challenges in and out of water. How do we know which concepts are "core?" Is it always obvious?

The work of the chapter authors, as well as the committee/author discussions that supported the volume's development, provides numerous insights about the identification of core concepts. The first is observed most explicitly in the work of Peter Lee (see Chapter 2): that two distinct types of core concepts must be brought to the fore simultaneously. These are concepts about the nature of the discipline (what it means to engage in doing history, math, or science) and concepts that are central to the understanding of the subject matter (exploration of the new world, mathematical functions, or gravity). Lee refers to these as first-order (the discipline) and second-order (the subject) concepts. And he demonstrates very persuasively in his work that students bring preconceptions about the discipline that are just as powerful and difficult to change as those they bring about the specific subject matter.

For teachers, knowing the core concepts of the discipline itself—the standards of evidence, what constitutes proof and disproof, and modes of reasoning and engaging in inquiry—is clearly required. This requirement is undoubtedly at the root of arguments in support of teachers' course work in the discipline in which they will teach. But that course work will be a blunt instrument if it focuses only on second-order knowledge (of subject) but not on first-order knowledge (of the discipline). Clarity about the core concepts of the discipline is required if students are to grasp what the discipline—history, math, or science—is about.

For identifying both first- and second-order concepts, the obvious place to turn initially is to those with deep expertise in the discipline. The concepts that organize experts' knowledge, structure what they see, and guide their problem solving are clearly core. But in many cases, exploring expert knowledge directly will not be sufficient. Often experts have such facility with a concept that it does not even enter their consciousness. These "expert blind spots" require that "knowledge packages"[3]—sets of related concepts and skills that support expert knowledge—become a matter for study.

A striking example can be found in Chapter 7 on elementary mathematics. For those with expertise in mathematics, there may appear to be no "core concept" in whole-number counting because it is done so automatically. How one first masters that ability may not be accessible to those who did so long ago. Building on the work of numerous researchers on how children come to acquire whole-number knowledge, Griffin and Case's[4] research conducted over many years suggests a core conceptual structure that supports the development of the critical concept of *quantity*. Similar work has been done by Moss and Case[5] (on the core conceptual structure for rational number) and by Kalchman, Moss, and Case[6] (on the core conceptual structure for functions). The work of Case and his colleagues suggests the important role cognitive and developmental psychologists can play in extending understanding of the network of concepts that are "core" and might be framed in less detail by mathematicians (and other disciplinary experts).

The work of Stewart and his colleagues described in Chapter 12 is another case in which observations of student efforts to learn help reshape understanding of the package of related core concepts. The critical role of natural selection in understanding evolution would certainly be identified as a core concept by any expert in biology. But in the course of teaching about natural selection, these researchers' realization that students underestimated the variation in populations led them to recognize the importance of this concept that they had not previously identified as core. Again, experts in evolutionary biology may not identify population variation as an important concept because they understand and use the concept routinely—perhaps without conscious attention to it. Knowledge gleaned from classroom teaching, then, can be critical in defining the connected concepts that help support core understandings.

But just as concepts defined by disciplinary experts can be incomplete without the study of student thinking and learning, so, too, the concepts as defined by teachers can fall short if the mastery of disciplinary concepts is shallow. Liping Ma's study of teachers' understanding of the mathematics of subtraction with regrouping provides a compelling example. Some teachers had little conceptual understanding, emphasizing procedure only. But as Box 13-1 suggests, others attempted to provide conceptual understanding without adequate mastery of the core concepts themselves. Ma's work provides many examples (in the teaching of multidigit multiplication, division of fractions, and calculation of perimeter and area) in which efforts to teach for understanding without a solid grasp of disciplinary concepts falls short.

SUPPORTING METACOGNITION

A prominent feature of all of the chapters in this volume is the extent to which the teaching described emphasizes the development of metacognitive skills in students. Strengthening metacognitive skills, as discussed in Chapter 1, improves the performance of all students, but has a particularly large impact on students who are lower-achieving.[7]

Perhaps the most striking consistency in pedagogical approach across the chapters is the ample use of classroom discussion. At times students discuss in small groups and at times as a whole class; at times the teacher leads the discussion; and at times the students take responsibility for questioning. A primary goal of classroom discussion is that by observing and engaging in questioning, students become better at monitoring and questioning their own thinking.

In Chapter 5 by Fuson, Kalchman, and Bransford, for example, students solve problems on the board and then discuss alternative approaches to solving the same problem. The classroom dialogue, reproduced in Box 13-2, supports the kind of careful thinking about why a particular problem-solv-

BOX 13-1 Conceptual Explanation Without Conceptual Understanding

Liping Ma explored approaches to teaching subtraction with regrouping (problems like 52 – 25, in which subtraction of the 5 ones from the 2 ones requires that the number be regrouped). She found that some teachers took a very procedural approach that emphasized the order of the steps, while others emphasized the concept of composing a number (in this case into 5 tens and 2 ones) and decomposing a number (into 4 tens and 12 ones). Between these two approaches, however, were those of teachers whose intentions were to go beyond procedural teaching, but who did not themselves fully grasp the concepts at issue. Ma[8] describes one such teacher as follows:

> *Tr. Barry, another experienced teacher in the procedurally directed group, mentioned using manipulatives to get across the idea that "you need to borrow something." He said he would bring in quarters and let students change a quarter into two dimes and one nickel: "a good idea might be coins, using money because kids like money. . . . The idea of taking a quarter even, and changing it to two dimes and a nickel so you can borrow a dime, getting across that idea that you need to borrow something."*
>
> *There are two difficulties with this idea. First of all, the mathematical problem in Tr. Barry's representation was 25 – 10, which is not a subtraction with regrouping. Second, Tr. Barry confused borrowing in everyday life—borrowing a dime from a person who has a quarter—with the "borrowing" process in subtraction with regrouping—to regroup the minuend by rearranging within place values. In fact, Tr. Barry's manipulative would not convey any conceptual understanding of the mathematical topic he was supposed to teach.*

Another teacher who grasps the core concept comments on the idea of "borrowing" as follows:[9]

> *Some of my students may have learned from their parents that you "borrow one unit form the tens and regard it as 10 ones". . . . I will explain to them that we are not borrowing a 10, but decomposing a 10. "Borrowing" can't explain why you can take a 10 to the ones place. But "decomposing" can. When you say decomposing, it implies that the digits in higher places are actually composed of those at lower places. They are exchangeable . . . borrowing one unit and turning it into 10 sounds arbitrary. My students may ask me how can we borrow from the tens? If we borrow something, we should return it later on.*

ing strategy does or does not work, as well as the relative benefits of different strategies, that can support skilled mathematics performance.

Similarly, in the science chapters students typically work in groups, and the groups question each other and explain their reasoning. Box 13-3 reproduces a dialogue at the high school level that is a more sophisticated version of that among young mathematics students just described. One group of students explains to another not only what they concluded about the evolutionary purpose of different coloration, but also the thinking that led them to that conclusion and the background knowledge from an earlier example that supported their thinking. The practice of bringing other knowledge to bear in the reasoning process is at the heart of effective problem solving, but can be difficult to teach directly. It involves a search through one's mental files for what is relevant. If teachers simply give students the knowledge to incorporate, the practice and skill development of doing one's own mental search is shortchanged. Group work and discussions encourage students to engage actively in the mental search; they also provide examples from other students' thinking of different searches and search results. The monitoring of consistency between explanation and theory that we see in this group discussion (e.g., even if the male dies, the genes have already been passed along) is preparation for the kind of self-monitoring that biologists do routinely.

Having emphasized the benefits of classroom discussion, however, we offer two cautionary notes. First, the discussion cited in the chapters is *guided* by teachers to achieve the desired learning. Using classroom discussion well places a substantial burden on the teacher to support skilled discussion, respond flexibly to the direction the discussion is taking, and steer it productively. Guiding discussion can be a challenging instructional task. Not all questions are good ones, and the art of questioning requires learning on the part of both students and teachers.[10] Even at the high school level, Bain (see Chapter 4) notes the challenge a teacher faces in supporting good student questioning:

Sarena	Does anyone notice the years that these were written? About how old are these accounts? Andrew?
Andrew	They were written in 1889 and 1836. So some of them are about 112 years old and others are about 165 years old.
Teacher	Why did you ask, Sarena?
Sarena	I'm supposed to ask questions about when the source was written and who wrote it. So, I'm just doing my job.

BOX 13-2 Supporting Skilled Questioning and Explaining in Mathematics Problem Solving

In the dialogue below, young children are learning to explain their thinking and to ask questions of each other—skills that help students guide their own learning when those skills are eventually internalized as self-questioning and self-explaining.

Teacher	Maria, can you please explain to your friends in the class how you solved the problem?
Maria	Six is bigger than 4, so I can't subtract here [pointing] in the ones. So I have to get more ones. But I have to be fair when I get more ones, so I add ten to both my numbers. I add a ten here in the top [pointing] to change the 4 to a 14, and I add a ten here in the bottom in the tens place, so I write another ten by my 5. So now I count up from 6 to 14, and I get 8 ones (demonstrating by counting "6, 7, 8, 9, 10, 11, 12, 13, 14" while raising a finger for each word from 7 to 14). And I know my doubles, so 6 plus 6 is 12, so I have 6 tens left. [She thought, "1 + 5 = 6 and 6 + ? = 12 tens. Oh, I know 6 + 6 = 12, so my answer is 6 tens."]
Jorge	I don't see the other 6 in your tens. I only see one 6 in your answer.
Maria	The other 6 is from adding my 1 ten to the 5 tens to get 6 tens. I didn't write it down.
Andy	But you're changing the problem. How do you get the right answer?
Maria	If I make both numbers bigger by the same amount, the difference will stay the same. Remember we looked at that on drawings last week and on the meter stick.
Michelle	Why did you count up?

Palincsar[11] has documented the progress of students as they move beyond early, unskilled efforts at questioning. Initially, students often parrot the questions of a teacher regardless of their appropriateness or develop questions from a written text that repeat a line of the text verbatim, leaving a blank to be filled in. With experience, however, students become productive questioners, learning to attend to content and ask genuine questions.

Maria	Counting down is too hard, and my mother taught me to count up to subtract in first grade.
Teacher	How many of you remember how confused we were when we first saw Maria's method last week? Some of us could not figure out what she was doing even though Elena and Juan and Elba did it the same way. What did we do?
Rafael	We made drawings with our ten-sticks and dots to see what those numbers meant. And we figured out they were both tens. Even though the 5 looked like a 15, it was really just 6. And we went home to see if any of our parents could explain it to us, but we had to figure it out ourselves and it took us 2 days.
Teacher	Yes, I was asking other teachers, too. We worked on other methods too, but we kept trying to understand what this method was and why it worked.
	And Elena and Juan decided it was clearer if they crossed out the 5 and wrote a 6, but Elba and Maria liked to do it the way they learned at home. Any other questions or comments for Maria? No? Ok, Peter, can you explain your method?
Peter	Yes, I like to ungroup my top number when I don't have enough to subtract everywhere. So here I ungrouped 1 ten and gave it to the 4 ones to make 14 ones, so I had 1 ten left here. So 6 up to 10 is 4 and 4 more up to 14 is 8, so 14 minus 6 is 8 ones. And 5 tens up to 11 tens is 6 tens. So my answer is 68.
Carmen	How did you know it was 11 tens?
Peter	Because it is 1 hundred and 1 ten and that is 11 tens.

Similarly, students' answers often cannot serve the purpose of clarifying their thinking for classmates, teachers, or themselves without substantial support from teachers. The dialogue in Box 13-4 provides an example of a student becoming clearer about the meaning of what he observed as the teacher helped structure the articulation.

BOX 13-3 Questioning and Explaining in High School Science

The teacher passes out eight pages of case materials and asks the students to get to work. Each group receives a file folder containing the task description and information about the natural history of the ring-necked pheasant. There are color pictures that show adult males, adult females, and young. Some of the pages contain information about predators, mating behavior, and mating success. The three students spend the remainder of the period looking over and discussing various aspects of the case. By the middle of the period on Tuesday, this group is just finalizing their explanation when Casey, a member of another group, asks if she can talk to them.

Casey	What have you guys come up with? Our group was wondering if we could talk over our ideas with you.
Grace	Sure, come over and we can each read our explanations.

These two groups have very different explanations. Hillary's group is thinking that the males' bright coloration distracts predators from the nest, while Casey's group has decided that the bright coloration confers an advantage on the males by helping them attract more mates. A lively discussion ensues.

Ed	But wait, I don't understand. How can dying be a good thing?
Jerome	Well, you have to think beyond just survival of the male himself. We think that the key is the survival of the kids. If the male can protect his

Group work and group or classroom discussions have another potential pitfall that requires teacher attention: some students may dominate the discussion and the group decisions, while others may participate little if at all. Having a classmate take charge is no more effective at promoting metacognitive development—or supporting conceptual change—than having a teacher take charge. In either case, active engagement becomes unnecessary. One approach to tackling this problem is to have students rate their group effort in terms not only of their product, but also of their group dy-

	young and give them a better chance of surviving then he has an advantage.
Claire	Even if he dies doing it?
Grace	Yeah, because he will have already passed on his genes and stuff to his kids before he dies.
Casey	How did you come up with this? Did you see something in the packets that we didn't see?
Grace	One reason we thought of it had to do with the last case with the monarchs and viceroy.
Hillary	Yeah, we were thinking that the advantage isn't always obvious and sometimes what is good for the whole group might not seem like it is good for one bird or butterfly or whatever.
Jerome	We also looked at the data in our packets on the number of offspring fathered by brighter versus duller males. We saw that the brighter males had a longer bar.
Grace	See, look on page 5, right here.
Jerome	So they had more kids, right?
Casey	We saw that table too, but we thought that it could back up our idea that the brighter males were able to attract more females as mates.

The groups agree to disagree on their interpretation of this piece of data and continue to compare their explanations on other points. While it may take the involvement of a teacher to consider further merits of each explanation given the data, the students' group work and dialogue provide the opportunity for constructing, articulating, and questioning a scientific hypothesis.

namics.[12] Another approach, suggested by Bain (Chapter 4), is to have students pause during class discussion to think and write individually. As students discussed the kind of person Columbus was, Bain asked them to write a 2-minute essay before discussing further. Such an exercise ensures that students who do not engage in the public discussion nonetheless formulate their ideas.

Group work is certainly not the only approach to supporting the development of metacognitive skills. And given the potential hazard of group

BOX 13-4 Guiding Student Observation and Articulation

In an elementary classroom in which students were studying the behavior of light, one group of students observed that light could be both reflected and transmitted by a single object. But students needed considerable support from teachers to be able to articulate this observation in a way that was meaningful to them and to others in the class:

Ms. Lacey	I'm wondering. I know you have a lot of see-through things, a lot of reflect things. I'm wondering how you knew it was see-through.
Kevin	It would shine just, straight through it.
Ms. Lacey	What did you see happening?
Kevin	We saw light going through the . . .
Derek	Like if we put light . . .
Kevin	Wherever we tried the flashlight, like right here, it would show on the board.
Derek	And then I looked at the screen [in front of and to the side of the object], and then it showed a light on the screen. Then he said, come here, and look at the back. And I saw the back, and it had another [spot].
Ms. Lacey	Did you see anything else happening at the material?
Kevin	We saw sort of a little reflection, but we, it had mostly just see-through.
Derek	We put, on our paper we put reflect, but we had to decide which one to put it in. Because it had more of this than more of that.
Ms. Lacey	Oh. So you're saying that some materials . . .
Derek	Had more than others . . .

dynamics, using some individual approaches to supporting self-monitoring and evaluation may be important. For example, in two experiments with students using a cognitive tutor, Aleven and Koedinger[13] asked one group to explain the problem-solving steps to themselves as they worked. They found that students who were asked to self-explain outperformed those who spent the same amount of time on task but did not engage in self-explanation on transfer problems. This was true even though the common time limitation meant that the self-explainers solved fewer problems.

Ms. Lacey	. . . are doing, could be in two different categories.
Derek	Yeah, because some through were really reflection and see-through together, but we had to decide which.
	[Intervening discussion takes place about other data presented by this group that had to do with seeing light reflected or transmitted as a particular color, and how that color compared with the color of the object.]
	[at the end of this group's reporting, and after the students had been encouraged to identify several claims that their data supported among those that had been presented previously by other groups of students]
Ms. Lacey	There was something else I was kinda convinced of. And that was that light can do two different things. Didn't you tell me it went both see-through and reflected?
Kevin & Derek	Yeah. Mm-hmm.
Ms. Lacey	So do you think you might have another claim there?
Derek	Yeah.
Kevin	Light can do two things with one object.
Ms. Lacey	More than one thing?
Kevin	Yeah.
Ms. Lacey	Okay. What did you say?
Kevin & Derek	Light can do two things with one object.

See Chapter 10 for the context of this dialogue.

Another individual approach to supporting metacognition is suggested by Stewart (Chapter 12). Students record their thinking early in the treatment of a new topic and refer back to it at the unit's end to see how it has changed. This brings conscious attention to the change in a student's own thinking. Similarly, the reflective assessment aspect of the ThinkerTools curriculum described in Chapter 1 shifts students from group inquiry work to evaluating their group's inquiry individually. The results in the ThinkerTools case suggest that the combination of group work and individual reflective assessment is more powerful that the group work alone (see Box 9-5 in Chapter 9).

PRINCIPLES OF LEARNING AND CLASSROOM ENVIRONMENTS

The principles that shaped these chapters are based on efforts by researchers to uncover the rules of the learning game. Those rules as we understand them today do not tell us how to play the best instructional game. They can, however, point to the strengths and weakness of instructional strategies and the classroom environments that support those strategies. In Chapter 1, we describe effective classroom environments as learner-centered, knowledge-centered, assessment-centered, and community-centered. Each of these characteristics suggests a somewhat different focus. But at the same time they are interrelated, and the balance among them will help determine the effectiveness of instruction.

A community-centered classroom that relies extensively on classroom discussion, for example, can facilitate learning for several reasons (in addition to supporting metacognition as discussed above):

- It allows students' thinking to be made transparent—an outcome that is critical to a learner-centered classroom. Teachers can become familiar with student ideas—for example, the idea in Chapter 7 that two-thirds of a pie is about the same as three-fourths of a pie because both are missing one piece. Teachers can also monitor the change in those ideas with learning opportunities, the pace at which students are prepared to move, and the ideas that require further work—key features of an assessment-centered classroom.
- It requires that students explain their thinking to others. In the course of explanation, students develop a disposition toward productive interchange with others (community-centered) and develop their thinking more fully (learner-centered). In many of the examples of student discussion throughout this volume—for example, the discussion in Chapter 2 of students examining the role of Hitler in World War II—one sees individual students becoming clearer about their own thinking as the discussion develops.
- Conceptual change can be supported when students' thinking is challenged, as when one group points out a phenomenon that another group's model cannot explain (knowledge-centered). This happens, for example, in a dialogue in Chapter 12 when Delia explains to Scott that a flap might prevent more detergent from pouring out, but cannot explain why the amount of detergent would always be the same.

At the same time, emphasizing the benefits of classroom discussion in supporting effective learning does not imply that lectures cannot be excellent pedagogical devices. Who among us have not been witness to a lecture from which we have come away having learned something new and important? The Feynman lectures on introductory physics mentioned in Chapter 1, for example, are well designed to support learning. That design incorporates a strategy for accomplishing the learning goals described throughout this volume.[14] Feynman anticipates and addresses the points at which students' preconceptions may be a problem. Knowing that students will likely have had no experiences that support grasping the size of an atom, he spends time on this issue, using familiar references for relative size that allow students to envision just how tiny an atom is.

But to achieve effective learning by means of lectures alone places a major burden on the teacher to anticipate student thinking and address problems effectively. To be applied well, this approach is likely to require both a great deal of insight and much experience on the part of the teacher. Without such insight and experience, it will be difficult for teachers to anticipate the full range of conceptions students bring and the points at which they may stumble.[15] While one can see that Feynman made deliberate efforts to anticipate student misconceptions, he himself commented that the major difficulty in the lecture series was the lack of opportunity for student questions and discussion, so that he had no way of really knowing how effective the lectures were. In a learner-centered classroom, discussion is a powerful tool for eliciting and monitoring student thinking and learning.

In a knowledge-centered classroom, however, lectures can be an important accompaniment to classroom discussion—an efficient means of consolidating learning or presenting a set of concepts coherently. In Chapter 4, for example, Bain describes how, once students have spent some time working on competing accounts of the significance of Columbus's voyage and struggled with the question of how the anniversaries of the voyage were celebrated, he delivers a lecture that presents students with a description of current thinking on the topic among historians. At the point at which this lecture is delivered, student conceptions have already been elicited and explored. Because lectures can play an important role in instruction, we stress once again that the emphasis in this volume on the use of discussion to elicit students' thinking, monitor understanding, and support metacognitive development—all critical elements of effective teaching—should not be mistaken for a pedagogical recommendation of a single approach to instruction. Indeed, inquiry-based learning may fall short of its target of providing students with deep conceptual understanding if the teacher places the full burden of learning on the activities. As Box 1-3 in Chapter 1 suggests, a lecture that consolidates the lessons of an activity and places the activity in the conceptual framework of the discipline explicitly can play a critical role in supporting student understanding.

How the balance is struck in creating a classroom that functions as a learning community attentive to the learners' needs, the knowledge to be mastered, and assessments that support and guide instruction will certain vary from one teacher and classroom to the next. Our hope for this volume, then, is that its presentations of instructional approaches to addressing the key principles from *How People Learn* will support the efforts of teachers to play their own instructional game well. This volume is a first effort to elaborate those findings with regard to specific topics, but we hope it is the first of many such efforts. As teachers and researchers become more familiar with some common aspects of student thinking about a topic, their attention may begin to shift to other aspects that have previously attracted little notice. And as insights about one topic become commonplace, they may be applied to new topics.

Beyond extending the reach of the treatment of the learning principles of *How People Learn* within and across topics, we hope that efforts to incorporate those principles into teaching and learning will help strengthen and reshape our understanding of the rules of the learning game. With physics as his topic of concern, Feynman[16] talks about just such a process: "For a long time we will have a rule that works excellently in an overall way, even when we cannot follow the details, and then some time we may discover a *new rule*. From the point of view of basic physics, the most interesting phenomena are of course in the *new* places, the places where the rules do not work—not the places where they *do* work! That is the way in which we discover new rules."

We look forward to the opportunities created for the evolution of the science of learning and the professional practice of teaching as the principles of learning on which this volume focuses are incorporated into classroom teaching.

NOTES

1. Egan, 1986.
2. Story summarized by Kieran Egan, personal communication, March 7, 2003.
3. Liping Ma's work, described in Chapter 1, refers to the set of core concepts and the connected concepts and knowledge that support them as "knowledge packages."
4. Griffin and Case, 1995.
5. Moss and Case, 1999.
6. Kalchman et al., 2001.
7. Palincsar, 1986; White and Fredrickson, 1998.
8. Ma, 1999, p. 5.
9. Ma, 1999, p. 9.

10. Palincsar, 1986.
11. Palincsar, 1986.
12. National Research Council, 2005 (Stewart et al., 2005, Chapter 12).
13. Aleven and Koedinger, 2002.
14. For example, he highlights core concepts conspicuously. In his first lecture, he asks, "If, in some cataclysm, all of scientific knowledge were to be destroyed, and only one sentence passed on to the next generation of creatures, what statement would contain the most information in the fewest words? I believe it is the atomic hypothesis that all things are made of atoms—little particles that move around in perpetual motion, attracting each other when they are a little distance apart, but repelling upon being squeezed into one another.
15. Even with experience, the thinking of individual students may be unanticipated by the teacher.
16. Feynman, 1995, p. 25.

REFERENCES

Aleven, V., and Koedinger, K. (2002). An effective metacognitive strategy: Learning by doing and explaining with a computer-based cognitive tutor. *Cognitive Science, 26,* 147-179.

Egan, K. (1986). *Teaching as story telling: An alternative approach to teaching and curriculum in the elementary school* (vol. iii). Chicago, IL: University of Chicago Press.

Feynman, R.P. (1995). *Six easy pieces: Essentials of physics explained by its most brilliant teacher.* Reading, MA: Perseus Books.

Griffin, S., and Case, R. (1995). Re-thinking the primary school math curriculum: An approach based on cognitive science. *Issues in Education, 3*(1), 1-49.

Kalchman, M., Moss, J., and Case, R. (2001). Psychological models for the development of mathematical understanding: Rational numbers and functions. In S. Carver and D. Klahr (Eds.), *Cognition and instruction: Twenty-five years of progress* (pp. 1-38). Mahwah, NJ: Lawrence Erlbaum Associates.

Ma, L. (1999). *Knowing and teaching elementary mathematics.* Mahwah, NJ: Lawrence Erlbaum Associates.

Moss, J., and Case, R. (1999). Developing children's understanding of rational numbers: A new model and experimental curriculum. *Journal for Research in Mathematics Education, 30*(2).

Palincsar, A.S. (1986). *Reciprocal teaching: Teaching reading as thinking.* Oak Brook, IL: North Central Regional Educational Laboratory.

Stewart, J., Cartier, J.L., and Passmore, C.M. (2005). Developing understanding through model-based inquiry. In National Research Council, *How students learn: History, mathematics, and science in the classroom.* Committee on How People Learn, A Targeted Report for Teachers, M.S. Donovan and J.D. Bransford (Eds.). Division of Behavioral and Social Sciences and Education. Washington, DC: The National Academies Press.

White, B., and Fredrickson, J. (1998). Inquiry, modeling and metacognition: Making science accessible to all students. *Cognition and Instruction, 6*(1), 3-117.

OTHER RESOURCES

National Academy of Sciences. (1998). *Teaching about evolution and the nature of science.* Working Group on Teaching Evolution. Washington, DC: National Academy Press: Available: http://books.nap.edu/catalog/5787.html.

National Academy of Sciences. (2004). *Evolution in Hawaii: A supplement to teaching about evolution and the nature of science* by Steve Olson. Washington, DC: The National Academies Press. Available: http://www.nap.edu/books/0309089913/html/.

Biographical Sketches of Committee Members and Contributors

Rosalyn Ashby is a lecturer in education in the History in Education Unit in the School of Arts and Humanities in the University of London Institute of Education. Her work focuses on designing history curricula, assessment systems, and support materials for teachers. She now leads a history teacher-training course. Prior to becoming a university lecturer, Ashby taught history, politics and economics, and then worked as a history adviser with primary and secondary teachers. She has published numerous articles and book chapters, including many coauthored with Peter Lee regarding children's ideas about history. She is an editor of the *International Review of History Education.* She has a degree in American history and government from the University of Essex.

Robert B. Bain is assistant professor in the school of education at the University of Michigan. He teaches social studies education and investigates history education, the intersection between the disciplines and social studies instruction, and professional development. Previously, he spent more than 25 years as a high school history teacher. Among other publications, he has coauthored an article on professional development of elementary school teachers.

John D. Bransford (*Chair*) is James W. Mifflin university professor and professor of education at the University of Washington in Seattle. Previously, he was centennial professor of psychology and education and codirector of the Learning Technology Center at Vanderbilt University. Early work by Bransford and his colleagues in the 1970s included research in the areas of human learning and memory and problem solving; this research helped shape the "cognitive revolution" in psychology. An author of seven books and hundreds of articles and presentations, Bransford's work focuses on the areas of cognition and technology. He served as cochair of the National Research Council (NRC) committee that authored *How People Learn: Brain, Mind, Experience, and School.* He received a Ph.D. in cognitive psychology from the University of Minnesota.

Susan Carey is a professor of psychology at Harvard University. Carey's research concerns the evolutionary and ontogenetic origins of human knowledge in a variety of domains, including number, lexical semantics, physical reasoning, and reasoning about intentional states. She studies conceptual change involving older children, and focuses on three domains of knowledge: number, intuitive biology, and intuitive physics. She received a Ph.D. from Harvard University.

Jennifer L. Cartier is an assistant professor in the Department of Instruction and Learning at the University of Pittsburgh. Her research interests include student learning in classrooms where modeling is a focus and teacher education—particularly the ways in which hands-on curriculum materials can be implemented to engage elementary school students in realistic scientific practices. She has published articles describing students' reasoning in genetics in *Science and Education* and *BioQUEST Notes* and she has coauthored a book chapter describing the use of black-box activities to introduce students to aspects of scientific argumentation.

M. Suzanne Donovan (*Study Director*) is also director of the NRC's Strategic Education Research Partnership (SERP) and coeditor of the project's two reports, *Strategic Education Research Partnership* and *Learning and Instruction: A SERP Research Agenda.* At the NRC, she served as director of the previous study that produced *How People Learn: Bridging Research and Practice,* and she was coeditor for the NRC reports *Minority Students in Special and Gifted Education* and *Eager to Learn: Educating Our Preschoolers.* Previously, she was on the faculty of Columbia University. She has a Ph.D. in public policy from the University of California at Berkeley.

Kieran Egan is a professor in the Faculty of Education at Simon Fraser University in Burnaby, Canada. Dr. Egan was the 1991 winner of the Grawemeyer Award in Education for his analyses of children's imaginations. His recent books include *The Educated Mind: How Cognitive Tools Shape Our Understanding* (University of Chicago Press) and *Getting It Wrong from the Beginning: Our Progressivist Inheritance from Herbert Spencer, John Dewey, and Jean Piaget* (Yale University Press).

Karen C. Fuson is a professor emeritus in the School of Education and Social Policy and in the Psychology Department at Northwestern University. After teaching high school mathematics to Chicago inner-city African-American students for 3 years, she began research to ascertain how to help all students enter high school with more knowledge of mathematics. She has conducted extensive research regarding children's learning of mathematical concepts from ages 2 through 12, focusing in on the development of effective teaching and learning materials, including the "Children's Math World's K through 5" curriculum, supporting effective learning for children from various backgrounds, and ambitious accessible learning paths through school mathematics. Fuson was a member of the NRC committee that authored *Adding It Up: Helping Children Learn Mathematics.*

Sharon Griffin is an associate professor of education and an adjunct associate professor of psychology at Clark University. She is coauthor of "Number Worlds," a research-based mathematics program for young children, coauthor of *What Develops in Emotional Development?* (Plenum), and author of several articles on cognitive development and mathematics education. For the past 10 years, she has sought to improve mathematics learning and achievement for young children by developing and evaluating programs to "provide the central conceptual prerequisites for success in school math to children at risk for school failure." Griffin is currently participating in an advisory capacity on national projects, in Canada and the United States, to enhance the cognitive, mathematical, and language development of "high-need" preschool children, from birth to 5 years.

Mindy Kalchman is an assistant professor in the School of Education at DePaul University. Her research interests include children's learning of mathematics, theory-based curriculum design, and the effect of discoveries from the field of developmental cognitive psychology on classroom practice. She has coauthored numerous articles regarding mathematics education and curriculum and has conducted workshops on how to teach functions. Kalchman also served as a consulting content editor for the development of the Ontario mathematics curriculum for grades 9–12. She received her Ph.D. from the Ontario Institute for Studies in Education, University of Toronto.

Kenneth R. Koedinger is an associate professor in the Human Computer Interaction Institute and Psychology Department at Carnegie Mellon University. His research interests include cognitive modeling, problem solving and learning, intelligent tutoring systems, and educational technology. Earlier in his career, Koedinger was a teacher in an urban high school. He has developed computer simulations of student thinking that are used to guide the construction of educational materials and are the core of intelligent software systems that provide students with individualized interactive learning assistance. He has developed such "cognitive tutors" for mathematics that are now in use in over 1700 schools.

Pamela Kraus is a research scientist and cofounder of FACET Innovations. She is currently working on the Diagnoser projects and related professional development projects and she is helping conduct the research and organize the facet clusters in the physical sciences. In addition, Kraus works closely with the resource teachers from across the state as they produce assessment tools. She received a Ph.D. from the University of Washington.

Peter J. Lee is a senior lecturer in education in the History Education Unit of the School of Arts and Humanities at the Institute of Education of The University of London. Previously, he taught history in primary and secondary schools. Lee has directed several research and curriculum development projects (the latter with Denis Shemilt). He has edited five books on history education, and published numerous chapters and articles exploring children's ideas about history, many of them coauthored with Rosalyn Ashby. He is an editor of the *International Review of History Education*. He received a history degree at Oxford University.

Shirley J. Magnusson is the Cotchett Professor of Science and Mathematics Teacher Education at the California Polytechnic State University. She has taught science to students at the elementary, middle school, high school, and college levels since 1980. She joined the faculty at the University of Michigan in 1991 as a science teacher educator, specializing in learning and instruction in science at the elementary school level. She collaborated with Annemarie Palincsar on a program of research that has sought to define and study the outcomes from an approach to inquiry-based science instruction known as Guided Inquiry supporting Multiple Literacies (GIsML). Publications of Magnusson's work have appeared in the *Journal of the Learning Sciences*, *Teaching and Teacher Education*, the *Journal of Science Education and Technology*, and *Learning Disabilities Quarterly*, as well as a number of books such as *Science Teacher Knowledge*, *Cognition and Instruction: Twenty-five Years of Progress*, and *Translating Educational Theory into Practice*.

James Minstrell is cofounder and research scientist at FACET Innovations, LLC. This position followed a lengthy career as a science and mathematics teacher and classroom researcher in the learning of physical science and mathematics. He received the Presidential Award for Excellence in Science and Mathematics Teaching from the National Science Foundation. Minstrell served on the U.S. Department of Education's Expert Panel on Science and

Mathematics Education. He has published numerous articles, with a major focus on understanding of mathematics and physics.

Joan Moss is an assistant professor in the Department of Human Development and Applied Psychology at the Ontario Institute for Studies in Education at the University of Toronto. Previously she worked as a master teacher at the Institute of Child Study Laboratory School. Her research interests include children's development and understanding of rational numbers and proportional reasoning. More recently, Moss has been working on classroom-based studies of children's development of algebraic thinking. Her work in professional development includes preservice training, as well as coordination of learning opportunities with novice elementary school mathematics teachers using a Japanese lesson study approach. She has published widely and is an author of a mathematics textbook series. Moss carried out postdoctoral research at the University of California at Berkeley.

Annemarie Sullivan Palincsar is the Jean and Charles Walgreen professor of reading and literacy at the University of Michigan's School of Education. She has conduced extensive research on peer collaboration in problem-solving activity, instruction to promote self-regulation, acquisition and instruction of literacy with primary students at risk for academic difficulty, and how children use literacy in the context of guided inquiry experiences. She was a member of the NRC committees that produced the reports *How People Learn: Bridging Research and Practice,* and *Preventing Reading Difficulties in young Children.* Palincsar is currently coeditor of *Cognition and Instruction.*

Cynthia M. Passmore is an assistant professor in the School of Education at the University of California, Davis. She specializes in science education and is particularly interested in student learning and reasoning about scientific models. Her research also focuses on preservice and in-service teacher professional development. She teaches the science methods courses for single and multiple subjects credential candidates, as well as graduate courses in science education. Earlier in her career she worked as a high school science teacher in East Africa, Southern California, and Wisconsin.

Denis Shemilt has worked at the University of Leeds for more than 25 years, where he has been evaluator of the Schools History Project 13-16, and codirector of the Cambridge History Project. Until recently, he was head of the School of Education at Trinity and All Saints, a constituent college of the university, devoting time to educational management at the expense of real work. He is now focusing on training history teachers and pursuing a long-postponed interest in the development of students' historical frameworks.

He has published numerous contributions to history education, including the *History 13-16 Evaluation Study* and papers on students' ideas about change, evidence, and empathy in history. He received a degree in education from the University of Manchester.

James Stewart is a professor in the School of Education's Department of Curriculum and Instruction at the University of Wisconsin-Madison. His research interests include student understanding, reasoning, and problem solving in science, particularly in the biological sciences. Stewart's recent publications include articles on student understanding in genetics and evolutionary biology in *Science Education* and the *Journal of Research in Science Teaching* and a book chapter, "Teaching Science in a Multicultural Perspective."

Suzanne M. Wilson is a professor in the Department of Teacher Education and director of the Center for the Scholarship of Teaching at Michigan State University. She was a history and mathematics teacher for 6 years; directed the Teacher Assessment Project at Stanford University; taught third-grade social studies in a professional development school; and has directed several research projects exploring the relationship of teachers' practice to curriculum mandates. Wilson teaches prospective and practicing teachers, as well as prospective teacher educators and researchers.

Samuel S. Wineburg is professor of education at Stanford University, where he directs the Ph.D. program in History Education. His research explores the development of historical thinking among adolescents and the nature of historical consciousness. Wineburg's book, *Historical Thinking and Other Unnatural Acts: Charting the Future and Past,* was awarded the 2002 Frederic W. Ness Prize for the "most important contribution to the understanding and improvement of liberal education" by the Association of American Colleges and Universities. He was a member of the NRC committee that wrote *How People Learn: Brain, Mind, Experience, and School.* He received his Ph.D. from Stanford University.

Index

O

T